FIFTH
EDITION

Philosophical Foundations of Education

HOWARD A. OZMON
SAMUEL M. CRAVER
Virginia Commonwealth University

Merrill,
an imprint of Prentice Hall

Englewood Cliffs, New Jersey   Columbus, Ohio

LIBRARY OF CONGRESS CATALOGING-IN-PUBLICATION DATA
Ozmon, Howard.
   Philosophical Foundations of Education/Howard A. Ozmon,
   Samuel M. Craver—5th ed.
     p. cm.
   Includes bibliographical references and index.
   ISBN 0-02-390311-2
   1. Education—Philosophy—History.
   I. Craver, Samuel M.
   II. Title.
   LA21.095   1995   94-25004
   370' .1—dc20   CIP

Cover photo: ©1992 Jeffrey M. Spielman/The Image Bank®
Editor: Debbie Stollenwerk
Production Editor: Julie Anderson Tober
Text Designer: Susan Frankenberry
Cover Designer: Brian Deep
Production Buyer: Deidra Schwartz
Electronic Text Management: Marilyn Wilson Phelps, Matthew Williams, Jane Lopez,
   Karen L. Bretz

This book was set in Century by Prentice-Hall and was printed and bound by
R.R. Donnelley and Sons Company. The cover was printed by Phoenix Color Corp.

 © 1995 by Prentice-Hall, Inc.
A Simon & Schuster Company
Englewood Cliffs, New Jersey 07632

Earlier editions © 1990, 1986, 1981, 1976 by Merrill Publishing Company.

Printed in the United States of America

10 9 8 7 6 5 4 3 2

ISBN: 0-02-390311-2

Prentice-Hall International (UK) Limited, *London*
Prentice-Hall of Australia Pty. Limited, *Sydney*
Prentice-Hall of Canada, Inc., *Toronto*
Prentice-Hall Hispanoamericana, S. A., *Mexico*
Prentice-Hall of India Private Limited, *New Delhi*
Prentice-Hall of Japan, Inc., *Tokyo*
Simon & Schuster Asia Pte. Ltd., *Singapore*
Editora Prentice-Hall do Brasil, Ltda., *Rio de Janeiro*

About the Authors

HOWARD A. OZMON is professor emeritus of education in the Division of Educational Studies at Virginia Commonwealth University. He received a B.A. in philosophy from the University of Virginia and a doctorate from Teachers College, Columbia University. Dr. Ozmon has taught in elementary and secondary schools as well as at several colleges and universities. He has published numerous books and articles dealing with philosophy and education.

SAMUEL M. CRAVER is professor in the Division of Educational Studies at Virginia Commonwealth University. He received his doctorate from the University of North Carolina at Chapel Hill. Dr. Craver has taught at both the secondary and university levels. He is the author of numerous papers on historical and philosophical issues in education, and presently teaches courses on history of education, philosophy of education, and professional ethics in education.

Preface

Throughout the centuries, philosophers have sought to discover many things, such as truth, meaning, coherence, clarity, or usefulness. They have also endeavored to transfer their knowledge and techniques to others. Philosophers, like thinkers in other fields, have often stood on the shoulders of those who came before them, and it is useful to see this kind of progression in thought and to understand the times and forces that influenced how philosophers developed their beliefs. Our purpose in this volume has been to show how philosophical ideas about education developed over a considerable period but with due regard to historical influences and settings and with emphasis on how these ideas continue to have relevance for education and life at present.

Some of the ideas included here are more than two thousand years old, yet they often appear today in the panoply of ideas that constantly surrounds and influences us. Old ideas as well as new ones are useful tools for evaluating our present world. Idealism, while not a particularly influential philosophy today, may be a useful counterpoint by which to compare and evaluate today's materialist culture. Marxism and existentialism, while declining in popularity, may still be useful frames of reference or "paradigms" for examining a person's intricate relationship with other persons and the larger society. Whereas certain philosophies may be more relevant to particular times and places than others, ideas often develop in relationship to a given time, and ever-changing conditions necessitate the development of different and newer ideas. Still, past ideas are useful tools in lighting the way because they almost always have a bearing on the present. Thus, we are concerned about the historical context in which ideas appear—not only because we think that people today may avoid the errors of the past, but also because old ideas often become useful again.

This book was conceived as an introductory text in the philosophy of education. We recognize that there are many variables to be considered in selecting ideas, philosophers, and format, but our guiding rule has been to select those we believe have had the most relevance for education. We examine a general philosophy, such as realism, and show its applications in aims, curriculum, and methods. We also provide a critical analysis of each philosophy, frequently including what other philosophers have said about them.

The philosophies of education presented here are essentially arranged in chronological order. We have tried to avoid unnecessary jargon, both in philosophical and educational ideas, but there is some terminology one needs to know in order to talk about ideas in philosophic fashion. However, we have tried to keep technical expression and jargon to a minimum. With regard to format, we realize that not all philosophers agree with a "systems" or "schools" approach, and that there are serious pros and cons to this issue. However, we feel that for beginning students, often those who may be encountering philosophy for the first time, the benefits of this organizational approach outweigh its disadvantages because it provides a useful way of synthesizing ideas.

We believe that the study of philosophy of education should help sharpen student ideas about education and also give them some tools to think about education in a very general sense. Not only do we think that the study of philosophy assists students in developing necessary analytical skills and encourages critical perspectives, but it also provides perspective or vision as to the importance of education. Although it is impossible to include in a volume of this size every philosopher or every leading philosophical idea that has had educational importance, we hope that the material presented will serve as a catalyst for students to explore further the interesting and important activity of education, and possibly even serve as a stimulus for students to be creative with ideas that can influence their future education and life.

ACKNOWLEDGMENTS

We wish to thank our colleagues Dr. Maike Philipson and Dr. Jon Wergin at Virginia Commonwealth University for their critiques of the new Postmodern coverage in Chapter 10.

In addition we appreciate the input from the following reviewers: Joseph Bronars, Jr., Queens College of CUNY; Lawrence D. Klein, Central Connecticut State University; and Elizabeth McAuliffe, Salve Regina University (RI). We also thank all those who have reviewed past editions and whose suggestions have helped improve each edition.

Howard Ozmon and Samuel Craver

Brief Contents

Table of Contents

2

REALISM AND EDUCATION   39

3

EASTERN PHILOSOPHY, RELIGION, AND EDUCATION   81

8

ANALYTIC PHILOSOPHY AND EDUCATION   281

9

MARXISM AND EDUCATION   321

10

PHILOSOPHY, EDUCATION, AND THE CHALLENGE OF POSTMODERNISM

Introduction

It can be said that the philosophy of education began when people first became conscious of education as a distinct human activity. Although preliterate societies did not have the long-range goals and complex social systems we find in modern times, and while they did not have the analytical tools that modern philosophers have, even preliterate education involved a philosophical attitude about life. Humanity had a "philosophy" of education long before we knew what it was or what it could mean in terms of educational development.

In earlier times, education was primarily for survival. Children were taught the skills necessary for living. Gradually, however, people came to use education for a variety of purposes. Today, education may be used not only for survival (though recent ecological studies show that it may still be used for such purposes) but also for better use of leisure time and refinements in social and cultural life. As the practice of education has developed, so also have philosophies about education; however, it has become easy for us to overlook the connection between theory and practice and to deal with practice apart from theory. We may be in a dilemma because we seem to be more involved with the "practical" aspects of education than we are with an analysis of educational theory and its connection with practice. What we need is not only better theorizing about education and better methods but also a concerted effort to join the two. Thinking about education without consideration for the "practical" world means that philosophers of education become web spinners of thought engaged in mere academic exercises. On the other hand, tinkering with educational methods without serious thought results in practices that have little substance or meaning.

THE NEED FOR A PHILOSOPHY OF EDUCATION

A study of philosophy of education seems imperative today, for we are in a critical era of transition. There has always been change but seldom at our present accelerated rate, creating in many individuals what Alvin Toffler called *future shock*. At a time when many observers say we are entering a "postmodern" era, it is easy for people either to embrace more and more change with little thought to eventual consequences or to resist change and keep old values no matter what. Educational philosophers, regardless of their particular theory, suggest that the solutions to our problems can best be achieved through critical and reflective thought.

We can say that philosophy of education is the application of philosophical ideas to educational problems. The practice of education, however, may lead to a refinement of philosophical ideas. Thus, educational philosophy is not only a way of looking at ideas but of learning how to use ideas in the best way. No intelligent philosophy of education is involved when educators do things simply because they were done in the past. A philosophy of education becomes significant when educators recognize the need to think clearly about what they are doing and to see what they are doing in the larger context of individual and social development.

Many major philosophers have written about education, probably because education is such an integral part of life that it is difficult to think about not having it. Humans are tool-making beings but can also be considered education-making beings because education has been closely connected with the development of civilization. Thinking about life in general has often been related to education in particular, and education has often been viewed as a way of bringing a better life into existence. This is as true today as it has ever been.

The study of philosophy does not guarantee that individuals will be better thinkers or educators, but it does provide valuable perspectives to help us think more clearly. The word *philosophy* literally means the love of wisdom and has traditionally implied the pursuit of wisdom. This is not to imply that philosophy provides no answers; rather, it offers an avenue for serious inquiry into ideas, traditions, and ways of thinking. Philosophers have been acute observers of human conditions and have articulated their observations in ways that can be instructive. Educators are not only aided by a careful and systematic approach to ideas that philosophers have fostered, but they also can gain ideas from philosophy that may help develop new insights into educational problems. While educators may choose to disregard the philosophical approach to problems, in doing so they ignore a vital and important body of thought.

One of the roles of philosophy in any era has been to examine critically the intellectual disputes of the time and to suggest alternative arguments or ways of viewing things. Another role has been to develop sensitivity to the logic and language used in constructing solutions to problems, whether in education or the larger society. It is possible to trace the history of ideas by tracing the development of philosophical thought, and the history of philosophy reflects some of humanity's best thinking—our collective wisdom, so to speak. It can be said that to think philosophically is to reflect upon who we are, what we are doing, why we are doing it, and how we justify all these things.

Education is involved with the world of ideas and the world of practical activity—good ideas can lead to good practices, and good practices can lead to good ideas. In order to behave intelligently in the educational process, the educator needs the things philosophy can provide—that is, an understanding of thinking processes and the nature of ideas, the language we use to describe education, criticism of cultural and social traditions, and perspective on how these may interact with practical affairs. For educators, philosophy is not simply a professional tool but a way of improving the quality and enjoyment of life because it helps us gain a wider and deeper perspective on human existence and the world around us.

Despite the depth of thought it provides, philosophy does not appeal to some people because it provides no clear-cut answers to pressing problems. Of course, philosophers disagree on many issues, but it is often from disagreements (including the philosophical sort) that the search for new social, political, economic, religious, and educational systems have developed. Those who avoid disagreement and prefer clear-cut answers may overlook important concerns about the development of civilization, because if there had been no disagreement about ideas, purposes, and methods, we probably would still be in the Stone Age. Disagreement has often brought about change, and it continues to do so.

Many differences in educational viewpoints have arisen because of changes in society. Social conditions often necessitate changes of viewpoint and behavior. This will probably always go on, but it would be gratifying if educational change resulted from people reflectively examining issues and clarifying direction. Many past events that affected social and cultural development, such as urbanization, were largely beyond human control. Although some people tried to study the changes, they had little influence over the direction events would take. Even more to the point, many social and cultural changes that could have been controlled with sufficient thought and foresight have wreaked havoc in history. Consequently, much philosophizing throughout history has been after the fact—and events ran their own capricious course.

As people sought to develop more control over social forces through education, however, they were faced with the problem of dealing with the direction of control. This problem has led to questions of whether the controls do more harm than good. For example, individuals and groups can be systematically controlled through psychological conditioning in the educational process, but whether such control is good is subject to argument and debate. Thus, the need arises for philosophical thought to examine the value of controls, to uncover the basic assumptions behind those controls, and to study the implications for human life and freedom.

People often approach philosophy looking for *the* answer to debatable issues—when they fail to find it, they reject philosophy, complaining that it is difficult to understand. Some question the value of studying philosophy at all, saying it has no relevance for practical life, but many of the problems philosophers have dealt with—the relation of individual freedom to social responsibility, the purposes of education, the meanings of terms and concepts, and so on—are relevant today.

Practically everything done in education reflects some point of view that may not be readily apparent to the pupil, the parent, or the educator. Perhaps the viewpoint itself is unclear or is a loose collection of ideas all lumped together without much logic or coherence, or it may be kept purposefully vague for hidden reasons. What is needed in such cases is a clarification and sorting out, but because many educators lack the understandings and skills that promote such clarification, they continue to drift in a sea of rhetoric and patchwork panaceas. Indeed, there is much dissatisfaction with education today, and much that goes on in contemporary schools attests to the drift. Attempts to solve such problems often result in a chaotic jumble of programs and superficial bickering among ideological camps.

"Practical" educators assume that we should throw out philosophical theory and get on with the "real" tasks at hand. The problem with this "practical" outlook is that its advocates approach educational problems with the same old attitudes and remedies. They assume that they can read the face of an intelligible universe unencumbered by "ivory tower" intellectual schemes. That outlook itself is a "theory," a set of assumptions for which the last word has yet to be said. It seems that educators, like everyone else, are caught up in their own humanity. There is no certainty with regard to all facets of life in *any* known approach to education, for the perfect approach has not yet been invented. We are left with the necessity to *think* about what we do, to attempt to reason out and justify our actions so that they are coherent, meaningful, and directed toward desirable educational ends.

Some maintain that no logical connections can be made between philosophical thought and the practical world of education; that is, philosophical reflection has no necessary logical connection with what ought to be done in a practical educational context. This may be true, but it has not kept philosophers and educators from attempting to make such connections. There may well be no logical connection between, for example, Plato's view of the good society and his construction of educational means to achieve this society. Many people have made such connections (whether logical or otherwise), however, and educational programs have been developed and instituted, drawing heavily upon Plato and other philosophers in the process.

This debt can be seen in recommendations put forward concerning the aims and purposes of education, curriculum content, teaching methods, and many other areas of educational endeavor. Although Plato lived over two thousand years ago, what he and his contemporaries said and thought about life and education still influence us—even if we are unaware of it. Part of the task of the student of education, then, is to become familiar with leading philosophical ideas about education and to understand the impact they have had and continue to have on our thinking.

Certain ideas and recommendations about education have a great deal of influence today, particularly in shaping public attitudes about "back to the basics" and "moral values" education. People who advocate such things may lack any philosophical sophistication or knowledge of the origin of these notions, but philosophers have often recommended certain "basics" and "values" that figure in educational recommendations. Philosophical traditions and recommendations are part of the working ideas and traditions of our society today. Many of us assume these things to be true and obvious without any clear idea of why. Thus, we may blindly accept many educational recommendations without knowing whether they are justified. The student who seeks to become an educator needs to be informed about these ideas and traditions in order to sift through rhetoric and argument and to reach a more intelligent understanding of the current scene.

THEORY AND PRACTICE IN EDUCATION

Some philosophers of education make little distinction between philosophy of education and educational theory. In 1942, for example, John S. Brubacher wrote that "several theories or philosophies" could be used as guides to solutions of educational problems. In this view, philosophy of education is a discipline "peculiarly competent to tell what should be done both now and later on." Philosophy of education, then, has much to offer in the way of theory, even though there may be a great deal of disagreement among philosophers as to what theory or theories to carry out. In Brubacher's view, the need for philosophy becomes apparent when the educator, parent, or learner confronts questions about the proper aims and means of education.

If we try to select content or choose a method, we must decide what we are trying to do and what aims or objectives are actually being proposed in the process. The development of educational aims, however, is complicated and gives rise to numerous philosophical questions: Are there "true" aims? Does the nature of life and the universe itself demand certain aims? Can we know what the "proper" aims of education are? Do aims flow from the practical activities of life and the problems confronting human beings in the everyday world?

In deciding what the aims should be, one is also confronted with determining what kinds of curricula and techniques will be most suitable for achieving those aims. Many new questions must then be confronted—philosophical questions concerning the nature of knowledge, learning, teaching, and so on. Brubacher felt that few educators could pursue such questions or give adequate responses about why schools should be operated in particular ways. He maintained that the study of philosophy of education would help educators build more adequate theoretical bases and hence more adequate education.

By 1955, Brubacher was attempting to get educators to focus their attention on pressing problems and use philosophical theory to deal with them. He identified six popular assumptions about education that philosophy of education could address: (1) anxiety that education is adrift; (2) concern that educational aims are vague, conflicting, and not conducive to loyalty; (3) beliefs that standards have been seriously relaxed; (4) uncertainty about the role of education in a democratic society; (5) concern that schools give students too much freedom and do not foster respect for authority and control; and (6) fears that schools have become too secular and neglect religion. These problems sound familiar because they are perhaps as significant today as they were when Brubacher wrote about them. His point that philosophy of education could help solve them may not be accepted on a much wider scale today than it was in 1955, but his insistence that these and other pressing issues cannot be treated satisfactorily without an understanding of philosophical theories that deal with the underlying assumptions about education in our culture still seems valid.

Brubacher, of course, did not originate the notion that philosophy and educational theory are connected. This connection has a long tradition, but perhaps the most thoroughgoing link between the two was made by John Dewey in *Democracy and Education*, first published in 1916. According to Dewey, the theory of education is a set of "generalizations" and "abstractions" about education. Most people probably think abstraction is useless in practical matters, but Dewey maintained that it can serve a useful purpose as "an indispensable trait in the reflective direction of activity." In this sense, theoretical abstractions or generalized meanings have a connection with actual, practical affairs. Things are generalized so that they may have broader application. A theory of education contains generalizations that are applicable to many situations. Theory becomes abstract in the remote sense when it ignores practical application. In the sense of useful theory, however, abstraction broadens meanings to include any person or situation in like circumstances.

For example, Dewey observed that a person may know many things that she cannot express. Such knowledge remains merely personal and cannot be shared unless it is abstracted or, to put it another way, expressed in some public language; then it can be shared and critically analyzed for improvement. In other words, for a person to share her thoughts and experiences she must consider the experience of others and put her ideas in language they can understand. Not only must experience be shared, it must be taken back into practice for testing. In this way, practice serves to expand theory and direct it toward new possibilities.

Practically everyone has had at least some experience with this because all of us have shared our experience of a particular thing or process with others. We may question friends or acquaintances about how they accomplished something, or we will tell them how we did it and recommend our way to them. Experienced teachers do this quite often. They exchange ideas and methods that they have found fruitful in achieving certain educational goals. In this sense, they are theorizing or building theory, even though it may not be very sophisticated. One person tries another's approach and afterward discusses it. They find ways to redefine goals and vary, expand, or redirect the approaches for future use.

The very "practical" matter of approaches and goals has been generalized, or abstracted. These approaches and goals have been tested and found successful, or they have been altered, improved, or found wanting. In this way, theory and practice may build upon each other. Look, for example, at Darwin's theory of the origin of species. Most of the central ideas of his theory had been enunciated by others. Even his investigations of flora and fauna during the famous voyage of the *Beagle*, while contributing to biological discoveries, did not add much to the theory itself. What was of major significance for theory was the manner in which Darwin connected the many disparate elements into a coherent, comprehensive, and logical system. Thus, the world gained a renowned theory that has influenced us all.

In the more sophisticated meaning of *theory*, the role of philosophy becomes crucial. In Dewey's view, philosophy deals with aims, ideas, and processes in a certain totality, generality, or ultimateness. It involves an attempt to comprehend varied details of life and the world and to organize them into an inclusive whole. It also involves a philosophical attitude, indicated by endeavors to achieve unified, consistent, and comprehensive outlooks on human experience. This is often what is meant by the "love of wisdom." Complete finality and certainty of knowledge are always lacking, however, because philosophy may also be characterized as "the pursuit of wisdom"; that is, it involves a continual search. Thus, terms like *totality* and *ultimateness* refer more to a consistency of attitude than to any final certainty of knowledge. Philosophy, then, is connected with thinking about and seeking what is possible, not arriving at complete knowledge. It does not furnish solutions so much as it defines difficulties and suggests methods for dealing with solutions or clarifying them.

The philosophical demand for a total attitude, Dewey held, arises out of the need to integrate activities among the conflicting interests of life. It is an effort to develop a comprehensive point of view with which to resolve conflicts and to restore some consistency in life. This is shown in philosophers' efforts to attack the puzzles of life and bring clarity to confused situations.

This kind of effort may also involve the struggles of individuals to bring continuity to their own lives, but philosophy at its most comprehensive level seeks to deal with discrepancies and puzzles that affect the community as a whole.

When coupled with education, this aspect of philosophy becomes clearer because education is one of those human activities that concern the whole community. To Dewey, education offers a vantage ground "from which to penetrate to the human, as distinct from the technical, significance of philosophic discussion." When philosophy is viewed from the standpoint of education, the life situations it studies are never far from view. As Dewey put it: "If we are willing to conceive education as the process of forming fundamental dispositions, intellectual and emotional, toward nature and our fellow men, philosophy may even be defined as *the general theory of education.*"

If we examine the basic points thus far discussed, we will see that certain elements stand out. First, there is the assertion that philosophy can enable us to build more adequate educational theory. This assertion is based on several points, one of which is philosophy's role in clarifying aims and methods and critically analyzing cultural assumptions about education. More central, however, is the role of philosophy in providing overall perspective and comprehensiveness. This role is illustrated by the philosophical attitude of "thinking about what is possible"; this effort is largely dominated by concern for integration and continuity. Philosophy, in this sense, may be considered as educational theory in the most general sense.

Educational theory, however, may also include more than philosophy because it uses relevant contributions from many fields. Theory serves as a guide to organize thought about education, and it helps provide order and clarity to the process. Theory serves as a directive to educational practice by helping educators clarify and organize educational practice reflectively. A common element in all of these points is that central to philosophical and theoretical discourse on education is (1) the necessity for reflection and (2) the organization of ideas for eventual practical activity.

A common assumption many people make is that *good* theory can be directly applied to practical matters—that it can be "plugged" into ongoing practical situations and yield direct results. If the theory does not work, it is obviously not a good theory. This assumption may be the reason that many people show disdain for theory and call it impractical, for few if any educational theories can be applied directly to practical conditions in the sense that one applies aspirin to a headache. Those who attempt such applications of theory seldom fail to be disappointed.

Why this is so relates to the characteristics of both theory and practice. The point has been made that theory and practice must be connected and that each can inform and expand the other. To affirm a connection, however, is far from saying that there is a direct or one-to-one relationship between theory and practice. Dewey, who said that philosophy is the general theory of education, also said, "It is an idea of what is possible, not a record of accomplished fact. Hence, it is hypothetical, like all thinking." In *Contemporary*

[Pratte]

Theories of Education (1971), Richard Pratte characterized educational theory as a directive for practice; but he also noted that "a theory is an instrument, a guide to thought, not necessarily a guide to direct practice."

Yet theory serves a practical function in many ways, and if the "plug-in" approach is usually doomed to failure, it is often not so much the fault of any given theory as it is its application. One practical feature of theory is its *general* nature. It contains ideas and propositions that allow for comparison, contrast, readjustment, and criticism from a variety of sources because they are stated in a public sense and are not locked into only the subjective thoughts of private individuals.

THEORY

Theoretical discourse invites argument and counterargument, for otherwise it ceases to be theoretical and passes into dogma or accepted "fact." Theory is also an aid in providing us with a more comprehensive perspective. It helps us evaluate or place in perspective what it is we are doing or could be doing. It helps us locate ourselves in relation to an overall or larger perspective. In addition, theory invites an attitude of seeking out possibilities, an attitude that constantly seeks a new or better way. Finally, theory aids in defining difficulties, clarifying confusions in thought and language, and sorting out and organizing plans for action. It provides rationale and gives direction to practical activity.

PRACTICE

Practice, on the other hand, provides both raw materials and testing grounds for theory. The value of a theory may well reside in what difference it makes in the practical world by helping us in our approach to everyday educational endeavor. William James was fond of quoting the biblical passage, "By their fruits shall ye know them"; it is the character of consequences or outcomes that helps determine the validity of any theory. If a theory does not help us communicate better, criticize our assumptions and actions, gain perspective, seek out new possibilities, and order and direct practice, then we had better let it go or revise it in new directions. It has lost its connection with practice, and the fruitful interchange has ceased.

These, then, are some of the practical aspects of theory. Prescription of detailed classroom activities, however, is seldom one of the practical applications. The reasons for this are obvious enough if we examine the characteristics of theory. A major characteristic is that theory suggests possibilities; however, this does not mean that any theory could foresee all the possible practical situations confronting an educator in the fluid world of ongoing activity. Conditions change, people come and go, and even individual persons change and develop; so it is virtually impossible to establish preexisting rubrics that will always be applicable. The suggestion of possibilities aids us in organizing and directing our thinking about educational activity: it does not dictate the activity.

What theory accomplishes is that it helps us organize specific practices or practical activities with a sense of direction, purpose, and coherence. It gives administration, curriculum, and our daily plans order and organization, and it aids us in constructing, for example, specific teaching and learning objectives and accompanying methods and techniques. This is the practical connection of educational theory to educational practice; and in this sense, educational theory can be applied to educational practice.

THE QUEST IN PHILOSOPHY OF EDUCATION

An era of transition from an old order to a new one seems to be appearing. Some observers say that we are suffering so much from the impact of rapid technological development that we are stumbling blindly from "future shock," unable to deal with our problems. Others say that we are leaving the modern era and are entering a postmodern era, a time of experimentation when old values are being altered in various aspects of life, including education. Perhaps every era faces similar difficulties of transition. Whatever the case, there is a great deal of confusion at present; and as far as we can tell, no synthesis or coalescence has been achieved. It often seems that negativeness, even disillusionment, is the rule rather than the exception. It has led some social theorists to call for redefinition and renewal of communal life. For example, Robert Bellah and his associates, in *The Good Society* (1991), call for a restoration of community.

The postmodern attitude has definitely shaken philosophy. A recent collection entitled *After Philosophy: End or Transformation?* (1987) gives an indication of the contemporary philosophical temperament. In Europe, for example, Jacques Derrida and Michel Foucault have forcefully criticized established philosophical and cultural assumptions. Critical philosophers, such as Jurgen Habermas, have sought to go beyond Marxism and understand the bases of human communication. In the United States, Richard Rorty has criticized old ways of thinking and has attempted to develop a new perspective that may be called *postmodern neopragmatism.* Such developments, which often start on the unorthodox fringes, have a way of dislodging what once seemed to be secure philosophical modes of thought. In the final analysis, perhaps the only thing we can be sure about is that changing times demand new ways of thinking.

Thus, uncertainty seems to be a fact of life, and old ideas are being challenged. Perhaps what it truly shows is that the philosophical task, despite contemporary movements this way or that, is still a search for wisdom. We believe that it is an inclusive search requiring many voices. From Plato down through history, there have been attempts to see humanity's development in some understandable, coherent, and orderly fashion. Descartes believed that he was beginning anew to construct an orderly way of thinking that would be incontestable. This same attitude is found in Kant, Hegel, Marx, and some contemporary philosophers. More recently, the feeling for such philosophical order and categorization has either vanished or has been seriously modified. Dewey talked about facts and propositions but couched them in the rhetoric of "warranted assertibility." His philosophical descendant, Richard Rorty, has left the analytic paradigm and has recommended a "conversation of culture" that includes many philosophical voices that may be admired or critiqued. Some observers say that we are in a postmodernist era when everything is subject to flux and change and old absolutes are deposed by new uncertainties.

The current mood in philosophy of education is generally toward understanding and dealing with problems and issues in context rather than a return to the idea that the individual, society, and education can be understood in an overriding system of thought. The conviction that a set of universal principles or a system of thought can explain the multitude of variables that pervade personal and social relations in education is gone. There is also an increased awareness of the danger that system-building itself can lead to circumstances in which we explain actions and events in terms of great and overriding principles (whether they be Kant's categorical imperatives or Descartes's "clear and distinct ideas") rather than in terms of the actual contexts of activities and events.

Thus, philosophical thinking in education has moved into a new arena. The emphasis is not on system development but rather on human predicaments in specific contexts. If philosophers no longer seek to provide general explanations and descriptions of the overriding scheme of things, a reasonable query may be "Who will?" Harry S. Broudy observed (in "Philosophy of Education Between Yearbooks" [1979]) that many people will continue to identify philosophy with the search for wisdom, and they will look to philosophy of education for more than "logical purity and wholesome skepticism." They are not and do not want educators and educational institutions to be neutral about their children's futures.

This expectation for philosophical guidance in education may be unwarranted, as recent developments in philosophy of education seem to declare; but as Broudy put it, "if the philosophy of education ignores or merely makes fun of this need, it will be satisfied by nonphilosophical sources." Broudy emphasized certain things that educators have a right to expect from philosophy of education, including attention to the problems of education in general and schooling in particular, clarification of educational concepts and issues, and rational discourse and freedom of inquiry. One direction educational discourse has been taking is represented by Stanley Aronowitz and Henry Giroux in *Postmodern Education: Politics, Culture, and Social Criticism* (1991); they advocate a radical reappraisal and change in our approaches to education.

Despite the uncertainties presented by the current state of philosophy of education, it is still evident that the philosophical task is one of constant probing and inquiry. It is participation in the questioning and challenging attitude of philosophy that this book hopes to encourage among educators. This inquisitive restlessness makes philosophy an enduring human enterprise, one that is never quite completed but is always in the making. In the final analysis, the search for wisdom may simply be an intensive search for better ways of thinking about human predicaments. This search involves education no less than other human concerns. Philosophy, when undertaken in this vein, is not a separate and exclusive search but is part of human life and education.

DEVELOPING A PHILOSOPHICAL PERSPECTIVE ON EDUCATION

Unless educators can see that philosophy of education makes a difference in their outlook or activity, they may fail to use it or may even ignore it altogether. Thus, they must translate philosophical ideas and thought patterns in ways that can lead to more consciously directed activity. This does not mean an uncritical acceptance of this or that principle or this or that system; rather, it means a responsible examination of philosophy of education in light of existing societal and educational conditions. As conditions change, the need to reexamine perspective and outlook may arise. Philosophy of education cannot be viewed in a vacuum but must be seen in the interplay with other forces.

Some philosophers of education have suggested a responsible eclecticism in building a personal philosophy of education. In suggesting this approach, they point out that no two people are at the same level in their intellectual and psychological development. Furthermore, perhaps no single educational philosophy may be suitable at any particular moment because philosophies have their ebb and flow and their value depends on particular needs of the times. This may mean striking out in new philosophical directions, but it may also include critical examination of older philosophies for the insights they may provide. It may also mean going to philosophy outside our own cultural traditions. Eastern philosophy, for example, provides contrasts to Western philosophical traditions and offers alternative vantage points from which to view education. Indeed, the postmodern temperament calls for inclusion of different and divergent ways of thinking.

Developing a philosophical perspective on education is not easy. It is, however, necessary if a person wants to become an effective professional educator. A philosophical perspective helps one see the interaction among students, curriculum, administration, and goals; thus, philosophy becomes very practical. Most importantly, however, educators need a philosophical perspective in order to give depth and breadth of meaning and direction to their personal and professional endeavors. This is not to say that they must have a particular philosophical perspective; instead, educators must think deeply about what they do. There is no one way to develop a philosophical perspective, yet some observations can be made that may assist in developing a perspective. One approach, adapted from Charles Marler (1975), is as follows:

1. *Becoming aware of education as more than school or classroom activities.* It is easy for a classroom teacher or school administrator to get bogged down in the day-to-day details of operating schools. There is little time for

reflection about what one does if one becomes enmeshed in meaningless details or loses sight of desirable objectives. An educator is often harried, and it is common to use this as an excuse for not thinking reflectively. For example, the classroom teacher may become convinced that the sum total of education is what happens in the classroom. The school principal may believe that the most important thing is an orderly master schedule or the administrative flow chart. However, education is interrelated with the development and direction a society takes, and a teacher must become aware of this. In the broadest sense, education involves at least two things: (1) passing on the cultural heritage from one generation to the next so that at least essential social and cultural continuity exists and (2) providing the skills, abilities, and understanding to develop new ways of doing things in light of changing conditions. Becoming aware of education in these terms is a necessary ingredient for developing a philosophical perspective.

2. *Becoming aware that philosophy provides a comprehensive view of education.* An educator may develop a broad understanding of education but may lack a sense of focus and organization. Philosophy as a disciplined study is concerned with developing a coherent, logical, and comprehensive outlook. Philosophy has traditionally involved itself with a wide range of issues and problems, and education has long been important to most philosophers. Thus, an extensive body of literature is available to help the educator develop understanding of education as a broadly based enterprise. When the educator becomes aware that philosophy contains comprehensive perspectives and tools for developing organized and structured views, the basic groundwork for a philosophical perspective on education has been laid.

3. *Studying the historical development of philosophical ideas and their relation to education.* The study of philosophical ideas does not guarantee that a person will become an accomplished philosopher or will be conscious of all of the various forces affecting education. It does provide, however, a chronological and systematic body of knowledge one can use to understand what has happened in educational thought up to the present. It shows how aims, objectives, and practices have evolved and how what we often consider new departures in education are really only restatements of ideas that go back for centuries. It may also help one to develop an appreciation of educational traditions and provide the basis for a more intelligent and critical evaluation of such traditions. Not only does it give us a sense of continuity, it provides a basis for developing new ideas and a vantage point from which to evaluate new aims and practices.

4. *Studying the philosophical treatment and analysis of specific issues in education.* Philosophically, there is a need for both a broad perspective and one that focuses on particular problems. Such problems as equality of educational opportunity, moral education, human sexuality, religion, and political ideologies may be looked at from the standpoint of psychology, theology, sociology, and political science. Yet philosophical analysis has a unique contribution in that it can provide a look at such problems in a critical, holistic, and

ethical fashion. It examines the interrelationship of the problem with other aspects of life and connects novel aspects of the problem with familiar traditions. It helps us organize the various elements of the problem in a clear and concise way so that we can treat it more intelligently. Philosophy helps us identify and express problems in clear and logical language.

5. *Engaging in continuing personal research, reading, and study in philosophy of education.* To appreciate the uses of philosophical thinking, an individual must become personally committed to continuing study. One way this can be accomplished is to become actively involved in "doing" philosophy. Such doing may involve creating new outlooks through combining, interrelating, and drawing connections from philosophical ideas. Although the classroom teacher may argue that professional duties do not allow time for such doing, professional and personal growth often depend on independent reading that provides a broader base for understanding educational problems and issues. An educator can also enhance educational perspectives by attending professional meetings where philosophical issues are discussed. Primarily, the educator must see the need for personal involvement in order to develop a philosophical attitude toward educational problems.

6. *Developing a philosophical perspective and internalizing it.* When a person becomes deeply engaged in philosophical activity, there is usually a continuous reassessment and reevaluation of one's value system, social mores, authority constructs, and educational beliefs. This internal-external process, in which personal values and beliefs are held up against other philosophical perspectives, enables us to begin to readjust and modify or strengthen our ideas. This process internalizes a philosophical perspective to the point where individuals not only think about philosophical ideas but where such ideas become a part of their mode of professional behavior and outlook on life.

ORGANIZATION OF THE BOOK

This book presents several philosophical positions or schools of thought. It is intended for introductory study and shows philosophical developments in an organized and orderly fashion. This approach enables the reader to grasp the essential elements and basic principles of each philosophy and to see how they have influenced educational theory and practice. However, the organization of the book by schools of thought is not meant to foster slavish emulation of any one school, combinations of schools, or even a school approach. The usefulness of our approach lies in showing how past philosophy developed, how it has been organized, and how it has been used to help devise educational policies and practices. After all, the major role of philosophy in education is not to formulate some grand scheme but to help develop the educator's thinking capacities.

As each chapter tries to show, it was the creative genius of individuals combined with particular cultural developments that produced philosophies of education. Individual philosophers seldom set out simply to construct a system, and many of them reject being identified with any system or school of thought. The cutting edge of philosophy is not a philosophical system but free and wide-ranging thought grappling with human problems. Perhaps the test of any era of human history is not whether it built a thought system to bind together irreconcilable conflicts but how it enabled conflicts to be resolved. However, each era must also write its own "philosophy" or consensus anew. This does not imply that old ideas are rejected but rather that thinking goes on, that a consideration of issues and problems is made, and that some common grounds are found.

Each of the chapters gives the historical development of a given philosophy, its current status, how it has influenced education, and a critique of its leading ideas. Taken together, these chapters provide a chronological development of philosophy of education. In addition, each chapter is followed by short selected readings from major philosophers who have been identified with that philosophy. The selections have been carefully chosen to illustrate leading themes in each chapter. They have also been selected to furnish students with primary source materials of sufficient length and depth to provide some firsthand acquaintance with leading works in the field. These selections are meant to give insight without overwhelming students and to whet their appetite to do further reading in philosophy of education.

The material presented in this book can be used in various ways, depending upon the previous background and knowledge of the readers, their motivations and interests, and the reciprocal relationship that exists between teacher and students. It is, however, introductory, and the development of a mature grasp of philosophy of education requires practical experience and concentrated study. This approach can help students establish foundations for future growth, for there are many sound and useful ideas from the past upon which to build. Students who attempt to understand education philosophically are certainly handicapped if they have no knowledge of what has been done before, and they may try to reinvent old educational wheels. The approach involves more than just schools of thought but includes critiques of each school and a general exploration of the connection between traditional and contemporary philosophy of education.

Finally, it should be noted that the text is intended as an introduction to the philosophical foundations of education and does not pretend to invite converts to any particular philosophy. It is designed for the student in education and is not written for the advanced student in philosophy. It attempts to be comprehensive in an introductory way and lays no claims to advanced specialization in philosophy of education. Numerous and excellent works are readily available for that purpose, many of which are cited in the chapter bibliographies and the Selected Bibliography.

The study of philosophy of education can be an exciting and challenging venture that allows us to encounter some of the great and enduring ideas of human thought. It enables us to understand what has gone on in the past in education and to develop the kind of perspective and intellectual tools that will help us deal with the educational problems of today and the years ahead.

SELECTED READINGS

Aronowitz, Stanley, & Giroux, Henry A. *Postmodern Education: Politics, Culture, and Social Criticism.* Minneapolis: University of Minnesota Press, 1991. A general treatment of a radical postmodern perspective on education. It provides an overview of the interdisciplinary approach to education favored by many postmodern educational theorists.

Baynes, Kenneth et al., eds. *After Philosophy: End or Transformation?* Cambridge, MA: The MIT Press, 1987. A collection of readings selected from the works of leading contemporary philosophers. It provides a good overview of the ferment in philosophical discourse.

Bellah, Robert N. et al. *The Good Society.* New York: Knopf, 1991. This is an influential work calling for the restoration of community and the need for a public philosophy attuned to the dynamics of social life.

Dewey, John. *Democracy and Education: An Introduction to the Philosophy of Education.* New York: Macmillan, 1961 (1916). A classic statement of pragmatism in philosophy of education, this book provides an important statement by Dewey that has exerted a great deal of influence on philosophy of education.

Educational Theory. 31(2):1–95, Winter 1981. This particular issue, devoted to a critical review of *Philosophy and Education: The Eightieth Yearbook of the National Society for the Study of Education,* contains review articles from philosophers of education and leaders from other fields of education. It is valuable in showing the variety of recent perceptions in philosophy of education.

Pratte, Richard. *Contemporary Theories of Education.* Scranton, PA: International Textbook, 1971. A treatment of the role philosophy can play in developing theory in education. Pratte's treatment is representative of an analytic approach in philosophy of education.

Soltis, Jonas, ed. *Philosophy and Education. Eightieth Yearbook of the National Society for the Study of Education, Part I.* Chicago: National Society for the Study of Education, 1981. A collection of essays on the field of philosophy of education in the 1980s, this volume purports to show the potential uses of philosophy for educators. It represents the status and development of the philosophy of education in the early 1980s.

———, ed. *Teachers College Record* 81(2):127–248, Winter 1979. A special issue edited by Jonas Soltis, in which all of the articles are devoted to the developments in the philosophy of education from midcentury to the late 1970s. This publication is particularly valuable in showing relatively recent historical changes in the field.

1

Idealism and Education

Idealism is perhaps the oldest systematic philosophy in Western culture, dating back at least as early as Plato in ancient Greece. Of course, there was philosophy and there were philosophers before Plato, but it was Plato who developed one of the most influential philosophies dealing with education.

Generally, idealists believe that ideas are the only true reality. It is not that all idealists reject matter (the material world). Rather, they hold that the material world is characterized by change, instability, and uncertainty while some ideas are enduring. Thus, *idea-ism* might be a more correct descriptive term for this philosophy. However, we must guard against oversimplification and attempt to get at a fuller and more wide-ranging understanding of this complex philosophy.

In order to achieve a more adequate understanding of idealism, it is necessary to examine the works of selected outstanding philosophers who are usually associated with this philosophy. No two philosophers ever agree on every point, so to understand idealism or any other school of thought properly, it is wise to examine the various approaches of individual philosophers. This will be accomplished by an exploration of three areas: Platonic idealism, religious idealism, and modern idealism and its characteristics.

THE DEVELOPMENT OF IDEALISM

One of the leading thinkers of ancient Greece was Socrates (469–399 BC), who challenged the material concerns of his contemporaries. Socrates went about Athens questioning its citizens, particularly the Sophists, for their "unexamined" way of life. Socrates saw himself as a kind of gadfly who prodded people into thinking. He was later brought to trial in Athens and executed for his beliefs. Although Socrates' ideas were only transmitted orally through a dialectic question-and-answer approach, Plato wrote them down and illustrated both the Socratic method and Socrates' thinking.

It has often been debated whether Plato added to these dialogues, since he wrote about them many years after they occurred. The general view is that Plato added a great deal and put the dialogues in a literary form that has had enduring value. Since the ideas of both Socrates and Plato are considered almost indistinguishable today, scholars generally refer to these writings as Platonic philosophy.

Platonic Idealism

Plato (427–347 BC)

Plato was a Greek philosopher who started as a disciple of Socrates and remained an ardent admirer throughout his life. Plato is largely known for his writings in which Socrates is the protagonist in a series of dialogues dealing with almost every conceivable topic. Two of his most famous works are the *Republic* and the *Laws*. After Socrates' death, Plato opened his own school, the Academy, where students and professors engaged in a dialectical approach to problems.

According to Plato, people should concern themselves primarily with the search for truth. Since truth is perfect and eternal, it cannot therefore be found in the world of matter, which is imperfect and constantly changing. Mathematics demonstrates that eternal truths are possible. Such concepts as $2 + 2 = 4$ or that all points of a perfect circle are equidistant from the center always have been true (even before people discovered them), are true, and always will be true. Mathematics shows that universal truths with which everyone can agree can be found, but mathematics constitutes only one field of knowledge. Plato believed that we must search for other universal truths in such areas as politics, religion, and education; hence, the search for absolute truth should be the quest of the true philosopher.

In the *Republic*, Plato wrote about the separation of the world of ideas from the world of matter. The world of ideas (or forms) has the Good as its highest point—the source of all true knowledge. The world of matter, the ever-changing world of sensory data, is not to be trusted. People need, as much as possible, to free themselves from a concern with matter so that they can advance toward the Good. This can be done by transcending matter through the use of the dialectic (or critical discussion) in which one moves from mere opinion to true knowledge.

We might describe the dialectic as follows: All thinking begins with a thesis or point of view, such as "War is evil." We might support this view by pointing out that war causes people to be killed, disrupts families, destroys cities, and has adverse moral effects. As long as we encounter only people of similar persuasion, we are not likely to alter our point of view. However, when we encounter the antithesis (or opposite point of view) that "War is good," we are forced both to reexamine and to defend our position. Arguments advanced to support the notion that war is good may include the belief that war promotes bravery, helps keep down population, and produces many technical benefits for us through war research. Simply put, the dialectic looks at both sides of an issue. Assuming that our antagonists are philosophers seriously interested in getting to the truth of the problem of whether war is good or evil, they will engage in a dialogue in which both advancement and retrenchment may occur.

Plato believed that, given ample time to argue their positions, the two discussants would come closer to agreement, or synthesis, and therefore closer to truth (which may be that war has both good and bad aspects). This kind of dialectic discussion could not be accomplished by those who simply argued to win or who would not maintain a critical perspective. It is for this reason that Plato thought preparation in the dialectic should involve a lengthy period of education beginning with studies in mathematics. He was particularly critical of inexperienced people who used the dialectic, for he believed that people are not mature enough for training in the dialectic until age thirty.

Plato saw the dialectic as a vehicle for assisting people in moving from a concern with the material world to a concern with the world of ideas. Supposedly, the dialectic crosses the "divided line" between matter and idea. The process begins in the world of matter with the use of the brain, the tongue, gestures, and so forth; but it ends in the world of ideas with the discovery of truth. In the Allegory of the Cave, Plato depicted prisoners chained in a world of darkness, seeing only shadows on a far cave wall that they took for reality. Imagine one of these prisoners freed from his chains, advancing up a steep slope and into the sunlight, and eventually able to see the sun, realizing it as the true source of heat and light. He would be happy in his true knowledge and would wish to contemplate it even more. Yet, when he remembers his friends in the cave and returns to tell them of the real world outside, they will not listen to someone who cannot now compete with them in their knowledge of shadows. If the fortunate one insists upon freeing the prisoners, they may even kill him.

The meaning of the allegory is this: we ourselves are living in a cave of shadows and illusions, chained by our ignorance and apathy. When we begin to loosen ourselves from our chains, it is the beginning of our education; the steep ascent represents the dialectic that will carry us from the world of matter to the world of ideas—even to a contemplation of the Good represented by the sun. Note Plato's admonition that the man, now the philosopher, who has advanced into the realm of true knowledge must return to the cave to bring enlightenment to the others. This points to Plato's strong belief that philosophizing should be not only an intellectual affair but that the philosopher also has a duty to share his learning with others, doing this even in the face of adversity or death.

Plato did not think that people create knowledge; rather, they discover it. In another interesting myth, he conjectured that the human soul once had true knowledge, but lost it by being placed in a material body that distorted and corrupted that knowledge. Thus, people have the arduous task of trying to remember what they once knew. This "Doctrine of Reminiscence" is illustrated by Socrates, who spoke of himself as a midwife who found men pregnant with knowledge, but knowledge that had not been born or realized. Through his discussions with people, Socrates sought to aid them in giving birth to ideas that in some cases they never knew they had. In the *Meno*, Plato described Socrates' meeting with a slave boy; through skillful questioning, Socrates shows that the boy knows the Pythagorean theorem even though he does not know that he knows it.

In the *Republic*, Plato proposed the kind of education that would help bring about a world in which individuals and society are moved as far as they are capable of moving toward the Good. He understood fully that most people do believe in matter as an objective reality, that there are individual differences, and that injustice and inhumanity are ways of life. He wished to create a world in which outstanding people, such as Socrates, could serve as models and would be rewarded instead of punished. Plato suggested that the state must take an active role in educational matters and that it must offer a curriculum leading bright students from a concern with concrete data toward abstract thinking.

It is interesting to note that Plato thought that girls and boys should be given an equal opportunity to develop themselves to the fullest in this respect, but those who showed little ability for abstractions should go into pursuits that would assist in the practical realities of running a society (such as industry, business, military affairs, and so forth). Those who demonstrated proficiency in the dialectic would continue their education and become philosophers in positions of power to lead the state toward the highest good. Plato believed that until philosophers were the rulers, states would never pursue the highest ideals of truth and justice.

Plato's idea was that the philosopher-king must be not only a thinker but a doer. He must supervise the affairs of the state, and like the philosopher who made his way out of the cave and yet returned to teach others, he must see that his wisdom pervades every aspect of state life. Needless to say, such a ruler would have no interest in materialism or even in ruling itself, but he would rule out of a sense of duty and obligation because he is the most fit to rule. Such a ruler could be either male or female, and Plato seriously championed the notion that women should occupy equal positions in the state, including all levels of military life. Plato's philosopher-king would not only be a person of wisdom but also a good person, since evil stems more from ignorance than from anything else.

Even though Plato's theories about society have never been fully implemented, he did attempt to establish such a society under the patronage of Dionysius II of Syracuse, but failed when the tyrant finally realized what Plato was doing. The value of Plato's ideas is that they have stimulated a great deal of thinking about the meaning and purpose of humanity, society, and education and have even entered into modern thinking and practice in many subtle ways. Who would not, for example, want the best person to lead our state,

[handwritten margin note: Connection to today]

assuming we knew what "best" really means. Today, we provide an educational system with great state involvement that has much to say about what occupation a person will eventually pursue as a result of the education he receives; and we recognize the tremendous influence of social class in education, as in Plato's utopian society, where he separated people into three classes: workers, military personnel, and rulers.

Plato influenced almost all philosophers who came after him, whether they supported or rejected his basic ideas. Indeed, there is a great deal of merit in the observation by philosopher Alfred North Whitehead that modern philosophy is but a series of footnotes to Plato.

Religious Idealism

Idealism has exerted considerable influence on Christianity. For one thing, Judaism, a precursor of Christianity, contained many beliefs compatible with idealism. The idea of one God as pure Spirit and the Universal Good can be readily recognized as compatible with idealism. For another, Greek culture was spread across the Mediterranean world by Alexander the Great. Wherever there was a solid Greek influence, there were also Greek schools; consequently, many of the writers of the New Testament had been at least partially influenced by Greek culture and philosophy. Paul, who wrote a considerable portion of the New Testament, was born Saul of Tarsus; and Tarsus was a city heavily influenced by Greek (or Hellenistic) culture and thought. One can find a heavy tinge of idealism in Paul's writings, stemming from both the Jewish and Greek traditions.

Augustine (AD 354–430)

The founders of the Roman Catholic church were also heavily influenced by idealism. Augustine was born into, and reared under, the influence of Hellenistic culture. In the *Confessions,* he described his early life of paganism and the debauchery of his youth until his conversion to Christianity. Although Augustine thought his conversion was a movement away from Greek paganism, one can find allusions to Greek philosophy and literature, specifically to Plato, interspersed throughout his Christian writings.

Augustine was very much concerned with the concept of evil and believed that since man inherited the sin of Adam, he was continuously engaged in a struggle to regain the kind of purity he had before the Fall. This idea is akin to Plato's myth about the star: souls that lived near the Good were exiled to the world of matter to suffer pain and death and struggle to return to the spiritual existence they once had.

[handwritten margin note: link to Plato]

He readily accepted Plato's notion of the "divided line" between ideas and matter, but he referred to the two worlds as the World of God and the World of Man. The World of God is the world of Spirit and the Good. The World of Man is the material world of darkness, sin, ignorance, and suffering.

Needless to say, Augustine believed one should, as much as possible, release oneself from the World of Man and enter into the World of God. Although no one was able to do this in any final sense until after death, a person could transcend this world by concentration on God, through meditation and faith.

Augustine, like Plato, felt that people do not create knowledge: God has already created it, but people can discover it through trying to find God. Since the soul is the closest thing people have to divinity, Augustine believed that we should look within our souls for the true knowledge that exists there. He thus promoted an intuitive approach to education and agreed with Plato that concentration on physical phenomena could lead us astray from the path of true knowledge. Like Plato, Augustine was a strong supporter of the dialectic method of learning: some written dialogues between Augustine and his illegitimate son Adeodatus use the dialectic to facilitate discovering true ideas about God and humanity.

Augustine's ideas about the nature of the true Christian found more acceptance among those who leaned toward a monastic conception of Christianity. Such monastics believed that the Christian should cut himself off from worldly concerns and meditate. There is an Augustinian monastic order still in existence today.

It is not surprising that idealism and religion have been closely inter-twined. Christianity, in particular, promotes the idea of God as transcendent and pure Spirit or Idea. Furthermore, there is the Christian concept that God created the world out of Himself or out of Spirit or Idea. This resembles the Platonic concept that true reality is, after all, basically idea.

Augustine's position was influenced by Plotinus, a philosopher of the third century. Plotinus believed that the primary purpose of teaching is to lead people back to an awareness of a union with the source from which all things come—the One or the Good. To achieve such a union requires perfect moral purity and intellectual effort. Plotinus believed that the Good (or God) is so great that it cannot contain itself and overflows into various levels, the highest level being pure spirit and the lowest level what we call matter. Such a view clearly indicates how the ideas of Plato might be applied to Christian thought, and Plotinus had considerable influence on Christian and Islamic philosophers.

It is not surprising that religious idealism exerted tremendous influence on education and schooling. Early Christians were quick to realize that Christianity would fare better if its adherents were given some kind of sys-tematic teaching. When they established schools, they established them in patterns with which they were familiar. Thus, many Jewish and Greek ideas about the nature of humanity, society, and God went into the Christian schools along with the distinctly Christian ideas. For centuries, the Christian church was the creator and protector of schooling; and the generations edu-cated in those schools were indoctrinated with the idealist point of view.

The mutuality of idealism and Judeo-Christian religion was brought together in a unity of European culture by the Middle Ages and afterward.

This may help explain several characteristics of modern thought. To Plato, ultimate reality is idea and our bridge to it is the mind. To the Judeo-Christian, ultimate reality is God and our bridge to it is the soul. It is a logical step to connect idea and God on the one hand, and mind and soul on the other. Thus, man's contact with ultimate reality is by means of mind and soul (or their congeners: self, consciousness, and subjectivity).

THE DEVELOPMENT OF MODERN IDEALISM

By the beginning of the modern period (here arbitrarily set with the rise of the scientific revolution in the fifteenth and sixteenth centuries), idealism had come to be largely identified with systematization and subjectivism; this identification was encouraged by the writings of René Descartes, George Berkeley, Immanuel Kant, Georg W. F. Hegel, and Josiah Royce.

René Descartes (1596–1650)

Born in the small town of La Haze, France, Descartes was educated by the Jesuits, for whom he retained admiration but with whom he developed dissatisfaction because of their doctrinaire teachings. Although his philosophical thinking challenged Catholic doctrine on many points, it seems that he remained sincere in his Catholicism.

It is difficult and misleading to classify such an original thinker as Descartes in one philosophical school. Certainly, much of his philosophy may be characterized as idealism, but he also contributed a great deal to philosophical realism and other thought systems. For present purposes, the significant works of Descartes to be considered are his celebrated *Discourse on Method* and *Meditations on the First Philosophy*.

It was principally in the *Discourse* that Descartes explored his "methodical doubt," whereby he sought to doubt all things, including his own existence. He was searching for ideas that are indubitable; he thought that if he could discover ideas that are "clear and distinct," then he would have a solid foundation upon which to build other true ideas. He found he could throw all things into doubt except one—that he himself was doubting or thinking. Although he could doubt that he was doubting, and although this factor was a mirrorlike infinite regression, Descartes could still not doubt that he was thinking. In this manner, he arrived at the famous Cartesian first principle: *Cogito, ergo sum,* "I think, therefore I am."

The Cartesian *cogito* has stimulated quite a bit of philosophical thought since Descartes's time. Traces of it may be found in many modern philosophies. However, the *cogito* is solidly in the tradition of idealism, for it reaffirms the centrality of mind in the relation of the human being to the world.

Descartes realized that even though the *cogito* was indubitable, he could not easily move from that stage to other indubitables. Objects outside the *cog-*

ito are grasped by the senses, and the senses are notoriously subject to error. Furthermore, any particular idea or thought depends upon other ideas. One cannot think of a triangle, say, without considering angles, degrees, lines, and so forth. Thus, Descartes encountered the necessity of one idea referring to another. He wanted to arrive at the idea at which further reference stopped. He found it impossible to arrive at any idea—even the indubitable *cogito*— that did not refer to something other than itself, except the idea of Perfect Being. Descartes thought he had, by arriving at Perfect Being, encountered God, the infinite and timeless Creator, the source of all things.

Thus, Descartes arrived at the two principles upon which he based his system: the *cogito* and the Deity. He had the indubitability of human thought in the *cogito,* and the foundation for all the objects of thought in the Deity. From these principles, he proceeded to build a philosophy that has, in one way or another, influenced practically all philosophy since. That some of these principles are within the tradition of idealism can be readily seen: there is finite mind contemplating objects of thought founded in God (in Platonic terms, human mind contemplating the ultimate reality of ideas). For Descartes, it was the manner in which he arrived at his principles, the method of his analysis, that brought new life into philosophy. The Cartesian method was extended into numerous fields of inquiry, including the natural sciences.

George Berkeley (1685–1753)

Berkeley was born and educated in Ireland and spent most of his professional life as a minister in the Episcopal Church of Ireland. While still a young man, he developed most of his innovative ideas, writing several treatises on philosophy, including *The Principles of Human Knowledge.* Berkeley contended that all existence depends on some mind to know it; if there are no minds, then for all intents and purposes nothing would exist unless it is perceived by the mind of God. Berkeley was attacking philosophical realism—that a material world exists independent of mind.

According to Isaac Newton, the universe is composed of material bodies moving in space and controlled by mathematical laws, such as the law of gravity. Berkeley held that no one had experienced such matter firsthand and, further, that such a theory is really a conception of mind. Berkeley thought people made a common error in assuming that such objects as trees, houses, and dogs exist where there is no mind to perceive them. Instead, to say that a thing exists means that it is perceived by some mind—*esse est percipi* (to be is to be perceived). To the classic question "Does a tree falling in the middle of a forest make some sound if there is no one around to hear it?" Berkeley would answer *no,* if we rule out the idea of it being perceived by God. There is no existence without perception, but things may exist in the sense that they are perceived by God.

Berkeley's philosophical views were strongly conditioned by his religious views. He held that immaterial substance (ideas or spirit) has been profaned by science, and science has brought on "the monstrous systems of atheists." What exists or has being is not matter: it is Spirit, Idea, or God. Berkeley's efforts may be viewed as a kind of "last-ditch" stand against the encroachments of science and scientific realism that holds to the materialistic thesis.

Berkeley refuted matter by showing that matter cannot exist except as a form of mind. We can know things only as we consciously conceive them, and when we think of the universe existing before finite minds can conceive it, we are led to assume the existence of an Omnipresent Mind lasting through all time and eternity. Thus, we might say that although people may not be conscious of the trees falling throughout eternity, God is. Berkeley was a champion of ideal realities and values whose main purpose is to make evident the existence of God and to prove that God is the true cause of all things.

It was the Scottish-born philosopher David Hume, however, who proved to be the greatest antagonist to the ideas of Berkeley. Hume was born in Edinburgh, Scotland, studied law, and later served in France as a member of the English embassy. His writings were not widely received at their inception and according to his own accounts "fell deadborn from the press." His major work, *Treatise upon Human Nature,* written when he was only twenty-six, was one of the strongest attacks on idealism ever written. While Hume began with an acceptance of the Berkeleian principle *esse est percipi,* he drew the conclusion that since all we can know are our own impressions and ideas, we have no real basis for asserting the reality of either material or spiritual substances; we cannot discover anything that justifies necessary connection or causation. To connect one occurrence with another, Hume pointed out, is merely the habit of expecting one event to follow another based upon an indefinite series of such happenings. All we can really know is that we have ideas and impressions, one following another in a kind of chaotic heap.

While Berkeley believed his philosophy had adequately dealt with atheism, Hume felt that there was no more justification for the existence of a deity than for the existence of matter. Thus, just as Berkeley thought he had destroyed atheism and materialism, so Hume believed he had also destroyed the concept of mind and God. Hume recognized that his theories resulted in skepticism that affected both religion and science, but he was unable to reconcile the paradox of a seemingly sensible world with the logic of human thought.

Today, Berkeley's ideas may appear strange, but the concepts he developed have influenced scholars in many fields. His notion of the centrality of subjective mind, and of the existence of anything being dependent upon a perceiving mind, has helped influence scholars to study further the nature of perception and the objects of thought.

Immanuel Kant (1724–1804)

The German philosopher Immanuel Kant was born in humble conditions, the son of a saddler. Educated in the schools of his hometown, Königsberg, he eventually rose to become perhaps the most famous professor that the University of Königsberg ever had. Kant is generally recognized as one of the world's great philosophers.

Among other things, Kant's work was a critique of past systems in which he sought to pull off a "Copernican revolution" in the field of philosophy. Two important works he accomplished in this effort were *Critique of Pure Reason* and *Critique of Practical Reason,* in which he sought to bring order to the divergent and warring philosophic camps of rationalism and empiricism.

The rationalists sought universal truths or ideas by which a coherent system and structure of knowledge could be deduced. They distrusted sense perception because its results are so individualized and erratic. On the other hand, the empiricists held to the immediate perceptions of experience because these are practical and connected with everyday life. They rejected rationalism because it is so abstract and disconnected from the practical.

Kant saw that the skirmishes between these divergent philosophic views were getting nowhere. He accepted the validity and reliability of modern science and believed that the constant bickering between the two positions was doing nothing to further science through the development of a compatible philosophic view of knowledge. This set the stage for Kant's philosophical task.

Kant's idealism comes from his concentration on human thought processes. The rationalist, he held, thinks analytically while the empiricist thinks synthetically. He worked out a system based on *a posteriori* (synthetic) and *a priori* (analytic) logical judgments that he called *synthetic a priori* judgments.

He thought he had arrived at a new system whereby we could have a valid knowledge of human experience established upon the scientific laws of nature. In short, we would have the best of both rationalist and empiricist insights gathered together in a unified system. This would give science the underpinnings it needed, for Kant recognized the scientific need for an empirical approach while at the same time acknowledging science's claim to discover universal laws. He recognized the importance of the human self or mind and its thought processes as a prime organizing agent in accomplishing this system.

Kant had to face the problem of the thinking subject and the object of thought. He rejected Berkeley's position that things are totally dependent on mind, for this notion would reject the possibility of scientific law. He was also caught by the problem of how subjective mind could know objective reality. He concluded that nature, objective reality, is a causal continuum, a world connected in space and time with its own internal order. Subjective mind cannot perceive this order in itself or in totality, for when subjective mind is conscious of something, it is not the thing-in-itself (*das Ding an sich*). Mind is conscious of the experience (the *phenomenon,* the aspect of the thing-in-itself). The thing-in-itself is the *noumenon.* Each experience (phenomenon) of a thing is one small additional piece of knowledge about the total thing (noumenon). Thus, all we know is the content of experience. When we go beyond this, we have entered into the rationalist argument and into speculation on the ultimate or noumenal reality of things-in-themselves, or else we have become engaged in moral and ethical considerations.

Kant explored the moral and ethical realm primarily in *Critique of Practical Reason.* His effort was to arrive at universal postulations concerning what we may call moral ideals, moral imperatives, or moral laws. This aspect of Kant's thinking was not tied to nature, so we might call this his "spiritual" side.

Many of Kant's efforts were directed toward refuting the skepticism of David Hume, for Kant wanted to show that real knowledge is possible. His efforts to do this were clouded by the uneasy manner in which he united apparently opposing themes, such as phenomenon and noumenon, the practical and the pure, and subjectivity and objectivity. The two *Critiques* illustrate this conflict, for one speaks to the logic of thought and the other to its "practical" applications. In the *Critique of Pure Reason,* the result ends up very close to Hume's skepticism, since Kant found it impossible to make absolutely universal and necessary judgments about human experience purely on rational and scientific grounds.

In his *Critique of Practical Reason,* he had to "switch gears" and go to the "practical" side, the moral and ethical side, where he thought that universal judgments could and should be made. Thus, his moral or "practical" philosophy consists of moral laws that he held to be universally valid, laws that he called "categorical imperatives"—such as, "act always so that you can will the maxim or the determining principle of your action to become a universal law."

This line of thinking permeates Kant's writings on education, a matter he considered to be of primary moral concern. He held that "the greatest and most difficult problem to which man can devote himself is the problem of education." One of the categorical imperatives he established in his moral philosophy was to treat each person as an end and never as a mere means. This imperative has greatly influenced subsequent thought about the importance of character development in education. Most of his educational statements are maxims derived from his categorical imperatives. He held that humans are the only beings who need education and that discipline is a primary ingredient of education that leads people to think and seek out "the good." Children should not simply be educated for the present but for the possibility of an improved future condition that Kant called the "idea of humanity and the whole destiny of mankind." For the most part, he thought education should consist of discipline, culture, discretion, and moral training.

The essence of education should not be simply training, however; for, to Kant, the important thing was "enlightenment" or teaching a child to think according to principles as opposed to mere random behavior. This is closely associated to his notion of will. The education of will means living according to the duties flowing from the categorical imperatives. In fact, Kant thought that an important part of the child's education was the performance of duties toward oneself and others.

We can readily see Kant's idealism in his concentration on thought processes and the nature of the relation between mind and its objects on the one hand and universal moral ideals on the other. Even though his attempts to bring about a "Copernican revolution" in philosophy failed, his systematic thought has been greatly influential on all subsequent Western philosophy, idealistic and otherwise.

Georg Wilhelm Friedrich Hegel (1770–1831)

Hegel is perhaps the capstone of idealistic philosophy in the modern era. He was born in Stuttgart, Germany, and led a rather normal and uneventful life as a youth, receiving his education until the age of eighteen in his native city. He then went to the University of Tübingen and majored in theology, graduating in 1793. He showed no particular promise as a budding philosopher, according to his professors, and for the next several years, he worked as a tutor with little economic success. He continued to study, and after he received a small inheritance from his father, his efforts became more successful. For a while, he was a lecturer at the University of Jena, then rector of a secondary school until 1816. He was a professor at the University of Heidelberg for two years and in 1818 became a professor of philosophy at the University of Berlin, remaining there until his death.

Although practically all of his major works were written before he went to Berlin, it was there that he became a prominent and overriding figure in philosophy. One can find elements of his thought in such disparate recent philosophies as Marxism, existentialism, and American pragmatism. In examining Hegel, we will look at three major aspects of his system: logic, nature, and spirit. Three of his important books are *Phenomenology of Mind, Logic,* and *Philosophy of Right.*

One of the striking characteristics of Hegel's philosophy is his logic. He thought he had developed a perfect logical system that corrected the inadequacies of Aristotelian logic. The word *dialectic* best fits Hegel's logic, and it has often been portrayed as a rather mechanical warring between thesis and antithesis, with the result being a synthesis. Yet his logic was not quite that inflexible, for it included many variations and shadings of the triadic categories. Even more to the point, Hegel conceived of thought as a continuum, not a series of mechanical synthetic unions. We could say that the continuum is characterized by a moving constant "synthesizing," a moving, growing, ever-changing thought process.

Hegel maintained that his logical system, if applied rigorously and accurately, would arrive at Absolute Idea. This is similar to the notion of unchanging ideas. The difference is that Hegel was sensitive to change (even though some of his critics charge that his explanation of change is a failure). Change, development, and movement are all central and necessary in Hegel's logic. Even Absolute Idea is really the final stage only as it concerns thought process, for Absolute Ideas have an antithesis—Nature.

To Hegel, Nature is the "otherness" of Idea, its opposite—or we may say, the difference between value and fact. He did not view Idea and Nature as finally separate, a dualism at which Descartes arrived, for to Hegel, dualisms are intolerable as any final stage: there must be a final synthesis. In holding this view, Hegel was not denying the ordinary facts, stones, and sticks of everyday life; rather, these are a lower order of reality, and not the final synthesis.

The final stage of synthesis of Idea and Nature is Spirit, and this is where the final Absolute is encountered. Absolute Spirit is manifested by the historical development of a people and by the finest works of art, religion, and philosophy. Yet, these manifestations are not Absolute Spirit—they are only its manifestations. Hegel did not think that this final and perfect end had been reached, but he did think that there was a final end toward which we move, however slowly and tortuously, and however many backslides we might make. It is in this view that Hegel's idealism is most apparent—the search for final Absolute Spirit.

One of the major features of the Hegelian system is movement toward richer, more complex, and more complete syntheses. To Hegel, history showed this movement just as much as logical thought processes did. It is as if all the universe, in Hegel's view, is moving toward completion and wholeness. Thus, in Hegel's system, if we examine any one thing, we are always referred to something else connected to it. Such was the case with the development of civilization; that is, history moved in a dialectic, rational process. Those who are familiar with the thought of Karl Marx will note similarities with Hegel, for Marx was very much indebted to him.

Hegel's thought no longer holds the preeminent position it once held. One reason for this is that his system led to a glorification of the state at the expense of individuals. It led some of his followers to believe in a mystical, foreordained destiny in the face of which individuals are powerless. In this view, individuals are mere parts or aspects of the greater, more complete and unified whole—the state.

Hegel has had considerable influence on the philosophy and theory of education. Ivan Soll has attempted to show some of Hegel's contributions to philosophy of education, contributions that must be viewed against the grand manner in which Hegel saw philosophical problems. Hegel seemed to think that in order to be truly educated, an individual must pass through the various stages of the cultural evolution of mankind. This idea is not as preposterous as it may seem at first glance, for he held that individuals benefit from all that has gone before them.

We can illustrate this idea by referring to the development of science and technology: to an individual who lived three hundred years ago, electricity was unknown except as a natural occurrence, such as lightning. Today, practically everyone depends on electric power for everyday use and has a working, practical knowledge of it entirely outside the experience of a person three hundred years ago. A contemporary person can easily learn elementary facts about electricity in a relatively short time; that is, he can "pass through" or learn an extremely important phase of our cultural evolution.

Hegel thought it was possible (if not always probable in every case) for at least some individuals to know everything essential in the history of man's collective consciousness. Today, because of the "knowledge explosion" and the increasing complexity and extent of human knowledge, such an encompassing educational ideal is naive. Yet Hegel's position retains some credibility, for there is still the need to pass on the cultural heritage and develop an understanding of people's paths to the present. Even to Hegel, the attainment of such a universal and encyclopedic knowledge was an ideal, possible only to the elite.

Josiah Royce (1855–1916)

One of the most influential spokesmen for Hegelian idealism at the beginning of the twentieth century in America was Josiah Royce. Royce maintained that the external meaning of a thing depends entirely on its internal meaning—that is, its "embodiment of purpose." He argued that "embodiment of purpose" is the criterion of "mentality," and thus the internal essence of anything is mental. Royce, like most idealists, saw his philosophical views as having great correspondence with religious teachings (the Christian religion in his case), and he spent much effort in demonstrating their compatibility.

Royce believed that ideas are essentially purposes or plans of action, and the ideas' fulfillment are plans that have been put into action. Thus, purposes are incomplete without an external world in which they are idealized, and the external world is meaningless unless it is the fulfillment of such purposes. Whose purposes are fulfilled? Royce answered in very Hegelian terms that it is the Absolute's purposes. He believed that one of the most important things for a person to develop is a sense of loyalty to moral principles and causes. This implies a spiritual overtone in which one achieves the highest good by becoming a part of the universal design. The influence of this kind of thinking is evident in the educational enterprise in terms of teaching people not only about the purposes of life but also about how they can become active participants in such purposes.

Following Kant and Hegel, there was a continuing interest in idealism in several countries. German idealism influenced an important movement in England, seen in the writings of Coleridge, Wordsworth, Carlyle, and Ruskin. The English school of idealism included such philosophers as Thomas Hill Green (whose writings included suggestions for ethical, political, and economic reforms) and Francis Herbert Bradley (who argued strongly against empiricism, utilitarianism, and naturalism).

In the United States (in addition to the work of Royce), transcendentalism (including the writings of Ralph Waldo Emerson) reflected idealist philosophy. William T. Harris was another American philosopher and educator involved with idealism. Harris later became the director of the Concord School of Philosophy, where he was active in an attempt to merge New England transcendentalism with Hegelian idealism.

IDEALISM AS A PHILOSOPHY OF EDUCATION

In general, idealists have shown a great concern for education, and many have written extensively about it. Plato made education the core of his utopian state, the Republic. Augustine gave extensive attention to the need for Christians to become aware of the importance of education. Kant and Hegel wrote about education or referred to it a great deal in their writings, and both made their living as teachers. More recently, such idealists as William Torrey Harris, Herman Horne, William Hocking, Giovanni Gentile, and J. Donald Butler have tried systematically to apply idealist principles to the theory and practice of education.

Aims of Education

Idealists generally agree that education should not only stress development of the mind but should also encourage students to focus on all things that are of lasting value. Along with Plato, they believe that the aim of education should be directed toward the search for true ideas. Another important idealist aim is character development, since the search for truth demands personal discipline and steadfast character. This aim is prevalent in the writings of Kant, Harris, Horne, Gentile, and others. What they want in society is not just the literate, knowledgeable person but the *good* person.

The Search for Truth

One of the major emphases of idealist philosophy is the search for truth. Plato thought that truth cannot be found in the world of matter because such a world is impermanent and ever-changing. At the Academy, students were encouraged to reach out toward the conceptual world of ideas rather than the perceptual world of sense data. The material world is not a real world anyway but is analogous to the shadows and illusions with which the prisoners in the cave contented themselves. Plato believed that one must break away from the chains of ignorance, greed, or apathy. Such a person would then be on the road to enlightenment and might become a philosopher. In Plato's view, philosophic wisdom or the conception of true ideas is the highest aim of education and one toward which all people should strive.

Idealists have always stressed the importance of mind over matter. Some idealists, such as Berkeley, reject the idea that matter exists by itself, whereas others, like Augustine, take the position that matter may exist in a generally detrimental way. Platonic idealists maintain that a proper education will include examining such areas as art and science, which should lead the student to the more speculative and abstract subjects of mathematics and philosophy. In any event, idealists place less stress on the study of physical and concrete areas than they do on the nonphysical and the abstract. The important thing for the idealist is to arrive at truth, and truth cannot be ever-shifting.

Some idealists, while not adhering strictly to the Platonic idea that truth is eternal and perfect, do believe that it is substantial and relatively permanent. Thus, for such idealists there may be many truths, even conflicting ones, but they are truths of a more lasting nature; consequently, many idealists favor studies in religion and the classics, two areas that contain enduring ideas.

Augustine, who was himself a Neoplatonist, agreed with Plato that the highest aim is a *search* for the truth, but he believed even more strongly than Plato that truth has overwhelming spiritual implications. The search for truth is a search for God. A true education leads one to God. Since God is pure idea, then God can be reached only through contemplation of ideas; therefore, a true education is one that is concerned with ideas rather than matter.

Other idealists have maintained that there may be levels of truth. Kant, for example, maintained the truths of both pure reason and practical reason. Hegel thought that truth is in development, moving from the simple to richer and more complex ideas. A great number of religions in the world claim that their ideas are true, even though they are in conflict with each other. This is why many idealists feel that it is not truth per se that is important but the search for truth. Even Socrates seemed to imply this position by stating that all ideas are open to challenge; a literal translation of the term *philosopher* is not a discoverer of truth but a lover of it, by implication a seeker of it.

Some modern educators who share many things with idealist philosophy have compiled lists of "Great Books" that contain disparate points of view ranging from the Bible to Marx's *Das Kapital* and from Augustine's *Confessions* to Voltaire's *Candide*. The idea behind using such books is not that any or all of them contain the final truth but rather that they contain some of the best and most lasting ideas conceived by humanity. Even though the books are different, many of the selections complement each other. What is most noticeable, however, (even with the books on science) is that they extol thinking and ideas rather than mere sense data and they concentrate on great concerns rather than on mere particulars.

One of the books often found on such lists is Herman Melville's *Moby Dick*. The reader would go awry if he found the book to be only a sea story or only concentrated on such things as the kinds of ships used or the number of fish caught. *Moby Dick* is a work containing great ideas about life, justice,

evil, and courage, truths that one needs to ponder. The aim is not to see this
or any other such book as a literal rendering of events but as something that
provides insight into ourselves and the universe of which we are a part. The
value of any major work in art or science lies in its carrying us to a higher
point in our thinking. We should not use literature and art only as vehicles for
moving us into the world of ideas, but into the realm of great ideas, ideas of
substantial value to us in understanding truth.

Idealists conceive of people as thinking beings, having minds capable of
seeking truth through reasoning and of obtaining truth by revelation. They
see them as beings who breathe, eat, and sleep but above all as thinking
beings whose thoughts can range from the ridiculous to the sublime. For
example, Plato believed that the lowest kind of thinking should be called
mere opinion. On this level, people's ideas are not well thought out and are
usually contradictory. People can aspire to wisdom, meaning they can
improve not only the way they think but also the quality of their ideas. They
can obtain ideas that are of substantial value and endurance, if not perfect
and eternal. People can come closer to this ideal by using the thinking of others or with the assistance of their writings. The important point is to direct
our thinking toward more universal concepts than those employed in the perfunctory matters of day-to-day living.

Reading the daily newspaper, for example, may be useful in learning
what is happening in the world, but the newspaper is not of great assistance
in understanding *why* something is happening. This not only demands
thought on our part but also the ability to relate the thinking of others to a
critical understanding of the problem. Some have contended that the Bible,
Moby Dick, and the *Republic* do not speak to our present concerns about pollution, weapons of mass destruction, and racial bigotry; but the idealist would
reply that although individuals may not find any particular answers to a particular problem in such works, they can find issues dealt with in a general
way that is more conducive to an understanding of specific problems and
their solutions. The Bible, for example, deals with the problems of war and
bigotry, and *Das Kapital* speaks at length about many economic problems
that are still significant. Our failure to deal adequately with our present problems is not from a lack of facts but from not using the facts in relationship to
great and encompassing ideas.

Self-Realization

The idealist emphasis on the mental and spiritual qualities of human beings
has led many idealist philosophers to concentrate on the concept of individuals and their place in education. This flavor of idealism gives it a subjectivist
orientation as opposed to its more objective aspects. The subjectivist side is
held by many to be one of idealism's most redeeming features, especially in
regard to education.

J. Donald Butler, a contemporary educator, holds that the concern for the individual is one of the primary characteristics that makes idealism still viable for modern people. His analysis of the problem, in *Idealism in Education,* indicates that self lies at the center of idealist metaphysics and (we may conclude) at the center of idealist education. Accordingly, he finds that the self is the prime reality of individual experience; that ultimate reality may be conceived as a self; and that it may be one self, a community of selves, or a Universal Self—hence, education becomes primarily concerned with self-realization. He quotes Giovanni Gentile that self-realization is the ultimate aim of education.

Such a theme has its roots deeply embedded in the idealist tradition. Descartes placed the thinking self at the very base of his metaphysical schema and his methodological search with his famous *cogito:* "I think, therefore I am." Some scholars date modern subjectivism from this development. Such thinkers as Berkeley further developed the notion of subjective reality that led to solipsism on the one hand or skepticism on the other. Berkeley's notion that things do not even exist unless perceived by the subjective individual mind, or the mind of God, gave impetus to the subjectivist trend of idealist educational thought. Since thinking and knowing are central in educational concerns, it is little wonder that idealism has exerted so much influence on educational views about individual mind and self.

Even though subjectivism is a major wing of idealism, we must not forget another equally powerful idealist notion—the relation of the part to the whole or the symbiotic relationship of the self to society. Plato could not even conceive of the individual apart from a specific place and role in society. This same theme, although enunciated differently, can be seen in Augustine's view of the connection of finite man to infinite God.

In the modern era, this theme was perhaps most fully developed by Hegel. He held that the individual must be related to the whole, for it is only in the setting of the total relationship that the real significance of a single individual can be found. This led Hegel to assert that an individual finds his true meaning in serving the state, a statement very close to Plato's idea. Hegel would even go so far as to say that one must relate oneself to the total of existence, the cosmos, in order to gain true understanding of oneself.

The impact of these ideas on education is readily apparent in the writings of Horne, Gentile, and Harris, all of whom have influenced modern education. Horne, an American idealist in the early twentieth century, maintained that education is an account of people finding themselves as an integral part of a universe of mind. The learner is a finite personality growing into the likeness of an infinite ideal. Because of the learner's immaturity, it is the role of the teacher to guide the learner along the correct paths toward the infinite. This calls for the teacher to be a well-informed person, one who must possess the knowledge and personal qualities necessary to accomplish this feat. The education of willpower becomes central here, for it is easy for the learner to be lured away from the desired path by the siren calls of corruption and untruth, a problem often discussed by Augustine and other religious thinkers. For Horne, education should encourage the "will to perfection" for the pupil and is an activity whereby one shapes oneself into the likeness of God—a task that requires eternal life for its fulfillment.

[Gentile] Gentile, the Italian idealist, thought that the individual is not only a part of a community of minds but connected with the mind of God; hence, all education is religious education. He maintained that one of the primary functions of education is to open the soul to God.

Harris, an American educator and philosopher, proposed that education should lead people to what he called "a third level of enlightenment." This involves the individual becoming aware of the spiritual nature of all things, including union with God and personal immortality. The influence of Hegel's thought is prominent in Harris's educational philosophy, particularly where he recommends taking the student up through insight into the personal nature of the Absolute. For Harris, human development and education are a series of dialectic experiences.

[Summary] Consequently, we may conclude that self-realization is a central aim of idealist education, but this does not imply that the self is realized in isolation. The individual self is a part and can only have meaning in the larger context.

Character Development

Idealists have given considerable attention not only to the search for truth but also to the persons involved in it. The teacher whom idealists favor is philosophically oriented, one who can assist students in choosing important material and infuse them with a desire to improve their thinking in the deepest possible way. Perhaps the best way to understand this is by looking at Socrates as a prototype of the teacher the idealist would like to have. Socrates spent a great deal of time analyzing and discussing ideas with others, and he was deeply committed to action based on reflection. The idealist-oriented teacher would seek to have these Socratic characteristics and would encourage students to better their thinking and to better their lives based upon such thinking. Idealists are, in general, greatly concerned with character development, which they believe should be one of the foremost goals of a good education.

Idealist philosophy is also very much concerned with the student as one who has enormous potential for growth, both morally and cognitively. The idealist tends to see the individual as a person whose moral values need to be considered and developed by the school. While the idealist may not always be willing to give "evil" an objective existence, it is present in the sense that students may choose things that are harmful. Therefore, idealists maintain that the school has an obligation to present students with models for development, and they would agree with Plato that religious ideas should be presented in ways that students can use them for guidance.

From the idealist's perspective, the teacher is in a unique and important position. The teacher's duty is to encourage students to ask questions and to provide a suitable environment for learning. The teacher exercises judgment about the kinds of materials that are the most important and encourages diligent study of material that is of more ultimate worth.

The idealist position has ramifications for the way we look at the individual. Rather than seeing people simply as biological organisms in nature, idealists see them as the possessors of an "inner light," a mind or soul. For religious idealists, the student is important as a creation of God and carries within some of the godliness that the school should seek to develop. Most idealists, whether religious or not, have a deep feeling about the individual's inner powers (such as intuition) that must be accounted for in any true education. Too much of what passes for education deals with filling the person with something rather than bringing out what is there—the truths that already exist. As discussed earlier, Plato speaks of the Doctrine of Reminiscence, whereby the soul regains the true knowledge it lost by being placed in the "prison house" of the body. The dialectic is the tool for regaining this lost wisdom.

Augustine thought that truth is inherent in the soul of the individual. Education is the process of bringing these truths to the surface; since many of these truths are directly related to God, education is the process of salvation. Education can be conceived as consisting of not only the dialectic but also the technique of meditation to bring out truths already possessed by the soul. This outlook on education was characteristic of medieval monastic education, in which salvation was to be achieved not by direct action but by meditation. Even today, many religious institutions practice such an approach as a part of the students' formal training. Some church schools still set aside a portion of time for pupils to meditate upon the ultimate meaning of things.

Many idealists are concerned with moral character as an outgrowth of thinking and thoughtful actions. The movement toward wisdom itself, the idealist would argue, results from a moral conviction. Augustine thought of God as the highest wisdom and the movement toward wisdom (or God) the highest moral principle. This concept is probably best expressed by Hegel, who described the dialectic as a movement going from the simple to the complex in terms of Spirit trying to understand itself. Hegel believed that the individual can know God, and he argued against theologians who say that God is unknowable. One achieves one's fullest stature when one understands the movement toward wisdom and fully participates in it.

One of the more prominent advocates of character development as a proper aim of education was Immanuel Kant. He made reason, not God, the source of moral law; consequently, the only thing morally valuable is a good will. Accordingly, people who have a good will know what their duty is and conscientiously seek to do that duty. Kant promoted what he called the "categorical imperative"; that is, one should never act in any manner other than how one would have all other people act. The proper function of education,

Golden Rule(?)

then, is to educate people to know and to do their duty in ways that respect the "categorical imperative." This is character education, and idealists generally agree, as J. Donald Butler has pointed out, that any education worthy of the name is character education. The education of character includes not only the sense of duty but also the development of willpower and loyalty.

Herman Horne emphasized the education of the will. By this, he meant that students should be educated to resist temptations and to apply themselves to useful tasks. The education of the will involves effort, for Horne believed that education is directly proportional to the effort expended. Whereas some educators maintain that children should only follow their interests, Horne held that the development of willpower enables a child to do things that may not be particularly interesting but are extremely valuable. Even though a person may not be particularly intelligent, Horne maintained that effort would enable one to achieve far beyond the point to which mere interest would have taken one.

Such idealists as Giovanni Gentile, who supported the Fascist regime of Benito Mussolini, have emphasized the development of loyalty as an important aspect of character education. Along with Hegel, Gentile thought that the destiny of the individual is tied to the destiny of the state; consequently, it is necessary for the individual to have a strong sense of loyalty to the state. Proper character education would thus develop the attribute of loyalty, for an individual without loyalty would be incomplete. When the teacher acts according to the interest of the state, the true interests of the student are being met. By the same token, a student's proper role is to abide by the authority of the teacher.

Methods of Education

Most idealists who look at our schools today are greatly dismayed at what they find. They see students regimented into studying facts, later becoming specialists of some kind, and using those specialties with little humane concern for their fellow human beings. Modern students seem like robots surveying bits and scraps of everything, thereby obtaining an "education" with little depth, operating on the basis of rules rather than on inner conviction.

Idealists lean toward studies that provide depth, and they would strongly suggest a modification of the view that things should be studied simply because they are "new" or "relevant." They find that much of the great literature of the past has more pertinence to contemporary problems than what is considered "new" and "relevant." Almost any contemporary problem, idealists would argue, has its roots in the past. Such problems as the relation of the individual to society have been debated extensively by great philosophers and thinkers. To ignore what great minds have to say in these areas is to ignore the most relevant writings about them.

As has been indicated in the aims of education, idealists do not favor specialized learning as much as learning that is holistic. They ask us to see the whole rather than a disjointed collection of parts. The holistic approach leads to a more liberal attitude toward learning. Although such subjects as the natural sciences are useful, they are of maximum value only when they help us to see the whole picture.

Plato believed that the best method of learning was the dialectic. Through this critical method of thinking, he believed the individual could see things *en toto.* The *Republic,* which is essentially the fruit of dialectic thinking, attempted to integrate a wide range of learning into a meaningful whole. Essentially, Plato believed that we can develop our ideas in ways that achieve syntheses and universal concepts. This method can be learned, but it requires a critical attitude, a background in mathematics, and extended study. The dialectic is a winnowing-out process in which ideas are put into battle against each other, with the more substantial ideas enduring the fray.

Although this method is not often used in schools today, the dialectic was widely used as an educational technique throughout the Middle Ages. Ideas were to be placed in the arena of battle; only if they emerged victorious would there be some reason for believing in them. Churchmen, such as Peter Abelard, used it in vindicating the truths of Christian doctrine. Abelard's famous *Sic et Non* was a way of looking at both sides of the question and allowing the truth to emerge.

In addition to dialectic method, some idealists maintain that truth is also received through intuition and revelation. Augustine practiced the dialectic, but he also put great stress upon the intuitive approach to knowledge. His argument was that God, the inner light of human beings, could speak to us if we made ourselves receptive. Augustine believed that we need to reject materialistic concerns as much as possible so we can attune ourselves with God. One still finds this approach used in monasteries or in contemplative religious orders.

Even outside strictly religious schools, most idealists advocate a conceptual method that includes both the dialectic and the intuitive approach to learning. Plato held that one does not learn as much from nature as from dialogues with other people. Augustine believed that though one be blind and deaf, incapable of any perception through his senses, one can still learn all the important truths and reach God.

Many modern idealists champion the idea of learning through the dialectic or contemplation, but these methods are not as widely applied as they once were. Today, some idealists lean more toward the study of ideas through the use of classical works or writings and art that express great ideas. The Great Books of the Western World, a program that began at the University of Chicago in the 1950s, achieved wide attention and is still in operation today. Although this program has been supported by contemporary adherents of classical realism, it is seen by some idealist educators as a vehicle for encouraging students toward learning of a more conceptual nature.

Idealists do believe, however, that any study of the Great Books should be undertaken with experienced leadership and with an emphasis upon the comprehension of ideas rather than the mere memorization and classification of information. They would insist on a seminar type of instruction with opportunity for ample dialogue between teacher and student. Furthermore, idealists attracted to a Great Books approach would emphasize those ideas that have perennial value; that is, ideas that have withstood the test of time across the centuries.

One recent theme that has resurrected the hopes of Great Books advocates has been *The Paideia Proposal* by Mortimer Adler. Adler has proposed a basic curriculum that would include a study of classic writings. Most notable about Adler's approach is that he is proposing this curriculum for *all* students, not just those who are academically gifted.

Although one might easily see how this idealist approach can be applied to college-level education, it may not be so apparent how it could be used in elementary and secondary schools. To begin with, one must be clear on the purpose of learning. The idealist is not primarily concerned with turning out graduates with specific technical skills but with giving students a broad understanding of the world in which they live. The curriculum revolves around broad concepts rather than specific skills. In elementary and preschool education, students are encouraged to develop habits of understanding, patience, tolerance, and hard work that will assist them later when they undertake more substantial studies. This is not to say that students cannot learn some important ideas at any age, but the earliest years of education prepare the student by developing the skills to undertake more in-depth work later.

The idealist emphasizes the importance of the teacher. The teacher should not only understand the various stages of learning but should also maintain constant concern about the ultimate purposes of learning. Some idealists stress the importance of emulation in learning, for they feel that the teacher should be the kind of person we want our children to become. Socrates has been used by idealists not only as a prototype of learning but also as a model for emulation.

Butler maintains that modern idealist educators like to think of themselves as creators of methods rather than as mere imitators. They prefer alternative ways of approaching learning, but they still like to see at least an informal dialectic in operation. In questioning and discussion sessions during which the dialectic operates, the teacher should help students see alternatives that they might otherwise have missed. Although the dialectic process may be informal, it should not become a mere pooling of the ignorance of immature students, for the teacher should participate to maintain the integrity of the process.

The lecture method still has a place in the idealist's methodology, but lecture is viewed more as a means of stimulating thought than as merely passing on information. In fact, some idealist teachers discourage note taking so that students will concentrate on the basic ideas. To the idealist, the chief purpose of a lecture is to help students comprehend ideas. Idealists also use such methods as projects, supplemental activities, library research, and art-work. Such diverse methods, however, grow out of the topic of study at hand. This illustrates the idealists' desire to show the unity of knowledge and their dislike for random and isolated activity.

One of the cardinal objectives of idealism and idealistic education is the ancient Greek directive to "know thyself." Self-realization is, as noted above, an important aim of education; hence, idealists stress the importance of self-directed activity in education. In essence, they believe that a true education occurs only within the individual self. Although teachers cannot get inside children's minds, they can provide materials and activities that influence learning. It is the response of the learner to these materials and activities that constitutes education. The sources of this action are personal and private; for in idealism, all education is self-education. The teacher must recognize that he cannot always be present when learning occurs and should attempt to stimulate the student so that learning continues even when the teacher is not present. The project method might be one concrete example of self-directed activity. The idealist insists only that the nature of any such activity be on a high plane of thought.

Curriculum

While not underemphasizing the development of a curriculum, idealists stress that the most important factor in education at any level is to teach students to think. The psychologist Jean Piaget and others have shown that it is reasonable to expect students to demonstrate some critical regard for the material they are exposed to at various stages of development, even with nursery tales that are read to them.

Idealists generally agree, however, that many of the educational materials used by children are inadequate. Although the materials may help teach such skills as reading, idealists do not understand why such skills cannot be taught in ways that also develop conceptual ability. One might argue that the McGuffey readers that were widely used in schools in the late nineteenth and early twentieth centuries taught the child something in addition to reading. They fostered ideas about parental relationships, God, morality, and patrio-tism. A counterargument might be that these are the wrong kinds of concepts, but are the more recent sterile readers exemplified by the Dick-and-Jane types an improvement?

Although most idealists claim that they are opposed to the use of reading material for indoctrination, they do not see why reading material cannot, while it is helping a child learn to read, encourage thinking about ideas involving brotherhood, truth, and fair play. Although there is a dearth of books and materials that express such ideas for children, idealists still believe that the teacher should encourage a consideration of ideas in the classroom.

Even with a Dick-and-Jane type of book, for example, a teacher should help a child to explore the materials for ideas about the purpose of family, the nature of peer pressures, and the problems of growing up.

With older children, one can use materials that are more appropriate to this kind of learning. *Treasure Island, The Adventures of Tom Sawyer,* and *Peter Pan* are well written and lend themselves admirably to a discussion of ideas. For high school students, even more idea-engendering material is available: *The Iliad; Hamlet; Twice-Told Tales;* and *Wind, Sand, and Stars.* Since these materials are already widely used, one might wonder what is so special about the way idealists would use them. Idealists charge that teachers are not always equipped to use such materials for the ideas contained in them. Such books may become, in the eyes of teachers and students, another hurdle to get over, another bench mark or list of books to be read.

Idealists believe that ideas can change lives. Christianity was once merely an idea, and so was Marxism, but such ideas have transformed whole societies. Idealists think that humans can become more noble and rational by developing the ability to think. The use of the classics for humanizing learning experiences has been encouraged by idealists. Whatever factors are involved in the human race's evolutionary past, the idealist holds that the most important part of one's being is one's mind. It is to be nourished and developed. It can accumulate facts, but it can also conceptualize and create.

Idealists charge that the schools neglect this important consideration of mind. Even when the classics are taught, students are often required to memorize dates and names without due attention to the creative aspects of the mind. Creativity will be encouraged when students are immersed in the creative thinking of others and when they are stimulated to think reflectively. This can come about only in an environment that promotes the use of the mind.

While idealist educators stress classical studies, this does not mean that such studies are all that they emphasize. Indeed, some idealists recommend studies that are distinctly modern. For example, William T. Harris developed a curriculum centered around five studies: (1) mathematics and physics, (2) biology, (3) literature and art, (4) grammar, and (5) history. Herman Horne suggested seven major studies: physics, biology, psychology, mathematics, grammar, literature, and history. Both Harris and Horne felt that these areas are important enough to be considered on every curriculum level and broad enough to contain even elective studies.

The sciences are heavily represented in both of these recommendations. This indicates that such idealists as Harris and Horne did not disregard the development of new knowledge or the needs of twentieth-century society. Neither Harris nor Horne saw any incompatibility between studies in the liberal arts and the natural sciences. In fact, they maintained that a more complete understanding of the universe necessitates studies in both the arts and the sciences.

CRITIQUE OF IDEALISM IN EDUCATION

Idealism is often considered a conservative philosophy of education because much of its thrust is to preserve the cultural traditions. This is borne out by examination of the idealists' concern for perennial and ultimate truths and their notion that education is largely a matter of passing on cultural heritage. Many adherents point to the strengths of idealism, such as the following:

1. The high cognitive level of education idealists promote
2. Their concern for safeguarding and promoting cultural learning
3. Their great concern for morality and character development
4. Their view of the teacher as a revered person central to the educational process
5. Their stress on the importance of self-realization
6. Their stress upon the human and personal side of life
7. Their comprehensive, systematic, and holistic approach.

Historically, the influence of idealism on education has been so strong that even today it is hard to find schools that do not in some way reflect idealist principles. While idealism's influence has suffered in recent decades, no other single philosophy has affected education for so long. Beginning with Plato in the fourth century BC, through scholasticism in the Middle Ages, to Kant and Hegel, and up to the twentieth century, idealism has been a dominant force. Several factors have contributed to a weakening of idealism in contemporary affairs: industrialization and technological advances have taken their toll, developments in science have brought about fundamental challenges to idealistic principles, the renewed vigor of realism and naturalistic philosophies has put more emphasis on the material as opposed to ideal aspects of life, and the contemporary emphasis on newness as opposed to cultural heritage and lasting values has eroded the idealist position.

Many idealists counter that certain ideas contained in traditional writings, some written over two thousand years ago, are as relevant today as ever. They maintain, with Ecclesiastes, that "There is nothing [really] new under the sun," for many problems we face today are problems philosophers and others faced long ago. Plato, for example, dealt extensively with the problems of democracy, individuality, and language. The Bible discusses such topics as human suffering, greed, wealth, and human purpose. When Herman Melville wrote *Moby Dick,* he drew upon central biblical themes of good and evil that still provide guidance.

Currently, seminars based on the Great Books program deal with such themes and many idealists believe that these seminars provide more insight than do most books on the best seller list. Such seminars have found their way into schools, libraries, reading circles, and even into adult education programs in many prisons. Many of the people who attended the Great Books program in the 1950s, when it began, still look back on their experience with nostalgia. Today, Encyclopaedia Britannica publishes the Great Books for home use; the accompanying Synopticon provides a key to help the reader locate and understand the central ideas of the books. Many people are amazed that so many issues we think are new, such as euthanasia and abortion, are treated extensively by even the ancient authors. Students of the Great Books often find flashes of insight from their readings that stimulate their thinking along new paths.

Opponents of idealism have long searched for ways to get around what to them is the lethargic nature of idealism. What they object to primarily are its fundamental premises. For example, the idealist notion of a finished and absolute universe waiting to be discovered has hindered progress in science and the creation of new ideas and processes. If one accepts the concept of absolute ideas, it is not possible to go beyond those ideas without questioning or doubting their absoluteness. This was one of the chief problems modern science had in gaining acceptance, for science is premised on tentativeness and hypotheses rather than on stability and axioms. Indeed, contemporary science is characterized by Heisenberg's indeterminacy principle, which holds that accurately measuring one quantity can produce uncertainties in related quantities—i.e., that the very act of observation can alter physical conditions. In addition, Einstein's theory of relativity has been used to challenge the idealist assertion of a fixed universe.

Still another cause of the weakening of idealism is the historical decline of the influence of traditional religion in contemporary affairs. Because idealism has been intimately linked with traditional religion, the weakening of the one has led to the weakening of the other.

There are, however, signs that the decline in religion may be changing. Although the influence of traditional organized religion has decreased, there has been a renewal of interest in mysticism, Eastern religious thought, and various forms of meditation that take new directions from the more traditional religious views. In addition, a resurgence in evangelical Christianity in recent years has placed considerable emphasis on education of the young. These developments usually have idealistic underpinnings, especially in their views on the proper aims and content of schooling.

From the standpoint of education, several issues need further scrutiny. The idealist influence on education has been immense, but that influence might not always have been beneficial. While idealist education has emphasized the cognitive side of humankind, it has tended toward intellectualism to the detriment of the affective and physical side. It has also often ignored the many people who find its cognitive emphasis narrow and pedantic. This has led to the charge that idealism leans toward an intellectual elite.

The problem of elitism goes deep into idealism's roots. Plato advocated an intellectual elite of philosopher-kings. Augustine argued for the superiority of the monastic life over the secular because of the higher quality of mind and intelligence to be found there: monks were a select group set aside for special treatment. Idealists have tended to view formal education not for the masses but for a chosen few who could understand and appreciate it properly; consequently, they have concentrated on education for the upper classes of society, particularly for those going into leadership positions in government or the church. This factor has often helped formal education to be viewed as a luxury, available only to the privileged few. To the extent that idealist regimes have tried to extend at least some formal schooling to the public, the view has been that vocational and technical studies are sufficient for the masses, while liberal studies are suitable only for the elite. While not all idealists have felt this way, the tendency toward elitism generally has been recognized.

John Paul Strain (1975) stated that one has to go back several years in the journals on education to find an article on idealism. One might think this conspicuous absence indicates that idealism is no longer a viable philosophy of education; yet the reverse is true, Strain stated. When people refer to idealism as a philosophy of education, they generally mean Hegelian idealism, which was dominant in the nineteenth century and influenced such thinkers as John Dewey and Herman Horne. Although it is difficult today to find philosophers of education who are true idealists, idealism does exist in the thought patterns of American education. These thought patterns influenced the writings and work of William T. Harris (who was a United States Commissioner of Education and Superintendent of the St. Louis Schools in the late nineteenth century) as well as "essentialists" who promoted strong traditional values in education. Strain believes that the philosophy of the Council of Basic Education is a perfect synopsis of idealism as a philosophy of education; that is, that education should focus on heritage and culture, reading and writing, intelligence and morality. We might also add to this list such things as respect for parental authority, law and order, discipline, and patriotism. Strain says that the thought pattern of idealism also encourages progress, strong institutions, self-control, discipline, and the importance of education.

Strain's views do reflect why many philosophers of education have not wished to be identified with idealism—with its religious character on the one hand and its subservience to political authority on the other. Hegel believed that the best form of government was a constitutional monarchy, and Strain favors a similar approach to government today. Strain is correct when he says that idealism still flourishes as a historical pattern of thought that exerts a powerful, often subtle influence on our thinking.

Despite its generalist approach to studies, idealism is susceptible to the charge of shortsightedness with regard to the affective and physical aspects of human nature. If we include in our definition of *affective* not only the aesthetic but also the emotional and personal-social side of life, then such a charge gains credence. The idealist curriculum is overly bookish; although attending to books is not bad in itself, if we fail to recognize emotional and social needs, then we are not really attending to the complete person. Idealists claim to be holistic and universal, yet in their extreme cognitive and bookish approach, they seem to fail to take their own advice in this regard.

For example, it is one thing to learn about human nature from reading enduring scholarly treatises on the subject but it is quite another to engage purposefully in social relationships with fellow human beings in the everyday
world. Consequently, idealist knowledge is often only "armchair" knowledge
rather than the deep insight that comes from interaction with other people.

In recent years, the idealist curriculum has increasingly come under
attack for lacking relevance. Idealists have offered some compelling defenses,
but an element of truth in the charge will not go away. To the extent that idealists concentrate only on works of the past, the charge gains credibility.
Certainly, the great writings of the past may provide insights, but they are
often too general to aid in dealing with specific contemporary problems. We
should study great ideas from the past, but this does not mean that we should
ignore contemporary ideas and writings. One of the criticisms leveled at such
educational institutions as St. John's of Annapolis is that they deal too much
with the past and too little with the present and the future. Although defenders of these programs maintain that there is allowance for more recent literature, most of the readings are hundreds or thousands of years old. This
approach tends to ignore or downgrade a large body of contemporary materials in many areas, such as art, science, philosophy, literature, and the mass
media.

One of the claims made by idealists is that they give more attention to
the development of character than do advocates of other philosophies. This is
probably true, but also raised are serious questions of why idealists are so
concerned with character development and what kind of character they want
to develop. Often, what purports to be character development in idealist philosophy is conformity and subservience on the part of the learner. Harris, for
example, said that the first rule to be taught to students is order; pupils
should be taught to conform to general standards and to repress everything
that interferes with the function of the school. More explicitly, pupils should
have their lessons ready on time, rise at the tap of the bell, and learn habits of
silence and cleanliness. One might well question whether this is character
development or training for docility.

This kind of character training may assist in educational and social stability, but it is often at the expense of creativity and self-direction. The kind of
character training idealists promote may also make students gullible—willing
to accept ready-made ideas without serious examination. Many of the so-
called great ideas, for example, rest on premises or assumptions that are
questionable and, in the final analysis, may be socially harmful. Giovanni
Gentile and Josiah Royce, for example, spent a great deal of time dealing
with the concept of loyalty as central to the development of character. While
loyalty may be socially useful in some cases, it can also be harmful when it
encourages the learner to submerge all questioning and intellectual independence with regard to concepts involving church, state, or school.

Some idealists, such as Butler, emphasize the self-realization aspect of
character education; yet such self-realization is often seen as a derivative of a

universal self. Hence, even under a softer idealist approach, the individual self is subsumed under a larger and more important concern—that is, the universal self or God. This line of reasoning can be traced back to Hegel, who saw the individual person achieving meaning by serving the state.

Another aspect of idealist philosophy that deserves attention is the contention that the primary function of philosophy is to search for and disseminate truths. One finds this view elaborated by Plato, who believed that truth is both perfect and eternal. Even today, idealists point out that the search for wisdom is really a search for truth—an ongoing pursuit each new generation of students must do—although the final answers may always be the same. This viewpoint leads to a type of staticism. The assumption is that we have the truth already at hand in great works of the past. The danger in this belief is that it discourages a search for new ideas and develops dogmatism and a false sense of security. Although idealists maintain that modern individuals are too relative and tentative in their thinking, the absoluteness of many idealists may be a more serious weakness.

While this attitude may characterize a number of idealists, some have a more pluralistic conception of truth, maintaining that there may be not one but many truths that people should ponder, not only for the sake of knowledge but for the intellectual stimulation provided. Idealism, of course, like all other philosophies, has many shades and meanings, and it would be grossly unfair to lump all idealists together. Each writer describes or reinterprets ideas in the light of his experiences, and thus no two are the same. Idealists do, however, share certain tendencies in such areas as character development and education in general; the purpose of this chapter has been to point out these general trends.

PLATO

THE REPUBLIC

The Republic has often been considered one of the greatest expressions of idealist philosophy and Plato's most thorough statement on education. Writing in the fourth century BC, *Plato described his utopian view of human society. It was not unusual for him to depict central ideas in allegorical format. In this selection,* he shows Socrates attempting to explain how achieving higher levels of thought (i.e., thinking philosophically), is akin to prisoners escaping from their shadowy prison in a cave. Plato demonstrates both the painful difficulty of the ascent toward wisdom and its potentially dangerous consequences. Many scholars believe that the story parallels Socrates' own life and death.*

Source: Plato, *The Republic,* translated by B. Jowett. New York: Dolphin Books, 1960, pp. 205–208.

And now, I said, let me show in a figure how far our nature is enlightened or unenlightened:— Behold! human beings living in an underground den, which has a mouth open towards the light and reaching all along the den; here they have been from their childhood, and have their legs and necks chained so that they can not move, and can only see before them, being prevented by the chains from turning round their heads. Above and behind them a fire is blazing at a distance, and between the fire and the prisoners there is a raised way; and you will see, if you look, a low wall built along the way, like the screen which marionette players have in front of them, over which they show the puppets.

I see.

And do you see, I said, men passing along the wall carrying all sorts of vessels, and statues and figures of animals made of wood and stone and various materials, which appear over the wall? Some of them are talking, others silent.

You have shown me a strange image, and they are strange prisoners.

Like ourselves, I replied; and they see only their own shadows, or the shadows of one another, which the fire throws on the opposite wall of the cave?

True, he said; how could they see anything but the shadows if they were never allowed to move their heads?

And of the objects which are being carried in like manner they would only see the shadows?

Yes, he said.

And if they were able to converse with one another, would they not suppose that they were naming what was actually before them?

Very true.

And suppose further that the prison had an echo which came from the other side, would they not be sure to fancy when one of the passers-by spoke that the voice which they heard came from the passing shadow?

No question, he replied.

To them, I said, the truth would be literally nothing but the shadows of the images.

That is certain.

And now look again, and see what will naturally follow if the prisoners are released and disabused of their error. At first, when any of them is liberated and compelled suddenly to stand up and turn his neck round and walk and look towards the light, he will suffer sharp pains; the glare will distress him, and he will be unable to see the realities of which in his former state he had seen the shadows; and then conceive some one saying to him, that what he saw before was an illusion, but that now, when he is approaching nearer to being and his eye is turned towards more real existence, he has a clearer vision,—what will be his reply? And you may further imagine that his instructor is pointing to the objects as they pass and requiring him to name them,—will he not be perplexed? Will he not fancy that the shadows which he formerly saw are truer than the objects which are now shown to him?

Far truer.

And if he is compelled to look straight at the light, will he not have a pain in his eyes which will make him turn away to take refuge in the objects of vision which he can see, and which he will conceive to be in reality clearer than the things which are now being shown to him?

True, he said.

And suppose once more, that he is reluctantly dragged up a steep and rugged ascent, and held fast until he is forced into the presence of the sun himself, is he not likely to be pained and irritated? When he approaches the light his eyes will be dazzled, and he will not be able to see anything at all of what are now called realities.

Not all in a moment, he said.

He will require to grow accustomed to the sight of the upper world. And first he will see the shadows best, next the reflections of men and other objects in the water, and then the objects themselves; then he will gaze upon the light of the moon and the stars and the spangled heaven; and he will see the sky and the stars by night better than the sun or the light of the sun by day?

Certainly.

Last of all he will be able to see the sun, and not mere reflections of him in the water, but he will see him in his own proper place, and not in another; and he will contemplate him as he is.

Certainly.

He will then proceed to argue that this is he who gives the season and the years, and is the guardian of all that is in the visible world, and in a certain way the cause of all things which he and his fellows have been accustomed to behold?

Clearly, he said, he would first see the sun and then reason about him.

And when he remembered his old habitation, and the wisdom of the den and his fellow-prisoners, do you not suppose that he would felicitate himself on the change, and pity them?

Certainly, he would.

And if they were in the habit of conferring honors among themselves on those who were quickest to observe the passing shadows and to remark which of them went before, and which followed after, and which were together; and who were therefore best able to draw conclusions as to the future, do you think that he would care for such honors and glories, or envy the possessors of them? Would he not say with Homer,

> "Better to be the poor servant of a
> poor master,"

and to endure anything, rather than think as they do and live after their manner?

Yes, he said, I think that he would rather suffer anything than entertain these false notions and live in this miserable manner.

Imagine once more, I said, such a one coming suddenly out of the sun to be replaced in his old situation; would he not be certain to have his eyes full of darkness?

To be sure, he said.

And if there were a contest, and he had to compete in measuring the shadows with the prisoners who had never moved out of the den, while his sight was still weak, and before his eyes had become steady (and the time which would be needed to acquire this new habit of sight might be very considerable), would he not be ridiculous? Men would say of him that up he went and down he came without his eyes; and that it was better not even to think of

ascending; and if any one tried to loose another and lead him up to the light, let them only catch the offender, and they would put him to death.

No question, he said.

This entire allegory, I said, you may now append, dear Glaucon, to the previous argument; the prison-house is the world of sight, the light of the fire is the sun, and you will not misapprehend me if you interpret the journey upwards to be the ascent of the soul into the intellectual world according to my poor belief, which, at your desire, I have expressed—whether rightly or wrongly God knows. But, whether true or false, my opinion is that in the world of knowledge the idea of good appears last of all, and is seen only with an effort; and, when seen, is also inferred to be the universal author of all things beautiful and right, parent of light and of the lord of light in this visible world, and the immediate source of reason and truth in the intellectual; and that this is the power upon which he who would act rationally either in public or private life must have his eye fixed.

I agree, he said, as far as I am able to understand you.

Moreover, I said, you must not wonder that those who attain to this beatific vision are unwilling to descend to human affairs; for their souls are ever hastening into the upper world where they desire to dwell; which desire of theirs is very natural, if our allegory may be trusted.

Yes, very natural.

And is there anything surprising in one who passes from divine contemplations to the evil state of man, misbehaving himself in a ridiculous manner; if, while his eyes are blinking and before he has become accustomed to the surrounding darkness, he is compelled to fight in courts of law, or in other places, about the images or the shadows of images of justice, and is endeavoring to meet the conceptions of those who have never yet seen absolute justice?

Anything but surprising, he replied.

Any one who has common sense will remember that the bewilderments of the eyes are of two kinds, and arise from two causes, either from coming out of the light or from going into the light, which is true of the mind's eye, quite as much as of the bodily eye; and he who remembers this when he sees any one whose vision is perplexed and weak, will not be too ready to laugh; he will first ask whether that soul of man has come out of the brighter life, and is unable to see because unaccustomed to the dark, or having turned from darkness to the day is dazzled by excess of light. And he will count the one happy in his condition and state of being, and he will pity the other; or, if he have a mind to laugh at the soul which comes from below into the light, there will be more reason in this than in the laugh which greets him who returns from above out of the light into the den.

That, he said, is a very just distinction.

But then, if I am right, certain professors of education must be wrong when they say that they can put a knowledge into the soul which was not there before, like sight into blind eyes.

They undoubtedly say this, he replied.

Whereas, our argument shows that the power and capacity of learning exists in the soul already; and that just as the eye was unable to turn from darkness to light without the whole body, so too the instrument of knowledge can only by the movement of the whole soul be turned from the world of becoming into that of being, and learn by degrees to endure the sight of being, and of the brightest and best of being, or in other words, of the good.

. . . .   **KANT**   . . . .

EDUCATION

Kant believed that education is "the greatest and most difficult problem to which man can devote himself"; in the following selection, he shows how education can be used to shape human character through maxims, or enduring principles for human activity. Although written in the eighteenth century, this essay shows a decidedly contemporary concern for child development and learning through activities. Kant stressed character development and a commitment to duty. This concern is illustrated in his descriptions of various maxims and how they should give certain results.*

Moral culture must be based upon "maxims," not upon discipline; the one prevents evil habits, the other trains the mind to think. We must see, then, that the child should accustom himself to act in accordance with "maxims," and not from certain ever-changing springs of action. Through discipline we form certain habits, moreover, the force of which becomes lessened in the course of years. The child should learn to act according to "maxims," the reasonableness of which he is able to see for himself. One can easily see that there is some difficulty in carrying out this principle with young children, and that moral culture demands a great deal of insight on the part of parents and teachers.

Supposing a child tells a lie, for instance, he ought not to be punished, but treated with contempt, and told that he will not be believed in the future, and the like. If you punish a child for being naughty, and reward him for being good, he will do right merely for the sake of the

Source: Immanuel Kant, *Education,* translated by Annette Charton. Ann Arbor: University of Michigan Press, 1960, pp. 83–94.

reward; and when he goes out into the world and finds that goodness is not always rewarded, nor wickedness always punished, he will grow into a man who only thinks about how he may get on in the world, and does right or wrong according as he finds either of advantage to himself.

"*Maxims*" ought to originate in the human being as such. In moral training we should seek early to infuse into children ideas as to what is right and wrong. If we wish to establish morality, we must abolish punishment. Morality is something so sacred and sublime that we must not degrade it by placing it in the same rank as discipline. The first endeavour in moral education is the formation of character. Character consists in readiness to act in accordance with "maxims." At first they are school "maxims," and later "maxims" of mankind. At first the child obeys rules. "Maxims" are also rules, but subjective rules. They proceed from the understanding of man. No infringement of school discipline must be allowed to go unpunished, although the punishment must always fit the offence.

If we wish to *form the characters* of children, it is of the greatest importance to point out to them a certain plan, and certain rules, in everything; and these must be strictly adhered to. For instance, they must have set times for sleep, for work, and for pleasure; and these times must be neither shortened nor lengthened. With indifferent matters children might be allowed to choose for themselves, but having once made a rule they must always follow it. We must, however, form in children the character of a child, and not the character of a citizen. . . .

Above all things, obedience is an essential feature in the character of a child, especially of a school boy or girl. This obedience is twofold, including absolute obedience to his master's commands, and obedience to what he feels to be a good and reasonable will. Obedience may be the result of compulsion; it is then *absolute:* or it may arise out of confidence; it is then obedience of the second kind. This *voluntary* obedience is very important, but the former is also very necessary, for it prepares the child for the fulfillment of laws that he will have to obey later, as a citizen, even though he may not like them.

Children, then, must be subject to a certain law of *necessity*. This law, however, must be a general one—a rule which has to be kept constantly in view, especially in schools. The master must not show any predilection or preference for one child above others; for thus the law would cease to be general. As soon as a child sees that the other children are not all placed under the same rules as himself, he will at once become refractory.

One often hears it said that we should put everything before children in such a way that they shall do it from *inclination*. In some cases, it is true, this is all very well, but there is much besides which we must place before them as *duty*. And this will be of great use to them throughout their life. For in the paying of rates and taxes, in the work of the office, and in many other cases, we must be led, not by inclination, but by duty. Even though a child should not be able to see the reason of a duty, it is nevertheless better that certain things should be prescribed to him in this way; for, after all, a child will always be able to see that he has certain duties as a child, while it will be more difficult for him to see that he has certain duties as a human being. Were he able to understand this also—which, however, will only be possible in the course of years—his obedience would be still more perfect.

Every transgression of a command in a child is a want of obedience, and this brings *punishment* with it. Also, should a command be disobeyed through inattention, punishment is still necessary. This punishment is either *physical* or *moral*. It is *moral* when we do something derogatory to the child's longing to be honoured and loved (a longing which is an aid to moral training); for instance, when we humiliate the child by treating him coldly and distantly. This longing of children should, however, be cultivated as much as possible. Hence this kind of punishment is the best, since it is an aid to moral training—for instance, if a child tells a lie, a look of contempt is punishment enough, and punishment of a most appropriate kind.

Physical punishment consists either in refusing a child's requests or in the infliction of pain. The first is akin to moral punishment, and is of a negative kind. The second form must be used with caution, lest an *indoles servilis* should be the result. It is of no use to give children rewards; this makes them selfish, and gives rise to an *indoles mercenaria*.

Further, obedience is either that of the child or that of the *youth*. Disobedience is always followed by punishment. This is either a really *natural* punishment, which a man brings upon himself by his own behaviour—for instance, when a child gets ill from overeating—and this kind of punishment is the best, since a man is subject to it throughout his life, and not merely during his childhood; or, on the other hand, the punishment is artificial. By taking into consideration the child's desire to be loved and respected, such punishments may be chosen as will have a lasting effect upon its character. Physical punishments must merely supplement the insufficiency of moral punishment. If moral punishment have no effect at all, and we have at last to resort to physical punishment, we shall find after all that no good character is formed in this way. At the beginning, however, physical restraint may serve to take the place of reflection.

Punishments inflicted with signs of *anger* are useless. Children then look upon the punishment simply as the result of anger, and upon themselves merely as the victims of that anger; and as a general rule punishment must be inflicted on children with great caution, that they may understand that its one aim is their improvement. It is foolish to cause children, when they are punished, to return thanks for the punishment by kissing hands, and only turns the child into a slave. If physical punishment is often repeated, it makes a child stubborn; and if parents punish their children for obstinacy, they often become all the more obstinate. Besides, it is not always the worst men who are obstinate, and they will often yield easily to kind remonstrance.

The obedience of the growing *youth* must be distinguished from the obedience of the *child*. The former consists in submission to rules of duty. To do something for the sake of duty means obeying reason. It is in vain to speak to children of duty. They look upon it in the end as something which if not fulfilled will be followed by the rod. A child may be guided by mere instinct. As he grows up, however, the idea of duty must come in. Also the idea of shame should not be made use of with children, but only with those who have left childhood for youth. For it cannot exist with them till the idea of honour has first taken root.

The second principal feature in the formation of a child's character is *truthfulness*. This is the foundation and very essence of character. A man who tells lies has no character, and if he has any good in him it is merely the result of a certain kind of temperament. Some children have an inclination towards lying, and this frequently for no other reason than that they have a lively imagination. It is the father's business to see that they are broken of this habit, for mothers generally look upon it as a matter of little or no importance, even finding in it a flattering proof of the cleverness and ability of their children. This is the time to make use of the sense of shame, for the child in this case will understand it well. The blush of shame betrays us when we lie, but it is not always a proof of it, for we often blush at the shamelessness of others who accuse us of guilt. On no condition must we punish children to force the truth from them, unless their telling a lie immediately results in some mischief; *then* they may be punished for that mischief. The withdrawal of respect is the only fit punishment for lying.

Punishments may be divided into *negative* and *positive* punishments. The first may be applied to laziness or viciousness; for instance, lying, disobedience. Positive punishment may be applied to acts of spitefulness. But above all things we must take care never to bear children a grudge.

A third feature in the child's character is *sociableness*. He must form friendships with other children, and not be always by himself. Some teachers, it is true, are opposed to these friendships in schools, but this is a great mistake. Children ought to prepare themselves for the sweetest enjoyment of life.

If a teacher allows himself to prefer one child to another, it must be on account of its character, and not for the sake of any talents the child may possess; otherwise jealousy will arise, which is opposed to friendship.

Children ought to be open-hearted and cheerful in their looks as the sun. A joyful heart alone is able to find its happiness in the good. A religion which makes people gloomy is a false religion; for we should serve God with a joyful heart, and not of constraint.

Children should sometimes be released from the narrow constraint of school, otherwise their natural joyousness will soon be quenched. When the child is set free he soon recovers his natural elasticity. Those games in which children, enjoying perfect freedom, are ever trying to outdo one another, will serve this purpose best, and they will soon make their minds bright and cheerful again. . . .

Children should only be taught those things which are suited to their age. Many parents are pleased with the precocity of their offspring; but as a rule, nothing will come of such children. A child should be clever, but only as a child. He should not ape the manners of his elders. For a child to provide himself with moral sentences proper to manhood is to go quite beyond his province and to become merely an imitator. He ought to have merely the understanding of a child, and not seek to display it too early. A precocious child will never become a man of insight and clear understanding. It is just as much out of place for a child to follow all the fashions of the time, to curl his hair, wear ruffles, and even carry a snuff-box. He will thus acquire affected manners not becoming to a child. Polite society is a burden to him, and he entirely lacks a man's heart. For that very reason we must set ourselves early to fight against all signs of vanity in a child; or, rather, we must give him no occasion to become vain. This easily happens by people prattling before children, telling them how beautiful they are, and how well this or that dress becomes them, and promising them some finery or other as a reward. Finery is not suitable for children. They must accept their neat and simple clothes as necessaries merely.

At the same time the parents must not set great store by their own clothes, nor admire themselves; for here, as everywhere, example is all-powerful, and either strengthens or destroys good precepts.

SELECTED READINGS

Butler, J. Donald. *Idealism in Education.* New York: Harper & Row, 1966. A compact and insightful treatment of philosophical idealism in contemporary education. A good starting point for examining idealism in education.

Horne, Herman H. *The Democratic Philosophy of Education.* New York: Macmillan, 1935. This book was written as a challenge to the growing strength of pragmatic philosophy in educational circles. It makes a case for returning to basic ideals and educational practices as the best way to achieve and maintain democracy.

Kant, Immanuel. *Education,* edited by Annette Charton. Ann Arbor: University of Michigan Press, 1960. A historically influential work that examines education as both a theoretical and practical endeavor, this book introduces the Kantian influence into many aspects of education from discipline to curriculum.

Plato. *Republic.* New York: Oxford University Press, 1945. One of the most famous treatises on education ever written, this work has influenced countless people across the centuries. It is a highly speculative and utopian approach to education as the basis of the good society.

Strain, John Paul. Idealism: A Clarification of an Educational Philosophy. *Educational Theory* 25:263–271, 1975. This article is a recent survey of the contributions of philosophical idealism to education in the twentieth century. Although the author recognizes the declining popularity of the idealist approach to philosophy, he points out that many people still hold an idealist philosophy of education that reveals itself in continuing traditions and practices.

2

Realism and Education

Like idealism, realism is one of the oldest philosophies in Western culture and dates back at least as early as ancient Greece. Because of its respectable age, realism has had a variety of spokesmen and interpretations. Consequently, there are several varieties of realism, ranging from classical and religious realism to scientific, natural, and rational realism. Because of this confusing array of variations, it seems most reasonable to approach this philosophy from common threads that are interwoven throughout its long history.

Perhaps the most central thread of realism is what may be called the principle or thesis of independence. This thesis holds that reality, knowledge, and value exist independent of the human mind. In other words, realism rejects the idealist notion that only ideas are real. The realist asserts, as fact, that the actual sticks, stones, and trees of the universe exist whether or not there is a human mind to perceive them. In one sense, we may say that for the realist, matter is real; however, this does not mean that all realists are rampant materialists. What is important is that matter is an obvious example of an independent reality. In order to understand this complex philosophy, we need to examine its development from classical times, how it was transformed by the scientific revolution, and what it is today.

CLASSICAL TRADITION

Aristotelian Realism

Aristotle (384–322 BC)

Plato believed that matter had no lasting reality and that we should concern ourselves with ideas. It was Plato's pupil Aristotle, however, who developed the view that while ideas may be important in themselves, a proper study of matter could lead us to better and more distinct ideas. Aristotle studied and taught at Plato's Academy for about twenty years and later opened his own school, the Lyceum. His differences with Plato were developed gradually, and in many respects, he never got out from under Plato's influence.

According to Aristotle, ideas (or forms) such as the idea of God or the idea of a tree can exist without matter, but there can be no matter without form. Each piece of matter has universal and particular properties. The particular properties of an acorn, for example, are those things that are peculiar to it and that differentiate it from all other acorns. These properties include its size, shape, weight, and color. No two acorns are exactly alike, so we can talk about some particular properties of any acorn as different from those of all other acorns. Each acorn, however, shares the universal property that can be called "acornness" with all other acorns.

Perhaps the difference between particular and universal properties can be understood better by referring to humans at this point. People, too, differ in their particular properties. They have different shapes and sizes, and no two are exactly alike. Yet all people do share in something universal, and this could be called their "humanness." Both humanness and acornness are realities, and they exist independently and regardless of any one particular human or acorn. Thus, we may say that forms (universals, ideas, or essences) are the nonmaterial aspects of each particular material object that relate to all other particular objects of that class.

Nonmaterial though form may be, we arrive at it by examining material objects that exist in themselves, independent of us. Aristotle believed we should be very much involved in studying and understanding the reality of all things. Indeed, he agreed with Plato on this position. They differed, however, in that Aristotle felt one could get to form by studying particular material things, and Plato believed form could be reached only through some kind of reasoning, such as the dialectic.

Aristotle argued that the forms of things, the universal properties of objects, remain constant and never change whereas particular components do change. The shell of an acorn may disintegrate and an acorn may be destroyed, but the form of all acorns, or acornness, remains. In terms of people again, though individual persons die, humanness remains. Even if all human beings should die, humanness would remain, just as the concept of circularity would remain even if all existing material circles were destroyed.

If we look at this in terms of the development of people, we can see that as children, individuals have the particular characteristics of children. As they grow, however, their bodies change and they enter the phase of growth called adolescence; later they become adults. Humanness remains even though the developmental process of the individual changes several times. Thus, form remains constant while particular matter changes. Aristotle and Plato agreed on the point that form is constant and matter is always changing, but Aristotle believed form was within particular matter and was even the motivating force of that matter. By the same token, the modern philosopher Henri Bergson spoke about an *élan vital*, or vital principle that each object has and that directs it in terms of fulfilling its purpose. This can be seen in the actual growth process of an acorn fulfilling its purpose in becoming an oak tree. It must take in the proper amount of sun and water, it must set its roots just so deep, and it must receive nourishment in the proper way. Each object, Aristotle thought, has a tiny "soul" that directs it in the right way.

Aristotle was both a scientist and a philosopher, and he believed that although we may separate science and philosophy artificially, there is a relationship between them in which the study of one aids us in the study of the other. For example, by studying the material aspects of an acorn (its shell, its color, and so forth) we should be led deeper into a contemplation of what the acorn really is—that is, its essence or form.

Of course, a great deal depends upon asking the right questions. There are scientific questions and there are philosophical questions, and they can overlap. If we went to the seashore and picked up a shell, we could ask ourselves many scientific questions about that shell. What is it composed of? How long has it been here? What lived in it? How much does it weigh? There are many such questions, and answering them would tell us quite a bit about the shell, but we would be asking only about its particular physical aspects.

We could also ask other kinds of questions. What is its meaning? Who or what created it? What is its purpose? These kinds of questions are basically philosophical, though they can be brought out by scientific investigation. It has been pointed out, for example, that *The Bulletin of Atomic Physicists* is becoming a more philosophically oriented journal each year. This would support Aristotle's claim that the deeper we go into matter, the more we are led to philosophy.

The most important questions we can ask about things relate to their purposes. Aristotle felt that each thing has a purpose or function. What is the purpose of a fish? If we examine it carefully, we might say that its purpose is to swim. The purpose of a bird is to fly. What, though, is humanity's purpose? Aristotle believed that since humans are the only creatures endowed with the ability to think, their purpose is to use this ability. Thus, we achieve our true purpose when we think, and we go against this end when we do not think or when we do not think intelligently.

According to Aristotle, there is design and order in the universe, for things happen in an orderly way. An acorn becomes an oak tree and not a sycamore. A kitten becomes a cat and not a dog. We can understand the universe by studying it in terms of its purposes. Thus, whatever happens can be explained according to purpose: the acorn follows its destiny and the kitten its destiny. With regard to humans, we have already seen that our purpose is to think, but we admitted that we can refuse to think or think poorly. We can avoid thinking by not paying attention, by misdirecting our thinking, or by otherwise subverting thinking. Aristotle believed that we can refuse to think and therefore go against the design of the universe and the reason for our creation; hence, we have free will. When we go against this purpose, however, we suffer the consequences of erroneous ideas, poor health, and an unhappy life, among other things.

Macrobiotics

Moderation ✗

For Aristotle, the person who follows a true purpose leads a rational life of moderation, avoiding extremes. There are two Aristotelian extremes: the extreme of too little and the extreme of too much. In terms of eating, if one eats too much, one will gorge oneself and suffer from obesity, lack of energy, poor health in general, or death. The moderate man or woman, the thinking person, avoids such excesses. For Aristotle, the proper perspective is the Golden Mean, a path between extremes.

Aristotle's concept of the Golden Mean is illustrated by his notion of the soul as an entity to be kept in balance. He spoke of the three aspects of the soul being vegetative, animative, and rational. We might say that when humans vegetate, they are following the extreme of too little; when they are angry and hostile the extreme of too much; but when they use reason to keep vegetative and animal aspects in harmony, they are following the path for which they were designed and are fulfilling their purpose. We might also relate this idea to Plato's concept of the ideal state where the good state is one where all of its classes, that is, brass (vegetative), silver (animal), and gold (rational) are in balance and harmony. Aristotle believed that a good education helps to achieve the Golden Mean and thereby promotes the harmony and balance of soul and body.

harmony,
balance

Balance is central to Aristotle's view. He saw all the universe in some balanced and orderly fashion. As far as humans are concerned, he did not view body and mind in opposition as Plato did; rather, body is the means by which data come to us through sense perception. The raw data of sense perception are organized by the reasoning of mind. Universal principles are derived by mind from an examination of the particulars by sense perception. Thus, body and mind operate together in a balanced whole with their own internal consistencies.

Aristotle did not separate a particular thing from its universal being. Matter and form are not two different kinds of being, but fundamental aspects of the same thing. Form is in matter; for formless matter is a false notion, not a reality. The important thing to see is that all matter is in some stage of actualization. Whereas Plato was primarily interested in the realm of forms or ideas, Aristotle tried to unite the world of matter with the world of forms. An example of this is his view of actuality and potentiality. Actuality is that which is complete and perfect—the form. Potentiality refers to the capability of being actualized or gaining perfection and form. It is the union of form and matter that gives concrete reality to things. In other words, an individual acorn contains both form and matter that make up the "real" acorn we experience.

This relationship between form and matter is further illustrated by Aristotle's conception of the Four Causes:

1. *The Material Cause*, the matter from which something is made;
2. *The Formal Cause*, the design that shapes the material object;
3. *The Efficient Cause*, the agent that produces the object;

4. ***The Final Cause***, the direction toward which the object is tending.

In common-sense language, when we talk about a house, the material it is made of (the wood, bricks, and nails) is its Material Cause; the sketch or blueprint followed in constructing it is its Formal Cause; the carpenter who builds it is its Efficient Cause; and its Final Cause is that it is a place in which to live, a house.

Matter is in process, moving to some end. In this respect, Aristotle's thought is similar to the modern view of evolution and the notion of an open-ended universe. The difference between Aristotle and this modern view is that Aristotle saw this movement headed toward a final end, so for him the universe is only so open ended. The power that holds all creation and process together is God, by which Aristotle meant the power or source to which matter points beyond itself, an Ultimate Reality; hence, God is the First Cause, the Final End, the Unmoved Mover, beyond all matter and form. In this respect, Aristotle's philosophy is as esoteric as Plato's. Yet for Aristotle, God is a logical explanation for the order of the universe, its organizational and operational principle.

Indeed, organization is essential to Aristotle's philosophy. Everything can be organized into a hierarchy. For example, human beings are biologically based and rooted in nature. However, they strive for something beyond themselves. If they are characterized by body, they are also characterized by soul, or a rational aspect, the capacity to move from within. If body and soul are balanced, they are also organized, and soul is of a higher order than body, more characteristically human than anything else. For Aristotle, human beings are the *rational* animals, most completely fulfilling their purpose when they think, for thinking is their highest characteristic. So it is, with Aristotle, that everything is capable of being ordered; for reality, knowledge, and value exist independent of mind, with their own internal consistency and balance capable of being comprehended by mind.

In order to search out the structure of independent reality, Aristotle worked on logical processes. Plato used the dialectic to synthesize opposing notions about truth. Aristotle was concerned with truth, too, and he sought access to it through attempting to refine the dialectic. The logical method he developed was the syllogism, which is a method for testing the truth of statements. A famous but simplistic version of it goes as follows:

> All men are mortal.
>
> Socrates is a man;
>
> therefore, Socrates is mortal.

The syllogism is composed of a major premise, minor premise, and conclusion. Aristotle used the syllogism to help us think more accurately by ordering statements about reality in a logical, systematic form that corresponds to the facts of the situation under study.

Aristotle's logical method is deductive; that is, it derives its truth from generalizations, such as "All men are mortal." One problem with this method is that if the major premise is false, the conclusion may be false. A catch comes in determining the truth of the major premise: by what method do we test its accuracy? If we continue to use the syllogism, we must also continue to rely on unproven general premises. Aristotle's logical method runs contrary to his insistence that we can better understand form (general principle) by studying specific material objects.

In this latter instance, Aristotle's thrust is inductive; that is, we come to truth by way of specifics, or the process goes from specifics to the general. His syllogism, however, goes from generalizations (all men are mortal) to specific conclusions (Socrates is mortal). This problem of logical method was a stumbling block to thinkers for centuries. The syllogistic approach led to many false or untenable positions. It was not until the sixteenth century that Francis Bacon devised a more suitable inductive approach.

The chief good for Aristotle is happiness; however, happiness depends on a virtuous and well-ordered soul. This can come about only as we develop habits of virtue that are shaped through the proper kind of education. Education necessitates the development of our reasoning capacity so that we can make the right kinds of choices. As already indicated, this means the path of moderation. An acceptance and following of such a principle becomes the core of Aristotle's educational proposals. Although Aristotle did not go into specific detail about his educational ideas, he felt that the proper character would be formed by following the Golden Mean. This would result in desirable social development and would assist the state in producing and nurturing good citizens. In the *Politics*, Aristotle further developed his view that there is a reciprocal relationship between the properly educated person and the properly educated citizen.

The Aristotelian influence has been immensely important and includes such things as recognizing the need to study nature systematically, using logical processes in thought, deriving general truths through a rigorous study of particulars, and emphasizing the rational aspects of human nature.

Religious Realism

Thomas Aquinas (1225–1274)

Thomas Aquinas was born near Naples, Italy, in 1225. His formal education began at age five when he was sent to the Benedictine monastery at Monte Cassino. Later, he studied at the University of Naples, and in 1244, he became a Dominican friar, dedicating his life to obedience, poverty, and intellectual toil. In 1245, he was sent to the University of Paris, where he studied under Albertus Magnus, a renowned scholar of Aristotelian philosophy. He studied and taught at the University of Paris until 1259, when the Dominicans sent him back to Italy to help organize the curriculum for Dominican schools. He returned to Paris in 1268 and served the remainder of his life as a professor of theology and as an educational leader for the Dominicans. He died on March 7, 1274.

Aristotle's ideas had a great impact upon the Christian religion; in many respects, they have tended to encourage the secularization of the church, as opposed to the monasticism engendered by the writings of Augustine. Gradually, the ideas of Aristotle were incorporated into Christianity and provided it with a philosophical base. Thomas Aquinas became the leading authority on Aristotle in the Middle Ages and found no great conflict between the ideas of the pagan philosopher and the ideas of Christian revelation. He argued that since God is pure reason, then the universe is reason; by using our reason, as Aristotle suggested, we could know the truth of things. Aquinas also put emphasis on using our senses in order to obtain knowledge about the world; his proofs of God's existence, for example, depend heavily upon sensory observation.

Aquinas believed that God created matter out of nothing and God is, as Aristotle stated, the Unmoved Mover who gives meaning and purpose to the universe. In his monumental work, *Summa Theologica,* he summed up the arguments dealing with Christianity. He used the rational approach suggested by Aristotle in analyzing and dealing with various religious questions. As a matter of fact, many of the supporting arguments in Christian religion are derived from the work of Thomas Aquinas, regardless of what branch of Christianity is considered. Roman Catholicism considers the philosophy of Thomas Aquinas (Thomism) to be its leading philosophy.

Thomas Aquinas was first of all a churchman. For him, all truths were eternally in God. Truth was passed from God to humans by divine revelation, but God had also endowed human beings with the reasoning ability to seek out truth. Being the churchman that he was, Aquinas would not subordinate revelation to reason, but he did want to give reason a proper place. He viewed theology as the primary concern and philosophy as the "handmaiden of theology." Thus, by recognizing the supremacy of theology, he was able to explore the philosophical development of religious thought more fully.

Aquinas agreed with Aristotle that we come to universals by a study of particulars. He accepted the thesis of independence and "form" as the principal characteristic of all being. He upheld the "principle of immanence" that is akin to Aristotle's view of each existence moving toward perfection in form. While he agreed that soul is the form of body, he held that soul is not derived from humanity's biological roots; rather, soul is a creation, immortal, and from God. Aquinas epitomized the scholasticism of the Middle Ages, an approach that emphasized the human's eternal soul and salvation. The scholastics integrated Aristotle's philosophy with the teachings of the church, and Aquinas fulfilled an important role in this task by working out the relationship between reason and faith.

The "Angelic Doctor," as Aquinas was sometimes called, was very interested in education, as his work with the Dominicans indicates. In addition to the educational ideas in *Summa Theologica,* he also wrote *De Magistro (On the*

Teacher), which dealt specifically with his philosophy of teaching. For example, he questioned whether one human can directly teach another or whether the role of teaching is God's alone. His view was that only God should be called Teacher in the ultimate sense: if a person teaches, however, teaching is accomplished (as Augustine pointed out at an earlier time) only by and through symbols. One human mind cannot directly communicate with the mind of another, but it can communicate indirectly.

It is often said that a physician heals the body; when in truth it is nature that really heals from the inside, and all the physician can do is apply external treatments and inducements. So it is with teaching: only God can touch the inside—the soul—directly. All the teacher can do is attempt to motivate and direct the learner through signs, symbols, and the techniques of encouragement. In other words, a teacher can only "point" the learner to knowledge and understanding with signs and symbols. Nevertheless, teaching is a way to serve humankind and it is part of God's work in this world. Leading the student from ignorance to enlightenment is one of the greatest services one person can give to another.

Central to the thought of Aquinas was the Judeo-Christian belief that each of us is born with an immortal soul. Continuing the thought of Platonic idealism as well as Aristotelian realism, he maintained that the soul possesses an inner knowledge that can be brought out to illuminate one's life more completely. The major goal of education, as Aquinas saw it, is the perfection of the human being and the ultimate reunion of the soul with God. To accomplish this, we must develop the capacity to reason and to exercise intelligence.

Here Aquinas' realism came to the forefront, for he held that human reality is not only spiritual or mental but also physical and natural. From the standpoint of the human teacher, the path to the soul lies through the physical senses; education must use this path to accomplish learning. Proper instruction directs the learner to knowledge that leads to true being by progressing from a lower to a higher form. This illustrates Aquinas' Aristotelianism, for his view includes a developmental cosmology of progressing from the lower to the higher, or movement toward perfection.

Aquinas' views on education are consistent with his philosophical position. Knowledge can be gained from sense data, and it can lead one to God provided the learner views it in the proper perspective. In essence, he believed that one should proceed from the study of matter to the study of form. He disagreed with Augustine that we could know God only through faith or some intuitive process; rather, Aquinas maintained that humans can use their reason to reach God through a study of the material world. Thus, he saw no inconsistency between the truths of revelation accepted on faith and the truths arrived at through careful rational observation and study. Aquinas believed the proper education is one that fully recognizes the spiritual and material nature of the individual. Since he thought the spiritual side was the higher and more important, Aquinas was strongly in favor of primary emphasis on the education of the soul.

In the view of Aquinas, the primary agencies of education are the family and the church, while the state—or organized society—runs a poor third. The family and the church have an obligation to teach those things that relate to the unchanging principles of moral and divine law. The mother is the child's first teacher. Because the child is easily molded, it is the mother's role to set the child's moral tone. The church stands as the source of knowledge of the divine and should set the grounds for understanding God's law. The state should formulate and enforce laws on education, but it should not abridge the educational primacy of the home and church.

Both Aristotle and Aquinas held to a dualistic doctrine of reality. This can be seen in Aristotle's view of matter and form and in Aquinas' view of the material and spiritual sides of humankind. This dualism was later carried on in the great conflict between a scientific and religious view of reality.

DEVELOPMENT OF MODERN REALISM

One of the chief problems of classical realism was its failure to develop an adequate method of inductive thinking. While the classicists had developed the thesis that reality, knowledge, and value may be ascertained by studying particulars, they were still caught in an essentially deductive style of thinking. They often had their truths in hand at the start, never really doubting that there was a First Cause or an Unmoved Mover. Modern realism developed out of attempts to correct such errors, and these corrective attempts were at the heart of what we today call the scientific revolution that swept Western culture. Of all the philosophers engaged in this effort, perhaps the two most outstanding realist thinkers were Francis Bacon and John Locke. They were involved in developing systematic methods of thinking and ways to increase human understanding.

Francis Bacon (1561–1626)

Francis Bacon was not only a philosopher but a politician in the courts of Elizabeth I and James I. Bacon was not very successful in his political efforts (he was removed from office in disgrace), yet his record in philosophical development is much more impressive. Bacon's philosophical task was ambitious if not pretentious in scope. He claimed to take all knowledge as his field of investigation. That he nearly accomplished this is testimony to his genius. Perhaps his most famous work is *Novum Organum,* in which he challenged Aristotelian logic.

Bacon attacked the Aristotelians for contributing to the lethargic development of science by their adoption of theological methods of thought. The problem with theology was that it started with dogmatisms and *a priori* assumptions and then deduced conclusions. Bacon charged that science could not proceed this way, for science must be concerned with inquiry pure and simple, inquiry not burdened with preconceived notions. Bacon held that science must begin in this fashion and must develop reliable methods of inquiry. By developing a reliable method of inquiry, we could be freed from dependence on the occurrence of infrequent geniuses and could develop knowledge through the use of the method. Bacon believed that "knowledge is power" and that through the acquisition of knowledge we could more effectively deal with the problems and forces that beset us on every side. In order to accomplish these things, he devised what he called the inductive method.

Bacon opposed Aristotelian logic primarily because he thought it yielded many errors, particularly concerning material phenomena. For example, religious thinkers (such as Thomas Aquinas and the Scholastics) accepted certain axiomatic beliefs about God—that He exists, is just, all powerful, and so forth—and then they deduced all sorts of things about the use of God's power, His intervention in human affairs, and so on. Bacon's inductive approach, which asked that we begin with observable instances and then reason to general statements or laws, counteracted the Scholastic approach, for it demands verification of specific instances before a judgment is made.

After observing instances of water freezing at 32° Fahrenheit, for example, we might state as a general law that water freezes at 32° Fahrenheit. This law is valid, however, only so long as water continues to freeze at that temperature. If, because of a change in atmospheric or terrestrial conditions, water no longer freezes at 32° Fahrenheit, then we would be obliged to change our law. People can also alter their beliefs through deduction, but they are less likely to change their beliefs when they begin with supposedly absolute truths than when they begin with neutral data.

A historical example of this conservatism involved the dispute between Galileo and the Catholic church about the position of the earth in the solar system. The church defended the Ptolemaic theory that the earth is the center of the universe and that the other celestial bodies, including the sun, revolve around it. This position was supported by several deductions. To begin with, since God created the earth, it was reasonable to assume that He would place it in the center. Also, since God chose to place man on earth, the earth must have had an important place in the plan of creation; this gives added weight to the importance of the earth being centrally located. The story in the Bible about Joshua fighting a difficult battle and asking God to make the sun stand still seemed to give even more support to this position.

Galileo, however, argued for the Copernican theory that the sun and not the earth is the center of the universe, for the earth rotates on its axis and revolves about the sun. The position of Nicolaus Copernicus (as set forth in *The Revolutions of the Heavenly Bodies*) was disputed by the church because it belittled the earth and God's plan and challenged the veracity of revelation. Galileo's use of a telescope to give empirical proof to the Copernican position increased the wrath of the church. It was reported that a Jesuit who had been invited into Galileo's study to look through the telescope for proof claimed that the devil was putting those things there for him to see. Church officials required that Galileo refute his position, yet his work was later substantiated in whole or in part by such scientists as Johann Kepler, Tycho Brahe, and Isaac Newton.

Since the scientific or inductive approach uncovered many errors in propositions that had originally been taken for granted, Bacon urged that we reexamine all our previously accepted knowledge. At the very least, we should attempt to rid our minds of various "idols" before which we bow down and cloud our thinking. Bacon described four such idols. There is the Idol of the Den, whereby we believe things because of our own limited experiences. If, for example, an individual had several bad experiences with men with mustaches, he might conclude that all mustached men are bad, a clear case of faulty generalization. Another idol is the Idol of the Tribe, whereby we tend to believe things because most people believe them. Numerous studies show that many people change their opinions to match those of the majority.

Another idol that Bacon believed interfered with our thinking is what he called the Idol of the Marketplace. This idol deals with language, for Bacon believed that words are often used in ways that prevent understanding. For instance, such words as *liberal* and *conservative* might have little meaning when applied to people because one could be liberal on one issue and conservative on another.

Bacon called his fourth idol the Idol of the Theatre. This is the idol of our religions and philosophies, which may prevent us from seeing the world objectively. He called for a housekeeping of the mind, in which we break away from the dead ideas of the past and begin again by using the method of induction.

Induction is the logic of arriving at generalizations on the basis of systematic observations of particulars. The general thrust of this view can be found in Aristotle, but Aristotle never developed it into a complete system. According to Bacon, induction involves the collection of data about particulars, but it is not merely a cataloging and enumeration of data. The data must be examined; where contradictions are found, some must be discarded. In addition, facts must be processed or interpreted at the same time. If the inductive method were well developed and rigorously applied, it would benefit us to the extent that it would give us more control over the external world by unlocking the secrets of nature.

John Locke (1632–1704)

Following somewhat in Bacon's footsteps, John Locke sought to explain how we develop knowledge. He attempted a rather modest philosophical task, to "clear the ground of some of the rubbish" that hindered people's gaining knowledge. In this respect, he was attempting to rid thought of what Bacon called idols.

Locke was born in England, the son of a country lawyer. He was educated at Westminster School and at Christ Church College at Oxford, where he was later a fellow. His education was classical and scholastic. He later turned on this tradition, attacking its Aristotelian roots and its scholastic penchant for disputations, which he thought were mere wrangling and ostentation.

Locke's contributions to realism were his investigations into the extent and certainty of human knowledge. He traced the origin of ideas to the object of thought, or whatever the mind entertains. For Locke, there are no such things as innate ideas. At birth, the mind is like a blank sheet of paper, a *tabula rasa*, upon which ideas are imprinted. Thus, all knowledge is acquired from sources independent of the mind or acquired as a result of reflection on data from independent sources. In other words, all ideas are derived from experience by way of sensation and reflection.

Locke did not overly concern himself with the nature of mind itself but concentrated on how ideas or knowledge are gained by mind. External objects exist, he argued, and they are characterized by two kinds of qualities: primary qualities (e.g., solidity, size, and motion) and secondary qualities (e.g., color, taste, smell, sound, and other "sense" qualities). We may call primary qualities *objective* (adhering or directly connected with the object) and secondary qualities *subjective* (dependent upon our experiencing them).

Locke was an empiricist. He respected the concrete and practical while he distrusted abstract idealisms; consequently, what we know is what we experience. We experience the qualities of objects, whether these are material or ideational qualities. The data with which the mind operates are *experienced* data, and while they come from without, mind can combine and order experience and can become aware of its operations. Thus, knowledge depends on sensation *and* reflection.

Concerning the nature of the external objective world, Locke had little to say. He basically assumed its existence, and he explained this existence with the "doctrine of substance"; that is, substance or external reality is a necessary support for experience. Thus, he assumed an independent reality but did not try to prove it. His major contribution to philosophy was the development of an acute awareness of experience. Rather than speculation about innate ideas or essences, or an independent material reality, his field of investigation was human experience and human knowledge.

Locke's views on education, as expressed in *Some Thoughts Concerning Education*, are not as theoretical as his speculations on epistemology. They are practical ideas about conduct, laziness, rewards and punishments, and other generalities in the educational process. Locke's ideas lead to the kind of "gentlemanly" education for which English education is noted. One might argue that despite Locke's philosophical penchant for democracy, his educational ideas lend themselves to an aristocratic elitism.

CONTEMPORARY REALISM

For the most part, contemporary realism has tended to develop most strongly around concerns with science and scientific problems of a philosophical nature. This movement has occurred mostly in the twentieth century and has been associated with the development of such new schools of thought as logical positivism and linguistic analysis. Yet within this development has been a continuance of the basic thesis of independence.

Two of the most outstanding figures in contemporary realism were Alfred North Whitehead and Bertrand Russell. These men had much in common, including the fact that both were English and they collaborated on mathematical writings. Eventually, they both came to teach in some of the outstanding universities in the United States and were interested in and wrote about education. With all this in common, they went in different philosophical directions. Whitehead's direction was almost Platonic in his search for universal patterns; Russell's went toward mathematical quantification and verification as the basis of philosophical generalization.

Alfred North Whitehead (1861–1947)

One of the most fruitful things creative philosophers do is to bring about reconciliation between contending systems of thought. Aquinas did this when he reconciled Aristotelianism with Christianity. Kant did this in trying to reconcile science and traditional values. Alfred North Whitehead sought to do this by attempting to reconcile some aspects of idealism with realism, thereby reconstructing the philosophical bases of modern science.

Whitehead came to philosophy through mathematics. He coauthored with Bertrand Russell a work titled *Principia Mathematica.* He was past sixty when he turned to philosophy on a full-time basis as a professor of philosophy at Harvard. One of his outstanding philosophical treatises is *Science and the Modern World,* and some of his major statements on education may be found in *The Aims of Education and Other Essays.*

Process is central to Whitehead's philosophy, for he held that reality *is* process. What a person encounters in this process are actual entities or *occasions* (the real "things" or objects), *prehensions* (relational processes between the experiencing person and experienced objects), and *nexus* (extended time sequences in which occasions and prehensions fit together in ongoing existence).

In many respects, Whitehead sought to unite philosophical oppositions, such as subjective perception and objective entities, and he believed that we must recognize both aspects. He rejected a bifurcated reality yet recognized the individuality of a thing in itself and the relational or universal aspects of things. What he objected to was going too far in one direction to the detriment of the other. He rejected the separation of the mental into a realm by itself, for mental activity had to be viewed in the context of experience. He preferred realism as a philosophy because he thought it helped people correct the excesses of subjective thought.

It may appear that Whitehead rejected the thesis of independence. This is true to the degree that he did not see objective reality and subjective mind as absolutely separate. They are together in an organized unity or pattern. Yet, at the same time, this organic unity itself can be seen as an active system, an ultimate reality so to speak, that operates according to its own principles in process. Philosophy is simply a search for pattern in the universe. Humans can never grasp pattern in any complete sense, although they may get aspects of it. Ultimately, the universe does have rationality to it and is not mere arbitrariness.

We may say that Whitehead was following solidly in the footsteps of Aristotle, for it is apparent that pattern in Whitehead's terms is similar to form. He also followed Aristotle in going to particulars to discern pattern, yet he deviated because he held that particulars are *events* that have to be viewed in terms of open-ended process. Thus, his events are not inert particulars but organic to, and moving with, process and according to pattern.

This brings us to a consideration of Whitehead's view of education. To him, the important things to be learned are ideas. In this sense, we may say he was Platonic. However, he was adamant in urging that education be concerned with "living ideas," ideas connected with the experience of learners—ideas that are useful and capable of being articulated. He warned against learning inert ideas simply because it had been done in the past. This shows his organic orientation that education should enable us to get into the flow of existence, the process-patterns of reality.

Ideas connected to experience

Bertrand Russell (1872–1970)

Bertrand Russell was born in Wales in comfortable economic circumstances. He received his degree at Cambridge University in philosophy and mathematics. One of the first-rate minds of the twentieth century, Russell exerted considerable influence as both a writer and teacher. Some of his books are *Our Knowledge of the External World, Religion and Science,* and the famous work he coauthored with Whitehead, *Principia Mathematica* (1910–1913). In education, he wrote *Education and the Social Order* and *Education and the Modern World* among other books. He taught at Cambridge, the University of Chicago, and the University of California.

Russell was a controversial figure. During World War I, he was imprisoned for his pacifist activities. His distaste for Victorian morality, especially his views on sex and marriage, often led him into conflict with others. In the 1960s, he was at the center of "Ban the Bomb" movements and anti–Vietnam War protests in England and Europe.

Russell was a maverick realist in some respects. Where Whitehead concluded that the universe is characterized by pattern, so did Russell; but Russell felt that these patterns can be verified with precision and analyzed mathematically. There is a need, he held, to merge the logical and mathematical so that pattern can be discerned both verbally and mathematically.

Russell held that the role of philosophy is both analytic and synthetic—that is, it should be critical in its analytic phase by showing the logical fallacies and errors in past systems and it should be constructive in its synthetic phase by offering hypotheses about the nature of the universe that science has not yet determined. However, Russell felt that philosophy should be mainly analytical. It should base itself upon science, since only science has any genuine claim to knowledge. From the standpoint of science, we can see Russell's adherence to realism and what we have called the thesis of independence. It was not so much the results of science as the methods that he accepted. By using these methods, he hoped to arrive at valid philosophical constructions—not constructions of large generalization, but rather piecemeal, detailed, verifiable constructions.

One could get two sorts of particular data on independent reality: hard data and soft data. Hard data refer to the facts of the situation, facts that can withstand the scrutiny of reflection and remain intact. Soft data are such things as beliefs, things that can neither be verified nor denied with any degree of certainty. Russell's stated purpose was to base his philosophical constructions as much as possible on the hard and verifiable side, the side of science; but he also recognized the soft side. This, he held, should make us more sensitive to overgeneralizing and its accompanying dangers of arriving at false certainties.

By using a cautious or more temperate approach to science, Russell hoped we could begin to solve such perplexing problems as poverty and ill health. He thought of education as the key to a better world. If we would use existing knowledge and apply tested methods, then through education we could eradicate such problems as poverty and thus transform the world. Russell even speculated that if this were done on a wide scale, the transformation could conceivably be accomplished in one generation.

For a time, Russell tried to put some of his educational ideas to work at the school he founded, called Beacon Hill. However, his radicalism met resistance, and his own driving inquisitiveness soon led him to other causes and reforms. Although his efforts in education at Beacon Hill met with limited success, Russell continued to the end of his life to try to bring about through education changes that he deemed beneficial to humanity.

REALISM AS A PHILOSOPHY OF EDUCATION

Realism is a confusing philosophy because there are so many varieties: classical realism, religious realism, scientific realism, and others. This confusion dates back to Aristotle, for although his prominence in philosophy was primarily derived from his differences with Platonic philosophy, there are probably more similarities overall than differences between Plato and Aristotle. The primary confusion over realism may be between a religious realism and a secular or scientific realism. Religious realism would show the similarities of Aristotle's philosophy to that of Plato and Thomas Aquinas; secular realism would relate Aristotle's work more to the development of scientific philosophy through the works of Bacon, Locke, and Russell. Whitehead may be said to incorporate aspects of each in his interpretation of realism.

Aims of Education

Plato, as an idealist, believed that such abstractions as truth, goodness, and beauty could be reached only through the study of ideas, primarily through the use of the dialectic. Aristotle, on the other hand, thought that ideas (forms) are also found by studying the world of matter. Plato and Aristotle end up at the same place, but the method of getting there is different. Plato believed that one acquires knowledge of ideas through contemplation of ideas; Aristotle believed that one could acquire knowledge of ideas or forms through a study of matter. Whereas Plato rejected matter as an object of study or as a real entity, Aristotle used matter as an object of study to reach something further.

For the religious realist, matter is not so important in itself unless it leads to something beyond itself. Aristotle recognized that one may look at any object simply as a scientific study, but this would be dealing only with one aspect of matter. A scientist finding a shell on the seashore may examine it descriptively in terms of size, shape, weight, and so on. Such concerns, however, should also lead to philosophical questions relating to the beginnings and purpose of the shell.

This process is illustrated by contemporary scientific efforts to study the moon. Specimens brought back by the astronauts are studied intensively. Many photographs and television compositions have been made on the natural makeup of the moon, but these have not been made simply to catalog its shape, size, and weight; rather, the purpose has been much deeper. Scientists and thinkers of various disciplines are interested in discovering knowledge about the very origins of our universe. This shows that scientific inquiry can lead to the most profound and ultimate kinds of philosophical questions. Thus, one can transcend nature and use it to venture into the realm of ideas.

For the religious realist, the prime reason for the study of nature is to transcend matter. The argument might run thus: God, who is pure spirit, created the world. He created it out of nothing; but He put himself into the world, giving it order, regularity, and design. By studying the world carefully, and by discovering its order and regularity, we can come to know about God. Religious realists, such as Thomas Aquinas, would say that this is our prime purpose—God created the world to provide a vehicle through which people could come to know Him.

Thomists (those who follow the teachings of Thomas Aquinas) maintain that the curriculum should include practical and speculative knowledge. For example, education helps the individual become self-aware so that one can think about one's actions. Through the practical study of ethics, one is led to the higher plain of ultimate reality, or metaphysics. Thomists believe that true education is always in process and never becomes complete. It is a process of the continuing development of the human soul.

Many thinkers (not necessarily philosophical realists) have believed that nature could provide us with something greater than itself. William

Wordsworth, Ralph Waldo Emerson, and Henry David Thoreau, all nineteenth century romanticists, used the theme that nature could be transcended by thinking and that individuals could venture into higher realms of thought. Religious realists believe that this kind of transcending should be the principal aim of education.

On the other hand, secular realists emphasize the sensory material world and its processes and patterns rather than the transcendent spiritual world to which sensory data might lead. Their approach is basically scientific. The scientific movement beginning with Francis Bacon ushered in an era of thought that stressed not only an understanding of the material world but control of it as well. It was Aristotle who pointed out the order and regularity of the material world; by this same process, scientists came to talk about the "laws of nature."

Secular realism stresses an understanding of the material world through the development of methods of rigorous inquiry. Bacon first suggested that people should clear their minds of the idols of generalization, language, and philosophy. Deduction, which was the prevailing method of thought prior to Bacon, was based primarily on rational thought. Reason alone, however, had led to many errors in Aristotle's thinking and to the metaphysical extravagances of the Scholastics. It was reason that produced such imaginings as mermaids, devils, centaurs, and the like. For the secular realist, the way out of this dilemma—that is, deciding which ideas are true—is to verify them in the world of experience.

John Locke gave great support to Bacon's empiricism by showing that no ideas are innate, but through reflection or reason we may create ideas, such as the idea of a purple cow, which does not exist in the world of experience. The empirical movement that Bacon and Locke encouraged requires that ideas must be subject to public verification. This means that ideas that cannot be proved through scientific experiment must be considered to be only hypotheses.

Secular realists promote a study of science and the scientific method. They believe that we need to know the world in order to use it to insure our own survival. This idea of survival is an important one. For example, Herbert Spencer, the nineteenth century British philosopher and social scientist, placed self-preservation as a primary and fundamental aim of education. In other words, the things children most need to know are those things that maintain their existence as individuals, as family members, and as citizens. The secular realist sees our control over nature as a vast improvement from our early beginnings when we were at the mercy of nature. Our misunderstanding of nature, such as the superstitious explanations for typhoons and floods, led to many false beliefs. Today, our continued advancement depends upon even greater understanding and control of nature. We might say that our technical skill has gotten us into the ecological mess, but the secular realist would add, it can also get us out of it.

Secular realism maintains that there are essential ideas and facts to know that can be learned only by a study of the material world. It places great stress on a study of basic facts, both for the purpose of survival and the advancement of technology and science. One could say that technical schools, such as the Massachusetts Institute of Technology, are "realist" in their approach to education. The former Soviet Union seemed to prefer this approach to education for technical and political purposes. In the United States, there has been strong support for a more technical and scientific education since the launching of Sputnik in 1957. Many education critics, such as Admiral Hyman Rickover, have argued that American education has become too "soft," dealing with "fads and frills," and that education needs to return to basic studies, like mathematics and science.

Realism as an educational philosophy has long been with us in one way or another, but it tends to assert itself most in times of turmoil. It is almost as if we have other educational philosophies when we can afford them, but realism is a necessity. The claim is that we will always have some need for basic factual data and such subjects as reading, writing, and arithmetic.

This tendency seemed to be pointed up particularly when the Soviets launched the first satellite. Many people believed that our second-place technical position in this respect was due in large measure to the schools, which were not teaching enough basic subject matter, particularly in science and mathematics. Rickover pointed to the dearth of competent scientists in this country as compared with the Soviet Union. He also praised Swiss education for its adherence to basics and believed that the American system should do likewise. He laid much of the blame for our lack of technical know-how and creativity at the door of John Dewey and the progressives, who were promoting an education that Rickover thought was not only superficial but actually dangerous in terms of our survival. An even more caustic critic was Max Rafferty, whose book *Suffer Little Children* was extremely popular and who believed that basic subject matter and other staples of American education, such as a concern for religion, patriotism, and capitalism, were being neglected.

A group of educators who were greatly concerned with the decline of basic subject matter in American schools formed an organization called the Council for Basic Education. This organization has fought strenuously to keep and add basic subject matter in schools, not only the three Rs, but such subjects as science and history. One of the leading spokesmen for the council, James Koerner, believes that part of the problem lies in the training of teachers, who are given survey courses instead of more basic studies and who come to the classroom intellectually impoverished.

A major problem, according to the realists, is a general cultural malaise caused by a lack of commitment to fundamental values. This is shown in the breakdown of discipline and disregard for basic traditions. Perhaps the best illustration of this is the fact that schools have drifted away from a concentration on the essentials of reading, writing, arithmetic, and character development.

Criticism

The "open education" movement is a recent example of this drift. Rather than having children study essential but not always exciting subjects, a "do-your-own-thing" ethic was instituted in which children were encouraged to "explore" and "discover" things that interested them personally. This creates a problem, many realists charge, because children seldom have clearly identified interests with enough focus to direct their needed educational development. In addition, they do not always know what is best for them or what they need, and this is confirmed by adults who in later life claim that such educational approaches failed to prepare them for the real world. Perhaps the crowning evidence of the failure of "discovery" and "open" approaches, realists argue, is the embarrassing number of high school graduates who are functionally illiterate.

The breakdown of commitment to basic cultural values is not limited just to education but is reflected in the larger society. The confusion surrounding the Vietnam War and the United States's role in it is but one example. Democracy depends on public debate of issues, but many realists feel that the willingness of organized society to allow young adults to rebel against authority when the country was engaged in military conflict reflects the extent of the breakdown and the failure of education to secure allegiance to basic values.

Perhaps the best illustration of the realist charge is the Watergate scandal, in which government officials, including the president, were involved in a cover-up of illegal and unethical political activities. Critics point to the fact that all of the people involved in this scandal went through American schools. Yet the schools apparently failed to instill those character traits and basic values necessary for ethical leadership. One wonders, even in the wake of Watergate, whether the schools have yet risen to meet the challenge. Despite all the talk about "back to the basics" and "accountability" in education, many observers of realist orientation question what is actually being done.

The failure can be seen at the local and national levels but is also present in international affairs. Many critics point to the erosion of America's political, economic, and military power. Americans have been held hostage by militarily weak foreign powers, and the United States has been virtually powerless to act. Other nations have been invaded by powerful neighbors, and the United States has been unable to reassert its once potent political leadership. Probably most frustrating of all is the decline in economic power, a much-vaunted strength in the past; so that American industrial might is at the mercy of small nations who control energy resources. Many nations have viewed education as a weapon to achieve economic, political, and military power, and critics wonder why Americans do not use this resource now by showing a commitment to education through expansion of funds and programs rather than the budgetary restraints currently fashionable.

One of the most tragic consequences of all of this, as frequently pointed out by such figures as Admiral Rickover, is that the talent of our most precious resource—the intellectually gifted—is being squandered. "Watered down" courses and "fads and frills" have limited the development of superior stu-

RE: gifted students

dents by bringing them down to the level of the common denominator. Textbooks reflect this by simplified reading material and content geared to the mythical "average" student. Instead of pulling students up to their academic capabilities, such practices only pull them down to the "accepted" average.

Modern exponents of a classical realist outlook have championed an approach called the Great Books of the Western World. Articulated by such figures as Robert Hutchins and Mortimer Adler, this approach stresses understanding perennial truths and knowledge that have been passed down through the ages. Thus, the curriculum should be organized around those great works that, even though some may be centuries old, still present fundamental knowledge about individual and social existence, human institutions, intellectual and moral endeavor, and the natural order. St. John's College at Annapolis has such a program in operation and is a good example of the kind of education advocates of classical realism would favor. At St. John's, students read the classics, analyze them, and then apply them to an understanding of current problems. Although no book less than fifty years old is on the official list of Great Books, students are encouraged to read such latter-day writers as Faulkner and Hemingway as supplementary reading. The emphasis in classical and modern readings, however, is upon universal truths that are germane to people in all times and places.

Following this line of reason, one proposal for educational reform that has elicited a great deal of interest since 1982 is *The Paideia Proposal* by Mortimer Adler on behalf of the members of the Paideia Group. In this proposal, the basic recommendations are that (1) schooling be a one-track system and (2) that it be general, nonspecialized, and nonvocational. Those who are familiar with Adler's previous writings and his long association with a Great Books approach to education will see this as a continuation of that aim. While Adler gives due consideration to skills (such as problem solving) and to subjects (such as mathematics, history, geography, and social studies), there is a strong emphasis on ideas found in books and art. Adler feels that all students should encounter these great ideas and that the best way of teaching them is through the Socratic (maieutic) method of questions and answers. In one exercise that Adler has used in demonstrations around the country, students analyze the words and statements contained in the Declaration of Independence.

Adler's proposals, while receiving a great deal of attention from the press, have not excited teachers and administrators to any great extent. Many educators feel that a track system is much more viable when there are students on diverse levels of ability and that the kind of education suggested by Adler promotes an elitist conception of education whereby only the "intelligent" students are able to master the material with any real depth. Another criticism has been that this is just another form of a "back to basics" movement. In *Paideia Problems and Possibilities,* a sequel to *The Paideia Proposal,* Adler argues that while there are some similarities to a "back to basics" movement, there is also a difference in that the "Paideia" approach emphasizes a discussion approach that is not generally used in teaching the basics. In response to the charge of being elitist, Adler affirms that his approach to learning is designed for *all* students, not just those who are college bound. If Adler's proposals have not resulted in widespread school reform, they still attract attention. For example, the Paideia Program, headed by Adler, continues to operate at the Institute for Philosophical Research at the University of Chicago, and the National Center for the Paideia Program was opened at the University of North Carolina in September 1988.

Critics of the advocates of "basic education" consider them alarmists crying wolf and say that their approach to education looks backward to the American schools of a bygone era. These critics assert that "basic education" is a conservative approach, a realism more interested in facts than in brotherhood, creativity, and human relations. Many educators maintain that facts can be taught in a pleasant atmosphere without the rote-style education associated with realism. Realists respond by saying this argument is often a cover-up for the schools' neglecting the hard tasks of education.

Between 1982 and 1984, several national reports on education appeared, such as *Making the Grade* (Twentieth Century Fund), *America's Competitive Challenge* (Business–Higher Education Forum), *Academic Preparation for College* (The College Entrance Examination Board), *Action for Excellence* (Education Commission of the States), *Education and Economic Progress: Toward a National Educational Policy* (The Carnegie Corporation), and *A Place Called School: Prospects for the Future* by John Goodlad. These reports emphasized the belief that American education is in trouble and that perhaps some radical surgery is needed to correct the situation.

The most widely discussed report, *A Nation At Risk,* was issued by Terrel H. Bell, former Secretary of Education. This report makes the following recommendations for all high school students: four years of English, three years of mathematics, three years of science, three years of social studies, and one-half year of computer science. For those going to college, two years of foreign languages is also recommended. Generally, the report supports more rigorous and measurable standards in the schools, a more effective use of the existing school day, and a longer day or a lengthened school year. In addition to this, the report also recommended higher teaching standards, an aptitude for teaching as well as demonstrated competence, and a leadership role by principals and superintendents.

Critics have also pointed out that there is nothing really new in these proposals and that they seem to reinforce many of the reforms recommended by conservative or "rightist" educational organizations. With regard to the report, perhaps the most significant thing is the title of the report itself—that is, that the National Commission on Excellence feels that unless such reforms are implemented, we face risk as a nation. Many interpret the risk to be one of not matching other countries economically and militarily.

When we look back over the long history of education, we are reminded of the story about the archaeologist who found an ancient clay tablet on which was written, "Why aren't they teaching them anything in schools anymore?" One of the functions of education from the earliest times has been to teach pupils the kinds of things society needs to know in order to survive. In ancient Egypt, students were expected to know the religious and political demands and how to prepare for an afterlife. In Greece and Rome, young men were taught oratory as a way of improving their stations in life. In the Middle Ages, a few were prepared for the priesthood while others were taught the code of chivalry. In the early history of our own country, the Native Americans had elaborate ceremonies through which to educate the young in the ways of the tribe.

Education has always been used as a way of teaching essential things to people; in this respect, it has served a valuable function. The need for knowing these essentials is no less today, argues the realist; in fact, it is probably greater, since there are more things to learn than ever before. When we fail to teach a child how to read and write, we doom that child to difficulty in finding a job, in knowing how to vote, or in developing socially. It is possible that because of this limitation, the child will become a liability rather than an asset to society. In the same way, when we fail to teach children the kind of preparation and skills needed for our technological maintenance and development, we are not using the schools to their fullest capacity. This may damage our status as a nation of power and influence in the world.

Although realists argue that education should develop technical skill and turn out specialists and scientists, they are not opposed to education in the humanities. However, they find that the schools are not teaching the humanities in ways conducive to cognitive development. It seems that teachers are more interested in turning out critics of literature than in teaching the literature itself.

Such educators as Harry Broudy would like teachers to take a critical look at what they are doing. When they see the negative effects the trend in contemporary education is having, it is hoped that they will reverse this trend by returning to more basic subject matter. Realists complain that they have been equated with such caricatures as Dickens's Mr. Gradgrind and Irving's Ichabod Crane. They say they are not for mere memorization and rote learning of facts, nor do they dismiss problem solving, projects, and enjoyable experiences in learning activities. They do feel, however, that such experiences should be fruitful in terms of producing students with needed knowledge and skills. They would very much like to see our institutions of higher education turn out capable teaching specialists who would serve as models for the future development of students. In today's world, we should equip students with information to understand current events and to assist in the advancement of knowledge in the future. Realists argue that we can do this only by providing students with basic and essential knowledge.

While realists share many concerns, there are also variations. If they agree that schools should promote the essentials, they each define *essential* from individual perspectives. For instance, Whitehead was almost idealistic in his recommendation that education be primarily concerned with ideas, but he condemned what he referred to as "scraps of information" and "inert ideas," for ideas should be learned in a practical and useful context. What makes his thought realistic is his view that one learns most truly from the material world in which one actually lives. He defended both classical and specialized studies if these studies have important applications *now*. Inertness, he held, is a central hazard in all education; consequently, Whitehead's view of the essentials might be very different from what someone else views as necessary, for he had a distinct notion of what education should contain.

Realists put great emphasis on the "practical" side of education, and their concept of practical includes education for moral and character development. John Locke, Johann F. Herbart, and Herbert Spencer all held that the chief aim of education should be moral education. Whitehead was close to this position when he said, "the essence of education is that it be religious." Spencer (in his essay "What Knowledge Is of Most Worth?") held that science provides for both moral and intellectual education because the pursuit of science demands integrity, self-sacrifice, and courage. For Locke, good character is superior to intellectual training; however, Locke's views on character education seem to have been directed primarily at the English gentry of his day, who were supposed to set examples for the rest of society. Herbart thought that moral education is founded on knowledge, and Spencer agreed with this theory.

Thus, we can see different approaches to a common thrust. Realists agree that education should be based on the essentials and the practical, but they vary in their individual approaches to these things. Regardless of these individual approaches, however, there is an underlying common element. The essentials and the practicalities of education lead to something beyond themselves, an element that is distinctly Aristotelian; that is, it proceeds from matter to form, from imperfection to perfection. Realists are Aristotelian in viewing education as the process of developing our rational powers to their fullest so that we can achieve the good life.

Methods of Education

The secular realist maintains that a proper understanding of the world requires an understanding of facts and ways of ordering and classifying knowledge. The establishment of scientific laws, for example, depends on verification of up-to-date factual data. The schools should teach such fundamental facts about the universe, and a good school program will present material in interesting and enjoyable ways. Not only facts but the method of arriving at facts must be taught. The realist places enormous emphasis upon critical reason aided by observation and experimentation.

Secular realism has had more recent impact upon the philosophy of education than has religious realism. It is not surprising, for example, that critics like Hyman Rickover and James Bryant Conant were also scientists. The kind of education they promote is primarily technical and leads to specialization. The idea of specialization, which is so repugnant to the idealist, arose out of the efforts to refine and establish definitive scientific knowledge. Secular realists charge that the generalist is prone to wide flights of fantasy, very little of which can be verified. It is very important to establish what we know, and this can be accomplished only by drawing together the efforts of many people, each one working on a small component of knowledge. The realists believe less in the personality of the teacher than in the effectiveness of the teacher to impart useful knowledge about the world.

Realists support the lecture method and other formal ways of teaching. Although such objectives as self-realization are valuable, realists maintain that self-realization best occurs when students are knowledgeable about the external world. Consequently, they must be exposed to facts, and the lecture method can be an efficient, organized, and orderly way to accomplish this objective. The lecture method is not the only one realists promote; for they insist that whatever the method used, it should be characterized by the integrity that comes from systematic, organized, and dependable knowledge.

Reflect for a moment on our chaotic history and how we have suffered because of ignorance of facts about such things as a balanced diet, diseases and their causes, and the causes of natural disasters—knowledge we take for granted today. Our grasp of knowledge and the enjoyment of a better life have come as a result of a slow but steady accumulation of facts. People could not exist for long without knowledge of at least some basic facts.

Realists think that the factual side of learning need not be painful or boring; in fact, they hold that learning should be enjoyable as well as useful. John Locke thought that play is a distinct aid to learning. He seems to have had a good grasp of child psychology, and he advocated methods that seem modern. In addition to asserting the usefulness of play, he urged that children should not be vexed by boring lessons, that they should not be pushed beyond their level of readiness (even if this means a year's delay in learning to read), that children should be given positive rewards to encourage further learning, and that the teacher should never push children beyond their natural inclinations. In many respects, Locke stands as a forerunner of much in modern educational theory. His recognition that children should not be pushed beyond their ability and readiness sounds current, and his sensitivity to a child's "natural inclinations" has a strong resemblance to the major tenets of modern theories of child growth and development.

While some realists, such as Locke, were systematic and organized from the standpoint of specific aspects of the child or the environment, others (such as Whitehead) looked to more general patterns in human activity.

Whitehead spoke of the "rhythmic" flow of education that can be discerned in three primary stages. First is the stage of romance (up to about the age of fourteen), in which the child's educational activity should be characterized mainly by discovering broad themes, shaping questions, and devising new experiences. The second stage (from the age of fourteen to eighteen) is the stage of precision, characterized by the disciplined study of specific and particular knowledge. Stage three is the stage of generalization, from eighteen to around twenty-two. It focuses on students becoming effective individuals capable of dealing with immediate experiences whereby they apply the principles of knowledge to life.

Despite the attention given to the nature of the child and the flow of experience by realist thinkers like Locke and Whitehead, critics of realism point out that in practice, realism is rigid. They charge that, in fact, realist theory results in such practices as Herbart's "five formal steps of learning": preparation, presentation, association, systematization-generalization, and application. Russell Hamm charges that such an approach leads mechanically to reviewing homework, presenting new material, having a question-and-answer period, doing desk work, and receiving new homework assignments. Herbart, for example, also recommended that children be kept occupied as much as possible and that corporal punishment be used when necessary. His recommendations could be due to the realist affinity for precision and order. The desire for order and precision is found in such practices as ringing bells, set time periods for study, departmentalization, daily lesson plans, course scheduling, increasing specialization in the curriculum, prepackaged curriculum materials, and line–staff forms of administrative organization.

Although all realists promote the importance of knowledge about the physical universe, there is a difference in the ends to which such knowledge is put. The religious realist believes that knowledge should ultimately lead to things beyond itself, such as God or Truth. One of the fundamental obligations of the teacher is to help the student know about the world and see the use of this knowledge as a way of reaching ultimates. In some parochial schools, for example, students study such areas as geography, history, and science; but these subjects are presented in ways that emphasize religious ideas or morality. The secular realist, however, tends to see knowledge about the physical world primarily in its use-value in improving technology and advancing civilization. Although realists may teach the same things, they may teach them for different purposes.

Many realists support competency, accountability, and performance-based teaching. They assume that educational growth in terms of competency, performance, and knowledge of the facts can be achieved and is measurable to a considerable extent. Furthermore, while it may be difficult to measure a student's growth in such areas as values, ethical considerations, and social relations, realists generally maintain that anything that exists, exists in some form capable of measurement. The best way to approach and deal with such problems as ethics is through our knowledge about the facts of ethics. It may be, for example, that the best ethics show us how to put ourselves in tune with the laws of the universe.

Realists emphasize the role of the teacher in the educational process. The teacher should present material in a systematic and organized way and should promote the idea that there are clearly defined criteria one can use in making judgments about art, economics, politics, and education. For example, realists would assert that a work of art, such as a painting, can be evaluated in terms of objective criteria, like the kind of brush stroke used, the shading of colors, the balance and quality of the subject matter, and the message conveyed. The same thing applies to the activity of education; there are certain objective criteria one can use to judge whether particular activities are worthwhile—for example, the type of material presented, how it is organized, whether or not it suits the psychological makeup of the child, whether the delivery system is suitable, and whether it achieves the desired results.

Contemporary realists emphasize the importance of scientific research and development. The "Scientific Movement in Education" has been accomplished primarily since 1900 and has brought about the advancement of knowledge in the psychology and physiology of education and developmental approaches to education. This movement has also been largely responsible for the extensive use of IQ tests, standardized achievement tests, diagnostic tests, and competency tests. Curricula have reflected the impact of the movement in the appearance of standard work lists, homogeneous grouping of students on the basis of intelligence, and standardized and serialized reading textbooks. The movement has also spawned the application of more precise and empirically based administrative techniques. A more recent development is the growing extent to which computer technology is used in the schools. While these developments have often met with sharp resistance and counterattacks, it seems that this aspect of realism in education has also met with increasing acceptance by many professional educators.

Contemporary critics of American education often strike at the widespread use of scientific technology as one of the prime evils in the schools. Others, while less acid in their criticism of technology and science itself, quarrel with the underlying realist theory as being the culprit behind the misuse of science and technology, largely because they think realists are too accepting and uncritical of things labeled "scientific." Whatever the position one wishes to take on the issue, the existence of such an issue is witness to the vitality realist ideas still have.

Curriculum

Although realists have different views about what subjects should constitute the curriculum, they agree that studies should be practical and useful. Locke, in *Some Thoughts Concerning Education*, approved of such practical studies as reading, writing, drawing, geography, astronomy, arithmetic, history, ethics, and law—with supplementary studies in dancing, fencing, and riding. Locke, as did Froebel, emphasized the educational value of play and physical activity. Locke believed that children should spend much time in the open air and accustom themselves to "heat and cold, shine and rain." He focused his attention upon the complete person and included not only intellectual concerns, but also diet, exercise, and recreation. He believed that instruction in reading should begin as soon as a child is able to talk. Writing should begin soon afterward. He promoted studies in languages, particularly French and Latin. He favored gardening and carpentry as useful educational experiences, as well as the idea of "a grand tour" with one's tutor.

When one peruses Locke's writings, one finds two curricula in his system: one for the rich and one for the poor. He proposed that all children between ages three and fourteen whose parents were on relief should be sent to a work school for as long as they resided with their parents. They should earn their way at this school so as not to burden the local government financially. While there, they should have a "belly-full of bread daily" and in cold weather "a little warm water gruel." They were to be taught the manual skills of spinning, knitting, and "some other part of woolen manufacturing," and "some sense of religion."

One of the historical features of the realist curriculum has been the great attention given to the use of didactic and object studies in education. For example, Comenius, a theologian and educator in the sixteenth century, was the first to introduce an extensive use of pictures in the educational process. He believed that it was possible for an individual to obtain all knowledge if provided with the proper kind of education. This proper kind of education should be based on a curriculum to perfect one's natural powers by training the senses. He stressed the importance of studying nature, and his curriculum included such subjects as physics, optics, astronomy, geography, and mechanics. In stressing this "pansophic" goal of achieving all knowledge, Comenius felt that schools should be enjoyable places with sympathetic teachers.

This idea of developing the senses in education was also adopted by Jean Jacques Rousseau, Johann Pestalozzi, and Friedrich Froebel, among others. Pestalozzi held that "sense impression of Nature is the only true foundation of human instruction, because it is the only true foundation of human knowledge." All that follows, he believed, is a result of this sense impression. Pestalozzi promoted such skills as spinning and gardening, with such subjects as arithmetic to be correlated with nature by having children apply numbers to objects. Froebel (the founder of the kindergarten), who studied at the Pestalozzian Institute of Frankfort, also believed in "object studies"; his primary educational methods focused on "gifts," songs, and games. Although Froebel's educational techniques began in the material world with material objects, he saw all things unified in God, who expresses Himself both in physical nature and in the human spirit.

Johann F. Herbart was another realist educator strongly influenced by Pestalozzi. Herbart criticized what he characterized as the atomistic curriculum of his day. He felt that there should be a system of "correlation and concentration" whereby each subject would bear upon, and be integrated with, other related subjects. Teaching, he believed, should be multilateral. Geography, economics, and history should be taught so that the student can see relationships that provide the basis for new knowledge. Herbart felt that ideas are kept alive through interest, and one function of education is to see that ideas are retained in the mind through books, lectures, and other teaching devices.

A more recent educator who promoted both interest and the use of objects in the educational process was Maria Montessori. The Montessori method provides all sorts of experiences with blocks, cylinders, and geometric patterns. These objects assist not only in cognitive development but in physical development as well.

Although her approach was originally designed for so-called mentally defective children, she later expanded it to include all children. Montessori believed that we can know children by observing them, and she felt that too many educators interfere with children's "spontaneous activity." In *The Secret of Childhood*, she maintained that children have a secret world of their own that educators can learn if they make the effort. Education means removing barriers from the path a child takes to discover the world and should therefore consist of a "prepared environment" with materials that children can use and that teach them how to learn. This method is solidly in keeping with the realist educational advocacy of sense perception and object lessons.

When we look at an overview of what realist educators propose for a curriculum, we see that it tends to be both mental and physical, places an emphasis on subject matter, and is highly organized and systematic in its approach.

CRITIQUE OF REALISM IN EDUCATION

Realism has steadily gained ground in American education. To say that this advance began with Sputnik and the accompanying clamor in 1957 and 1958 would not be true, although that event certainly accelerated the movement. Realism received its major thrust from the industrial and technological age that has characterized American society from the late nineteenth century to the present. It is little wonder that our schools would see as their major task the training and preparation of professionals and technicians in a society where professionalism and technical skill are so highly prized. Yet many critics decry this state of affairs as shortsighted and dehumanizing, pandering primarily to material concerns. Although classical and religious realists still recognize the higher ends of moral and spiritual values, critics charge that

Social control + order

scientific realists generally maintain a materialistic conception of human nature biased toward social control and social order.

While the problems of order and control are often laid at the door of secular and scientific realism, there is evidence that the bias toward order and control goes back to Aristotle and Thomas Aquinas. These thinkers tended to see the universe in terms of an independent reality with its own internal and systematic order. Thus, we must adapt and adjust to this reality; our dreams and desires have to be subsumed under its demands. The contemporary outcome of this view is the pressure to adjust to the needs of the corporate industrial state, totalitarian regimes, religious systems, and other overriding and apparently enduring world views.

John Dewey tried to counteract what he considered the negative aspects of both realism and idealism by showing that what we know as real is neither totally in the mind nor totally objective and external; rather, he argued that human reality consists of both individuality and environment. Instead of adjustment to environmental and social conditions as a one-way movement, Dewey advocated the use of intelligence to transform the world to be more in line with human values. Dewey's detractors have accused him of promoting the "life adjustment" movement in education, but this movement is more characteristic of realism than of Dewey's philosophy.

Perhaps the most vocal critics of realism are those with an existentialist orientation. They attack realism because it has advocated the idea of a fixed, intelligible universe, capable of being perceived objectively by the observing intellect. This view, they charge, has been promoted through the centuries, through the Age of Reason and the Enlightenment, and into the contemporary scene of the technological society. It has deified reason to the detriment of the total human by ignoring passion, emotion, feeling, and irrationality. If we want truly to understand the human being in the world, we must consider the totality or entirety of the individual, a totality that realism tends to ignore or hide. Realists claim that they do view human beings in their entirety and their entirety is one of dependence on a universe much larger than themselves. The critics reply that the realist view of the totality of the human being in the world is conditioned by preconceived notions about the universe.

These preconceived notions often lead realists to conclusions about humanity that create difficulties in the field of education. For instance, Whitehead disparages "the dull average student." Although such "average" students may constitute a majority of the school-age population, realists seem more concerned with the necessity of students measuring up to the standard curriculum than seeing them as individuals. Russell believed in the love of knowledge for its own sake, despite all of his talk about individuality, subjectivity, and humanistic concerns. He spoke of "excellencies" as the desirable things to achieve in education, a view that would probably meet with little resistance except that the underlying assumption is that achievement of these "excellencies" has to be measured against external criteria. The net result of views expressed by both Whitehead and Russell is that students come to be seen in terms of subservience to a superior entity, such as the curriculum or standards of excellence. This problem is central to the criticism of the purported dehumanizing effects of realism.

This point of contention is further illustrated by the controversy over liberal and vocational education. While many realists support the need for both, they seem to view liberal education as intensive studies in the arts and sciences for superior students and feel that slower students should be given a more narrow technical-vocational training. James Bryant Conant, for example, studied the social conditions of our inner cities and concluded that the conditions faced by the urban poor, particularly the black poor, are breeding grounds for "social dynamite." Critics point out that while Conant could have devised uplifting, sensitive, and humanitarian reform proposals, he recommended that poor people be given vocational education. Such outlooks all too often result in one kind of education for the "superior" people and another kind of education for everybody else.

Despite the historical insistence of realists on holism, they have for good or bad encouraged a movement in education toward specialism. This may be a corollary of the knowledge explosion we are all facing, and realists, like others, are caught up in this problem. Their tendency to concentrate on specialized, piecemeal modules of knowledge does little to cure the problem. Comenius advocated a "pansophist" approach in education to enable individuals to use reason to gain all knowledge. This idea has been promoted historically by many realists, but their proclivity for the piecemeal approach does not lend itself to holistic and unified conclusions.

Today, the realist ideal of the scientist and technician shows little recognition of the unity of knowledge, for scientists often work on one small component of a larger entity without understanding that larger entity or appreciating its implications for humanity. Thus, it is possible for a scientist to work on a project that may have antisocial or antihuman implications without being aware of it. The highly trained technician working on expensive space technology at Cape Canaveral may ignore the fact that his expensive gadgetry takes up resources that could otherwise be used to alleviate human misery.

Realism displays a bias in favor of a fact-based approach to knowledge. While this has its laudable aspects, it is also susceptible to various errors. What was once thought to be indisputable fact in so many cases is now considered to be interesting myth and outright ignorance, such as the Ptolemaic cosmology once supported by religious realism. Even the "laws" of modern physics, which have tremendous research and experimentation behind them, may fall to new ideas in the future.

There is also confusion over what is meant by "fact," for there are "facts of reason" and "facts of empirical research." Aristotle thought it self-evident that objects of different weights fall at different speeds. It was not until

Galileo that this "fact of reason" was overturned by empirical research; he reportedly tested the proposition and found it false. Keeping these problems in mind, it is understandable that a "factual" approach may lead to closed-mindedness and narrowness. If one already has the truth in hand (whether religious or scientific), one is hardly motivated to search further. This point of view is antiphilosophical to the extent that it discourages an open mind and the unshackled search for wisdom.

One current controversy that has its roots in the realist tradition is the problem of testing. A realist assumption (as expressed by E. L. Thorndike) that anything that exists, exists in some quantity and can be measured has led to a plethora of standardized tests ranging from the IQ tests of young children to college board and national teachers' examinations. The testing movement has been touted as "scientific" and "fact based," and it has gained an almost uncritical acceptance in some quarters.

The same kind of criticism can be directed toward statistical research studies, such as opinion surveys and other kinds of data sampling. The assumption is that what one finds by statistical research is "scientific" and "factual"; this, in turn, leads the researcher to believe that his findings really reveal some truth. What can happen is the "pygmalion effect"; that is, the data influence the way a teacher views the members of the class. The dangers of such a faith in "factual data" have received widespread attention in various professional journals, but it seems that testing is hardly abating and may even be growing. It is almost as if educators are caught in the clutches of a blind faith in anything labeled "scientific fact."

It is often claimed that the testing movement is one of the areas where science has had its greatest impact on education. This movement has accelerated in recent years in conjunction with the clamor for "cost-effectiveness" and a "systems approach" to education. The movement has been directed toward finding some way to gauge teacher effectiveness and student performance more efficiently. Many states already require students to pass competency tests before graduation.

Some school systems also make competency tests mandatory for prospective teachers. The National Teachers Examination is another kind of test designed to assure that teachers have a grasp of the fundamentals of the profession before being licensed. Such a trend can provide valuable objective support to those concerned with educational quality, but some critics argue that such tests are culturally biased and are punitive against various social groups. Perhaps, in light of controversies over testing, we should consider the other extreme, presented by the Russian educator Makarenko, who said that whenever he received a file on a student, he threw it into the fire lest it color his objective opinion of that person.

Finally, the realist advocacy of discipline and hard work can be criticized for various internal difficulties. Religious realism has supported the doctrine of original sin, a view that has led to a belief that the human being is by nature corrupt, lazy, and prone to wrongdoing. While modern secular realists may reject this view, there are still remnants of it in education, for hard work and discipline are considered "good" for us and students' heads should be filled with "factual truth" so that they do not come to a bad end.

The "hard work and discipline" syndrome and the emphasis on "factual truth" have been vigorously attacked and disputed by thinkers from Rousseau to contemporary proponents of "open education." These advocates maintain that it makes just as much sense to take an opposite view: that people are basically good, energetic, and naturally inquisitive. Education should not be forced upon people; rather, it should be made available in a palatable and enjoyable fashion recognizing our basic makeup. Both of these positions are extreme and susceptible to the same basic error; that is, they are too sure that human nature can be determined or that it is basically oriented toward good or bad behavior. The point is that realism has been criticized for the weakness of a narrow, restrictive view of human nature and that this view has had a debilitating effect on schooling and educational theory.

Despite its shortcomings, a realist philosophy of education often finds strong support from many educators, parents, business and religious institutions, and grass-roots America. The realist approach appears to be a "no-nonsense" education that concentrates on things that most people consider important. A large percentage of the public believes that lack of discipline is the number one problem found in schools today; the emphasis on discipline in realist philosophies of education appeals to this sector of the public.

The emphasis on discipline includes not only behavior but a disciplined approach to subject matter, learning, and life activities. When one seriously examines existing school practices here and abroad, one may find that more schools are following realist educational principles than those of any other single philosophy.

ARISTOTLE

THE POLITICS AND ETHICS OF ARISTOTLE

Aristotle thought that a primary aim of education is to produce a virtuous person. He believed education should not be limited to the schoolroom but is a function of the state as well. His approach to wisdom was "practical," using the method of science as well as philosophy. A major concern was to shape understanding and "correctness of thinking." Aristotle's educational writings have had a significant impact on the development of Western education. His thought has greatly influenced our conceptions of education in both the humanities and the sciences, and his ideas have found favor with secular and religious thinkers in education.

What constitution in the parent is most advantageous to the offspring is a subject which we will hereafter consider when we speak of the education of children, and we will only make a few general remarks at present. The temperament of an athlete is not suited to the life of a citizen, or to health, or to the procreation of children, any more than the valetudinarian or exhausted constitution, but one which is in a mean between them. A man's constitution should be inured to labor, but not to labor which is excessive or of one sort only, such as is practised by athletes; he should be capable of all the actions of a freeman. These remarks apply equally to both parents.

Women who are with child should be careful of themselves; they should take exercise and have a nourishing diet. The first of these prescriptions the legislator will easily carry into effect by requiring that they shall take a walk daily to some temple, where they can worship the gods who preside over birth. Their minds, however, unlike their bodies, they ought to keep unexercised, for the offspring derive their natures from their mothers as plants do from the earth.

As to the exposure and rearing of children, let there be a law that no deformed child shall live, but where there are too many (for in our State population has a limit), when couples have children in excess, and the state of feeling is averse to the exposure of offspring, let abortion be procured before sense and life have begun; what may or may not be lawfully done in these cases depends on the question of life and sensation.

And now, having determined at what ages men and women are to begin their union, let us also determine how long they shall continue to beget and bear offspring for the State; men who are too old, like men who are too young, produce children who are defective in body and mind; the children of very old men are weakly. The limit, then, should be the age which is the prime of their intelligence, and this in most persons, according to the notion of some poets who measure life by periods of seven years, is about fifty; at four or five years later, they should cease from having families;

and from that time forwards only cohabit with one another for the sake of health, or for some similar reason.

As to adultery, let it be held disgraceful for any man or woman to be unfaithful when they are married, and called husband and wife. If during the time of bearing children anything of the sort occur, let the guilty person be punished with a loss of privileges in proportion to the offence.

After the children have been born, the manner of rearing them may be supposed to have a great effect on their bodily strength. It would appear from the example of animals, and of those nations who desire to create the military habit, that the food which has most milk in it is best suited to human beings; but the less wine the better, if they would escape diseases. Also all the motions to which children can be subjected at their early age are very useful. But in order to preserve their tender limbs from distortion, some nations have had recourse to mechanical appliances which straighten their bodies. To accustom children to the cold from their earliest years is also an excellent practice, which greatly conduces to health, and hardens them for military service. Hence many barbarians have a custom of plunging their children at birth into a cold stream; others, like the Celts, clothe them in a light wrapper only. For human nature should be early habituated to endure all which by habit it can be made to endure; but the process must be gradual. And children, from their natural warmth, may be easily trained to bear cold. Such care should attend them in the first stage of life.

The next period lasts to the age of five; during this no demand should be made upon the child for study or labor, lest its growth be impeded; and there should be sufficient motion to prevent the limbs from being inactive. This can be secured, among other ways, by amusement, but the amusement should not be vulgar or tiring or riotous. The directors of education, as they are termed, should be careful what tales or stories the children hear, for the sports of children are designed to prepare the way for the business of later life, and should be for the most part imitations of the occupations which they will hereafter pursue in earnest. Those are wrong who [like Plato] in the Laws attempt to check the loud crying and screaming of children, for these contribute towards their growth, and, in a manner, exercise their bodies. Straining the voice has an effect similar to that produced by the retention of the breath in violent exertions. Besides other duties, the directors of education should have an eye to their bringing up, and should take care that they are left as little as possible with slaves. For until they are seven years old they must live at home; and therefore, even at this early age, all that is mean and low should be banished from their sight and hearing. Indeed, there is nothing which the legislator should be more careful to drive away than indecency of speech; for the light utterance of shameful words is akin to shameful actions. The young especially should never be allowed to repeat or hear anything of the sort. A freeman who is found saying or doing what is forbidden, if he be too young as yet to have the privilege of a place at the public tables, should be disgraced and beaten, and an elder person degraded as his slavish conduct deserves. And since we do not allow improper language, clearly we should also banish pictures or tales which are indecent. Let the rulers take care that there be no image or picture representing unseemly actions, except in the temples of those gods at whose festivals the law permits even ribaldry, and whom the law also permits to be worshipped by persons of mature age on behalf of themselves, their children, and their wives. But the legislator should not allow youth to be hearers of satirical Iambic verses or spectators of comedy until they are of an age to sit at the public tables and to drink strong wine; by that time education will have armed them against the evil influences of such representations.

We have made these remarks in a cursory manner—they are enough for the present occasion; but hereafter we will return to the subject and after a fuller discussion determine whether such liberty should or should not be granted, and in what way granted, if at all. Theodorus, the tragic actor, was quite right in saying that he would not allow any other actor,

not even if he were quite second-rate, to enter before himself, because the spectators grew fond of the voices which they first heard. And the same principle of association applies universally to things as well as persons, for we always like best whatever comes first. And therefore youth should be kept strangers to all that is bad, and especially to things which suggest vice or hate. When the five years have passed away, during the two following years they must look on at the pursuits which they are hereafter to learn. There are two periods of life into which education has to be divided, from seven to the age of puberty, and onwards to the age of one and twenty. [The poets] who divide ages by sevens are not always right: we should rather adhere to the divisions actually made by nature; for the deficiencies of nature are what art and education seek to fill up.

Let us then first inquire if any regulations are to be laid down about children, and secondly, whether the care of them should be the concern of the State or of private individuals, which latter is in our own day the common custom, and in the third place, what these regulations should be.

No one will doubt that the legislator should direct his attention above all to the education of youth, or that the neglect of education does harm to States. The citizen should be moulded to suit the form of government under which he lives. For each government has a peculiar character which originally formed and which continues to preserve it. The character of democracy creates democracy, and the character of oligarchy creates oligarchy; and always the better the character, the better the government.

Now for the exercise of any faculty or art a previous training and habituation are required; clearly therefore for the practice of virtue. And since the whole city has one end, it is manifest that education should be one and the same for all, and that it should be public, and not private—not as at present, when everyone looks after his own children separately, and gives them separate instruction of the sort which he thinks best; the training in things which are of common interest should be the same for all. Neither must we suppose that anyone of the citizens belongs to himself, for they all belong to the State, and are each of them a part of the State, and the care of each part is inseparable from the care of the whole. In this particular the Lacedæmonians [Spartans] are to be praised, for they take the greatest pains about their children, and make education the business of the State.

That education should be regulated by law and should be an affair of state is not to be denied, but what should be the character of this public education, and how young persons should be educated, are questions which remain to be considered. For mankind are by no means agreed about the things to be taught, whether we look to virtue or the best life. Neither it is clear whether education is more concerned with intellectual or with moral virtue. The existing practice is perplexing; no one knows on what principle we should proceed—should the useful in life, or should virtue, or should the higher knowledge, be the aim of our training; all three opinions have been entertained. Again, about the means there is no agreement; for different persons, starting with different ideas about the nature of virtue, naturally disagree about the practice of it. There can be no doubt that children should be taught those useful things which are really necessary, but not all things; for occupations are divided into liberal and illiberal; and to young children should be imparted only such kinds of knowledge as will be useful to them without vulgarizing them. And any occupation, art, or science, which makes the body or soul or mind of the freeman less fit for the practice or exercise of virtue, is vulgar; wherefore we call those arts vulgar which tend to deform the body, and likewise all paid employments, for they absorb and degrade the mind. There are also some liberal arts quite proper for a freeman to acquire, but only in a certain degree, and if he attend to them too closely, in order to attain perfection in them, the same evil effects will follow. The object also which a man sets before him makes a great difference; if he does or learns anything for his own sake or for the sake of his friends, or with a view to excellence, the action will not appear illiberal;

but if done for the sake of others, the very same action will be thought menial and servile. The received subjects of instruction, as I have already remarked, are partly of a liberal and partly of an illiberal character.

The customary branches of education are in number four; they are—(1) reading and writing, (2) gymnastic exercises, (3) music, to which is sometimes added (4) drawing. Of these, reading and writing and drawing are regarded as useful for the purposes of life in a variety of ways, and gymnastic exercises are thought to infuse courage. Concerning music a doubt may be raised—in our own day most men cultivate it for the sake of pleasure, but originally it was included in education, because nature herself, as has been often said, requires that we should be able, not only to work well, but to use leisure well; for, as I must repeat once and again, the first principle of all action is leisure. Both are required, but leisure is better than occupation; and therefore the question must be asked in good earnest, what ought we to do when at leisure? Clearly we ought not to be amusing ourselves, for then amusement would be the end of life. But if this is inconceivable, and yet amid serious occupations amusement is needed more than at other times (for he who is hard at work has need of relaxation, and amusement gives relaxation, whereas occupation is always accompanied with exertion and effort), at suitable times we should introduce amusements, and they should be our medicines, for the emotion which they create in the soul is a relaxation, and from the pleasure we obtain rest. Leisure of itself gives pleasure and happiness and enjoyment of life, which are experienced, not by the busy man, but by those who have leisure. For he who is occupied has in view some end which he has not attained; but happiness is an end which all men deem to be accompanied with pleasure and not with pain. This pleasure, however, is regarded differently by different persons, and varies according to the habit of individuals; the pleasure of the best man is the best, and springs from the noblest sources. It is clear then that there are branches of learning and education which we must study with a view to the enjoyment of leisure, and these are to be valued for their own sake; whereas those kinds of knowledge which are useful in business are to be deemed necessary, and exist for the sake of other things. And therefore our fathers admitted music into education, not on the ground either of its necessity or utility, for it is not necessary, nor indeed useful in the same manner as reading and writing, which are useful in money-making, in the management of a household, in the acquisition of knowledge and in political life, nor like drawing, useful for a more correct judgment of the works of artists, nor again like gymnastic, which gives health and strength; for neither of these is to be gained from music. There remains, then, the use of music for intellectual enjoyment in leisure; which appears to have been the reason of its introduction, this being one of the ways in which it is thought that a freeman should pass his leisure; as Homer says—

"How good is it to invite men to the pleasant feast,"

and afterwards he speaks of others whom he describes as inviting

"The bard who would delight them all."

And in another place Odysseus says there is no better way of passing life than when "Men's hearts are merry and the banqueters in the hall, sitting in order, hear the voice of the minstrel." It is evident, then, that there is a sort of education in which parents should train their sons, not as being useful or necessary, but because it is liberal or noble. Whether this is of one kind only, or of more than one, and if so, what they are, and how they are to be imparted, must hereafter be determined. Thus much we are now in a position to say that the ancients witness to us; for their opinion may be gathered from the fact that music is one of the received and traditional branches of education. Further, it is clear that children should be instructed in some useful things—for example, in reading and writing—not only for their usefulness, but also because many other sorts of knowledge are required through them. With a like view they may be taught drawing, not to

prevent their making mistakes in their own purchases, or in order that they may not be imposed upon in the buying or selling of articles, but rather because it makes them judges of the beauty of the human form. To be always seeking after the useful does not become free and exalted souls. Now it is clear that in education habit must go before reason, and the body before the mind; and therefore boys should be handed over to the trainer, who creates in them the proper habit of body, and to the wrestling-master, who teaches them their exercises.

The happy man will need external prosperity, so far forth as he is man; for human nature is not sufficient of itself for contemplation; but the body must be in health, and it must have food and all other care and attendance. We must not however imagine that the person who is to be happy will want many and great goods, because we say that without external good he can be blessed; for self-sufficiency does not consist in excess, nor does action. But it is possible to perform honourable things without being lord of earth and sea; for a man may be able to act according to virtue with moderate means. We may see this plainly: for private individuals are thought to perform good acts no less than men in power, but even more so. And it is sufficient to have a competence, for the life of that man will be happy, who energizes according to virtue. Solon also perhaps gave a good description of the happy man, when he said, that in his opinion it was he who was moderately supplied with external goods, who had done the most honourable deeds, and lived temperately; for it is possible that men who have moderate possessions should do what they ought. Anaxagoras also seems to have conceived the happy man to be neither rich nor powerful, when he said, that he should not be surprised if he was thought absurd by the multitude; for they judge by externals, having a perception of such things only.

The opinions of wise men, therefore, seem to agree with what has been said; such statements, therefore, carry with them some weight. But we judge of truth, in practical matters, from facts and from life, for on them the decisive point turns; and we ought to try all that has been said by applying it to facts and to life; and if our arguments agree with facts, we may receive them; but if they are at variance, we must consider them as mere words. He also who energizes according to intellect, and pays attention to that, and has it in the best state, is likely to be most beloved by the gods; for if any regard is paid to human affairs by the gods, as it is thought that there is, it is reasonable to suppose that they would take pleasure in what is the best and nearest allied to themselves: but this must be the intellect; and that they would be kind in return to those who love and honour this most, as to persons who pay attention to their friends, and who act rightly and honourably. But that all these qualities especially belong to the wise man, is quite clear; it is probable, therefore, that he is at the same time most dear to the gods, and most happy; so that even in this way the wise man must be the happiest man. . . .

[It] is thought that men become good, some by nature, others by practice, others by teaching. Now it is plain that whatever belongs to nature is not in our own power, but exists by some divine causes in those who are truly fortunate. But reasoning and teaching, it is to be feared, will not avail in every case, but the mind of the hearer must be previously cultivated by habits to feel pleasure and aversion properly, just as the soil must, which nourishes the seed. For he who lives in obedience to passion, would not listen to reasoning which turns him from it; nay, more, he would not understand it. And how is it possible to change the convictions of such a man as this? On the whole, it appears that passion does not submit to reasoning, but to force. There must, therefore, previously exist a character in some way connected with virtue, loving what is honourable, and hating what is disgraceful. But to meet with right education in the path of virtue from childhood is difficult, unless one is brought up under such laws: for to live temperately and patiently is not pleasant to the majority, and especially to the young. Therefore, education and institutions ought to be regulated by law; for they will not be painful when they have become familiar.

Perhaps it is not sufficient that we should meet with good education and attention when young; but since when we arrive at manhood we ought also to study and practise what we have learnt, we should require laws also for this purpose: in short, we should want laws relating to the whole of life; for the masses are obedient to compulsion rather than to reason, and to punishments rather than to the principle of honour. Therefore, some think that legislators ought to exhort to virtue, and to urge men on by appealing to the principle of honour, since those who are good in their practice will obey when they are led; but to impose chastisements and punishments on those who are disobedient and naturally indisposed to virtue, and to banish altogether the incurable; because he who is good, and lives with regard to the principle of honour, will obey reason; but the bad man desires pleasure, and is corrected by pain, like a beast of burthen. Therefore, it is a common saying, that the pains ought to be such as are most opposed to the pleasures which are loved.

Now, then, as has been said, he that is to be a good man must have been educated well, and have been made to form good habits, and thus continue to live under good institutions, and never practise what is bad, either involuntarily or voluntarily; and this is to be done by living in obedience to some intelligent principle, and some right regulation, which has the power of enforcing its decrees. But the paternal authority has no strength, nor compulsory force; nor, in short, the authority of any one man, unless he is a king, or some one of that sort; but the law does possess a compulsory power, since it is reason proceeding from a certain prudence and intelligence; and besides, men hate those individuals who oppose their appetites, even if they do it rightly; but the law is not odious when it prescribes what is good. In the city of Lacedæmon [Sparta] alone, with a few others, the legislator seems to have paid attention to education and institutions; whilst in most states such matters have been neglected, and each lives as he pleases, like the Cyclops,

> Administering the law for his children and wife.

It would therefore be best that the state should pay attention to education, and on right principles, and that it should have power to enforce it: but if neglected as a public measure, it would seem to be the duty of every individual to contribute to the virtue of his children and friends, or at least to make this his deliberate purpose.

Source: Aristotle, *The Politics*, translated by B. Jowett. New York: The Colonial Press, 1899, pp. 192–199; Aristotle, *The Nicomachean Ethics*, translated by R. W. Browne. London: Henry G. Bohn, 1853, pp. 284–288.

. . . .   L O C K E   . . . .

SOME THOUGHTS CONCERNING EDUCATION

Locke's educational writings are classics of pedagogy that dominated the eighteenth century and still influence us today. Basing his observations on experience, Locke's educational proposals were aimed at producing the well-mannered, well-informed English gentleman. In addition to being a philosopher, Locke was also a physician; and it is not surprising that he included, in addition to intellectual concerns, health, exercise, and physical growth and development. He presented a liberal and humane view of education, especially as compared with what existed in his day, but while he advocated democracy, his educational recommendations were aimed primarily at the children of the upper classes. He emphasized individuality, self-discipline, the importance of reasoning with the child, and development of character as well as intellect.

A sound mind in a sound body, is a short, but full description of a happy state in this world; he that has these two, has little more to wish for; and he that wants either of them, will be but little the better for any thing else. Men's happiness, or misery, is most part of their own making. He whose mind directs not wisely, will never take the right way; and he whose body is crazy and feeble, will never be able to advance in it. I confess, there are some men's constitutions of body and mind so vigorous, and well framed by nature, that they need not much assistance from others; but, by the strength of their natural genius, they are, from their cradles, carried towards what is excellent; and, by the privilege of their happy constitutions, are able to do wonders. But examples of this kind are but few; and I think I may say, that, of all the men we meet with, nine parts of ten are what they are, good or evil, useful or not, by their education. It is that which makes the great difference in mankind. The little, or almost insensible, impressions on our tender infancies, have very important and lasting consequences: and there it is, as in the fountains of some rivers, where a gentle application of the hand turns the flexible waters into channels, that make them take quite contrary courses; and by this little direction, given them at first, in the source, they receive different tendencies, and arrive at last at very remote and distant places.

I imagine the minds of children, as easily turned, this or that way, as water itself; and though this be the principal part, and our main care should be about the inside, yet the clay cottage is not to be neglected. I shall therefore begin with the case, and consider first the health of the body, as that which perhaps you may rather expect, from that study I have been thought more peculiarly to have applied myself to; and that also which will be soonest dispatched, as lying, if I guess not amiss, in a very little compass.

How necessary health is to our business and happiness; and how requisite a strong constitution, able to endure hardships and fatigue, is, to one that will make any figure in the world; is too obvious to need any proof. . . .

This being laid down in general, as the course ought to be taken, it is fit we come now to consider the parts of the discipline to be used a little more particularly. I have spoken so much of carrying a strict hand over children, that perhaps I shall be suspected of not considering enough what is due to their tender age and constitutions. But that opinion will vanish, when you have heard me a little farther. For I am very apt to think, that great severity of punishment does but very little good; nay, great harm in education: and I believe it will be found, that, ceteris paribus, those children who have been most chastised, seldom make the best men. All that I have hitherto contended for, is, that whatsoever rigour is necessary, it is more to be used, the younger children are; and, having by a due application wrought its effect, it is to be relaxed, and changed into a milder sort of government. . . .

Manners, as they call it, about which children are so often perplexed, and have so many goodly exhortations made them, by their wise maids and governesses, I think, are rather to be learned by example than rules; and then children, if kept out of ill company, will take a pride to behave themselves prettily, after the fashion of others, perceiving themselves esteemed and commended for it. But, if by a little negligence in this part, the boy should not put off his hat, nor make legs very gracefully, a dancing-master will cure that defect, and wipe off all that plainness of nature, which the à-la-mode people call clownishness. And since nothing appears to me to give children so much becoming confidence and behaviour, and so to raise them to the conversation of those above their age, as dancing; I think they should be taught to dance, as soon as they are capable of learning it. For, though this consist only in outward gracefulness of motion, yet, I know not how, it gives children manly thoughts and carriage, more than any thing. But otherwise I would not have little children much tormented about punctilios, or niceties of breeding.

Never trouble yourself about those faults in them, which you know age will cure. . . .

I place virtue as the first and most necessary of those endowments that belong to a man or a gentleman, as absolutely requisite to make him valued and beloved by others, acceptable or tolerable to himself. Without that, I think, he will be happy neither in this nor the other world. . . .

When he can talk, it is time he should begin to learn to read. But as to this, give me leave here to inculcate again what is very apt to be forgotten, viz. that great care is to be taken, that it be never made as a business to him, nor he look on it as a task. We naturally, as I said, even from our cradles, love liberty, and have therefore an aversion to many things, for no other reason, but because they are injoined us. I have always had a fancy, that learning might be made a play and recreation to children; and that they might be brought to desire to be taught, if it were proposed to them as a thing of honour, credit, delight, and recreation, or as a reward for doing something else, and if they were never chid or corrected for the neglect of it. . . .

Thus children may be cozened into a knowledge of the letters; be taught to read, without perceiving it to be any thing but a sport, and play themselves into that which others are whipped for. Children should not have any thing like work, or serious, laid on them; neither their minds nor bodies will bear it. It injures their healths; and their being forced and tied down to their books, in an age at enmity with all such restraint, has, I doubt not, been the reason why a great many have hated books and learning all their lives after: it is like a surfeit, that leaves an aversion behind, not to be removed. . . .

The Lord's prayer, the creed, and ten commandments, it is necessary he should learn perfectly by heart; but, I think, not by reading them himself in his primer, but by somebody's repeating them to him, even before he can read. But learning by heart, and learning to read, should not, I think be mixed, and so one made to clog the other. But his learning to read should be made as little trouble or business to him as might be. . . .

When he can read English well, it will be seasonable to enter him in writing. And here the first thing should be taught him, is to hold his pen right; and this he should be perfect in, before he should be suffered to put it to paper: for not only children, but any body else, that would do any thing well, should never be put upon too much of it at once, or be set to perfect themselves in two parts of an action at the same time, if they can possibly be separated. . . .

As soon as he can speak English, it is time for him to learn some other language: this nobody doubts of, when French is proposed. And the reason is, because people are accustomed to the right way of teaching that language, which is by talking it into children in constant conversation, and not by grammatical rules. The Latin tongue would easily be taught the same way, if his tutor, being constantly with him, would talk nothing else to him, and make him answer still in the same language. But because French is a living language, and to be used more in speaking, that should be first learned, that the yet pliant organs of speech might be accustomed to a due formation of those sounds, and he get the habit of pronouncing French well, which is the harder to be done, the longer it is delayed.

When he can speak and read French well, which in this method is usually in a year or two, he should proceed to Latin, which it is a wonder parents, when they have had the experiment in French, should not think ought to be learned the same way, by talking and reading. Only care is to be taken, whilst he is learning those foreign languages, by speaking and reading nothing else with his tutor, that he do not forget to read English, which may be preserved by his mother, or some body else, hearing him read some chosen parts of the scripture or other English book, every day. . . .

At the same time that he is learning French and Latin, a child, as has been said, may also be entered in arithmetic, geography, chronology, history, and geometry too. For if these be taught him in French or Latin, when he begins once to understand either of these tongues, he will get a knowledge in these sciences, and the language to-boot.

Geography, I think, should be begun with; for the learning of the figure of the globe, the situation and boundaries of the four parts of the world, and that of particular kingdoms and countries, being only an exercise of the eyes and memory, a child with pleasure will learn and retain them: and this is so certain, that I now live in the house with a child, whom his mother has so well instructed this way in geography, that he knew the limits of the four parts of the world, could readily point, being asked, to any country upon the globe, or any county in the map of England; knew all the great rivers, promontories, straits, and bays in the world, and could find the longitude and latitude of any place before he was six years old. These things, that he will thus learn by sight, and have by rote in his memory, are not all, I confess, that he is to learn upon the globes. But yet it is a good step and preparation to it, and will make the remainder much easier, when his judgment is grown ripe enough for it: besides that, it gets so much time now, and by the pleasure of knowing things, leads him on insensibly to the gaining of languages.

When he has the natural parts of the globe well fixed in his memory, it may then be time to begin arithmetic. By the natural parts of the globe, I mean several positions of the parts of the earth and sea, under different names and distinctions of countries; not coming yet to those artificial and imaginary lines, which have been invented, and are only supposed, for the better improvement of that science.

Arithmetic is the easiest, and consequently the first sort of abstract reasoning, which the mind commonly bears, or accustoms itself to: and is of so general use in all parts of life and business, that scarce any thing is to be done without it. This is certain, a man cannot have too much of it, nor too perfectly. . . .

As nothing teaches, so nothing delights, more than history. The first of these recommends it to the study of grown men; the latter makes me think it the fittest for a young lad, who, as soon as he is instructed in chronology, and acquainted with the several epochs in use in this part of the world, and can reduce them to the Julian period, should then have some Latin history put into his hand. The choice should be directed by the easiness of the style; for wherever he begins, chronology will keep it from confusion; and the pleasantness of the subject inviting him to read, the language will insensibly be got, without that terrible vexation and uneasiness which children suffer where they are put into books beyond their capacity, such as are the Roman orators and poets, only to learn the Roman language. When he has by reading mastered the easier, such perhaps as Justin, Eutropius, Quintus Curtius, & c. the next degree to these will give him no great trouble: and thus, by a gradual progress from the plainest and easiest historians, he may at last come to read the most difficult and sublime of the Latin authors, such as are Tully, Virgil, and Horace....

Though the systems of physics, that I have met with, afford little encouragement to look for certainty, or science, in any treatise, which shall pretend to give us a body of natural philosophy from the first principles of bodies in general; yet the incomparable Mr. Newton has shown, how far mathematics, applied to some parts of nature, may, upon principles that matter of fact justify, carry us in the knowledge of some, as I may so call them, particular provinces of the incomprehensible universe. And if others could give us so good and clear an account of other parts of nature, as he has of this our planetary world, and the most considerable phenomena observable in it, in his admirable book "Philosophiæ naturalis principia mathematica," we might in time hope to be furnished with more true and certain knowledge in several parts of this stupendous machine, than hitherto we could have expected. And though there are very few that have mathematics enough to understand his demonstrations; yet the most accurate mathematicians, who have examined them, allowing them to be such, his book will deserve to be read, and give no small light and pleasure to those,

who, willing to understand the motions, properties, and operations of the great masses of matter in this our solar system, will but carefully mind his conclusions, which may be depended on as propositions well proved....

Though I am now come to a conclusion of what obvious remarks have suggested to me concerning education, I would not have it thought, that I look on it as a just treatise on this subject. There are a thousand other things that may need consideration; especially if one should take in the various tempers, different inclinations, and particular defaults, that are to be found in children; and prescribe proper remedies. The variety is so great, that it would require a volume; nor would that reach it. Each man's mind has some peculiarity, as well as his face, that distinguishes him from all others; and there are possibly scarce two children, who can be conducted by exactly the same method. Besides that, I think a prince, a nobleman, and an ordinary gentleman's son, should have different ways of breeding. But having had here only some general views in reference to the main end and aims in education, and those designed for a gentleman's son, who being then very little, I considered only as white paper, or wax, to be moulded and fashioned as one pleases; I have touched little more than those heads, which I judged necessary for the breeding of a young gentleman of his condition in general; and have now published these my occasional thoughts, with this hope, that, though this be far from being a complete treatise on this subject, or such as that every one may find what will just fit his child in it; yet it may give some small light to those, whose concern for their dear little ones makes them so irregularly bold, that they dare venture to consult their own reason, in the education of their children, rather than wholly to rely upon old custom.

Source: John Locke, "Some Thoughts Concerning Education," in *The Works of John Locke*, vol. X. London: W. Otridge and Son et al., 1812, pp. 6–7, 35, 50, 128, 143–144, 147–148, 150, 152, 172–173, 175–176, 186–187, 204–205.

SELECTED READINGS

Aristotle. *Politics.* New York: Modern Library, 1943. A well-developed and classic statement of the realist approach to education. The author relates educational reform to social and political aims.

Broudy, Harry S. *Building a Philosophy of Education.* Englewood Cliffs, NJ: Prentice-Hall, 1961. This book presents a strong case for realism in modern education and an appeal for more fundamental and basic approaches and studies in the schools. It is regarded as one of the better, more recent statements of realism in education.

————. *The Real World of the Public Schools.* New York: Harcourt Brace Jovanovich, 1972. The author provides a critical analysis of the public schools at a time when public dissatisfaction with them is mounting. He argues for more discipline, rigor, and respect in schools and a recovery of their central mission of providing a knowledge base for a mature society.

Locke, John. *John Locke on Education,* edited by Peter Gay. New York: Teachers College Bureau of Publications, 1964. This work contains some of Locke's best-known thoughts on education. It deals with educational problems ranging from individual learning experiences to the importance of environment. It is an empirical approach to education and is representative of early modern realism.

Russell, Bertrand. *Education and the Good Life.* New York: Boni and Liverright, 1926. This is the leading educational statement of one of the foremost spokesmen for modern realist philosophy. The book is somewhat polemical in its urgings for social reform. It shows Russell's reformist tendencies and demonstrates his view of the importance of education.

Whitehead, Alfred N. *The Aims of Education and Other Essays.* New York: Free Press, 1957. A collection of wide-ranging essays on education, this volume shows Whitehead's approach to philosophical patterns of thought. It is particularly incisive in its critique of inertness in education and attention to the creative process.

3

Eastern Philosophy, Religion, and Education

Eastern philosophy has a long and varied history. Its range not only in terms of years but in terms of ideas is enormous, and it is a fascinating study in the historical development of human thinking. This fascination increases when one compares and contrasts it with Western thinking.

Eastern philosophy consists of four major areas of thought: Indian, Chinese, Japanese, and Middle Eastern. While there are many different philosophical beliefs within each culture, there are also common threads. If any one idea is paramount, it is a concentration on the inner rather than the outer life. Eastern philosophy, unlike our Western, more empirical approach, stresses intuition, inner peace, tranquility, attitudinal development, and mysticism. Eastern beliefs, often because of their very early origins, have had a significant historical impact upon Western thought. The influence of Judaism and Christianity is an obvious case in point. The appeal of Eastern beliefs remains important today, particularly as an antidote to Western philosophical complacency.

THE DEVELOPMENT OF EASTERN THOUGHT

Most studies of Western philosophy begin with the Greeks. Greek philosophy, as a systematic development of thought, began in the sixth century BC with Thales, who was later followed by Pythagoras and Socrates. Yet there is some support for the view that Platonic philosophy owed much to Indian philosophy, with its emphasis on the illusory quality of matter and other idealist tendencies. At the time when ancient Greek thought began, philosophy had already reached a high stage of development in both India and China.

Perhaps Greek philosophy was unique in its emphasis on rationality rather than mysticism and supernaturalism. Western philosophy tended to emphasize logic and materialism; while Eastern philosophy in general

81

stressed the inner rather than the outer world, intuition rather than sense, and mysticism rather than scientific discoveries. This has certainly differed from school to school, and Chinese philosophy is as a whole much less mystical than Indian; but overall they begin with the inner world that then reaches out to the outer world of phenomena.

It is sometimes charged, however, that most Indian and Chinese philosophies are not philosophies at all but religions. Because of the very early beginnings of these philosophies, they showed a strong bent toward gods and goddesses, much like Greek mythology. Unlike Greek philosophy, which separated philosophy and religion, Indian and Chinese religion and philosophy were more closely intertwined. Religious doctrines were often merged with philosophical views about the nature of the world and one's interaction with it.

Some Westerners argue that philosophical and religious studies should be separated, but think how difficult it would be to separate Thomas Aquinas the theologian from Thomas Aquinas the philosopher. It is true that religious thought, rather than philosophy, has tended to rely more on deduction, faith, intuition, and mysticism; but many philosophies, even modern ones, laud these approaches today. The separation is difficult, particularly when we look so far back. One can hardly expect early civilizations to have a sophisticated or scientific idea about the nature of the universe and humanity's place in it. Perhaps we should not attempt such a strict delineation but rather ask how these ideas have contributed to a growing understanding of the world and its people—a world that to Eastern philosophers was sometimes hostile but also benevolent and understandable.

FAR EASTERN AND INDIAN THOUGHT

The Far East or Eastern Asia, which includes China, Korea, Japan, and India, comprises an enormous land area of immense populations. In this area, the indigenous peoples have lived in the same geographical area for a long time. Eastern and Southern Asia are noted for their relatively stable traditions, in contrast to the West. In these areas, traditions and taboos encourage an attitude skeptical of change that might undermine religious and social mores; however, there is still great social diversity. In the past, cultures in the Far East were often better organized, more advanced technologically, and richer than in the West.

Eastern thought has always seemed somewhat mysterious and exotic to Westerners: an abject sense of duty in some cases, an emphasis on a rigid class structure, strong familial ties and ancestor veneration, and punishment of the body are not generally found or promoted in Western society. Needless to say, Eastern philosophers are equally repulsed by the West's excessive concern for material goods, social advancement, and changing moral standards. The differences between East and West often seem so great that one may wonder if any bridge is possible between these viewpoints. Perhaps the great stumbling blocks are a lack of understanding between these two cultures, their enormous historical diversity, and their differences in expectations and motivations.

The West has greatly influenced the East politically and economically; the East, in turn, has served to enrich the West philosophically and spiritually. Because of the ethnocentrism prevalent in both cultures, there has not been as much serious dialogue as there should have been. To understand the Eastern position, we must set aside Western biases and Western aims. When we do, we find that there is much to admire and to learn from these philosophies.

Indian Thought

Indian philosophy has a long and complex history. Almost every shade of thought can be found, ranging from idealism to materialism, pluralism to monism, and asceticism to hedonism. Great emphasis is placed on a search for wisdom in Indian philosophy, but this need not mean a rejection of worldly pleasures. Though it emphasizes speculation, Indian philosophy has a very practical character. It began as a way to solve the basic problems of life, as well as to improve life. For example, early people faced both mental and physical suffering and sought to understand the reasons for this. Speculation helped to provide remedies for such suffering. Indian philosophers seem to insist that knowledge be used to improve both social and communal life and that people should live according to their ideals. There is also a prevailing sense of universal moral justice in Indian philosophy, in which individuals are responsible for what they are and what they become.

Hinduism

This philosophy has no known founder and no definite set of doctrines. Its growth parallels the growth of the races that settled in India, and it is more a way of life than a dogma. Hinduism does not generally encourage asceticism or a renunciation of the world; consequently, it does not discourage desire but believes that one should be able to control and regulate it. Basically, one should not devote his life to either sensual pleasure or worldly success.

The beginnings of Hindu philosophy are found in three basic texts: the Vedas, the Upanishads, and the Epics. These writings appeared from about 1200 BC to AD 200.

Vedas. The Vedas were a group of hymns, chants, and treatises of Aryan people. Early Vedic religion was a worship of nature with anthropomorphic overtones. To the Vedic Indian, the universe consisted of three entities: earth, atmosphere, and heaven. A flood meant that the rivers were angry; when there was nice weather, the gods were pleased. This polytheistic view of the universe consisted of thirty-three gods, such as Agni, god of fire; Indra, god of thunder and rain; and Varuna, who controls and regulates the seasons. The first section of the Vedas consists of mantras that praise and propitiate the gods. The gods are also supplicated with sacrifices and oblations. There are good spirits, such as the spirit of the dawn; and there are bad ones, such as the demons of drought and darkness. The gods and demons fight continual battles, with the gods generally overpowering the demons. In Vedic literature is a continuing attempt to effect a harmony between people's material quests and needs and their spiritual lives.

To the Vedic believer, the following were the fundamental spiritual truths of the Vedas:

1. There is an Ultimate Reality that is all-pervading and is the final cause of the universe
2. This Reality is an uncreated, self-luminous, and eternal spirit
3. Religion or Dharma consists of meditating on this Spirit and leading a life of virtue and righteousness
4. The human soul is divine, with the entire universe a manifestation of the Supreme Spirit.

The Vedic seers believed that humans are spirit and not merely body or mind. As spirit, human beings are divine in essence. Unlike other animals, we can realize our divinity, for God is within us. We cannot see this when we are motivated by lust, anger, or greed; hence, these evils must be removed and the heart and mind purified. This purification process may take several lifetimes of reincarnation.

Upanishads. The Upanishads, which literally means "secret teachings," were built on the Vedas but carried Vedic thought to a new dimension. The Upanishads were much more lofty and intellectual than the Vedas, and the gods receded into the background. No matter how crude, they marked the beginning of real philosophical speculation in India. In the Upanishads, sacrifices are looked down upon, contemplation rather than worship is extolled, and divine knowledge is the important thing. The message is to merge self (Atman) with the supreme (Brahman), whereby Atman and Brahman come together. Whereas women occupied an inferior role in Vedic literature, in the Upanishads they were elevated to equal status with men.

The Upanishads promote a monistic conception of the deity. The Brahman is all powerful, all pervading, infinite, eternal, impersonal, and an indescribable Absolute. All creatures find their beginning and their end in Him. The Upanishads tell of a life full of miseries continued by transmigration to new lives as a result of one's actions (Karma). Deliverance can be achieved only by a true knowledge of Brahman obtained by a purity of life and meditation. When true knowledge comes, the individual soul merges with the universal soul.

All of the Upanishads support the quest for a true understanding of the nature of Brahman. Brahman is the supreme reality, just as God is central in

Christian thought. It is that on which all depends and is the source of all things: seas, mountains, rivers, plants, and the essences of all things. Since Brahman is in everything that exists, to deny Brahman is to deny one's own being.

Since Brahman is the only absolute reality, one must be absorbed into Brahman to achieve liberation. The best way to accomplish this task is to find a teacher, a knower of Brahman. Instruction, however, is secret and to be imparted only to qualified students. The student is advised to approach humbly a spiritual teacher (guru) who is well versed in Vedic scriptures as well as knowledge of Brahman. Such a teacher can then impart knowledge of the imperishable truth. In the Vedic literature, one sees the development of religious thought from polytheism to monotheism. The idea of monotheism is even more pronounced in the Upanishads, where "Brahman is everywhere and Brahman alone."

Another aspect of Hinduism is the development of laws. These laws exercised great weight in Hindu life and established codes that still influence Hindu social life today. One of the great law-givers of Hindu thought was Manu, said to be one of the chief authors of *Laws of Righteous Conduct*, which was probably completed within the first few centuries of the Christian era, as Westerners date history.

Manu placed the Brahmin class at the top of the social hierarchy. Brahmins are men of learning, thinkers, priests, teachers, and seekers of Brahman and are expected to lead a life of simplicity and austerity. Beneath the Brahmins are the Kshatriyas, men of courage and energy but without the intelligence of Brahmins. Beneath the Kshatriyas are the Vaisyas, those who desire wealth and power but who often see this as an end in itself. The Sudras are the lowest caste. Beneath the Sudras are the "untouchables"—people considered not much above the level of lower animals. Although Manu did not believe that caste was necessarily inherited, a hereditary caste system did develop; the four major castes Manu described, as well as many sub-castes, became a rigid part of Hindu society.

Manu established three desired stages in a man's life. In the first stage, the student learns training and discipline of mind and body under a guru or teacher who requires no fee. There is no prescribed course of study or method, and learning is determined by the capacity of the student. Learning is to be for its own sake and not for gain. In the second stage (around twenty-five years of age), a man is expected to marry and family becomes an important consideration. At this stage, men realize their duty to the sage, the gods, their ancestors, animals, and the poor. In the third stage (around fifty years of age), a man gives up his household to his son and either retires to a forest hermitage or assists the community as a wise counselor or advisor.

Manu also established three desired stages in the lives of women. A female is first subject to her father or brothers, then to her husband, and after her husband's death to her sons. She must never be independent and must constantly worship her husband as a god, even if he is "devoid of good qualities." She must always be cheerful and clever in the management of household affairs. Women may never perform a sacrifice, vow, or fast apart from their husbands. Although Manu's plan has lost its vitality because of modern social and economic constraints, it is still considered to be the ideal life plan for a Hindu.

(3) *Epics.* In Indian philosophy, the two greatest epics are Ramayana and Mahabharata. The more significant of these is the Mahabharata, which contains the Bhagavad-Gita, written between 200 BC and AD 200. In the Gita, the first section advocates the pursuit of yoga, the second elaborates pantheistic doctrine, and the third expounds principles of Porusha and Prakrit, the five senses, and other tenets of this philosophy. The Gita promotes the idea that the whole world of nature and the universe of name and form are all illusion. The only reality is Spirit, and there should be stern devotion to duty, as well as an emphasis on the functions allotted to each caste at birth. In the Gita, God speaks to humans more intimately and in more detail, thus achieving a greater personal form.

The Bhagavad-Gita, a poem of some seven hundred verses in eighteen chapters, describes a great war that took place before 1000 BC between the Kauravas and the Pandavas for succession to the throne. One of the great warriors, Arjuna, pondered the consequences of war. The questions posed by Arjuna are answered by Krishna (identified with the god Vishnu), who explains to Arjuna why he should fight. Arjuna is told that he must fulfill his Dharma, the obligations of his life. Only in this way can salvation be achieved. The deeper concerns of their discussion involve motivation, purpose, and the meaning of any human action. The ideal individual accepts pain and pleasure with equal tranquillity. With unshakable resolve, one is no longer swayed by joy, envy, anxiety, and fear. One is patient, steadfast, and forgiving.

The Bhagavad-Gita expresses divine compassion for humanity. Krishna does not stress intellectual qualities as much as he does feelings of devotion and duty. In the Way, which is the path to wisdom, there is a simplicity in salvation, and God and humanity are not enemies but companions. An important major theme of the Gita is that salvation is open to all and that Brahman accepts all.

The notion of yoga is most clearly associated with the Bhagavad-Gita, which discusses the sage who through serenity ascends into yoga. It is frequently interpreted as a "union with the Absolute," whereby one might "yoke" one's soul with the world-soul. Historically, the most significant form of yoga has been the classical system of Patanjali, founded in the second century AD, as described in the *Yoga Sutras.* Patanjali did not state a philosophy as much as a method of instruction on how to induce certain psychological states. The yoga belief is that the mind can be trained to function at higher levels.

The three external steps of yoga are (1) right posture, (2) right breathing, and (3) control of the senses. The body is to be so controlled that it will offer no impediment to the serious practice of meditation. One learns to pay no attention to sounds, sights, skin sensations, or to any other distraction. There is also control of the emotions so that concentration may be fixed toward reaching freedom and illumination.

Modern Hinduism

A modern renaissance of Hinduism has been led by such men as Rabindranath Tagore, Sri Aurobindo, Dr. S. Radhakrishnan, and Mahatma Gandhi. Gandhi was born in Porbandar, Northwest India, where his father was a provincial prime minister. In 1891, he received a degree in law from University College in London; he returned to India, where he turned his law practice to one for social reform. He was prominent in civil disobedience protests that resulted in independence for India from Great Britain in 1947.

According to Gandhi, religion should be practical. God is not to be realized by meditating in some cave but by living in the world. God is truth, and the best way to seek truth is by practicing nonviolence (*ahimsa*) in word, thought, and deed. We should lead a life of love and service toward others, and religion should mold our social, economic, educational, and political life. Gandhi was opposed to the traditional concepts of untouchability, enforced widowhood, and child marriage. He advocated equal rights for women, promoted admission to temples and schools for all people, endorsed the kind attitude toward lower animals generally practiced by Hindus, and strongly encouraged manual labor for everyone.

He believed that God is not an abstraction but a living presence, "an indefinable mysterious power that pervades everything." Gandhi believed that one cannot know God completely in this life and can at best achieve only a partial vision of the Truth, which should encourage in us a tolerant attitude toward the views of others. One should, however, be willing to suffer for one's own convictions without making others suffer. Gandhi realized that absolute nonviolence may not be possible, but one can achieve and realize a relative nonviolence.

Buddhism

Siddhartha Gotama (563–483 BC) was born within the present boundary of Nepal. These dates are somewhat uncertain, as is information about the life and teachings of the Buddha ("Enlightened One"), as he was called. The Buddha wrote nothing down, and most writings about him arose a considerable time after his death.

According to tradition, when the Buddha was born, the trees of Lumbini Park burst into bloom. He was born a prince named Gotama, the son of a rich Hindu raja, and was destined for rulership. He was cared for by thirty-two nurses in three palaces, and his father surrounded him with luxury and attempted to shield him from all unpleasantness during his youth. At nineteen, Gotama was married to a princess, Yasodhara, who bore him a son named Rahula. It would appear that Gotama had a perfect life, but he saw in succession a wrinkled and toothless old man bent over a stick, a diseased man with fever, and a corpse wrapped in cloth being carried in procession to the funeral pyre. These experiences caused Gotama to search for serenity in the face of the evils of existence: old age, sickness, and death.

Gotama studied under a succession of teachers and took up the role of an ascetic, living, they say, on one grain of rice a day. While seated under a pipal tree (bo tree) one day, Gotama achieved illumination or enlightenment and entered nirvana. His first sermon was the "Sermon on the Turning of the Wheel of the Law," which dealt with the problem of suffering and how to overcome it. He believed that personal gratification is the root and cause of suffering in the world. In another of his sermons, he put forth the Four Noble Truths and the Noble Eightfold Path:

1. Life is suffering.
2. The cause of this suffering is desire.
3. Suffering can be eliminated when desire is extinguished.
4. Desire can be eliminated through the eightfold path, consisting of:
   a. *Right understanding*—understanding things as they are and having knowledge of where we are and where we want to go.
   b. *Right speech*—not telling lies, backbiting, slandering, engaging in foolish gossip or harsh or abusive language. We must not speak carelessly. If we can't say anything useful we should keep "noble" silence.
   c. *Right conduct*—avoiding destruction to life and property. We should promote harmonious and peaceful living, adopt an honorable profession, and have no dishonest dealings or illegitimate sexual intercourse.
   d. *Right vocation*—a desire to follow the correct path and put knowledge into practice.
   e. *Right effort*—our energies must be directed toward wholesome states of mind.
   f. *Right mindfulness*—a vigilant attitude toward desire, anger, hope, and fear.
   g. *Right concentration*—a disregard for passionate desires and evil thoughts and a development of spiritual awareness.
   h. *Right thought*—a selfless renunciation and detachment, with thoughts of love and nonviolence.

Buddhism holds with Hinduism that the universe is a samsara, a stream without end in which the law of Karma operates. We must overcome samsara, and the only way we can do this is to obtain freedom from the cycle of births and deaths by realizing nirvana.

The Buddha rejected the notion of ritual and ceremonies, as well as the knowledge and religious authority maintained by the Brahmins. He also objected to mystery, speculation, and the concept of a personal God. He eschewed worship and never prayed, though ironically enough he was to become a god worshiped through prayer by millions of people.

The Buddha spent much of his life teaching and directing his disciples to (1) use ordinary discourse and make points gradually, (2) observe a proper sequence of ideas, (3) use words of compassion, (4) avoid irrelevant matters, and (5) avoid caustic remarks against others. He did not believe that one should explain the tenets of Buddhism all at once but should begin with that which is elementary and related to the student's condition. More difficult ideas should be put forth in stages followed by the higher teachings.

Before beginning a discussion, the Buddha tried to form an idea of a person's view by posing appropriate questions. He utilized similes, parables, fables, and verses. In addition to meticulous attention to his own style of teaching, the Buddha gave studious attention to the conduct and training of his disciples, correcting their weaknesses through patience and advice.

It was only with great misgiving that the Buddha later received women into discipleship. His early teachings encouraged his followers to shun women, even their gaze. Female disciples who became nuns were to keep a certain distance from the master and to remain in a totally submissive role. For those men who were to become Buddhist monks, the Buddha established an order, the Sangha. This order lived under definite rules and regulations known as the "Monk's Rules," which constituted an important part of Buddhist scripture. There were some 227 rules governing a monk's conduct, including four great prohibitions. An ordained monk could not (1) have sexual intercourse, (2) take what has not been given to him, (3) deprive any creature of life, not even a worm or an ant; or (4) boast of any superhuman perfection. Monks were to meet regularly and examine themselves for any lapse in standards. If a member felt that he was guilty of some infraction, he was expected to make a public confession of it.

Today some Buddhist monks continue the teachings of Gotama. They argue that suffering occurs when one is not in harmony with the universe. Suffering is the result of a wrong attitude, and the craving for things results in unhappiness. When one follows the "middle path" and renounces desire, happiness will ensue.

While adherents to Hinduism are found mostly in India, Buddhists are found in Burma, Sri Lanka, China, Tibet, Korea, Japan, Kampuchea, and Laos as well as in India. Buddhism, after flourishing in India for fifteen hundred years, lost its foothold there and was driven away by Hinduism or absorbed by it. It has persisted for over twenty-five hundred years but has undergone profound changes during that time. Many newer schools of thought have developed, some coexisting with older ones, and many writings composed centuries after the Buddha's death have been ascribed to him. In its first phase, Buddhism stressed nonattachment; in its second phase, it stressed concern for humanity and the desire to become Buddhalike; and in the third, it emphasized a sense of harmony with the universe, in which one is under no constraint to change forces within or without. With all its changes, however, it has maintained a recognizable character and continuity.

Jainism

Like Buddhism, the Jain religion is an offshoot of Hinduism. Jains are followers of the Jinas. The term *Jina* is an appellation given to one who has
attained enlightenment. Jainism is similar to Buddhism in that both originated in the same part of India, opposed prevailing orthodox views, rejected the
caste system and a personal God, used many identical terms, and gave great
importance to the concept of noninjury. Both also rejected Vedic literature
and extolled nirvana—release from the birth–death cycle. Unlike Buddhism,
however, Jainism is mostly confined to India.

   Traditional belief is that the development of Jainism was primarily connected with Vardhamana Mahavira. The scion of a princely family, Mahavira
was born at Kshatriyakundagrama, a suburb of Vaisali (modern Basarh,
Bihar state), near modern Patna. The traditional date of his birth is 599 BC,
but scholars believe that this date is forty or more years too early because
Mahavira appears to have been a younger contemporary of Gotama. When
Mahavira was thirty, certain gods appeared and urged him to renounce the
world. According to legend, he stood beneath a holy asoka tree and
renounced all possessions, removed all clothing, and pulled out his hair by
hand, indicating an end of concern for the body and a willingness to face
pain. He is considered to be the last prophet, and the religion is older than his
dates would suggest. Jains believe that theirs is the oldest religion in the
world, even antedating Hinduism. A prophet named Parsvanatha lived 250
years before Mahavira, and a predecessor of Parsvanatha supposedly died
84,000 years before Mahavira's nirvana. Thus, adherents believe the religion
is eternal.

   After the death of his parents, Mahavira became an ascetic for twelve
years and is said to have attained nirvana at Pava around 527 BC. The oral
teachings of Mahavira were later put into written form and consist of the following philosophical and ethical doctrines:

1. The human being is dual in nature, both spiritual and material.
2. One must control the material world by one's spiritual nature.
3. One can separate one's soul from karmic matter by one's own efforts.

Before taking vows, each Jain must give up certain faults. A Jain must not (1)
entertain any doubts about the soundness of Jain theory, (2) adopt another
faith, (3) question the reality of the fruits of Karma, and (4) associate with
hypocrites. The vows that the Jain then takes are

1.   To avoid injury to any form of life; not to hurt anyone by word or deed.
One should cover one's mouth to prevent injury to the air, and one should
avoid stepping on any living thing. One should not scratch for fear of injuring
a parasite and should avoid agriculture that may injure animals, such as
worms in the soil. One should also avoid the killing of all animals, including
fish. Jains have been active in providing hospitals for sick animals and for

putting numerous bird feeders in the streets. Jains also feel that we should avoid psychological injury as well and that if we follow this doctrine we could achieve a world of peace and brotherhood.

2. To speak no untruths; not to utter falsehoods, rash or harsh speech; not to speak ill of others or give bad advice.

3. To steal nothing; not to become a victim of greed or envy.

These vows are to be accepted by all Jains. For those who are to be in the highest order (known as Yatis) there are two additional vows:

4. To practice chastity, either fidelity in marriage or the renouncing of all sexual contact.

5. To renounce all attachments and neither love nor hate any object.

Other vows, primarily for householders, include avoiding unnecessary travel, limiting things in daily use, guarding against evils, keeping specific times for meditation, maintaining special periods of self-denial, serving occasional days as monks, using no alcohol or drugs, and giving alms in support of Yatis. The Jains put such an emphasis on following these vows that despite their great concern for life, they feel that a Jain should commit suicide by starvation if he is incapable of following them.

Jains believe that the universe has existed from all eternity, undergoing an infinite number of revolutions produced by the powers of nature without the intervention of any external deity. The world is both uncreated and indestructible. They believe that trying to prove God's existence is a hopeless cause, yet they recognize a higher deity (paramadevata) as the object of veneration—namely, the Jina, the teacher of sacred law, who (being free from all passions and delusions and being omniscient) has reached perfection after annihilating all his karma.

The Jains have a philosophy that rejects systems as absolutes and affirms them only as partial truths. This is known as the doctrine of *Syaduada* or "maybe." No judgment is absolutely true or absolutely false.

Jains promulgate seven propositions about reality:

1. Maybe, reality is.
2. Maybe, reality is not.
3. Maybe, reality is and is not.
4. Maybe, reality is indescribable.
5. Maybe, reality is and is indescribable.
6. Maybe, reality is not and is indescribable.
7. Maybe, reality is, is not, and is indescribable.

During the twelfth and thirteenth centuries, the Jain community experienced great Hindu opposition to their "atheistic" and anti-Vedic doctrines. Through the centuries, Jainist views have suffered several schisms; the most serious involves the doctrine of absolute nonviolence. Dr. Albert Schweitzer, who was one of the best known Jains, declared that he killed germs only when they attacked a higher organism (humans); he did not go around indiscriminately killing germs. Other questions are raised, such as "If a snake were about to kill me, could I kill the snake?" Although the Jains are firmly entrenched in views of tolerance and nonviolence, many have questioned whether these views really can succeed in a world where violence may seem necessary under certain extreme conditions.

Chinese Thought

As in India, religion has been a powerful force in Chinese thought. Ancient Chinese governments drew heavily upon religious thought in framing their governmental decrees, and social and economic life was tied in with religious convictions. Religion, philosophy, government, and social life were all inter-twined in an attempt to help humanity achieve harmony with the universe and with life.

Much of Western philosophy emphasizes conflict, such as the conflict between philosophy and religion, the conflict between humans and nature, and the conflict between individual rights and government. In Chinese phi-losophy, the emphasis is more on harmony, and correct thinking should help one to achieve harmony with life. This harmony of government, business, and family should then lead toward a higher synthesis.

Confucianism

Confucius (551–479 BC) was born in the state of Lu, of a poor and common background. As a youth, he was given responsibility in the house of Baron Chi. He later became a magistrate in the model town of Chung-tu, then a Grand Secretary of Justice, and finally Chief Minister. During his lifetime, he traveled and taught disciples government and the way of a gentleman. After his death, his disciples collected his ideas and put them together in a manual known as the _Analects._

At the peak of Confucius' career, approximately three thousand students gathered around him. He taught them philosophy and music, with a particu-lar emphasis on ethics. The word Confucius used to describe the moral order was li. Many talked of li, but few lived it. The Confucian ideal of the superior individual is one who lives a life of rightness, virtue, and propriety. Confucius realized that his views were at variance with those of the nobility, who believed that one was a gentleman because of birth. Confucius argued that being a gentleman was a question of conduct and character. His students came from the nobility as well as the poor, and Confucius stated that he never refused instruction to anyone.

Confucius believed that humans are social beings. They must interact with society without necessarily surrendering to it, and the moral individual will attempt to change others to conform to the moral path. Confucius even exhorted his followers to criticize a ruler if they found him to be unjust. He was very interested in political authority and established Five Constant Virtues that he believed a ruler should follow in governing his people:

1. *Benevolence.* Always think first of what is good for the people.
2. *Righteousness.* Do not do to your subjects what you would not want them to do if you were in their place.
3. *Propriety.* Always behave with courtesy and respect toward your subjects.
4. *Wisdom.* Be guided by knowledge and understanding.
5. *Sincerity.* Be sincere and truthful in all you do.

For over two thousand years, Confucian thought dominated education, government, and culture in China. Confucius believed that people needed standards or rules for life, and rules were developed for a wide range of social activities. He also believed that the self should not come before society because people had overriding obligations to parents, ancestors, and society as a whole.

Confucius stressed the importance of education, but he believed that building moral character was more important than merely teaching skills or imparting information. This moral approach emphasized practicality, part of which dealt with one's relationship with one's parents. Sons should obey and defer to their parents and respect the wisdom they gained in their journey through life. If one followed these and other correct principles he could become *chün-tzu*, the true gentleman, as a result of his moral development. The chün-tzu was distinguished by faithfulness, diligence, and modesty. He would not serve an evil prince or seek mere personal profit. He would lay down his life for the good.

Confucius believed that the superior individual develops Five Constant Virtues: Right Attitude, Right Procedure, Right Knowledge, Right Moral Courage, and Right Persistence. These virtues, if practiced, would lead to a new society based on the principles of justice and wisdom.

Confucius never intended to start a religion, nor is there any emphasis on God, a savior, sacrifice, or even salvation; instead, he emphasized the here and now and service to humanity. His aim was to educate the person to be a good father, mother, son, daughter, friend, and citizen. Confucius believed that every person should strive for the continual development of self until excellence is achieved.

Taoism

Lao-tzu (circa fifth century BC) served for some time in the imperial court and saw its corruptive nature. He was aware of Confucian thought but criticized its "self-sufficient air [and] overweening zeal; all that is of no use to your true person." Lao-tzu set down his teachings in a small volume known as *Tao Te Ching*. It has had a great influence in China and has provided guidance in troubled times. Whereas Confucianism greatly emphasizes the fulfillment of external obligations, the Taoist seeks to develop the inner life whereby one can meet any difficulty.

The central concept of Taoism is *Tao,* which means the Way or Path. It is the way the universe moves, the way of perfection and harmony. It is conformity with nature. Perhaps the most significant quality of the Tao is nonaction, letting things alone, not forcing one's personal desires into the natural course of events. It is a noncompetitive approach to life. The best leader is one who rules by letting things alone and using moderation. The Taoists believe that conflict and war represent a basic failure in society, for they bring ruin to states and a disrespect for life.

In the Tao Te Ching, Lao-tzu says that "Man conforms to earth; Earth conforms to Heaven; Heaven conforms to Tao; and Tao conforms to the way of Nature." When things are allowed to take their proper course, there is perfection and harmony in the universe. People were originally happy but suffer now as a result of the changes brought by civilization. The best thing to do, therefore, is to live in tranquil communion with nature. This applies even to death, for it is part of the vast cosmic changes whereby all things ebb and flow. Taoism became a kind of mystical philosophy—a nature mysticism—for nature possesses something greater than logic. We need to share in nature's truth and seek union with the Absolute, the Tao, something that cannot be really known or seen or even talked about. To be close to nature, the early Taoists led solitary lives in remote parts of China, while later sects achieved a sort of compromise between nature and societal life.

Lao-tzu believed that one should not rebel against the fundamental laws of the universe. "Do nothing," *wu wei,* is the famous injunction of Taoists. This does not mean doing nothing at all but doing nothing that is unnatural or not spontaneous. Most importantly, we should not strain or strive after anything but let things come naturally.

There is a strong sense of relativism in Taoist philosophy. Lao-tzu tells us that beauty, the taste of foods, and the location of one's residence fit no absolute standards. Deer eat grass, snakes like centipedes, owls enjoy mice. With moral problems, also, there is a "thus" and a "not thus," and who is to say which is correct? Things should be allowed to run their course within the all-embracing universe.

Taoism also speaks to political practice. When there is no interference with freedom and special privilege, then happiness and peace will ensue. The Taoists denied rulership by divinity or birth and often engaged in nonresistance against power and militarism. They believed that a proper individual would give up his life to achieve social justice. Taoists believed that people can govern themselves, and there is a strong sense of anarchy in their writings. They felt that governments tend to impose on the people rules that are inconsistent with the natural flow of life. They opposed both war and repressive government and argued that the more laws there are, the more thieves and bandits multiply. Nor does a death penalty work, for the people do not fear death. The best ruler would be the Taoist Sage, who governs in the interests of the people as a whole and who is beyond good and evil and above emotion. He might destroy a city and kill its inhabitants with impunity if he felt this action was in the interest of the totality.

Another major figure in the development of Taoism was Chuang-tzu (399–295 BC). In the book *Chuang-tzu,* he advocated transcending the world rather than reforming it. To achieve such emancipation one should engage in "free and easy wandering," "fasting of the mind," and "forgetting." The Tao, as Chuang-tzu saw it, means a detachment from the self and the world. Both life and death must be accepted as a part of nature. Thus, an individual should face life with great indifference and with humor.

Japanese Thought

The major historical base for Japanese philosophy is to be found in Shinto. This early religion of Japan lives on today but is not as influential as it once was. Shintoism encouraged nature worship, which meant the worshiping of trees, mountains, rocks, and waves. There was also emperor worship and the use of rituals, sorcery, divination, and purification rites. By AD 1000, there were three thousand shrines in Japan where Shintoists worshiped three thousand deities. The center of Shinto worship is the Sun Goddess, Amaterasu, who is the symbol of the things most sacred in Japanese life.

The Japanese perspective is one of acceptance and enjoyment of life and kinship with nature. Intuition is often prized over intellectualization, and religious views are often interwoven with ideas about nature and family. There is a strong feeling for loyalty, purity, and nature.

Today, the Japanese are a remarkable people who have utilized Eastern and Western influences while maintaining much of their cultural and philosophical heritage. They have been successful in fusing Confucian, Buddhist, and Taoist beliefs and practices in ways that incorporate them with a distinctly Japanese perspective. One example is the development of Buddhism, which began in India, flourished in China, and was adapted and transformed to fit a Japanese perspective, thus becoming Zen Buddhism.

Zen Buddhism

Buddhism probably entered Japan around AD 552. It was encouraged as a way of promoting national and political unity. Prince Shotoku Taishi (573–621) was deeply devoted to Buddhism and believed it would assist in developing social harmony. He encouraged Buddhist priests to lecture in Japan and helped to create Buddhist temples. In time, however, the Japanese modified Indian Buddhism considerably, adapting it to Japanese culture and contributing to the development of Zen Buddhism. Zen consists of a highly mystical approach to reality. It was founded in China around the sixth century by an Indian monk named Bodhidharma, who was popularly known as Daruma. It did not reach Japan until 1191, when several schools of Zen were established, such as the Rinzai and Soto schools.

Zen has no saviors, paradise, faith, or God. It has no books or scriptures, nor does it teach: it only points. It proposes to discipline the mind and seeks the freedom of mind. Its advocates emphasize that Zen is neither a philosophy nor a religion in the Western sense: It does not preach a doctrine; it does not proselytize. It promotes the idea that one can explore new paths without giving up one's own religious beliefs or philosophies.

Zen emphasizes a dependence on oneself rather than on an outside source for answers and wisdom. It depends more on intuition than intellectual discovery and holds that logical thinking and verbalization may actually prevent enlightenment. The insight obtained from any experience cannot be taught or communicated, yet there are disciplines and techniques that can orient one toward enlightenment (satori). The important thing is to develop a "third eye." This third eye helps us to see things in addition to what our two eyes show us and should be attuned to the things around us.

Enlightenment is not obtained only in isolated meditation but can be achieved at any time—while we work, walk in the fields, or converse with a friend. Even ordinary things in our daily lives can hide some deep meaning that the third eye uncovers. Suzuki said that the question "What is Zen?" is at once easy and difficult to answer. You lift a finger and there is Zen. You sit in silence and there too is Zen. Everything you do or say is Zen and everything you do not do or say is Zen. There is Zen in the garden, and Zen in you and me. Zen is in, with, and around everything.

Zen emphasizes silent meditation, aiming to awaken the mind in each person. Enlightenment comes through an immediate and intuitive understanding of reality that awakens our Buddha nature. Zen Buddhists insist that one cannot realize this through intellect, reason, or logic; rather, one must transcend the framework of rational thinking.

The methods of Zen are zazen, koan, and sanzen. These methods are designed to help one reach satori. Zazen is seated meditation in which one sits in a lotus position with half-open eyes looking straight ahead in contemplation. A koan is a statement or riddle on which Zen students meditate, such as "What was the appearance of your face before your ancestors were born?" The koan helps one acquire a radically different perspective on life. Sanzen is meditation with consultation. The student may meditate on a koan and consult privately with a master. The master helps to correct the student's false conceptions and prejudices.

Zen methods may also include physical violence, such as striking the student on the side of the head with a stick of bamboo to unlock the mind. The master may also utilize shouting and finger exercises. These methods are encouraged as a way to awaken the student by cutting off the reasoning process and the desire to rationalize the universe. These awakening experiences are for the purpose of making something happen. When they are successful, they trigger an experience of enlightenment.

As Zen flourished and its followers increased, monasteries where Zen ideals could be realized were instituted. The monks stress the importance of work, an ascetic way of life without possessions or waste, and a life devoted to a realization of all their faculties. There is no real literary education but a "learning by doing." There is no definite timetable for becoming a Zen master, for one lifetime might not be enough. No amount of reading, teaching, or contemplation is enough to become a Zen master. It is something that is the life of wholeness responding to wholeness, an unconditional union with all that is.

The influence of Zen Buddhism has been widely felt in Japanese culture, in its literature (Haiku), drama, painting, archery, judo, swordsmanship, karate, and the tea ceremony. As they are often practiced, these arts emphasize concentration of the mind and the harmony of people and nature.

MIDDLE EASTERN THOUGHT

The Middle Eastern nations include Egypt, Turkey, Iran, Israel, and the Arab countries of Asia Minor. For many centuries, this area has been commercially significant, and the history of the Middle East has been one of great conflict and influence. Many philosophies and religions owe their origins to thought that began in the Middle East, and Middle Eastern thought still stands as a challenge to Western ideas and traditions. Many thinkers have seen the Middle East historically as a meeting ground between the civilizations of the East and the West. The predominant language of the Middle East today is Arabic, and although there are a variety of philosophies and religions, the predominant religious view is Islamic.

Islam

Muhammad (AD 571–632) was born in Mecca. His parents died when he was young, and he was brought up by a succession of relatives. He was employed by a wealthy widow to look after her camels while she was trading in Damascus. He became her steward and then her husband.

Muhammad entered into an ascetic phase during which he would spend many hours in a cave on Mt. Hira, a hill near Mecca. He would endure long fasts and vigils, praying and meditating. When Muhammad was in his fortieth year, Allah spoke to him through Gabriel, the angel of revelation. The angel commanded that Muhammad call upon all the people to worship Allah, the one true God. Gabriel appeared to Muhammad again and told him that his mission was to restore to the Arabs the pure faith of their father Abraham and to free them from bondage and idolatry. Muhammad told his people that they had to give up the worship of many gods and goddesses and follow the will of Allah, the one true God.

Muhammad's revelations were not well received by the local populace; and in 622, in order to avoid persecution, he was forced to depart from Mecca to Yathrib, now known as Medina. This movement of the Moslems to Medina has since been called the Hegira. In this new community, Muhammad exercised great authority and power.

Eight years after he had left Mecca, Muhammad returned and conquered the city with his armies. He stripped all idols from the Ka'aba, and Mecca became the holy city of Islam. He then sought to unify the Arab tribes and bring them together in one nation governed by the will of Allah. After the death of Muhammad, Abu-Bakr began to collect his speeches and sermons into a book entitled the *Koran*, which means "The Reading." To the Moslem, every word in the Koran is the word of God as revealed by the angel Gabriel. It is written in classical Arabic, and most Moslems believe that it should not be translated into other languages.

The enormous growth of Islam can be attributed in part to the ideas of the Koran, which speaks to the hopeless, the poor, and the outcast, regardless of race, color, or nationality. The Koran also did away with intermediaries between God and humans. Any person, no matter how sinful, can bring a plea before God. One does not even have to go to a mosque to speak with Allah.

Muhammad taught that Allah is a purposeful God who created things to reach certain desired goals. The Koran tells the Moslem that each person will be tried in the Last Judgment, when Allah will judge all souls. Those who have followed the will of Allah will be eternally rewarded in paradise, an oasis of flowing waters, pleasant drinks, food, and sensual delights. For those who have not followed the will of Allah, there is eternal suffering in fire and heat.

The basic beliefs of the orthodox Islamic religion consist of the following:

1. One God
2. Sacred ground (All the earth belongs to Allah, so wherever one prays is holy ground.)
3. Equality before God
4. A life hereafter
5. A prohibition on intoxicating drink
6. Truthfulness
7. The sinfulness of adultery
8. Charity
9. Duty to animals (Treat animals with kindness and compassion.)
10. Limited polygamy (A Moslem is allowed to marry four wives, provided he can take care of them.)

The religious duties of Moslems are stated in the "Five Pillars" of Islam:

1. *Belief.* Moslems profess faith as "I bear witness that there is no God but Allah, and that Muhammad is the prophet of Allah."

2. *Prayer.* Muhammad required formal prayer five times a day at sunrise, noon, midafternoon, sunset, and nightfall.

3. *Fasting.* A fast during the month of Ramadan is required for all. During this time, one cannot take food or drink between sunrise and sunset.

4. *Almsgiving*. One is encouraged to share goods and money with the poor and to support Moslem schools and mosques.

5. *Pilgrimage*. Muhammad urged his followers to travel each year to the sacred city of Mecca. At the very least, one should do this once during his life-time.

Like other religions, Islamic religion has also experienced great reform. Two major changes have been the reform of Muslim higher education and the putting of Islamic doctrines into acceptable terms for the modern world. The seeming conflict between scientific and religious authority has been minimized, and secular education has grown. H. A. R. Gibb said that the orthodox positions in Islam resemble eighteenth-century positions in relation to Christian doctrine and that during the past hundred years the extension of secular education has exposed Moslems to the same influences that revolutionized Western thought.

JUDAISM AND CHRISTIANITY

Today, Judaism and Christianity are viewed within the Western cultural tradition, although Judaism still exerts an important Middle Eastern influence in the modern nation-state of Israel. Indeed, when someone speaks of Western culture, we often hear the term "Judeo-Christian" applied to it. However, both Judaism and Christianity had their origins in an Middle Eastern cultural setting. It can be argued, for example, that one cannot fully understand either the Old Testament or the New Testament unless one tries to perceive them in terms of their Middle Eastern cultural and geographical roots.

Judaism

Judaism traces its beginnings from Hebraism, beginning with the call of Abraham (circa 1750 BC), through Yahwehism and the giving of the Torah to Moses and the people, through biblical Judaism, and through the Mishnaic and the Talmudic period. The classical age of Judaism began with Moses and extended until the completion of the Talmud some centuries later.

The first Hebrew was Abraham, who wandered around the "fertile crescent" area of the Tigris and Euphrates valleys. As a legendary hero, Abraham was said to have come from Mesopotamia into Palestine about 2000 BC. He believed in a god who had a special interest in humanity, a tribal god who was a benefactor of his people. His grandson Jacob, or Israel, took up residence in Egypt, where the Israelites eventually were put into slavery. Under the leadership of Moses, the Israelites escaped from Egypt into the desert; and forty years later, they reached the edge of Canaan. After Moses' death, Joshua led the Hebrews into Canaan, where they established a monarchy under Saul. Under Kings David and Solomon, Palestine became the Israelite Empire. Judaism still has many roots in its early development as a religion and philosophy of wandering tribes. It antedates Christianity and Islam and contributed greatly to the development of each.

According to the Bible, God gave the Law and the Ten Commandments to Moses on Mt. Sinai. The Law is called the *Torah* ("Teaching") and consists of five books: Genesis, Exodus, Leviticus, Numbers, and Deuteronomy. Another part of the Bible is known as "The Prophets" and another "The Writings." In addition to the Torah, there is the Talmud, which is an extension of the Torah.

Philo of Alexandria, who was a Jewish philosopher, put the basic beliefs of Judaism into five fundamental concepts:

1. Belief in God.
2. Belief that there is only one God.
3. Belief that God created the world but the world is not eternal.
4. Belief that there is only one universe.
5. Belief that God cares for the world and all its creatures.

In earlier conceptions of Judaism, God was viewed anthropomorphically—with physical attributes the same as humans' and with such similar feelings as hate, jealousy, love, and vindictiveness. In later conceptions, God becomes more idealized, incorporeal, and mystical. He is "I am who am." Not only is this new God a spiritual entity but a God who is omniscient, omnipotent, and eternal. God is a just God, who metes out justice to people for the character of their lives, sending some to heaven or hell. There is also a belief in the coming of a Redeemer—a Messiah—who will establish heaven on earth and create the holy city of Zion.

In terms of practices, the Jewish religion makes observance of the Sabbath prominent. It is a day of great spiritual significance and rejoicing, a day of bodily rest. In addition, there are ceremonial observances, such as the Day of Atonement, the Festival of Passover, the Feast of Tabernacles, and Pentecost. There are also many festivals and holy days that celebrate both joy and suffering.

In Judaism, each congregation governs itself. Rabbis are not priests but individuals who teach the people and clarify the laws. Today, there is Orthodox Judaism, which attempts to be faithful to the ancient traditions; Conservative Judaism, which promotes a reinterpretation of the Torah; and Reform Judaism, which attempts to adapt Judaism to modern life.

The Jewish faith is currently centered around the nation of Israel, which many Jews feel has a divine and prophetic role to play in international life. It is in Israel that the ancient words come to life: "Israel chose Yahweh to be their God, and Yahweh chose Israel to be his people."

Christianity

Christianity began as a Jewish sect, organized and centered in Jerusalem around a small group of followers proclaiming Jesus of Nazareth as the Messiah. Jesus is reputed to have been born under King Herod around 6 BC.

(This date conflicts with the beginning of the Christian calendar, which is based on a miscalculation of Herod's death by medieval monks.) The career of Jesus began with his baptism by John the Baptist. Afterwards, he gathered his own disciples, who accepted him as "Christ," the chosen one, sent to fulfill God's promise. Jesus was a teacher who also performed miracles and forgave sins.

According to the Bible, Jesus was born in Bethlehem of a virgin mother and was crucified by Pontius Pilate, the Roman procurator of Judea, in AD 30. After suffering death, he arose from the dead on the third day and ascended into heaven. The words and deeds of Jesus form the basis for the New Testament, which is said to be the word of God. At the time of Jesus' death, there were no more than a hundred followers; and this new faith met such hostility in Jerusalem that its members withdrew to Samaria, Damascus, and Antioch. Yet the Christians showed enormous zeal, and Saul of Tarsus (or St. Paul) spent more than thirty years establishing churches in Asia Minor and Greece. Christianity appealed to the poor and oppressed, and by AD 150, many churches were established throughout Asia Minor. Christians continued to suffer persecution for three centuries, particularly in Rome under Nero, Domitian, and Diocletian. After Constantine I came into power, he established Christianity as the quasiofficial state religion of the Roman Empire in 324.

Religious philosophy dominated Europe after the decline and fall of the Roman Empire and into that period known as the Dark Ages, perhaps reaching its pinnacle of social control in the thirteenth century. According to Gibbon and other historians, Christianity was one of the factors that caused the fall of the Roman Empire.

Although Christianity is based largely on the works and life of Christ as recorded by Matthew, Mark, Luke, and John, it was later given a more philosophical background through various reflections and writings. Christianity incorporated from Judaism its beliefs of divine creation and providence but placed greater emphasis on the fatherhood of God and in God's concern for humanity. Belief in Jesus as a divinity has always been the crucial difference between Judaism and Christianity, and the New Testament represents a distinctly more loving and caring God than the Old Testament.

Augustine (AD 354–430)

One of the earliest philosophers of the Christian Church was Augustine, who was born in North Africa. He was educated in classical schools in the area and later described his early life as one of excess and debauchery. He came into contact with the Manichean religion, which stressed the dominance of evil, but later was converted to Christianity in 386, became a priest in 391, and in 395 was appointed Bishop of Hippo. His *Confessions* detail his early life and conversion to Christianity.

Augustine connected the philosophy of the Platonists and Neoplatonists to Christian beliefs. In *The City of God*, he described the City of God and the City of Man as divisions of the universe parallel to Plato's schemata of the

World of Ideas and the World of Matter. Like Plato, Augustine believed that the senses were unreliable and belief in God rests ultimately on faith. "We must first believe," he wrote, "in order that we may know." In Plato's philosophy, the soul has knowledge that is obscured by being imprisoned in the body. In Augustine's interpretation, the soul was blackened by Adam's fall from grace, which resulted in human doubt and uncertainty.

The doctrine of Original Sin is one of the most significant points in Augustinian philosophy. Humans were sinless in the beginning, as the Platonic notion implies, but they later became corrupt. Now the soul must become purified by an ascent of the mind toward God. This ascent occurs not only through the dialectic, which Augustine used extensively, but also through faith. Our earthly existence is like an intellectual and faith-engaging pilgrimage of which we must be a part in order to reach the City of God.

Augustine patterned his educational philosophy after the Platonic tradition. He believed that worldly knowledge gained through the senses was full of error but reason could lead toward understanding, and he held that, ultimately, it was necessary to transcend reason through faith. Only through faith, or intuition, can one enter the realm of true ideas.

Augustine believed that the kind of knowledge to be accepted on faith would be determined by the Church. The Church would not only determine unquestioned beliefs (such as the idea of the Trinity) but the proper kind of education. Augustine did not believe that the right kind of learning was easy. The child, an offspring of Adam, is prone to sin, and his evil nature must be kept under control to develop the good that is deep inside. Studies should concentrate on acceptance of the Church's truths.

One of the questions Augustine pondered in *De Magistro* was "Can one man teach another?" He believed that one cannot teach another in the traditional sense but can direct the learner with words or other symbols or "signs." Learning must come from within, and all true knowledge ultimately comes from God. Augustine was the greatest of the Christian Platonists, and his stress on the role of the learner's spontaneous and God-directed intelligence had great implications for Christian education for many centuries.

Thomas Aquinas (c. 1225–1274)

A later Christian philosopher-theologian was Thomas Aquinas, who was born near Naples in southern Italy. He attended the University of Naples and also studied under Albertus Magnus at the universities in Paris and Cologne. In 1256, he was appointed to the chair of theology at the University of Paris.

Aquinas first encountered the work of Aristotle while studying in Naples. This began a lifelong passion of attempting to reconcile Aristotelian philosophy with Christian concepts. He accepted Aristotle's realistic view that man is a combination of matter and mind, or body and soul. Aristotle taught that man is a natural being with a natural function but that our highest good comes through thinking. Aquinas connected this with the idea of

Christian revelation and maintained that since we are children of God, our best thinking should agree with Christian tenets. He spent much of his intellectual life showing that the word of God as represented by revelation is consistent with the thinking of Aristotle.

Aquinas agreed with Augustine that man is born with original sin and that life is a testing period, but he disagreed with the idea that we can only know truths through faith. Aquinas believed that God is pure reason and that when God created the world He made it possible for us to acquire true knowledge by studying the world through the use of observation and reason. God gave man reason so that he could know Him better and discern the true purpose and meaning of life. Aquinas believed that faith may be used for things we cannot yet understand but that ultimately all religious truths can be understood and reaffirmed through reason. He also believed that most things could already be proved through reason, such as God's existence, and that faith was only necessary when reason had reached its limits.

In his *Summa Theologica*, Aquinas debated the primary questions that faced Christian thought and used Aristotelian philosophy to provide insight into such questions. Both Augustine and Aquinas helped fuse the Middle Eastern religious beliefs of Judaism and Christianity with Western philosophical traditions derived from Plato and Aristotle.

In his disputation entitled "Concerning the Teacher," Aquinas maintained that the teacher is an agent who, with the help of God, can elevate the intellect. He advocated learning knowledge through the senses but believed that it should always be geared toward the higher knowledge of Christianity. He maintained that intellectual and theoretical knowledge was superior to practical knowledge. Where Augustine held that one man cannot really teach another because God is the ultimate teacher, Aquinas maintained that learners could learn some things on their own. The teacher, like the physician who helps the body to heal itself, can help the student to improve upon what is already known by suggesting order and relationships in learning. These philosophical and religious views later were called Thomism and became the basis for Roman Catholic education.

Martin Luther (1483–1546)

As the Old and New Testaments of Christianity became more plentiful in Europe because of the development of printing, more people had access to them and new interpretations began to be found. This sparked the Protestant Reformation, which was spearheaded by Martin Luther.

Martin Luther was born in Thuringia, Germany. He was extensively educated and earned both the master's and doctorate degrees. In 1505, he joined the Augustinian order and became an instructor in logic and physics at the University of Wittenberg. He later objected to certain practices of the Catholic Church and challenged Church doctrine through the Ninety-Five Theses he posted on the door of the Castle Church of Wittenberg.

Luther set out to rebuild the church in accordance with his conception of the Gospel and translated the Bible into German in order to make it easier for people to read. He believed that people should read the Bible and interpret it for themselves, with "everyman his own priest." Luther championed education for everyone to read the Bible, and he sponsored an educational movement that opened Lutheran schools to be under the authority of the princes rather than the Church. However, Luther's belief in an individual interpretation of the Bible led to many independent positions and schisms in Christianity under such leaders as John Calvin, John Knox, and Huldreich Zwingli. In the United States today, there are more than 300 different Christian religions that use the teachings of Christ as their basic orientation.

Despite the many different divisions and sects of Christianity, most believers seem to agree, with some variations, on the following:

1. God is the creator of all things.
2. Jesus is the Messiah, Christ, son of God.
3. The human being is a sinner who requires redemption.
4. The Trinity includes the Father, Son, and the Holy Ghost (Spirit).
5. Christ came down to earth to help humankind.
6. The soul is immortal.
7. The Old and New Testaments are our best guides.
8. Baptism is necessary for salvation.
9. Sinners must repent of their sins.
10. There is life hereafter.

Judeo-Christian thought continues to be an important religious and philosophical force in the world today. Most of the ethical and social mores, as well as laws, found in Western society today are based on Judeo-Christian principles.

EASTERN THOUGHT AND PHILOSOPHY OF EDUCATION

Much in Eastern philosophy speaks to our concern for education. All too often today, Western education is seen primarily as a way of acquiring a job or social advancement. Many Westerners are so immersed in their material concerns that they see little value in lofty speculation, mysticism, or anything that takes a great deal of time. Our educational institutions emphasize order, regularity, science, and the importance of "facts." It is true that much of the secularism and neutrality of Western thought developed as a reaction to speculative thought, particularly the religious speculations of the Middle Ages; but Western philosophy may have lost something of importance in its quest for objectivity.

Eastern thinking spawned many of the ideas that have found their way into Western philosophy, and Eastern philosophy still serves as a useful antithesis to our present beliefs. The concept of progress, for example, when looked at by Eastern and Western thinkers, is quite different. For the Western thinker, progress may be measured in terms of better bridges and a more practical and efficient social and political system. For the Eastern philosopher, progress may mean nonattachment and the development of one's inner being.

One thing is clear, however, and that is that Eastern thinkers have always concerned themselves with education. They have seen education as a way of achieving wisdom, maintaining the family structure, establishing the law, and providing for social and economic concerns. Eastern philosophy extols education, especially the role of the teacher, for many of the great Eastern thinkers were teachers as well as theorists. They saw the importance of the teacher in acquainting people with new doctrines and providing instruction in the things one must do to achieve the good life. Eastern philosophers see education as necessary not only for this life but for achieving the good life in the hereafter.

Aims of Education

There is certainly no one aim of education for Eastern philosophy. The aim of the earliest writers was to provide information about the forces of nature so that one could best deal with them. These forces were often capricious and demanding. The authors of the Vedic writings made the forces more understandable in their anthropomorphic guise and thus acceptable to village people who believed that nature, like humankind, was not to be trusted. These writings also suggested ways one could cope with or propitiate these forces to mitigate or assuage their fury.

Later writings of Indian and Chinese philosophers became more sophisticated, and increasingly less attention was focused on gods and ceremonies than on ways to live. A feeling developed that the way one lives is the important thing, and the way one lives may change things. Eastern philosophers pay much attention to the sufferings of life, and in our narrow framework of thinking today, we may be like the Buddha, who did not see suffering in the beginning. For example, when there is a terrible automobile accident, it is cleared away so quickly that few get to see the blood and pain. Old people are shunted out of sight to die, and asylums incarcerate those who might be a nuisance or cause physical harm to others. We are thus shielded from much suffering.

In Eastern philosophy, suffering is to be accepted as a way of life; but suffering has its causes, and these causes may be external, internal, or both. Those who lived a dissolute existence in a previous life may now be paying for their misdeeds. Perhaps, also, we need to see suffering as being beneficial to one's development in wisdom. Some philosophers think we can mitigate suffering, but it requires following a way, a path, something that is difficult and long.

Eastern philosophy has not been as singular in its development as Western philosophy. One has to take it system by system, culture by culture, and school by school. Often these schools, such as Confucianism, lasted long periods of time and influenced large numbers of people, including emperors. Sometimes these schools vied with each other for influence, and some served as stepping stones to new and different ideas. The fact that so many of them still exist and have such large followings attests to their continued vitality. Unlike the Western approach, most Eastern philosophies begin with sense experience and carry it backward to consciousness. In the Western view, the belief is that one should steadily increase the number of sensory experiences one has in order to amass a mountain of facts and data. The Eastern approach often seeks to diminish sense experience, or at least to downplay its role in the achievement of wisdom.

Eastern educational philosophy also tends to place a greater emphasis on the teacher–student relationship and to see great change forthcoming from this relationship. The student is changed as a result of contact with the guru, the master, the prophet, or the spiritual leader. Change is important because most Eastern philosophies emphasize that one cannot live a good life without thought. Education may also be necessary for salvation, and thus it takes on a spiritual quality. There is an emphasis on transformation, for the individual must be transformed in order to be able to face life or suffering with equanimity. Attitude shaping is important, and Eastern philosophers emphasize that the attitude one holds toward life is often the deciding factor. If one has an attitude that encourages the accumulation of goods, the Buddhists point out, then one will never achieve happiness.

There is an underlying aim of social change in most Eastern philosophies, but this larger social change often begins with individual change. The individual seeks and is changed, and as many individuals are changed, so too will society be changed. It is true that people are weak, that they seek pleasure and materiality; but they can be changed so that they do not seek these things. There is failure, but it is individual failure; and one can overcome this through meditation, through giving, through fasting and prayer.

One of the recurring educational aims of Eastern philosophy is to put humanity in tune with nature. There is a great emphasis on observing nature and learning through wanderings and pilgrimages. The art of the East tends to reflect a deep longing and even spiritual consideration of nature. But a study of nature should serve to promote introspection and emphasize the inner life. The importance of achieving wisdom, satori, enlightenment, or nirvana is supreme. All paths must lead to this, and from wisdom springs virtue, right living, and correct social and political behavior.

Methods and Curriculum

Eastern philosophy uses many education methods, ranging from an oral tradition to today's modern methods of communication. In comparison with

Western philosophy, Eastern philosophy has probably provided a greater variety of approaches in education for the purpose of living well, alleviating suffering, achieving enlightenment, or reaching nirvana. Hinduism, for example, emphasizes oral traditions and the reading of sacred literature. The 250 Upanishads represent its spiritual and philosophical basis. In Hinduism, beliefs grew through a succession of stages and as a result of certain leaders who gathered together the thoughts of the day in the form of Sutras, which often required some commentary to make them intelligible. Each stage had to develop its views, challenge criticisms, and provide answers to new problems.

When one thinks of a primary method connected with Indian philosophy (Hinduism), it is yoga, although this is certainly only one method. In Patanjali yoga, the mind enters a trance in which it is emptied of all content, unaware of subject or object, and absorbed into the ultimate, where it becomes one with the One. Through yoga, the mind is liberated from the body and achieves an inner freedom that transcends the material world of the senses. Chinese philosophy also emphasizes yoga (Buddhism), as well as attention to the teaching of rules of right conduct (Confucianism), and to attitude shaping (Taoism). Thus, Chinese philosophy emphasizes the here and now more than the supernatural views found in Hindu philosophy.

The Chinese were never preoccupied with supernatural views or with preparing for the next world, and many observers believe that this is why communism, with its materialist philosophy, was able to make easy inroads into Chinese life. Chinese philosophy has been characterized by a sense of proportion, with people suitably arranging their attitudes and actions in sequence with proper priorities. One of these priorities has traditionally been the family and one's ancestors, who are to be remembered and honored. In connection with this, there has been a great emphasis placed on rules of order and rules of right conduct within the family and society.

While one may pursue the search for nirvana on one's own, many sects promote the importance of a guru, or teacher, who has already obtained knowledge and can lead the student along the true path. Some aspirants to the role of the guru might prepare themselves for as long as thirty-two years, as in the case of Prajapati's students. The potential guru is to be carefully selected and through a variety of techniques properly educated. The guru occupies a central place in the student's life and is revered for the wisdom provided. In some cases, the guru may encourage students to do things that seem meaningless and absurd to them but that actually lead to enlightenment. Thus, students must be able to place much confidence in their teacher.

Japanese thought places greater emphasis on being in harmony with nature than does Chinese thought, but in both there is a great reverence for the teacher. Zen Buddhism, as one example, places the teacher in a position of great prominence. There is, through the teacher, the possibility of sudden enlightenment by the use of the koan, which consists of cryptic questions and sudden blows intended to shock the student. Often, students wander about seeking the perfect Zen master from whom they can obtain enlightenment.

In addition to the koan, there is an emphasis on tranquillity from meditation and the absence of thought. Zen has also influenced such arts as archery. *Zen in the Art of Archery* shows that a study of archery can lead to a knowledge of self and the meaning of existence.

Middle Eastern philosophies tend to extol sacred literature; and Judaism, Islam, and Christianity all have their sacred books. In most cases, these writings demand explanation or clarification; and a class of priests, rabbis, or prophets is necessary to explain these writings to the people. There are also sacred rites, prayers, and sacrifices to be made at certain observed times and under rather specific conditions. As modern-day beliefs, these religions are often challenged by changing social and political events in a fast-paced world. Unlike Western philosophies, however, which seem to change with every social upheaval, Eastern philosophies have remained more intact. The role of the school, for example, has often been to encourage doctrinal purity rather than to explore alternatives in a changing world. Eastern education has tended to remain apart from the Western educational traditions, which many Easterners believe do not promote desirable philosophical and religious ideals.

CRITIQUE OF EASTERN PHILOSOPHY IN EDUCATION

One good reason to study Eastern philosophy is that it represents a vantage point from which to examine Western thought. It encourages us to question seriously our most basic commitments to science, materialism, nature, religious traditions, education, and notions of the meaning of progress and the good life. This is not to say that Eastern philosophies do not deal with these things, but they generally do not view them as ends in themselves.

Western belief also differs from Eastern belief in the emphasis on upward social mobility without any order or rules. Getting to the top is the most important thing for many Westerners, and they promote the view that anyone can do it. They are taught that they should get to the top even if this alienates or separates them from family, friends, or community life. Priorities, rules of order, and decorum are often ignored or ridiculed if they block achievement of the desired material end. In Eastern philosophy, order, regularity, and patience are generally prized; and it is an order that is proportional and in harmony with the law of nature.

There is much to be critical of in Eastern philosophy, such as its emphasis on an unyielding supernaturalism as in Hindu philosophy; and some Western philosophers see the danger of dogmatism in the close relationship between Eastern religion and philosophy. Unlike Western philosophies, Eastern views are also often characterized by a sense of vagueness, splits between various factions, and an individualistic attitude toward salvation. In many cases, they also seem to promote a callous disregard for human life through such devices as the caste system. Western philosophies have tended increasingly to extol freedom and a democratic approach to government, whereas many Eastern philosophies still promote a slavish worship of rulership and a belief in one's fixed and ordered place in the universe.

Another aspect of Eastern philosophy that bothers Western philosophers, particularly contemporary ones, is the great reliance placed on codes, rules, and prescriptive ways of life, such as Buddhism with its eightfold path, the Jains with their five vows, the "correct principles" of Confucianism, and the commandments of Judaism and Christianity. People may need help and direction in their lives, but these lists of rules often strike thinkers as too contrived to be of any real use in modern life. The older philosophies indicate the need for structure, which may have been important in an emerging civilization but does not fit today's world, with its complex social and moral dilemmas. One also faces difficulty in interpretation regarding rules, such as whether to kill germs (Jain) or whether to kill an attacker (Christian). Codes that seem simple on the surface are often difficult to apply in real situations. It is not surprising, therefore, that many modern philosophies have promoted a situational or contextual approach to problems rather than a reliance on such seemingly strict and narrow rules.

With regard to education, one finds a great respect and concern for it throughout Eastern cultures. Teachers have occupied an important and central role in the development of thought, and the great religious and philosophical leaders were above all else teachers. There is an emphasis in Eastern philosophy not only upon knowing but upon teaching this knowledge to others. Buddha was a teacher, as were Confucius, Jesus, and Muhammad.

While Westerners are critical of approaches to learning that are primarily theoretical, Eastern ideas are a contrast to the view that education should be primarily concerned with social and vocational skills. There also seems to be undue emphasis, in the minds of many Western educators, on the role of the teacher in the learning process versus the role of students in learning on their own. The emphasis on perfection also seems misplaced to many Western thinkers, who believe the important thing is not to achieve perfection but to improve one's present state in terms of livelihood, material gain, or happiness.

Although many millions of people still abide by Eastern beliefs, there is little likelihood that those beliefs will greatly change the course of Western development. Indeed, it seems likely to be the other way around as the West enlarges its spheres of influence, power, and communications. There is every evidence that this has been happening for some time, as Western and Marxist philosophies challenge traditional views. Japan, in particular, and China and India are fast becoming great industrial and banking centers, and this is changing the character of their beliefs as well as the character of their socioeconomic institutions.

For some Westerners, the appeal of Eastern philosophy is more romantic than real. Many have turned to Eastern philosophy as an escape from a hectic, constantly changing, and highly industrialized society. Jack Kerouac, for example, spoke of fasting and solitary excursions in the mountains in his *Dharma Bums*. Today, Eastern philosophy has already found a place in religion, psychoanalysis, and rock music; and it has often provided us with a refreshing and original look at these fields. Despite the criticisms leveled against it, Eastern philosophy remains a fascinating study that emphasizes a wide variety of views. It is an important study not only because of its historical significance, and large following, but also because it forces us to reexamine the meaning and purpose of life.

BHAGAVAD-GITA

The Bhagavad-Gita, or Gita, was written sometime between the fourth and third centuries BC; it is one of the best known and loved of Indian writings. Its title means "the Song of the Lord" or "the Song Celestial," and it is still chanted in Hindu temples today. The Gita is basically a dialogue between Arjuna (Arjun), the great warrior, and Krishna, the Lord, who is an embodiment of the Supreme. Arjuna is asking Krishna about responsibility and the mastery of oneself in the face of life's challenges. The dialogue between Arjuna and Krishna shows some of the distinctive ethical ideals to come out of Indian philosophy.

Sanjaya:
Him, filled with such compassion and such grief,
With eyes tear-dimmed, despondent, in stern words
The Driver, Madhusudan, thus addressed:

Krishna:
How hath this weakness taken thee? Whence springs
The inglorious trouble, shameful to the brave,
Barring the path of virtue? Nay, Arjun!
Forbid thyself to feebleness! it mars
Thy warrior-name! cast off the coward-fit!
Wake! Be thyself! Arise, Scourge of thy Foes!

Arjuna:
How can I, in the battle, shoot with shafts
On Bhishma, or on Drona—O thou Chief!—
Both worshipful, both honourable men?

Better to live on beggar's bread
    With those we love alive,
Than taste their blood in rich feasts spread,
    And guiltily survive!
Ah! were it worse—who knows?—to be

> Victor or vanquished here,
> When those confront us angrily
>   Whose death leaves living drear?
> In pity lost, by doubtings tossed,
>   My thoughts—distracted—turn
> To Thee, the Guide I reverence most,
>   That I may counsel learn:
> I know not what would heal the grief
>   Burned into soul and sense,
> If I were earth's unchallenged chief—
>   A god—and these gone thence!

Sanjaya:
So spake Arjuna to the Lord of Hearts,
And sighing, "I will not fight!" held silence then.
To whom, with tender smile, (O Bharata!)
While the Prince wept despairing 'twixt those hosts,
Krishna made answer in divinest verse:

Krishna:
Thou grievest where no grief should be! thou
    speak'st
Words lacking wisdom! for the wise in heart
Mourn not for those that live, nor those that die.
Nor I, nor thou, nor any one of these,
Ever was not, nor ever will not be,
For ever and for ever afterwards.
All, that doth live, lives always! To man's frame
As there come infancy and youth and age,
So come there raisings-up and layings-down
Of other and of other life-abodes,
Which the wise know, and fear not. This that irks—
Thy sense-life, thrilling to the elements—
Bringing thee heat and cold, sorrows and joys,
'Tis brief and mutable! Bear with it, Prince!
As the wise bear. The soul which is not moved,
The soul that with a strong and constant calm
Takes sorrow and takes joy indifferently,
Lives in the life undying! That which is
Can never cease to be; that which is not
Will not exist. To see this truth of both
Is theirs who part essence from accident,
Substance from shadow. Indestructible,
Learn thou! the Life is, spreading life through all;
It cannot anywhere, by any means,
Be anywise diminished, stayed, or changed.
But for these fleeting frames which it informs
With spirit deathless, endless, infinite,
They perish. Let them perish, Prince! and fight!

He who shall say, "Lo! I have slain a man!"
He who shall think, "Lo! I am slain!" those both
Know naught! Life cannot slay. Life is not slain!
Never the spirit was born; the spirit shall cease to be
    never;
  Never was time it was not; End and Beginning are
    dreams!
  Birthless and deathless and changeless remaineth the
    spirit for ever;
  Death hath not touched it at all, dead though the
    house of it seems!

    Who knoweth it exhaustless, self-sustained,
    Immortal, indestructible,—shall such
    Say, "I have killed a man, or caused to kill?"

      Nay, but as when one layeth
        His worn-out robes away,
      And, taking new ones, sayeth,
        "These will I wear to-day!"
      So putteth by the spirit
        Lightly its garb of flesh,
      And passeth to inherit
        A residence afresh.
  I say to thee weapons reach not the Life;
Flame burns it not, waters cannot o'erwhelm,
Nor dry winds wither it. Impenetrable,
Unentered, unassailed, unharmed, untouched,
Immortal, all-arriving, stable, sure,
Invisible, ineffable, by word
And thought uncompassed, ever all itself,
Thus is the Soul declared! How wilt thou, then,—
Knowing it so,—grieve when thou shouldst not
    grieve?
How, if thou hearest that the man new-dead
Is, like the man new-born, still living man—
One same, existent Spirit—wilt thou weep?
The end of birth is death; the end of death
Is birth: this is ordained! and mournest thou,
Chief of the stalwart arm! for what befalls
Which could not otherwise befall? The birth
Of living things comes unperceived; the death
Comes unperceived; between them, beings perceive:
What is there sorrowful herein, dear Prince?
  Wonderful, wistful, to contemplate!
    Difficult, doubtful, to speak upon!
  Strange and great for tongue to relate,
    Mystical hearing for every one!
  Nor wotteth man this, what a marvel it is,
    When seeing, and saying, and hearing are done!

This Life within all living things, my Prince!
Hides beyond harm; scorn thou to suffer, then,
For that which cannot suffer. Do thy part!
Be mindful of thy name, and tremble not!
Nought better can betide a martial soul
Than lawful war; happy the warrior
To whom comes joy of battle—comes, as now,
Glorious and fair, unsought; opening for him
A gateway unto Heav'n. But, if thou shunn'st
This honourable field—a Kshattriya—
If, knowing thy duty and thy task, thou bidd'st
Duty and task go by—that shall be sin!
And those to come shall speak thee infamy
From age to age; but infamy is worse
For men of noble blood to bear than death!
The chiefs upon their battle-chariots
Will deem 'twas fear that drove thee from the fray.
Of those who held thee mighty-souled the scorn
Thou must abide, while all thine enemies
Will scatter bitter speech of thee, to mock
The valour which thou hadst; what fate could fall
More grievously than this? Either—being killed—
Thou wilt win Swarga's safety, or—alive
And victor—thou wilt reign an earthly king.
Therefore, arise, thou Son of Kunti! brace
Thine arm for conflict, nerve thy heart to meet—
As things alike to thee—pleasure or pain,
Profit or ruin, victory or defeat:
So minded, gird thee to the fight, for so
Thou shalt not sin!

       Thus far I speak to thee
As from the "Sânkhya"—unspiritually—
Hear now the deeper teaching of the Yôg,
Which holding, understanding, thou shalt burst
Thy Karmabandh, the bondage of wrought
    deeds.
Here shall no end be hindered, no hope marred,
No loss be feared: faith—yea, a little faith—
Shall save thee from the anguish of thy dread.
Here, Glory of the Kurus! shines one rule—
One steadfast rule—while shifting souls have laws
Many and hard. Specious, but wrongful deem
The speech of those ill-taught ones who extol
The letter of their Vedas, saying, "This
Is all we have, or need;" being weak at heart
With wants, seekers of Heaven: which comes—
    they say—
As "fruit of good deeds done;" promising men
Much profit in new births for works of faith;

In various rites abounding; following whereon
Large merit shall accrue towards wealth and
     power;
Albeit, who wealth and power do most desire
Least fixity of soul have such, least hold
On heavenly meditation. Much these teach,
From Veds, concerning the "three qualities;"
But thou, be free of the "three qualities,"
Free of the "pairs of opposites," and free
From that sad righteousness which calculates;
Self-ruled, Arjuna! simple, satisfied!
Look! like as when a tank pours water forth
To suit all needs, so do these Brahmans draw
Texts for all wants from tank of Holy Writ.
But thou, want not! ask not! Find full reward
Of doing right in right! Let right deeds be
Thy motive, not the fruit which comes from them.
And live in action! Labour! Make thine acts
Thy piety, casting all self aside,
Contemning gain and merit; equable
In good or evil: equability
Is Yôg, is piety!

       Yet, the right act
Is less, far less, than the right-thinking mind.
Seek refuge in thy soul; have there thy heaven!
Scorn them that follow virtue for her gifts!
The mind of pure devotion—even here—
Casts equally aside good deeds and bad,
Passing above them. Unto pure devotion
Devote thyself: with perfect meditation
Comes perfect act, and the right-hearted rise—
More certainly because they seek no gain—
Forth from the bands of body, step by step,
To highest seats of bliss. When thy firm soul
Hath shaken off those tangled oracles
Which ignorantly guide, then shall it soar
To high neglect of what's denied or said,
This way or that way, in doctrinal writ.
Troubled no longer by the priestly lore,
Safe shall it live, and sure; steadfastly bent
On meditation. This is Yôg—and Peace!

Arjuna:
What is his mark who hath that steadfast heart,
Confirmed in holy meditation? How
Know we his speech, Keśava? Sits he, moves he
Like other men?

Krishna:
When one, O Prithâ's Son!—
Abandoning desires which shake the mind—
Finds in his soul full comfort for his soul,
He hath attained the Yôg—that man is such!
In sorrows not dejected, and in joys
Not overjoyed; dwelling outside the stress
Of passion, fear, and anger; fixed in calms
Of lofty contemplation;—such an one
Is Muni, is the Sage, the true Recluse!
He who to none and nowhere overbound
By ties of flesh, takes evil things and good
Neither desponding nor exulting, such
Bears wisdom's plainest mark! He who shall draw
As the wise tortoise draws its four feet safe
Under its shield, his five frail senses back
Under the spirit's buckler from the world
Which else assails them, such an one, my Prince!
Hath wisdom's mark! Things that solicit sense
Hold off from the self-governed; nay, it comes,
The appetites of him who lives beyond
Depart,—aroused no more. Yet may it chance,
O Son of Kunti! that a governed mind
Shall some time feel the sense-storms sweep, and
        wrest
Strong self-control by the roots. Let him regain
His kingdom! let him conquer this, and sit
On Me intent. That man alone is wise
Who keeps the mastery of himself! If one
Ponders on objects of the sense, there springs
Attraction; from attraction grows desire
Desire flames to fierce passion, passion breeds
Recklessness; then the memory—all betrayed—
Lets noble purpose go, and saps the mind,
Till purpose, mind, and man are all undone.
But, if one deals with objects of the sense
Not loving and not hating, making them
Serve his free soul, which rests serenely lord,
Lo! such a man comes to tranquillity;
And out of that tranquillity shall rise
The end and healing of his earthly pains,
Since the will governed sets the soul at peace.
The soul of the ungoverned is not his,
Nor hath he knowledge of himself; which lacked,
How grows serenity? and, wanting that,
Whence shall he hope for happiness?
        The mind
That gives itself to follow shows of sense

Seeth its helm of wisdom rent away,
And, like a ship in waves of whirlwind, drives
To wreck and death. Only with him, great Prince!
Whose senses are not swayed by things of sense—
Only with him who holds his mastery,
Shows wisdom perfect. What is midnight-gloom
To unenlightened souls shines wakeful day
To his clear gaze; what seems as wakeful day
Is known for night, thick night of ignorance,
To his true-seeing eyes. Such is the Saint!

And like the ocean, day by day receiving
    Floods from all lands, which never overflows;
Its boundary-line not leaping, and not leaving,
    Fed by the rivers, but unswelled by those;—

So is the perfect one! to his soul's ocean
    The world of sense pours streams of witchery;
They leave him as they find, without commotion,
    Taking their tribute, but remaining sea.

Yea! whoso, shaking off the yoke of flesh
Lives lord, not servant, of his lusts; set free
From pride, from passion, from the sin of "Self,"
Toucheth tranquillity! O Prithâ's Son!
That is the state of Brahm! There rests no dread
When that last step is reached! Live where he
        will,
Die when he may, such passeth from all 'plaining,
To blest Nirvâna, with the Gods, attaining.

Source: The Bhagavadgita, translated by Edwin Arnold. London:
Kegan-Paul, Trench, Traubner, and Co., Ltd., 1899, pp. 9–24.

. . . .   H E R R I G E L   . . . .

ZEN IN THE ART OF ARCHERY

*This classic work is concerned with a German philosopher who came to Japan and stud-
ied archery as a pathway to Zen. In this illuminating account, the author comes to understand that in a study of archery, the hitter and the hit are not two opposing objects, but
one. Under the Zen master, archery can train the mind and bring it into contact with ultimate reality.*

*The Japanese pupil brings with him three things: good education, passionate love for
his chosen art, and uncritical veneration of his teacher. The teacher–pupil relationship
has belonged since ancient times to the basic commitments of life and therefore presupposes, on the part of the teacher, a high responsibility which goes far beyond the scope of
his professional duties.*

Nothing more is required of the pupil, at first, than that he should conscientiously copy what the teacher shows him. Shunning long-winded instructions and explanations, the latter contents himself with perfunctory commands and does not reckon on any questions from the pupil. Impassively he looks on at the blundering efforts, not even hoping for independence or initiative, and waits patiently for growth and ripeness. Both have time: the teacher does not harass, and the pupil does not overtax himself.

Far from wishing to waken the artist in the pupil prematurely, the teacher considers it his first task to make him a skilled artisan with sovereign control of his craft. The pupil follows out this intention with untiring industry. As though he had no higher aspirations he bows under his burden with a kind of obtuse devotion, only to discover in the course of years that forms which he perfectly masters no longer oppress but liberate. He grows daily more capable of following any inspiration without technical effort, and also of letting inspiration come to him through meticulous observation. The hand that guides the brush has already caught and executed what floated before the mind at the same moment the mind began to form it, and in the end the pupil no longer knows which of the two—mind or hand—was responsible for the work.

But, to get that far, for the skill to become "spiritual," a concentration of all the physical and psychic forces is needed, as in the art of archery—which, as will be seen from the following examples, cannot under any circumstances be dispensed with.

A painter seats himself before his pupils. He examines his brush and slowly makes it ready for use, carefully rubs ink, straightens the long strip of paper that lies before him on the mat, and finally, after lapsing for a while into profound concentration, in which he sits like one inviolable, he produces with rapid, absolutely sure strokes a picture which, capable of no further correction and needing none, serves the class as a model.

A flower master begins the lesson by cautiously untying the bast which holds together the flowers and sprays of blossom, and laying it to one side carefully rolled up. Then he inspects the sprays one by one, picks out the best after repeated examination, cautiously bends them into the form which exactly corresponds with the role they are to play, and finally places them together in an exquisite vase. The completed picture looks just as if the Master had guessed what Nature had glimpsed in dark dreams.

In both these cases—and I must confine myself to them—the Masters behave as if they were alone. They hardly condescend to give their pupils a glance, still less a word. They carry out the preliminary movements musingly and composedly, they efface themselves in the process of shaping and creating, and to both the pupils and themselves it seems like a self-contained event from the first opening maneuvers to the completed work. And indeed the whole thing has such expressive power that it affects the beholder like a picture.

But why doesn't the teacher allow these preliminaries, unavoidable though they are, to be done by an experienced pupil? Does it lend wings to his visionary and plastic powers if he rubs the ink himself, if he unties the bast so elaborately instead of cutting it and carelessly throwing it away? And what impels him to repeat this process at every single lesson, and, with the same remorseless insistence, to make his pupils copy it without the least alteration? He sticks to this traditional custom because he knows from experience that the preparations for working put him simultaneously in the right frame of mind for creating. The meditative repose in which he performs them gives him that vital loosening and equability of all his powers, that collectedness and presence of mind, without which no right work can be done. Sunk without purpose in what he is doing, he is brought face to face with that moment when the work, hovering before him in ideal lines, realizes itself as if of its own accord. As with the steps and postures in archery, so here in modified form other preparations have the same meaning. And only where this does not apply, as for instance with religious dancers and actors, are the self-recollection and self-immersion practiced *before* they appear on the stage.

As in the case of archery, there can be no question but that these arts are ceremonies. More clearly than the teacher could express it in words, they tell the pupil that the right frame of mind for the artist is only reached when the preparing and the creating, the technical and the artistic, the material and the spiritual, the project and the object, flow together without a break. And here he finds a new theme for emulation. He is now required to exercise perfect control over the various ways of concentration and self-effacement. Imitation, no longer applied to objective contents which anybody can copy with a little good will, becomes looser, nimbler, more spiritual. The pupil sees himself on the brink of new possibilities, but discovers at the same time that their realization does not depend in the slightest degree on his good will.

Assuming that his talent can survive the increasing strain, there is one scarcely avoidable danger that lies ahead of the pupil on his road to mastery. Not the danger of wasting himself in idle self-gratification—for the East has no aptitude for this cult of the ego—but rather the danger of getting stuck in his achievement, which is confirmed by his success and magnified by his renown: in other words, of behaving as if the artistic existence were a form of life that bore witness to its own validity.

The teacher foresees this danger. Carefully and with the adroitness of a psychopomp he seeks to head the pupil off in time and to detach him from himself. This he does by pointing out, casually and as though it were scarcely worth a mention in view of all that the pupil has already learned, that all right doing is accomplished only in a state of true selflessness, in which the doer cannot be present any longer as "himself." Only the spirit is present, a kind of awareness which shows no trace of egohood and for that reason ranges without limit through all distances and depths, with "eyes that hear and with ears that see."

Thus the teacher lets his pupil voyage onward through himself. But the pupil, with growing receptivity, lets the teacher bring to view something of which he has often heard but whose reality is only now beginning to become tangible on the basis of his own experiences. It is immaterial what name the teacher gives it, whether indeed he names it at all. The pupil understands him even when he keeps silent.

The important thing is that an inward movement is thereby initiated. The teacher pursues it, and, without influencing its course with further instructions which would merely disturb it, helps the pupil in the most secret and intimate way he knows: by direct transference of the spirit, as it is called in Buddhist circles. "Just as one uses a burning candle to light others with," so the teacher transfers the spirit of the right art from heart to heart, that it may be illumined. If such should be granted to the pupil, he remembers that more important than all outward works, however attractive, is the inward work which he has to accomplish if he is to fulfill his vocation as an artist.

The inward work, however, consists in his turning the man he is, and the self he feels himself and perpetually finds himself to be, into the raw material of a training and shaping whose end is mastery. In it, the artist and the human being meet in something higher. For mastery proves its validity as a form of life only when it dwells in the boundless Truth and, sustained by it, becomes the art of the origin. The master no longer seeks, but finds. As an artist he is the hieratic man; as a man, the artist, into whose heart, in all his doing and not-doing, working and waiting, being and not-being, the Buddha gazes. The man, the art, the work—it is all one. The art of the inner work, which unlike the outer does not forsake the artist, which he does not "do" and can only "be," springs from depths of which the day knows nothing.

Steep is the way to mastery. Often nothing keeps the pupil on the move but his faith in his teacher, whose mastery is now beginning to dawn on him. He is a living example of the inner work, and he convinces by his mere presence.

How far the pupil will go is not the concern of the teacher and master. Hardly has he shown him the right way when he must let him go on alone. There is only one thing more he can do to help him endure his loneliness: he turns him away from himself, from the Master, by exhorting him to go further than he himself has done, and to "climb on the shoulders of his teacher."

Wherever his way may take him, the pupil, though he may lose sight of his teacher, can never forget him. With a gratitude as great as the uncritical veneration of the beginner, as strong as the saving faith of the artist, he now takes his Master's place, ready for any sacrifice. Countless examples down to the recent past testify that this gratitude far exceeds the measure of what is customary among mankind.

More than five years went by, and then the Master proposed that we pass a test. "It is not just a question of demonstrating your skill," he explained. "An even higher value is set on the spiritual deportment of the archer, down to his minutest gesture. I expect you above all not to let yourself be confused by the presence of spectators, but to go through the ceremony quite unperturbed, as though we were by ourselves."

Nor, during the weeks that followed, did we work with the test in mind; not a word was said about it, and often the lesson was broken off after a few shots. Instead, we were given the task of performing the ceremony at home, executing its steps and postures with particular regard to right breathing and deep concentration.

We practiced in the manner prescribed and discovered that hardly had we accustomed ourselves to dancing the ceremony without bow and arrow when we began to feel uncommonly concentrated after the first steps. This feeling increased the more care we took to facilitate the process of concentration by relaxing our bodies. And when, at lesson time, we again practiced with bow and arrow, these home exercises proved so fruitful that we were able to slip effortlessly into the state of "presence of mind." We felt so secure in ourselves that we looked forward to the day of the test and the presence of spectators with equanimity.

We passed the test so successfully that the Master had no need to crave indulgence of the spectators with an embarrassed smile, and were awarded diplomas on the spot, each inscribed with the degree of mastery in which we stood. The Master brought the proceedings to an end by giving two masterly shots in robes of surpassing magnificence. A few days later my wife, in an open contest, was awarded the master title in the art of flower arrangement.

From then on the lessons assumed a new face. Contenting himself with a few practice shots, the Master went on to expound the "Great Doctrine" in relation to the art of archery, and to adapt it to the stage we had reached. Although he dealt in mysterious images and dark comparisons, the meagerest hints were sufficient for us to understand what it was about. He dwelt longest on the "artless art" which must be the goal of archery if it is to reach perfection. "He who can shoot with the horn of the hare and the hair of the tortoise, and can hit the center without bow (horn) and arrow (hair), he alone is Master in the highest sense of the word—Master of the artless art. Indeed, he is the artless art itself and thus Master and No-Master in one. At this point archery, considered as the unmoved movement, the undanced dance, passes over into Zen."

When I asked the Master how we could get on without him on our return to Europe, he said: "Your question is already answered by the fact that I made you take a test. You have now reached a stage where teacher and pupil are no longer two persons, but one. You can separate from me any time you wish. Even if broad seas lie between us, I shall always be with you when you practice what you have learned. I need not ask you to keep up your regular practicing, not to discontinue it on any pretext whatsoever, and to let no day go by without your performing the ceremony, even without bow and arrow, or at least without having breathed properly. I need not ask you because I know that you can never give up this spiritual archery. Do not ever write to me about it, but send me photographs from time to time so that I can see how you draw the bow. Then I shall know everything I need to know.

"I must only warn you of one thing. You have become a different person in the course of these years. For this is what the art of archery means: a profound and far-reaching contest of the archer with himself. Perhaps you have hardly noticed it yet, but you will feel it very strongly when you meet your friends and acquaintances again in your own country: things will no longer harmonize as before. You will see with other eyes and measure with other measures. It has happened to me too, and it happens to all who are touched by the spirit of this art."

In farewell, and yet not in farewell, the Master handed me his best bow. "When you shoot with this bow you will feel the spirit of the Master near you. Give it not into the hands of the curious! And when you have passed beyond it, do not lay it up in remembrance! Destroy it, so that nothing remains but a heap of ashes."

Source: Eugen Herrigel, *Zen in the Art of Archery.* New York: Pantheon Books, 1953, pp. 62–69, 89–93.

. . . .

SELECTED READINGS

Baird, Robert D., and Bloom, Alfred. *Indian and Far Eastern Religious Traditions.* New York: Harper & Row, 1972. A thoroughgoing look at a broad range of philosophies from early Vedic religion to Japanese Buddhism.

Feibleman, James K. *Understanding Oriental Philosophy.* New York: Horizon Press, 1976. A popular account of oriental philosophy for the Western world.

Fung, Yu-Lan. *The Spirit of Chinese Philosophy.* Westport, CT: Greenwood Press, 1947. An interesting account of growth and changes in Chinese beliefs.

Gibb, H. A. R. *Modern Trends in Islam.* Chicago: University of Chicago Press, 1947. Examines the foundation of Islamic thought and the impact of its transformation into a modernist religion.

Harshbarger, Luther H., and Mourant, John A. *Judaism and Christianity (Perspectives and Traditions).* Boston: Allyn and Bacon, 1968. An introduction to the implementation of an interreligious dialogue that deals with the historical and social development of Judaism and Christianity.

Organ, Troy Wilson. *Western Approaches to Eastern Philosophy.* Athens, OH: Ohio University Press, 1975. A comprehensive look at the values, attitudes, and varying structures of Eastern philosophy.

Suzuki, Daisetz T. *The Essentials of Zen Buddhism.* Westport, CT: Greenwood Press, 1962. A general overview of Zen and its impact on Japanese culture.

Pragmatism and Education

The root of the word *pragmatism* is a Greek word meaning "work." Pragmatism is a philosophy that encourages us to seek out the processes and do the things that work best to help us achieve desirable ends. Since this idea is so sensible, one might wonder why people insist on doing things and using processes that do not work. Of course, there are any number of reasons why such impracticality exists; among these are the weight of custom and tradition, as well as fear and apathy. Some habitual ways of thinking and doing in the past worked very well in their own time, but many of them have lost value for today's world. Pragmatism seeks to examine traditional ways of thinking and doing and, where possible and desirable in today's context, to reconstruct our approach to life more in line with human needs.

While pragmatism is primarily viewed as a twentieth-century philosophy developed by Americans for the most part, its roots can be traced back to British, European, and ancient Greek philosophic traditions. One important element of this tradition is the developing world view brought about by the scientific revolution. The questioning attitudes fostered by the Enlightenment and the development of a more naturalistic humanism have been outgrowths of this movement. The background of pragmatism can be found in the works of such figures as Francis Bacon, John Locke, Jean-Jacques Rousseau, and Charles Darwin. But the philosophical elements that give pragmatism a consistency and system as a philosophy in its own right are primarily the contributions of Charles Sanders Peirce, William James, and John Dewey.

ROOTS OF THE PRAGMATIST WORLD VIEW

The antecedents of the philosophy of pragmatism are many and varied, but some basic elements are vitally important. These are induction, the importance of human experience, naturalistic humanism, and the relations between science and culture.

Induction: A New Way of Thinking

Francis Bacon (1561–1626)

Francis Bacon's chief concern was with the ways by which we think. He believed that the method used before his time—deduction—was primarily the method of religion and speculative philosophy, and it yielded many errors, particularly with material phenomena. Deduction began with certain axiomatic statements or premises, and other statements or conclusions were deduced from them. Aristotle's syllogism is a good example of the method of deduction.

An instance of the problems generated by a purely deductive approach can be seen in Aristotle's belief that if objects of different weights are dropped from a given height they fall at different speeds. Instead, Bacon tried to get people to cease putting their faith in old beliefs, generalizations from the past (which may or may not have validity and reliability). He urged us to think, to develop valid knowledge. Induction would allow people to be experimental in their approach to the world. In essence, Bacon's ideas put a premium on human experience of and within the world of everyday life.

Bacon's influence on pragmatism has been significant. The inductive method that he suggested has served as the basis for the scientific method, which in turn has been of fundamental importance to pragmatism. While Bacon thought that science should be concerned primarily with material things, the pragmatists extended its range to include problems in economics, politics, psychology, education, and even ethics. For instance, in *How We Think,* John Dewey set forth the process of scientific thinking as central to the method of education. Indeed, according to Dewey, when we think in an orderly and coherent fashion, we are really thinking along the lines of scientific method, although we may not be conscious of it as such. If the nature of the thinking process were made conscious—if we were all educated in it—then our thinking would more likely be characterized by orderliness, coherence, and desirable consequences.

The general thrust of pragmatism is toward a heightened sensitivity to consequences as the final test for thought. Hence, pragmatist results are not always "practical" in the ordinary sense. First, pragmatists hold that there can be no artificial separation of means from ends; that is, the means used always dictate to some degree the actual ends achieved. In this case, sensitivity to consequences calls for an increased vigilance over the means used. Second, the consequences of thinking are not always "practical" in the ordinary sense, for the consequences may be aesthetic, or moral, or even religious. Thus, pragmatists, while enthusiastic advocates of the scientific method, are no recluses in sterile laboratories; rather, they wish to apply their version of the scientific method to the problems of humanity to secure a more satisfying life for all.

The inductive approach that is so characteristic of pragmatism is illustrated by the thought of George Herbert Mead. Mead applied induction to social and psychological behavior in a more thoroughgoing manner than had been accomplished previously. His view of the self as social particularly influenced Dewey and other pragmatist thinkers in education. Mead thought that if we viewed the child inductively, we would see that children do not learn to be social; rather, they have to be social even to learn. In other words, for Mead the self is by nature social and not some mental inner thing hidden from view.

William James applied inductive method to moral and religious questions. For him, the consequences that follow the application of a moral belief determine the truth or falsity, the rightness or wrongness of that belief. This view shows James extending the inductive method far beyond previous attempts, since to him the method was capable of extension to human experiences not included in ordinary empiricism. James was inductive to the extent that he rejected old assumptions about the nature of things and built his ideas on the basis of experience. In matters of religion, he held that religious beliefs had value if they provided suitable consequences. Belief in God, for example, could not be rejected if that belief provided personal meaning and value.

Thus, we can see that some pragmatists did not narrowly construe the meaning of induction so as to restrict it only to physical and material studies. Mead applied it to social and psychological areas; James used it in explaining religious and moral beliefs; while Dewey, learning from his predecessors, applied it to education and society in broad terms. A complicating factor involved in the pragmatist use of induction refers to pragmatism's "hard" and "soft" sides. James represents the "soft" side by such things as his investigations in religion. The "hard" side of pragmatism is seen where it insists on a rigorous application of induction that yields objective and verifiable data. Some aspects of both the "soft" and the "hard" sides can be seen in Dewey's work as he addressed a wide range of social and political issues.

The Centrality of Experience

Human experience is an important ingredient of pragmatist philosophy. This ingredient and the central emphasis it receives have helped give pragmatism a decidedly environmental orientation. The emphasis on experience, however, had its precedent in British and European philosophic traditions.

John Locke (1632–1704)

John Locke investigated the ways in which human beings experience and come to know things, and his examination led him to the view that the individual's mind at birth is blank, a *tabula rasa.* Ideas are not innate, as Plato maintained; rather, they come from experience—that is, sensation and reflection. As people are exposed to experiences, these experiences are impressed on the mind; thus, a baby soon has the idea of milk acquired through the sense of taste, perfume through the sense of smell, velvet through the sense of touch, green through the sense of sight. These experiences are all imprinted on the mind through one or more of the five senses. Once in the mind, they can be related in various ways through reflection. Therefore, one can create the idea of green milk or perfumed velvet.

Locke believed that as people have more experiences, they have more ideas imprinted on the mind and more to relate. He argued, however, that one can have in one's mind false ideas as well as true ones. A person can have a true idea of an apple or of a horse but also the idea of a mermaid created by erroneously relating the ideas of a woman and a fish, both obtained from the sensory world. The only way we can be sure our ideas are correct is by verifying them in the world of experience. We can find physical proof for a horse or an apple, but we cannot do the same for a mermaid.

One might think of the human mind as a kind of computer: until something is programmed in, one can get nothing out. Consequently, Locke emphasized the idea of placing children in the most desired environment for their education and pointed to the importance of environment in making people what they are. His book, *Some Thoughts Concerning Education,* describes the ideal education of a gentleman, who is to be exposed to many varied experiences, including extensive travel among people of different cultures. Locke's heightened sensitivity to the importance of experience and its relation to thought processes and personal development stimulated many thinkers who came after him.

Locke's notion of experience, however, contained internal flaws and caused difficulties. His insistence that mind is a *tabula rasa* established mind as a passive, malleable instrument buffeted by a weltering conflict of impressions received through the senses. When carried to its logical conclusion, Locke's notion leads to the separation of mind from body with the result that one can know only ideas. This lay at the base of George Berkeley's conclusion that "to be is to be perceived" (i.e., the existence of anything is dependent upon mind). David Hume took Locke's view and developed it to the point of skepticism regarding the existence and meaning of both ideas and matter. Thus, we arrive at the philosophical problems generated by the notion of a passive mind and uncertainty regarding the nature of reality.

According to John Dewey, it was Charles Peirce who opened the road leading out of the impasse generated by Locke. Ideas are not to be perceived as only isolated impressions on a blank tablet but as interrelated parts of experience. Dewey took this to mean that ideas have to be defined functionally in reference to a particular problem, rather than as mere mental constructs. Locke's view of mind was too passive for Dewey, for it meant that one's ideas are formed primarily by external sources.

Dewey, like Kant, pointed to the importance of mind as an active agent in the formulation of ideas as well as an instrument to effect changes in the environment that in turn affect us. Dewey constantly stressed the transactional nature of the relations between the organism and the environment. Empirically, we experience things as beautiful, ugly, and so forth; but we do not experience such things as projections of a subjective mind on objective reality; rather, they result from the connection and continuity of experience and nature.

Dewey rejected not only Lockean epistemology but also Locke's social theories, which contributed to the philosophy of liberalism in the classic sense. Locke's notion of freedom was the *power to act* in accordance with choice. This view of freedom, combined with his concern for economic factors, led to a laissez-faire theory of property, industry, and trade that encouraged the limitation of government and police functions and a free hand to economic exploiters.

Dewey held that Locke's laissez-faire view resulted in so-called popular philosophies of "self-expression" in which the "self-expression" of a few impeded the self-expression of the many. Classic Lockean liberals believed that individuals were endowed with ready-made capacities that if unobstructed would lead to freedom. Dewey maintained, however, that such a movement assisted the emancipation of only those having a privileged antecedent status while providing no general liberation of the majority.

Dewey also challenged the notion (advanced by Baruch Spinoza) that real freedom can be achieved only when each individual gains power by acting in accord with the whole, "being reinforced by its structure and momentum." This idea of the individual acting in accordance with "the whole" leads to a kind of Hegelian subservience of individuals to the state or other such external agencies. Dewey argued, however, that we should act intelligently in terms of the practical world in which we find ourselves because we cannot act in isolation from other people, from nature, or from human institutions.

Because of Dewey's cognizance of such social forces, many interpreters have believed that this gives support to a social-adjustment or "life-adjustment" view of education (i.e., that one should be taught to adjust to the way things are). Dewey did promote an awareness of contemporary conditions as well as interaction with them, but this did not preclude one's working constantly to improve existing institutions or to abolish them and establish new ones. Indeed, rather than advocating the kind of conservatism identified with Spinoza, Locke, and classical liberals, Dewey's views reflect a kind of underlying radicalism with regard to individuality and social action.

Jean-Jacques Rousseau (1712–1778)

Another figure whose philosophical views influenced pragmatism was Jean-Jacques Rousseau. Along with Locke, Rousseau wrote extensively about the relation of education and politics. His *Social Contract* and *Émile*, both of which appeared in 1762, antagonized so many of those in power that Rousseau had to leave Paris and seek refuge in Bern, Switzerland.

Although he was born in Geneva, Switzerland, Rousseau lived most of his life in France. His first philosophical work was a prize-winning essay on a subject proposed by the Academy of Dijon in 1749: "Has the Restoration of the Sciences and the Arts Contributed to Purify Morals?" Rousseau's answer was an emphatic *no*, for he followed Locke's insistence on the importance of environment in shaping human experience and thought. He maintained that civilization in its present form (that is, art and science) was harmful because it had led us away from nature.

Rousseau thought that individuals are basically good but corrupted by civilization. He did not believe that people would give up all of their artistic and technological developments, but he did think these should be controlled, particularly where they prevented us from being natural. Simply put, Rousseau argued for those aspects of civilization that are not corrupting to a natural life. He chose Daniel Defoe's story of Robinson Crusoe as representative of the kind of "Noble Savage" he envisioned, and he used it as the basis for *Émile*. In Defoe's story, Robinson Crusoe is shipwrecked on a deserted island, and he visits his shipwrecked vessel many times to remove civilized implements he needs for survival. Yet, these things do not interfere with his natural life: he builds his own house, kills his own food, and devises his own means of transportation. Other similar Noble Savage types from literature would include the Swiss Family Robinson, Natty Bumppo in the James Fenimore Cooper stories, and Thoreau at Walden Pond.

Rousseau's proposals for education are found in *Émile*, where he describes a child taken out of civilization and brought up in the country. Once in the country, Émile has a private tutor who sees to it that he lives naturally, and the tutor tries to arrange things so that Émile learns from nature. Rousseau did not think highly of books, which he felt only reinforced the artificial nature of civilization; and in *Émile*, he ignores books altogether until Émile reaches age twelve. He gave little attention to the education of women but did have one or two chapters dealing with Sophy, who is Émile's counterpart. As Rousseau viewed it, Sophy is to be Émile's helpmate, and she should have the kind of education that would complement Émile's.

His major contribution to pragmatism was not romanticism but the connection he saw between nature and experience. It is upon this intimate connection that he largely built his theory of education. While many modern observers may tend to dismiss Rousseau as a romantic because of his views on the Noble Savage, his views have appeal in light of the ever-increasing complexity of modern technological society. Certainly, his connection of nature and experience influenced many educational theorists, including Johann H. Pestalozzi, Friedrich Froebel, Francis W. Parker, G. Stanley Hall, and John Dewey.

Rousseau's emphasis on the place of naturalism in education affected the way pragmatist thinkers viewed the child. Children are no longer seen as miniature adults but as organisms going through various stages of development. This conception of the child as a developing person particularly influenced such psychologists as G. Stanley Hall, who is regarded as the founder of scientific child psychology. Rousseau's views helped educators to pose questions concerning what is natural for children. In other words, it is unnatural for children to sit still for long periods, to concentrate on abstractions, to remain quiet, or to exhibit refined muscle control. Rousseau helped educators to become more sensitive to the physiological, psychological, and social developmental stages of childhood. His attention to the physiological aspects of learning directly influenced the theories of such people as Maria Montessori.

Rousseau's attention to the nature of child development and his belief in the inherent goodness of people set the stage for contemporary "child-centered" education. Although this theme is found in the educational theory and practice of some pragmatists, others object to the sentimental romanticism that has grown up around Rousseau's works—a romanticism that has often been identified as uninhibited permissiveness. While this sentiment has often been attributed to Rousseau, not even Rousseau believed in the kind of license some present-day permissiveness suggests. One hears the charge of license leveled against the educational theories of pragmatists, but the charge is unfounded when one carefully examines the writings of leading thinkers, particularly John Dewey or Sidney Hook.

One of the hallmarks of Rousseau's philosophy is that education should be guided by the child's interests. An interest is not the same thing as a whim, however; by "interest," Rousseau meant children's native tendency to find out about the world in which they live. He believed in the child's autonomy but regarded it as a natural autonomy in which children have to suffer the natural consequences of their behavior. Even twentieth-century writers, such as A. S. Neill, whose Summerhill School strongly reflected a Rousseauist bias, advocate freedom but not license. Rousseau's impact on pragmatism is his sensitivity to the part of nature in education and the natural developmental process involved in one's learning experiences.

Science and Society

Modern science has dramatically changed our views of human destiny. That a scientific revolution has occurred is undeniable, for old metaphysical views, religious views, and social and political philosophies have been altered or have fallen before the juggernaut. The advance of science has not only affected theoretical views of society but the practical area of social structures and social relations as well. The social problems resulting from this scientific advance have been of central concern to pragmatism, for its social philosophy has not developed in a vacuum. In this regard, pragmatism has been influenced by such persons as Bacon, Locke, and Descartes. While science has helped contribute to many contemporary social problems, pragmatists believe that it can also help alleviate these problems.

Auguste Comte (1798–1857)

One of the most intensive philosophical efforts to apply science to society was by Auguste Comte. Although not a pragmatist, Comte, like Bacon, influenced the early development of pragmatism by helping thinkers become sensitive to the possibilities of using science to help solve social problems. For example, Dewey told how he was attracted to Comte's notion that Western civilization is disorganized because of a rampant "individualism," in which only a few are truly individuals while the many are submerged. From Comte, he drew the idea that science can be a regulative method in social life.

Comte's dream was to reform society by the application of science. Accordingly, science deals with both the organic and inorganic. Inorganic matter is handled by such sciences as physics and chemistry, while organic considerations are dealt with by physiology and sociology; thus, all matter is the province of science. While theology and metaphysics once served a useful function in helping to explain things, the rise and perfection of scientific thinking have surpassed them. The secrets of humankind and nature can now be unlocked, and we can live in harmony with ourselves and all other matter.

Today we might say that Comte was too optimistic, for we have discovered that scientific and positivistic thought often produces results that threaten to destroy us. Comte did help establish the application of science more directly to society rather than to just physical matter. Indeed, Comte was one of the fathers of modern sociology. His willingness to view social structures and relationships as capable of systematic study and control helped usher in elements of social theory that are distinct to pragmatism.

Charles Darwin (1809–1882)

Perhaps the single most important influence on pragmatism from the standpoint of science, however, was the work of Charles Darwin. Darwin first studied medicine at the University of Edinburgh and then studied divinity at Cambridge. Afterward, he was given the opportunity to go on a scientific expedition to the Southern Hemisphere. He spent five years aboard the *Beagle* and returned home in 1838. Thereafter, he devoted his life to developing his scientific theories, which were based largely on the data he collected during the voyage.

His major work, *On the Origin of Species* (1859), rocked the intellectual and religious communities of the Western world. Religionists attacked Darwin's theory because it challenged biblical creation. Intellectuals were stunned because it challenged old cosmological beliefs.

The underlying cosmological theory Darwin used was that nature operates by a process of development without predetermined directions or ends. Elements of Darwin's theory had been expressed by predecessors, but it was Darwin who gathered quantities of evidence and who painstakingly put it together in a most revealing way. Although his research was highly scientific, he wrote his findings in such a way that practically any literate person could understand them. He argued that species arise naturally through what he called a universal struggle for existence. This "descent with modification" occurs in an interplay between organism and environment. Food supply, geographical conditions, presence or absence of predators—all these set the stage on which natural selection occurs. Favorable characteristics persist, and unfavorable characteristics die out. Through this process, some species (such as dinosaurs) arise and then disappear as conditions alter; this selection process operates over a considerable time span.

Darwin's theory caught the popular imagination because he enunciated something every livestock farmer who practices selective breeding knows. It is not a high-blown philosophical utopia but something connected with ordinary experience. These conditions have helped foster an examination of many areas of intellectual inquiry; and the cosmology of development, spurred by Darwin's efforts, has become more widely applied in fields that even Darwin himself never envisioned.

In philosophy, the cosmology of development directly attacked the Platonic notion of essences and universals. This helped foster philosophical views that the universe itself is in process of development: Reality is not to be found in Being, but in Becoming. Gradually, such ideas have led to the rejection of a block universe and to notions that see reality as fixed or capable of being comprehended in entirety by intellect alone. For the pragmatists, this came to mean that reality is open-ended, in process, with no fixed end. These views of open-endedness further encouraged the view in pragmatism that a person's education is directly tied to biological and social development. From this standpoint, both William James and John Dewey attempted to weld humanism together with naturalism in a more integrated manner.

THE AMERICAN PRAGMATISTS

It has been said that the philosophy of pragmatism is "as American as apple pie." This is true in part, but as we have just seen, pragmatism had its roots in European philosophical traditions. In addition, F. C. S. Schiller developed a British version of pragmatism. By and large, however, pragmatism received its fullest treatment from three Americans: Charles Sanders Peirce, William James, and John Dewey.

Charles Sanders Peirce (1839–1914)

In many respects, Peirce was never given the recognition in his own day that he deserved. Although he was friends with such leading American intellectuals as William James, he never received a permanent post at any university and his major ideas never won public acclaim. For most of his life, he was a lonely and reclusive man, and he died in straitened economic circumstances.

What he achieved philosophically was primarily in his influence on later figures. His works got an eventual posthumous publication, but probably his most influential work was in an article titled "How to Make Our Ideas Clear" (which appeared in *Popular Science Monthly* in January 1878), in which he attempted to attack head-on the problem of the dualism of mind and matter, or the subjective and the objective. For the most part, he accepted the proposition that mind is different from material reality. In this respect, he agreed with Aristotle's view, but he also maintained that what we know about objective reality resides in the idea we have of any given object. The important thing, consequently, is to make sure our ideas are as clear and precise as possible. He argued that we should always remain extremely sensitive to the consequences of conceiving an idea in any particular fashion. In fact, Peirce maintained that *it is the concept of practical effects that makes up the whole of our concept of an object.*

We might say that our mental grasp of any object is nothing more than the meaning we apply to that object in terms of consequences. As Peirce put it, "Our idea of anything is our idea of its sensible effects." Thus, ideas or concepts cannot be separated from human conduct, for to have an idea is to be aware of its effects and consequences or their probability in the arena of human affairs.

Peirce concluded that true knowledge of anything depends upon testing our ideas in actual experience. In and of themselves, ideas are little more than hypotheses until tried upon the anvil of experience. Although Peirce's complete thought system was very complex, even going into speculations about the nature of God, immortality, and the self, it was his work on the nature of ideas and the necessity for testing them in experience that most influenced pragmatism.

William James (1842–1910)

Although Peirce was largely ignored during his lifetime, another figure brought the philosophy of pragmatism to a wide public audience: William James. The son of a prominent family, James rather leisurely tried his hand at several vocations, including medicine, but he made his mark in psychology and philosophy. He was not a particularly systematic thinker; rather, his contribution to philosophy lay in the power of his ideas, which ranged from psychology to the nature of religious experience.

James took Peirce's admonition about the practical consequences of ideas seriously, for this lay at the heart of James's theory of truth. He viewed the truth of an idea in terms of that idea's "workability." Truth is not absolute and immutable; rather, it is *made* in actual, real-life events. Truth does not belong to an idea as some property adhering to it, for it is found in acting on ideas, in the *consequences* of ideas. Truth is not always objective and verifiable; it is also found in concrete individuality. For James, there is the "inexpugnable reality" of individual existence.

In the life of an individual, experiences occur that have meaning and truth to that individual but that cannot necessarily be verified objectively to someone else. This view of truth—verifiability or "workability" and inexpugnable reality—is what James called "radical empiricism." In effect, he held that truth is inseparable from *experience*; in order to get at truth, we must study experience itself, not some immutable, otherworldly Absolute, extraneous to experience.

Thus, for James the primary datum is human experience. He concentrated on what he called the "stream" of experience, the sequential, serial course of events. Experience, he cautioned, is a "double-barreled" word, for there is experien*cing*, the actual lived, undergoing aspect; and there is the experien*ced*, the things of experience or the experience itself. Thus, experience is the *primary datum* and is capable of being studied cross-sectionally (the experiencing), and longitudinally (the experienced). James called upon thinkers to concentrate on experience in lieu of essences, abstractions, and universals. There is no Truth, Reality, or Absolute; but as his study of experience revealed to him, the universe is open-ended, pluralistic, and in process.

John Dewey (1859–1952)

James popularized pragmatism, and John Dewey "systematized" it and carried its leading ideas to far-reaching development. Dewey was born in 1859, the same year that Darwin's *Origin of Species* was published, and Darwin's thought was to play an important part in Dewey's philosophy, for the cosmology of development was central to his beliefs. Like James, he believed that there are no immutable absolutes or universals and his primary datum was experience; and like Peirce, he sought to clarify ideas in terms of their consequences in human experience. Dewey's contributions were not ignored, as Peirce's were; and while his ideas certainly had power and impact, as did James's, Dewey had the additional virtue of being able to pursue the most intricate problems doggedly and to search out their practical implications.

Dewey owed a great deal to Darwin, Peirce, and James; but he began his philosophical journey mainly in the Hegelian tradition. The most influential part of Hegel was, for Dewey, the Hegel who studied historical development and who sought an emerging unity from contending historical forces—not the Hegel who arrived at Absolute Spirit. Dewey once remarked that, "acquaintance with Hegel has left a permanent deposit in my thinking." If Dewey was taken with anything, it was the growing, developing, dynamic nature of life, not its speculative ultimates. He accepted James's notion of experience as a stream, and from this basis, Dewey was launched upon a wide-ranging philosophical career that spanned from horse-and-buggy days through World War II and into the atomic age.

The Nature of Experience

For Dewey, experience is not just an isolated happenstance—it has depth and reaches into nature. Experience and nature are not two different things separated from each other; rather, experience itself is *of* nature. Experience could, in the reflective sense, be divided into the experiencing being and the experienced things; but in the primary sense of the word, experience is of nature. People do not experience "experience" but the world in which they live, a world of things, ideas, hopes, fears, and aspirations—all rooted in nature. What had misled previous philosophy, he claimed, was the confusion over experience itself and our thoughts about it. Too many thinkers had concentrated on the reflective products of experience and had held these to be the ultimate reality. Unfortunately, such philosophers settled upon abstractions and not genuine experience.

The centrality of experience and the extent to which Dewey used it is revealed by the titles of some of his major books: *Essays in Experimental Logic, Experience and Nature, Art as Experience, Experience and Education.* His investigations into experience were not just speculative adventures, for he directed his efforts primarily toward real-life problems. Dewey took Peirce to heart and looked at the practical consequences of ideas. He held that genuine thought begins with a "problematic situation," a block or hitch in the ongoing stream of experience. In encountering these blocks, consciousness is brought to focus and one is made more acutely aware of the situation. It is in dealing with these real problems, Dewey argued, that creative intelligence is capable of development. Older philosophies had taken "problematic situations" and attempted to fit them to a preexisting set of abstractions. He urged that each situation be looked upon as unique and dealt with experimentally by investigating the probable consequences of behaving in particular ways. This approach shows Dewey's position that the world—experience and nature—cannot be understood in a monolithic way. The consequences are that we must be sensitive to novelty and variation and we must seek to be creative in dealing with our problems. Dewey headed in the direction of developing an experimental methodology and believed that method takes precedence over explanatory metaphysical schemes.

According to Dewey, experience is *of* and *in* nature. Nature consists of stones, plants, diseases, social conditions, enjoyments, and sufferings. In short, Dewey maintained we cannot separate experience and nature. Nature is what we experience, and we must view our experience in terms of its natural connections. In this respect, Dewey viewed nature as both precarious and stable, problematic and determinate; that is, some things change rapidly and make life precarious, whereas other things change very slowly and provide a sense of stability. Some experiences are stable, while others are in fluctuating confusion.

For example, natural changes in plant and animal species take place over long stretches of time, and it often takes centuries for the physical contours of land masses to change; however, some forms of life, such as certain kinds of bacteria, are capable of fairly rapid evolution, and land masses may be rapidly altered by volcanic action. Nature, therefore, has certain characteristics that are fairly stable and others that fluctuate, and the same can be said for human affairs, which Dewey considered to be a part of nature.

Some types of human behavior relating to family life seem to endure across the ages, while others are rapidly changing. We speak of the so-called sexual revolution as an indication of change, but certain human needs relating to child rearing and family life seem to endure. By the same token, broad social and political upheavals, such as the Marxist Revolution in Russia in 1918, appear to be cataclysmic. Closer examination reveals, however, that the causes of such events often go back for centuries. Thus, Dewey believed that some things are fairly stable and some are subject to rapid change, whether we are speaking of biology, social institutions, or politics.

Dewey followed Rousseau's lead in seeing the importance of nature in education, although he rejected Rousseau's romanticism. Rousseau established three sources of education: (1) nature, the spontaneous development of our organs and capacities; (2) human beings, the social uses to which we put this development; and (3) things, the acquisition of personal experience from surrounding objects. Dewey thought Rousseau regarded these three factors as separate operations, independent of the use to which they were put. His naturalism differs from Rousseau's in that he believed that the three factors have to be viewed in terms of their interrelationships. While Rousseau thought a child should be removed and educated "naturally" in the formative years, Dewey maintained that the child should not be removed from a social environment conducive to proper education. Thus, Dewey held that nature does not include just physical entities but social relationships as well.

Dewey argued that if one accepts the hypotheses of the open-ended universe and a pluralistic reality, it becomes less important to develop abstract explanations and more important to examine natural human processes. Acceptance of the open-ended nature of things does not necessarily lead to an overly optimistic view of life, for some processes lead to human goods and some lead to human ills. However, we *can* control our own affairs, even if not in an absolute sense and even if controlling any one state of affairs gives respite only momentarily. Dewey was not a wild-eyed optimist as some of his critics charge—he was fully sensitive to the tragic side of human affairs—but he did steadfastly maintain that we have it within our power to attain a more satisfying life. This can be done intelligently by using processes that yield desired results, that help solve the problems of humankind. Scientific method and experimental thinking can, if used properly, help us achieve desirable ends. In fact, thinking processes are of utmost importance because Dewey felt that most human difficulties result from faulty thinking. He was mostly concerned with connecting thinking processes with social processes, and this is shown in his emphasis on social action and education.

Experimentalism and Instrumentalism

Dewey's attention to social action and education gave his philosophy a decidedly practical orientation. Instead of dealing only with unchanging theoretical constructs, he urged that philosophy should concern itself with human problems in a changing and uncertain world. He felt that most thinkers embarked upon a "quest for certainty" in which they sought true and eternal ideas, when what is needed are practical solutions to practical problems. This view is in accord with modern science, in which ideas are not immutable but are accepted on the basis of how well they solve a perplexing problem.

Dewey believed that we should use philosophy to help us be more "experimental" in our approach to social problems by testing ideas and proposals reflectively before acting on them, and by critical appraisal and reflective assessment of results after trying them out in practice. In this sense, ideas are *instruments* in the solution of human problems, and those solutions should be tried on an experimental basis so that we can learn from our efforts and redirect them to better effect. Thus, he sometimes preferred the terms "experimentalism" and "instrumentalism" rather than "pragmatism" to designate his philosophy.

In *How We Think* (1910), Dewey showed how ideas can be used as instruments in the solution of real-life problems. He described his view in five stages:

1. *A felt difficulty* that occurs because of a conflict in our experience or a hitch or block to ongoing experience
2. *Its location and definition,* establishing the limits or characteristics of the problem in precise terms
3. *Suggestions of possible solutions,* formulating a wide range of hypotheses
4. *Development by reasoning of the bearings of the suggestions,* reflecting on the possible outcomes of acting on these suggestions—in short, mulling things over
5. *Further observation and experiment leading to its acceptance or rejection,* testing hypotheses to see if they really yield the desired results.

Although these five steps are presented in an orderly sequence, this does not mean that they are independent in a given situation or occur in any special order. They can occur together in such ways that the various steps interact with each other or become fused.

In this regard, Dewey viewed *method* rather than abstract answers as a central concern. If the universe is open-ended, if existence is precarious and uncertain, we cannot expect to locate enduring solutions; instead, we have to take each human problem as it arises. This is not to say that answers are unimportant, but it does recognize that they must be couched in terms of real-life situations, no two of which are exactly alike. Consequently, we must view the place of ideas in an experimental and instrumental sense. Like Peirce, we understand something as true or false on the basis of what it does and what effects it has in human activity. Dewey's work at the Laboratory School at the University of Chicago not only demonstrated his concern for education but also his belief that ideas should be tested in the crucible of real-life experience.

Individuality and Social Relations

One of the areas of Dewey's philosophy around which controversy has swelled is his treatment of individuality in the social world. This controversy is somewhat surprising and lends credence to the observation that Dewey is much "cussed" and discussed but little read. On one hand are those who claim that he exalted individuality at the expense of organized society. On the other hand, some critics charge that he submerged the individual under a stifling objectivity represented by the scientific consciousness and centralized social institutions. The controversy is surprising because, if one gives Dewey a fair reading, it is difficult to find that he maintains either position.

Rather than accepting the extremes of subjectivity or objectivity, Dewey tried to show that experience is first and primarily gross and macroscopic and that distinctions of subjectivity (or individuality) and objectivity (or the social and physical environment) come out of experience. In short, the one is not necessarily more real than the other because Dewey viewed subject and object or individual and society in a precarious balance, a *transactional* relationship. Of course, individuality can be submerged or lost by rigid institutional restrictions, and sociality can be denied by a rampant individualism of the economic laissez-faire variety. What Dewey actually said is that individuality and sociality are interrelated: both are possibilities and not guarantees. In other words, we have to work to see that they are in fact actualities and not just theoretical propositions.

Dewey thought that modern industrial society had submerged both individuality and sociality. Because of the confusion of modern society, he argued, the school should be an institution where both the individual and the social capabilities of children can be nurtured. The way to achieve this is through democratic living. Individuality is important because it is the source of novelty and change in human affairs. Dewey defined individuality as the interplay of personal choice and freedom with objective conditions. To the extent that personal choice is intelligently made, then individuals exercise even greater control over their personal destinies and the objective world surrounding them; that is, they have more freedom.

Sociality refers to a milieu or medium conducive to individual development. In Dewey's mind, there could be no genuine individuality without humane, democratic, and educative social conditions; consequently, the category of the social is the *inclusive* philosophic idea because it is the means by which the distinctly human is achieved. Therefore, individuality and sociality cannot be divorced in Dewey's system. They are interdependent and interrelated.

In this respect, we can better understand Dewey's ideal for the school and his rejection of those philosophies that promote a separation of individuals from institutions. The school, through democratic education, must enhance the interplay of individuality and sociality, the one supporting and enlarging the other, as in an ever-widening spiral.

Religious Experience

Dewey's views on religious experience can be found in several of his works but are most succinctly stated in *A Common Faith*, published in 1934. Dewey felt that being "religious" did not require the acceptance of supernatural beliefs or of organized religion. He thought most religions have a negative effect because they tend to separate and classify people, an untenable practice in a democratic society. He rejected both supernaturalism and militant atheism and promoted instead a consideration of the human being in the realm of nature. Religious ideas are rooted in humanity's natural needs.

Dewey thought that there are two schools of social and religious reform. One holds that people must be constantly watched, guided, and controlled to see that they stay on the right path, whereas the other believes that people will control their own actions intelligently. Dewey sympathized with the latter, but he pointed out that there are no guarantees that we will exercise control intelligently. However, we *can* do so; that is, freedom is a *possibility* and not a guarantee. Human existence occurs in a context and not in a vacuum. An individual's actions are influenced by the social context, for when an individual acts, she always acts in some socially connected way. When human beings understand the connecting links between themselves and their social context, when they act to promote the desirable elements of this connection, they achieve a "religious" character. An "unreligious" attitude is that which attributes human purpose and achievement to the individual in isolation from the physical and social environment.

Pragmatist philosophy is under frequent attack today from the fundamentalist religious right for being a leading thought system behind a "secular humanist" movement in public education, and Dewey is frequently accused of being a chief offender. These critics charge that the secular humanist denies the importance of prayer and does not think that the Bible should be treated differently from any other piece of literature. Secular humanists are also charged with favoring Darwinist evolution and for holding that the biblical story of Creation is an interesting but wholly imaginary theory without scientific justification. Finally, critics take secular humanists to task for promoting a worldly education rather than emphasizing the spiritual nature of humankind.

One of the problems of applying the term *secular humanism* to pragmatist philosophy is that many fundamentalist critics see secular humanism as another religion. If prayer and Bible reading can be banned from public schools, they reason, then secular humanism should also be banned. In addition, the term has become an epithet for a wide range of educational reforms and practices that fundamentalists oppose. Critics of the fundamentalists say that secular humanism is a red herring the fundamentalists use to taint any position with which they disagree.

If we go to the pragmatist philosophers themselves, such as James and Dewey, we find an abiding concern for religious experience. One of James's leading works is *The Varieties of Religious Experience* (1902), which has been influential in philosophical and theological thought. Dewey's *A Common Faith* (1934) has not been as influential, but it is a concise statement of a position that underlies much of his thought on education, democratic theory, and religion. However, neither James nor Dewey embraced either supernaturalism or organized religion. Certainly both were humanists in the long tradition of the Western humanities, as were many past thinkers on religion, such as Desiderius Erasmus.

A problem is that some fundamentalists have misused the word *humanist*, causing some people to see all humanistic thought as dangerous and antireligious. It has even led a few followers to suggest censoring the *humanities* or eliminating them from public school curricula! Such a development, if it ever came to pass, would certainly endanger the integrity of education, for it would deprive students of familiarity with a long and valued cultural heritage encompassed in the academic study of history, philosophy, literature, languages, and even religion itself.

Moral Development

In *Human Nature and Conduct,* Dewey proposed a "broad sweep" of morals as these relate to all the social disciplines connected with the study of humankind. He thought that not only analyzing morals but looking at them constructively was in the tradition of Hume's skepticism. Moral rules should be considered in light of particular situations and in terms of their consequences; hence, each action may be judged good or bad in terms of its moral outcomes. Essentially, this is an educative process, for an awareness of and concern for consequences are to be arrived at only through careful and reflective thinking. Dewey rejected moral theory based on a priori reasoning or divine precept. Basically, he thought that moral traits are to be acquired by individual participation in the social context and its cultural heritage or by learning about morality through living and reflective inquiry.

A recent development that has stimulated a great deal of critical comment is the work of Lawrence Kohlberg, who claimed that his theory, at least in part, is an elaboration of Dewey's views on moral education. Kohlberg maintained that the key to understanding a person's moral character lies in understanding that person's "moral philosophy." Every person is a moral "philosopher," and while there are variations from one individual to another, there are *universal* forms of moral thinking that may be described as "cognitive developmental stages." Stage development occurs in an invariant sequence, although the rate of development may vary and some children may be arrested at any stage. Stages consist of "structured wholes," total ways of thinking rather than mere attitudes toward particular situations. An individual is not always at a given stage but may be in transition from a past stage to a future one.

Kohlberg's work has its critics. One point of contention has been on how he interpreted Dewey's theory. Certainly Dewey thought that development occurs sequentially, or in "stages." His view that the aim of education is *growth* is indicative of this sequential development, but he did not see development in terms of discreet, invariant stages along Kohlberg's lines; rather, it flowed out of the experience of individuals in social contexts. In schools, it could be purposefully developed with the proper organization of curriculum, methods, and social life. In the final analysis, it seems that Kohlberg's approach to moral education owes more to Immanuel Kant than to John Dewey. Where Kohlberg's stage theory points toward a kind of fixed, ultimate end (justice), Dewey had no fixed end. The closest thing to it in Dewey's philosophy is the concept of growth, a growth that is open-ended in the sense that proper growth in one context may lead to further growth in other contexts.

From Dewey's perspective, the chief role of the educator from the standpoint of moral education is to see that students acquire vital ideas that become "motive forces in the guidance of conduct" or result in a "widening and deepening of conscious life." In *Democracy and Education* (1916), Dewey held that "All education which develops power to share effectively in social life is moral"; and in *Moral Principles in Education* (1909), Dewey asserted that apart from participation in social life, the school has no moral end. For ideas to become motive forces in conduct, they must affect how an individual relates ethically with others. As Dewey put it, "Ultimate moral motives and forces are nothing more or less than social intelligence." For growth in social intelligence to occur, the school must be organized and arranged so that the education it provides relates to the personal experience of the students, enters into their personal life, and helps shape their judgment—or what Dewey called "social power" and "force of character." Individuals achieve this only to the extent that they are "continually exercised in forming and testing judgments." For Dewey, then, *the* aim of education is growth, and its moral importance resides in its social consequences—growth in personal judgment and social intelligence.

Aesthetic Development

According to Dewey, art is a marriage between form and matter; that is, artists attempt to incorporate their ideas into the object being created. Thus, they engage in their work until they achieve the desired end. The artist is not only the creator but also the perceiver. However, Dewey did not believe that art and aesthetic experiences are to be left only to the realm of the professional artist. Everyone can achieve and enjoy aesthetic experiences, provided that creative intelligence is developed through education. Therefore, art need not be the possession of the few but can be available to everyone and can be applied to the ordinary activities of life.

Dewey believed that a truly aesthetic experience is one in which people are unified with their activity. It is an experience that is so engaging and fulfilling that there is no conscious distinction of self and object in it; the two are so fully integrated that such distinctions are not needed. In short, an aesthetic experience is one in which the contributions of both the individual and the environment or the internal and the external are in harmony. This kind of experience is what Dewey called "consummatory experience," or experience that provides unity and completion. This is human experience at its highest point.

Like the Greeks, Dewey thought that we should project art into all human activities, such as the *art* of politics, and the *art* of education. Although he was very much in favor of using science and technology in the educational enterprise, Dewey still believed that education is primarily an artistic activity as opposed to a strictly scientific or technical one. The desirable educator, from Dewey's point of view, is one who seeks to unify the mind and body of the student, or thinking and doing. When this is achieved, education becomes the supreme art form—the art of education.

Resurgent Pragmatism

Philosophical pragmatism never really died out with the passing of John Dewey, but it surely suffered a decline, particularly in academic philosophy. Nevertheless, it still had adherents; and the reports of its death, like those of Mark Twain's, were greatly exaggerated. Pragmatism, or *neo*pragmatism, now seems to be revived in interesting and exciting new ways. It is also difficult to say at the moment exactly what impact this "resurgent" pragmatism will have, if any, on the theory and practice of education. Writings specifically devoted to education from leading figures of the new movement to date have been scant, but an examination of some highlights may give an indication.

Richard Bernstein is one of those philosophers who has kept pragmatism an active philosophy. In "The Resurgence of Pragmatism" (1992), Bernstein briefly summarized the decline and renewal of pragmatism. The so-called philosophical "revolution" afforded by logical positivism and Anglo-American analytic philosophy (see Chapter 8) led many philosophers to de-emphasize pragmatism and take "the analytic turn," beginning shortly before World War II and spreading rapidly afterward.

Despite this success, many thinkers in philosophy and in other disciplines eventually found analytic philosophy to be rather narrow. Then, too, such philosophers as Bernstein continued to explore pragmatist themes. In any event, pragmatism is now experiencing a resurgence, and Bernstein notes some of the themes that continue to make it vital:

1. A persistent criticism of the idea that philosophy (or any field of inquiry for that matter) rests upon certainty and fixed foundations of knowledge
2. A strong sense that human existence is precarious and fallible
3. An ethical and political commitment to the amelioration of human suffering
4. A positive commitment to ongoing egalitarian democratic social reform
5. A resistance to cynicism, fashionable forms of despair, and beliefs in social and political impotence.

Bernstein's own writings reflect a major concern with these themes. For example, in *Praxis and Action* (1971), he explored contemporary philosophies that had *praxis* central to their thought—Marxism, existentialism, pragmatism, and analytic philosophy. All of them held that the end result of philosophizing about ethics and politics should be to promote the ideal of free human activity. He concluded that pragmatism, however, offered some badly needed correctives of open and mutual criticism, rather than dogma, and a more optimistic view regarding opportunities for amelioration of human ills, rather than a slide into subjectivism and nihilism.

Some twenty years later, in *The New Constellation* (1992), he examined modernity/postmodernity (see Chapter 10) and the attraction of many contemporary philosophers to what is called "critical theory." Where traditional philosophy was intent on fixed principles and universals, postmodern philosophy seems intent on negation of unity and the elevation, even celebration, of differences. Critical analysis must go on, Bernstein believes, but it must also include criticism for *reconciliation* as well. Thus, he returns to a theme of pragmatism that says however much we are committed to our own views, we must also listen to others. This involves an ideal of a *community* of inquirers or interpreters, an ethical ideal reflecting a sense of optimism and a recognition of important common bonds of democracy.

Perhaps the most significant figure in the resurgence is Richard Rorty, formerly a professor of philosophy at Princeton University and now a professor of humanities at the University of Virginia. Rorty was trained in the analytic mode of philosophy, but finding this restrictive, he sought to break out of the mold. Among his best known works are *Philosophy and the Mirror of Nature* (1979), *The Consequences of Pragmatism* (1982), and *Contingency, Irony, and Solidarity* (1989). In what is probably his most important work, *Philosophy and the Mirror of Nature*, he related how we need an intellectual effort that is "therapeutic," that attempts to "break the crust of tradition" so that we do not become stuck on singular vocabularies or particular philosophical modes of thought.

Rorty's villains are the Cartesian and Kantian traditions—and their recent manifestations in positivism and analytic philosophy—that view the mind as a great mirror, knowledge as accurate representation, and philosophy as the foundation upon which to polish and repair the mirror in order to get more accurate representations. His heroes are Ludwig Wittgenstein, Martin Heidegger, and John Dewey—philosophers whom Rorty calls the "great edifying, peripheral thinkers" who taught us that when we think we have true beliefs about anything, we may actually have no more than "conformity to the norms of the day" and that words and vocabularies acquire their meanings in human usage rather than "their representative character" and "their transparency to the real."

As Rorty sees it, a healthy departure for philosophy is to cease trying to become the foundation of knowledge from which to critique the remainder of culture and to view philosophical activity as part of a "conversation of culture," where knowing is not having an essence to be described by scientists or philosophers but rather a right to believe based on the best current standards. Such a conversation of culture, Rorty maintains, is the appropriate context in which to understand knowledge as "alternative standards of justification," and ongoing changes in those standards is what makes up intellectual history.

Perhaps the best part of Rorty's philosophical work is how he assesses intellectual history (those past voices in the conversation of culture) and how he urges us to draw back from being stuck on hopeless disputes about the "problems of philosophy"—as if philosophy can eventually discover some timeless method or form of analysis that will stand alone outside the historical flow. In "Intellectuals in Politics" (1991), he pushed for extending the best of our traditions (such as using democratic means to prevent the rich from ripping off the poor and keeping alive the hope of democratic reform) but being cognizant while doing so that we are fallible. These thrusts are clearly along lines followed by Dewey, who warned against the "quest for certainty."

The quest to be the foundation of knowledge is, to Rorty, akin to what Jean-Paul Sartre called "bad faith" and "self-deception"; that is, we deceive ourselves when we think that by knowing "what's out there" we will better know ourselves. Rorty takes the view that the vocabulary of the philosophical search for objective knowledge is just another set of descriptions, but the quest has so permeated our philosophical tradition that it has become "normal" discourse. What is needed, he believes, is "abnormal" discourse, a criticism of our comfortable assumptions to shake us loose and to develop new and more creative approaches to thought. This "edifying philosophy" merely aims to keep the conversation of culture going, not the establishment of an objective foundation for knowledge. Rorty fears that an objectified foundational description would freeze over culture and dehumanize it with a single vocabulary. However, he warns that we need to understand the "normal" discourse before we can proceed to the "abnormal." The value of the abnormal is that it shakes us loose from believing we have at last found a permanent foundation from which to critique our culture.

Is Rorty's direction one that would be useful in the philosophy of education? Perhaps, because the tradition in philosophy of education is part and parcel of the Western philosophical tradition Rorty criticizes. However, we should approach any Rorty-like philosophizing carefully. As Bernstein, in *Philosophical Profiles* (1986), noted, Rorty's critique is an effort to recover

Aristotle's notion of *phronesis*, or practical reasoning not based on eternal standards or foundations. If, like Rorty, we approach rationality as no more than various forms of rational persuasion, this does not mean that "anything goes." Bernstein defended Rorty as not denigrating truth and objectivity but as trying to demystify such labels and to justify claims to knowledge or truth by appealing to social practices hammered out in history. When all is said and done, it is through these claims that we distinguish what is true and false. But again, this does not mean that "anything goes."

On the other hand, Bernstein continued, if Rorty sees Dewey as only "therapeutic rather than constructive" and "edifying rather than systematic," then this is a gross exaggeration of Dewey. As Bernstein sees it, Dewey was primarily concerned with the role that philosophy might play after one had been liberated from the obsessions of outmoded thinking. Dewey would agree with Rorty that knowledge claims involve existing social practices and that philosophy has no special knowledge or access to truth; but for Dewey, this is where the real work begins. To what social practices should we appeal, and which ones need to be discarded, criticized, and reconstructed? Rorty never quite gets to these kinds of questions. As Bernstein saw it, Rorty too quickly leaves the matter at the conversation of culture level without filling in some needed blank space. In the final analysis, and as Dewey understood so well, we must deal with present conflicts with courage and with creative democracy as our goal.

In a novel and interesting interpretation of the philosophy of pragmatism, Cornel West proposed a new twist that he calls prophetic pragmatism. In *The American Evasion of Philosophy* (1989), West anchored pragmatism's American lineage in Ralph Waldo Emerson; and he analyzed such luminaries as Peirce, James, Dewey, Hook, and Rorty—but he also gave places to W. E. B. Du Bois, Reinhold Niebuhr, C. Wright Mills, and Lionel Trilling. West's background with the African-American tradition of Christianity and his interest in liberation theology are connected with philosophical pragmatism in ways that promise some new directions.

For example, West sees Ralph Waldo Emerson as an overlooked and rarely examined precursor of pragmatism, and he promotes the idea that Emerson's *theodicy* (his belief in goodness despite the presence of evil) and his evasion of epistemology-centered philosophy are central themes underlying pragmatism. For example, Dewey's own study of Emerson, which has been little noticed by most scholars, led Dewey to characterize Emerson as *the* philosopher of democracy, an accolade usually applied to Dewey himself; but West argues that the Emersonian optimism and assumption of goodness help account for the optimism that underlies pragmatism itself.

The evasion of traditional epistemological problems led pragmatists to seek new ways of analyzing social and political life, ways that helped them steer around the dead ends of the traditional problems of philosophy. A case in point is the pragmatists' insistence that social change should come through peaceful means, especially through education, public dialogue, and an experimental approach to social and political problems—what Dewey called the method of intelligence and which shows this humane optimism. Rather than armed struggle and violence, the pragmatists say, let us reason together, try things out, and evaluate them to gain new ends and a better, happier life for all. This does not mean that there is no tragic side of life; rather, a proper philosophical approach seeks to avoid despair and the paralysis that comes from being overwhelmed by the tragic.

West's injection of the "prophetic" and an African-American perspective into pragmatism are important contributions to the tradition. He believes that pragmatism offers the more promising intellectual route for Americans at this stage because of its commitments, such as Dewey's insistence on critical intelligence in social action or Du Bois' concern for the conditions of "the wretched of the earth." Prophetic pragmatism embraces philosophy as "a political form of cultural criticism," and it sees politics from the standpoint of "the everyday struggles of ordinary people."

Unlike traditional pragmatism, prophetic pragmatism uses Marxist forms of social analysis, but like traditional pragmatism, it shuns the dogmatic elements of Marxism. Prophetic pragmatism does not try to sidestep the tragic, the brutalities and atrocities of human life but takes a "third-wave left romantic approach"; that is, it faces tragedy but seeks ways and means to achieve progress and betterment through social transformation rather than violence, through praxis and action rather than despair. West uses the term "prophetic" because he seeks to unite pragmatism with the Jewish and Christian tradition of prophets who, through the urgency of compassionate criticism of the evils of their day, sought to bring about social transformation, a philosophical role not unlike those played by Dewey, Mills, and Du Bois.

One can see the need for some of Rorty's "abnormal discourse" and West's "prophetic" cultural criticism in education today. The "science of education" uses a vocabulary based in the self-confident claims of the physical and behavioral sciences. We hear boasts about "research-based education" and how much we know about the educational process, but there is a dearth of compelling evidence that we know much more about education than we did in the past or that "scientific" analysis is a significant improvement over philosophical criticism. Perhaps we are overdue for some serious but helpful criticism.

Too many times in the past, the field of education has been awash with sweeping reform claims that could not be sustained and would-be reformers were left high and dry. In the 1960s and 1970s, for example, there were calls for "radical reform" and "revolution" in education. Many practitioners in elementary and secondary schools simply ignored would-be reformers and went on about the more mundane business of traditional schooling. Still, talk about "revolution" and "radicalism" in educational theory helped to project the schools toward angry public criticisms spearheaded by right-wing political interests, a loss of faith in educational institutions, and the recent imposition of reactionary "reforms." If educators want to undertake a new criticism akin to what Rorty or West suggest, we must understand our educational traditions, learn the lessons of the present (of which radical educational theory can help inform us), and proceed with a philosophical discourse that challenges entrenched ways of thinking about education in thoughtful and helpful ways.

Certainly, education must involve traditional knowledge because this includes not only the contemporary vocabulary of knowledge but the intellectual traditions that helped establish that vocabulary, the heart of the traditional curriculum. If we take pragmatism seriously, this means to explore with students those traditional and newer subjects in the curriculum—history, language, science, math, cultural differences, etc.—in terms of present circumstances and help prepare students in ways that develop critical and creative intelligence to help them change the status quo and move toward a more humane, democratic society.

PRAGMATISM AS A PHILOSOPHY OF EDUCATION

The impact of pragmatism on American education has been considerable. Today, many schools have implemented elements of pragmatist ideas in one way or another, but this influence is not always consciously connected with the philosophy. One reason is that pragmatism in its most influential period was often identified with radical social reform, particularly progressive education. Many educators thought that this identification was a detriment to getting pragmatist ideas accepted into basically conservative and traditional schools; therefore, they were more interested in the practical use of pragmatist ideas than having those ideas identified with the philosophy of pragmatism or with progressivism. In a sense, therefore, elements of pragmatism came in through the back door of schools, and this factor helps to explain why pragmatist ideas and methods are often used (and misused) but are not always identified with the philosophy.

Although pragmatic philosophy greatly influenced progressivism, it would be a mistake to link progressivism too closely with pragmatism. While it is certainly true that most progressivists claimed to agree with the philosophy of John Dewey, Dewey himself was often critical of the excesses of progressivism. His book *Experience and Education* (1938) was directed as much at progressivist "child-centered" excess as it was at tradition-bound, old-style American education. It has been pointed out many times that Dewey's name was often invoked but his works seldom studied and that his ideas were taken out of context by many progressive zealots.

Progressive education as a movement began because many liberal thinkers in the late nineteenth and early twentieth centuries felt that American education did not reflect the ideas of justice and freedom found in democratic theory. Progressivism had its "hard" and "soft" wings. The soft wing identified with a romanticized view of the goodness of the child, and it sought a "child-centered" education that put few restraints on behavior or eschewed rigorous levels of academic performance. This led to charges of "permissiveness" being leveled against progressive theory and (since many progressives claimed Dewey as their philosophical leader) against Deweyan pragmatism, too. The "hard" wing of the movement believed that education should reflect advances made in the physical sciences, the social sciences, and technology. However, some of these "hard" progressives thought that scientific procedures should be used to measure, categorize, and separate children by "ability" and "intelligence" to meet demands in the economy. This view led to grouping practices that aggravated social differences in school and society and resulted in Deweyan pragmatism being criticized as crassly materialistic and wedded to industrial capitalism.

Not all progressive ideas can be linked to pragmatism, however. Locke's view that no ideas are innate and that experience is the primary shaper of human existence found ready acceptance in the progressive movement. Some advocates came to believe that schooling was primarily a matter of encouraging children to experience a variety of things. Pragmatism, however, stresses the importance of seeing the child in relation to the variety of experiences encountered in the environment, not just school experiences. Pragmatists feel that children must be looked at in terms of mental, physical, and emotional development and also in light of all the other social and cultural factors that serve to influence and shape their lives.

Rousseau influenced progressive thinking with his emphasis on nature, and some progressives took this to mean that "natural" education should be free from all societal restraints. Pragmatists maintain that education should be natural and related to the development of the human as a complex kind of animal. They have long championed schools where children can move about, where there is an open and stimulating environment that brings the natural element into education. However, this is a far cry from Rousseau's romantic naturalism, which encouraged many "soft" progressives to develop educational theories that sentimentalized the "natural goodness" of the child and severely limited adult guidance and direction.

Dewey did not champion either of the extremes on the "soft" or "hard" wings of progressivism, and so the identification of progressivism with Dewey and pragmatism should be made carefully.

Aims of Education

Dewey and the pragmatists believed that education is a necessity of life. It renews people so that they can face the problems encountered through their interaction with the environment. Civilized society exists, Dewey pointed out, because education is transmitted from generation to generation, occurring by means of the communication of habits, activities, thoughts, and feelings from the older to the younger. Without this, social life cannot survive; therefore, education should not be looked upon merely as schooling and the acquisition of academic subject matter but as a part of life itself.

Education is basically an art, and teachers express the highest concept of this art when they keep it from becoming routinized and lethargic. All living educates, but social living helps us to extract the net meaning from our education. Dewey, like Plato, believed that society is a necessary part of people's learning experiences, and we must guard against schools treating subject matter as if it were a thing apart from social life itself.

Pragmatists do not believe that "training" is the same thing as education. We can train children, through such methods as behavioral conditioning, to like or avoid things without their really understanding *why* they should do so. Most of the habits of animals are the result of training; but humans, unlike horses, can *understand* and *act* upon that understanding. Therefore, the educative process is fulfilled only when we promote understanding and intelligent action. Helping the child to think and do becomes *education* as opposed to mere training. In doing this, we may appeal to language as a means of conveying ideas and helping others to reason and provide a setting where they can act upon and test their understanding. This approach to education must be framed in the proper environment that has been regulated deliberately so as to achieve maximum educative effect.

Dewey felt that the school should provide just this kind of environment. The school should be the place where the other environments that the child encounters—the family environment, the civic environment, the work environment, and others—are coordinated in meaningful ways for the child to study.

In the pragmatist view, then, education should not be looked upon as a preparation for life but as life itself. The lives of children are as important to children as the lives of adults are to the adults. Thus, educators should be aware of the interests and motivations of children as well as the environment from which they come. In "My Pedagogic Creed," Dewey set forth the belief that education has two fundamental sides: the psychological and the sociological. One could not be subordinate to the other because the child's own instincts and powers provide the material and starting point of all education, and the educator's knowledge of social conditions is necessary to interpret the child's powers. An educator does not know what these powers and instincts are until she can translate them into their social equivalents for students and project them into the future lives of students for insight into the consequences.

In sum, Dewey believed that individuals should be educated as social beings, capable of participating in and directing their own social affairs. This means a freer interaction among social groups as well as attention given to developing all the potentialities an individual may have for future growth. He looked upon education as a way to free the individual to engage in continuous growth directed toward appropriate individual and social aims.

Whatever the specific aims of schooling and learning, pragmatists stress the importance of the way in which we arrive at those aims. According to

Dewey, aims should (1) grow out of existing conditions. They should (2) be tentative, at least in the beginning, and maintain flexibility. Perhaps most important of all, the aim must (3) always be directed toward a freeing of activities, an "end in view." This last suggestion is central to Dewey's idea of education. Properly speaking, Dewey thought people (parents, students, and citizens) and not the process of education are the ones who have educational aims. Yet there is still a sense of meaningfulness about the aims of education.

As stated in *Democracy and Education*, the aim of education is growth: "Since growth is the characteristic of life, education is all one with growing; it has no end beyond itself." In this regard, Dewey was speaking of growth as an enlargement of the capacity to learn from experience and to direct future experience in a meaningful way. Here rests the importance of the third point, that education should free our activities and make us more capable of directing individual and social life, for only in this way can proper growth in democratic living occur.

Sidney Hook, in *Education for Modern Man* (1963), maintained that education for growth goes together with education for a democratic society. In fact, the ideals of democracy establish the direction in which growth should occur, and resulting growth should support and develop a more democratic society. Intelligence is significant because it enables us to break the bonds of habit and makes it possible to devise alternatives that are more satisfying and desirable. Hook pointed out that growth, democracy, and intelligence are the inclusive and related aims of education.

William Heard Kilpatrick was an influential educator and one of Dewey's students and colleagues. In *Education for a Changing Civilization* (1927), he maintained that the overriding concern of each individual should be that all people have "the fullest and finest life possible." What we have accomplished and the possibility of future accomplishments are always uncertain; therefore, continued progress demands intelligent effort. Education becomes involved in teaching children how to live. This is accomplished in three steps: (1) provision of opportunity to live, (2) provision for learning experiences, and (3) provision of conditions for proper character development.

The function of education, then, is to help people direct, control, and guide personal and social experience. Pragmatists argue that we need to make persons aware of the consequences of their actions so they may guide their actions more intelligently, whether this action is at the personal or societal level. In this way, individuals learn to direct and control their own actions and require less outside support and direction. They learn to have greater effect in the larger social context, even to the point of social change and reform. Educated people grow in this manner, and their growth depends on a good environment shared with others as well as the natural flexibility inherent in the individual. Schools should foster habits of thought, invention, and initiative that will assist people in growing in the right direction—that is, toward democratic living.

According to the pragmatists, education should be an experimental enterprise as well as something that assists in social renewal. It should promote a humane spirit in people as well as the desire to explore and find new answers to our present-day problems in economics, politics, and other social life. Education should promote our true individualism, which will result in a diminishing of our reliance upon mere custom and tradition in the solving of our problems and cause us to rely more upon intelligence to achieve our goals and interests. This does not mean that valuable customs and traditions are not to be respected and preserved; rather, it means that we must learn to solve pressing problems intelligently rather than mindlessly rely on traditions.

Dewey pointed out that a "philosophy of education" is not the application of ready-made ideas to every problem but rather the formation of right mental and moral attitudes to use in attacking contemporary problems. Philosophy itself is "the theory of education in its most general phases." When fundamental changes occur in social life, we must reconstruct our educational program to meet these challenges. Thus, our ideas will have a pragmatic function. Learning helps us to meet environmental changes and affects our character as well. In this way, education has a moral influence and should play a vital part in helping us become the kind of moral persons who are interested not only in promoting our own growth but also in promoting the growth of others.

Methods of Education

Pragmatist educators prefer flexible methods that can be used in various ways. By the same token, they like functional school buildings and furnishings. Movable furniture, furniture that fits children, folding walls, and large print in books all came out of Dewey's work at the Laboratory School in Chicago. The same is true with methods, for pragmatists maintain that there is no single way to educate children; consequently, we should be aware of a variety of elements that can be used, including settings and situations from inside the school to the wider community outside.

Some pragmatists urge that teachers and students see that all knowledge is related. Reading, writing, and spelling can be combined as language arts. We can put history, geography, government, multicultural studies, and economics under social studies because we can see the relationship between these areas. Furthermore, relationships can be found between social studies and language arts and between other areas of the curriculum. This can be done by developing a "core" approach to curriculum so that students can understand how things are related. We may then have students select an area of concentration or "core" for a period of study, such as "exploration," and all the subject areas would revolve around this.

The language arts, for example, would deal with the literature of exploration, including the biographies of famous explorers past and present, accounts dealing with the impact on native peoples, science fiction that gives exploration themes, and work written by students in which they express themselves creatively or by which they report the results of their inquiry into the theme of exploration. In addition, they could investigate the important place of mathematics in exploration, ranging from the practical mathematics of circumnavigating the globe to mathematical explorations of the kind done from the time of Pythagoras down to Albert Einstein and contemporary mathematicians.

One could hardly study exploration without becoming involved in social studies and the sciences. In social studies, students would inquire into the history, the economics and politics, and the geographical considerations involved in exploration, as well as the social outcomes exploration has had. Science itself has been one of the frontier areas of exploration and would, of course, serve as a fundamental area of study (as suggested in some of the preceding examples)—not only in terms of the past, but of the present and projected future.

Students would even examine the art of exploration, ranging from paintings with exploratory themes to students doing their own exploratory compositions. By so doing, they would be exposed to several relevant bodies of knowledge that could be brought to bear on the theme of exploration. They would be involved with the fundamentals of knowledge in a practical and applied way so that the usefulness of knowledge would be more apparent. This approach demonstrates the relation of the various disciplines and shows students the wholeness of knowledge and helps them learn to use it in attacking problematic situations in novel and creative ways.

The teacher should constantly be aware of motivation. Dewey held that children are naturally motivated and that the teacher should capture and use the motivation that is already there. There should be an understanding, however, that all children are not at the same point and cannot be educated in the same way. Although there may be projects that motivate some students for group work, there may have to be individual projects for others.

Pragmatists are adherents of action-oriented education; therefore, they would suggest an activity-oriented approach to curriculum, so not only would students learn that they can relate various kinds of knowledge and use them to attack a problem but that they can act on them as well. To understand exploration more fully, students might visit historical sites of exploration or contemporary sites, such as the Kennedy Space Center. At school, they could reconstruct past events and life situations in order to appreciate the difficulties involved in the actual occurrence and examine both positive and negative effects exploration had. For example, the arrival of Europeans in the Americas had a profound impact on both Europe and the Americas, with positive and negative outcomes that continue to have effects today. Reconstructing this part of human experience (that is, questioning and studying this phase of human history) would help students gain better understanding not only of the past but of their world today. These reconstructions could involve readings, lectures or presentations, field trips, and videos; but they could also take the form of student-constructed dramatizations, role playing, and model building.

Since pragmatists are concerned with teaching children how to solve problems, they feel that real-life situations encourage problem-solving ability in a practical setting. For example, the conservation and wise use of energy is a leading problem today. Let us suppose that in a particular science class the children want to understand the energy problem. Some of them suggest that they should plan an energy allocation system. This becomes the specific problem, and the children will need to look at the history of energy, how various sources of energy have been used for human needs, how the need for energy aggravates world problems, what the science of energy offers for understanding, and what resources and plans are available.

Of course, the materials gathered must be appropriate for the age of the children, and the teacher must provide direction to keep the activities within reasonable limits. The motivation is there in student interest, and the teacher serves as a resource person concerned with helping children get the maximum educational advantages out of the situation. However, the children do the work themselves, and they run into various problems about what kinds of allocation schemes to use, how to construct an equitable allocation basis, what social and economic issues must be considered, what possible alternative energy sources may be tapped, or how modern society could conserve energy better. In tackling such problems and trying to provide solutions, children come to appreciate actual hurdles to be overcome and to gain important understanding that will help them control their own destinies better, such as helping conserve energy resources at home and in school and understanding the need to share energy and its allocation around the world.

In some respects, the method of learning is as important to pragmatists as what is learned. They feel that if one knows how to go about understanding and tackling problems, then one is equipped to handle more remote things with which school may not be able to deal, since the school does not know what kinds of life problems a person will face. Pragmatists think, however, that where problems (such as those relating to the community, the family, cultural origin, gender, the workplace, leisure time, citizenship, and questions of peace and war) may be identified or predicted in general ways, the school should help to prepare the person to cope with them. Hunger, overpopulation, and environmental degradation are only a few problems that must be addressed now and in the future, and they must be addressed in the educational sense if students are to be adequately prepared.

Pragmatist educators advocate meeting the needs and interests of the child. This has sometimes been interpreted to mean letting children do anything they want. "Interests and needs" do not necessarily mean the dictates of whim. Suppose a child wants to build model airplanes. Pragmatists would point out that this child's interest could be used as a motivational basis by which basic areas of the curriculum could be related. For example, one could be taught mathematics and physics by examining the principles of the airfoil. One could do this by studying people's dreams to fly and the eventual realization of it. In Dewey's Laboratory School at Chicago, the principle followed was to start children in some activity of direct interest and then as they encountered practical problems in the activity to involve them in particular knowledge of the activity that in turn would lead to more general knowledge.

Pragmatists tend toward a broad education rather than a specialized one. This is why they endorse a more general education as opposed to narrow specialization. They maintain that when one breaks knowledge down into discrete elements and does not put it back together, one faces the danger of losing perspective. The research chemist working on a specialized project may not be able to see the social consequences of her action. After World War II, for example, many nuclear physicists became disillusioned because their work was used mainly for destructive war-making purposes, a highly specialized purpose.

In today's knowledge explosion, it is impossible for a person to know everything, but one can understand the general operating principles of nature and social conditions that serve as guides for participation. The pragmatist approach is supposed to correct the excesses of narrow specialization. It does not oppose breaking knowledge down into its constituent elements, but it encourages us to put them back into a reconstructed whole that gives new direction and insight. It is in achieving this new wholeness that pragmatism becomes humanistic and holistic.

The concept of experimentation is basic to pragmatist philosophy. The fact that Dewey called his school at Chicago the "Laboratory School" illustrates his view that education is by its very nature experimental. Even though there are numerous guides, precepts, and maxims with regard to education, pragmatists hold that in the final analysis education is a process of experimentation because there are always new things to learn and different things to experience. Life does not stand still, and there is a constant need for improvement. This concept illustrates the pragmatist assumption of the open-ended universe in which new development is a distinct possibility. Experimental education is therefore necessary because it meets the need for flexibility in an ever-changing world and gives individuals security and a sense of constancy by helping them learn to understand and exercise control over the directions of change. Thus, pragmatist methods of education are not fixed "cookbook" methods but can be changed to fit changing circumstances.

Experimental method recognizes that there are no fixed or absolute conclusions; consequently, pragmatist education is really "discovery" education. Even the teacher does not always know what specific conclusions students will draw from their inquiry, although general possibilities may be known. Dewey gave the example of seven-year-old students who were cooking eggs and comparing them with vegetables and meats. If cooking eggs were simply the end, the children could have used only a cookbook. They raised this very point; but in cooking the eggs, asking questions, and seeking answers, they discovered that albumen is a characteristic feature of animal foods corresponding to starches in vegetables. Thus, they had learned an important lesson in nutrition by discovery. The teacher could have given them this information beforehand, but the lively manner of discovery established the knowledge in a much more profound way than mere telling could ever have accomplished. The students were learning the process of discovery as much as the facts uncovered. This type of learning is of twofold value: an important piece of knowledge is learned, and the skills of inquiry and self-sufficiency are developed that will benefit individuals for years to come.

One of the approaches suggested by such pragmatist educators as William Heard Kilpatrick is the "project approach" to learning. This is a systematization of the general approach Dewey used at the Laboratory School. According to Kilpatrick, a project approach results in the student's receiving a general education. Projects are decided by individual and group discussion, with the teacher as moderator. Children cooperate in pursuing the goals of the project. The essential features are those used by Dewey, but the approach is less structured; for in some cases, the teacher has no idea what the outcome will be. Kilpatrick carefully pointed out that teachers can and should veto projects that are too ambitious or for which resources are lacking. He advocated that the entire time of the elementary school be devoted to the project method and that it be extended into the secondary school but in diminishing amount to make room for some specialization.

Although there may be some individual variations among pragmatists on specific aspects of method, they all agree that the proper method of education is experimental, flexible, open-ended, and oriented toward developing the individual's capacity to think and to participate intelligently in social life.

Curriculum

Pragmatists have rejected the tendency of traditional approaches to curriculum in which knowledge is separated from experience and is fragmented or compartmentalized. When this happens, facts are torn away from experience and made to fit general principles that may or may not be helpful. In *The Child and the Curriculum*, Dewey maintained that the result of fragmentation has usually been to focus primary attention upon subject matter rather than on the contents of the child's own experience. In such an approach, children may be able to quote passages from Shakespeare without seeing how these can inform them about their own lives. The schools present materials to children in almost total neglect of their actual experiences. Children are often egotistic, self-centered, and impulsive, and their experiences confused, vague, and uncertain; yet the materials they encounter in school present the world as well-ordered, certain, and predictable. On the other hand, Dewey criticized those who made children the only starting point, the center, and the end of education. He did not believe that everything should be subordinate to the personality and whims of children.

According to Dewey, there are two major concerns in such cases: the logical and the psychological. The first emphasizes "discipline" and the second "interest." The error is to see a gap between a child's interest and necessary subject matter, for appropriate subject matter is not something fixed and ready-made outside a child's interest. The problem resides in how subject matter is organized and presented to students. For example, history is traditionally taught as something students should study simply because it is "good" for them, yet it may be remote and alien to their everyday experiences. What the study of history should do is enable children to connect their own experiences, customs, and institutions with those of the past. It should liberate and enrich personal life by furnishing it with context, background, and outlook. Dewey thought that the practice of divorcing history from the present is a grievous error because it robs historical study of the capacity to provide intelligent insight into the present. A divorced history loses its value for ethical instruction. It does not give understanding of the fabric of present life and may produce callous indifference to why things become what they are.

When we look upon what a child learns as fixed and ready-made, attention is directed too much upon outcome and too little upon process. Pragmatists want to focus at least some attention on process because ends should not be divorced from means. They assert that the means used to accomplish something dictate what the actual ends, the outcomes, really are. For example, to say that the American school should produce democratic citizens and then establish the school in such a way that the students have almost no choice, judgment, or decision-making opportunity is, in actuality, to produce virtually anything but democratic citizens. The older generation then sits back and wonders why the young do not participate more in social and political activities. According to the pragmatists, there is little doubt as to why such conditions exist.

Pragmatists believe in a diversified curriculum. This has helped American education extend itself into many areas not previously considered its domain. For example, pragmatists have advocated studies in occupations and hygiene and in such topics as the family and the economy. Today, schools have courses in health, physical education, family life, and sex education, but the actual outcome has not always been what the pragmatists want. For example, sex education courses are often taught only from a biological or physiological point of view. This is important, but pragmatists would say that human sexual behavior permeates many other human activities and should be integrated with them. How can one properly understand the meaning of so much of our great literature, for instance, without some understanding of sexual behavior?

Consequently, many pragmatists have advocated what is sometimes referred to as "problems-centered learning," the "core curriculum," the "project method," and the "problems approach." Essentially, such approaches to curriculum start with a central question, "core," or problem. Students are to attack the problem in diverse ways according to interest and need. Some may work independently, others in groups, and still others in various combinations and contexts. Information and ideas are drawn from whatever source is applicable. Resources include books, periodicals, videos, travel, field trips, experts, and other community or human sources. The materials are then sifted and evaluated for importance, and the students draw conclusions and construct suitable generalizations concerning the problem. They evaluate their own growth and development, which sets the stage for the next phase of education.

In many respects, the pragmatist curriculum is a process as much as a distinct body of subject matter. Traditional disciplines are not ignored; rather, they are studied and used for the light they throw on the problem and for their significance in aiding student growth. Pragmatist curriculum is composed of both process and content, but it is not fixed or an end in itself.

CRITIQUE OF PRAGMATISM IN EDUCATION

Pragmatism has been influential in twentieth-century America. It has influenced not only education but such other areas as law, art, economics, psychology, and religion. It is difficult, however, to separate a philosophy from the prevailing culture, so it is hard to determine whether pragmatism shaped America or America shaped pragmatism. American culture is generally pragmatic in the popular sense of the word because Americans are concerned with workability, the "show me" attitude, and the "cash value" of propositions. It is also difficult to say that these things flow from philosophical pragmatism. Dewey's pragmatism, for example, called for a rigorous attention to consequences in terms of moral and social goods and not in the crassly materialistic way in which many people interpret the word "pragmatism."

The place of pragmatism in philosophy of education today is not easy to assess. By the mid-twentieth century, few philosophers identified themselves as pragmatists, one reason being that associating oneself with an "ism" was out of philosophical fashion. Yet there seems to be a resurgence of pragmatism today, and particularly the work of John Dewey continues to wield important influence. Even a casual review of a leading journal in philosophy of education, such as *Educational Theory*, reveals a steady publication of articles on Dewey's philosophy, either in support of his views or against them. Even more numerous are the citations of Dewey's works in numerous scholarly publications to illustrate particular philosophical arguments.

For example, there is the issue of multicultural education, which revolves around how best to treat educationally the many cultural and ethnic identities found in pluralistic societies, such as the United States. Because Dewey spoke out against schemes to Americanize the immigrants and against the notion of the "melting pot" theory of cultural assimilation and because he wrote so consistently and forcibly on the connection of democracy and education, his ideas continue to have a significant bearing on this approach.

There is disagreement, however, on just what Dewey's significance is, and debate has swirled around where Dewey stood on various issues. One camp accuses him of using education to shape a pluralistic society without due regard for unique cultural differences. Another sees him as downgrading individualism in his advocacy of cultural pluralism. Still another views him as narrowly supporting cultural pluralism only to the extent that it promotes the Deweyan version of democracy.

Part of the difficulty resides in the fact that Dewey was an active philosopher for a considerable period of time and the volume of his writings is lengthy. Naturally, he changed some of his ideas during a long and productive career. Although he did not confront the term *cultural pluralism* until his middle fifties, when the term was coined by Horace Kallen, he produced a respectable number of writings on the issue of cultural differences. The point is, however, that whatever position or positions Dewey may have taken, what he thought on the issue is still important. Understanding how Dewey grappled with cultural diversity, how he analyzed the concept of cultural variety and sorted out its side issues, is important to scholars today in coming to grips with the theoretical dimensions of education in a culturally diverse society.

Another measure of the continuing influence of Dewey and philosophical pragmatism is the work being accomplished at the Center for Dewey Studies at Southern Illinois University at Carbondale. The Center houses Dewey's papers, correspondence, and other documents as well as his published works. It has produced a widely acclaimed definitive edition of his collected works, which consists of about forty volumes of material. This is contributing to a better, more systematic understanding of Dewey's philosophy and has helped raise the level of scholarship on Dewey's impact.

There is, however, continuing debate over just what influence pragmatist philosophy, and the works of John Dewey in particular, had and continue to have on American education. This is difficult to say because so many variables come into play in the question of Dewey's influence. Some critics lump progressivism and Dewey together, overlooking the fact that the progressive movement was not a single thing but a loosely joined movement encompassing several philosophic persuasions.

Joe Burnett maintains that progressive education has at least two philosophical roots, one being the romantic naturalism of Rousseau and the other being pragmatist philosophy in the Peirce-James-Dewey tradition. When both James and Dewey began writing on education, the progressive movement already had an established place in American educational reform, dating back to at least the mid-nineteenth century. Horace Mann and Henry Barnard both showed an interest in the child-centered philosophy of Rousseau and in the works of Pestalozzi, who was a follower of Rousseau and who, in turn, influenced such figures as Froebel and Herbart.

Thus, when Dewey came on the educational scene, he joined forces with this nascent progressivism as a *political* movement to overthrow the old education in favor of a new, more humane education. In Burnett's view, then,

Dewey accepted the romantics as political rather than philosophical allies. The romantics, in turn, borrowed and selected certain elements of Dewey's philosophy to justify their own position rather than following Dewey in any systematic fashion. Dewey tolerated rather than embraced this borrowing, as indicated by his criticism of the excesses of progressivism.

Many observers equate pragmatism with progressivism and progressivism with John Dewey. However, others had as much if not more to do with developing the progressive education movement than did Dewey. Colonel Francis Parker and G. Stanley Hall certainly loom large in the movement, both in practical and theoretical terms. The followers of Dewey, such as William Heard Kilpatrick, John Childs, Boyd Bode, and Gordon Hullfish, were also influential. Dewey was often critical of those who accepted his philosophy uncritically. At one point in his career, he openly criticized progressive educators he thought had misinterpreted his philosophy. In his nineties, and shortly before his death, Dewey looked back on the history of progressive education and lamented that his ideas had been taken as ready-made rubrics to be applied like mustard plaster to educational problems and not in the experimental sense that they were offered.

During the early twentieth century, when pragmatist and progressive ideas were being developed, some people identified Dewey and his followers as subversive to the American system. For this reason, many educators repudiated pragmatist aims and techniques as too radical. Thus, pragmatists found it difficult to get their ideas widely accepted in secondary and higher education, but they were more successful at the elementary level. In many cases, the pragmatist ideas accepted were of the less threatening sort and were not recognized as being related to a philosophy. Such things as colored chalkboards, gaily colored surroundings, movable furniture built specifically for children, greater involvement of students in decision making, and increased community involvement and support were all advocated by the pragmatists. Although Dewey designed his ideas primarily for public schools, many private and parochial schools were also influenced by his philosophy.

By the late 1930s, progressive methods were sufficiently widespread and a massive national study was launched to compare traditional and progressive schools. Known as the "Eight Year Study" and conducted between 1932 and 1940, the investigation showed that high school students in progressive schools did as well or better than those attending traditional institutions. This study, involving thirty high schools and three hundred colleges, aided in the adoption of progressive methods in American elementary and secondary schools. The final report on the study, however, came out in the hectic days of World War II so that the study never received the attention it deserved.

As progressive ideas gained more acceptance, reaction to them also grew. Americans had to put education on the back burner during World War II, but the reaction blossomed again after the war. Criticisms about "soft-headed" pedagogy, "fads and frills," and "permissiveness" in progressive education were tossed about. A "back to the basics" movement gained momentum with the launching of Sputnik by the Soviet Union in 1957. This stimulated Congress to pass the National Defense Education Act in 1958. This act poured millions of dollars into the schools to support the basic studies of science, mathematics, and foreign languages. Such critics as James Bryant Conant, Admiral Hyman Rickover, Max Rafferty, Arthur Bestor, and James D. Koerner spearheaded the movement for basic education. They criticized progressivism for its alleged lack of patriotic and religious fervor, its emphasis on change and relativism, and its excessive freedom and lack of discipline. While many of these criticisms are shallow and directed at the straw man called progressivism, they also reflect on some of pragmatism's fundamental philosophical tenets.

One of the criticisms directed against progressivism/pragmatism in education is that it deprecates acquisition of knowledge and cognitive development. It "waters down" the curriculum by advocating a "problems" approach that takes a piece of this and a bit of that discipline without ever fully exploring either one. Consequently, students may be shortchanged in terms of knowledge. Furthermore, critics charge, pragmatist educators are oriented toward organizing studies around student interests. The result is that students often lack the discipline that comes from study in the basic subject areas. Pragmatists have replaced history with "social studies," English with "language arts," and biology with "life sciences." The effort, critics say, is to cater to students' interests and not to give them the basic disciplines they need. Pragmatists are too permissive in the way they bend to students' whims; therefore, students leave school lacking judgment, with no depth, and with an almost total lack of direction or commitment to basic values.

Some of this criticism has merit because curriculum reform based on pragmatist ideas has usually been implemented too hastily and without adequate preparation of the teaching staff. In addition, many progressive educators were too shallow in their interpretation of what student interests are, what is relevant, and what a problematic approach really involves. It has been pointed out on numerous occasions that Dewey's works were grossly distorted. When he said "interest," he did not mean whim or mere desire. Children have interests in understanding the society they live in whether they recognize that interest or not. It is the duty of the teacher to help students recognize these kinds of interests and to help them make these interests personal and operative.

This is a symptomatic problem of interpreting Dewey's ideas, and it lies at the heart of his attack on dualistic thinking. He rejected any approach that went solely to the subjective side (student choice) or to the objective side (the subject matter). He argued against false separations of mind and body or individual and society. To meet student interest from Dewey's standpoint is to respect both subjective desires and objective demands, and both should be integrated into the educative process so that they are not at odds but are supportive of each other.

The same kind of problem exists with regard to Dewey's view of the place of intellectual development. Some educators have taken Dewey to mean that the intellectual and cognitive side of education are unimportant. The fact is that Dewey placed intelligence and thinking in a central position in his philosophy. He thought that intelligence is developed in purposeful activity dealing with problems and arriving at solutions. He did not ignore books, subject matter, and the need for periodic drill. He simply rejected that these are the only important things in education. Dewey believed that every purposeful human activity has potential for intellectual, emotional, aesthetic, and moral growth.

Indeed, there is a wide gap between what Dewey urged and what has often transpired in his and other pragmatist philosophers' names. A case in point is the "life adjustment" movement. Some critics argue that pragmatists, and particularly Dewey, promoted an ethic of adjusting personal desires and interests to existing social and economic conditions. They say that such an outlook promotes monopolistic economics, status quo social divisions, and a general deadening effect. In fact, there once was an educational movement called "life adjustment," but there is no evidence that Dewey or any other leading pragmatist ever supported it. Dewey used the word *adjustment,* but he used it in terms of people adjusting objective conditions to themselves as much as the other way around. He pointed out that people, in order to reconstruct and reorient society, first have to interact with existing conditions. In this sense, they have to adjust like any other organism, but they do it for the purpose or end of strengthening some existing conditions and changing others—*not* simply to conform to status quo authority and power relations.

Conservative critics have often attacked pragmatism for its "relative" and "situational" approach to life problems. They maintain that pragmatism rejects traditional values in religion, ethics, and society and tends toward values that are uncertain, changeable, and impermanent. While there is an element of truth in these charges, part of the criticism may relate to pragmatist philosophers' efforts to address social, cultural, and educational contexts rather than the general or metaphysical topics of traditional philosophy. Moreover, despite critics' charges about relativism, pragmatists (such as Dewey) did not think that one should reject traditional ideas and values out of hand but that they should be important considerations in philosophical inquiry. He did feel, however, that one could not afford to rely only on hand-me-down values and that one should be constantly searching for new ideas and values in every area of human activity. This problem is particularly apparent in the pragmatist approach to education, in which pragmatists support the idea that schools should maintain a constant "experimental" approach to learning. This does not mean that workable approaches no matter how ancient in origin are to be scrapped, but that new ideas and approaches should be sought, developed, and implemented to solve perplexing human problems.

Several factors account for some of the difficulty found in the application of pragmatist thought to education: the writings of some pragmatists, such as Dewey, may lend themselves too easily to misinterpretation; the breadth and the lack of specificity in pragmatist philosophy make it difficult to apply; zealous followers have attempted to apply broad ideas to specific educational problems and, hence, have oversimplified basic propositions; and there has been a woeful lack of energetic attention to pragmatist philosophy itself—particularly Dewey's portions of it—in lieu of reliance on second-hand interpretations of it.

In the closing decade of the twentieth century, the debate over the merits of pragmatism in education continues. For example, William Paringer, in *John Dewey and the Paradox of Liberal Reform* (1990), took a Marxist orientation in criticizing Dewey for not being radical enough. In Paringer's view, Dewey's philosophy is too anchored in Enlightenment concepts and too lacking in ideological and political analysis. While Dewey examined power relations in classrooms, he failed to provide adequate treatment of power relations in the wider society—power relations that maintain racism, sexism, violence, and class division. On the contrary, Sanford Reitman argued (in *The Educational Messiah Complex* [1992]) that American progressives and social reconstructionists who borrowed from Dewey were too radical. They came to view the school as an instrument of salvation from all the social ills that plague society and lost sight of Dewey's view that all social contexts have educational potential and that the educational task is to insure that desirable educational results flow from those contexts.

These kinds of analyses show that pragmatist philosophy continues to engage educational theorists, but in some respects, Dewey's philosophy of education has not had a truly systematic criticism because most critics have taken on only piecemeal aspects, have made polemical attacks rather than critical analyses, or have used particular aspects of pragmatism to support other partisan philosophical views. Nevertheless, the philosophy of pragmatism has made important contributions to educational theory and practice and will continue to do so.

. . . . JAMES . . . .

TALKS TO TEACHERS

William James wrote little on education, but what he did produce reflected many of his central ideas. The following selection illustrates some of those ideas, notably the "stream of consciousness" and the child as a "behaving organism." Consciousness is complex and cannot be divided neatly into the intellectual and the practical, nor can it be divorced from the formation of habitual patterns of behavior. According to James, the process of education is both the acquisition of important habits of behavior and the acquisition of ideas in ever higher and richer combinations.

The Stream of Consciousness

. . . The most general elements and workings of the mind are all that the teacher absolutely needs to be acquainted with for his purposes.

Now the immediate fact which psychology, the science of mind, has to study is also the most general fact. It is the fact that in each of us, when awake (and often when asleep), *some kind of consciousness is always going on.* There is a stream, a succession of states, or waves, or fields (or whatever you please to call them), of knowledge, of feeling, of desire, of deliberation, etc., that constantly pass and repass, and that constitute our inner life. The existence of this stream is the primal fact, the nature and origin of it form the essential problem, of our science. . . .

We have thus fields of consciousness,—that is the first general fact; and the second general fact is that the concrete fields are always complex. They contain sensations of our bodies and of the objects around us, memories of past experiences and thoughts of distant things, feelings of satisfaction and dissatisfaction, desires and aversions, and other emotional conditions, together with determinations of the will, in every variety of permutation and combination.

In most of our concrete states of consciousness all these different classes of ingredients are found simultaneously present to some degree, though the relative proportion they bear to one another is very shifting. One state will seem to be composed of hardly anything but sensations, another of hardly anything but memories, etc. But around the sensation, if one considers carefully, there will always be some fringe of thought or will, and around the memory some margin or penumbra of emotion or sensation. . . .

In the successive mutations of our fields of consciousness, the process by which one dissolves into another is often very gradual, and all sorts of inner rearrangements of contents occur. Sometimes the focus remains but little changed, while the margin alters rapidly. Sometimes the focus alters, and the margin stays. Sometimes focus and margin change places. Sometimes, again, abrupt alterations of the whole field occur. There can seldom be a sharp description. All we know is that, for the most part, each field has a sort of practical unity for its possessor, and that from this practical point of view we can class a field with other fields similar to it, by calling it a state of emotion, of perplexity, of sensation, of abstract thought, of volition, and the like. . . .

The Child as a Behaving Organism

I wish now to continue the description of the peculiarities of the stream of consciousness by asking whether we can in any intelligible way assign its *functions.*

It has two functions that are obvious: it leads to knowledge, and it leads to action.

Can we say which of these functions is the more essential?

An old historic divergence of opinion comes in here. Popular belief has always tended to estimate the worth of a man's mental processes by their effects upon his practical life. But philosophers have usually cherished a different view. "Man's supreme glory," they have said, "is to be a *rational* being, to know absolute and eternal and universal truth. The uses of his intellect for practical affairs are therefore subordinate matters. 'The theoretic life' is his soul's genuine concern." Nothing can be more different in its results for our personal attitude than to take sides with one or the other of these views, and emphasize the practical or the theoretical ideal. In the latter case, abstraction from the emotions and passions and withdrawal from the strife of human affairs would be not only pardonable, but praiseworthy; and all that makes for quiet and contemplation should be regarded as conducive to the highest human perfection. In the former, the man of contemplation would be treated as only half a human being, passion and practical resource would become once more glories of our race, a concrete victory over this earth's outward powers of darkness would appear an equivalent for any amount of passive spiritual culture, and conduct would remain as the test of every education worthy of the name.

It is impossible to disguise the fact that in the psychology of our own day the emphasis is transferred from the mind's purely rational function, where Plato and Aristotle, and what one may call the whole classic tradition in philosophy had placed it, to the so long neglected practical side. The theory of evolution is mainly responsible for this. Man, we now have reason to believe, has been evolved from infra-human ancestors, in whom pure reason hardly existed, if at all, and whose mind, so far as it can have had any function, would appear to have been an organ for adapting their movements to the impressions received from the environment, so as to escape the better from destruction. Consciousness would thus seem in the first instance to be nothing but a sort of superadded biological perfection,—useless unless it prompted to useful conduct, and inexplicable apart from that consideration.

Deep in our own nature the biological foundations of our consciousness persist, undisguised and undiminished. Our sensations are here to attract us or to deter us, our memories to warn or encourage us, our feelings to impel, and our thoughts to restrain our behavior, so that on the whole we may prosper and our days be long in the land. . . .

No one believes more strongly than I do that what our senses know as 'this world' is only one portion of our mind's total environment and object. Yet, because it is the primal portion, it is the *sine qua non* of all the rest. If you grasp the facts about it firmly, you may proceed to higher regions undisturbed. As our time must be so short together, I prefer being elementary and fundamental to being complete, so I propose to you to hold fast to the ultra-simple point of view.

The reasons why I call it so fundamental can be easily told.

First, human and animal psychology thereby become less discontinuous. I know that to some of you this will hardly seem an attractive reason, but there are others whom it will affect.

Second, mental action is conditioned by brain action, and runs parallel therewith. But the brain, so far as we understand it, is given us for practical behavior. Every current that runs into it from skin or eye or ear runs out again into muscles, glands, or viscera, and helps to adapt the animal to the environment from which the current came. It therefore generalizes and simplifies our view to treat the brain life and the mental life as having one fundamental kind of purpose.

Third, those very functions of the mind that do not refer directly to this world's environment, the ethical utopias, aesthetic visions, insights into eternal truth, and fanciful logical combinations, could never be carried on at all by a human individual, unless the mind that produced them in him were also able to produce more practically useful products. The latter are thus the more essential, or at least the more primordial results.

Fourth, the inessential 'unpractical' activities are themselves far more connected with our behavior and our adaptation to the environment than at first sight might appear. No truth, however abstract, is ever perceived, that will not probably at some time influence our earthly action. You must remember that, when I talk of action here, I mean action in the widest sense. I mean speech, I mean writing, I mean yeses and noes, and tendencies 'from' things and tendencies 'toward' things, and emotional determinations; and I mean them in the future as well as in the immediate present. . . .

You should regard your professional task as if it consisted chiefly and essentially in *training the pupil to behavior;* taking behavior, not in the narrow sense of his manners, but in the very widest possible sense, as including every possible sort of fit reaction on the circumstances into which he may find himself brought by the vicissitudes of life.

Education and Behavior

. . . [Education] consists in the organizing of *resources* in the human being, of powers of conduct which shall fit him to his social and physical world. An 'uneducated' person is one who is nonplussed by all but the most habitual situations. On the contrary, one who is educated is able practically to extricate himself, by means of the examples with which his memory is stored and of the abstract conceptions which he has acquired, from circumstances in which he never was placed before. Education, in short, cannot be better described than by calling it the *organization of acquired habits of conduct and tendencies to behavior....*

... So it is with the impressions you will make ... on your pupil. You should get into the habit of regarding them all as leading to the acquisition by him of capacities for behavior,—emotional, social, bodily, vocal, technical, or what not. And, this being the case, you ought to feel willing, in a general way, and without hairsplitting or farther ado, to take up for the purposes of these lectures with the biological conception of the mind, as of something given us for practical use. That conception will certainly cover the greater part of your own educational work.

The Laws of Habit

It is very important that teachers should realize the importance of habit, and psychology helps us greatly at this point. We speak, it is true, of good habits and of bad habits; but when people use the word 'habit,' in the majority of instances it is a bad habit which they have in mind. They talk of the smoking-habit and the swearing-habit and the drinking-habit, but not of the abstention-habit or the moderation-habit or the courage-habit. But the fact is that our virtues are habits as much as our vices. All our life, so far as it has definite form, is but a mass of habits,—practical, emotional, and intellectual,—systematically organized for our weal or woe, and bearing us irresistibly toward our destiny, whatever the latter may be....

I believe that we are subject to the law of habit in consequence of the fact that we have bodies. The plasticity of the living matter of our nervous system, in short, is the reason why we do a thing with difficulty the first time, but soon do it more and more easily, and finally, with sufficient practice, do it semi-mechanically, or with hardly any consciousness at all. Our nervous systems have ... *grown* to the way in which they have been exercised, just as a sheet

of paper or a coat, once creased or folded, tends to fall forever afterward into the same identical folds.

Habit is thus a second nature....

So far as we are thus mere bundles of habit, we are stereotyped creatures, imitators and copiers of our past selves. And since this, under any circumstances, is what we always tend to become, it follows first of all that the teacher's prime concern should be to ingrain into the pupil that assortment of habits that shall be most useful to him throughout life. Education is for behavior, and habits are the stuff of which behavior consists.

... The great thing in all education is to *make our nervous system our ally instead of our enemy.* It is to fund and capitalize our acquisitions, and live at ease upon the interest of the fund. *For this we must make automatic and habitual, as early as possible, as many useful actions as we can,* and as carefully guard against the growing into ways that are likely to be disadvantageous. The more of the details of our daily life we can hand over to the effortless custody of automatism, the more our higher powers of mind will be set free for their own proper work. There is no more miserable human being than one in whom nothing is habitual but indecision, and for whom the lighting of every cigar, the drinking of every cup, the time of rising and going to bed every day, and the beginning of every bit of work are subjects of express volitional deliberation. Full half the time of such a man goes to the deciding or regretting of matters which ought to be so ingrained in him as practically not to exist for his consciousness at all. If there be such daily duties not yet ingrained in any one of my hearers, let him begin this very hour to set the matter right.

... Two great maxims emerge.... The first is that in the acquisition of a new habit, or the leaving off of an old one, we must take care to *launch ourselves with as strong and decided an initiative as possible.* Accumulate all the possible circumstances which shall reinforce the right motives; put yourself assiduously in conditions that encourage the new way; make engagements incompatible with the old; take a public pledge, if the case allows; in short, envelope your resolution with every aid you know. This will give your new beginning such a momentum that the temptation to break down will not occur as soon as it otherwise might; and every day during which a breakdown is postponed adds to the chances of its not occurring at all. . . .

The second maxim is, *Never suffer an exception to occur till the new habit is securely rooted in your life.* Each lapse is like the letting fall of a ball of string which one is carefully winding up: a single slip undoes more than a great many turns will wind again. Continuity of training is the great means of making the nervous system act infallibly right. . . .

We all intend when young to be all that may become a man, before the destroyer cuts us down. We wish and expect to enjoy poetry always, to grow more and more intelligent about pictures and music, to keep in touch with spiritual and religious ideas, and even not to let the greater philosophic thoughts of our time develop quite beyond our view. We mean all this in youth, I say; and yet in how many middle-aged men and women is such an honest and sanguine expectation fulfilled? Surely, in comparatively few; and the laws of habit show us why. Some interest in each of these things arises in everybody at the proper age; but, if not persistently fed with the appropriate matter, instead of growing into a powerful and necessary habit, it atrophies and dies, choked by the rival interests to which the daily food is given. . . . We forget that every good that is worth possessing must be paid for in strokes of daily effort. We postpone and postpone, until those smiling possibilities are dead.

I have been accused, when talking of the subject of habit, of making old habits appear so strong that the acquiring of new ones, and particularly anything like a sudden reform or conversion, would be made impossible by my doctrine. Of course, this would suffice to condemn the latter; for sudden conversions, however infrequent they may be, unquestionably do occur. But there is no incompatibility between the general laws I have laid down and the most startling sudden alterations in the way of char-

acter. New habits *can* be launched, I have expressly said, on condition of there being new stimuli and new excitements. Now life abounds in these, and sometimes they are such critical and revolutionary experiences that they change a man's whole scale of values and system of ideas. In such cases, the old order of his habits will be ruptured; and, if the new motives are lasting, new habits will be formed, and build up in him a new or regenerate 'nature.' . . .

The Association of Ideas

You remember that consciousness is an ever-flowing stream of objects, feelings, and impulsive tendencies. We saw already that its phases or pulses are like so many fields or waves, each field or wave having usually its central point of liveliest attention, in the shape of the most prominent object in our thought, while all around this lies a margin of other objects more dimly realized, together with the margin of emotional and active tendencies which the whole entails. Describing the mind thus in fluid terms, we cling as close as possible to nature. At first sight, it might seem as if, in the fluidity of these successive waves, everything is indeterminate. But inspection shows that each wave has a constitution which can be to some degree explained by the constitution of the waves just passed away. And this relation of the wave to its predecessors is expressed by the two fundamental 'laws of association,' so-called, of which the first is named the Law of Contiguity, the second that of Similarity.

The *Law of Contiguity* tells us that objects thought of in the coming wave are such as in some previous experience were *next* to the objects represented in the wave that is passing away. The vanishing objects were once formerly their neighbors in the mind. When you recite the alphabet or your prayers, or when the sight of an object reminds you of its name, or the name reminds you of the object, it is through the law of contiguity that the terms are suggested to the mind.

The *Law of Similarity* says that, when contiguity fails to describe what happens, the coming objects will prove to *resemble* the going objects, even though the two were never experienced together before. In our 'flights of fancy,' this is frequently the case. . . .

. . . [As] teachers, it is the *fact* of association that practically concerns you, let its grounds be spiritual or cerebral, or what they may, and let its laws be reducible, or non-reducible, to one. Your pupils, whatever else they are, are at any rate little pieces of associating machinery. Their education consists in the organizing within them of determinate tendencies to associate one thing with another,—impressions with consequences, these with reactions, those with results, and so on indefinitely. The more copious the associative systems, the more complete the individual's adaptations to the world.

The teacher can formulate his function to himself therefore in terms of 'association' as well as in terms of 'native and acquired reaction.' It is mainly that of *building up useful systems of association* in the pupil's mind. This description sounds wider than the one I began by giving. But, when one thinks that our trains of association, whatever they may be, normally issue in acquired reactions or behavior, one sees that in a general way the same mass of facts is covered by both formulas.

It is astonishing how many mental operations we can explain when we have once grasped the principles of association. . . .

To grasp these factors clearly gives one a solid and simple understanding of the psychological machinery. The 'nature,' the 'character,' of an individual means really nothing but the habitual form of his associations. To break up bad associations or wrong ones, to build others in, to guide the associative tendencies into the most fruitful channels, is the educator's principal task. But here, as with all other simple principles, the difficulty lies in the application. Psychology can state the laws: concrete tact and talent alone can work them to useful results. . . .

The Acquisition of Ideas

The images of our past experiences, of whatever nature they may be, visual or verbal, blurred and dim, vivid and distinct, abstract or con-

crete, need not be memory images, in the strict sense of the word. That is, they need not rise before the mind in a marginal fringe or context of concomitant circumstances, which mean for us their *date*. They may be mere conceptions, floating pictures of an object, or of its type or class. In this undated condition, we call them products of 'imagination' or 'conception.' Imagination is the term commonly used where the object represented is thought of as an individual thing. Conception is the term where we think of it as a type or class. For our present purpose the distinction is not important; and I will permit myself to use either the word 'conception,' or the still vaguer word 'idea,' to designate the inner objects of contemplation, whether these be individual things, like 'the sun' or 'Julius Caesar,' or classes of things, like 'animal kingdom,' or, finally, entirely abstract attributes, like 'rationality' or 'rectitude.'

The result of our education is to fill the mind little by little, as experiences accrete, with a stock of such ideas. . . . The sciences of grammar and of logic are little more than attempts methodically to classify all such acquired ideas and to trace certain laws of relationship among them. The forms of relation between them, becoming themselves in turn noticed by the mind, are treated as conceptions of a higher and more abstract order, as when we speak of a 'syllogistic relation' between propositions, or of four quantities making a 'proportion,' or of the 'inconsistency' of two conceptions, or the 'implication' of one in the other.

So you see that the process of education, taken in a large way, may be described as nothing but the process of acquiring ideas or conceptions, the best educated mind being the mind which has the largest stock of them, ready to meet the largest possible variety of the emergencies of life. The lack of education means only the failure to have acquired them, and the consequent liability to be 'floored' and 'rattled' in the vicissitudes of experience.

Source: William James, *Talks to Teachers on Psychology: and to Students on Some of Life's Ideals.* New York: Henry Holt and Co., 1916, pp. 15–19, 22–31, 64–69, 72–73, 76–84, 144–146.

DEMOCRACY AND EDUCATION

Perhaps the single most important work Dewey wrote on education was Democracy and Education, *published in 1916. His understanding of education was very detailed and complex, and he struggled to express his ideas in a language ordinary people could understand; however, he was not always successful because complex ideas are often difficult to express simply. The following selection is a lucid but general statement of Dewey's views. In it he reflects on the social nature of education and how it is necessary for individuals to enter into social relations to become educated. Communication is central to the education of individuals in social contexts because communication enlarges experience and makes it meaningful. Education occurs in both formal and informal settings, and philosophy's role is to help achieve a proper balance between the two.*

1. Renewal of Life by Transmission

The most notable distinction between living and inanimate beings is that the former maintain themselves by renewal. A stone when struck resists. If its resistance is greater than the force of the blow struck, it remains outwardly unchanged. Otherwise, it is shattered into smaller bits. Never does the stone attempt to react in such a way that it may maintain itself against the blow, much less so as to render the blow a contributing factor to its own continued action. While the living thing may easily be crushed by superior force, it none the less tries to turn the energies which act upon it into means of its own further existence. If it cannot do so, it does not just split into smaller pieces (at least in the higher forms of life), but loses its identity as a living thing.

As long as it endures, it struggles to use surrounding energies in its own behalf. It uses light, air, moisture, and the material of soil. To say that it uses them is to say that it turns them into means of its own conservation. As long as it is growing, the energy it expends in thus turning the environment to account is more than compensated for by the return it gets: it grows. Understanding the word "control" in this sense, it may be said that a living being is one that subjugates and controls for its own continued activity the energies that would otherwise use it up. Life is a self-renewing process through action upon the environment.

In all the higher forms this process cannot be kept up indefinitely. After a while they succumb; they die. The creature is not equal to the task of indefinite self-renewal. But continuity of the life process is not dependent upon the prolongation of the existence of any one individual. Reproduction of other forms of life goes on in continuous sequence. And though, as the geological record shows, not merely individuals but also species die out, the life process continues in increasingly complex forms. As some species die out, forms better adapted to utilize the obstacles against which they struggled in vain come into being. Continuity of life means continual readaptation of the environment to the needs of living organisms.

We have been speaking of life in its lowest terms—as a physical thing. But we use the word "life" to denote the whole range of experience, individual and racial. When we see a book called the *Life of Lincoln* we do not expect to find within its covers a treatise on physiology. We look for an account of social antecedents; a description of early surroundings, of the conditions and occupation of the family; of the chief episodes in the development of character; of signal struggles and achievements; of the individual's hopes, tastes, joys and sufferings. In precisely similar fashion we speak of the life of a savage tribe, of the Athenian people, of the American nation. "Life" covers customs, institutions, beliefs, victories and defeats, recreations and occupations.

We employ the word "experience" in the same pregnant sense. And to it, as well as to life in the bare physiological sense, the principle of continuity through renewal applies. With the renewal of physical existence goes, in the case of human beings, the re-creation of beliefs, ideals, hopes, happiness, misery, and practices. The continuity of any experience, through renewing of the social group, is a literal fact. "Education, in its broadest sense, is the means of this social continuity of life." Every one of the constituent elements of a social group, in a modern city as in a savage tribe, is born immature, helpless, without language, beliefs, ideas, or social standards. Each individual, each unit who is the carrier of the life-experience of his group, in time passes away. Yet the life of the group goes on.

The primary ineluctable facts of the birth and death of each one of the constituent members in a social group determine the necessity of education. On one hand, there is the contrast between the immaturity of the newborn members of the group—its future sole representatives—and the maturity of the adult members who possess the knowledge and customs of the group. On the other hand, there is the necessity that these immature members be not merely physically preserved in adequate numbers, but that they be initiated into the interests, purposes, information, skill, and practices of the mature members: otherwise the group will cease its characteristic life. Even in a savage tribe, the achievements of adults are far beyond what the immature members would be capable of if left to themselves. With the growth of civilization, the gap between the original capacities of the immature and the standards and customs of the elders increases. Mere physical growing up, mere mastery of the bare necessities of subsistence will not suffice to reproduce the life of the group. Deliberate effort and the taking of thoughtful pains are required. Beings who are born not only unaware of, but quite indifferent to, the aims and habits of the social group have to be rendered cognizant of them and actively

interested. Education, and education alone, spans the gap.

Society exists through a process of transmission quite as much as biological life. This transmission occurs by means of communication of habits of doing, thinking, and feeling from the older to the younger. Without this communication of ideals, hopes, expectations, standards, opinions, from those members of society who are passing out of the group life to those who are coming into it, social life could not survive. If the members who compose a society lived on continuously, they might educate the new-born members, but it would be a task directed by personal interest rather than social need. Now it is a work of necessity.

If a plague carried off the members of a society all at once, it is obvious that the group would be permanently done for. Yet the death of each of its constituent members is as certain as if an epidemic took them all at once. But the graded difference in age, the fact that some are born as some die, makes possible through transmission of ideas and practices the constant reweaving of the social fabric. Yet this renewal is not automatic. Unless pains are taken to see that genuine and thorough transmission takes place, the most civilized group will relapse into barbarism and then into savagery. In fact, the human young are so immature that if they were left to themselves without the guidance and succor of others, they could not even acquire the rudimentary abilities necessary for physical existence. The young of human beings compare so poorly in original efficiency with the young of many of the lower animals, that even the powers needed for physical sustenance have to be acquired under tuition. How much more, then, is this the case with respect to all the technological, artistic, scientific, and moral achievements of humanity!

2. Education and Communication

So obvious, indeed, is the necessity of teaching and learning for the continued existence of a society that we may seem to be dwelling unduly on a truism. But justification is found in the fact that such emphasis is a means of getting us away from an unduly scholastic and formal notion of education. Schools are, indeed, one important method of the transmission which forms the dispositions of the immature; but it is only one means, and, compared with other agencies, a relatively superficial means. Only as we have grasped the necessity of more fundamental and persistent modes of tuition can we make sure of placing the scholastic methods in their true context.

Society not only continues to exist by transmission, *by* communication, but it may fairly be said to exist *in* transmission, *in* communication. There is more than a verbal tie between the words common, community, and communication. Men live in a community in virtue of the things which they have in common; and communication is the way in which they come to possess things in common. What they must have in common in order to form a community or society are aims, beliefs, aspirations, knowledge—a common understanding—like-mindedness as the sociologists say. Such things cannot be passed physically from one to another, like bricks; they cannot be shared as persons would share a pie by dividing it into physical pieces. The communication which insures participation in a common understanding is one which secures similar emotional and intellectual dispositions—like ways of responding to expectations and requirements.

Persons do not become a society by living in physical proximity, any more than a man ceases to be socially influenced by being so many feet or miles removed from others. A book or a letter may institute a more intimate association between human beings separated thousands of miles from each other than exists between dwellers under the same roof. Individuals do not even compose a social group because they all work for a common end. The parts of a machine work with a maximum of cöoperativeness for a common result, but they do not form a community. If, however, they were all cognizant of the common end and all interested in it so that they regulated their specific activity in view of it, then they would form a community. But this would involve communication. Each would have to know what the other was about and would have to have some way of keeping the other informed as to his own purpose and progress. Consensus demands communication.

We are thus compelled to recognize that within even the most social group there are many relations which are not as yet social. A large number of human relationships in any social group are still upon the machine-like plane. Individuals use one another so as to get desired results, without reference to the emotional and intellectual disposition and consent of those used. Such uses express physical superiority, or superiority of position, skill, technical ability, and command of tools, mechanical or fiscal. So far as the relations of parent and child, teacher and pupil, employer and employee, governor and governed, remain upon this level, they form no true social group, no matter how closely their respective activities touch one another. Giving and taking of orders modifies action and results, but does not of itself effect a sharing of purposes, a communication of interests.

Not only is social life identical with communication, but all communication (and hence all genuine social life) is educative. To be a recipient of a communication is to have an enlarged and changed experience. One shares in what another has thought and felt and in so far, meagerly or amply, has his own attitude modified. Nor is the one who communicates left unaffected. Try the experiment of communicating, with fullness and accuracy, some experience to another, especially if it be somewhat complicated, and you will find your own attitude toward your experience changing; otherwise you resort to expletives and ejaculations. The experience has to be formulated in order to be communicated. To formulate requires getting outside of it, seeing it as another would see it, considering what points of contact it has with the life of another so that it may be got into such form that he can appreciate its meaning. Except in dealing with commonplaces and catch phrases one has to assimilate, imaginatively, something of another's experience in order to tell him intelligently of one's own experience. All communication is like art. It may fairly be said, therefore, that any social arrangement that remains vitally social, or

vitally shared, is educative to those who participate in it. Only when it becomes cast in a mold
and runs in a routine way does it lose its educative power.

In final account, then, not only does social
life demand teaching and learning for its own
permanence, but the very process of living
together educates. It enlarges and enlightens
experience; it stimulates and enriches imagination; it creates responsibility for accuracy and
vividness of statement and thought. A man
really living alone (alone mentally as well as
physically) would have little or no occasion to
reflect upon his past experience to extract its
net meaning. The inequality of achievement
between the mature and the immature not only
necessitates teaching the young, but the necessity of this teaching gives an immense stimulus
to reducing experience to that order and form
which will render it most easily communicable
and hence most usable.

3. The Place of Formal Education

There is, accordingly, a marked difference
between the education which every one gets
from living with others, as long as he really
lives instead of just continuing to subsist, and
the deliberate educating of the young. In the
former case the education is incidental; it is
natural and important, but it is not the express
reason of the association. While it may be said,
without exaggeration, that the measure of the
worth of any social institution, economic,
domestic, political, legal, religious, is its effect
in enlarging and improving experience; yet this
effect is not a part of its original motive, which
is limited and more immediately practical.
Religious associations began, for example, in
the desire to secure the favor of overruling
powers and to ward off evil influences; family
life in the desire to gratify appetites and secure
family perpetuity; systematic labor, for the
most part, because of enslavement to others,
etc. Only gradually was the by-product of the
institution, its effect upon the quality and
extent of conscious life, noted, and only more
gradually still was this effect considered as a
directive factor in the conduct of the institution. Even to-day, in our industrial life, apart
from certain values of industriousness and
thrift, the intellectual and emotional reaction of
the forms of human association under which
the world's work is carried on receives little
attention as compared with physical output.

But in dealing with the young, the fact of
association itself as an immediate human fact,
gains in importance. While it is easy to ignore
in our contact with them the effect of our acts
upon their disposition, or to subordinate that
educative effect to some external and tangible
result, it is not so easy as in dealing with adults.
The need of training is too evident; the pressure to accomplish a change in their attitude
and habits is too urgent to leave these consequences wholly out of account. Since our chief
business with them is to enable them to share
in a common life we cannot help considering
whether or not we are forming the powers
which will secure this ability. If humanity has
made some headway in realizing that the ultimate value of every institution is its distinctive-
ly human effect—its effect upon conscious
experience—we may well believe that this lesson has been learned largely through dealings
with the young.

We are thus led to distinguish, within the
broad educational process which we have been
so far considering, a more formal kind of education—that of direct tuition or schooling. In
undeveloped social groups, we find very little
formal teaching and training. Savage groups
mainly rely for instilling needed dispositions
into the young upon the same sort of association which keeps adults loyal to their group.
They have no special devices, material, or institutions for teaching save in connection with initiation ceremonies by which the youth are
inducted into full social membership. For the
most part, they depend upon children learning
the customs of the adults, acquiring their emotional set and stock of ideas, by sharing in what
the elders are doing. In part, this sharing is
direct, taking part in the occupations of adults
and thus serving an apprenticeship; in part, it is
indirect, through the dramatic plays in which
children reproduce the actions of grown-ups

and thus learn to know what they are like. To savages it would seem preposterous to seek out a place where nothing but learning was going on in order that one might learn.

But as civilization advances, the gap between the capacities of the young and the concerns of adults widens. Learning by direct sharing in the pursuits of grown-ups becomes increasingly difficult except in the case of the less advanced occupations. Much of what adults do is so remote in space and in meaning that playful imitation is less and less adequate to reproduce its spirit. Ability to share effectively in adult activities thus depends upon a prior training given with this end in view. Intentional agencies—schools—and explicit material—studies—are devised. The task of teaching certain things is delegated to a special group of persons.

Without such formal education, it is not possible to transmit all the resources and achievements of a complex society. It also opens a way to a kind of experience which would not be accessible to the young, if they were left to pick up their training in informal association with others, since books and the symbols of knowledge are mastered.

But there are conspicuous dangers attendant upon the transition from indirect to formal education. Sharing in actual pursuit, whether directly or vicariously in play, is at least personal and vital. These qualities compensate, in some measure, for the narrowness of available opportunities. Formal instruction, on the contrary, easily becomes remote and dead—abstract and bookish, to use the ordinary words of depreciation. What accumulated knowledge exists in low grade societies is at least put into practice; it is transmuted into character; it exists with the depth of meaning that attaches to its coming within urgent daily interests.

But in an advanced culture much which has to be learned is stored in symbols. It is far from translation into familiar acts and objects. Such material is relatively technical and superficial. Taking the ordinary standard of reality as a measure, it is artificial. For this measure is connection with practical concerns. Such material exists in a world by itself, unassimilated to ordinary customs of thought and expression. There is the standing danger that the material of formal instruction will be merely the subject matter of the schools, isolated from the subject matter of life-experience. The permanent social interests are likely to be lost from view. Those which have not been carried over into the structure of social life, but which remain largely matters of technical information expressed in symbols, are made conspicuous in schools. Thus we reach the ordinary notion of education: the notion which ignores its social necessity and its identity with all human association that affects conscious life, and which identifies it with imparting information about remote matters and the conveying of learning through verbal signs: the acquisition of literacy.

Hence one of the weightiest problems with which the philosophy of education has to cope is the method of keeping a proper balance between the informal and the formal, the incidental and the intentional, modes of education. When the acquiring of information and of technical intellectual skill do not influence the formation of a social disposition, ordinary vital experience fails to gain in meaning, while schooling, in so far, creates only "sharps" in learning—that is, egoistic specialists. To avoid a split between what men consciously know because they are aware of having learned it by a specific job of learning, and what they unconsciously know because they have absorbed it in the formation of their characters by intercourse with others, becomes an increasingly delicate task with every development of special schooling.

Source: John Dewey, *Democracy and Education.* New York: Macmillan, 1916, pp. 1–9. Reprinted with the permission of the Center for Dewey Studies, Southern Illinois University at Carbondale.

SELECTED READINGS

Dewey, John. *Democracy and Education.* New York: Macmillan, 1916. Dewey believed that this work was the most complete statement of his philosophy. It has been one of the most influential books on education written in the twentieth century.

————. *Experience and Education.* New York: Macmillan, 1938. In this, one of Dewey's most concise statements on education, he criticizes excesses of the progressive movement and misinterpretations of his ideas. He attacks either/or thinking as debilitating to educational theory and maintains that a philosophy of experience must be central.

Jervis, Kathe, and Montag, Carol, eds. *Progressive Education for the 1990s: Transforming Practice.* New York: Teachers College Press, 1991. A collection of essays that provides both historical and contemporary viewpoints on progressive education and its continuing role in American education.

Kilpatrick, William H. *Education for a Changing Civilization.* New York: Century, 1926. Kilpatrick promotes the use of pragmatic method in educational practices. He sees the use of this philosophy as a way of improving both man and society.

Putnam, Hilary, and Putnam, Ruth. Education in a Multicultural Democracy: Two Deweyan Perspectives. *Educational Theory* 43(4):361–376, Fall 1993. An exploration that connects Dewey's thought with the debate over multicultural education, a debate in which the authors believe Dewey's thought has much to offer.

Wirth, Arthur G. *John Dewey as Educator: His Design for Work in Education (1894–1904).* New York: John Wiley and Sons, 1966. A historical and philosophical study of a crucial period of Dewey's life, this volume shows how Dewey worked out some of his leading ideas in philosophy and education during the Chicago years.

5

Reconstructionism and Education

The philosophy of reconstructionism contains two major premises: (1) society is in need of constant reconstruction or change, and (2) such social change involves both a reconstruction of education and the use of education in reconstructing society. It is not unusual for those who are involved with change, particularly the kinds of immediate and necessary changes that every age seems to require, to turn to education as the most effective and efficient instrument for making such changes in an intelligent, democratic, and humane way. Reconstructionists advocate an attitude toward change that encourages individuals to try to make life better than it was or is. In our own age, particularly, reconstructionism could strike a responsive chord because we are faced with a bewildering number of problems regarding race, poverty, war, ecological destruction, and technological inhumanity—problems that call for an immediate reconstruction of all our existing religious and philosophical value systems.

Ideas and values that once seemed workable for religion, family life, and education no longer seem as viable as they once were. Individuals are bewildered not only by the changes that have already taken place but also by the prospect of future changes that must be made if we are to cope adequately with these problems. While there have always been persons of intelligence and vision who thought about and promoted social change, only in recent times has there been the development of a systematic outlook called *reconstructionist philosophy.*

HISTORICAL BACKGROUND OF RECONSTRUCTIONISM

Reconstructionist ideas in one form or another have existed throughout history. Plato, in preparing his design for a future state (the *Republic*), was a "reconstructionist" philosopher. He outlined a plan for a just state in which education would become the building material for a new and better society. Plato believed that his state would be eminently desirable. He proposed radical departures from the customs of his Greek contemporaries, such as sexual equality, communal child rearing, and rule by a philosopher-king. In the

171

Laws, he envisioned a time when interest charges would be forbidden, profits would be limited, and human beings would live friend to friend. Although Plato's attempts to establish such a society failed, perhaps he was simply ahead of his time.

The Stoic philosophers, particularly in their concern for a world state, promoted a "reconstructionist" ideal. Marcus Aurelius, a Roman emperor and philosopher, maintained that he was a citizen of the world, not of Rome. This concept is one that reconstructionists articulate today in their attempts to minimize nationalistic fervor and chauvinism.

Many of the Christian philosophers, such as Augustine, preached reconstructionist reforms in order to bring about an ideal Christian state. The kinds of reforms Augustine asked for in *The City of God* were intended for the human soul rather than material being, but they had ramifications that carried over to the material world as well. Theodore Brameld, a major contemporary reconstructionist, stated that Augustine raised several difficult questions that later utopian philosophers endeavored to answer, such as whether history encourages us to believe that our ideal goals can be reached. Thomas More, Thomas Campanella, Johann Valentin Andreae, Samuel Gott, and other Christian utopian writers also proposed things we might do to bring the state into better accord with Christian thinking.

The writings of eighteenth- and nineteenth-century utopian socialists, such as Comte de Saint-Simon, Charles Fourier, and François Noël Babeuf advocated reconstructionist ideals through the development of various forms of socialism. Robert Owen and Edward Bellamy were greatly influenced by the Industrial Revolution and saw the use of technology not for the production of wealth per se but for improving the lot of humanity throughout the world. It was Karl Marx, decrying the harm done to workers by the dehumanization of the industrial system, who pictured a reconstructed world based upon an international communism.

Karl Marx received a Ph.D. degree in philosophy yet wrote extensively about economics. Marx deplored armchair philosophical thinking and, like the reconstructionists, believed that education should not be an ivory-tower affair but a method of changing the world. In his *Thesis on Feuerbach,* Marx wrote: "Philosophers have only interpreted the world differently; the point, however, is to change it."

Marx had studied Hegel intensively, but where Hegel saw the dialectical movement of the Universe in idealist terms, Marx saw it in terms of the clash of economic forces. These forces manifest themselves today by pitting the worker against the capitalist system. Education has been used as a way of maintaining the status quo because it has supported the interests of the ruling class. However, Marx believed that education can also be used to overthrow those interests and place the proletariat in control. At such a time, Marx felt, the power of the state will begin to wither and eventually will be replaced by a true rule of the people.

According to Marx, education has been an insidious device used to indoctrinate people into accepting and supporting the attitudes and outlooks of the moneyed interests. Although money is seemingly neutral, laborers are robbed of their freedom by exchanging work and production for money, a condition of which workers are usually unaware. Thus, workers are exploited by the system, their productive abilities appropriated in exchange for the symbolic value of money.

Education is a means to entrench this system by promoting the interests of the ruling class using both the formal and the informal or "hidden" curriculum that encourages subservience and docility. This is accomplished through the ways schools are controlled by elite governing authorities, and the schools in turn control students through rules and regulations, discipline procedures, and the curriculum. Textbooks are censored when they challenge conventional views on economics and government as well as sex, religion, and other touchy issues. Teachers, often without even realizing it, promote conventional biases, attitudes, and practices in many subtle ways. Students control each other through peer group pressures that can be powerful and unconscious influences.

Just as education can be used to enslave us, however, it can also be used, if properly understood, to free us. To do this would mean overthrowing our present economic system and instituting a new kind of education oriented toward raising social consciousness of economic controls that would enable each person to be an end and not a means.

Although World Wars I and II turned people's thoughts away from optimistic pictures of future worlds and spawned such dysutopias as Aldous Huxley's *Brave New World* and George Orwell's *1984*, there were still reformers and optimists, such as Bertrand Russell, whose *Principles of Social Reconstruction* listed steps that we might take in order to avoid the holocaust of war. Today, various groups propose ways to change the world and eliminate racism, poverty, and war. Some advocate the use of conditioning or "behavioral engineering" (as in B. F. Skinner's *Walden Two*) to make important and significant changes in everyday life through advancing technical skills. In *Beyond Freedom and Dignity,* Skinner maintains that we cannot afford "freedom" in the traditional sense and we must resolutely engineer a new social order based on the technology of behavior.

When we examine proposals from Plato to Skinner, we find that they recommend education as a primary instrument for social change. Plato, for example, thought of education as the *sine qua non* of the good society; Marx saw it as a way to help the proletariat develop a sense of "social consciousness"; Christian writers advocated the use of education as a means of inculcating religious faith and ideals, and modern technocrats see it as a way to promote technical change and provide individuals with the necessary skills for living in an advanced technological society. In *Walden Two,* Skinner depicted a community of highly trained technicians, engineers, artists, and agronomists who are educated or conditioned to a high level of proficiency. This is certainly a far cry from the romantic heritage of Henry David Thoreau's *Walden* and Jean Jacques Rousseau's *Émile,* but even Rousseau saw his finished product (as did John Locke in *Some Thoughts Concerning Education*) as a person who would later guide society along newer and better paths. Locke's "gentleman" was to lead by virtue of his breeding and education, while Rousseau's "Noble Savage" would lead because of his purity and naturalness. They all looked for social change through education.

In the United States, a number of people have seen education as a tool for social reform: Horace Mann, Henry Barnard, William Torrey Harris, Francis Parker, and John Dewey. Dewey saw education as an instrument for changing both individuals and society, and particularly during the 1920s and 1930s, his philosophy became identified with radical social reform. Dewey's pragmatism was linked with a rejection of absolutes and an acceptance of relativism, and it rankled many who thought (and some who still do) that education was in the grip of forces destined to lead American society down the liberal path to eventual destruction. Though Dewey's philosophy is more readily identified today with moderate "progressivism," at its peak it was often identified with radicalism.

Modern reconstructionism is basically pragmatic and owes a tremendous debt to Dewey. Reconstructionists promote such things as the scientific method, problem solving, naturalism, and humanism. Reconstructionists diverge from pragmatists in how they believe the pragmatic method should be used. Although pragmatism advocates continuous change and a forward-looking approach to the problems of people and society, it has become (in the hands of many who call themselves progressivists) a tool for helping people to "adjust" to society rather than to change it. One can explain this attitude partly by reference to the immigrants coming to America in the early 1900s who needed to be "adjusted" to American language and customs to bring them more into the "mainstream" of American society. There was and always will be a need for education to "adjust" people to social and cultural values, but reconstructionists do not believe that this is the primary role education should undertake. Education, from the reconstructionist's point of view, is to serve as a tool for immediate and continuous change.

Although much has been written about Dewey's radicalism in politics, philosophy, education, and other areas, he has also been interpreted to have viewed education as a way of making evolutionary as opposed to revolutionary progress toward social change. Dewey envisioned these changes occurring within the democratic fabric of society as it existed, or as it would evolve, rather than through the major revolutionary changes many reconstructionists believe are necessary. Whereas some pragmatists support the idea of dealing with problems within the existing framework of society, many reconstructionists hold that while this may be a reasonable approach for some problems, it is often necessary to get outside the general bounds of the contemporary value system in order to look at our problems afresh without traditional restraints. Utopian writers have pointed out, and perhaps understood better than anyone else, that many of the great problems of society cannot be solved without changes in the structure of society itself. Many utopians and reconstructionists (and in all fairness, Dewey himself) believe that some of the things we consider evil are really part of the institutions to which we give allegiance, and we cannot hope to eradicate such evils without fundamental changes in these institutions.

Many of us are perplexed when we hear that Socrates, the "gadfly of Athens," chose to face death rather than oppose the laws of Athens as they then existed. Some reconstructionists charge that pragmatists appear to have accepted the Socratic compromise: pragmatists have championed change, but not at the price of alienating those who gradually need to be persuaded into accepting orderly and systematic movement through established democratic institutions. Dewey, for example, seemed to be somewhat reluctant to advance education much faster than society itself could be advanced. The reconstructionists maintain that modern individuals may not have the luxury of such delay. Thus, while reconstructionism has its roots in past philosophical systems and philosophers, it attempts to strike out in more radical directions than its predecessors.

PHILOSOPHY OF RECONSTRUCTIONISM

Reconstructionism is not a *philosophy* in the traditional meaning of the term; that is, it does not seek to make detailed epistemological or logical studies. As indicated, reconstructionism is more concerned with the broad social and cultural fabric in which we exist. We might say that reconstructionism is almost a purely social philosophy. Its leading exponents are not so much professional philosophers as they are educational and social activists. They concentrate on social and cultural conditions and how these can be made more palatable for full human participation.

George S. Counts and Theodore Brameld have exemplified this outlook. Brameld has come closer to the more traditional role of the philosopher, having written in considerable depth about the philosophical nature of reconstructionism. Counts was the educational activist–scholar whose interests were wide ranging; while not lacking in philosophical knowledge, his writings and professional activities were more broadly concerned with social activism.

George S. Counts (1889–1974)

Counts came from a rural background and spent most of his adult life in some of America's major universities and intellectual circles. He engaged in extensive travel and study abroad, especially in Russia during the time of the Soviet Union. He was an acquaintance of John Dewey and was greatly influenced by that philosopher's social activism.

Counts' major work on reconstructionism is a small but widely read book, *Dare the Schools Build a New Social Order?* First delivered as three public lectures before a national group of educators, the central theme of *Dare the Schools* struck American educators with force. Counts had returned from the Soviet Union in 1930, where he had made a detailed study of that country's struggles. Seeing the United States bogged down in the social confusion of the Depression (a condition Counts thought was inexcusable and needless), he sought to awaken educators to their strategic position in social and cultural reconstruction.

Counts' central message was that while education had been historically used as a means of introducing people to their cultural traditions, social and cultural conditions were so altered by modern science, technology, and industrialization that education must now be used as a positive force for establishing new cultural patterns and eliminating social evils. He implied that educators must envision the prospects for radical social change and actually implement those prospects. Counts argued that educators should give up their comfortable role of being supporters of the status quo and should take on the more difficult tasks of social reformers. Further, he expressed some dissatisfaction with the course of progressive education, charging that it had identified itself with the "liberal-minded upper middle class." He stated:

> If Progressive Education is to be genuinely progressive, it must emancipate itself from the influence of this class, face squarely and courageously every social issue, come to grips with life in all of its stark reality, establish an organic relation with the community, develop a realistic and comprehensive theory of welfare, fashion a compelling and challenging vision of human destiny, and become less frightened than it is today at bogies of *imposition* and *indoctrination*.

Counts' thesis that the school should take responsibility for social renewal met with heated opposition. He was criticized and condemned as a Soviet sympathizer. Critics pointed out that the school, a relatively weak institution, could not accomplish so great a task; but Counts' view was not tied solely to the school, and his radicalism went much deeper. Indeed, he pointed out that the school should not promote any one reform but rather it should "give our children a vision of the possibilities which lie ahead and endeavor to enlist their loyalties and enthusiasms in the realization of the vision." To him, all social institutions and practices should be scrutinized critically, and the school serves as a reasonable means whereby a rational scrutiny can be made. The actual reform, however, must be culture-wide and thorough.

Counts was the author of numerous books (over nine of them on Soviet culture and education) and hundreds of articles. He influenced many students, educators, and social reformers. His philosophical influence, although confined primarily to philosophy of education and within that to the philosophy of reconstructionism, has nevertheless been considerable.

Theodore Brameld (1904–1987)

The person who was most influential in building reconstructionism into a more fully developed philosophy of education was Theodore Brameld. The author of many books, including *Toward a Reconstructed Philosophy of Education, Education as Power,* and *Patterns of Educational Philosophy,* Brameld taught philosophy and philosophy of education, lived and taught in Puerto Rico, and held posts in some of America's major universities.

Brameld viewed reconstructionism as a crisis philosophy, not only in terms of education but of culture as well. He saw humanity at the crossroads—one road leads to destruction, and the other to salvation only if we make the effort. Above all, he saw reconstructionism as a philosophy of values, ends, and purposes. While he had definite ideas about which road we *should* take, he pointed out that he was by no means sure which road we *will* take.

According to Brameld, we are confronted with mass confusion and contradictions in modern culture. We have at our disposal immense capacity for good on the one hand and a terrifying capacity for destruction on the other. We must establish clear goals for survival. In broad terms, this calls for a world unity. We must forego narrow nationalistic bias and embrace the community in a worldwide sense. This will involve world government and world civilization "in which peoples of all races, all nations, all colors, and all creeds join together in the common purpose of a peaceful world, united under the banner of international order." One major activity for philosophy would be an inquiry into the meanings of different conceptions of this central purpose of world unity. We need a democratic value orientation, an orientation in which "man believes in himself, in his capacity to direct himself and govern himself in relation to his fellows." It would involve, in terms of world government, majority policy making and provision for minority criticism. A basic means by which these goals may be achieved is through education.

Brameld attempted to provide us with alternative possibilities for a new society. In *The Open Society and Its Enemies,* Karl Popper wrote about a piecemeal engineering approach versus the utopian approach to the problems of society. Popper was clearly in favor of the former, which fosters the view of an open society where many possibilities are explored. He opposed the utopian approach because he felt that long-range goals may become fixed and unyielding. Brameld, however, saw value in both approaches—that is, utopian ends and piecemeal means. He recognized the need for piecemeal engineering on a daily basis, but this should be directed toward some goal, even though goals may be changed from time to time. It is true, as Popper showed, that goals can become inflexible; but for Brameld, this did not have to be true, and he was as opposed to absolutes in goal setting as he was to absolutes in anything else. He was a dreamer as well as a worker, and his proposals were more visceral than provable in any complete sense; he had certain presuppositions about the continued perfectibility of individuals and society. Brameld was active in advancing proposals for consideration and implementation, and he saw the utopian concept as a technique for establishing useful goals and orienting people toward an acceptance of change itself.

Reconstructionists tend to look upon problems holistically. They understand that problems overlap, and in solving one problem we may only create new ones; however, they maintain that if people can be encouraged to see problems in a broader perspective, the chances of eliminating the problems are greatly enhanced. Reconstructionists charge that the piecemeal engineers, for all their good intentions, are often only tinkering with problems rather than solving them, and perhaps unwittingly preparing the ground for other problems to come.

The argument has often been advanced that there is no empirical way to determine what the good society should be and that the reconstructionist operates on premises that are more a matter of wish fulfillment than anything else. No one, Brameld included, can say definitively what the good society should be. While he was aware and appreciative of the empirical approach, he maintained that the results of scientific achievement should be used as broadly as possible for the benefit of humankind. However, he was quite critical of the fact that science—no less than politics, education, and economics—is often dealt with too narrowly.

Scientific technology is involved in making war and killing more efficient than ever before. In our own country, horrible deaths through automobile and industrial accidents are another part of the price we pay for living in a highly mechanized society. Scientific technology is also used in making cigarettes and alcohol and in developing harmful chemicals used on food and crops. Technology is often used in industry in ways that belittle and dehumanize workers. Brameld certainly was not opposed to the advancement of science and technology, but he felt that their advancement should depend upon humane use. He was aware that the determination of what is humane is difficult, but maintained that through education we can be encouraged to see human events in a much broader fashion.

Reconstructionists, such as Brameld, are future-oriented and optimistic. This is not to state that there is any certainty that the future can be made better than the present or that underlying forces of class struggle or spirit, such as in the Marxian or Hegelian sense, are propelling us toward a higher point; rather, reconstructionists hold the belief that the future *can* be better *if* people adopt an attitude to work to make it better.

Recently, some individuals and organizations have continued to push for ideas and reforms in accord with a reconstructionist philosophy. Brameld maintained that although Saul Alinsky was hardly regarded as an "educator" in the professional sense, he may have contributed far more richly to the education of grass-roots Americans than any number of superintendents of schools and professors of education. For example, in Buffalo, Alinsky taught poor people to unite against unemployment in favor of equal opportunity for every employable adult.

There are several others who serve as change-agents of democracy. Ralph Nader has long fought for consumer protection and has maintained that there can be an end to mass injustice if enough private citizens become *public* citizens. John Gardner and Common Cause have shown how individuals can work together to eliminate social injustices and improve the political process. Buckminster Fuller was widely applauded for developing plans for future awareness and control of technology. Lewis Mumford dedicated a great deal of time to analyzing contemporary civilization and suggesting alternatives.

Some organizations agree with many of the reconstructionists' ideas. The Council for the Study of Mankind has been seeking to analyze and interpret the meaning of a "planetary" notion of the human species. The World Law Fund has developed "world order models" as designs for world law. Both the Council for the Study of Mankind and the World Law Fund have enlisted a variety of students in schools and colleges for their projects. The World Future Society is another organization consistently seeking to examine futuristic trends as well as to develop models in government, marriage, and education as guides to human behavior. Basically, this organization is concerned with a study of alternative futures and receives private and public support for its activities. There are also many grass-roots organizations, such as Greenpeace, that have a futurist perspective.

Reconstructionist philosophy is strongly inclined toward utopian or futuristic thinking. Reconstructionists have a penchant for utopian thinking, which manifests itself in their desire for an ideal world free of hunger, strife, and inhumanity. They believe that planning and thinking about the future is a good way of providing alternative societies for people to consider, and they feel that this kind of thinking should be promoted in schools, where teachers can encourage students to become future oriented.

Alvin Toffler, who coined the term *future shock*, points out that people are suffering mental and physical breakdowns from too much change in too short a time. These breakdowns are revealed in the number of heart attacks, ulcers, nervous disorders, and similar ailments of modern people. To combat future shock, Toffler feels that "future studies" should be part of the curriculum on every level of schooling. Some forms that this curriculum could take might include students preparing scenarios, engaging in "think-tank" thinking, role playing, computer programming of "futures games," and conducting futures fairs and clubs.

Toffler's *The Third Wave* is an appropriate sequel to *Future Shock*. In *The Third Wave*, Toffler describes three major changes or "waves" that have greatly affected human life. The first wave was brought about by the development of agriculture, changing our nomadic existence. According to Toffler, this wave existed from 8000 BC to around AD 1650 to 1750. The second great change, the Industrial Revolution (or industrial wave), began after this time and lasted until about 1955. This wave not only brought us industry and technology but changed our thinking accordingly. It encouraged schools to adopt routinized lock-step methods of instruction that paralleled factory life. Now, Toffler says, we are in a Third Wave that emphasizes individuality, "hot relationships" where people work together at home, and a service economy. Toffler believes that our homes are now "electronic cottages"; because of this, more and more learning is taking place within the home.

In *Learning for Tomorrow*, Toffler says, "So long as the rate of technological change in such a community stays slow, so long as no wars, invasions, epidemics or other natural disasters upset the even rhythm of life, it is simple for the tribe to formulate a workable image of its own future, since tomorrow merely repeats today." Today we know that this is no longer true, yet our educational systems often deal with the world as a static system. The problem is reminiscent of that recounted in Peddiwell's *The Saber-Tooth Curriculum*, in which the author shows that little or no change is necessary in education until the encroaching glacier makes current practices out of date. Today, we still continue to teach theories and practices that are no longer useful in improving or maintaining the life of the tribe. Toffler says that even now "most schools, colleges and universities base their teaching on the usually tacit notion that tomorrow's world will be basically familiar: the present writ large." We realize that this is most unlikely. It is more probable that the future will be radically different from the world as we now know it. Still, we continue to educate people not for a future time, not even perhaps for a present time, but for a past time.

One contemporary approach in education is the application of business management theory to education. Some advocate the method of Japanese management technique extolled in a provocative book by Paul S. George, entitled *The Theory Z School*. George designates the successful Japanese corporation as a "Type J," the unsuccessful American corporation as "Type A," and the best of both Japanese and American corporations as "Type Z." He believes that we should emulate successful business practices by applying them to schools. This involves setting forth a vital philosophy, curriculum alignment, classroom congruence, group involvement, and spirited leadership. One of the basic aspects of the Theory Z approach is that it treats people as part of a family. Management listens to workers and pays attention to their concerns, fears, and motivations. Although George thinks that it may be difficult if not impossible to apply Japanese management theory to education carte blanche, many aspects of it could be utilized to make schools more effective, vital, and cooperative ventures than they now are.

James Herndon, in *How to Survive in Your Native Land*, noted that while his classes were engaged in new and creative activities, other classes in the same school slaved over lessons about Egypt. One could compile a lengthy catalog of obsolete courses that should be replaced with those more germane to today's and tomorrow's needs. For example, schools emphasize penmanship instead of typing, forbid students to use calculators in mathematics classes, teach spelling and the diagramming of sentences instead of creative writing, drill pupils in phonics instead of teaching speed-reading,

Alverno

and so on. The inordinate attention they give to maintaining the status quo may represent the attitude of those who really run the schools—our school boards and our state legislatures. Frequently, such organizations promote a more conservative viewpoint and fail to see the need for change in education if it is to keep up with changes in society at large. This idea has been stressed by such educational reconstructionists as George Counts and Theodore Brameld, who emphasize the change aspect.

Reconstructionists, understandably enough, are critical of contemporary society. They point out the contradictions and hypocrisies of modern life. Education, they feel, should help students deal with these problems by trying to orient them toward becoming agents of change. Counts, for example, suggested that educators should enter areas, such as politics, where great change can be achieved. He also suggested that teachers run for political office or become active in organizations that promote change. Reconstructionists feel that students should think more about such things as world government, a world without schools, and approaches to ending war, bigotry, and hunger.

Although most educators have not seriously heeded the philosophy advocated by reconstructionists, some have become aware of the great need for change. During the 1960s and 1970s, a rash of school programs was sparked by cries of "relevance" and "innovation." Teachers were encouraged to innovate, although innovation was often of the most trivial kind and relevance was interpreted to mean relevance to a system that was in decay. Few of the programs developed during this period changed education in any lasting way. Their lack of seriousness has today led to a counterreaction among parents and other laypeople who are calling for a return to basics and the kind of authoritarian school structure that existed some fifty years ago.

In many quarters, however, a more sober assessment is being made of the needs of education, not only for today but also for tomorrow. The World Future Society has sponsored numerous workshops for teachers in an effort to get them to think about the future. Such workshops have spawned some of the programs on the future found in elementary and secondary schools. Educators are now becoming increasingly aware that classroom activities are not an end in themselves and that, years after their days in the classroom, students may face conditions for which they had not been specifically prepared. This concern led Dewey to point out that the facts we teach children today may be out of date by the time they graduate. Thus, he emphasized a problem-solving method that he felt would be as useful in the future as it is in the present.

There has been a great deal of speculation about where our schools are headed as well as about what course they should follow in the years ahead. Some futurists have suggested such things as longer hours for preschoolers, extending formal education from birth to death, selective breeding to raise IQs, and increased use of electronic media to aid learning.

Long-range predictions usually start with birth technology. It is possible that future prospective parents will be able to predetermine the sex of their child and to program its intelligence, looks, and personality. In-vitro fertilization will become commonplace, and embryo transfers will be widespread. Parents may be able to select twins or triplets. Children may be gestated in artificial wombs. Parents may one day purchase embryos in a "babytorium." Some children may even have more than two biological parents. (Experiments with the embryos of mice have shown that if several embryos are placed into a dish they form a single embryo. This embryo, when implanted in another mouse, produces offspring having the characteristics of each mouse and all of their accompanying genetic traits.) There is also the possibility of cloning, the production of several people or even an infinite number who are genetically identical. Such developments most certainly would have a profound effect upon education and would necessitate changes in the way we look at children.

As future children grow up, they may receive more of their education at home through various media, such as computers, television, tapes, radio, and movies. There may also be twenty-four–hour day-care centers where parents can leave children for extended periods, visiting them only when they choose.

Ivan Illich goes even further in *Deschooling Society*. He suggests that we need no schools at all. Illich, who makes a distinction between schooling and education, believes that education should be spread throughout society rather than being conducted only in special buildings provided for that purpose. He feels that people could be educated on the job, at home, and wherever they may be during their day-to-day activities. Illich has also proposed the use of "learning webs" through which people can pool information and talents with others. Some critics point out that we once went through a period in our history without schools or with few schools. Others see Illich's idea as having great implications for the future; they contend that special buildings set aside for elementary, secondary, and higher education may be passé. Certainly, many changes are on the way for education; undoubtedly, efficiency and quality will be enhanced.

Illich's interests have always been wide-ranging: education, transportation, revolution, medicine, and poverty. In the last few years, he has not written much on education, but much attention is still given to ideas expressed in his writings, particularly *Deschooling Society*. This "smart, silly book," as Sidney Hook has called it, has caused educators, particularly educators concerned with social inequalities, to reassess the role that education plays in a society—that is, that education is not always a positive benefit.

Some critics say that what Illich is doing is assessing the role of education in a "just society", the kind of medieval ideal that stressed the cooperative ties between the individual, the social community, and nature. Education, from Illich's viewpoint, should be a "convivial" affair whereby institutions encourage a concern for others as individuals. A more recent work is *Medical Nemesis*, in which Illich points out that the human ability to cope with pain and death has been appropriated by the medical profession, which serves the needs not of the individual but of the corporate industrial society.

Educators including Neil Postman point out that they have an "Ivan Illich Problem"—that Illich has caused them to reassess how conservative they really are and to reconsider the question of intellectual cowardice, or even worse, obtuseness. Illich raises the crucial issue of how effective schools are in seeing the complete student as well as the needs of humanity; in so doing, he asks us to ponder how well schools serve the cause of a just and moral universe.

Educators may approach the teaching of the future in various ways. In order to get students to think about the future, some courses raise such questions as these: Where will you be in ten years? What are some long-range projections regarding the status of the family? What major changes do you see occurring in the years ahead? In some schools, there is even a game called "What If?" It asks such questions as "What if your eyes were closed and you opened them in the future? What would be the first thing you would see?" or "What if there were no schools and everyone had to find his own education? Where would you begin?"

In experiments in some schools, students work on projects that examine their possible life on Mars. Questions are posed about what laws they would enact. How would they manage limited food and air supplies? What activities might they engage in on Mars? Students can be asked to develop an ideal society, focusing on such areas as economics, politics, social patterns, and so forth. They might even prepare a wheel showing how all of these various activities would interrelate to develop an efficient and harmonious society. At one school, students were asked to write their own obituaries, stating the cause of death, the year they died, and major activities performed during their lifetimes. (One creative student reported that his death was caused by a monkey wrench dropped by a careless robot.)

Students can engage in making short- and long-range forecasts using various forecasting techniques. As part of this assignment, they could evaluate the forecasts of others. Students can be asked to write scenarios or science fiction stories. They might even be encouraged to think about the future in terms of such present-day facts as the following: (1) The United States has only 6 percent of the world's population but consumes 30 percent of the world's energy output; (2) 10 percent of the world's population is white while 90 percent is nonwhite; (3) the average length of time people of the United States spend in any large city is four years. These and other facts may encourage interest in the future and serve as the basis for report writing and discussion. Students might also use these facts as springboards for dramatizations and role playing. Many students seem to have a natural interest in the future, and teachers can use this interest for motivation in the study of mathematics, science, and art. Some children who are not "turned on" by traditional approaches may be motivated by the novel and direct appeal of future concerns.

Since the world of tomorrow will be run by the children of today, it is vital that we encourage young people to be concerned about the future and instill in them the idea that they can help shape that future according to their own goals and aspirations. Rather than view it as something that just happens, we need to look at the future as something that we can, by our own efforts, make into a world of beauty and infinite promise.

As a recent movement in education, reconstructionism has influenced educators in thinking anew about the role of education. Reconstructionists have been in the vanguard of those seeking to make education a more active social force. They have championed the role of the educator as a primary change-agent and have sought to change schools in ways that would contribute to a new and better society. Since reconstructionism is a relatively new movement in education, it is difficult to assess its impact fully at this time.

RECONSTRUCTIONISM AS A PHILOSOPHY OF EDUCATION

Perhaps the most outstanding characteristics of reconstructionist educators are their views that modern society is facing a grave crisis of survival, that the educator must become a social activist, and that the school occupies a strategic position in meeting the crisis and providing a necessary foundation for action.

Education and the Human Crisis

Numerous educators call themselves reconstructionists. The Society for Educational Reconstruction (SER) was established in 1969 to further reconstructionist ideals on a wider scale. A policy statement released by SER sets forth the two basic objectives of reconstructionism: democratic control over the decisions that regulate human lives and a peaceful world community. They believe that educators everywhere ought to be helped to present their deepest social concerns to their students with optimum effectiveness. They encourage leaders who are able to apply reconstructionist values to experimental educational programs in the school and community.

The members of SER believe that most approaches to educational and social reform are luxuries we can no longer afford. From their perspective, we cannot wait for the kinds of gradual reform advocated by most philosophies, particularly when our very survival may depend on the immediate steps needed to make society more humanistic and productive. Indeed, it appears that we are living in an age of crisis, and progressivism, which once promised so much, seems to be an outmoded way of dealing constructively with present issues. As reconstructionists point out, we now have the power to extinguish ourselves and all living creatures from the face of the earth, and unless some way is found to integrate our technological developments with the highest principles of human rights, all our cogitations and discussions will become as mere rhetoric. Our schools have failed to take on this task. As one reconstructionist has put it, "What academic concept will students be 'discovering' when the computers press the nuclear button?"

The reconstructionists see the primary struggle in society today as being between those who wish to preserve society as it is, or with little change, and those who believe that great changes are needed to make society more responsive to the needs of the individual. Such a struggle is not limited to the United States; it is a major international crisis. This crisis demands concerted and well-planned action. Central to this needed action, the reconstructionists believe, is the crucial role of the educator and the schooling institution.

If we assess the role of educators nationally and internationally in this time of crisis, we may conclude with the reconstructionists that most educators are, at their worst, linked with the forces of reaction and, at their best, only liberalized. Many teachers come from the middle class, from families in which the parents seldom suffered loss of income from unemployment; they seldom had to worry about where the next meal was coming from, and their parents could afford to send them to college. Most of them attended schools that taught traditional "genteel" attitudes toward life and society. As a reward for their endeavors, they obtained positions in which they have continued the teaching of preestablished materials in preestablished ways. Such teaching has failed to reach minority groups, to change racial attitudes, to create change-oriented individuals, to develop humane attitudes, or to solve the problems of poverty, repression, war, and greed. One might even argue that instead of solving such problems, education has actually helped perpetuate these problems. It has provided specialists for warfare and for Wall Street, and it has aided the conspicuous consumer. Reconstructionists maintain that we have indeed forgotten that education should create change and argue that we use it to keep things as they are.

For educators to make real changes in society, reconstructionists urge them to become involved in affairs outside their own classrooms and schools. In a book entitled *The Nature of Teaching*, Peter Schrag challenged Counts' treatise of 1932 by the fact that educators are not located at those points in society where fundamental political and economic decisions are made. Although Counts did suggest that teachers run for political office and engage in social issues outside the classroom, the number of teachers who have done so is pitiably small; those who have seem to have acted not for the purpose of advancing the cause of education or enacting great social reforms but for achieving personal gain or some other self-interest.

Some critics feel that teachers should not take part in social and political affairs because schools should be neutral places and teachers may lose objectivity by playing a partisan role. However, as the French philosopher Jean-Paul Sartre has pointed out, there are no neutral positions; not to act is to act by default. Teachers by their deliberate nonaction stand responsible for the absurdities all around us in the same sense that good Germans were responsible for Nazi atrocities. There are no neutral positions; even if there were, most reconstructionists would agree that "the hottest spot in hell is reserved for those who in times of moral crisis remain neutral."

Nobuo Shimahara, who challenged the neutrality in higher education after the student uprisings at Columbia University in the late 1960s, also explored this issue. In an article appearing in the January 1969 issue of *School and Society,* Shimahara stated that the appeal to neutrality as an attempt to resolve the dilemma was futile and obsolete. Why? Colleges and universities are politically influenced to a significant degree and occasionally adulterated by politicians. Research in an advanced university, for example, is more or less determined by the structure of investments of private industries and the order of political priorities in government. University trustees and alumni usually influence local or national political and economic power and strongly influence university direction and basic policies. The university inevitably reflects the national political and economic structures, a factor that should not be concealed.

Reconstructionist educators tend to think of themselves as radical educational reformers rather than reactionary conservatives, timid moderates, or weak-hearted liberals. In the past few decades, an increasing number of educators have called for radical changes in our educational aims and methods; among them are Herbert Kohl, Kenneth Clark, Paul Goodman, A. S. Neill, Ivan Illich, and Neil Postman. However, only a few seem to have fully comprehended that radical changes in education cannot occur without radical changes in the structure of society itself. Such sociologists as Christopher Jencks point out that educational reforms cannot be made apart from wider social reforms. It is generally true that educational reform follows social reform and rarely if ever precedes or causes it. For educators to engage in educational reform effectively, they must perform a dual role: educator and social activist. There should be no separation between the two roles, for the reconstructionist educator is committed enough to act upon those things taught in the classroom. This is also what it means to be a *citizen* in the fullest sense of that term, although what we are talking about here is world citizenship rather than national citizenship. Acting as a citizen implies that one is not only a participating member of society but also a person who continually searches for better values and an end to degrading and harmful aspects of society. It also implies becoming willing to act in ways to bring society more in line with those better values.

The idea of an educator as an action-agent, particularly as a social activist, disturbs some people. Reconstructionists explain that there is no real need to separate knowledge and action. Knowledge should lead to action, and action should clarify, modify, and increase knowledge. This point is illustrated by a painting that hangs on the third floor of the New York Public Library in New York City. It shows some monks busily working on their Bible safe inside the monastery, while outside knights are burning down houses and cutting off the noses of the slower taxpayers. The monks saw no need to use what knowledge they had for the improvement of humanity in *this* world.

Action without thought does lead to detrimental ends, but thought without action is no more defensible. Thus, educators, because of their nonintervention in the course of human affairs, have contributed to some extent to the problems facing us worldwide. Actions are no more perfect than ideas, but placing an idea into action allows us, as Dewey argued, to reassess it in the world of human experience and through subsequent thought make it a better idea. Reconstructionists would like to link thought with action, theory with practice, and intellect with activism.

The Role of the School

Americans have asked a lot from their schools. When driver education needed to be taught, the schools took it on, just as they have taken on sex education, home economics, drug education, and many other tasks. However, the belief that educators and the schools are thus leading society in some better way may be erroneous. The schools are fulfilling a need that by virtue of their organized and specialized structure they can do better than any other institution. Yet schools have remained basically the same, and the idea that we are advancing society by making education more "relevant" or "accountable" is only to say that we are making it more "relevant" to the needs of the status quo or more "accountable" to vested interests as they presently exist. To think that the changes recently undertaken to make school curricula more open or flexible will also result in necessary societal changes may be called wishful thinking. Such changes do not often succeed in altering the power structure as much as in maintaining or advancing it.

There is a great need in education today to view the schools in much wider perspective. Such a movement cannot simply be a movement in "life adjustment," "relevancy," "accountability," or "open education," since these only prolong ideas and institutions that are in need of change. To be effective, this movement must be a more radical approach that seeks through a variety of methods to change existing social institutions, including the school, in ways that make them more responsive to human needs.

Such a movement must begin with the view that the school does not exist apart from society but within it, and the reconstruction of society will occur not *through* the school but *with* it. This requires educators who are willing to explore new possibilities through action. It requires teachers who can see alternatives and who have some conception of a better world. It demands a school institution freed from the traditional ideological framework so that it can project new goals and values. It needs individuals—teachers and students—who are moral in the sense that there is no conflict between the well-thought ideas and well-planned actions they are willing to perform on a daily basis. This means insisting on the idea that people can change society through individual and collective effort, for not to be involved is to assist in the perpetuation of values and systems that are archaic, unworkable, and dehumanizing. We live in a world where nuclear destruction is possible at any moment; where there is air, water, and noise pollution; where the population explosion grows more threatening every day—a world where there are worsening racial relations, international misunderstandings, and political idiocy on an international scale.

America embarked upon a program of mass education unparalleled in human history. It has succeeded to the extent that we have taught a vast number of people who would have been denied schooling in many other countries. Our methods of teaching, while still far from ideal, have vastly improved. Reconstructionists maintain, however, that our schools are still looking backward rather than forward. In 1900, about 60 percent of our human power rested on physical strength. Today, only about 6 percent is manual. Education was slow to move in a direction that enabled it to cope with such changes. It must now redouble its efforts to face the time ahead when even greater changes will occur. As difficult as the task may be, we need to provide people with education for a future we do not know—one that will most likely be more complex than our present circumstances.

The problem of goal setting in society and in the schools is important because although we have many people who are busily engaged in the affairs of life, much of what they do is harmful to themselves and others. We have people working to turn out missiles, new methods of warfare, unnecessary luxuries, and all the rest. They do not lack initiative, drive, and productivity. However, is there any real purpose in all this? The problem is a moral one. Reconstructionists view all our actions in a moral context, for everything we do has consequences for the future. Actions in the schools must be directed toward humane goals that result in better social consequences for all.

Ivan Illich, a priest turned social reformer, recently struck a new radical note. In Cuernavaca, Mexico, Illich founded the Center for Intercultural Documentation (CIDOC), where he and other scholars studied and explored radical alternatives. In *Deschooling Society*, he charged that modern societies, such as the United States, have become too dependent upon established institutions, particularly with regard to education. Schools certify and license parasitical interests. They hold a monopoly over the social imagination, controlling standards for what is valuable through their degree-granting powers. It has come to the point that knowledge is suspect unless certified by schooling. The social and human results create psychological impotence and the inability to fend for ourselves.

What we must do, Illich maintained, is to detach learning from teaching and create a new style of education based on self-motivation and new linkages between learners and the world. Educational institutions have become too "manipulative"; what is needed is a "convivial" system of education that promotes, rather than selectively controls, educational access by helping learners arrange for their own education. This new system would have "learning networks" of information storage and retrieval systems, skill exchanges, and peer-matching capacities. It would provide learners with available resources at any time in their lives, it would recognize those who want to share what they know and connect them with those who want to learn it, and it would provide opportunities for the open examination of public issues. "Deschooling" would liberate access to education, promote the sharing of knowledge and skills, liberate individual initiative, and free individuals from institutional domination.

While Illich's book did not bring forth a massive disestablishment of the schools, it did help many persons reevaluate their beliefs about education and schooling. The idea that there are many paths to education and that formal schooling is not the only or even the best way in every instance received a renewed emphasis.

A similar cry for reform was heard from Paulo Freire, who is currently the Secretary of Education of Brazil. In his *Pedagogy of the Oppressed*, Freire shows how education has been used to exploit poor people. Freire suggested that ideal teachers are friends of those they educate. Through subtle techniques, he enables adult students to become cognizant of the forces that exploit them and to become aware of how they can use education and knowledge as a means to improve their lives. Freire criticized the traditional or what he called the "banking" concept of education, in which people learn something they may then recall for future use. Students are not required really to *know* anything; they just memorize information presented by the teacher. Instead, Freire wanted education to be involved with the real and present everyday problems of people. If poor people need better health, then education ought to help them comprehend or construct ways in which to secure it.

Aims of Education

Reconstructionism emphasizes the need for change. It is utopian in the idea of goals directed toward a world culture or civilization. Yet it is also flexible because it holds that goals can be modified in process as we see problems and blocks along the way. Whatever the specific educational goals, one thing seems fairly certain: we need social *change* and social *action*.

The idea of promoting change is based on the notion that individuals and society can be made better. One may see in this idea the kind of evolutionary development or Hegelianism connected with Dewey's philosophy; that is, we can assist in the process of moving things from a less desirable to a more desirable state. Thus, reconstructionists would like to involve people more as change-agents, to change both themselves and the world around them. They are opposed to abstract or armchair philosophies where the emphasis is more on knowing than on doing. Reconstructionists do not believe that there is any conflict between knowing and doing, for all actions should be well thought out in advance. Dewey once said that burly sinners rule the world while saints sit in their ivory towers. Reconstructionists would like to see an end to the ivory tower mentality, with everyone involved in some way in social action. They see education as something that includes both individuals and society. The education that one generally receives in today's schools, based as it is on competition, tends to isolate and separate people. Reconstructionists do not think we can separate school from the rest of society or individuals from each other. They strive for unity rather than fragmentation.

When Counts wrote *Dare the Schools Build a New Social Order?* he provided a rallying cry for reconstructionists. He criticized the direction progressivism had taken in its life-adjustment phase and its failure to act on critical issues of the day. He argued for a new progressivism that would be more active and take the lead in social change. When we look at the situation today, we find that schools and educators are still not leaders of change and often serve to prevent it. Even when society has moved ahead in accepting new social customs, the school often continues to preserve the outmoded styles. Counts urged educators to begin taking the lead in obtaining power and exercising that power for the good of society. Educators should become more involved in social causes. In this way, they would be involved in improving their own education and would serve to educate others far more than in any classroom activity.

World community, brotherhood, and democracy are three ideals that reconstructionists believe in and desire to implement in schools and in society. Schools should foster these ideals through curricular, administrative, and instructional practices. While schools cannot be expected to reconstruct society by themselves, they can serve as models for the rest of society by adopting these ideals.

Methods of Education

Reconstructionists are critical of most of the methods currently used in all levels of schooling. This is because the old methods reinforce traditional values and attitudes underlying the status quo and resistance to change. In such circumstances, the teacher becomes an unwitting agent of entrenched values and ideas. The "hidden curriculum" underlies the educational process, and students are shaped to fit preexisting models of living. To the extent that teachers are ignorant of this factor, they continue to nurture and sustain the system through the teaching techniques and processes they use. For example, school boards or states approve the textbooks that teachers must use in their classrooms, and teachers who accept and use these adopted materials without question become party to a devious kind of indoctrination. Often, such textbooks are approved because they are noncontroversial or contain distortions, such as subtle economic, racist, or sexist ideas that are popular in the dominant culture.

Instructional tools, such as texts and teaching techniques and processes, are guilty of subtle influences on learners. For example, where teachers are viewed as dispensers of knowledge and students as passive recipients, the way is paved for students to accept uncritically whatever is presented.

Passivity on the part of students deprives them of any creative role in analyzing and constructing materials or in making judgments and decisions. Perhaps this kind of problem is most readily seen in the area of social studies. What often passes as social studies is really little more than nationalistic bias that reinforces chauvinistic tendencies. Prefabricated teaching materials with the questions and answers already established result in making students think alike about society, the economy, and the political structure. Social studies are designed to encourage good citizenship, but a built-in bias of what good citizenship is almost guarantees a narrow and provincial outlook among students.

It is regrettable that fewer than half of the citizens of the United States bother to vote in national elections. Usually, not more than 70 percent of the *registered* voters actually go to the polls, and they make up only a portion of citizens who *could* vote if they bothered to register. Local elections are even more poorly attended, and some issues do not receive even a 15 percent turnout. Polls show that few citizens know who their United States senators are, and even fewer know the names of their congressmen. Studies have shown that citizens do not know what the branches of government are. Citizens, for the most part, take a passive attitude toward government. Although they may complain about high taxes, inefficient government, and the low quality of public officials, they do not often exercise their rights to change these things.

The failure to vote is only an indication of a deeper problem, according to the reconstructionist. In addition to voting, citizens need to work for candidates they believe in or to run for office themselves. Reconstructionists want to see activism rather than the passivity that currently exists.

Education should be directed toward arousing interest in public activism. For example, one political science professor allowed his class to spend a semester working for the candidates of their choice. These students learned more about the political process through active participation than they could have by reading sterile books or attending lectures. Reconstructionists would heartily endorse this kind of approach for at least a portion of the students' formal education.

In order to carry out this kind of activist educational program, teachers must be freed from their own passivity and fears about actively working for change. They must begin focusing on critical social issues not usually found in textbooks or generally discussed in schools. One useful tactic would be propaganda analysis or what Neil Postman and Charles Weingartner call "crap detecting." Rather than being passive purveyors of knowledge, teachers must become critical, analytical, and discriminating in judgment. They should also encourage this same kind of development on the part of students. In this way, reconstructionism helps develop democratic approaches to social problems by allowing students to cope with social life intelligently. In fact, democratic procedures should be used on every level of schooling. This means that the student will play an active part in the formulation of objectives, methods, and curricula used in the educational process. Perhaps the most important facet of a student's education is the development of decision-making abilities, and reconstructionists maintain that this cannot be accomplished outside democratic educational practices.

Curriculum

Reconstructionists favor, first, that students get out as much as possible into society, where they can both learn and apply learning. Brameld recommends that as much as half of a student's time be spent outside the traditional school structure, learning at some place other than a school. Reconstructionists favor such programs as the Parkway Plan in Philadelphia and Metro in Chicago where this method has been in operation. The traditional classroom setting may have some value, but the important thing is to get students to use what they learn, and traditional schools do not always encourage this.

One of the ways of organizing curriculum is to modify the core plan advocated by progressivists into what Brameld calls "the wheel" curriculum. According to Brameld, the core may be viewed as the hub of the wheel, the central theme of the school program. The spokes represent related studies, such as discussion groups, field experiences, content and skill studies, and vocational studies. The hub and the spokes support each other, while the rim of the wheel serves in a synthesizing and unifying capacity. While each school year would have its own "wheel," there would be continuity from year to year, with each "wheel" flowing into and strengthening the other. Although each year would be different, it would also inherit the problems and solutions from previous years and would move on to new syntheses. Brameld thinks that the reconstructionist curriculum is both a "centripetal" and "centrifugal" force. It is centripetal because it draws the people of the community together in common studies and centrifugal because it extends from the school into the wider community. Thus, it has the capacity to help bring about cultural transformation due to the dynamic relationship between school and society.

In terms of curriculum, reconstructionists favor a "world" curriculum with emphasis on truth, brotherhood, and justice. They are opposed to narrow or parochial curricula that deal only with local or community ideas and ideals. They favor studies in world history as well as explorations into the contemporary work of the United Nations and other world agencies. The curriculum should be action oriented by engaging students in such projects as collecting funds for worthy causes, informing citizens about social problems, and using petitions and protests. Students can learn from books, but they can also learn from such activities as voter registration drives, consumer research, and antipollution campaigns, in which they can make a genuine social contribution while they are learning.

One important development in recent years is how much attention schools are giving to the variety of cultures in American society. *Cultural pluralism* is the term generally used to describe this cultural diversity, and *multicultural education* is the term most often applied for educational programs designed to study it. The issue of multicultural education is so important that accrediting organizations, such as the National Council for Accreditation of Teacher Education, have encouraged it in studies for prospective teachers. These organizations have made multicultural education a necessary part of every accredited teacher education program. Their rationale is based on the historical and contemporary facts that American society is a conglomeration of many cultures and that this diversity needs to be recognized properly rather than ignored.

Originally, state systems of public schools had a cultural "melting pot" role in which schools were viewed as instruments to Americanize immigrant children by "melting" away cultural differences so that newcomers would fit into mainstream American society. More recently, however, there has been an increasing awareness that many cultural differences did not disappear, that these differences added strength to the American social fabric, and that such differences needed to be preserved. Thus, school curricula now include anthologies with stories about many cultural settings, and American history textbooks have been revised to include content on African-American history, the history of women, and Native Americans. Immigration to the United States has long been a fact of American life, and now attention has been given not only to the older immigrant groups from Europe and Asia but also to the newer groups, such as those from Hispanic cultures or Southeast Asia.

Reconstructionists champion and welcome such developments. The recognition of the diversity of American origins is long overdue, and they look to this development as a fundamental way to promote peace and understanding among people. Indeed, they believe that multicultural education—if approached with proper care and understanding—should help change the ways Americans view themselves, both as individuals and as members of groups. Multicultural education should result in views that are in line with the actual facts of American historical and contemporary life.

One social problem that reconstructionists would like schools to address is the problem of nuclear war. A number of educational organizations, such as the National Education Association, have prepared materials explaining the dangers and horrors of nuclear war for teachers to use in classrooms. These materials have been strongly resisted by others who feel that they scare children and may promote a defeatist attitude that encourages aggression from national enemies. Reconstructionists believe that nothing is to be gained by hiding one's head in the sand, and that knowledge about the possibilities and dangers of nuclear war may be our best hope for eliminating future conflicts. Many reconstructionists are in the forefront of those opposing nuclear war because of their belief in a "spaceship earth" mentality that points to the interconnectedness of all nations and all peoples.

Reconstructionists realize that it is all too easy to be enculturated so that we are not aware of the problems of other nations. They would encourage learning the language and the mores of other peoples. They would also encourage reading the literature of other nations as well as newspapers and magazines that deal with issues on a worldwide basis. In some schools, considerable attention is given to other nations, with special activities designed to inform students about other cultures and customs. Sometimes students dress up in the costumes of other nations, serve their food, and engage in activities that provide better understanding of cultural relationships.

Reconstructionists want teachers to be internationally oriented and humanitarian in their outlook. They should be experts in getting students engaged in action projects of all kinds. When a student is involved in some social activity, then that curriculum can produce far more learning than most classroom lectures.

Not only should students become oriented to other cultures, but they should also become future oriented and should study proposals for future development. They need to plan activities that lead to future goals. Most of our schools today, as Alvin Toffler points out, are backward looking and do not face the future properly. People must learn to confront the future; consequently, teachers should encourage students to construct plans for future societies with some cognizance of problems regarding population, energy, transportation, and so on. They could visit with various communal organizations where futuristic alternative life-styles are being practiced.

Reconstructionists reason that if people are sincerely interested in society and education, then they will be at those pivotal places where decisions are made. They strongly urge community action and promote the kind of education to assist people in obtaining social and human rights. Saul Alinsky in Chicago demonstrates this kind of education. Alinsky helped people to participate in activities designed to raise social consciousness about their problems and to learn how to attack such problems effectively. Likewise, reconstructionists think people should be involved in both community and world affairs and they should become efficient and effective activists for continuous social reform.

CRITIQUE OF RECONSTRUCTIONISM IN EDUCATION

Reconstructionists believe their approach is a radical departure from pragmatism. This is true in terms of the positions many pragmatists have taken on social, economic, and political issues. However, it is misleading to say that Dewey did not champion radical solutions. He argued that solutions to social problems must be thought out carefully and experimentally with an ever-watchful eye on possible consequences. The results of his approach may be that Dewey was a cautious radical, a reflective champion of social change. Critics have often attacked reconstructionism for a lack of Dewey's caution, charging that the reconstructionist analyses of social problems and the accompanying remedies do suffer from shallowness and superficiality.

Often reconstructionists, in their strong desire for change, are precipitous in their recommendations for reform. The charge has been made that this precipitousness results in a great deal of talk and controversy concerning aims and methods in education but little effect. One can point to the actual effects pragmatism has had on schools, but it is extremely difficult to discern any concrete impact from reconstructionism. Perhaps this occurs because pragmatists' recommendations are easier to accept and less radical on the surface, but it may be due to the depth and feasibility of their proposals. By the same token, the reconstructionists' lack of impact may be directly attributable to the fact that their recommendations are not popular with the mass of people or with the majority of educators.

It appears that the recent attention to multicultural education represents a reconstructionist advance. Certainly, reconstructionists championed cultural pluralism over the years, and any assessment of their impact must include multicultural education. However, it is also true that ethnic groups promoting their own interests have been as responsible for the development of multicultural education as any organized reconstructionist effort. For example, Hispanic Americans, rather than seeking radical change in American thought and institutions, have championed recognition of their cultural identity in order to gain acceptance in society as it exists. The same may be said of women, African-Americans, and Native Americans. This is not to say that philosophical reconstructionism has not been a part of the agenda of some proponents of multicultural education; rather, it is to observe that the effect of reconstructionism on multicultural education has not been nearly so obvious as that of pragmatism on progressive education. However, perhaps a philosophical outlook is successful when its ideas become commonplace and its postulates are accepted by others without recognition of the source. Perhaps reconstructionism has lost its punch as a philosophy of education because many people accept the need to promote just change and work for unmet needs, as reconstructionists have tirelessly expounded. The problem with this latter view, however, is that justice and change have not been the exclusive properties of reconstructionism.

In many respects, reconstructionists have a romantic notion of what the schools can do. Recent studies by such historians as Michael Katz and David Tyack and by such sociologists as James Coleman and Christopher Jencks show that our expectations of what the schools can do have far outstripped the actual benefits accrued. Indications are that schools cannot directly affect income, racial acceptance, and equality of opportunity. Counts believed that great social reforms could be achieved when educators banded together, but it is questionable whether teachers could ever obtain such power or use it in the best way. Counts argued that teachers should engage in political action and thus provide a moral basis for social change. However, when one considers the educators who do run for and achieve political office, such a premise can be seriously questioned. Educators are rarely different from other politicians, or they are generally coopted by the very forces they seek to change.

Another charge leveled against the reconstructionists is that their view of democracy and decision making is questionable. They start with the premise that change is needed, and often they state the goals before they start the journey. This is quite different from Dewey's conception of open-endedness and of the intimate relation between means and ends. Reconstructionists advocate world law, but there is evidence that people accept laws to the extent that the laws respect basic cultural patterns and are formulated by the people themselves or their representatives. Because of the diversity of world cultures, it is doubtful that a universal code to which every cultural group would pay allegiance could be constructed at this time. Not only does a world law code disregard cultural diversity, but it assumes that it is good to centralize the regulation of human behavior. Reasonable and intelligent objections to such centralization may be raised by people of a different philosophical persuasion. There is the notion that change and novelty itself come about because of individual variation, and any centralization on a world scope may have detrimental consequences for social change. Indeed, it may result in the destruction of cherished ideals in reconstructionism itself concerning change. We do not really know if world law is possible or desirable, for there has not yet been sufficient study and experimentation. The United Nations is perhaps humanity's most notable experiment in this regard, but its power of control in terms of warfare, international intrigue, and even starvation and economic injustice is almost negligible. Reconstructionism's noticeable utopianism has some advantages, but it also may take our eyes off immediate problems to focus them on some ideal end.

There is evidence that reconstructionists and liberal reformers have been coopted by the very forces they once sought to overcome. They once fought vigorously for the social welfare programs of the liberals of the early and mid-twentieth century. They argued for unemployment insurance, welfare, unionism, the graduated income tax, social security, and the extension of tax-supported education beyond public elementary and secondary schools to community colleges and state universities. They have accomplished their aims, and these programs are now part of the status quo; however, reconstructionists have failed to come up with new programs and goals to capture the imagination and nerve of the activist sector. In effect, the World Future Society has presented more alternative solutions to the world's problems in recent years than has reconstructionism. As a consequence, many of reconstructionism's thrusts now have the sound of a tired refrain, and its forcefulness has been dissipated.

Despite reconstructionism's less noticeable profile, its call for action remains. Despite liberal reform efforts of an earlier time, problems seem to endure and may even be more complex than they were. Today, people do not speak about crises, but "megacrises" that seem immune to the best planned reforms. Americans traditionally have been opposed to long-range planning, and we seem to "muddle" through with a "crisis mentality" that does not act until a problem is upon us.

Computer simulation of world trends shows us moving toward a series of mounting crises as world population and runaway industrialization deplete natural resources and spoil the environment. The Club of Rome report is only one notable call to action about this kind of problem. This group of one hundred industrialists, scientists, economists, educators, and statesmen attempted to stimulate concerted and international political action in a rational and humane direction. They established graphic projections of impending disasters in population, food supply, and nonrenewable resources unless direct action was taken in the near future. *The Limits of Growth,* a book based on their initial work, predicts global catastrophe within the next century if present rates of growth continue.

In their second report, *Mankind at the Turning Point,* they describe two great gaps—one between human beings and nature and the other between the rich countries of the Northern Hemisphere and the poor countries of the Southern Hemisphere. These findings and conclusions stress the need for the immediate and radical worldwide changes that are advocated by the reconstructionists. The crises and impending disasters on the horizon have been anticipated by reconstructionists for many years and really should not take us by surprise. Those critics who have accused reconstructionists of being alarmists may now need to reconsider. If anything, it appears that the reconstructionists erred not by being alarmists but by failing to sound a stronger warning. Today, many people are unaware of the extent and depth of our problems, and reconstructionists can rightly claim that schools and educators have not been forthright in informing the public of the nature of the difficulties.

Reconstructionist philosophy has been an available antidote to the easy virtues of materialism, established cultural values, and social adjustment. While reconstructionist theories are not always accepted, they can stimulate and provoke thinking about critical issues. They have provided visions of a more perfect world and have suggested means of attaining them. It is, perhaps, a shortcoming of other philosophies that they do not have future goals, either short-range or long-range. Concern for social values, humane justice, the human community, world peace, economic justice, equality of opportunity, freedom, and democracy are all significant goals for reconstructionism, things in which the world is sadly lacking. If it is true that reconstructionists are impatient and precipitous in their desire to eliminate social evils, it is understandable in a world still filled with hate, greed, bigotry, and war.

DARE THE SCHOOLS BUILD A NEW SOCIAL ORDER?

George S. Counts, many of whose ideas loom large in reconstructionism, was one of the most radical progressive educators. He thought the aim of education should be social reform and urged teachers to throw off their "slave psychology" and work for the good of the people. Counts was identified with the progressive movement in education and became disenchanted with its rhetoric for change but reluctance to act. In the following selection, written in 1932 in the depths of the Great Depression, Counts calls to educators to "reach for power" and initiate changes in society. The words still have a modern ring.

[Education] . . . must . . . face squarely and courageously every social issue, come to grips with life in all of its stark reality, establish an organic relation with the community, develop a realistic and comprehensive theory of welfare, fashion a compelling and challenging vision of human destiny, and become less frightened than it is today at the bogies of *imposition* and *indoctrination*. . . .

This brings us to the most crucial issue in education—the question of the nature and extent of the influence which the school should exercise over the development of the child. The advocates of extreme freedom have been so successful in championing what they call the rights of the child that even the most skillful practitioners of the art of converting others to their opinions disclaim all intention of molding the learner. And when the word indoctrination is coupled with education there is scarcely one among us possessing the hardihood to refuse to be horrified. . . .

I believe firmly that a critical factor must play an important role in any adequate educational program, at least in any such program fashioned for the modern world. An education that does not strive to promote the fullest and most thorough understanding of the world is not worthy of the name. Also there must be no deliberate distortion or suppression of facts to support any theory or point of view. On the other hand, I am prepared to defend the thesis that all education contains a large element of imposition, that in the very nature of the case this is inevitable, that the existence and evolution of society depend upon it, that it is consequently eminently desirable, and that the frank acceptance of this fact by the educator is a major professional obligation. I even contend that failure to do this involves the clothing of one's own deepest prejudices in the garb of universal truth and the introduction into the theory and practice of education of an element of obscurantism. . . .

There is the fallacy that the school should be impartial in its emphases, that no bias should be given instruction. We have already observed how the individual is inevitably molded by the culture into which he is born. In the case of the school a similar process operates and presumably is subject to a degree of conscious direction. My thesis is that complete impartiality is utterly impossible, that the school must shape attitudes, develop tastes, and even impose ideas. It is obvious that the whole of creation cannot be brought into the school. This means that some selection must be made of teachers, curricula, architecture, methods of teaching. And in the making of the selection the dice must always be weighted in favor of this or that. Here is a fundamental truth that cannot be brushed aside as irrelevant or unimportant; it constitutes the very essence of the matter under discussion. Nor can the reality be concealed beneath agreeable phrases. . . .

If we may now assume that the child will be imposed upon in some fashion by the various elements in his environment, the real question is not whether imposition will take place, but rather from what source it will come. If we were to answer this question in terms of the past, there could, I think, be but one answer: on all genuinely crucial matters the school follows the wishes of the groups or classes that actually rule society; on minor matters the school is sometimes allowed a certain measure of freedom. But the future may be unlike the past. Or perhaps I should say that teachers, if they could increase sufficiently their stock of courage, intelligence, and vision, might become a social force of some magnitude. About this eventuality I am not over sanguine, but a society lacking leadership as ours does, might even accept the guidance of teachers. Through powerful organizations they might at least reach the public conscience and come to exercise a larger measure of control over the schools than hitherto. They would then have to assume some responsibility for the more fundamental forms of imposition which, according to my argument, cannot be avoided.

That the teachers should deliberately reach for power and then make the most of their conquest is my firm conviction. To the extent that they are permitted to fashion the curriculum and the procedures of the school they will definitely and positively influence the social attitudes, ideals, and behavior of the coming generation. In doing this they should resort to no subterfuge or false modesty. They should say neither that they are merely teaching the truth nor that they are unwilling to wield power in their own right. The first position is false and the second is a confession of incompetence. It is my observation that the men and women who have affected the course of human events are those who have not hesitated to use the power that has come to them. Representing as they do, not the interests of the moment or of any special class, but rather the common and abiding interests of the people, teachers are under heavy social obligation to protect and further those interests. In this they occupy a relatively unique position in society. Also since the profession should embrace scientists and scholars of the highest rank, as well as teachers working at all levels of the educational system, it has at its disposal, as no other group, the knowledge and wisdom of the ages. . . .

This brings us to the question of the kind of imposition in which teachers should engage, if they had the power. Our obligations, I think, grow out of the social situation. We live in troublous times; we live in an age of profound change; we live in an age of revolution. Indeed it is highly doubtful whether man ever lived in a more eventful period than the present. In order to match our epoch we would probably have to go back to the fall of the ancient empires or even to that unrecorded age when men first abandoned the natural arts of hunting and fishing and trapping and began to experiment with agriculture and the settled life. Today we are witnessing the rise of a civilization quite without precedent in human history—a civilization founded on science, technology, and machinery, possessing the most extraordinary power, and rapidly making of the entire world a single great society. Because of forces already released, whether in the field of economics, politics, morals, religion, or art, the old molds are being broken. And the peoples of the earth are everywhere seething with strange ideas and passions. If life were peaceful and quiet and undisturbed by great issues, we might with some show of wisdom center our attention on the nature of the child. But with the world as it is, we cannot afford for a single instant to remove our eyes from the social scene or shift our attention from the peculiar needs of the age. . . .

Consider the present condition of the nation. Who among us, if he had not been reared amid our institutions, could believe his eyes as he surveys the economic situation, or his ears as he listens to solemn disquisitions by our financial and political leaders on the cause and cure of the depression! Here is a society that manifests the most extraordinary contradictions: a mastery over the forces of nature, surpassing the wildest dreams of antiquity, is accompanied by extreme material insecurity; dire poverty walks hand in hand with the most extravagant living the world has ever known; an abundance of goods of all kinds is coupled with privation, misery, and even starvation; an excess of production is seriously offered as the underlying cause of severe physical suffering; breakfastless children march to school past bankrupt shops laden with rich foods gathered from the ends of the earth; strong men by the million walk the streets in a futile search for employment and with the exhaustion of hope enter the ranks of the damned; great captains of industry close factories without warning and dismiss the workmen by whose labors they have amassed huge fortunes through the years; automatic machinery increasingly displaces men and threatens society with a growing contingent of the permanently unemployed; racketeers and gangsters with the connivance of public officials fasten themselves on the channels of trade and exact toll at the end of the machine gun; economic parasitism, either within or without the law, is so prevalent that the tradition of honest labor is showing signs of decay; the wages paid to the workers are too meager to enable them to buy back the goods they produce; consumption is subordinated to production and a philosophy of deliberate waste is widely proclaimed as the highest economic wisdom; the science of psychology is employed to fan the flames of desire so that men may be enslaved by their wants and bound to the wheel of production; a government board advises the cotton-growers to plow under every third row of cotton in order to bolster up the market; both ethical and aesthetic considerations are commonly over-ridden by "hard-headed business men" bent on material gain; federal aid to the unemployed is opposed on the ground that it would pauperize the masses when the favored members of society have always lived on a dole; even responsible leaders resort to the practices of the witch doctor and vie with one another in predicting the return of prosperity; an ideal of rugged individualism, evolved in a simple pioneering and agrarian order at a time when free land existed in abundance, is used to justify a system which exploits pitilessly and without thought of the

morrow the natural and human resources of the nation and of the world. One can only imagine what Jeremiah would say if he could step out of the pages of the Old Testament and cast his eyes over this vast spectacle so full of tragedy and of menace.

The point should be emphasized, however, that the present situation is also freighted with hope and promise. The age is pregnant with possibilities. There lies within our grasp the most humane, the most beautiful, the most majestic civilization ever fashioned by any people. This much at least we know today. We shall probably know more tomorrow. At last men have achieved such a mastery over the forces of nature that wage slavery can follow chattel slavery and take its place among the relics of the past. No longer are there grounds for the contention that the finer fruits of human culture must be nurtured upon the toil and watered by the tears of the masses. The limits to achievement set by nature have been so extended that we are today bound merely by our ideals, by our power of self-discipline, by our ability to devise social arrangements suited to an industrial age. If we are to place any credence whatsoever in the word of our engineers, the full utilization of modern technology at its present level of development should enable us to produce several times as much goods as were ever produced at the very peak of prosperity, and with the working day, the working year, and the working life reduced by half. We hold within our hands the power to usher in an age of plenty, to make secure the lives of all, and to banish poverty forever from the land. The only cause for doubt or pessimism lies in the question of our ability to rise to the stature of the times in which we live.

Our generation has the good or the ill fortune to live in an age when great decisions must be made. The American people, like most of the other peoples of the earth, have come to the parting of the ways; they can no longer trust entirely the inspiration which came to them when the Republic was young; they must decide afresh what they are to do with their talents. Favored above all other nations with the resources of nature and the material instrumentalities of civilization, they stand confused and irresolute before the future. They seem to lack the moral quality necessary to quicken, discipline, and give direction to their matchless energies. In a recent paper Professor Dewey has, in my judgment, correctly diagnosed our troubles: "the schools, like the nation," he says, "are in need of a central purpose which will create new enthusiasm and devotion, and which will unify and guide all intellectual plans."

Source: George S. Counts, *Dare the Schools Build a New Social Order?* New York: Arno Press and the New York Times, 1969, pp. 9–12, 19, 27–29, 31–37.

TOFFLER

EDUCATING THE YOUNGEST FOR TOMORROW

Harold Shane and June Grant Shane are well known for their writings on the future. The following selection reflects the reconstructionist belief that the school should be on the "frontiers of social change." Education is viewed as perhaps the only sane way to prepare for the future and bring about the major changes that are needed if we are to achieve a civilized future. It should also be noted that this selection is taken from a book edited by Alvin Toffler, the author of the influential work Future Shock *(1970). Reconstructionists/futurists, like the Shanes and Toffler, would like to see the future, as a topic of study, brought into schools at all levels of instruction. They promote efforts to change schools to promote more futuristic thinking.*

Learning for Tomorrow: The Role of the Future in Education

From earliest times there have been divided opinions as to the purpose of schooling. In somewhat oversimplified terms, the major split has been between persons of conservative persuasion, those who are satisfied to support teaching that will reflect and preserve the status quo, and those who believe that the schools should be outposts on the frontiers of social change. Between these polar positions, of course, there are infinite nuances of opinion.

To accept the idea of a future-oriented education is to enter the ranks of those who believe that education must be an agent of cultural change. It is from this action viewpoint that we explore possible educational developments that promise better to school our children by teaching the future.

Any meaningful approach to conceptions of the future (when working with children of twelve or below) has at least two dimensions:

(1) an image of the kind of world to be sought in the future, including the future-focused role-image with which the child identifies himself in this world, and (2) a perspective of the content and the educational conditions or "climate" which (hopefully) will create changes in the individual behavior of boys and girls—changes congruent with the self-image they have of themselves in the future.

Development of an image of a "good" future world implies a number of new teaching methods. Thus, it requires preparation without indoctrination, the extensive use of inquiry as a method of instruction, and the continuing development of the open-mindedness which is a prerequisite to inquiry. It also involves an understanding of the meaning of "duty" to one's society (as one of many world cultures of comparable respectability), instrumental skills that make one useful to himself and to his fellows, expressive skills that lend meaning to the individual human life, and the will to laugh (with kindness and compassion as needed) at and with a world in which individual humor—

and even pleasant irony—have become diminished by the canned "overkill humor" or puerile farce poured out each season by mass media.

A "futurizing" education implies that the learner will begin to sense and to accept both the constraints and the advantages of freedom. Finally, future-directed teaching and learning should emphasize the ineluctable fact that education will increase rather than decrease inequality! To the degree that it personalizes, it will increase inequalities in the ability of different individuals to contribute to society, rather than suppress the differences and, in that way, create dull, egalitarian intellectual **bidonvilles**. (One important qualification must be voiced, however, with respect to education that "increases inequality". Such future-directed learning should **decrease** inequality in the ability of all persons to engage in effective, receptive, and expressive **communication** in their many forms, including the inaudible but eloquent languages of gesture and expression.)

These educational methods and targets are too important to postpone until students reach the secondary level, and, indeed, even to delay until the primary-school years. In an appropriate fashion they can be used with children under the age of three.

The Content of Learning

If one probes beneath the surface of a generalization such as "the school should make extensive use of inquiry as a method of instruction", what does such a phrase really mean when interpreted or applied with young learners? How shall we change the **content** (what is learned) and the **climate** (the spirit or tone) of the teaching-learning situations that we endeavor to develop?

Since most schooling up to the 1970s has tended to preserve the traditions of the past and to maintain much of the status quo, one might contend that the best future-oriented education could be based on a reversal of contemporary practice. Such a switch would create or accelerate curriculum trends and changes that carried us

From	To
Mass teaching	Personalized teaching
Single learnings	Multiple learnings
Passive answer-absorbing	Active answer-seeking
Rigid daily programs	Flexible schedules
Training in formal skills and knowledge	Building desirable appreciations that stimulate a questing for knowledge
Teacher initiative and direction	Child initiative and group planning
Isolated content	Interrelated content
Memorized answers	Problem awareness
Emphasis on textbooks	Use of many media in addition to texts
Passive mastery of information and so on	Active stimulation of intellect and so on

But to advocate or acquiesce in the mere reversal of present practices in elementary education is both simplistic and likely to build a false sense of success in teaching *for* and *of* the future. What is needed, in addition to many basic 180-degree turns, is a new conception of what constitutes fitting content and of the qualities of a suitable psychoemotional and social climate for learning.

We need a better understanding of the educational experiences that will implant, without numbing indoctrination, a wholesome future-focused self-image in the mind of the child. We also need to conceive of a desirable psychological field and an emotionally stabilizing matrix in which young learners become secure and self-directive in the acceptance and pursuit of a satisfying role-image.

The genuinely important content of instruction eventually resides in a body of skills, knowledge, attitudes, and convictions that govern the learner's behavior after he has forgotten many of the details of the input that he has absorbed through his schooling. What we propose is not a downgrading of such individual content-bred competencies but a closer linkage of the individual to the purposes of his experiencing, and to the acceptance of these purposes because he recognizes and accepts them as relevant to his personal future-focused role-image. . . .

We noted earlier that "teaching the future" was a twofold task. In addition to a reinterpreted approach to content which provides a more suitable role-image for the future with which a child can identify, there is the matter of maintaining a sound, affective milieu for learning: an emotionally wholesome climate that will mediate thinking and behaving in childhood in ways that are consistent with the objectives of education.

Competent teachers long have recognized that there is such a thing as a "good" or "right" setting and tone for learning experiences. Among familiar attributes of such a milieu are encouragement of inquiry, respect for the learner, an atmosphere of freedom, stimulating content, flexible teaching procedures, and so on. The climate of future-focused schooling is especially important because of the need to motivate children to make a sustained effort both to attain a better world of tomorrow and to create a realistic place for themselves in such a world.

This is not to imply that each child should be prepared for his slot in an Orwellian future. Rather, his learning experiences should free him to "create himself" in terms of a viable self-image of the finest, most contributive, joyful person he can become. Patently, a supportive environment that will help children accomplish this delicate task is tremendously important. But what are its characteristics? Here is a brief list of some of the important, often neglected, components of a psychological climate that promise to help free children for cumulative self-realization:

An affective approach is made to cognitive experiences. The learner should feel ready to learn. His attitude, his readiness, rather than a prescriptive curriculum guide or course of study, provide the clues as to the timing, the sequence, and the breadth of what is experienced.

Participation is encouraged. A suitable climate helps prepare the child of twelve and below for future effectiveness by ensuring that he is "in" on things, that his opinions are valued, and that they will govern decisions to whatever degree that they have merit. Confrontation, as a technique of forcing issues, thus becomes needless. Even very young children can develop this understanding. They also can begin to sense that genuine broad-based participation makes it unnecessary to support an elite to think for others in the years ahead.

Pressures for uniform "Protestant Ethic" behavior are sharply reduced. At least some Americans have long been persuaded that unpleasant or hard school tasks had disciplinary value. They "helped make a man of you". Long, cold winter walks to school, penalties for being tardy, bell-regulated schedules, busywork that "kept idle hands from becoming the Devil's Workshop", and arduous, drill-type homework were some of the educational expressions of this Protestant Ethic.

Teaching for maximum self-realization as children grow older will more clearly recognize that it is unwise to attempt to pour human individuality into an eighteenth-century New England mold. The future requires flexibility and the power to adapt quickly, rather than an ability to respond to behavioral problems in terms of carefully transmitted, rigid conduct codes. This is not to suggest that elementary education will be without standards, but that the tone of teaching and learning will reflect an appreciation for a number of different values. Respect for human individuality—in recognition of the fact that children best do different things in different ways at different times—implies varied school entrance ages, perhaps different hours spent in learning, certainly a large number of personalized experiences, and new thinking as to the desirable limits of compulsory attendance at the secondary level.

Society rather than child or school is held accountable. Until recently children were held personally accountable for behavior and achievement in school. Punishment and report cards were the agents, respectively, for preserving order and for recording academic performance. In the late 1960s and 1970s there was much talk about the schools being held accountable, especially with respect to measurable academic skills. When teaching for the future, it probably will be desirable to do so in a classroom climate in which the child himself is not the fall guy who is blamed if he learns less than demanded for a "C" or better!

At the same time, there is considerable doubt in our minds as to whether the teacher of the school can be made accountable for formal discipline and uniform academic performance—particularly if an emotionally comfortable atmosphere is sought. Only in a comfortable atmosphere, free of unreasonable or premature academic pressure, can youngsters have experiences that will enable them to move into the future with a positive self-concept and a healthy future-focused role-image. Neither the teacher nor the learner can be held

fully accountable. Society, itself, must once again accept some responsibility for the educative experiences of children.

When Tom Sawyer was a lad, virtually all of the adults in his riverfront town on the Mississippi felt responsible for *all* children's progress toward adult maturity. Recall how quickly someone took action or informed Aunt Polly when Tom strayed from the path of rectitude! In a broader, more dynamic sense, the community today needs once again to take on the responsible role it has played in most of mankind's history in being accountable for the next generation.

Source: Learning for Tomorrow: The Role of the Future in Education, edited by Alvin Toffler. New York: Random House, copyright © 1974, pp. 183–186, 192–194. Reprinted by permission of Curtis Brown, Ltd.

· · · · · · · ·

SELECTED READINGS

Brameld, Theodore. *Toward a Reconstructed Philosophy of Education.* New York: Dryden, 1956. This book is one of the most complete statements by a leading reconstructionist and explores the development and uses of reconstructionism as a philosophy of education.

————. *Patterns of Educational Philosophy: Divergence and Convergence in Culturological Perspective.* New York: Holt, Rinehart and Winston, 1971. The author connects the need for philosophy with the contemporary "crisis in culture," that reflects his deep interest in philosophical and cultural anthropology and their relation to education. An attempt is made to establish a critical perspective for reconstructionism in contrast to other philosophies.

Counts, George S. *Dare the Schools Build a New Social Order?* New York: John Day, 1932. This work is a challenging attack on the status quo and the misuses and distortions of progressive educational thought. The book is still timely, and its well-written contents continue to stimulate thought.

Illich, Ivan. *Deschooling Society.* New York: Harper and Row, 1970. In a radical departure, Illich argues that society has become too dependent on institutionalized education. Just as society had to be "de-churched" by the Reformation, so it is now in need of deschooling.

Shimahara, Nobuo, ed. *Educational Reconstruction: Promise and Challenge.* Columbus, OH: Merrill Publishing Co., 1973. This collection of reconstructionist writings deals with significant educational and social problems and is one of the most complete statements of recent reconstructionist thought.

Stanley, William B. *Curriculum for Utopia: Social Reconstructionism and Critical Pedagogy in the Postmodern Era.* Albany: State University of New York Press, 1992. An overview of the history of reconstructionism and a connection of that tradition with recent developments, including feminist scholarship, neopragmatism, poststructuralism, and critical theory.

Toffler, Alvin. *The Third Wave.* New York: William Morrow and Co., 1980. A leading treatise on futuristics that attempts to explain the dramatic changes that have affected human society. The author focuses on educational changes he believes will come in the near future.

6

Behaviorism and Education

Behaviorism is not generally considered a philosophy in the same sense that idealism, realism, pragmatism, and other such thought systems are. It is most often classified as a psychological theory, a more specialized and less comprehensive theory than a systematic philosophy. At the same time, behaviorism has been given increasing attention and acceptance in the field of education, so that in many instances it has extended into areas ordinarily considered the domain of philosophy. These extensions include theoretical considerations dealing with the nature of the human being and society, values, the good life, and speculations or assumptions on the nature of reality.

Perhaps no psychological theory can escape dealing with philosophical assumptions and implications. For a long time, psychology was thought to be a philosophical study; only in recent times have most psychologists come to think of themselves as scientists. Indeed, the leading proponents of behaviorism do consider themselves scientists, perhaps more justifiably laying claim to that title than some other schools of psychology. Be that as it may, most psychologists at some point in their endeavors encounter philosophical questions. Much psychological theory rests upon assumptions about human nature that have had a long career in the history of philosophy. Behaviorism, even though it lays claim to an objective scientific orientation, is no less involved with philosophical questions than are other psychological theories.

This chapter shows some of the connections of behaviorism with past philosophical systems and how these systems have influenced modern behavioristic theory. It also explores philosophical themes in behaviorism, primarily as these are given in the works of B. F. Skinner. Finally, it considers the educational uses and implications of behaviorism—what might be more appropriately called behavioral engineering.

PHILOSOPHICAL BASES OF BEHAVIORISM

Behaviorism has roots in several philosophical traditions. It is related to realism: the realists' thesis of independent reality resembles the behaviorists' belief that behavior is caused by environmental conditions. Behaviorism also is indebted to materialistic philosophy, such as that promoted by Thomas Hobbes, who held that reality is primarily matter and motion and all behavioral phenomena can be explained in those terms.

Realism

Behaviorism's connection with realism is primarily with modern realism and its advocacy of science. However, there are some similarities to classical realism. For example, Aristotle thought we reached form or essence through the study of particulars. Behaviorists believe that we can understand human behavior by a meticulous study of particular behaviors. Indeed, they expand this approach to the effect that human "nature" (if there be such) can be explained by what traditionally has been thought to be only a particular aspect of human nature—behavior. In addition, there is no "internal" reality hidden from scientific discovery for behaviorists because what is real is external, factual, and observable behavior capable of being known.

Thus, one of the realist elements of behaviorism includes going from particular, observable facts (particular behaviors) to "forms," or the laws of behavior. Behaviorists think the human traits of personality, character, integrity, and so forth are the results of behaving in certain ways. These traits are not internally determined by each individual but come about by behavior patterns developed through environmental conditioning. The emphasis on environment shows another realist leaning toward the importance of the discernible, factual, observable aspects of the universe. In other words, by understanding particular behaviors and how they are caused by environmental circumstances, we can detect the patterns and processes by which behavior comes about. Thus it is possible, behaviorists maintain, to discern the laws of behavior and thereby come to exercise control over human behavior. It is possible, then, to construct a technology of behavior.

Of course, these notions about behavior would be foreign to Aristotle, but it is possible to see similarities between him and the behaviorists in at least the basic framework. The connection becomes even more apparent with more recent versions of realism, especially the realism that came about with the advent of modern science. For example, Francis Bacon, in his efforts to develop an inductive scientific method, held that we must reject indubitable dogmas in favor of an inquiry approach that seeks meaning in the facts as we find them. Behaviorism holds that we should cease accentuating the mind, consciousness, or soul as the causal agent of behavior and look rather to the facts of behavior, or that which is observable and capable of empirical verification. This consideration is not only Baconian but is representative of contemporary realism.

The idea of the "laws" of behavior, while having similarities to Aristotelian and Baconian realism, is akin to Alfred North Whitehead's contention that the philosopher should seek out the patterns of reality. Behaviorists do this by seeking the processes and patterns through which behavior is shaped. Once they have sufficient understanding of these, they maintain, it will be possible to engineer more effectively the kinds of people and social conditions we want.

"Engineer" people / social conditions

Materialism

Materialism has its roots in Greek philosophy, but as it exists today, it is essentially the theory developed along with modern science in the sixteenth and seventeenth centuries. Materialism is the theory that reality can be explained by the laws of matter and motion. We can see that behaviorism is definitely a kind of materialism, for most behaviorists view human beings in terms of their neurological, physiological, and biological contexts. Beliefs about mind, consciousness, and soul, they say, are relics of a prescientific age. The behaviorists seem to be saying that body is material and that behavior is motion. Thus, humans can be known from the standpoints of matter and motion.

Elements of behaviorism are akin to some aspects of mechanistic materialism. This philosophical perspective also dates back several centuries. For the materialist, human beings are not partially supernatural beings above nature (as some religious persons might hold); rather, they are a part of nature. Even though they are one of the more complex natural organisms, they can be studied and are governed by natural law like any other natural creature.

Agree to some extent →

Thomas Hobbes (1588–1679)

Thomas Hobbes was an exponent of mechanistic materialism. He was personally acquainted with some of the greatest figures of his day, including Descartes, Galileo, and Kepler. He learned a great deal about philosophy and science from these men but was also a first-rate thinker in his own right. Hobbes was a thoroughgoing determinist, and he rejected the elements of self-determination and free will in the thought of Descartes. In most respects, he was more at home with the thinking of Galileo and Kepler. He applied some of their ideas about the physical universe to human beings and social institutions. Life is simply motion, Hobbes held; one can say that a machine has life, albeit artificial. By the same token, an organized society is like a machine: it has an artificial life that has to be maintained. Even biological natural life is mechanistic in the sense that it operates according to its own design.

A machine has "life" ..... *Life is "mechanistic"*

For Hobbes, an individual's psychological makeup can be explained in mechanistic terms. We experience objects by their qualities (color, odor, texture, and so forth) through sensation. Sensation is physical, what is sensed is quality, and quality is motion. Even imagination, according to Hobbes, is motion. The same can be said for thinking. Therefore, all that truly exists is matter and motion and all reality can be explained in terms of mathematical precision.

Behaviorism's close affinity with mechanistic materialism lies in several areas. For one thing, both materialists and behaviorists believe that we behave in certain ways according to our physical makeup. Bodily functions occur in certain objectively describable and predictable ways. Because of this physical makeup, we are capable of numerous motor responses. Organs and limbs operate according to known physiological processes. The brain, for instance, contains no soul but does contain physiological and neurologic materials and processes because chemical and electrical processes make up a large part of the brain's functions. However, it is body-in-situation that is significant, for here there is *human* behavior or motion. The significant thing is to observe behavior (motion) of a body in an environment (supporting material conditions). While this is not precisely what the behaviorists say, the similarity to mechanistic materialism is obvious. One difference is that for the behaviorists, human behavior or motion is *the* significant datum and knowledge of matter is crucial because it helps us understand behavior itself.

Early Behaviorists

Ivan Pavlov (1849–1936)

Pavlov was an eminent experimental psychologist and physiologist in pre-Soviet Russia. He was noted for his studies of the reflex reaction in humans and animals and devised a number of conditioning experiments. He found that when a bell is rung each time a dog is fed, the dog is conditioned to associate the sound of the bell with food. Consequently, when the bell is sounded, the dog physiologically anticipates food. Pavlov was the father of conditioning theory and was also a strong opponent, throughout his life, of the Freudian interpretation of neuroses.

Pavlov's conditioning studies show how both realism and materialism are related. For a dog, bodily response is not based on something mental going on inside the dog; rather, the response is made on the basis of conditioning and conditioning can be explained by external circumstances. This lay at the heart of Pavlov's opposition to Freudianism. Of course, it could be argued that Freud recognized conditioning by his extensive work on the influence of early childhood and family training. The difference is, however, that Freud claimed that this influence resides in a mentalistic unconscious, an "inner" thing. Pavlov wanted an explanation based on controllable external conditions that require no inner source of action. This illustrates both realism's affinity for an independent reality and materialism's claim that things can be explained in terms of matter and motion.

Modern behaviorists hold that Pavlov was headed in the right direction but that his explanations were too simplistic. Pavlov considered only conditioned reflex behavior, whereas modern behaviorists use operant conditioning that includes action on the part of the organism being conditioned. The organism can act to change its environment, and the resulting changes reinforce the behavior of the organism in some way. The modern view tends more toward a two-way flow, while Pavlov showed it only one way. Nevertheless, his pioneering was of crucial importance.

John B. Watson (1878–1958)

Watson repudiated the introspective method in psychology as delusive and unscientific. He relied solely on an observational technique restricted to behavior. He believed that fears are conditioned responses to the environment. In experiments, he conditioned people to be fearful and then deconditioned them. He thought of the environment as the primary shaper of behavior and maintained that if he could control a child's environment he could then engineer that child into any kind of person desired. Following his work with infants in the maternity ward of Johns Hopkins Hospital in Baltimore, he announced

> The behaviorists believe that there is nothing within to develop. If you start with a healthy body, the right number of fingers and toes, and the few elementary movements that are present at birth, you do not need anything else in the way of raw material to make a man, be that man a genius, a cultured gentleman, a rowdy, or a thug.

Watson was very influential, and the strong movement in American psychology toward behaviorism is often directly attributed to him.

Watson was even more materialistic than preceding behaviorists. He thought the chief function of the nervous system is simply to coordinate senses with motor responses. Thus, the brain is only a part of the nervous system and not the seat of mind or consciousness or a self-active entity. He thought that the senses not only gain knowledge of the world but are also instruments in guiding activity for successful maintenance of life. In rejecting mentalistic notions of mind and consciousness, Watson also rejected such concepts as purpose, feeling, satisfaction, and free will because they are not observable and therefore not capable of scientific treatment or measurement.

Behaviorism and Positivism

Watson's penchant for giving acceptance only to directly observable things set a pattern for those who came after him. E. L. Thorndike was solidly within Watson's outlook when he proclaimed that anything that exists, exists in some quantity capable of being measured. These kinds of thinking have been influential in psychology and have had their parallels and influences in and from philosophy. One movement that has given a philosophical basis to such positions as Watson's and Thorndike's is known as positivism.

Philosophical positivism was initiated by Auguste Comte, often referred to as the founder of modern sociology. His objective was to reform society, and he argued for a positive social science to achieve this end. He thought that by applying scientific principles to social conditions systematically, we would be able to recognize the laws constituting the social order, their evolution, and the ways to apply them more systematically. This could be accomplished through discovering the real and exact knowledge of society. The test of value of this knowledge would be the extent to which it helps us change the material world and society to more desirable conditions.

Comte divided history into three periods, each characterized by a particular way of thinking. The first is the *theological*, in which things are explained by references to spirits and gods. The second period is the *metaphysical*, in which events are explained by causes, inner principles, and substances. The third or *positive* period is the highest stage, in which one does not attempt to go beyond observable and measurable fact.

Comte's thought influenced subsequent thinkers to use science in devising social policy. Behaviorists are squarely in this tradition because Watson's statements concerning how he could produce any kind of person from a reasonably healthy child have been taken seriously by contemporary behaviorists. No longer is science the province of intellectuals and individuals of leisure; it is now viewed as the key to the better society. In some quarters, psychology, sociology, and similar disciplines are no longer referred to as the *social* sciences but as the *behavioral* sciences. This change in terms has occurred because behavior is the objective, observable human element susceptible to scientific manipulation.

While earlier positivism was founded on the science of the nineteenth century, contemporary positivism has been more interested in the logic and language of scientific concepts. This has been exemplified most by the school of thought called logical positivism. It has dealt with areas familiar to both behaviorism and the older positivism, but it is primarily known for its work on the logic of propositions and the principle of verification.

The movement began in the early decades of the twentieth century and has often been identified with a group of European philosophers, mathematicians, and scientists known as the Vienna Circle. It included such figures as Rudolf Carnap, Herbert Feigl, Felix Kaufmann, and others. Bertrand Russell and Ludwig Wittgenstein, although not members of the group, had close philosophical ties to it. The circle has since dissolved, and its members dispersed in several different directions.

The impetus of logical positivism has been to develop a unity among the sciences by devising a consistent set of logical or linguistic phrasings and structures. This effort has come about in order to rectify the language difficulties encountered in scientific investigation. An investigation can often be sidetracked or misled by the words and statements used. For example, our words and statements should reflect the facts of the situation under discussion.

Suppose we are studying an educational problem, and our problem is largely involved with self-concept. Suppose we cannot discover that there really is such a thing as self in the sense of mind or consciousness. Then what we need to do is examine what we really mean by the term *self*. This word is so colored by prescientific and metaphysical considerations that its usage is vague, even with tinges of the theological soul. If we are truly scientific, we want an objective statement of the problem in such terms that an objective resolution can be made. In other words, we must specify clearly what we are talking about.

The connection of this philosophical school of thought with behaviorism is that behaviorists seek a language framework that more accurately reflects the facts of behavior. Rather than using the word *self* to signify personal identity or the characteristics of an individual, the behaviorists speak of "conditioned" or "reinforced behavior," "repertoire of behavioral responses," or perhaps "operant conditioning" in regard to the specific organism we may call John Jones. Self or self-concept are too much tied to mentalistic constructs, and we are in danger of being misled in the direction of imputing certain mysterious, internal, driving forces to John Jones to explain his behavior.

Logical positivists are sensitive to the fallacies that the wrong uses of language can foster. What we should do, they maintain, is make meaningful statements conveying information regarding the observable, verifiable facts of the situation. In the context of behaviorism and logical positivism, it is one thing to make such a statement as, "There are matches in this box," and quite another thing to state, "There is a self-concept in John Jones." We can verify whether there are matches in this box by opening the box and examining it. Either there are matches or there are no matches. We cannot operate on John Jones and find that self is a fact. First, it would be ridiculous to cut John Jones open. Second, it makes more sense to observe John Jones' behavior to see what stimulates him to behave as he does.

The behaviorist maintains that because we know little about behavior—because of our lack of knowledge—we wrongly impute meaning to behavior by reference to an "inner being," a self, mind, consciousness, soul, or some such hidden entity that "causes" the behavior. Even the most meticulous and rigorous scientific experiments have not been able to locate this "inner being." Behaviorists and logical positivists alike would agree with the British philosopher Gilbert Ryle, who maintained that traditional meanings of mind really imply a "ghost in the machine" (or a mind in the body).

Coupled with their concern for more linguistic precision, logical positivists have also championed what is called "the principle of verifiability." This principle means that no statement should be taken as truthful unless it can be verified empirically or it is at least capable of being verified. For example, a statement about angels is not verifiable in any scientific way, nor can it be verified at some future date because of the very nature of the statement.

Even those who believe in angels do not maintain that angels can be verified by science. However, such a statement as "There is life in outer space" may not be capable of immediate verification; but it is certainly within our technical capacity to verify that statement in the near future. Thus, logical positivists try to discourage nonsense statements and promote language and thought that are more controllable and rigorous. The behaviorist, mindful about careless linguistic and logical statements, seeks to avoid absurd theories. There are observable, factual behavior and environmental conditions, and we must describe them in objective, logical, and accurate terms.

Summary

PHILOSOPHICAL ASPECTS OF BEHAVIORISM

B. F. Skinner (1904–1990)

Burrhus Frederic Skinner was born in Susquehanna, Pennsylvania. He studied at Hamilton College and Harvard University and later taught at the University of Minnesota and at Indiana University (where he was chairman of the department of psychology) before returning to Harvard as professor of psychology. He was sometimes called the high priest of behaviorism. Others more sympathetically refer to him as one of the most important twentieth-century psychologists. Skinner's work and influence have certainly caught attention and comment, even though opinions have ranged from bitter criticism to disciplelike emulation. Few of the persons knowledgeable about Skinner's work are neutral about it.

Skinner himself often debunked philosophical approaches to psychology. He thought that much error and misunderstanding have come about because philosophers have tried to deduce an understanding of human beings from a priori generalizations (i.e., they have been "armchair scientists" content with introspection). He claimed, on the other hand, to base his findings on observations and controlled scientific experiment. Yet he often found it necessary to make statements about such traditional philosophical topics as human nature and the good society. In fact, Skinner was not necessarily the sterile scientist in the laboratory, for he was also a dreamer and a utopian. It is possible to discern a strong element of social radicalism in his writing. The following overview of his thought (taken largely from his book, *Beyond Freedom and Dignity*), explores some of these ideas.

Human Nature

Traditionally, the study of human nature has been an important aspect of philosophical endeavor. It has been central to the metaphysics of many great philosophers and has been influential in the philosophical treatment of ethics. Skinner maintained that less philosophical speculation and more "realistic" observation of behavior are necessary, but he still posed the question, "What is man?"

Skinner attacked what he called the traditional views of humanity. Those views have imputed all kinds of internal drives, forces, or otherwise mysterious actions to the "autonomous person"—such forces as aggression, industry, attention, knowing, perceiving, and so on. Traditionally, such capacities were assumed to be there somewhere, hidden from direct scrutiny, and were said to make up (at least in part) the very essence of human nature. Skinner, on the other hand, maintained that aggression, for example, is not inherent in our nature in the sense that we will automatically harm or damage others. It makes just as much sense to say that we behave in a manner we call aggressive because that behavior is reinforced by particular environmental contingencies. For Skinner, the contingencies of reinforcement themselves explain the aggressive behavior quite apart from some assumed internal or genetic force within us.

Let us explore an example. In wartime, some persons commit acts that we call depraved. During the Vietnam War, some American soldiers indiscriminately killed noncombatant women and children. When one such event was made known in America, there were outcries of disbelief and horror. In searching for explanations, some observers said that these actions only indicated an evil human nature. A widely publicized court martial was held, and an officer was found guilty of having participated in the massacre. From a Skinnerian point of view, we could say that however deplorable the behavior, finding a guilty culprit and punishing him does not get at the real problem. Punishment may extinguish certain kinds of behavior, but it is usually ineffective.

Does a soldier under combat conditions kill others because he is basically evil? Or does it make more sense to observe his behavior in terms of the environmental contingencies and the reinforcement of particular aggressive behaviors under those conditions? Although not all soldiers kill noncombatant civilians, it also seems likely that noncombatant civilians would not have been killed by combatant soldiers if there had been no war, no behaviors of combatant soldiering, and no existing environmental conditions that would make warlike behavior rewarding. We may say that the evil lies in making war, training people to kill, and maintaining and securing conditions that make such behavior rewarding—not in some innate evil within people.

Let us take another example: knowing. Skinner said that the traditional view sees an autonomous individual who, in perceiving the world, reaches out or acts upon that world in order to know it, to "take it in," to "grasp it." The implication is that the action and initiative come from the autonomous person, but Skinner maintained that the reverse is the case. Knowing is really a case of the environment acting on us. We perceive and know to the extent that we respond to stimuli from environmental contingencies. For instance, we may respond to heat, light, color, and so forth according to the arrangement of contingencies. As Skinner put it, we move in or out of sunlight depending upon how hot or cold it is. Thus, we come to know sunlight, heat, and cold. Sunlight figures in how we arrange time, set schedules, and perform certain activities. Our knowledge of the sun, heat, and light is expanded to the extent that we behave in relation to these environmental conditions and are reinforced by that behavior. Too often, we think knowing is a cognitive process, but it is behavioral and environmental, neurologic, and even physiological.

Some critics say behaviorism cannot deal with individual consciousness—with awareness of oneself. They insist that there is an "inner realm" that the behaviorist ignores. Perhaps Skinner's best-known critic on this issue is Carl Rogers, another psychologist who approached his work philosophically. Rogers maintained that there *is* a reality to the "inner realm," a reality characterized by freedom. He agreed that humans are conditioned by outside factors and that they respond to external stimuli, but Rogers felt that Skinner did not explain how free and responsible choice can be exercised in the way a person responds to externals. An individual does not have to respond to a stimulus in a preestablished and set way but can examine the alternatives or even create new ones in the way she responds. In other words, an individual can choose a direction, be responsible in pursuing it, and give commitment to sustaining it. This, Rogers argued, shows that the person has freedom of choice and freedom of responsible commitment, and this freedom springs from the inside. Freedom is a subjective, inner thing.

Skinner said that this charge is serious and cannot be lightly passed over and held that, thus far, self-observation must be included in any comprehensive analysis of human behavior. What is at stake, however, is what an individual knows when she does this self-analysis. For Skinner, what one knows in this respect is difficult to comprehend because it is largely a matter of responding to the natural contingencies of individual circumstances. We respond to our own internal stimuli (without much awareness), as in such behavior as walking, jumping, and running. To the extent that we really *know* these behaviors and their causes, we must do more than merely respond to them. This kind of knowing would involve systematic study beyond a mere internal soliloquy and would include bodily functions, environmental conditions, and contingencies.

Knowing one's desires, beliefs, and feelings, the things usually thought to be most private, is more difficult. For one thing, we lack the necessary verbal tools to accomplish this. Without some form of verbalization, behavior is largely unconsciousness; Skinner maintained that consciousness in the verbal awareness sense is a social product and not within the range of a solitary individual. Really knowing this "inner realm" is difficult because we have not developed appropriate verbalization of it. We are too prone to rest the case on our conviction of an inner or autonomous person. We have not effectively uncovered the contingencies of reinforcement in order to describe this personal awareness. It is as if, we may say, we hug our privacy to us and refuse to understand it.

Skinner attempted not to deny personal awareness but to affirm that when and if we really come to know it, *what* we know will not be essentially different from external objects. That is, the *what* or content of the knowledge will be that which is observable. In Skinnerian terminology, that content will be knowledge of behavior and contingencies of reinforcement and not the old catchall of a mind, soul, consciousness, or an "inner man."

Skinner's reply to the charges of his critics that he was destroying or abolishing humanity was that a scientific analysis in no way destroys us, for no theory destroys that which it is a theory about. What is too often destructive is actual human behavior, not a theory. Skinner put it thus: "What is being abolished is autonomous man—the inner man, the *homunculus*, the possessing demon, the man defended by the literature of freedom and dignity." What is left is the real, observable human organism who is biological and animal. Although Skinner maintained that humans are not machines in the classic sense, he held that we are machinelike in the sense that we are a complex system behaving in lawful, observable ways. But even if humans are simply animal and mechanical, Skinner was fascinated by their complexity, their uniqueness, and their intricacy.

Skinner believed that the importance lies in human behavior and how it makes us what we are. Perhaps the most accurate description of Skinner's view is that we are both controller and controlled. Another way of putting it is that, in a very real sense, we are our own makers. It is Skinner's position that we have developed through two processes of evolution; one is the biological process from which we evolved, and the other is the cultural process of evolution that we have largely created. The latter process was more important and intriguing for Skinner. He pointed out that our environment is largely contrived, not natural, and it is an environment we have wrought. This environment contains the significant contingencies of reinforcement that make us human. In this respect, we may say that we are our own makers, and while we are doing the making, we are being made or we are in the making.

The Good Society Through Cultural Design

Skinner was paradoxical. On one hand, he appeared to be a hard-nosed scientist, dealing only with factual, observable behavior. On the other, he seemed to be a utopian dreamer. Perhaps the best statement of Skinner's utopian ideals is expressed in his work *Walden Two,* a fictional account of a futuristic social experiment.

In *Beyond Freedom and Dignity,* however, Skinner gave a nonfictional descriptive account of his views. Accordingly, the important thing is the social environment. We may even say that for Skinner, social environment *is* culture. This position is in opposition to those who say that culture is essentially ideas or values apart from human behavior. Behavior carries the ideas and values of a culture, and it transforms, alters, and changes a culture. In a large sense, cultural evolution is an evolution of behavioral practices that are established within a social milieu or a milieu of contingencies of reinforcement. So we may say that in cultural evolution, what actually evolves are practices set in a social context.

Skinner makes a strong case for controlled cultural evolution. In the past, we had a confused sort of control, often as not blind and accidental. We did not fully understand the nature of the control or how it could be more effectively used. Skinner maintained that controls are needed to make us more sensitive to the consequences of our behavior. Reinforcement follows behavior; it does not precede it (even though most human behavior is conditioned by previous reinforcement). Behavior develops in directions that are positively reinforced; consequently, we should be controlling, devising, or using contingencies that reinforce desired behaviors. In short, control lies at the crux of sensitivity to the consequences of our behavior.

Skinner admitted that we do not really know the *best* way to rear children, to educate effective citizens, or to build the good society; but he did maintain that we can develop *better* ways than we now have. If we want to change culture or individuals, we must change behavior, and the way to change behavior is to change the contingencies (i.e., culture or social environment).

What are contingencies of reinforcement? Simply put, contingencies are the conditions in which behavior occurs; they reinforce it and influence the future direction and quality of behavior. For example, we cannot drive an automobile unless an automobile actually exists. The behavior of automobile driving is contingent upon an actual automobile. Furthermore, the manner in which we drive is contingent upon numerous other conditions, such as the functions and capacities of that particular automobile, road and traffic conditions, and a host of other supporting conditions. Finally, driving an automobile does things for us. It gets us to a desired destination, helps us earn a living, increases our range of mobility. What an automobile does for us is rewarding, and our behavior of driving automobiles is reinforced. Some of these conditions serve as particularly strong contingencies. Much of the trouble with the operation of motor vehicles, such as speeding, comes about because of a lack of understanding and control of the contingencies.

Skinner stated that contingencies of reinforcement are hard to discern in many instances. For one thing, we are not used to viewing human situations in behavioral terms (or else we fail to recognize the behavioral point of view). For another, our understanding is at least hampered, if not misled, by holding to such notions as the autonomous individual. We have not developed sensitivity to the *conditions*, the contingencies, in and with which behavior occurs. But Skinner maintained that contingencies *are* accessible (even if with difficulty), and as we progressively come to understand the relation between behavior and environment, we will discover new ways of controlling behavior. It is possible, as further understanding is developed, to design and control not just isolated behaviors and their contingencies but a whole culture.

Skinner viewed the educational process as one of the chief ways of designing a culture, and his attention was also directed at numerous other institutions. He believed that positive reinforcement can induce us to begin to alter and control our schools and other institutions. Our behavior is shaped in the direction of reward; that is, behavior is reinforced to the extent that its consequences are good or bad. Good consequences are positive reinforcement, and bad consequences are aversive reinforcement. A problem arises in that humanity is too often ignorant of long-range consequences. What is immediate positive reinforcement may have negative effects later. We need to examine cultural contingencies critically in light of likely consequences.

The critical analysis of culture is not to be taken lightly. It is easier to proceed piecemeal because planning and foresight of consequences are simplified. Thus, it is easier to change particular teaching practices than a whole educational establishment, and it is easier to change one institution than a whole culture. For Skinner, the greatest mistake is to stop trying.

The big questions, however, are What is the good society? How do we get it? Who is to say what is good? and Who controls the good society? Such questions have been the stumbling blocks to social or cultural reconstruction throughout history. Recently, these questions have been considered to be outside the realm of science; for as the claim goes, science deals with what is, while questions about a "good society" deal with what ought and ought not to be. Such questions involve value judgments and not matters of fact. This would seem to rule out any part for the behavioral scientist or other scientists.

On the contrary, Skinner rejected the claim that value judgments are more remote from scientists than from any other human beings. He posed this question as a more suitable one: "If a scientific analysis can tell us how to change behavior, can it tell us what changes to make?" To Skinner, this is a question about the behavior of those who advocate and promote changes. In other words, people act to effect changes for reasons, and among these reasons are behavioral consequences. To say we would like a culture in which war-making is absent is to say we would like to eradicate war-making behavior. Whatever the behavioral consequences considered in efforts to effect change, these consequences include things people call *good* or *valuable*. Thus, we can see that, for Skinner, the good society and values are within the domain of the behavioral scientist precisely because those goods and values are involved in behavior, even based in it and coming out of it.

As a behavioral scientist, Skinner may have been solidly involved with the good and value, but it makes just as much sense to say that he was also behaving like a philosopher and dealing with philosophical issues. Many quibble over what label should be applied to Skinner, but he did become involved in the areas of the good and value, and these are intricately woven into his views of achieving a better culture or social environment.

What, then, is good and of value from the Skinnerian standpoint? Simply put, to classify something as "good" is to classify it as a positive reinforcer. We say certain foods are "good" because they give us positive reinforcement (they are pleasing, delicious, palatable, healthful, and so forth), and we tend to seek out and eat "good" food. By the same token, some foods are "bad" because they do not taste good, are unhealthful, and are undesirable—so we avoid them. But tastes vary, and what is positively reinforcing to one may be aversive to another. This applies in many areas, such as things that feel good or bad, look good or bad, sound good or bad, and so on. Skinner calls these goods "personal goods."

There are other goods to be considered, those which Skinner called "goods of others," and they refer to more social-like behaviors even though they may also flow from personal goods. Most societies have found rampant dishonesty to be aversively reinforcing. Although the dishonest individual may find it rewarding, measures have been instituted by the social group to control individual behavior to the extent that dishonesty is met with aversive measures while honesty is praised and rewarded. (Of course, there have been and are some groups in which dishonesty is rewarded when it is conducted against an outsider or enemy.)

There is still one further kind of good that Skinner called "the good of culture." This good induces the members of a culture to work for the survival and enhancement of that culture. Generally, such goods may have dim cultural and genetic roots. We do not always know why we work to support our culture or to change it for what is deemed a better state of affairs. As Skinner pointed out, we are faced with so many enormous problems today that immediate changes are needed for our very survival. We are confronted with warfare, overpopulation and starvation, and environmental pollution, all of which, if allowed to run rampant, can mean disaster.

Change does not occur simply because of the passage of time but because of what *occurs* while time passes. Thus, we are thrown back to behavior. All change is not necessarily good and valuable, and neither is all behavior. But directed and intended change depends upon behavior aware of its consequences. We may phrase the behavioral context of the goods of culture in this way: If we are reinforced by human survival, and if human survival depends upon the cultural and physical environment in which we exist, then we will work for human survival by designing culture to that end. Skinner seems to say there is little choice. We must act.

What, then, is good? That which is positively reinforcing in terms of the personal, social, and cultural survival contexts. What is of value? That which has desired reinforcing effects. The good society is one that gives personal satisfaction, supports social interaction, and furthers our survival. The good society is valuable, and the way to achieve it is through the proper design of the culture; that is, through the proper arrangement and development of the contingencies of reinforcement.

Skinner maintained that we need a sophisticated science and technology of human behavior. Although such a development would be morally neutral and could be misused and abused, he believed that it has a definite survival value. The survival value will not insure against abuse, but he felt that survival will go a long way in aiding desirable usage. When we survey the plight of the modern world and the brink on which we totter, we may be strongly inclined to agree with Skinner.

BEHAVIORISM AS A PHILOSOPHY OF EDUCATION

The principles of behaviorism and the techniques of behavioral engineering go back at least to Pavlov and Watson, but B. F. Skinner pioneered their implementation in many fields of contemporary life. Skinner saw behaviorism extending into politics, economics, and other social organizations. He strongly championed it as an educational method that is more practical and produces greater results than any other. It has grown in popularity and is used frequently, particularly in areas of special education and with disadvantaged children.

Aims of Behaviorism

Although many people disapprove of the concept of behavioral engineering, it has increasingly become part of our educational process. One might even argue that conditioning has always gone on in education, though it has not been labeled as such. Teachers have conditioned students to sit up straight and to be quiet through looks, grades, and physical punishment. When students are emotionally disturbed, conditioning is one way to develop a step-by-step program through rewards (or punishment) so that they are led to achieve complex patterns of behavior. At some institutions for the emotionally disturbed, students can earn tokens and use them to buy things: a drink, playtime, or even time away from the institution. Students may acquire tokens in diverse ways. They may obtain them for staying in their seats, for doing a certain amount of required work, or for approved social behavior. Critics often consider it undesirable for children to be rewarded extrinsically for every action, but Skinner responds by saying that extrinsic rewards are necessary when other methods do not work or do not work as well, though they should be replaced by more intrinsic rewards at a later date.

Behaviorists consider the child as an organism who is already highly programmed before coming to school. This programming is accomplished by, among other influences, parents, peers, siblings, and television. Most of the programming may have been bad, but the child has been receptive to it and has absorbed a lot of it. For example, Skinner believed that one of the reasons people have trouble making moral decisions is that the programming they have received on morality has been contradictory.

Skinner would have liked to replace the erratic and haphazard conditioning that most people receive with something systematic and meaningful. First, some kind of agreement about just what is meaningful and important (toward which children ought to be conditioned) must be reached. This point raises a storm of controversy since it seems to indicate that *some* people will decide how *other* people will be conditioned. Skinner maintained that one of our obligations as adults, and particularly as educators, is to make educational decisions and then to use whatever methods we have at our disposal (conditioning being the best) to achieve them. He believed that we should try to create a world of brotherhood and justice; if conditioning can help, it should be used.

We can easily see that the way children are currently being conditioned in school is unsatisfactory. Either the teacher does not condition systematically or else reinforcement does not follow immediately. Skinner wanted teachers to see that what they are doing generally involves some kind of conditioning; hence, they had best learn how to do it more effectively.

Many people see education and conditioning as two different things. Education presumably represents a free mind being exposed to ideas that one may look upon critically and accept or not accept, whereas conditioning is seen to represent the implementation of certain specific ideas in the pupil's mind with or without her critical consent. Skinner, however, drew no distinction between education and conditioning. He did not feel that the mind is free to begin with. Whatever kinds of critical judgment or acceptance of ideas students make are already predicated on ideas with which they have been previously conditioned.

Since so much of our education at present involves rote or memory learning, Skinner felt that mechanical electronic devices also have a useful part to play. Usually, the programs prepared for electronic devices (such as teaching machines or computers) have been structured in ways that provide for a more systematic learning, and they provide the kinds of immediate reinforcement that Skinner feels is lacking in present-day education. Teaching machines may take very different forms, but they are all based on the theory that we should reward the kinds of responses we want, and we should do it immediately.

Behavioral engineering, one might argue, has been based primarily on experiments with laboratory animals. Some claim that Skinner's experiments with animals are inapplicable to humans and to human education, but Skinner argued that the human being is an animal, although more advanced, and the difference between humans and other animals is of degree and not of kind.

The primary aim of behavioristic techniques is to change behavior and point it in more desirable directions. The question of whether one should go in a special direction is immediately raised: who decides what changes and what direction? Skinner replied that we are already largely controlled by genetic forces, parental upbringing, schooling, peer groups, the media, the church, and society. He argued that the question of control is not a good one; that is, we may feel free and even actually be relatively free, but we are always controlled by something—though we may assist in the control that is exercised over us. Thus, Skinner does away with the concept of innate freedom by saying that people have always been controlled, though we have not always been aware of the control and the direction in which it leads.

One thing primarily wrong with control is not that it has always existed but that it has been random and without any real direction. We have been controlled by politicians for their own ends and purposes and by business interests for their own profits, but such controls have been directed toward base ends and, unfortunately, in ways that served for self-negation. Skinner advocated control and thought that a new society can be shaped through control. This means that someone must be in charge to make sure the control is exercised efficiently toward the highest aims we can establish. At present, we have many kinds of control, but they are directed toward war, consumerism, superstition, and greed. Skinner pointed out that we have been talking for years about a world directed toward peace, brotherhood, and freedom and that now, for the first time, we have in our hands a method for bringing about such things. Not to use control for such high purposes would be immoral.

Skinner was a strong advocate of education, although many critics argue that what he meant by education is not education but "training." Skinner charged that much of what passes for education is not good education because it is not reinforcing, it does not properly motivate students to progress, and does not deal with immediate reinforcement. When children take a spelling test, for example, they are interested in knowing what responses are right or wrong at the time of the test. When the test is returned to them a week later, they have usually lost interest. Skinner maintained that the children should know immediately when they are right or wrong, and this is why he has championed such methods of immediate reinforcement as programmed learning and teaching machines.

Although many behaviorists use positive and negative methods of reinforcing behavior, Skinner advocates positive reinforcement. Aversive (or negative) reinforcement, although it may be effective, often has many bad side effects. The same results can be achieved through rewarding good behavior rather than punishing bad behavior. For example, in experiments to train pigeons to perform certain activities, the pigeons are rewarded with food when they peck the proper square. To discontinue such behavior, it is simply a matter of stopping the reward. The behavior may continue for a short time after it is no longer rewarded, but eventually it will cease. Some behaviorists would punish the pigeon with shocks or similar devices, but Skinner maintains that the most effective procedure is to withdraw reward. It could be argued that depriving the organism of reward for a particular task is punishment, but in most situations, Skinner would have disagreed: it is simply a matter of ceasing to reward a specific behavior.

Many people argue that the aim of behavioral engineering is to turn out robots, people who are at the beck and call of others who control them. Skinner countered that this is not true; for when we look around at our present world, we find that most people are controlled by forces of which they are unconscious. He believed that we live in a world where advanced technology in conditioning can be used to improve human life if we use it in the right way. In *Walden Two*, we are shown a world where technology is used to make people better, more humane, creative, and even more individualistic. Skinner did not believe that individuality can exist apart from social development.

The title *Walden Two* suggests that Waldens like Thoreau's are somewhat romantic and impractical today. Skinner attempted to show us what technology can do when it is used wisely.

In *Walden Two*, the only unhappy person is Frazier, who is the conditioner of others. He is aware that he is in control, and whatever decisions he makes involve numerous conflicts. Skinner pointed out that one who is conditioned may not assent to or be aware that she is conditioned. We are all conditioned anyway, and we could even assist in our own conditioning. We do this when we reward ourselves for doing something right and punish ourselves for doing something wrong. The development of personal habits depends largely on conditioning techniques that we ourselves use.

Methods of Behaviorism

According to the behaviorist, teachers have many rewards or reinforcers at their disposal: praise, a smile, a touch, stars, candies, or what have you. In some schools, paper money or tokens are used as reinforcing mechanisms. Many people have questioned the use of such extrinsic rewards, but behaviorists claim they are only to be used in place of intrinsic ones that should be encouraged later. Studies indicate that rewards need not be given every time, for they can also be effective on an intermittent basis. One example might be a situation in which a child would be called upon three successive times to spell words but then would not be called upon again. We see the child raise a hand to answer the first question and answer it correctly. This is repeated for the second spelling word and the third. However, she is not to be called on again. The child may continue to raise a hand several times without being called upon. If we called upon the same child only occasionally, we could probably get as strong a response as if we called upon that child every time.

One might briefly describe a procedure for behavior modification in the ordinary classroom as follows: (1) specify the desired outcome, what needs to be changed, and how it will be evaluated; (2) establish a favorable environment by removing unfavorable stimuli that might complicate learning; (3) choose the proper reinforcers for desired behavioral manifestations; (4) begin shaping desired behavior by using immediate reinforcers for desired behavior; (5) once a pattern of desired behaviors has begun, slacken the number of times reinforcers are given; (6) evaluate results and reassess for future development.

Suppose, for example, that a student runs in the hallways, endangering other students and herself. For safety, the teacher wants to modify the behavior so that running ceases; the objective will be achieved when the student stops running. Investigation shows that the student runs partly because she must go all the way to the other end of the building for her next class and fears that the time for class change is too short. Also, she seems to like to run. The teacher works to get the student's class time shortened so she can be excused early. He begins to compliment the student when she does not run, and the student's classmates are less hostile toward her because she is not constantly bumping and jostling them in the hall. Because the student gets more positive reinforcement from her peers, the teacher finds it less necessary to compliment her. In addition, the student finds that she can make it to class on time if she does not dawdle, even without extra time. Finally, because she now finds walking more rewarding than running, extrinsic reinforcers are no longer needed or can be reduced.

Evaluation by the teacher shows that the desired behavior has been fairly well achieved and that it may eventually be possible to stop all external reinforcers. This does not mean that the teacher loses interest in the problem, for he may check periodically to see if the student's desired behavior is being continued. One might also observe that this approach has reinforced the teacher's behavior. The positive success reinforces the teacher to use this technique in similar instances.

Teaching machines

Skinner thought that one of the most effective kinds of instruction may be done through the use of teaching machines, including small computers. He is often referred to as the "father of the teaching machine" and has done significant research in this area. One type of machine may ask "Who was the first president of the United States?" There is a place for students to write in their answer, and their answer appears under a glass case at the top of the machine when they push a button. The students can then check their answer against the machine; if they answered correctly, they are rewarded by the machine, which reinforces them to remember the answer.

The questions in a teaching machine are interrelated and are usually arranged in sequences of increasing complexity. Skinner thought that learning should take place in small steps and succeeding questions should have some relationship to the preceding ones. He preferred that students have nothing but success. They should simply go on if they miss a question or two. If they miss too many questions, then they probably do not belong on that particular program. Some of the early teaching machines rewarded the children with candy or spoke to them, but recent studies indicate that getting the right answer is often reward enough.

Other more sophisticated teaching machines and computers are designed primarily for adults. One machine has a large amount of material on microfilm that the student must read. After reading the material, the student is asked to choose one of several possible answers. If the correct answer is chosen, one goes on to the next frame. If the wrong answer is chosen, however, there are two contrasting views about what should happen. Skinner thought that to make the student repeat the materials is too much punishment and that if one misses the answer the machine should still go on to the next frame. Other behaviorists, such as S. J. Pressey, maintain that repeating the material is not too much punishment and that the student should get the right answer before the machine moves to the next frame. Some machines make this process as painless as possible, and if the student presses the wrong button, the machine will go to a frame that tells why the wrong answer was selected and then refer back to the material to be reread.

Some teaching machines are also "branching" machines; that is, they contain programs for average, slow, and bright students. A student who completes exercises one through ten without making a mistake may be able to skip the next ten lessons because they are repetitious. A student who makes a single mistake will have to do the next ten, and one who makes two mistakes may be referred to a remedial program before beginning at lesson one again.

According to the behaviorists, the advantages of machine learning are many: immediate reinforcement is given, the programmed material is written by competent people, and the learning takes place in many small steps so that the student can avoid making mistakes. One major objection to the teaching machine is that while it might be good in teaching factual material, it cannot teach material of a more conceptual or creative nature. Skinner disputes this and claims that we can develop programs to teach very complicated ideas as well as create machines that provide reinforcement every time the child gives what is considered a more creative answer.

Behavioral engineering has many implications for modern education and raises many important philosophical questions regarding control and democratic procedures. Its increasing application and apparent effectiveness, however, may make it a vital force in the educational process. Nothing seems to bring out more ire among educators than a discussion of behavioral engineering as applied to education. Skinner was always interested in education, wrote about it, spoke to educational groups, and did pioneering work in the field. In one interview, he remarked that he had planned to put more about education in *Walden Two* but had misplaced the section he had written on it.

Skinner's views about education must be seen as an integral part of his overall views concerning the individual and society. He believed that education must be seen not simply as giving people information but as a controlling power over people's lives. Many have related Skinner's ideas to those of Aldous Huxley (*Brave New World*) and George Orwell (*1984*). Although Skinner maintained that his ideas about conditioning are different and more humanitarian, he did not deny that the forces for control (as discussed by Huxley and Orwell) exist.

We might even be inclined to think, if we observe modern life closely, that many of the things discussed by Huxley and Orwell have existed for some time. Some of the things in *1984*, such as video cameras to watch people's daily lives, have been used in industry, education, and government. Skinner is not so much opposed to the controls that have been developed or proposed as to the misuse of them.

Today, we can see wide varieties of behavioral techniques already in use. All of these methods rest essentially on a particular theory: we first determine the kind of behavior we want, and then we get it repeated by reinforcing it through various rewards. In classrooms, the same process may be employed by using praise or tangible rewards, such as candy or tokens. Some educators seriously question the use of such rewards, but behavioral engineers argue that they are to be used sparingly and only to the point where the student learns to reward herself without outside tangible rewards. One finds, for example, tangible rewards used with special education students, who are rewarded for staying in their seats for a certain time or doing a particular amount of work. Carl Bereiter and Siegfried Engelmann have used behavioral techniques with disadvantaged students who supposedly have poor learning abilities. Other psychologists have used such techniques for purposes ranging from toilet training to piloting aircraft. The essential thing about any of these techniques, however, is that whatever reward is used should be systematic and immediate. Skinner and others believe that a primary problem with most education at present is a definite lack of immediate reinforcement.

In recent years, there has been a shift away from mechanistic, passive models of behavior modification to ones that emphasize self-management and the active role of the participants in shaping their own behavior. Earlier Watsonian or Skinnerian models utilized a "person as machine" approach in which manipulation of the environment was the critical factor. Today, many behaviorists are concentrating on the environment–organism interplay whereby the subject contributes to her own treatment. This can be done in part by training people to become better problem solvers and analysts of their own condition.

What this points to is that many behaviorists now concentrate on "processes in the head"—that is, people's belief systems, thinking, and self-control. Individuals can be induced to study their own behavior, detect elements of danger, and take appropriate steps to prevent negative actions from taking place or at least to mitigate their effects. This approach might well remind one of the Lockean notion of the mind as a passive receiver versus Kant's notion of the mind as an active agent in the transformation of ideas. Thus, many behaviorists now study the philosophical question of how we think and how thinking in turn shapes our behavior.

This recent approach to behavior modification is characterized by an emphasis on the inner person. "Cognitive theory" stresses the human qualities in people and says that people can change their lives through their own thinking, creativity, and willpower. Many destructive and upsetting emotions and behaviors are caused by what people believe of themselves. A mentally healthy person is one who has an accurate perception of things and who can act intelligently on the basis of such perceptions.

Those who promote a cognitive approach insist that it is a more "humanistic" method because it looks at the individual not as a passive mechanism to be manipulated by the environment but as a thinking, willful, emotional being. One's existence can be shaped by the power of one's own thinking and thus not controlled by divine power, unconscious drives, or demons. Individuals can shape their own destiny and improve and create themselves through their own power. It is in using this power that they best express what it is to be human.

CRITIQUE OF BEHAVIORISM IN EDUCATION

Interest in the use of behavioral engineering has been steadily increasing in many walks of life. Business, churches, the military, and schools have felt its impact, and it is becoming more and more prevalent for such institutions to assess growth by their success with behavioral techniques.

Probably the most outstanding feature of this approach is that it is "scientific." It is based on a great deal of research, and researchers can point to measurable success with this method. It has been increasingly used in education since the 1960s, and many educators are zealous supporters of behavioral techniques that they are using in their classrooms. In such areas as special education, teachers find the concept of immediate reinforcement particularly useful in controlling and directing children with motor and mental handicaps. Even within the ordinary classroom, however, one hears about candies, a token economy, and positive and negative reinforcements as effective aids in the educational process. Skinner's air crib, designed as a behavior-reinforcing mechanism for the early life of the child, has been used by some parents in an effort to influence child behavior at the earliest stages of life.

Behaviorism's popularity arose because its techniques seem to work when so many other approaches fail. Furthermore, the approach used by many behavioral engineers, Skinner in particular, tries to avoid any aversive methods of education, and this fact appeals to many modern educators. Children also seem to respond well to a method that provides both incentives and rewards for their achievements. Teaching machines are popular with some teachers and students and are effective and efficient ways of imparting knowledge in a given area, with the range of areas steadily increasing.

Behavioral engineers suggest the use of their methods not only in education but in social life as well. Skinner, for example, took the possibilities of his theories into the area of social and cultural reform. He saw behavioral engineering as applicable on a global scale, maintaining that it is possible to solve problems of hunger, warfare, and economic upheaval if we will do so through the development of a technology of behavior.

Many people scoff at Skinner's recommendations and launch vitriolic attacks on his theories, particularly where he held that the individual has no inherent freedom and dignity. They say that if his suggestions are followed, Orwell's *1984* will be a certainty. Skinner replied that his theory is perhaps the only hope for survival in our technologically complex age. We have come to the point where we can no longer afford the old luxuries of self-centeredness, violence as a way of life, the wealth of a few at the expense of the many, and the old philosophical and theological notions about the human being's inner makeup that support these old luxuries.

Freedom and dignity in the old sense are emotive ideas that generate strong support, but Skinner maintained that these ideas are too often used for hiding a multitude of sins. Aggressiveness, for example, is often said to be a part of the human being's inner makeup and nothing can be done about it because "you can't change human nature." Skinner considered such easy escapes and superficial assumptions regrettable. The net result is to give up before we begin because aggressiveness is a learned behavior and can be unlearned or extinguished if we take an intelligent approach in controlling it.

Many critics charge that Skinner's theories belittle and limit humanity, but there is a strong argument that his views are optimistic, holding the promise that we can become practically anything through proper behavioral engineering. From the Skinnerian standpoint, little in people's inner makeup limits development in a variety of creative ways. For these reasons, the Skinnerians maintain that it is possible to build the good society with good people in the foreseeable future if we have the fortitude to plan and cooperate in this venture. When all is said and done, the controls will be on the environment, on the contingencies of reinforcement; in this way, individuals are indirectly controlled. While some critics see Skinner's *Walden Two* as the kind of Brave New World Huxley wrote about, Skinner maintained that it is an idealization of the behaviorally engineered society, where happiness and good will prevail.

Behavioral techniques are successful in the laboratory, but legitimate questions may be raised about their applicability to human society, where so many variables and unknowns exist. In the laboratory, rigorous control can be maintained, but control is difficult in the rough-and-tumble out-of-doors world. Behaviorists are probably on soundest grounds when they are dealing with the step-by-step procedures of learning. It is certainly reasonable to construct a theory that ignores or discounts human inner nature because such a theory may open up new insights into the study of human beings. It may work and work beautifully, but this still does not mean that there may not be innate human capacities or characteristics that are being overlooked. Skinner said that "no theory destroys what it is a theory about," and this idea cuts both ways. To say that the individual has no inner freedom and dignity does not destroy such inner freedom and dignity if they do exist.

While behaviorists make some questionable assumptions about human beings, they also make them about the nature of the universe. One assumption undergirding much of their thinking is that the universe operates mechanistically. They view the scheme of things as orderly, regular, predictable, and thus controllable. Serious questions have been raised as to whether the universe operates this way or whether behaviorists impose this notion of order upon the inscrutable face of the universe. This penchant for order and regularity is most noticeable in behaviorists' efforts to develop a technology of behavior patterns. They may be trying to make an exacting approach out of something based on highly questionable assumptions. This drive for exactness seems to be modeled after the physical sciences, but there are those knowledgeable in the physical sciences who maintain that exactness is much overrated even within their disciplines. In other words, behaviorists may be constructing their theory on the shifting sands of the quest for certainty.

One of the most glaring weaknesses critics point to is the social-policy recommendations of behaviorists, such as Skinner. They may be on solid ground when they are describing how learning takes place or how behavior is altered in small, sequential steps in the laboratory or classroom. But when they take the quantum leap from the laboratory to broad social, political, and economic conditions, critics begin to flinch. Skinner recommends a group of planners and controllers for the reshaping of the individual and society, but there does not seem to be sufficient and systematic work to back up such a recommendation. The controllers sound very much like the psychologist in the laboratory, but again, there is much difference between the laboratory and society at large. History is replete with examples of individuals and groups who thought that they and only they could lead society in the proper direction. History is also replete with the disastrous effects of such thinking. In so many respects, there seems to be little difference between deriving the powers of government from divine authority, the laws of dialectical material- ism, or the laws of behavior.

One recurring question is "Who controls the controllers?" Skinner maintained that the controlled exert influence over the controllers, just as the behavior of schoolchildren affects the teacher's behavior. In other words, the directions of the behavior of the controlled set the conditions to which the controllers react. This argument seems weak because the initiative is loaded in favor of the controllers, who have social, political, intellectual, and eco- nomic power concentrated in their hands. It seems predictable that the pow- erless of the Skinnerian society will be just as manipulated (even if "for their own good") as the powerless in any other authoritarian structure.

Although Skinner and other behaviorists strongly maintain that their aims and methods do not belittle us or eclipse inner feelings and purposes, the charge that their programs result in a robotization of humanity has some basis. Some critics feel that behaviorists ignore what is truly human in favor of a new, more mechanistic view of human nature. Frazier, the character Skinner depicted as the founder of *Walden Two*, says that he is the only unhappy one in the controlled society because he is the only one who was not reared there. Given the option of being Frazier, with all his frustrations, hopes, and fears, or the new engineered individual of *Walden Two*, who is in blissful ignorance of the controls exerted, many people would choose the former.

THE LEVIATHAN

Thomas Hobbes, the seventeenth-century English philosopher, was not a behaviorist, but his materialist philosophy contains many ideas central to behaviorism. The following selection is from Leviathan, or the Matter, Form, and Power of a Commonwealth Ecclesiastical and Civil, *first published in 1651. Hobbes thought that the human mind connects with environmental objects (the behaviorist's "stimuli") by way of the senses. Motion (or behavior) is both "vital" (inborn or genetic) and "acquired" (learned). His notions of "appetite" and "aversion" have close affinity with positive and negative reinforcement. Hobbes' belief that science and reason could be used to build the good society is akin to behavioral engineering. Finally, like such behaviorists as Skinner, Hobbes saw liberty or freedom as depending upon external conditions.*

The Introduction

Nature, the art whereby God has made and governs the world, is by the *art* of man, as in many other things, so in this also imitated—that it can make an artificial animal. For seeing life is but a motion of limbs, the beginning whereof is in some principal part within, why may we not say that all *automata* (engines that move themselves by springs and wheels as does a watch) have an artificial life? For what is the *heart* but a *spring*, and the *nerves* but so many *strings*, and the *joints* but so many *wheels* giving motion to the whole body such as was intended by the artificer? *Art* goes yet further, imitating that rational and most excellent work of nature, *man*. For by art is created that great LEVIATHAN called a COMMONWEALTH or STATE—in Latin, Civitas—which is but an artificial man, though of greater stature and strength than the natural, for whose protection and defense it was intended. . . .

Of Sense

Concerning the thoughts of man, I will consider them first singly and afterwards in train or dependence upon one another. Singly, they are every one a *representation* or *appearance* of some quality or other accident of a body without us which is commonly called an *object.*

Which object works on the eyes, ears, and other parts of a man's body, and by diversity of working produces diversity of appearances.

The original of them all is that which we call sense, for there is no conception in a man's mind which has not at first, totally or by parts, been begotten upon the organs of sense. The rest are derived from that original. . . .

The cause of sense is the external body or object which presses the organ proper to each sense, either immediately as in the taste and touch, or mediately as in seeing, hearing, and smelling; which pressure, by the mediation of the nerves and other strings and membranes of the body continued inward to the brain and heart, causes there a resistance or counterpressure or endeavor of the heart to deliver itself, which endeavor, because *outward*, seems to be some matter without. And this *seeming or fancy* is that which men call *sense*, and consists, as to the eye, in a *light* or *color figured*; to the ear, in a *sound*; to the nostril, in an *odor*; to the tongue and palate, in a *savor*; and to the rest of the body, in *heat, cold, hardness, softness,* and such other qualities as we discern by *feeling*. All which qualities, called *sensible*, are in the object that causes them but so many several motions of the matter by which it presses our organs diversely. Neither in us that are pressed are they anything else but divers motions, for motion produces nothing but motion. But their appearance to us is fancy, the same waking that dreaming. And as pressing, rubbing or striking the eye makes us fancy a light, and pressing the ear produces a din, so do the bodies also we see or hear produce the same by their strong, though unobserved, action. For if those colors and sounds were in the bodies or objects that cause them, they could not be severed from them as by glasses, and in echoes by reflection, we see they are, where we know the thing we see is in one place, the appearance in another. And though at some certain distance the real and very object seem invested with the fancy it begets in us, yet still the object is one thing, the image or fancy is another. So that sense, in all cases, is nothing else but original fancy, caused, as I have said, by the pressure—that is, by the motion—of external things upon our eyes, ears, and other organs thereunto ordained. . . .

Of Reason and Science

. . . [It] appears that reason is not, as sense and memory, born with us, nor gotten by experience only, as prudence is, but attained by industry: first in apt imposing of names, and secondly by getting a good and orderly method in proceeding from the elements, which are names, to assertions made by connection of one of them to another, and so to syllogisms, which are the connections of one assertion to another, till we come to a knowledge of all the consequences of names appertaining to the subject in hand; and that is it men call SCIENCE. And whereas sense and memory are but knowledge of fact, which is a thing past and irrevocable, *science* is the knowledge of consequences and dependence of one fact upon another, by which out of that we can presently do we know how to do something else when we will, or the like another time; because when we see how anything comes about, upon what causes and by what manner, when the like causes come into our power we see how to make it produce the like effects. . . .

To conclude, the light of human minds is perspicuous words, but by exact definitions first snuffed and purged from ambiguity; *reason* is the *pace*; increase of *science*, the *way*; and the benefit of mankind, the *end*. . . .

Of The Interior Beginnings of Voluntary Motions Commonly Called the Passions. . .

There be in animals two sorts of *motions* peculiar to them: one called *vital*, begun in generation and continued without interruption through their whole life—such as are the *course* of the *blood*, the *pulse*, the *breathing*, the *concoction, nutrition, excretion*, etc.—to which motions there needs no help of imagination; the other is *animal motion*, otherwise called *voluntary motion*—as to *go*, to *speak*, to *move* any of our limbs in such manner as is first fancied in our minds. That sense is motion in the organs and interior parts of man's body caused by the action of the things we see, hear, etc., and that fancy is but the relics of the same motion remaining after sense, has been already said in the first and second chapters. And because *going, speaking*, and the like voluntary motions depend always upon a precedent thought of *whither, which way*, and *what*, it is evident that the imagination is the first internal beginning of all voluntary motion. And although unstudied men do not conceive any motion at all to be there where the thing moved is invisible or the space it is moved in is, for the shortness of it, insensible, yet that does not hinder but that such motions are. For let a space be never so little, that which is moved over a greater space, whereof that little one is part, must first be moved over that. These small beginnings of motion within the body of man, before they appear in walking, speaking, striking, and other visible actions, are commonly called endeavor.

This endeavor, when it is toward something which causes it, is called appetite or desire, the latter being the general name and the other oftentimes restrained to signify the desire of food, namely *hunger* and *thirst*. And when the endeavor is fromward something, it is generally called AVERSION. These words, *appetite* and *aversion,* we have from the Latins; and they both of them signify the motions, one of approaching, the other of retiring. . . . For nature itself does often press upon men those truths which afterwards, when they look for somewhat beyond nature, they stumble at. . . .

That which men desire they are also said to LOVE, and to HATE those things for which they have aversion. So that desire and love are the same thing, save that by desire we always signify the absence of the object, by love most commonly the presence of the same. So also by aversion we signify the absence, and by hate the presence of the object.

Of appetites and aversions, some are born with men, as appetite of food, appetite of excretion, and exoneration, which may also and more properly be called aversions from somewhat they feel in their bodies; and some other appetites, not many. The rest, which are appetites of particular things, proceed from experience and trial of their effects upon themselves or other men. For of things we know not at all, or believe not to be, we can have no further desire than to taste and try. But aversion we have for things, not only which we know have hurt us, but also that we do not know whether they will hurt us or not.

Those things which we neither desire nor hate we are said to *contemn,* CONTEMPT being nothing else but an immobility or contumacy of the heart in resisting the action of certain things; and proceeding from that the heart is already moved otherwise by other more potent objects or from want of experience of them.

And because the constitution of a man's body is in continual mutation, it is impossible that all the same things should always cause in him the same appetites and aversions; much less can all men consent in the desire of almost any one and the same object.

But whatsoever is the object of any man's appetite or desire, that is it which he for his part calls *good;* and the object of his hate and aversion, *evil;* and of his contempt, *vile* and *inconsiderable.* For these words of good, evil, and contemptible are ever used with relation to the person that uses them, there being nothing

simply and absolutely so, nor any common rule of good and evil to be taken from the nature of the objects themselves—but from the person of the man, where there is no commonwealth, or, in a commonwealth, from the person that represents it, or from an arbitrator or judge whom men disagreeing shall by consent set up and make his sentence the rule thereof.

As in sense that which is really within us is, as I have said before, only motion caused by the action of external objects, but in appearance to the sight light and color, to the ear sound, to the nostril odor, etc., so when the action of the same object is continued from the eyes, ears, and other organs to the heart, the real effect there is nothing but motion or endeavor, which consists in appetite or aversion to or from the object moving. But the appearance or sense of that motion is that we either call *delight* or *trouble of mind.*

This motion, which is called appetite, and for the appearance of it *delight* and *pleasure,* seems to be a corroboration of vital motion and a help thereunto; and therefore such things as caused delight were not improperly called *jucunda, à juvando,* from helping or fortifying, and the contrary, *molesta, offensive,* from hindering and troubling the motion vital.

Pleasure, therefore, or *delight* is the appearance or sense of good; and *molestation* or *displeasure* the appearance or sense of evil. And consequently all appetite, desire, and love is accompanied with some delight more or less, and all hatred and aversion with more or less displeasure and offense.

Of pleasures or delights, some arise from the sense of an object present, and those may be called *pleasures of sense*—the word *sensual,* as it is used by those only that condemn them, having no place till there be laws. Of this kind are all onerations and exonerations of the body, as also all that is pleasant in the *sight, hearing, smell, taste,* or *touch.* Others arise from the expectation that proceeds from foresight of the end or consequence of things, whether those things in the sense please or displease. And these are *pleasures of the mind* of him that draws those consequences, and are generally called JOY. In the like manner, displeasures are some in the sense, and called PAIN; others in the expectation of consequences, and are called GRIEF.

These simple passions called *appetite, desire, love, aversion, hate, joy,* and *grief* have their names for divers considerations diversified. As first, when they one succeed another, they are diversely called from the opinion men have of the likelihood of attaining what they desire. Secondly, from the object loved or hated. Thirdly, from the consideration of many of them together. Fourthly, from the alteration or succession itself.

Of The Virtues Commonly Called Intellectual. . .

Virtue generally, in all sorts of subjects, is somewhat that is valued for eminence, and consists in comparison. For if all things were equal in all men, nothing would be prized. And by *virtues intellectual* are always understood such abilities of the mind as men praise, value, and desire should be in themselves and go commonly under the name of a *good wit,* though the same word *wit* be used also to distinguish one certain ability from the rest.

These *virtues* are of two sorts: *natural* and *acquired.* By natural, I mean not that which a man has from his birth for that is nothing else but sense, wherein men differ so little one from another and from brute beasts as it is not to be reckoned among virtues. But I mean that *wit* which is gotten by use only and experience, without method, culture, or instruction. This NATURAL WIT consists principally in two things: *celerity of imagining*—that is, swift succession of one thought to another—*and steady direction* to some approved end. On the contrary, a slow imagination makes that defect or fault of the mind which is commonly called DULLNESS, *stupidity,* and sometimes by other names that signify slowness of motion or difficulty to be moved.

And this difference of quickness is caused by the difference of men's passions that love and dislike, some one thing, some another; and therefore some men's thoughts run one way,

some another, and are held to and observe differently the things that pass through their imagination. And . . . in this succession of men's thoughts there is nothing to observe in the things they think on but either in what they be *like one another* or in what they be *unlike,* or *what they serve for* or *how they serve to such a purpose.* . . .

As for *acquired wit*—I mean acquired by method and instruction—there is none but reason, which is grounded on the right use of speech and produces the sciences. . . .

The causes of this difference of wits are in the passions, and the difference of passions proceeds partly from the different constitution of the body and partly from different education. For if the difference proceeded from the temper of the brain and the organs of sense, either exterior or interior, there would be no less difference of men in their sight, hearing, or other senses than in their fancies and discretions. It proceeds, therefore, from the passions, which are different not only from the difference of men's complexions, but also from their difference of customs and education.

The passions that most of all cause the difference of wit are principally the more or less desire of power, of riches, of knowledge, and of honor. All which may be reduced to the first— that is, desire of power. For riches, knowledge, and honor are but several sorts of power.

And therefore a man who has no great passion for any of these things but is, as men term it, indifferent, though he may be so far a good man as to be free from giving offense, yet he cannot possibly have either a great fancy or much judgment. For the thoughts are to the desires as scouts and spies, to range abroad and find the way to the things desired, all steadiness of the mind's motion, and all quickness of the same, proceeding from thence; for as to have no desire is to be dead, so to have weak passions is dullness. . . .

Of The First and Second Natural Laws. . .

The RIGHT OF NATURE, which writers commonly call *jus naturale,* is the liberty each man has to use his own power, as he will himself, for the preservation of his own nature—that is to say, of his own life—and consequently of doing anything which, in his own judgment and reason, he shall conceive to be the aptest means thereunto.

By LIBERTY is understood, according to the proper signification of the word, the absence of external impediments; which impediments may oft take away part of a man's power to do what he would, but cannot hinder him from using the power left him according as his judgment and reason shall dictate to him.

A LAW OF NATURE, *lex naturalis*, is a precept or general rule, found out by reason, by which a man is forbidden to do that which is destructive of his life or takes away the means of preserving the same and to omit that by which he thinks it may be best preserved. For though they that speak of this subject use to confound *jus* and *lex*, *right* and *law*, yet they ought to be distinguished; because RIGHT consists in liberty to do or to forbear, whereas LAW determines and binds to one of them; so that law and right differ as much as obligation and liberty, which in one and the same matter are inconsistent. . . . Consequently it is a precept or general rule of reason *that every man ought to endeavor peace, as far as he has hope of obtaining it; and when he cannot obtain it, that he may seek and use all helps and advantages of war.* The first branch of which rule contains the first and fundamental law of nature, which is *to seek peace and follow it.* The second, the sum of the right of nature, which is, *by all means we can to defend ourselves.*

From this fundamental law of nature, by which men are commanded to endeavor peace, is derived this second law: *that a man be willing, when others are so too, as far forth as for peace and defense of himself he shall think it necessary, to lay down this right to all things, and be contended with so much liberty against other men as he would allow other men against himself.* For as long as every man holds this right of doing anything he likes, so long are all men in the condition of war. But if other men will not lay down their right as well as he, then there is no reason for anyone to divest himself of his, for that were to expose himself to prey, which no man is bound to, rather than to dispose himself to peace. This is that law of the gospel: *whatsoever you require that others should do to you, that do ye to them.*

Source: Thomas Hobbes, *Leviathan, Parts I and II*, edited by Herbert W. Schneider. New York: The Liberal Arts Press, copyright © 1958, pp. 23, 25–26, 49, 50–55, 64, 68, 109–110. Reprinted by permission of The Bobbs-Merrill Company.

· · · · · · · · · · S K I N N E R · · · · · · · · · ·

BEYOND FREEDOM AND DIGNITY

Of all the behaviorists, Skinner has probably been the most important. Following the leads of Pavlov and Watson, he constructed a science of behavior based on operant conditioning. While much of his work was based on laboratory experiments, he took considerable pains to discuss the social and political consequences of his theory. In the following selection, Skinner argues against traditional notions of the freedom and dignity of the human being, views that are often supported by various philosophies. His claim is that such notions can be socially harmful, particularly the notions of permissiveness championed by some philosophical and educational schools of thought. At the same time, his rejection of permissiveness does not imply resort to punishment; instead, he argues for control based on the principles of a technology of behavior.

Those who champion freedom and dignity do not, of course, confine themselves to punitive measures, but they turn to alternatives with diffidence and timidity. Their concern for autonomous man commits them to only ineffective measures, several of which we may now examine. . . .

A method of modifying behavior without appearing to exert control is represented by Socrates' metaphor of the midwife: one person helps another give birth to behavior. Since the midwife plays no part in conception and only a small part in parturition, the person who gives birth to the behavior may take full credit for it. Socrates demonstrated the art of midwifery, or maieutics, in education. He pretended to show how an uneducated slave boy could be led to prove Pythagoras' theorem for doubling the square. The boy assented to the steps in the proof, and Socrates claimed that he did so without being told—in other words, that he "knew" the theorem in some sense all along. Socrates contended that even ordinary knowledge could be drawn out in the same way since the soul knew the truth and needed only to be shown that it knew it. The episode is often cited as if it were relevant to modern educational practice. . . .

Intellectual, therapeutic, and moral midwifery is scarcely easier than punitive control, because it demands rather subtle skills and concentrated attention, but it has its advantages. It seems to confer a strange power on the practitioner. Like the cabalistic use of hints and allusions, it achieves results seemingly out of proportion to the measures employed. The apparent contribution of the individual is not reduced, however. He is given full credit for knowing before he learns, for having within him the seeds of good mental health, and for being able to enter into direct communication with God. An important advantage is that the practitioner avoids responsibility. Just as it is not the midwife's fault if the baby is stillborn or deformed, so the teacher is exonerated when the student fails, the psychotherapist when the patient does not solve his problem, and the mystical religious leader when his disciples behave badly.

Maieutic practices have their place. Just how much help the teacher should give the student as he acquires new forms of behavior is a delicate question. The teacher should wait for the student to respond rather than rush to tell him what he is to do or say. As Comenius put it, the more the teacher teaches, the less the student learns. The student gains in other ways. In general, we do not like to be told either what we already know or what we are unlikely ever to know well or to good effect. We do not read books if we are already thoroughly familiar with the material or if it is so completely unfamiliar that it is likely to remain so. We read books which help us say things we are on the verge of saying anyway but cannot quite say without help. We understand the author, although we could not have formulated what we understand before he put it into words. There are similar advantages for the patient in psychotherapy. Maieutic practices are helpful, too, because they exert more control than is usually acknowledged and some of it may be valuable.

These advantages, however, are far short of the claims made. Socrates' slave boy learned nothing; there was no evidence whatever that he could have gone through the theorem by himself afterward. And it is as true of maieutics as of permissiveness that positive results must be credited to unacknowledged controls of other sorts. If the patient finds a solution without the help of his therapist, it is because he has been exposed to a helpful environment elsewhere.

Another metaphor associated with weak practices is horticultural. The behavior to which a person has given birth grows, and it may be guided or trained, as a growing plant is trained. Behavior may be "cultivated."

The metaphor is particularly at home in education. A school for small children is a child-garden, or kindergarten. The behavior of the child "develops" until he reaches "maturity." A teacher may accelerate the process or turn it in slightly different directions, but—in the classical phrase—he cannot teach, he can only help the student learn. The metaphor of guidance is also common in psychotherapy.

Freud argued that a person must pass through several developmental stages, and that if the patient has become "fixated" at a given stage, the therapist must help him break loose and move forward. Governments engage in guidance—for example, when they encourage the "development" of industry through tax exemptions or provide a "climate" that is favorable to the improvement of race relations.

Guidance is not as easy as permissiveness, but it is usually easier than midwifery, and it has some of the same advantages. One who merely guides a natural development cannot easily be accused of trying to control it. Growth remains an achievement of the individual, testifying to his freedom and worth, his "hidden propensities," and as the gardener is not responsible for the ultimate form of what he grows, so one who merely guides is exonerated when things go wrong.

Guidance is effective, however, only to the extent that control is exerted. To guide is either to open new opportunities or to block growth in particular directions. To arrange an opportunity is not a very positive act, but it is nevertheless a form of control if it increases the likelihood that behavior will be emitted. The teacher who merely selects the material the student is to study or the therapist who merely suggests a different job or change of scene has exerted control, though it may be hard to detect.

Control is more obvious when growth or development is *prevented*. Censorship blocks access to material needed for development in a given direction; it closes opportunities. De Tocqueville saw this in the America of his day: "The will of man is not shattered, but softened, bent, and guided. Men are seldom forced ... to act, but they are constantly restrained from acting." As Ralph Barton Perry put it, "Whoever determines what alternatives shall be made known to man controls what that man shall choose *from*. He is deprived of freedom in proportion as he is denied access to *any* ideas, or is confined to any range of ideas short of the totality of relevant possibilities." For "deprived of freedom" read "controlled."

It is no doubt valuable to create an environment in which a person acquires effective behavior rapidly and continues to behave effectively. In constructing such an environment we may eliminate distractions and open opportunities, and these are key points in the metaphor of guidance or growth or development; but it is the contingencies we arrange, rather than the unfolding of some predetermined pattern, which are responsible for the changes observed.

Jean-Jacques Rousseau was alert to the dangers of social control, and he thought it might be possible to avoid them by making a person dependent not on people but on things. In *Émile* he showed how a child could learn about things from the things themselves rather than from books. The practices he described are still common, largely because of John Dewey's emphasis on real life in the classroom.

One of the advantages in being dependent on things rather than on other people is that the time and energy of other people are saved. The child who must be reminded that it is time to go to school is dependent upon his parents, but the child who has learned to respond to clocks and other temporal properties of the world around him (not to a "sense of time") is dependent upon things, and he makes fewer demands on his parents. ...

Another important advantage of being dependent on things is that the contingencies which involve things are more precise and shape more useful behavior than contingencies arranged by other people. The temporal properties of the environment are more pervasive and more subtle than any series of reminders. A person whose behavior in driving a car is shaped by the response of the car behaves more skillfully than one who is following instructions. ...

But things do not easily take control. The procedures Rousseau described were not simple, and they do not often work. The complex contingencies involving things (including people who are behaving "unintentionally") can, unaided, have very little effect on an individual in his lifetime—a fact of great importance for reasons we shall note later. We must also remember that the control exercised by things may be destructive. The world of things can be tyrannical. Natural contingencies induce people to behave superstitiously, to risk greater and greater dangers, to work uselessly to exhaustion, and so on. Only the counter control exerted by a social environment offers any protection against these consequences.

Dependence on things is not independence. The child who does not need to be told that it is time to go to school has come under the control of more subtle, and more useful, stimuli. The child who has learned what to say and how to behave in getting along with other people is under the control of social contingencies. People who get along together well under the mild contingencies of approval and disapproval are controlled as effectively as (and in many ways more effectively than) the citizens of a police state. Orthodoxy controls through the establishment of rules, but the mystic is no freer because the contingencies which have shaped his behavior are more personal or idiosyncratic. Those who work productively because of the reinforcing value of what they produce are under the sensitive and powerful control of the products. Those who learn in the natural environment are under a form of control as powerful as any control exerted by a teacher.

A person never becomes truly self-reliant. Even though he deals effectively with things, he is necessarily dependent upon those who have taught him to do so. They have selected the things he is dependent upon and determined the kinds and degrees of dependencies. (They cannot, therefore, disclaim responsibility for the results.)

It is a surprising fact that those who object most violently to the manipulation of behavior nevertheless make the most vigorous efforts to manipulate minds. Evidently freedom and dignity are threatened only when behavior is changed by physically changing the environment. There appears to be no threat when the states of mind said to be responsible for behavior are changed, presumably because autonomous man possesses miraculous powers which enable him to yield or resist. . . .

Beliefs, preferences, perceptions, needs, purposes, and opinions are other possessions of autonomous man which are said to change when we change minds. What is changed in each case is a probability of action. A person's belief that a floor will hold him as he walks across it depends upon his past experience. If he has walked across it without incident many times, he will do so again readily, and his behavior will not create any of the aversive stimuli felt as anxiety. He may report that he has "faith" in the solidity of the floor or "confidence" that it will hold him, but the kinds of things which are felt as faith or confidence are not states of mind; they are at best by-products of the behavior in its relation to antecedent events, and they do not explain why a person walks as he does.

We build "belief" when we increase the probability of action by reinforcing behavior. When we build a person's confidence that a floor will hold him by inducing him to walk on it, we might not be said to be changing a belief, but we do so in the traditional sense when we give him verbal assurances that the floor is solid, demonstrate its solidity by walking on it ourselves, or describe its structure or state. The only difference is in the conspicuousness of the measures. The change which occurs as a person "learns to trust a floor" by walking on it is the characteristic effect of reinforcement; the change which occurs when he is told that the floor is solid, when he sees someone else walking on it, or when he is "convinced" by assurances that the floor will hold him depends upon past experiences which no longer make a conspicuous contribution. For example, a person who walks on surfaces which are likely to vary in their solidity (for example, a frozen lake) quickly forms a discrimination between surfaces on which others are walking and surfaces on which no one is walking, or between surfaces called safe and surfaces called dangerous. He learns to walk confidently on the first and cautiously on the second. The sight of someone walking on a surface or an assurance that it is safe converts it from the second class into the first. The history during which the discrimination was formed may be forgotten, and the effect then seems to involve that inner event called a change of mind.

Changes in preference, perceptions, needs, purposes, attitudes, opinions, and other attributes of mind may be analyzed in the same way. We change the way a person looks at something, as well as what he sees when he looks, by changing the contingencies; we do not change something called perception. We change the relative strengths of responses by differential reinforcement of alternative courses of action; we do not change something called a preference. We change the probability of an act by changing a condition of deprivation or aversive stimulation; we do not change a need. We reinforce behavior in particular ways; we do not give a person a purpose or an intention. We change behavior toward something, not an attitude toward it. We sample and change verbal behavior, not opinions.

Another way to change a mind is to point to reasons why a person should behave in a given way, and the reasons are almost always consequences which are likely to be contingent on behavior. Let us say that a child is using a knife in a dangerous way. We may avoid trouble by making the environment safer—by taking the knife away or giving him a safer kind—but that will not prepare him for a world with unsafe knives. Left alone, he may learn to use the knife properly by cutting himself whenever he uses it improperly. We may help by substituting a less dangerous form of punishment—spanking him, for example, or perhaps merely shaming him when we find him using a knife in a dangerous way. We may tell him that some uses are bad and others good if "Bad!" and "Good!" have already been conditioned as positive and negative reinforcers. Suppose, however, that all these methods have unwanted by-products, such as a change in his relation to us, and that we therefore decide to appeal to "reason." (This is possible, of course, only if he has reached the "age of reason.") We explain the contingencies, demonstrating what happens when one uses a knife in one way and not another. We may show him how rules may be extracted from the contingencies ("You should never cut *toward yourself*"). As a result we may induce the child to use the knife properly and will be likely to say that we have imparted a knowledge of its proper use. But we have had to take advantage of a great deal of prior conditioning with respect to instructions, directions, and other verbal stimuli, which are easily overlooked, and their contribution may then be attributed to autonomous man. A still more complex form of argument has to do with deriving new reasons from old, the process of deduction which depends upon a much longer verbal history and is particularly likely to be called changing a mind.

Ways of changing behavior by changing minds are seldom condoned when they are clearly effective, even though it is still a mind which is apparently being changed. We do not condone the changing of minds when the contestants are unevenly matched; that is "undue influence." Nor do we condone changing minds surreptitiously. If a person cannot see what the would-be changer of minds is doing, he cannot escape or counterattack; he is being exposed to "propaganda." "Brainwashing" is proscribed by those who otherwise condone the changing of minds simply because the control is obvious. A common technique is to build up a strong aversive condition, such as hunger or lack of sleep and, by alleviating it, to reinforce any behavior which "shows a positive attitude" toward a political or religious system. A favorable "opinion" is built up simply by reinforcing favorable statements. The procedure may not be obvious to those upon whom it is used, but it is too obvious to others to be accepted as an allowable way of changing minds.

The illusion that freedom and dignity are respected when control seems incomplete arises in part from the probabilistic nature of operant behavior. Seldom does any environmental condition "elicit" behavior in the all-or-nothing fashion of a reflex; it simply makes a bit of behavior more likely to occur. A hint will not itself suffice to evoke a response, but it adds strength to a weak response which may then appear. The hint is conspicuous, but the other events responsible for the appearance of the response are not.

Like permissiveness, maieutics, guidance, and building a dependence on things, changing a mind is condoned by the defenders of freedom and dignity because it is an ineffective way of changing behavior, and the changer of minds can therefore escape from the charge that he is controlling people. He is also exonerated when things go wrong. Autonomous man survives to be credited with his achievements and blamed for his mistakes. . . .

The freedom and dignity of autonomous man seem to be preserved when only weak forms of nonaversive control are used. Those who use them seem to defend themselves against the charge that they are attempting to control behavior, and they are exonerated when things go wrong. Permissiveness is the absence of control, and if it appears to lead to desirable results, it is only because of other contingencies. Maieutics, or the art of midwifery, seems to leave behavior to be credited to those who give birth to it, and the guidance of development to those who develop. Human intervention seems to be minimized when a person is made dependent upon things rather than upon other people. Various ways of changing behavior by changing minds are not only condoned but vigorously practiced by the defenders of freedom and dignity. There is a good deal to be said for minimizing current control by other people, but other measures still operate. A person who responds in acceptable ways to weak forms of control may have been changed by contingencies which are no longer operative. By refusing to recognize them the defenders of freedom and dignity encourage the misuse of controlling practices and block progress toward a more effective technology of behavior.

Source: B. F. Skinner, *Beyond Freedom and Dignity*. New York: Alfred A. Knopf, Inc. Copyright © 1971 by B. F. Skinner. Reprinted by permission of Alfred A. Knopf, Inc.

SELECTED READINGS

Bereiter, C., and Engelmann, S. *Teaching Disadvantaged Children in the Preschool.* Englewood Cliffs, NJ: Prentice-Hall, 1966. This is a well-known attempt to develop behavioral techniques for use with disadvantaged children in preschool settings. While not basically philosophical in scope, the book shows how aspects of behaviorism can be applied to education.

Meichenbaum, Donald. *Cognitive-Behavior Modification.* New York: Plenum Press, 1977. This look at conditioning techniques takes into account more than simple environmental factors. Cognitive-behavioral modification includes not only organism-environment relations but also the ways in which the organism modifies and changes the environment through its belief system.

Pavlov, I. P. *Conditioned Reflexes.* London: Oxford University Press, 1927. Pavlov's work is a classic study of conditioning and has had great influence on the historical development of behaviorism.

Skinner, B. F. *Beyond Freedom and Dignity.* New York: Knopf, 1971. This book attacks the notion that freedom or dignity in its present forms are inherent or necessary for human fulfillment. It is a comprehensive exposition of the implications of Skinner's theories for individuals and society.

————. *Walden Two.* New York: Macmillan, 1948. Skinner presents a picture of what behavioral engineering might be like in communal form. It is a fictional treatise that has attracted a wide audience of readers from scientists to utopian-minded thinkers.

Thoresen, Carl E., ed. *Behavior Modification in Education. The Seventy-Second Yearbook of the National Society for the Study of Education, Part One.* Chicago: The National Society for the Study of Education, 1973. This volume is a readable collection of scholarly essays that offer critical analyses of behavior modification. They range from techniques of classroom teaching to a philosophical study of behaviorism.

7

Existentialism, Phenomenology, and Education

Existentialism is one of the newer modern philosophies; hence, it has had only recent application to educational theory and the problems of education. The roots of this philosophy may be traced as far back as the Sophists, but existentialism as such began with the works of Søren Kierkegaard and Friedrich Wilhelm Nietzsche in the nineteenth century. In the twentieth century, it was further developed by such figures as Martin Buber, Karl Jaspers, and Jean-Paul Sartre. Phenomenology is usually attributed to Edmund Husserl in the early twentieth century, and it was greatly extended by such figures as Martin Heidegger and Maurice Merleau-Ponty.

Although there are differences between existentialism and phenomenology, the two have much in common. Sartre, as much as anyone, was identified with existentialism, yet he also wrote as a phenomenologist. Heidegger, who rejected the existentialist label, wrote philosophy that many existentialists have found compatible with their views. As these philosophies have been used in philosophy of education, they have been so closely allied that some advocates refer to their work as "existential phenomenology."

In philosophy of education, traditional philosophers consider questions about the nature of knowledge, truth, and meaning, while the existentialist is concerned with how these things are educationally significant within the lived experience of individuals. Phenomenologists see their inquiry more specifically focused on the phenomena of consciousness, the significance of education in perception, and the development of meaning in concrete individual experience.

EXISTENTIALIST PHILOSOPHERS AND THEIR THOUGHT

Existentialism offers a puzzling array of interpretations, so it is often difficult to sort out a consistent set of meanings. Part of this difficulty occurs because

243

it is such a new philosophy and is spread across so many different nationalities and cultural contexts. Its seemingly tortured and mixed varieties may be due to the very nature of the existentialist credo—the lonely, estranged, and alienated individual caught up in a meaningless and absurd world.

In some respects, the nature of individualism studied by existentialists was influenced by the works of Friedrich Wilhelm Nietzsche (1844–1900), a German philosopher. Nietzsche attempted to establish a new morality that went beyond traditional Judeo-Christian morality, for he felt that traditional morality had tamed us too much, making us weak. In *Thus Spake Zarathustra,* he explored the individual transcending conventional social values and becoming a "superman," a being beyond the confines of the conventional. This theme was expanded in *Beyond Good and Evil* and *Toward a Genealogy of Morals.* In *The Will to Power,* he explored the political ramifications of his ideas and favored a leadership of exceptional people who would create and define values for others, a position that Nazi Germany later tried to use to its advantage.

The difference between Nietzsche and the existentialists, however, is that existentialism displays a deep sense of moral reservation, even moral uncertainty, about individual responsibility. Rather than moral certitude and a drive to be a Nietzschean overlord, the individualism of existentialism is characterized by anxiety and a lack of definition and certainty. In order to understand what the existentialists themselves are attempting to say, we shall examine the particular thought systems of four representative existentialist philosophers: Kierkegaard, Buber, Heidegger, and Sartre.

Søren Kierkegaard (1813–1855)

Kierkegaard's childhood was spent in close association with his father, who demanded that his children excel in intellectual matters. Under the eye of his father, young Kierkegaard learned to act out the plots of literary works, became proficient in Latin and Greek, and developed the habit of pursuing ideas for intellectual satisfaction. As a young man, he studied Hegel and revolted against his systematization and adherence to a society-oriented outlook. Kierkegaard chose instead to search out individual truth by which he could live and die.

His ideas were largely passed over in his own time because of his eccentric views and his ascetic nature. For one thing, he was a devout Christian who attacked conventional Christianity with a vengeance, producing biting literary works, such as *Attack Upon Christendom.* For another, he believed that Christianity had become warped by modern times, for modern conventional Christianity seemed to perpetuate such human absurdities as war. Obviously, these views did not endear him to the religious establishment. He called for a "leap of faith" in which the modern individual would accept the Christian deity, even though there is no proof that such a God exists and even though there is no rational way to know Him. It is only through the "leap of faith" that one can begin to restructure one's life and truly live out the principles of Christianity.

Kierkegaard's category of philosophical study was the lonely individual against an objective and science-oriented world. He was acid in his criticism of science and what it has wrought, and he felt that it is the scientific penchant for objectivity that has largely driven modern society away from a viable Christian belief. People have embraced objectification, and this has led them to become group centered or, in the words of some contemporary American sociologists, "other-directed." Instead, Kierkegaard argued for the subjective individual who makes personal choices, eschewing the scientific demand for objective proof. This unfounded subjectivity calls for a "leap of faith" in which one must abandon reason and accept groundless belief.

Kierkegaard was not concerned with "being" in general but with individual human existence. He believed that we need to come to an understanding of our souls, our destiny, and the reality of God. He attacked Hegelian philosophy and other abstract speculation for depersonalizing individuals by tending to emphasize thought rather than the thinker. He believed that individuals are confronted with choices in life that they alone can make and for which they must accept complete responsibility. Kierkegaard described three stages on "life's road." The first is the aesthetic stage, where we live in sensuous enjoyment and where emotions are dominant. The second, the ethical stage, occurs when we arrive at the "universal human" and achieve understanding of our place and function in life. The third stage is the religious, which for Kierkegaard was the highest, where we stand alone before God.

There is an unbridgeable gulf between God and the world that we must somehow cross through faith. This takes passion, and passion is sorely lacking in modern life. We achieve such passion not through reflection but through understanding ourselves as creatures of God. Kierkegaard believed that education should be subjective and religious, devoted toward developing individuality and the individual's relationship with God. He opposed vocational and technical studies because they are directed primarily toward the secular world of objectivity.

Although Kierkegaard was largely ignored in his own time, his writings and thoughts were revived in the twentieth century because it was then that Kierkegaard's fears of an unchecked and raging objectification and technological revolution seem to have become largely realized. World wars, with their ever-increasing engines of death and destruction, characterized the twentieth century, and the rise of totalitarianism and loss of individuality seem to go along with this objectification. Thus, Kierkegaard's thought appears to many European and American intellectuals to point the finger most aptly at the true condition of the modern individual. Through the efforts of such thinkers, the word *existentialism* has gained familiarity with increasing numbers of people.

Martin Buber (1878–1965)

Martin Buber, the Israeli philosopher-theologian, was one who took Kierke-gaard seriously and began to develop his own system of thought. Although born and educated in Europe, Buber immigrated to Palestine to join in the attempt of the Jewish people to reclaim their homeland. Perhaps this strug-gle epitomized the human predicament for Buber, because his writings reflect the need for mutual respect and dignity among all human individuals. Buber's best-known book is *I and Thou*, a work that seeks to get at the heart of human relations.

In *I and Thou*, Buber described how the individual is capable of relating and identifying with the outside world. There is an objective relationship characterized as "I–It." In this relationship, one views something outside one-self in a purely objective manner, as a thing to be used and manipulated for selfish ends. One needs to look upon one's fellow human beings in terms of the "I–Thou" relation; that is, one must recognize that each and every indi-vidual has an intense, personal world of meaning. To the extent that this per-sonal or subjective reality of each individual is discounted or ignored, then human beings will continue to suffer from the absurdities in which they are caught. It is from the standpoint of I–It that inhumanity, death, and destruc-tion are foisted upon one person by another.

Buber found people treated as objects (Its) in business, religion, science, government, and education. Many students today feel that they are only social security numbers stored in a computer. In college classes of two hun-dred or more, it is not surprising that this concern becomes reinforced when the teacher cannot remember a student's name or perhaps not even know who is enrolled in the class. The teacher assigns material, marks papers, and gives grades; but student and teacher each go their own separate ways. When the students leave that class, they are replaced by other equally anonymous organisms. Buber did not feel that it had to be this way. In a proper relation-ship between teacher and student, there is a mutual sensibility of feeling: there is empathy. This is not a subject-to-object relationship as in an I–It rela-tionship but rather a subject-to-subject relationship—one in which there is a sharing of knowledge, feelings, and aspirations. It is a relationship in which each person involved is both teacher and learner, sharing in a personal way with the other. Buber believed that this kind of relationship should pervade the educational process at all levels as well as society at large.

Buber thought that a series of I–Thou relationships constitute a continu-um with humanity at one end and God at the other. People do not turn aside from the course of that life to find God. The divine and the human are relat-ed, and through one's communication with fellow human beings, one experi-ences a reciprocal subjectivity that makes life more spiritual. The existence of mutuality between God and humanity cannot be proven, just as God's exis-tence cannot be proven. Yet one's faith both in God and in one's fellow human beings is witness of one's devotion to a higher end.

Buber's humanism has had a profound impact on many thinkers, not only in philosophy and theology but in psychology, psychiatry, literature, and education. In fact, Buber was one of the few existentialists who wrote specifically about education, especially the nature of the relations between teacher and student. He was careful to point out that education, like many other areas, could also consist of an I–It relationship in which the student is treated as an object. What Buber really wanted was the kind of education where the teacher and student, while differing in kinds and amounts of knowledge, were on an equal footing in terms of humanity and where each person in the relationship is both teacher and learner. Buber believed that the most desirable educational situation is one where friendship–the epitome of an I–Thou relationship—can exist.

[handwritten margin note: Summary "I–thou" in Ed.]

Martin Heidegger (1889–1976)

Heidegger was born in Messkirch, Germany, and was reared in the Catholic faith. He spent much time wandering in the hills and woods of the Black Forest and later did much writing and thinking there. He attended the University of Freiburg, where he was influenced by Kantian philosophy and later by the teachings of the philosopher Edmund Husserl, who developed the philosophical method known as phenomenology. Heidegger adopted this methodology and extended its usage with *hermeneutics,* or the interpretation of lived experience. In his mature years, he became famous as a professor of philosophy at the University of Freiburg, where he taught many young philosophers, including Jean-Paul Sartre, who probably was his most renowned student. His teachings and works, particularly his major work, *Sein und Zeit (Being and Time)*, published in 1927, have influenced many philosophers.

Although Heidegger did not accept the label "existentialist" for his thought, many observers have credited him with extending existentialist thinking into new areas. On several occasions, he took pains to state that his major category of investigation was Being, and not the lonely, estranged individual. Be that as it may, Heidegger's starting point was what he called "being-in-the-world," or lived experience at the individual-environment (world) level. The individual existent is *Dasein;* Heidegger devotes considerable space to the analysis of dasein. Thus, although Heidegger's intent and purpose is to investigate Being, his analysis largely rests on the individual interpreting and constructing a personal world of meaning.

Individual existence, or being-in-the-world, consists of three basic aspects. The first of these is the individual experiencing the world as a surrounding environment (*Umwelt*). *Umwelt* is not just the physical environment in the objective sense; rather, it is the environment *as experienced* by the individual. Thus, umwelt is not strictly an objective experience. The second aspect of being-in-the-world is the experience of others, or fellow individuals

(*Mitwelt*). Mitwelt is the complicated ground of social relations; for not only does the individual experience others subjectively, but others are also subjectivities with their own personal viewpoints. The third aspect of being-in-the-world is that in which one becomes aware of oneself as a distinct and subjective existent (*Eigenwelt*). This is the intensely personal level encountered when one poses such a question as "Who am I?" It is in encountering such a fundamental question that the individual comes face to face with existential anguish and anxiety, for there is no apparent answer at the level of lived experience. No laws, guidelines, or objective reality automatically give us the answer: each person must answer the question as an individual.

This brief exposition of Heidegger's dasein analysis in no way does justice to his complex philosophy. In fact, he himself found it extremely difficult to find words adequate to describe the intricacies of Being from the standpoint of the individual existent, and he has been roundly criticized for the terminology and style in which he wrote. The weighty and intricate particular meanings he had to attach to such words as *dasein* and *eigenwelt* complicate any understanding of his thought. This complexity is further heightened for those who must read him in English translation, for one will encounter many words, such as *dasein*, that have no accurate English equivalent. Nonetheless, there is no substitute for a thorough study of Heidegger's works for those who wish to understand some of the ideas of this philosophical pioneer.

Heidegger did not write specifically about education, but his thought has a great deal of promise in helping the educator better understand the intense personal side of existence. The question "Who am I?" is a profound and troubling question, one that most of us face more or less in a blind panic during the adolescent years and one that is probably never fully answered. We might say that this condition lies at the heart of the identity crisis each person encounters at various times in his life.

Jean-Paul Sartre (1905–1980)

Of all the leading existentialist philosophers, probably the best known is Jean-Paul Sartre. Born in France, he was brought up in a home where he was encouraged to develop his intellectual talents. At a very early age he began to write, emphasizing the predicaments of the human condition. Influenced a great deal by his grandfather, who was a language teacher, Sartre himself aspired to become a teacher of philosophy. He was an excellent student, and after completing his education in France, he went to Germany where he studied with Martin Heidegger in the 1930s. He later settled in Paris, where he became a professor of philosophy.

At the same time, he pursued his literary ambitions, writing several novels and plays that became best sellers in Europe. But Sartre, like so many others, was caught up in the destructive web of World War II. He joined the French Army and was captured by the Germans early in the war. After the fall of France, he was allowed to return to Paris on parole, and it was there that he joined the underground French Resistance. The Nazis were brutal and swift in their punishment of captured Resistance fighters: men and women in the Resistance were constantly faced with instant death, and it was in this kind of situation that Sartre's thinking on the absurdity and meaninglessness of individual existence was sharpened.

Even in the face of the Nazi death machine, Sartre was able to write and publish a major philosophical work in 1943, *L'Être et le néant* (*Being and Nothingness*). It stands as one of the most original philosophical treatises to be written in the twentieth century, and it is Sartre's most thorough philosophical statement. It investigates consciousness (being-for-itself) and the objects of consciousness (being-in-itself). Consciousness, or being-for-itself, is the reflection and negation of the objective world. It is as if human consciousness tries to be its objects, as in the case of the self-conscious person who, in playing a role, literally tries to be the other person, or the "dedicated" teacher who tries to be the essence of all teachers. Such attempts, of course, are always failures; for consciousness, or individuality, cannot really be what it is not. Being-for-itself always transcends, negates, or goes beyond being-in-itself. This means that human consciousness or individuality is free. In a sense, it could be said that consciousness deals with the *meaning* of things and not with *raw* objectivity or things-in-themselves.

In his philosophical works, Sartre viewed the human predicament in terms of the lonely individual in an absurd world. He viewed human existence as primarily meaningless, for we are thrown into the world totally without meaning and any meaning that we encounter in the world we must construct ourselves. The development of meaning is an individual matter, and since both the world and the individual are without meaning, we have no justification for existing. There is no God to give existence meaning (Sartre was an atheist), nor is there any realm of ideas or independent physical reality with its own independent and immutable meaning. Humanity, individually and collectively, exists without any meaning or justification except what we ourselves make.

Sartre's point of view is very austere, at least when compared with, say, idealism or realism, and it is very pessimistic when compared with pragmatism. Yet it would be an error to take this notion too far. Sartre stated that "existence precedes essence" and meant that if we are indeed without meaning when we are born, we can fashion our own meaning in the world in any way we see fit. According to Sartre, if there is no God, no First Cause, then there is nothing to prevent us from becoming whatever we desire because there is no predetermined self or essence.

The same can be said for physical reality and science, for Sartre saw science as a human creation, no better or no worse in and of itself than any other creation. Thus, when we step back and view ourselves as we really are, we see that *nothing* determines us to do anything; for all the absolutes, rules, and restrictions are simply the puny and absurd creations of humans. If there are no primal restrictions, then there is no determinism. Everything is possi-

ble. Humanity is absolutely free; or as Sartre put it in his characteristic terminology, "man is condemned to be free."

Human freedom is awesome, for if we are totally free, we are also totally
responsible for our choices and actions. In other words, we cannot do something and then claim it was God's will, or was caused by the laws of science,
or that society made us do it. We are free; therefore we are totally responsible. We have no excuse, as Sartre tried to show in his play, *No Exit*.

If one thinks seriously about this existentialist proposition, he may come
to understand that human existence is a sword that cuts two ways. Existence
today may be characterized by war, disease, hunger, or starvation on the part of
many and conspicuous consumption on the part of a few. There is ignorance,
racial strife, and a host of the most severe and depressing conditions that make
up the human predicament, but who is responsible? Is it God? Is it the law of
supply and demand? National honor? No. People themselves are responsible.
If we can create war, we can also create peace. And if we can, through absurd
economics, create conditions of starvation by allowing a few individuals to control the wealth of a country, we can also likewise redistribute the wealth so that
no one need starve. In other words, if we are the creators of our ills, we can also
create a better and more humane way of living. It is up to us. All we have to do
is make our choices and act accordingly. However, these choices and actions
are not easy; for if we attempt to change these conditions, those who benefit
from them will resist us. Sartre did not disregard existing society and customs,
for he was well aware that many individuals do not see anything wrong with
war, or the surplus controlled by a few, or even starvation.

We may argue that while all of this is true, we do have to contend with
nature and scientific law. Sartre would answer by pointing out that "nature,"
"law," and "science" are themselves meanings created by humans. We may
then object that while this is true for science and scientific laws, surely we
cannot ignore nature, our oldest enemy that thwarts us at every turn. But that
which we call "nature" is itself meaningless and without justification, and it is
people who give it meaning as "nature." Witness how the "laws" of nature
have changed through the ages: once it was accepted that the world was flat,
but this has changed. No one would want to stake his life on the proposition
that people will view the world a thousand years from now in the same way
they do at the present. What this points to is that even nature itself is endowed
with meaning by human beings. Through this endowment, we come to control
nature, however limited this control may be. We say we cannot control nature
because we do not understand it, but it makes just as much sense to say we do
not control nature because we have not given it sufficient meaning. Scientific
investigation is, after all, nothing more than the striving to endow the natural
world with meaning so that we can control our own lives better. Here again,
we are even responsible for the meaning of nature.

Lest we begin to think that Sartre makes the human being into God, it
should be pointed out that this is just the opposite of his view. Instead, he
says we try to be God; but since God does not exist, this is only further evi-

dence of our absurdity. In fact, Sartre calls humans a "useless passion" when they try to set themselves up as God.

Much of the foregoing may sound strange to our ears. We are used to thinking differently about existence, if we bother to think about it at all. We may tend to view life as a "bowl of cherries," or we may go the other way and become cynical pessimists who bemoan our fate. Sartre is really trying to call our attention to what is obvious: we *can* make a difference, but not without choosing our goals and working toward them. It could be said that every advance humans have made, every humane act committed, has happened because some individual or group of individuals chose to make it happen and then struggled to achieve that choice. Few if any of the things we achieve come about by accident. Even those events that occur by accident show Sartre's insight, because they are *accidents,* meaningless in and of themselves. They depend on humans to experience them, suffer, undergo, endure, or enjoy them. It is *humanity* who gives them their meaning *for* humanity.

Critics have pointed out that existentialism in general, and Sartre's philosophy in particular, lacks an adequate social base to treat institutions, such as the school, and this factor has hampered more thorough application of existentialist thought to the problems of education. Sartre, who was perhaps the most individualistic of all the existentialist philosophers, eventually came to align himself with Marxist theory, although he did not adopt a doctrinaire Marxist position and preferred to think of himself as an independent. This happened primarily because (as Sartre put it) his theory could not stand alone, for it needed Marxism for completion; and Marxism needed the humanizing influence of the existential perspective. Apparently, Sartre came to agree that individuals may find value in participation in the social and political process as long as the individual defines that participation.

EXISTENTIALISM IN MODERN LIFE

Existentialism has affected many areas of thought. There has been the development of a strong movement in existential psychiatry, and there is even a journal by that name. Essentially, it is a nondirective approach and is similar to the thought espoused by Carl Rogers and Abraham Maslow.

Rogers, for example, believed that teachers should risk themselves for their students in classroom experimentation. The teacher should look for the "potentiality and wisdom of the person" and work for self-directed change on the part of the learner. The risk involves not only the individual teacher's sense of self but a willingness to trust the learner. This means that the teacher must be a "facilitator of learning" to help release students' potential. Rogers is against the concept of teaching as showing, guiding, or directing; rather, the teacher should "prize" the learner and make him feel worthwhile. This can be accomplished through prizing the feelings and opinions of the student, and it involves the development of what Rogers calls "empathic understanding." The result of successful education and living should be a "fully functioning person."

Maslow talks about a hierarchy of needs and differentiates between basic needs and "metaneeds." Basic needs are primary: the need for air, food, protection from danger, and a familiarity with the environment. Metaneeds transcend these basic needs and involve a personal reaching or growing to realize one's potential. These metaneeds include such things as belongingness, esteem, and aesthetic needs. They are necessary, in Maslow's view, to help us become "self-actualized" persons who are realistically oriented, autonomous, and creative. Maslow also differentiates between pseudo–self-actualization and authentic self-actualization. Pseudo–self-actualization is the undisciplined release of impulses in which, for example, someone behaves like a spoiled child. An authentic self-actualized person says "I've considered my feelings and yours too." The central idea is that people should be encouraged to make their own decisions, respect themselves, and treat others with compassion. Life is full of paradox and contradiction, and no single life-style is necessarily the true one. To recognize the existentialist frame of reference is to recognize individual differences and variation.

The intensity of modern life has brought on increasing tension and anxiety. The nature of individual choice, individual action, and commitment is such that anxiety is real and present in all human beings, regardless of their station in life or their particular ideology. This feature of modern life is of great concern to existentialists and has been treated extensively in their works. Some critics have castigated the existentialists for their inordinate amount of attention to anxiety, charging that they dwell too much on the tragic, the perverse, and the morbid side of life and exclude the more hopeful and optimistic themes. Existentialists reply that too many people wrongly emphasize the optimistic, the good, and the beautiful—all of which create a false impression of existence. For example, if friends from out of town visit, the host usually takes them to the beautiful spots—the parks, the museums and art galleries, and the best restaurants. One does not take a guest to the slums, the depressing areas of poverty, and places where extensive suffering is going on. Without experiencing these things, visitors get a one-sided picture of the city as it really is. Existentialists feel that it is time to balance the scales, but even more fundamentally, they think that the tragic side of life more nearly illustrates human existence where "the chips are down" and the individual must face up to his condition. We have no recourse but ourselves. Our very existence is one of anxiety.

Strange as it may sound, Christian theologians have found existentialism to be a fresh breeze in a musty environment. It was Nietzsche, one of the early architects of existentialism, who proclaimed that God is dead. In addition, Christianity has traditionally had a strong streak of optimism in its promise of eternal salvation. Many existentialists agree with Karl Marx that religion is the opiate of the masses, pointing toward some supposed heaven and keeping our attention diverted from the real problems of the world. The result is that the masses are brutally exploited by the few. It will be recalled that another founder of existentialism—Kierkegaard—found Christian belief to be characterized by anxiety, anguish, and doubt. Christian existentialist theology has embraced these themes, holding out to the believer the proposition that anxiety and doubt are real and necessary experiences to be encountered in living the Christian life.

Gabriel Marcel, a French religious existentialist, wrote about the Christian experience of the "subjectivity" or "presence" of others. This presence should not be treated as a mere object of experience but as a fellow human in line with, perhaps, the theme of the Golden Rule. The idea of "presence" has similarities to Buber's I–Thou concept. It also resembles Sartre's "being-for-itself" (subjectivity) and "being-in-itself" (objectivity), but Marcel was more attuned to the characteristics and necessities of social relations than was Sartre. Marcel recognized anxiety and "baseless" choice, and he held that while a person's belief is always subject to doubt and questioning, one is not totally isolated from all other existence and needs to be open to the "presence" of others.

Other Christian thinkers, such as Paul Tillich, examined human nature in all its ambiguity. Tillich questioned what humanity ought to be in an "age of anxiety." His answer was that we must have "the courage to be" despite fate, death, meaninglessness, and despair. The "courage to be" is based on a belief in God when God has "disappeared," and it involves a faith undermined by resulting doubt. Thus, courage becomes a necessary characteristic of the believer in order to sustain belief. The impact of existentialism upon modern Christianity has been notable. It has thrown new light on the mystical aspects of religion and reduced the emphasis on the material side of life, and it has helped many persons to make religion more a matter of personal commitment and inner conviction.

Some critics have even questioned whether existentialism should be considered a philosophy. Certainly it is not systematic in the traditional pattern, but it still has a strong claim as a philosophy in the tradition of Socrates. Just as Socrates was the "gadfly" of Athens, pricking the consciences and "shells of decency" of the Athenians, so also do the existentialists call us to examine our personal lives and break away from superficial beliefs and uncommitted action.

PHENOMENOLOGICAL PHILOSOPHERS AND THEIR THOUGHT

Edmund Husserl (1859–1938)

Husserl was born in Czechoslovakian Moravia and was educated in schools and universities in Austria and Germany. Although he received a doctorate in mathematics, he was drawn to philosophy after studying under Franz Brentano. He taught philosophy at several universities, including Göttingen and Freiburg. The term *phenomenology* was used earlier by both Kant and Hegel. However, the use of this term today to designate a particular philosophical method is generally attributed to Husserl.

Husserl was influenced by Kant and Hegel, but he saw his work as a radical departure from theirs, similar to Descartes's call for philosophy to be grounded on insight beyond the possibility of doubt. In *Ideas*, Husserl's main work, his aim was to use phenomenology to help make philosophy into a rigorous science, but a science different from the physical and behavioral sciences. The latter take what Husserl called "the thesis of the natural standpoint"; that is, the thinker's perception is attuned wholly toward things of the environment or of overt behavior. Traditional science, then, assumes an autonomous world outside human thought. Husserl, on the other hand, wanted to study the *original intuition* of the things outside; that is, he wanted to study our original conscious grasp of things before we begin to impute meaning or interpretation to them. His field of investigation was the preconceptual level of awareness, the original and immediate data of consciousness. The phenomenologist, then, seeks to understand "original experience," or the primordial phenomenon of consciousness, prior to our bringing our previous learning or prejudices to bear on the perception of subsequent meanings. Husserl's call to go "back to the things themselves" means to return to these original, immediate data of consciousness.

Husserl thought that if the phenomenological method were rigorously applied and executed, it would make philosophy scientific but different from the traditional sciences. Traditional scientific realism teaches us that the objects of experience—the sticks, stones, and events of life—are just what they are, independent of conscious perception. This "reality" is outside consciousness and may be understood or brought to consciousness by the exacting description of scientific method. However, Husserl argued that scientific descriptions are really abstractions filtered from scientific methodology; they are not the stuff of primordial conscious perception. Consequently, if we want to understand primordial conscious experience, we have to perform a "phenomenological reduction"; that is, we must strip away or "bracket" the assumptions and presuppositions of culture (of which traditional science is but one part) and get back to the immediate or original consciousness.

In many respects, Husserl's philosophy is a form of transcendental idealism. He took Descartes's notion of the *cogito*, an idealistic view of subjective thought, and transformed it into a transcendental ego—that is, a consciousness that transcends natural conditions and confronts pure Being. This is seen in his belief that the bracketing of the cultural world was possible. On the other hand, there is also a sense of realism in his thought; for his phenomenology can be seen as a form of empiricism, of trying to arrive at meaning through conscious experience.

Heidegger and Phenomenology

Husserl's interpreters took his thought in new directions, and of these inter-preters, Heidegger stands out. Heidegger served for a time as Husserl's assis-tant, and he accepted the notion of phenomenology as a method and as a sci-ence of the phenomena of consciousness. An analysis of the term *phenomenol-ogy* provides a better idea of Heidegger's conception: "phenomenon" is that which shows or presents itself, and "logos" is rational discourse about phe-nomena. For Heidegger, the task was not, however, simply an effort to describe phenomena but to get at what lies behind them—their *being*. Thus, for Heidegger, phenomenology was the science of Being—ontology.

To get to the being of phenomena, Heidegger concentrated his analysis on *dasein*, a term that has no exact English equivalent but that signifies human *being* in the sense of "being there," situated within a historical con-text. This helps show why Heidegger resisted being lumped with existential-ism, for dasein is not the isolated ego many existentialists write about. The human being is indelibly historical, he argued, and history is the indelible determinant of our nature. Individual dasein has a past and is oriented toward a future, and while phenomenology looks at the immediate present, this historical background colors any given situation of dasein, for dasein is always arriving out of a past and anticipating a future. Thus, Heidegger changed Husserl's notion of bracketing in any absolute sense; for to under-stand immediate dasein, it is necessary to consider its history. With Heidegger, this meant that historical background needs interpreting, and this steered him toward hermeneutics, or historical interpretation. However, his focus was on concrete history, not history writ large as Hegel or Marx would view it.

Two developments by Heidegger would help steer phenomenology away from Husserl's transcendentalism, and these were the importance of lan-guage (after the *logos,* or discourse, aspect of phenomenology) and hermeneutics. Heidegger's major work was *Being and Time* (1927), which concentrated on dasein analysis. However, in *The Basic Problems of Phenomenology* (1975, English translation 1982), a work published shortly before his death, one can see certain directional changes in his thought. The study of the philosophic concept of time becomes more important than mere dasein analysis, and this gives added importance to hermeneutics and the need for interpretation.

Maurice Merleau-Ponty (1908–1961)

Where Husserl looked for a complete bracketing of the world through phe-nomenological reduction, Merleau-Ponty maintained that there could be no denial of the world and hence no complete bracketing. Where Heidegger sought to understand Being, Merleau-Ponty concentrated on the primacy of perception. Where Sartre saw a radical dichotomy between consciousness and the world, Merleau-Ponty saw perception as always a part of the world. For Merleau-Ponty, perception is in and of the world. Since reflection is carried out in the temporal flux of the world, the only way to view it with any accuracy is to accept this worldly base in philosophical work. He saw the roots of the mind in the body and the world and maintained that perception is not simply the result of the action of external things on us, for there is no pure interiority or exteriority.

Merleau-Ponty was attempting to devise a philosophical program that would enable him to lay down a new base for research on imagination, language, culture, ethics, and politics. Unfortunately, his untimely death in 1961 prevented him from carrying out this objective, and we have only hints of what his plans might have produced. His major work was *Phenomenology of Perception* (1945), and several of his more important papers and articles were published posthumously as *The Primacy of Perception* (1962). It has been said that he used the fundamental concepts of phenomenology but interpreted them in his own unique way.

For Merleau-Ponty, our "facticity," our worldly existence, cannot be escaped. We must recognize that human consciousness itself is a project of the world, a world that it neither possesses nor embraces but without which it cannot exist. Consciousness is perpetually directed toward the world of things, ideas, events, persons, or experience. Perception is not a purely intellectual synthesis; rather, perception is experienced bodily and in the world at the prereflective level. Reflection comes after perception and helps "solidify" or clarify perception, for a perception that is not followed by thought is soon lost. Reflection involves language, and this puts us even farther away from immediacy. As Merleau-Ponty put it, to use language, to name a thing or describe it in language, is to tear oneself away from a thing's individual and unique characteristics and to see it as representative of an essence or category. It is to go from the concrete to the categorical, where words establish meaning.

Nevertheless, for Merleau-Ponty, perception is primary. He felt that previous philosophy had erred in viewing our primary relation to the world as that of a thinker to an object of thought. Thinking, thought, and the objects of thought are not concrete but abstract. Perception occurs in a concrete, temporal world of flux, and what we think about it later may not hold for similar future perceptions. In other words, perception is immediate and prereflective; and in the final analysis, "every perception takes place within a particular horizon. . . . We experience a perception and its horizon 'in action' rather than by 'posing' them or explicitly 'knowing' them." The significance of this realization, which inserts a note of skepticism into Merleau-Ponty's philosophy, is that we cannot view perceptions as pure, unified abstractions or theorems—for there is no transcendent Cartesian *cogito* that grasps truths, nor is truth immanent in perception. These things come secondarily, not primarily. Certainty may be had in reflection, but it is a certainty that is abstract, categorical, and secondary. In other words, abstract truth is not self-evident in perception, but perception has within it the potential for arriving at truth in a more suitable fashion as it is sensed or experienced rather than as it is filtered through the philosophical dogmatisms and assumptions of the past.

Phenomenology and Hermeneutics

Where phenomenology seeks an ordered description of the objects of consciousness, hermeneutics concentrates on the interpretation and meaning of conscious experience over time. Language is central to hermeneutics because it is through language that fruitful interpretation and meaning are secured. What Heidegger was striving for in his analyses of both dasein and time was rational understanding of human existence or human *being*, and this could not be secured without attention to language. As he put it in *The Basic Problems of Phenomenology*, "In speaking about something, the dasein speaks itself out, expresses itself, as existent being-in-the-world, dwelling with and occupying itself with beings." In effect, when we contemplate or mull over something, we are projecting ourselves into a future understanding of ourselves and the world. To project oneself into some new understanding is, so to speak, to redefine oneself and to strike out in new directions. This is how the self (or dasein) grows and evolves; and it was just this history, this concept of time, that Heidegger was attempting to understand. Furthermore, understanding (and thought itself) is carried on through some form of language or symbolization. To gain clarity or rational understanding, we must be attentive to language. We must engage in hermeneutics.

Two philosophers who have been prominent in developing hermeneutics are Hans-Georg Gadamer (b. 1900) and Paul Ricoeur (b. 1913). Gadamer has taken the position that Heidegger's later philosophy was not concerned with just the being of dasein, but rather the being of dasein that understands itself, or self-understanding. This is shown in Heidegger's concentration on historicity and time. In effect, consciousness and selfhood, in and of themselves, are banished in favor of self-understanding in the historical sense. Interpretation establishes the essential unity of self-understanding. This is not, however, the same as focusing our gaze inward. Rather, it is a self-understanding that comes from trying to understand ourselves and the world, from trying to be as rational as possible about the things around us. Hence, hermeneutical phenomenology does not embrace the radical (and perhaps self-centered) individualism that some existentialists dwell upon.

Hermeneutics does, however, focus on the "internal" process of using language; for as Gadamer puts it, "hermeneutics is primarily of use where making clear to others and making clear to oneself has become blocked." In Gadamer's view, a chief value of hermeneutical philosophy is the educational value of self-formation (or *Bildung*). It is his belief that this self-formation is a more important goal for philosophical study than traditional epistemology.

Paul Ricoeur, in some respects like Gadamer, shifts the point of departure of phenomenology from the perceptualist mode to the linguistic mode. He maintains the concrete subject as the focus of inquiry but does not believe that one can know oneself directly or introspectively. The only course is to seek understanding indirectly, and this explains his concentration on language. His linguistic and phenomenological hermeneutics is based on the notion that it is through language that one expresses one's self-understanding. It is through words, through language, that people bring into the open whatever understanding they have of themselves. His phenomenology, then, focuses on a description of the phenomena of consciousness indirectly, as these phenomena are revealed through language; and hermeneutic interpretation is brought to bear on the question of how the comprehension of signs (language) relates to the comprehension of self.

EXISTENTIALISM AND PHENOMENOLOGY IN PHILOSOPHY OF EDUCATION

Existentialism is one of the most individualistic philosophies. There are many kinds of existentialism, and existentialist writers often resent being lumped together; however, there are many areas of similarity in their thinking as well as specific differences. Because existentialism is a protest type of philosophy, its adherents have not been overly concerned with methodology and systematic exposition. Some philosophers have seen phenomenology as providing a rigorous methodology for describing lived experience and its concern with hermeneutics as providing an interpretive approach to individual experience.

Aims of Education

Existentialists believe that most philosophies of the past have asked people to think deeply about abstractions that had little or no relationship to life. Scholastic philosophy, in which thinkers debated such questions as how many angels could sit on the head of a pin, might be a case in point. The answers to such questions provided nothing except perhaps some psychological satisfaction at winning a debate through argumentation. Even then the answers were unprovable. Existentialists reject this approach to ideas. They feel that their philosophy is one in which the individual is drawn in as a participant. We explore our own feelings and relate ideas to our own lives. Consequently, in an existentialist education the emphasis is not on scholarly debate but on creation; that is, one can create ideas relevant to one's own needs and interests.

Existentialists, such as Sartre, tell us that "existence precedes essence." First comes the individual and then the ideas the individual creates. Ideas about heaven, hell, and God are all human inventions. Even theistic existentialists admit that ideas about God are unprovable, although they might parallel something in existence. Thus, the individual can be given credit for the creation of concepts like peace, truth, and justice but blamed for things like bigotry, war, and greed. Since people are the creators of all ideas, this

Emphasis on creation [handwritten margin note]

focuses as much attention on humans as on the ideas themselves; and if it is true that we have created ideas that are harmful in practice, then likewise we can create new ideas to replace them.

Because the individual human is so important as the creator of ideas, existentialists maintain that education should focus upon individual human reality. It should deal with the individual as a unique being in the world—not only as a creator of ideas, but as a living, feeling being. Most philosophies and religions, existentialists charge, tend to focus on the individual only as a cognitive being. The individual is this, but he is also a feeling, aware person; and existentialists think that this side deserves attention.

Existentialists assert that a good education would encourage individuals to ask such questions as "Who am I?" "Where am I going?" "Why am I here?" In dealing with these questions, we would have to recognize that the individual is an emotional and irrational creature as much or more than an unemotional and rational one. The individual is always in transition, so that the moment one believes he knows himself is probably the moment to begin the examination all over again.

Most educational philosophies up to this point have emphasized the concept of a person as a rational being in a rational world. Much of this stems from the Aristotelian notion that we can understand our place in the universe and that this understanding is primarily a result of sharpening our powers of intellect through the use of reason and observation. Even through the Age of Enlightenment, there was a strong conviction that we could steadily increase our knowledge and power over the universe. Yet, with this rise of rationality, we continued to be plagued by wars, inhumanity, and irrationality—often perpetrated by those who believed that they had attained a mastery of logic and philosophy.

For the modern existentialists, World War II was a watershed in such irrationality and inhumanity, and existentialists, particularly in France and Germany, began to take a new look at human nature. They reexamined such things as death, courage, and reason. Reason, often used to justify the great amount of death and destruction inflicted by war, was particularly scrutinized. Existentialists found that reason was used to justify cruelty and aggression to the extent that millions of Jews were sent to the gas chambers through what some Nazis thought were rational motives. Reason was used to defend these actions—so that a person could say he was only following orders, that it was not his decision, or that it was done for better worlds to come.

Existentialists believe that a good education is one that emphasizes individuality. It attempts to assist each of us in seeing ourselves with our fears, frustrations, and hopes, as well as the ways in which we use reason for good and ill. The first step in any education, then, is to understand ourselves.

Existentialists maintain that the "absurd" side of life needs serious exploration. Perhaps what we take to be a rational explanation of the universe is our own application of what we think is rational. It is difficult to see things as they really are, objectively, as if we came from another planet. Yet if we did so, how strange many things would seem that we take for granted, such as women walking on little stilts that they call shoes, and men wearing around their collars flashy colored material that they call ties. Further areas of absurdity might be explored, such as the pierced ear from which to dangle bright shiny objects or the efforts of some who hate blacks but want to change their skin coloring to dark tan in the summer. Are these rational acts, or do we use our reason to say that they are rational?

One area of drama is known as theater of the absurd. Eugene Ionesco, Samuel Beckett, Edward Albee, and others wrote plays in this genre. Theater of the absurd is about life, magnifying and emphasizing certain aspects of it in ways to show its irrationality and absurdity. In the play *Who's Afraid of Virginia Woolf,* we see a married couple who spend a great deal of time attacking each other and who have become very skillful at it through practice. Seemingly, such people remain together for the purpose of developing greater ways of hurting each other.

We are not encouraged through our own kind of education to see the absurdities of life; rather, the good side is emphasized. For example, most reading books for children focus upon the uniformity and reliability of existence. They show children in settings where there is no marital conflict, war, hunger, or death. Existentialists feel that a vital part of one's education is to examine the perverted and ugly side of life, the irrational as well as the good side. Yet in education we are always covering up. Apparently, we do not believe that a child should be exposed to such human realities as death, and so we tell him that his dead grandfather went on a long trip or that he is away. We lie to children about birth, about sex, about money, and about a host of other things. Existentialists believe in a truthful kind of education where there is no cover-up, where children learn about many facets of life, whether good or bad, rational or irrational.

Existentialists feel that education should foster an understanding of anxiety. Many people certainly are frustrated by life, but this frustration is often caused by the kind of education that did not prepare them for a world of conflict. What existentialists mean by anxiety is an awareness of the tension of existence. When one is involved in life, when one is an acting person, she is bound to feel some tension through involvement. Existentialists point out that there is no tension after death and that some people are trying to make their own lives like death by avoiding conflict at all cost. The opposite of death is life, and life for the existentialist requires some degree of tension. Though Marx talked of religion as the opium of the people, Christian existentialists say that true Christians are people in conflict, people who must constantly wonder if what they believe is really true, and if they are acting enough in support of those beliefs.

One of the distinguishing features of existential phenomenological philosophy of education is the emphasis on *possibility* as a goal of education. It could be said that the emphasis on human *being* is really an emphasis on *becoming,* for human consciousness can never be static. This is reminiscent of Sartre's argument that human consciousness (being-for-itself) can never become a substance, an objective *thing* (being-in-itself). Hence, when one speaks of the aims of education from an existential phenomenological perspective, possibility takes on central importance.

As Gordon Chamberlin put it in *The Educating Act,* "The life-world out of which we interpret what happens to us has been constituted through our interpretations of what has happened to us in the past." This life-world interpretation may be characterized by adequacy or inadequacy, but each of us reacts to a new experience in terms of this interpreted background. This life-world "history" is the history that Heidegger wanted to understand in his hermeneutics. It is what Gadamer was seeking to understand in his notion of education as *Bildung,* or edification. In short, each new experience adds to the funded meaning of experience that each of us has and sets the stage for present and future possibilities. Educators, then, must be cognizant of their own and their students' life worlds. Indeed, it could be said that the chief goal of the educator is to help learners construct the best life-worlds possible. The emphasis is not simply on the past, however, but on the present and future, on *possibility.* As Chamberlin points out, "Education always leads to action. Education always follows action. Indeed, education is an activity."

The point is further illustrated by Paulo Freire, in *Pedagogy of the Oppressed.* Freire asserts that often people are oppressed because they serve as "hosts" for the oppressors. The oppressor is whoever or whatever serves as an overriding influence that is uncritically accepted or chosen by the oppressed. In Freire's view, oppression will be present wherever one's consciousness is characterized by the condition "in which *to be* is *to be like,* and *to be like* is *to be like the oppressor.*" Oppression is, or forces, passivity, and there may be a degree of security in passivity, for nothing is risked. For Freire, however, an education that liberates is painful, for like a childbirth it brings a new person into the world. It is an education that cannot be achieved in idealistic terms or simply by talking about it; rather, it is something to be achieved through purposeful action.

From the phenomenological standpoint, liberating education initially results in the perception that the world of oppression is not a closed world from which there is no escape; instead, oppression is a limiting situation that can be transformed. This perception is tentative, however, for it must result in action that seeks to change existing conditions. The phenomenological import of this educational view resides in how we perceive conditions, or how conditions present themselves to consciousness. On the one hand, the oppressive perception is fatalistic, believing that the given cannot be changed. On the other hand, liberated perception does not accept the given as inevitable but looks to *possibilities,* to a world to be born through *praxis* or purposeful action.

Maxine Greene's expression for education for possibility is *wide-awakeness.* The aim is to enable learners to become attentive, perceptive, or wide-awake to possibilities. Many things in contemporary life hinder wakefulness. Many people live in societies that are characterized by stifling bureaucracies and mindless consumerism. Others suffer from grinding poverty and ignorance. These and other forces almost guarantee passivity in conditions of domination and powerlessness. Greene forcefully suggests, however, that such feelings can largely be overcome through the conscious effort of individuals to keep themselves alert, to think about their worldly condition, to inquire into the forces that seem to dominate them, and to interpret their daily experiences. Education can help tremendously in achieving this wide-awakeness, but it must be conceived and conducted in the right way. For the educator it means not accepting dominating administrative hierarchies as inevitable. It means becoming aware that hierarchies are made by human beings and are not a part of the inevitable order of the universe. It means developing awareness about such things as state-adopted classroom material, mandated testing programs, or curriculum censorship instigated by politically powerful interest groups. It means becoming aware of the moral issues involved in such things as mandated testing programs that unfairly discriminate or any host of institutionalized practices that interfere in free educational activity. Finally, it means that the educator should develop phenomenological and hermeneutical competence to "demystify" such conditions and help learners develop similar competence. People must learn to evaluate comfortable conventions and pressure to "go along with the gang" against carefully chosen moral principles. They must become attuned to possibility, to being wide awake.

Despite the seeming fascination of existentialists with the irrational, they have rarely if ever advocated irrationality as a goal. To the contrary, their effort has been to confront irrationality as an aspect of the human condition and to put it in proper perspective. Many existentialists have talked about the "tragic side of life," and a large part of that tragedy is irrationality. Phenomenology helps put the irrational in proper perspective, for the thrust of phenomenology is toward rational description. As phenomenology has been applied to education, emphasis has been put on helping learners understand and comprehend lived experience. As Donald Vandenberg put it, education involves becoming as reasonable a person as humanly possible. Thus, reasonableness should be added as one of the goals of an existential phenomenological philosophy of education.

Greene makes the point that one of the problems of the contemporary world is the polarization of those who embrace an authority of science and those who embrace an authority of affect and "life-style." On one hand, we have those who extol scientific knowledge as the objective and final answer to fundamental questions; while on the other, there are those who extol the subjective and private inner world as the only source of answers. Although educators may not accept either side of the argument, they cannot remain unaffected by this kind of polarization, or what has been called "the crisis of culture." Buffeted by such polarizations, young people may throw up their hands in discouragement about trying to sort out the conflicting claims. They may throw themselves into trying to "fit into the groove" and being accepted by their peers. What often results from the frustration of such culture conflict is anti-intellectualism. But what the educator must do is to help enable the young to conceptualize and develop a rational perspective of their worlds.

The rational understanding sought by the phenomenologist, however, is not that of an older rational empiricism that looked solely on the impact of the outer world; instead, the phenomenologist looks toward a rationality that proceeds from primal consciousness that thrusts toward the outer world and engages with it. From Greene's point of view, phenomenology does not glorify inwardness and introspection. It concerns itself with how the individual comes into touch with the outer world through perceiving, judging, believing, remembering, and imagining. What composes the inner "stream of experience" has to do with the outer world and involves what the phenomenologists call "intentionality."

Let us explore this notion further, for it lies at the heart of any phenomenological concept of education. Much of our conscious life occurs without our being explicitly conscious of being conscious; that is, our consciousness is absorbed with everyday events and we take for granted the common-sense reality of things. Occasionally, however, we become explicitly conscious of things on the horizon of consciousness that become suddenly questionable and throw barriers before the flow of everyday events (similar to the Jamesian–Deweyan "hitch" or "block" to the flow of conscious experience). As a consequence, we must try to sort things out through existential critique, phenomenological description, and hermeneutical interpretation. We must try to be as reasonable as we can, not in the sense of "objective" and removed rationalism, but in the sense of a rationalism that is ever cognizant of the human condition. If we are going to be open to possibility and wide awake, we must also be reasonable.

Methods of Education

The first thing that most existentialists want is a change in our attitude about education. Instead of seeing it as something a student is filled with, measured against, or fitted into, the existentialist suggests that we first look at students as individuals and that we allow them to take a positive role in the shaping of their own education and life. Every student brings to school a background of experiences that will influence personal decisions, but by and large, existentialists urge that schools and other institutions be free places where students are encouraged to do things because they want to do them. Some writers, such as Van Cleve Morris, look at *Summerhill* as a sketch of the kind of education existentialists prefer. At Summerhill, students do not have to attend class if they do not want to and there are no grades or examinations unless students request them. It is an environment where students are encouraged to make their own choices and are free to do so. Summerhill has its rules and regulations, some made by the children and some made by the administration; but basically it is a free institution as compared with most other schools.

For the existentialist, no two children are alike. They differ in the information, personal traits, interests, and desires they have acquired. It is ridiculous to think they should have the same kind of education. Yet all too often we find children not only lumped together but taught the same things that are supposedly appropriate to their grade level. There has been much concern with "mass society," "the lonely crowd," and "a nation of sheep," but our educational institutions still foster conformity and obedience.

Many existentialists are disturbed by the emphasis that some educators put upon education for adjustment. Although Dewey believed that education should be in the forefront of change, he also recognized the need to prepare the child for existing society while working for change. Some "progressive" educators, however, under the guise of pragmatic philosophy, made "life adjustment" the primary focus of education and promoted education that stifled both individuality and social change.

Existentialists would like to see an end to the manipulation of the student. Teachers control children along predetermined paths using behavioral techniques of reward and punishment. Existentialists would like the children to choose their own paths from the number of options available to them. Schools often contain uniform materials, curriculum, and teaching. Although educators have talked quite a bit about promoting individuality in education, most programs and teaching methods have tended to become more alike. Existentialists argue for diversity in education—not only in curriculum but in the way things are taught. Some students, they point out, learn well through one approach and others through another. Many options for learning should be open to them.

Existentialists are concerned with the role of the teacher or educator in the learning process. They believe that every teacher should be a student and every student a teacher. Martin Buber discussed this in detail in his description of the I–Thou and I–It concepts. In the I–It relation, a teacher treats a student as someone to direct and fill up with knowledge. The student is an object to be manipulated. Followers of Buber support an I–Thou approach where both student and teacher learn from each other and where the relation is more friend to friend.

Donald Vandenberg, in *Being and Education*, has given a phenomenological description of traditional pedagogic methods as characterized by dominance/submission and commanding/obeying relations. The teacher dominates and commands, and it is the role of the student to submit and obey. In such relations, teachers and students are drawn away from what could be a more satisfying educational relationship into playing roles that defeat education. In other words, the teacher is drawn into spending much time trying to control students and students are drawn into trying to defeat teacher control. Educational method is not used to help students be open to possibilities for growth by understanding their "being-in-the-world" (their individual histories and ways of responding), nor is it used to help them secure a better understanding of their own potentials upon which to engage in educational activity. As a result, they are alienated from the teacher. What phenomenologist-educators must seek, then, is to construct educational methods that provide an openness to the world for both themselves and students. This does not imply a laissez-faire role for the teacher; rather, because of the greater experience, knowledge, and phenomenological understanding of the teacher, it is that person's responsibility to develop an educational environment that promotes awareness of the past and present, and of future possibilities.

This is somewhat akin to a Buberian reciprocal relationship between teacher and student. It is also sensitive to phenomenological time—that is, to the past–present–future nature of conscious life. Proper educational method, then, brings the possibilities of the world before teacher and student—to the teacher in rediscovering the excitement of learning and to the student in opening up a whole new world of possibility.

In practical terms, this involves, for example, methodology that helps a student gain greater command of a language and realize more effective ways to communicate, ways that make the student more articulate and capable of comprehension and self-expression. Another example would be an openness to human history and the development of a greater understanding of why human culture has developed as it has. Students become educated into a better understanding of the human adventure and their own circumstances within it. They become more sensitive to human possibility and understand that they themselves are not necessarily and fully determined by the past. Every present is conditioned by the past, but every present is also pregnant with future possibility for change and new direction. To accomplish this kind of educational approach and outcome, the teacher must understand that the chief requirement is to help the student explore the world and to open up the possibilities of the world for the student.

In a sense, what the phenomenologist seeks is a method that helps students internalize the world and make it their own, but it is always more than a mere internalizing. Gordon Chamberlin has described the educational experience as "the meeting of two complex streams of experience," the stream of the teacher and the stream of the learner. While the teacher's experience may be greater than the learner's simply because of maturity and extent, both are complex; the educational process is essentially one of bringing these streams together. The student is dependent because of immaturity, lack of understanding, or other factors, but this does not mean that all the initiative is on the side of the teacher. The teacher's role is that of an enabler who helps the student appropriate, internalize, and make over. The teacher takes a cue from the responses of the learner, whether these responses are active or passive. The learner may initiate new directions by posing questions and expressing desire, or even by novel departures.

As Chamberlin sees it, the teacher may make authority claims over the learner, but that authority derives from an understanding of the educational process and the phenomenological world of the learner. The learner also has authority—the authority to interpret the teacher's intent and the authority to interpret how learning is appropriated and meaning imputed within the learner's own life-world.

The convergence of the two streams of experience of teacher and learner, then, depends to some degree on the antecedents each brings to an educational encounter. It also depends on the present and on the interpretation each makes of ongoing activity. Finally, the convergence depends on ensuing action—that is, on how the teacher becomes more effective and how the learner grows and is more capable of managing personal affairs and the affairs of the world.

In *Teacher as Stranger*, Maxine Greene has set forth the kinds of questions an educator must ask in confronting the phenomenological conditions of human relationships between a teacher and student. The teacher must ask not only the existentialist question Who am I? but also How am I to conceive *the other?* as a student, fellow human being, and the outside world. It is simply not enough to know the scientific characteristics of a fellow being, such as biological and psychological characteristics; one must know also the phenomenological conditions. The teacher must confront phenomenologically what he understands (and feels and imagines) as significant fact, as useful knowledge, or as serious belief. Contemporary life seems to be a time of uncertainty and confusion, and this is even more reason for the educator to seek rational understanding and comprehension—not from some all-encompassing, "objective" platform removed from living experience but from a phenomenological standpoint that attempts to understand the primary world of consciousness that each of us brings to the educational situation. Consequently, the educator will not view the educational process as simply something to be imposed from the outside onto impressionable students but will strive to understand how each of us approaches learning from a unique background.

This is not to say that structured knowledge will not be presented by the teacher and by learning materials or that students will not have to struggle with difficult ideas. As Greene sees it, educators must be capable of both "tough mindedness" and "tender mindedness"; that is, they must be able to comprehend the educational process both from the standpoint of subject matter to be learned and from the lived experience perspective of the learner. Of course, no educator can ever climb into the consciousness of the learner and see the world as it is actually presented to and experienced by the learner; however, each of us is a learner, and each of us is presented with situations that are difficult to embrace and understand. Educators, by trying to understand rationally their own experience and the learning difficulties presented by so many actual experiences of life, will also have a better understanding of the proper methods of education by understanding the difficulties, mysteries, uncertainties, and joys experienced by the learner.

The phenomenologist's concern with educational method is not so much with specific techniques, although these are certainly important, but with clearing the way for a pedagogic encounter. In the words of Vandenberg, the concern is "to lay the groundwork so that being can clear a space for itself within the teacher–pupil relation."

Curriculum

It is interesting that most existentialist and phenomenological philosophers have had lengthy and rigorous educations. Most of them taught at one time or another, usually in a university setting. They have been concerned primarily with the humanities and have written extensively in that genre. Through the humanities, the existentialists have tried to awaken modern individuals to the dangers of being swallowed up by the megalopolis and a runaway technology. This seems to have taken place because the humanities contain greater potential for introspection and the development of self-meaning than other studies.

The humanities loom large in an existentialist curriculum because they deal with the essential aspects of human existence, such as the relations between people, the tragic side of human life as well as the happy, the absurdities as well as meaning. In short, existentialists want to see humankind in its totality—the perverted as well as the exalted, the mundane as well as the glorious, the despairing as well as the hopeful—and they feel that the humanities and the arts do this better than the sciences. Existentialists, however, do not have any definite rules about what the curriculum should comprise. They believe that the student-in-situation making a choice should be the deciding factor.

Although existential phenomenologists have been more interested in understanding the lived experience of the learner than in the specific content of things to be learned, some of them have given attention to curriculum organization and content. The tendency, however, is to view curriculum from the standpoint of the learner rather than as a collection of discrete subjects. Donald Vandenberg has suggested that an appropriate way to conceive of the tasks involved in curriculum decision-making is to see the learner in terms of "landscape" and "geography." "Landscape" is the correlate of the learner's prereflective consciousness. It is unorganized, even chaotic; and education should proceed in such a way as to expand continually the horizons of this landscape within the limits of the learner's own finitude. "Geography" involves bringing order and logic to this landscape and providing the learner with structured education, as represented by the organized curriculum. "Landscape" is the original setting of our being-in-the-world, and "geography" is the world of fact and universal concept, a world of abstraction. Authentic existence is in neither the one nor the other but is, in a sense, having a foot in each, or residing in between. To ignore "landscape" is to court alienation of the learner. To ignore "geography" is to court a disorganized and chaotic conscious life. The educator, then, must deal with what Vandenberg calls the "pedagogic paradox." What the educator must seek is a context in which the student can unite his originality, his "landscape," with the "geography" of organized curriculum so that originality gains power and direction.

Maxine Greene makes a similar point, although in a different manner. She has spoken more explicitly about specific subject matter, for she is a steadfast advocate of the humanities and the arts and has also given attention to the basics. Greene believes that the disciplines that constitute the curriculum should be presented as opportunities for individual "sense-making." It is difficult in many circumstances to arouse student interest in traditional curriculum because so many youth exist in conditions of dominance and alienation. If the teacher attempts to introduce students to dogmatic "truth" and if students are cut off from using the curriculum to make meaning in their own lives, then there is a real possibility that students will only become more alienated from organized educational activity. This is a difficult path for the teacher, who is obligated at some point to take the student out of the familiar into the realm of more remote subject matter. In some cases, this is not all that difficult—for the subject matter lends itself, with appropriate interpretation, to the lived experience of learners.

Greene has illustrated many ways in which literature, for example, can be used to help students interpret the moral dilemmas we face as a society and as individuals. In addition to literature, other art forms express meanings that can be interpreted fruitfully for the lives of learners. Some subject areas, such as linear algebra or chemistry, do not readily lend themselves to such application and may seem remote to many students, but they also have the capacity to help students gain meaning. Whatever the subject, and whatever the nature of the students with whom the teacher works, it is necessary for the teacher to confront the task of education and to balance as well as humanly possible the tension between the demands of individual learners and their need to understand a variety of subjects.

Certainly one responsibility of the teacher is the transmission of cherished values and ideals and another the communication of the skills and concepts needed to survive and thrive. Students, however, may not appreciate abstract justifications for education and, in fact, may resist them. Furthermore, there seems to be little social consensus about what education should be, and so there is no clear support from the wider society for what should be in the curriculum. This further complicates the teacher's task, but Greene maintains that the task is not impossible.

She recommends that a dialogue be initiated to involve the community in conversation and shared activity regarding education. While there is no absence of public talk about education, it is as if one group speaks past another. For example, some advocates of the "basics" seem to want to go back to an idealized earlier time. Some debate the merits of computers in the classroom, vocational education, or the humanities. In Greene's view, there is a need to build community understanding of the complexities of curriculum issues, for their importance is too great simply to be settled by professional educators.

In the meantime, the teacher must decide what to include and how to approach it within the restrictions of requirements, time, and circumstance. This means that the educator must be knowledgeable about students' needs and students' perceptions of the world. The teacher must study and wrestle with the moral choices involved in curriculum selection and arrangement and the difference those choices may make in the lives of students. It is not an easy task, but an existential phenomenological understanding of education is an invaluable source of insight. One of those insights is that considerable freedom is needed by students to merge their own perceived possibilities with those of the organized curriculum and to synthesize their own courses of action with the best of communal life.

CRITIQUE OF EXISTENTIALISM AND PHENOMENOLOGY IN EDUCATION

Existentialist philosophy has been hailed as a helpful antidote to American education, especially where that education has become dominated by an organizational mentality and the continuing bureaucratization of the American school. Existentialism's challenge that we must not be beguiled by the technological society has been heeded by many members of society, the so-called counterculture described by Theodore Roszak. This challenge has awakened us to the tragedy and absurdity of life and to the lonely, baseless existence of the modern individual. It has been a needed medicine for contemporary Americans who have never experienced the direct effects of widespread hunger, devastating war, or wide-scale genocide. Most American philosophies have an optimistic tone, and existentialism has served the purpose of sounding a sobering note—sobering but not hopeless.

If it is sobering, it also calls us to reexamine our culture in terms of its rampant materialism, its robotization of the worker, its anti-intellectualism, and its devastating effect on individuality. Probably no modern philosophy devotes as much concern to individuality in political, social, and economic life as existentialism. It speaks to us in terms that belong distinctly to the twentieth century and the enduring human predicament. It encourages us toward self-examination in a world that tends to force us outward to nonpersonal concerns.

We are constantly bombarded by advertisements that induce us to be something other than what we are. Individuals are manipulated by church, school, family, business, industry, government, and other institutional forces. Existentialism points to the possibility that we *can* refuse these enticements and seductions, that we are *free* to choose ourselves if we will but exhibit the courage. We do not have to be pawns buffeted about like helpless victims without succor. Even though our efforts to resist may be puny, may end in death, the individual human being is forged in the struggle to overcome such forces.

With regard to education, existentialists and phenomenologists have been among the most severe critics. They have condemned the school as a dehumanizing force that indoctrinates the individual and steals personal initiative. It is as if the school's main function is to process human beings as a canning factory processes tuna. Everyone comes out alike. While the analogy may exaggerate the actual case with schools, the existentialist criticism calls our attention to a definite problem of magnitude. Teachers and students are both victims of this condition, and modern society cannot hope to find itself if its educational institutions are aligned against individual identity, personality, and well-being. Rather than uplifting individuality, the schools have all too often submerged it.

These conditions helped give rise to a popularization of existentialist thought, mainly because it vigorously protested against such conditions. But popularization has also had its drawbacks, perhaps best shown by the glorification of "the individual" (meaning, in this case, an abstract individual). We glorify "the individual" to the exclusion of the real-life needs of particular, concrete, live children. Some educators have rejected all order, discipline, and study in the guise of promoting true individuality. They have preached an individualism that is often harmful to real individuals because it promotes selfishness, egoism, and disregard for others. "Spoiled brats" have sometimes been the result.

"Spoiled brats" [margin note]

The existentialists have called upon us to become aware of our existence as authentic beings, but this has been corrupted by the "do your own thing" ethic. These corrupters seem to be ignorant of Sartre's reminder that while an individual may do anything, personal actions are a message to others that they may do likewise. If one is totally free, Sartre cautioned, one is also totally responsible, and this is an awesome responsibility for any individual.

Repeated criticisms of the individualistic and nihilistic character of existential thought have led some adherents to strike off in new directions. Phenomenology has been used as a more adequate method to investigate educational problems from an existential perspective. Donald Vandenberg, a leading figure in this methodological movement, advocates analyzing problems from the standpoint of the lived experience of the child—that is, the child's world, existence, and experiences. The phenomenological method tries to understand and develop a more adequate theory of what Vandenberg has called "the chronological development of inwardness and outwardness"—that is, understanding how people's consciousness is developed or educated from their own perspective. This method investigates phenomena related to the expansion, development, and integration of conscious existence through learning. By *learning* is meant a "coming to know things," and "being aware of something of which one was not previously aware." Thus, educational phenomena are those things generating awareness of conscious existence. There is still an individual emphasis on the lived world of the child, but the focus is not so much on doctrinaire notions of a nihilistic life-style as on methodological steps toward understanding how an individual comes to be whatever he is in the modern world.

"New" approach [margin note]

Despite its promise of more methodological rigor for existentialist educational theory, the phenomenological movement presents some persistent problems. One of these is the difficulty many people have with phenomenological terminology. Its reliance on hard-to-translate German terms and its penchant for hyphenated expressions create comprehension problems for many readers. Critics argue that these devices obfuscate and that a theory is useful only to the extent that it clarifies rather than confuses. Supporters reply that while phenomenological theory is complex, this is because the nature of the human condition it seeks to clarify is itself complex. Furthermore, the ideas uncovered by phenomenology seem strange to people enamored with "objective" scientific terminology, and more familiarity with phenomenological philosophy would help solve many comprehension difficulties. Finally, supporters maintain, the difficulties of comprehension are a small price to pay for the greater understanding phenomenology can bring to human education and the lived experience of the learner.

Existentialist and phenomenologist ideas of education do not mean that individuals cannot learn from others, cannot profit from discipline, or cannot gain from formal study in school. However, they insist that these are not the only ways we can create new avenues and identities. While existentialism and phenomenology have helped foster the movement known as "alternative education," proponents sometimes seem to forget that formal study—even the three Rs—is an alternative open to consideration. Existentialist and phenomenological philosophers have sought and are seeking to open our eyes to human possibility and not necessarily to make narrow, doctrinaire ideologues out of us. Such an outcome would be anathema to both the letter and spirit of existentialism and phenomenology.

SARTRE

EXISTENTIALISM AND HUMANISM

Jean-Paul Sartre was a prolific writer and produced major works in many different areas, including novels, plays, and formal philosophical treatises. In the following selection, he offers a defense of some of his ideas and in the course of this defense presents some central themes of his philosophical views. He claims that existentialism is indeed humanistic and provides insight into human freedom and human responsibility. Although Sartre did not write directly about education, his views have been applied to learning, curriculum, and the ethical aspects of education.

My purpose here is to offer a defense of existentialism against several reproaches that have been laid against it.

First, it has been reproached as an invitation to people to dwell in quietism of despair. For if every way to a solution is barred, one would have to regard any action in this world as entirely ineffective, and one would arrive finally at a contemplative philosophy. Moreover, since contemplation is a luxury, this would be only another bourgeois philosophy. This is, especially, the reproach made by the Communists.

From another quarter we are reproached for having underlined all that is ignominious in the human situation, for depicting what is mean, sordid or base to the neglect of certain things that possess charm and beauty and belong to the brighter side of human nature: for example, according to the Catholic critic, Mlle. Mercier, we forget how an infant smiles. Both from this side and from the other we are also reproached for leaving out of account the solidarity of mankind and considering man in isolation. And this, say the Communists, is because we base our doctrine upon pure subjectivity—upon the Cartesian "I think": which is the moment in which solitary man attains to himself; a position from which it is impossible to regain solidarity with other men who exist outside of the self. The *ego* cannot reach them through the *cogito*.

From the Christian side, we are reproached as people who deny the reality and seriousness of human affairs. For since we ignore the commandments of God and all values prescribed as eternal, nothing remains but what is strictly voluntary. Everyone can do what he likes, and will be incapable, from such a point of view, of condemning either the point of view or the action of anyone else.

It is to these various reproaches that I shall endeavour to reply to-day; that is why I have entitled this brief exposition "Existentialism and Humanism." Many may be surprised at the mention of humanism in this connection, but we shall try to see in what sense we understand it. In any case, we can begin by saying that existentialism, in our sense of the word, is a doctrine that does render human life possible; a doctrine, also, which affirms that every truth and every action imply both an environment and a human subjectivity. The essential charge laid against us is, of course, that of overemphasis upon the evil side of human life. I have lately been told of a lady who, whenever she lets slip a vulgar expression in a moment of nervousness, excuses herself by exclaiming, "I believe I am becoming an existentialist." So it appears that ugliness is being identified with existentialism. That is why some people say we are "naturalistic," and if we are, it is strange to

see how much we scandalise and horrify them, for no one seems to be much frightened or humiliated nowadays by what is properly called naturalism. Those who can quite well keep down a novel by Zola such as *La Terre* are sickened as soon as they read an existentialist novel. Those who appeal to the wisdom of the people—which is a sad wisdom—find ours sadder still. And yet, what could be more disillusioned than such sayings as "Charity begins at home" or "Promote a rogue and he'll sue you for damage, knock him down and he'll do you homage"? We all know how many common sayings can be quoted to this effect, and they all mean much the same—that you must not oppose the powers-that-be; that you must not fight against superior force; must not meddle in matters that are above your station. Or that any action not in accordance with some tradition is mere romanticism; or that any undertaking which has not the support of proven experience is foredoomed to frustration; and that since experience has shown men to be invariably inclined to evil, there must be firm rules to restrain them, otherwise we shall have anarchy. It is, however, the people who are forever mouthing these dismal proverbs and, whenever they are told of some more or less repulsive action, say "How like human nature!"—it is these very people, always harping upon realism, who complain that existentialism is too gloomy a view of things. Indeed their excessive protests make me suspect that what is annoying them is not so much our pessimism, but, much more likely, our optimism. For at bottom, what is alarming in the doctrine that I am about to try to explain to you is—is it not?—that it confronts man with a possibility of choice. To verify this, let us review the whole question upon the strictly philosophic level. What, then, is this that we call existentialism?

Most of those who are making use of this word would be highly confused if required to explain its meaning. For since it has become fashionable, people cheerfully declare that this musician or that painter is "existentialist." A columnist in *Clartés* signs himself "The Existentialist," and, indeed, the word is now so loosely applied to so many things that it no longer means anything at all. It would appear that, for the lack of any novel doctrine such as that of surrealism, all those who are eager to join in the latest scandal or movement now seize upon this philosophy in which, however, they can find nothing to their purpose. For in truth this is of all teachings the least scandalous and the most austere: it is intended strictly for technicians and philosophers. All the same, it can easily be defined.

The question is only complicated because there are two kinds of existentialists. There are, on the one hand, the Christians, amongst whom I shall name Jaspers and Gabriel Marcel, both professed Catholics; and on the other the existential atheists, amongst whom we must place Heidegger as well as the French existentialists and myself. What they have in common is simply the fact that they believe that *existence* comes before *essence*—or, if you will, that we must begin from the subjective. What exactly do we mean by that?

If one considers an article of manufacture— as, for example, a book or a paper-knife—one sees that it has been made by an artisan who had a conception of it: and he has paid attention, equally, to the conception of a paper-knife and to the pre-existent technique of production which is a part of that conception and is, at bottom, a formula. Thus the paper-knife is at the same time an article producible in a certain manner and one which, on the other hand, serves a definite purpose, for one cannot suppose that a man would produce a paper-knife without knowing what it was for. Let us say, then, of the paper-knife that its essence—that is to say the sum of the formulae and the qualities which made its production and its definition possible—precedes its existence. The presence of such-and-such a paper-knife or book is thus determined before my eyes. Here, then, we are viewing the world from a technical standpoint, and we can say that production precedes existence.

When we think of God as the creator, we are thinking of him, most of the time, as a supernal artisan. Whatever doctrine we may be considering, whether it be a doctrine like that of Descartes, or of Leibnitz himself, we always

imply that the will follows, more or less, from the understanding or at least accompanies it, so that when God creates he knows precisely what he is creating. Thus, the conception of man in the mind of God is comparable to that of the paper-knife in the mind of the artisan: God makes man according to a procedure and a conception, exactly as the artisan manufactures a paper-knife, following a definition and a formula. Thus each individual man is the realisation of a certain conception which dwells in the divine understanding. In the philosophic atheism of the eighteenth century, the notion of God is suppressed, but not for all that, the idea that essence is prior to existence; something of that idea we still find everywhere, in Diderot, in Voltaire and even in Kant. Man possesses a human nature; that "human nature," which is the conception of human being, is found in every man; which means that each man is a particular example of an universal conception, the conception of Man. In Kant, this universality goes so far that the wild man of the woods, man in the state of nature and the bourgeois are all contained in the same definition and have the same fundamental qualities. Here again, the essence of man precedes that historic existence which we confront in experience.

Atheistic existentialism, of which I am a representative, declares with greater consistency that if God does not exist there is at least one being whose existence comes before its essence, a being which exists before it can be defined by any conception of it. That being is man or, as Heidegger has it, the human reality. What do we mean by saying that existence precedes essence? We mean that man first of all exists, encounters himself, surges up in the world—and defines himself afterwards. If man as the existentialist sees him is not definable, it is because to begin with he is nothing. He will not be anything until later, and then he will be what he makes of himself. Thus, there is no human nature, because there is no God to have a conception of it. Man simply is. Not that he is simply what he conceives himself to be, but he is what he wills, and as he conceives himself after already existing—as he wills to be after that leap towards existence. Man is nothing else but that which he makes of himself. That is the first principle of existentialism. And this is what people call its "subjectivity," using the word as a reproach against us. But what do we mean to say by this, but that man is of a greater dignity than a stone or a table? For we mean to say that man primarily exists—that man is, before all else, something which propels itself towards a future and is aware that it is doing so. Man is, indeed, a project which possesses a subjective life, instead of being a kind of moss, or a fungus or a cauliflower. Before that projection of the self nothing exists; not even in the heaven of intelligence: man will only attain existence when he is what he purposes to be. Not, however, what he may wish to be. For what we usually understand by wishing or willing is a conscious decision taken—much more often than not—after we have made ourselves what we are. I may wish to join a party, to write a book or to marry—but in such a case what is usually called my will is probably a manifestation of a prior and more spontaneous decision. If, however, it is true that existence is prior to essence, man is responsible for what he is. Thus, the first effect of existentialism is that it puts every man in possession of himself as he is, and places the entire responsibility for his existence squarely upon his own shoulders. And, when we say that man is responsible for himself, we do not mean that he is responsible only for his own individuality, but that he is responsible for all men. The word "subjectivism" is to be understood in two senses, and our adversaries play upon only one of them. Subjectivism means, on the one hand, the freedom of the individual subject and, on the other, that man cannot pass beyond human subjectivity. It is the latter which is the deeper meaning of existentialism. When we say that man choos-

es himself, we do mean that every one of us must choose himself; but by that we also mean that in choosing for himself he chooses for all men. For in effect, of all the actions a man may take in order to create himself as he wills to be, there is not one which is not creative, at the same time, of an image of man such as he believes he ought to be. To choose between this or that is at the same time to affirm the value of that which is chosen; for we are unable ever to choose the worse. What we choose is always the better; and nothing can be better for us unless it is better for all. If, moreover, existence precedes essence and we will to exist at the same time as we fashion our image, that image is valid for all and for the entire epoch in which we find ourselves. Our responsibility is thus much greater than we had supposed, for it concerns mankind as a whole. If I am a worker, for instance, I may choose to join a Christian rather than a Communist trade union. And if, by that membership, I choose to signify that resignation is, after all, the attitude that best becomes a man, that man's kingdom is not upon this earth, I do not commit myself alone to that view. Resignation is my will for everyone, and my action is, in consequence, a commitment on behalf of all mankind. Or if, to take a more personal case, I decide to marry and to have children, even though this decision proceeds simply from my situation, from my passion or my desire, I am thereby committing not only myself, but humanity as a whole, to the practice of monogamy. I am thus responsible for myself and for all men, and I am creating a certain image of man as I would have him to be. In fashioning myself I fashion man.

Source: Jean-Paul Sartre, *Existentialism and Human Emotions.* New York: Philosophical Library, 1957, pp. 9–18.

LANDSCAPES OF LEARNING

Maxine Greene has been an important contributor to an existential phenomenology of education. She has urged educators to use the creative products of human struggle to help youngsters come to grips with their own lives. To be "wide awake" is to be open to the possibilities of human existence; but it is also to be aware of the needs for meaning. In this selection, Greene sketches ways in which the arts and humanities can be used to help students become more acutely conscious of their existential situation. Literature is Greene's special concern, and she proposes to use it to help students gain personal meaning through a phenomenological interpretation of human predicaments as portrayed in literature.

In an ironic account of how he "became an author," Søren Kierkegaard describes himself sitting in the Frederiksberg Garden one Sunday afternoon asking himself what he was going to do with his life. Wherever he looked, he thought, practical men were preoccupied with making life easier for people. Those considered the "benefactors of the age" knew how to make things better "by making life easier and easier, some by railways, others by omnibuses and steamboats, others by telegraph, others by easily apprehended compendiums and short recitals of everything worth knowing, and finally the true benefactors of the age ... (making) spiritual existence systematically easier and easier...." He decided, he says, "with the same humanitarian enthusiasm as the others," to make things harder, "to create difficulties everywhere."

Writing that way in 1846, Kierkegaard was anticipating what certain contemporary thinkers speak of as a "civilization malaise" reflecting "the inability of a civilization directed to material improvement—higher incomes, better diets, miracles of medicine, triumphs of applied physics and chemistry—to satisfy the human spirit." He saw the individual subsumed under abstractions like "the Public," lost in the anonymity of "the Crowd." Like others responding to the industrial and then the technological age, he was concerned about depersonalization, automatization, and the bland routinization of life. For him, human reality—the *lived* reality—could only be understood as a difficult, indeed a dreadful freedom. To make things harder for people meant awakening them to their freedom. It meant communicating to them in such a way that they would become aware of their "personal mode of existence," their responsibility as individuals in a changing and problematic world.

Henry David Thoreau was living at Walden Pond in 1846, and, when he wrote about his experience there, he also talked (in the first person) of arousing people from somnolence and ease. *Walden* also has to do with making life harder, with moving individuals to discover what they lived for. Early in the book, Thoreau writes passionately about throwing off sleep. He talks about how few people are awake enough "for a poetic or divine life." And he asserts that "To be awake is to be alive." He speaks personally, eloquently, about what strikes him to be the requirements of the truly moral life. But he never prescribes; he never imposes his own ethical point of view. The *point* of his kind of writing was not simply to describe a particular experiment with living in the woods; it was to move others to elevate their lives by a "conscious endeavor," to arouse others to discover—each in his or her own terms—what it would mean to "live deliberately."

The theme has been developed through the years as technology has expanded, fragmentation has increased, and more and more people have felt themselves impinged upon by forces they have been unable to understand. As time has gone on, various writers and artists have articulated experiences of being conditioned and controlled. Contemporaneous with the advance of scientific and positivistic thinking, therefore, an alternative tradition has taken shape, a tradition generated by perceptions of passivity, acquiescence, and what Thoreau called "quiet desperation." It is what may now be called the humanist tradition, if the human being is understood to be someone always in search of himself or herself, choosing himself or herself in the situations of a problematic life. There are works of art, there are certain works in history, philosophy, and psychology, that were deliberately created to move people to critical awareness, to a sense of moral agency, and to a conscious engagement with the world. As I see it, they ought—under the rubric of the "arts and humanities"—to be central to any curriculum that is constructed today.

My argument, as has been suggested, has to do with wide-awakeness, not with the glowing abstractions—the True, the Beautiful, and the Good. Like Nick Henry in Ernest Hemingway's *Farewell to Arms,* I am embarrassed by, "Abstract words such as glory, honour, courage, or hallow. . . ." Wide-awakeness has a concreteness; it is related, as the philosopher Alfred Schutz suggests, to being in the world:

> By the term "wide-awakeness" we want to denote a plane of consciousness of highest tension originating in an attitude of full attention to life and its requirements. Only the performing and especially the working self is fully interested in life and, hence, wide-awake. It lives within its acts and its attention is exclusively directed to carrying its project into effect, to executing its plan. This attention is an active, not a passive one. Passive attention is the opposite to full awareness.

This goes beyond ordinary notions of "relevance" where education is concerned. Schutz is pointing out that heightened consciousness and reflectiveness are meaningful only with respect to human projects, human undertak-

ings, not in a withdrawal from the intersubjective world. He is also pointing out that human beings define themselves by means of their projects and that wide-awakeness contributes to the creation of the self. If it is indeed the case, as I believe it is, that involvement with the arts and humanities has the potential for provoking precisely this sort of reflectiveness, we need to devise ways of integrating them into what we teach at all levels of the educational enterprise; we need to do so consciously, with a clear perception of what it means to enable people to pay, from their own distinctive vantage points, "full attention to life."

It is, at least on one level, evident that works of art—*Moby Dick,* for instance, a Hudson River landscape painting, Charles Ives' *Concord Sonata*—must be directly addressed by existing and situated persons, equipped to attend to the qualities of what presents itself to them, to make sense of it in the light of their own lived worlds. Works of art are, visibly and palpably, human achievements, renderings of the ways in which aspects of reality have impinged upon human consciousness. What distinguishes one art form from another (music from poetry, say, the dance from painting) is the *mode* of rendering, the medium used, and the qualities explored. But all art forms must be encountered as achievements that can only be brought to significant life when human beings engage with them imaginatively.

For all the distinctiveness of the arts, there is a characteristic they share with certain kinds of history. I have in mind, as an example, Edward Hallet Carr's conception of history as dialogue. Carr talks about the historian's provisional interpretations of provisionally selected facts and about the subtle changes that take place through the "reciprocal action" of interpretation and the ordering of those facts.

> And this reciprocal action also involves reciprocity between present and past, since the historian is part of the present and the facts belong to the past. The historian and the facts of history are necessary to each other. The historian without his facts is rootless and futile; the facts without their historians are dead and meaningless. My first answer therefore to

the question, What is history?, is that it is a continuous process of interaction between the historian and his facts, an unending dialogue between the present and the past.

What is striking here is the emphasis on selecting, shaping, and interpreting, the ordering of raw materials according to distinctive norms. The process itself is not unlike the process of art-making. The crucial difference is that the historian is in quest of truth, in some degree verifiable, while the artist strives for coherence, clarity, enlargement, or intensity.

Even more important: in the aesthetic experience, the mundane world or the empirical world must be bracketed out or in some sense distanced, so that the reader, listener, or beholder can enter the aesthetic space in which the work of art exists. Captain Ahab's manic search for the white whale cannot be checked in any history of the whaling industry; its plausibility and impact have little to do with a testable truth. Thomas Cole's painting, "The Ox-Bow," may look in some way like the river, but, if it is not encountered as a drama of color, receding planes, and light, it will not be experienced as a work of art. A historical work—Thucydides' *The Pelopponesian War*, John B. Bury's *The Idea of Progress,* or Richard Hofstadter's *The Age of Reform*—refers beyond itself to events in time past, to the changing situations in humankind's ongoing experience, to whatever are conceived to be the "facts."

Most significant of all, however, is the possibility that these histories, like Carr's own history, can involve their readers in dialogue. Reading any one of them, readers or students cannot but be cognizant of a distinctive individual behind the inquiry. They cannot but gain a sense of a living human being posing questions to the past from his own standpoint and the standpoints of those he chooses to be his fellow-historians, working at different moments in time. Students may well come upon the insight Jacob Burckhardt describes when he speaks of history as "the break with nature caused by the awakening of consciousness." They may begin, from their own vantage points to confer significance on moments in the past, to push back the horizons of the meaning-

ful world, to expand the scope of lived experiences. Maurice Merleau-Ponty, speaking of what this kind of awareness can mean, writes, "My life must have a significance which I do not constitute; there must be strictly speaking an intersubjectivity. . . ." Engaging with the kind of history I have been describing, individual human beings can locate themselves in an intersubjective reality reaching backwards and forwards in time.

These are the reasons why I would include certain works of history in an arts and humanities program—works that provoke wide-awakeness and an awareness of the quest for meaning, which has so much to do with feeling alive in the world. I would exclude from the program (although not from the total curriculum) mathematicized or computerized history, exemplified by, say, *Time on the Cross*.

I would approach my choices in philosophy, criticism, and psychology in the same fashion: those works that engage people in posing questions with respect to their own projects, their own life situations. William James, John Dewey, George Herbert Mead, George Santayana, Alfred North Whitehead, Jean-Paul Sartre, Maurice Merleau-Ponty: these, among the modern philosophers, are likely to move readers to think about their own thinking, to risk examination of what is presupposed or taken for granted, to clarify what is vague or mystifying or obscure. To "do" philosophy in this fashion is to respond to actual problems and real interests, to the requirements of sense-making in a confusing world. It may also involve identification of lacks and insufficiencies in that world—and some conscious effort to repair those lacks, to choose what *ought* to be. Some of the humanistic or existential psychologies may function similarly as they engage students in dialogue about what it is to be human, to grow, to *be*.

If the humanities are indeed oriented to wide-awakeness, if dialogue and encounter are encouraged at every point, it might be possible to break through the artificial separations that make interdisciplinary study so difficult to achieve. If students (and their teachers as well) are enabled to pose questions relevant to their life plans and their being in the world, they might well seek out answers in free involvement with a range of disciplines. Once this occurs, new perspectives will open up—perspectives on the past, on cumulative meanings, on future possibilities.

The important thing is for these perspectives to be sought consciously and critically and for meanings to be perceived from the vantage points of persons awake to their freedom. The arts are of focal significance in this regard, because perceptive encounters with works of art can bring human beings in touch with themselves. Jean-Paul Sartre writes that literature addresses itself to the reader's freedom:

> For, since the one who writes recognizes, by the very fact that he takes the trouble to write, the freedom of his readers, and since the one who reads, by the mere fact of his opening the book, recognizes the freedom of the writer, the work of art, from whichever side you approach it, is an act of confidence in the freedom of men.

I believe this may be said, in essence, about all the arts. Liberating those who come attentively to them, they permit confrontations with the world as individuals are conscious of it, *personally* conscious, apart from "the Crowd."

I would want to see one or another art form taught in all pedagogical contexts, because of the way in which aesthetic experiences provide a ground for the questioning that launches sense-making and the understanding of what it is to exist in a world. If the arts are given such a central place, and if the disciplines that compose the humanities are at the core of the curriculum, all kinds of reaching out are likely. The situated person, conscious of his or her freedom, can move outwards to empirical study, analytic study, or quantitative study of all kinds. Being grounded, he or she will be far less likely to confuse abstraction with concreteness, formalized and schematized reality with what is "real." Made aware of the multiplicity of possible perspectives, made aware of incompleteness and of a human reality to be pursued, the individual may reach "a plane of consciousness of highest tension." Difficulties will be created everywhere, and the arts and humanities will come into their own.

Source: Maxine Greene, *Landscapes of Learning.* New York: Teachers College Press, 1978, pp. 161–166. Originally published in *Teachers College Record,* Fall 1977. Copyright © 1978 by Teachers College, Columbia University. All rights reserved. Reprinted by permission of the publisher.

· · · · · · · ·

SELECTED READINGS

Gadamer, Hans-Georg. *Hans-Georg Gadamer on Education, Poetry, and History: Applied Hermeneutics.* Edited by Dieter Misgeld and Graeme Nicholson. Translated by Lawrence Schmidt and Monica Reuss. Albany: State University of New York Press, 1992. The author's ideas on higher education are provided in several essays and recent interviews. Gadamer focuses on the need to find human solidarity and possibilities for freedom.

Greene, Maxine. *Teacher as Stranger: Educational Philosophy for the Modern Age.* Belmont, CA: Wadsworth, 1973. This is an engaging work that combines a literary analysis of existentialist themes with philosophical and educational concepts. It is an exploratory work that many readers will find stimulating.

Kneller, George F. *Existentialism and Education.* New York: Philosophical Library Inc., 1958. One of the first efforts to give a systematic treatment to the relationship of existentialism to education, this work has been widely used but also widely criticized for its systematization of the philosophy.

Morris, Van Cleve. *Existentialism in Education.* New York: Harper & Row, 1966. A comprehensive overview of existentialism as a philosophy of education, this work tries to provide some insight into possible uses of existential thought. Like Kneller, Morris has been vigorously criticized for treating existentialist thought as another "ism."

Sartre, Jean-Paul. *Existentialism and Human Emotions.* New York: Philosophical Library, 1974. This is a short compilation of writings from among some of Sartre's best-known philosophical works. It is an excellent introduction to Sartre's ideas as well as to his style of philosophizing.

Troutner, Lee. Making Sense out of "Existential Thought and Education": A Search for the Interface, in *Philosophy of Education, 1975. Proceedings of the Thirty-First Annual Meeting of the Philosophy of Education Society.* San Jose, CA: Philosophy of Education Society, 1975, pp. 185–199. This paper explores the contributions of existential thought to education. The author sketches possible future contributions existentialism can make.

Vandenberg, Donald. *Being and Education: An Essay in Existential Phenomenology.* Englewood Cliffs, NJ: Prentice Hall, 1971. This work is different in that it does not present existentialist thought as another "ism." Instead, it attempts to apply phenomenological method to selected problems in education.

8

Analytic Philosophy and Education

One recent development in philosophy is called the analytic movement. Analytic philosophy is not a systematic philosophy like idealism or realism. Indeed, most analytic philosophers take pains to repudiate identity with a systematic philosophy, for they say that the "systems" approach in philosophy has brought more problems than solutions to human affairs. For the most part, analytic philosophers seek to clarify the language, concepts, and methods we use in the more precise activities of life, such as science. Analytic efforts at clarification have also been extended into less defined kinds of activity, such as education.

Clarification is the one simple unifying theme in analytic philosophy. The underlying assumption of the analysts is that most philosophical problems of the past were not really problems concerning ultimate reality or truth, goodness, and beauty, but problems located in confused language, warped or unclear meanings, and conceptual confusion. Genuine knowledge, most analysts claim, is the business of science, not philosophy. The true role of philosophy is critical clarification.

There are several kinds of approaches within the general movement of analytic philosophy, and the general movement itself has undergone a somewhat puzzling historical evolution. Basically, philosophical analysis has always gone on. Socrates was analyzing when he investigated the meaning of justice. But the modern movement of analytic philosophy has its more immediate roots in several recent philosophical developments. To try to fit these developments into any one mold is to alter the actual facts of the situation. Consequently, what follows may at times appear connected and at other times disconnected. This, however, only reflects what has occurred and is still occurring in the analytic movement.

The first part of this chapter attempts to show the evolution of analytic philosophy from the late nineteenth and early twentieth centuries to the present, and the second part concerns the way that philosophical analysis has been applied to educational theory and philosophy of education.

THE ANALYTIC MOVEMENT IN PHILOSOPHY

The analytic movement has undergone an evolution stemming in part from the influence of contemporary realism as it was being shaped at the turn of the century by G. E. Moore and Bertrand Russell. Furthermore, analysis has been developed largely in the Anglo-American cultural context, although several of its exponents, primarily of Germanic-Austrian origin, came from Continental Europe. This latter aspect, however, was to have its impact mainly in Britain and the United States, for the Germanic-Austrian figures came to these two countries as they found Naziism repulsive and Continental social conditions restrictive. An important aspect of the influence that came from the Continent and finally merged for the most part with the Anglo-American analytic movement was logical positivism. This was a philosophical school originally identified with a group of philosophers known as the Vienna Circle.

More recently, the analytic movement, composed of persons of various persuasions (including many individuals formerly associated with logical positivism), has often been identified with the name "linguistic analysis," and most of its advocates were greatly influenced by Ludwig Wittgenstein. Overall, these developments are sometimes referred to as "the linguistic turn" in philosophy, a turn away from traditional philosophy (such as concern with absolute knowledge and truth) toward examining the way we discuss and describe our conceptions of things and ideas.

This part of the chapter will explore the roots of analysis in realism, as represented by Moore and Russell; the impact of logical positivism on analysis, as represented by A. J. Ayer; and its evolution into linguistic and conceptual analysis, as represented by the later writings of Ludwig Wittgenstein and the work of Gilbert Ryle.

Realism and the Early Analytic Movement

Realism is not the sole parent of the analytic movement, but the family resemblance is strong. Nor did G. E. Moore and Bertrand Russell invent the analytic movement; for some of their contemporaries were equally capable, aware, and involved—but Moore and Russell are perhaps the most representative of this train of thought.

George Edward Moore (1873–1958)

Moore, an Englishman, was instrumental in the development of twentieth-century realism and one of its outgrowths, philosophical analysis. He influenced Bertrand Russell and is often credited with heading Russell toward a realist orientation when Russell had become infatuated with Hegelian idealism. Moore and Russell became good friends and philosophical colleagues, but gradually a difference emerged. Moore's realism went toward common sense philosophy and ordinary language while Russell's went toward science, mathematics, and formal language.

A Defense of Common Sense is one of Moore's better known works. Primarily, he was interested in the things we say in ordinary life. He believed that most common-sense things are true and that we know what we are talking about in ordinary, common-sense language. Many philosophers, on the other hand, had made a career out of disputing common sense. In both ordinary language and in philosophy, however, are many statements that can neither be proved nor disproved, and Moore saw as his task not the discovery of the truth or falsity of the propositions of ordinary language and philosophy but an analysis of the meaning of propositions. He thought that analysis would clear the way toward a better understanding of the truth and propriety of what we say and write.

Moore's investigations went primarily into ordinary language because he felt that there were better reasons for accepting it than philosophical propositions. For one thing, ordinary language deals with the common-sense, everyday world. Its statements and propositions are about commonly encountered matters of fact and real-life experiences. Ordinary language and common sense deal with the real and have done so over the centuries, withstanding the test of time. Moore sought to analyze commonly used terms, such as *good*, *know*, and *real*. We all know what these words mean when we use them in ordinary language. Moore believed that we have a concept of *good* already in mind before we use it, but knowing the meaning (or having the concept) and analyzing the meaning are two different things. Analysis of the meaning would help us clarify the propriety of the meaning—or we might say, its "goodness of fit."

This illustrates the value of Moore's philosophical task: how often are we thrown into all kinds of difficulties and troubles because of our confusion over meaning? Many, if not most, of the problems of the modern world are due to misunderstanding and confusion over ideological positions, political beliefs, and so forth, all of which depend heavily on key word meanings and concepts. Moore sought to analyze the meanings of key words so as to shed light on the nature of the confusion. Consequently, he became very much involved in ethical meanings. In his *Principia Ethica,* he analyzed the various meanings we have in mind when we use the word *good*.

Let us explore this further in light of the above statement about ideological and political confusion. It is probably safe to assume that most serious-minded political theories incorporate notions or concepts about what is good. What one theory holds to be good is often different from what another theory may hold. Consider economic considerations in political theories. Marxist theory holds that collective ownership of the means of production results in certain desirable ends or goods. Other political theories maintain that private ownership is one of the supreme goods. In other instances, a political theory may contain internal inconsistencies and even contradictions about what is good. Perhaps a great deal of human strife results from such confusions over the various meanings of the word *good*.

While the preceding examples in no way show the sophisticated manner in which Moore carried out his analysis, they do shed light on the nature of the problem he was tackling. From Moore's standpoint, the philosophers themselves were often guilty of the confusion because they attempted to wrest meaning from common sense and ordinary language and make that meaning remote and abstract. Moore believed that common sense knows "where the shoe pinches" while abstract theories do not. He accused philosophers of abusing language when they took it away from common, ordinary usage and meaning. But it was not just meaning that Moore was after; he was after the *analysis* of meaning. His characteristic approach was to analyze a given concept (or meaning) in light of similar concepts and to distinguish one from another more precisely.

Moore's influence receded for some time due to the development of Russell's more formalistic analytic approach and later that of the logical positivists. Recently, however, people have been returning to elements of Moore's work.

Bertrand Russell (1872–1970)

Whereas Moore regarded analytic philosophy as the analysis of meanings in ordinary language and common sense, Russell developed a more formal logical analysis akin to the exact sciences and necessitating a precise vocabulary. In *Principia Mathematica,* by Russell and Alfred North Whitehead, mathematics was reduced to a logical language. Russell held that mathematics gives us a clarity and a logic that is not found in the general uses of language; since language is such an important part of our lives, we must try to make it more precise and clear.

Aristotle had been responsible for the development of classical logic, using principally the syllogistic method, which was a logic of classes. Russell's logic, however, dealt with the relationship of propositions to each other: "If it is raining, then the streets are wet." The clauses *it is raining* and *the streets are wet* both express propositions that have a certain relationship, or what Russell called *implication. Principia Mathematica* attempted to demonstrate that mathematics is, in fact, a part of logic. Russell further held that language has a basic logical structure similar to that of mathematics. Thus, he hoped that mathematical logic could be used to provide philosophy with an instrument for precisely clarifying the meaning of language.

Russell distinguished between what he called *atomic sentences* and *molecular sentences.* An atomic sentence has no parts that are themselves sentences. Thus, "Mary is human" is an atomic sentence; and the sentence "Mary and Betty are going shopping" is a molecular sentence since it is a complex sentence containing two parts, each of which is itself a sentence: "Mary is going shopping," and "Betty is going shopping." Molecular sentences are created out of atomic sentences by connective words, such as *and, or,* and *if.* Russell thought we could analyze any molecular sentence into a set of atomic sentences with the logical connectives. Thus, the meaning of a molecular sentence could be explained by breaking it down into its constituent atomic sentences. This is often referred to as Russell's *logical atomism.*

Accordingly, when an atomic sentence is true, the subject denotes an individual thing or object and the predicate refers to some characteristic of this thing or object. In showing that atomic sentences refer to such objects and characteristics, we are informed that the world is made up of *facts* and that all facts are *atomic* and can be described by an atomic sentence. Russell believed that there are no *molecular* facts in nature since connectives *and, or,* and *if . . . then* are only linguistic devices used to combine atomic sentences in various ways. Atomic sentences are "syntactic" only. There are no general facts either, such as "All humans are mortal," since this can be reduced to the atomic sentences "Mary is mortal," "Betty is mortal," and so on for every individual.

Russell dealt with what he called the "Theory of Descriptions," in which he attempted to show that philosophers, through the faulty analysis of language, had been led by specious arguments into believing that the sorts of things that ordinary people regard as fiction, or nonexistent, in some sense actually exist. For example, we seem to be making a true statement when we say "Captain Ahab pursued the white whale." This is true in a sense even though there really was no Captain Ahab or white whale. Russell put it this way: "How is it possible for there to be such a sentence as 'The present king of France is wise,' when there is no king of France?" Russell dealt with this kind of problem by making a distinction between the "grammatical form" of a sentence and its "logical form." Thus, the grammatical structure leads us to believe that the phrase "the present king of France" is logically the subject term and "is wise" is the predicate term and that this is an atomic sentence. But this sentence is not "logically" of the subject–predicate form. When analyzed, we have the following three sentences:

1. Something is current monarch of France.
2. Not more than one thing is current monarch of France.
3. Whatever is current monarch of France is wise.

Each of these three sentences is a "general" sentence, not an atomic one. There are no proper names; instead, we have such generalities as "something," "whatever," and so forth. Thus, "the present king of France" is not logically a proper name, though it might function to form a grammatical point of view. In pointing out that "the present king of France" is logically a "general" sentence and not an atomic one, Russell showed that such a phrase has no relationship to any object in the world and thus has no meaning on its own. If we translate a sentence into logical language, its meaning becomes clear. If it turns out not to be of the subject–predicate form, then its grammatical subject refers to nothing directly, since in the perfect language every subject term denotes an actual object in the world and every predicate term denotes an actual characteristic of that subject.

His efforts to construct a logical language, or a more perfect language that is objective and oriented to the facts of science, show the difference between Moore and Russell. Russell wanted a formal, logical language. In fact, he preferred to call his approach *logical analysis.*

The term *analytic* takes on special meaning for Russell. Much of the philosophy of the past had been *synthetic*—that is, it had tried to take disparate parts or issues and synthesize them into a "great answer" or a "block system." Russell argued that philosophers already had their great answers in hand and that they erroneously tried to make the disparate parts fit into the answers. He believed that the way out of trouble is to discard block universe conceptions in favor of taking on issues one at a time. By reducing each issue or problem to its smallest parts (its "atoms," so to speak), clarity and precision of meaning could be gained.

This is Russell's analytic approach—to whittle each problem down to its constituent parts and then to examine each part in detail to pick out its essential features. Thus, rather than arriving at great answers or syntheses, we have small but significant and well-worked analyses. We get to the truth this way. Science does this, according to Russell, and philosophy should do it, too. Russell's analytic approach is *reductive*. It reduces propositions to their smallest bare-bones significance. It is also *empirical*, for the bare-bones significance of a proposition must square with reality or with the facts of the case. This is demonstrated by the example about the king of France. It is useless to talk about the king of France if there is, in fact, no king. If there is no king, this nonexistent king cannot possibly be wise. This, in effect, illustrates Russell's condemnation of the synthetic, "grand manner" philosophy of the past. There has been too much talk and system building around nonexistent, nonwise "kings" or great answers.

In fact, this aversion to a "systems" or "grand manner" approach to philosophy fairly well characterizes the analytic movement. Analysts oppose categorization of ideas into philosophical systems, preferring to view ideas as overlapping and not belonging to any single viewpoint. Thus, they feel a "systems" or "ism" approach defeats the purpose of the kind of thinking philosophy should promote. They prefer to analyze language meaning and to clarify ideas rather than to categorize them.

Although Russell helped to develop philosophical analysis, his interest in analysis was primarily methodological. His orientation was strongly in realism. Russell's emphasis on fact, his insistence on going to the atomic as opposed to molecular and general propositions, show his acceptance of the realist's thesis of independence. We should point out that a figure of Russell's stature is difficult to pin into any school. He willingly gave up positions and renounced views when he discovered what to him were errors. At the end of his life, he was still making the philosophical quest, still searching for wisdom wherever that search led and whatever sacred ox was gored. That his influence has extended in many directions is testimony of his virtue as a thinker.

Both Moore and Russell show the strong roots that analysis has in realism: Moore for his insistence on anchoring analysis in the ordinary world of facts and sense experience and Russell for his insistence on the scientific model of a logical, orderly, and systematic treatment of particulars. The analytic movement still has much of this realist orientation, although most modern analysts reject identity with any system.

Logical Positivism and Analysis

Logical positivism originated with a group of European philosophers, scientists, and mathematicians. In 1929, they formally designated themselves the "Vienna Circle" and began publishing a journal, *Erkenntnis*. Members included Moritz Schlick, Rudolph Carnap, Herbert Feigl, Felix Kaufmann, and A. J. Ayer. The works of Bertrand Russell, especially the *Principia Mathematica*, exerted some influence on this group, as did the earlier works of Ludwig Wittgenstein, especially his *Tractatus Logico-Philosophicus*. Perhaps the most notable feature of the members of the group was their fascination with the progress of modern scientific method (especially the theory of relativity) and what has been called the *principle of verification*; that is, no proposition can be accepted as meaningful unless it can be verified on formal grounds (that is, logic and mathematics) or verified on empirical or sense-data grounds. The former shows their indebtedness to modern mathematics and logic and the latter their indebtedness to modern empirical science.

After several years, however, they encountered difficulties with the principle of verification; for in their zeal, they had given it a narrow and rigorous application that ruled out any consideration of unverifiable propositions. It was found that some of the fundamental assumptions of science itself are unverifiable in the rigorous application the logical positivists used. The important weight given to empirical sense-data presented problems, too; for such data depend on human beings observing some phenomenon, and this lets in the subjective element of perception. What one encounters is the *observation* of the object or phenomenon and not the objective reality of the thing itself, as Kant maintained with *das Ding an sich*. Thus, there is always this probable error of subjectivism, and this particularly sticky problem led to various splinterings within logical positivism.

For this reason, few people subsequently identified themselves with logical positivism—for its assumptions have proved to be perhaps too simple and its methodology too rigid. Nonetheless, its influence should not be discounted, even though its career as a philosophical position was short lived.

In terms of its influence on the analytic movement, several things need to be pointed out about logical positivism. Two leading figures will be used for illustration: Ludwig Wittgenstein and A. J. Ayer.

Ludwig Wittgenstein (1889–1951)

Wittgenstein's connection with logical positivism stems from his earlier works, primarily the *Tractatus Logico-Philosophicus*. In this book, he argued that the natural sciences are the primary source of true propositions and the primary means of finding new facts. Philosophy should not be seen as the discovery of truth but rather as an activity to solve dilemmas, elucidate problems, and clarify ideas obtained from other sources. A true proposition might be referred to as an "atomic proposition" that reveals the particular structure and arrangement of objects and facts. Philosophers should not concern themselves with the *truth* of the data but should deal with the *language* and *state-*

ments made about the data. Thus, we need to specify what we can and cannot say—that is, the limits of language.

Wittgenstein was born in Austria and raised by rather rigid parents who expected only excellence from their children. His father wanted Ludwig to become an engineer, so he studied engineering first in Berlin and later in Manchester, England. He specialized in aircraft propulsion and consequently developed a deep interest in pure mathematics as an outgrowth of his work.

While in England, he was introduced to the mathematical logic of Russell and soon went to Cambridge and became a student and personal friend of Russell. His studies, philosophical research, and association with Russell were interrupted by World War I. He returned to Austria, served in the Austrian army, and was captured on the Italian front. He completed most of the work on *Tractatus Logico-Philosophicus* while serving in the army. It was also during this time that he apparently had some sort of mystical experience; for after the war, he returned home, gave away his considerable wealth, and became an elementary school teacher.

The Wittgenstein of the *Tractatus* was an even more rigorous empiricist than Russell, and this may account for his appeal to logical positivism. He thought that the only significant use of language was to picture the facts or to state tautologies—beyond this, he thought language was nonsensical. During the 1920s, he again came into contact with Cambridge intellectual circles, and in 1929, he moved to Britain and became a British subject. He began revising his philosophy and by the mid 1930s arrived at an altered position that was to have profound effects on Anglo-American philosophy thereafter.

Although in his later works Wittgenstein repudiated or revised some of the above views, the members of the Vienna Circle understood his early views to mean that philosophy should be primarily an activity that tries to clarify concepts. They, too, believed that philosophy does not produce propositions; it merely clarifies the meaning of statements, showing some to be scientific, some mathematical, and some nonsensical. Thus, every significant statement is either a statement of formal logic (which includes mathematical statements) or a statement of science. Other statements may be "partial," "emotive," "pictorial," or "motivational" but are not cognitive. Philosophy should show the limits of language, try to make propositions intelligible, and provide clarity. Again, the insistence is not on the development of truth, but on the meaning of propositions as they currently exist.

The principle of verification was adopted by the Vienna Circle and stands as one of its chief devices. The members believed that all propositions must be verifiable by either logic or sense perception statements. An example of a logical statement would be "Fathers are males"—a logically true statement based on the terms employed. On the other hand, "Fathers are workers" is not necessarily true or meaningful. This kind of proposition is meaningful only if it can be verified empirically by sense experience. Proponents of logical positivism made a distinction between what they called "analytic" and "synthetic" sentences. Sentences whose truth logically follows from their meaning, such as the statement "All bald-headed men have no hair," are called analytic. Sentences that have some sort of empirical investigation for their confirmation are called "synthetic," such as the statement "John has brown hair." Kant made this distinction between analytic and synthetic in his *Prolegomena to Any Future Metaphysics* and insisted that synthetic a priori statements are only permissible in mathematics.

The positivists believed that all analytic sentences are in the realm of formal logic—they are true because of their structure—and all synthetic statements belong to science, requiring empirical investigation for their validity. It should be pointed out that analytic sentences do not refer to the world the way synthetic sentences do. We cannot, for example, infer that the items mentioned by the terms of an analytic sentence actually exist. Thus, from the analytic statement "Mermaids are women," we cannot infer that any actual mermaids exist; but the statement "This cat is white" can be verified by checking the facts of the situation. The logical positivists thought that analytic sentences are "trivial," whereas synthetic ones are "informative." Analytic statements are only true by definition, while synthetic statements make actual claims about reality that can be verified as true or false.

Care should be taken here with the terms *analytic* and *synthetic*. The positivists were not using the term *synthetic* in the older meaning. They, too, were as suspicious as Russell had been of the old "philosophy in the grand manner" that sought to construct "great answers" and elaborate systems out of a synthesis of conflicting ideas.

To Wittgenstein and the logical positivists, the old manner of synthesis was too metaphysical. For Wittgenstein, metaphysical statements are nonsensical. The only *sayable* propositions are the propositions of natural science. The logical positivists took Wittgenstein's position to mean that true propositions must be capable of empirical verification. Wittgenstein, however, was interested in the limits of language—what is sayable. He himself did not anchor his position on empirical verification. Apparently, the logical positivists understood his statement about natural science to mean "the empirically discoverable" or "what can be verified by the senses." At any rate, they arrived at the "principle of verification"; consequently, they gave a rather exalted position to "synthetic," "informative" statements because these can be verified empirically.

Alfred Jules Ayer (1910–1989)

A. J. Ayer was one who seriously sought further to combine logical positivism with analytic approaches. He was educated at Eton and Oxford, taught for several years at the University of London, and became a professor at Oxford in 1959. He was a prominent member of the Vienna Circle and sought to interpret logical positivism to the English-speaking world not only through teaching and writing but also through radio and television.

Ayer attempted to reconcile and order the principal doctrines of analysis from the works of Russell, Wittgenstein, and the Vienna Circle. He considered that the task of philosophy is to classify language, distinguish genuine propositions from others, and explain the meaning and justification of propositions by their reductive analysis into basic statements about immediate experience. Ayer used the principle of verification to show that religious, evaluative, and metaphysical utterances are not propositions.

In *Language, Truth and Logic*, Ayer used the verifiability criterion of meaning. Accordingly, a sentence can be factually significant to a given person if and only if she knows how to verify the propositions that it purports to express; that is, if she knows what observation would lead her under certain conditions to accept the proposition as being true or to reject it as being false. Thus, it must be possible to describe what sorts of observations would have to be made in order to determine whether a sentence is true or false. If some observations can be made that will be relevant in determining the truth or falsity of a sentence, then the sentence is significant; if not, it is meaningless. In the sentence "Angels have silver wings," there would not seem to be any *observation* that could confirm or deny this proposition, and thus it is meaningless. This is quite different from such a statement as "There are intelligent beings on another planet," for while it is not verifiable at present, it is at least capable of being verified at some point in the future.

Ayer thought philosophy would do well to abandon the metaphysical "grand manner" approach, especially where that approach starts with first principles and then constructs a deductive system from them as a complete picture of reality. The problem with this approach is that first principles are taken to be logically certain. What makes more sense, according to Ayer, is the inductive approach, in which any derived generalizations are viewed as only probable and hypothetical. More to the point, the most valuable thing philosophy can do is to reveal the criteria that are used in showing whether a proposition is true or false. The truth or falsity of any proposition must be determined by empirical verification, not philosophical clarification.

Ayer softened somewhat on the finality of the verification principle because of the criticism directed at the rigorous application he and the logical positivists used. Consequently, he ceased to identify himself with any definable school of thought, but he did retain some elements of the empirical approach of logical positivism. It has been suggested that Ayer could most aptly be called an "analytically minded empiricist."

Linguistic Analysis

Linguistic analysis is the name many observers prefer when discussing the current state of analytic philosophy. This is due to a general trend away from trying to construct an ideal language as precise as the scientific model of mathematics or trying to construct too rigid a set of rules for ordinary language. Perhaps tacking the word *linguistic* in front of analysis is still a far from accurate way to describe the current scene. Indeed, many kinds of analysis are going on and development is under way in many directions, but *linguistic* still rings true. The task is as much linguistic as it is a matter of formal logic or some brand of positivism.

The trend noted above may be credited to the later works of Ludwig Wittgenstein as much as to any one figure; for in his mature stage, his viewpoint opened considerably to recognize many uses of language. Hence, *linguistic* becomes an apt term to signify this approach to philosophy.

Wittgenstein's Later Works

Wittgenstein was mentioned earlier in this chapter, yet his ideas deserve additional attention because of the complexities of his career and thought as well as the confusing development of philosophical analysis. The "later Wittgenstein" set new directions in philosophy; these new directions had a profound impact on linguistic analysis.

These views first came to light in written form as mimeographed notes on lectures he had delivered to students in the early 1930s. Called the *Blue and the Brown Books*, they were not published until after his death. The basic ideas of these works appeared in a much expanded and revised form as *Philosophical Investigations*, also published posthumously. Of all his writings, perhaps the most simple and easiest to read is the *Blue Book*.

Wittgenstein's revised philosophy no longer took the narrow view of language but saw language consisting of indefinite possibilities of usage. In effect, he was saying that we must get at the context of any language usage, and in order to understand the meaning of a language, we may construct "language games." He thought that most philosophical "problems" were not really problems at all but puzzlements brought about by linguistic confusions. The proper issue was these puzzlements and how most of us early in life had gotten locked into certain language uses from which we could not readily escape. We are, in Wittgenstein's view, like flies in a bottle, haphazardly flitting about and banging against the walls in our confusion. The role of philosophy, then, should not be to construct explanations about reality and so forth but to solve the puzzles of linguistic confusion. Philosophy should be viewed as a method of investigation (although no specified, singular method) that results in pure description, and language should be seen as having no necessary or ideal form.

Historically, philosophy has posed such questions as "What is real?" "What is meaning?" and so forth. Wittgenstein thought these kinds of questions only led to mental cramp. It is better to ask "What is an explanation of meaning?" than "What is meaning?" Thus, he focused on the explanation of meaning, or the meaning of meaning. According to Wittgenstein, we get into problems when, upon hearing a word, we immediately begin to look for its meaning in some corresponding object. What we ought to do is look at the word itself, the sign, the statement, and examine the context of its usage.

Usage depends on the meaning of signs (that is, names or words) in relation to other signs within a system of signs; in short, within a language. According to Wittgenstein, understanding a sentence involves understanding a language. (By language, he did not mean English, French, or German—for any of these can have many languages within them in terms of usage and context.)

Let us take an example of a word over which philosophers have long argued: *thinking*. According to Wittgenstein, the meaning of *thinking* varies. When confronted with the word, most of us may associate it with mind and mental activity. However, what happens when we begin to explain what we mean by the sign *thinking*? Is it hidden away inside the cranium? If we could open people's heads while they were thinking, could we see it? Likely, we would see physiological things. What do we do when thinking is going on? Some suggestions may come easily to mind: writing, reading, speaking. Is thinking done by the mouth and larynx? Why do we say *mind* is doing the thinking? Where is its locus, its seat? Really, we can explain thinking only by signifying such agents as the brain, hand, and larynx.

Wittgenstein did not question that thinking also went on in the brain, but he maintained that when we try to describe thinking in words and statements, we signify agents of thinking and draw *analogies* from them. We try to sum all these up into a general term such as *mind* and then relate this to a thing or object. For centuries, philosophers have argued about mind, mental, and thinking and have tried to locate and delineate them. Wittgenstein suggested that the puzzle is really linguistic. We became fascinated with a linguistic form when we thought we had a problem with a thing.

Part of this difficulty, Wittgenstein maintained, is that we have come to crave generality, a concept that is linked to many philosophical puzzlements. Philosophers have taught that we should look for commonality in all things that can be brought under a general term. The tendency to generalize is rooted in our forms of expression. Words have come to possess the meaning of a general image of things associated with, or corresponding to, the words. The result is a confusion of the things named with the names themselves—the words. We have also come to confuse, as in the case of *thinking*, mental processes and mechanisms with states of consciousness or awareness. Part of this is due, Wittgenstein thought, to our preoccupation with the method of science, which seeks to reduce the explanations of natural phenomena to the smallest possible number of natural "laws" or principles—or if you will, scientific generalizations. He stated that this preoccupation is the source of metaphysics in philosophy. For Wittgenstein, it is not the proper business of philosophy to reduce anything, to produce generalizations, or to offer grand explanations. Philosophy's business is to be purely descriptive.

Wittgenstein believed that the problem with modern philosophy is the "contemptuous attitude towards the particular case." For example, we use the word *kind* a great deal. This shows our penchant for generalization, for we quickly want to subsume something under a larger heading. When confronted with strange words about something, a quick reaction is to ask, "What kind of thing is it?" as if we had to subsume it under some heading of animal, vegetable, or mineral before we could understand the meaning of the word properly. Let us go back to the philosopher's plight with the word *thinking*. We want to locate it, and in our analysis we describe several cases of thinking. But there is still something lacking, because it is virtually impossible to define *thinking* in a manner to cover all cases so that the word truly designates a general class. In actual usage, the word has no sharp boundary. To Wittgenstein, the idea that we must find a common element in all applications of a word or statement is a hindrance to philosophical investigation. It has led philosophers to the grievous error of dismissing the concrete particular.

Furthermore, Wittgenstein held that the explanation of the meaning of a word depends upon the actual context of usage and the language structure being used. If we attempt to construct generalizations, then we are thrown into the pit of drawing analogies from one context to another, relying on conventions rather than specifics of behavior, devising criteria and symptoms of usage, and then arbitrarily picking one convention, criterion, or symptom as more important than another. In effect, we are reduced to constructing arbitrary and abstract rules and procedures that get away from the concrete usage and meaning in context. We come to view language according to the mathematical rules of calculus. However, actual language is rarely like calculus. The craving for generality leads to abstract exactness that gives rise to philosophical puzzlements and linguistic confusion.

Wittgenstein believed that in actuality words have no true meaning given to them by some independent power. They have the meanings *people* give them. Thus, we cannot scientifically investigate what a word *really* means, and we cannot tabulate strict rules of usage. It is also fruitless to construct an ideal language to replace ordinary language: rather, an ideal language should remove the trouble of thinking that one had gotten *the* exact usage of an ordinary word. Thus, Wittgenstein rejected any *necessary* form of language.

In actual usage, we construct and play "language games," or "systems" of communication. The understanding of language is as varied as the games. What makes anything a language, anyway? Commonality or generality is necessarily involved, but it is a commonality like a family resemblance and not the complete picture of the family. Wittgenstein thought we could invent our own language games to help us understand actual usage by showing the similarities and differences of a language. These constructed games would be used to examine actual and possible uses of language in various contexts.

Wittgenstein had no systematic doctrine, no rules of procedure, and no lock-step "grand manner" approach to philosophizing. This makes his philosophy difficult to comprehend because we are accustomed to seeing answers put forth and explanations offered for the world's origin and destiny. Wittgenstein would have none of this and asserted that philosophy needs to be purely descriptive. We may say his view recommends uncorking the bottle and letting the fly out to see where it will go.

Gilbert Ryle (1900–1976)

Ryle was born, reared, and educated in England. Early in his philosophical career, he was attracted to certain aspects of Continental philosophy, especially Husserl's work, but by the age of thirty-one, Ryle had become well versed in philosophical analysis. He viewed analysis as a matter of finding the sources of linguistic confusion by examining some of the continually perplexing problems in philosophy, such as the mind–body dualism. His work on the use of the words *mind, mental, thinking, knowing* and related words made him one of the most influential and widely read contemporary British philosophers. His best-known work is *The Concept of Mind*, which is one of the most famous books in twentieth-century philosophy.

In *The Concept of Mind*, Ryle attacked the Cartesian doctrine of splitting off body and mind. The doctrine holds that body is in the realm of matter, susceptible to and subject to the laws of matter. It can be studied objectively, and its behavior can be publicly observed and measured. In contrast, the mind is hidden from view—a private, secret realm. It is subjective, and while one may have access to his own mental operations, he cannot examine another's objectively. Thus, while the material body can be scientifically studied, mind is not available to science but is amenable to a special subjective method of investigation called introspection. Ryle disputed these contentions, calling the theory "the dogma of the Ghost in the Machine." It is false in principle, he maintained, because it is a "category mistake," and the dogma he referred to as "the philosopher's myth."

According to Ryle, a "category mistake" occurs when one allocates concepts to logical types to which they do not belong. He gave the example of the visitor who came to Oxford and was shown the various colleges, laboratories, libraries, offices, and so forth. The visitor then asked, "But where is the university?" This is a category mistake, for the visitor was allocating the concept of university to the same logical type as its constituent colleges. In the case of Oxford, *university* is a collective logical type and *college* is a "constituent element" logical type. A similar kind of category mistake can be made with the word *institution*. We speak of marriage as an institution and we speak of Harvard University as an institution, but there is a world of difference between the logical meanings of the term *institution* in these cases.

How did the mind–body confusion come about? According to Ryle, the science developed by Galileo and others maintained that certain mechanical laws of matter governed every object occupying space. Descartes, being concerned with science, could accept such laws; but as a philosopher, he could not accept a mechanistic theory for human mind. Mental was not the same as mechanical but its exact opposite. This is a category mistake because it puts body and mind under the same logical type in the manner of exact opposites. Both are things, but things of entirely different natures. If body is a machine, then mind is a "nonmachine." The belief that mind and body (or mind and matter) are at polar positions came about because of the belief that they are both of the same logical type, although opposites. Ryle was not trying to absorb the one into the other by saying it is either all material or all mental. He held that while the dogma is absurd, we *are* justified in making distinctions between physical activity and mental activity. It all hinges on the *sense* in which we are speaking.

Perhaps most of the problem belongs to the confusion engendered by such words as *mind, mental, thinking,* and similar mentalistic terms. Certainly, Ryle maintained, we may legitimately describe "doing long division" or "thinking things over" as mental activity. We err, however, when we ascribe any sense of place to mental activity. We picture "in the head" when we say mental activity. This is what Ryle called the "intellectualist legend" that intelligence is some internal operation. Yet we can be justified in speaking of mental activity "in the head" if we understand that we are speaking metaphorically. One does not necessarily do arithmetic "in the head," for one can do it just as well (if not better) by speaking it out loud or writing it on a paper. The same can be said of imagined noise. We can "hear" music "in our heads." Who has not heard a tune over and over "in the mind"? If someone else placed an ear against the head of the subject, the tune would not be heard; but if the subject were actually speaking or singing out loud, it could be heard by means of cranial bone vibrations. The tune that we metaphorically say is "in our minds" is not really in our heads. A great deal of confusion over the mind–body "problem" results from mixing the literal sense with a metaphorical one.

A related problem is associated with the term *knowing.* "Knowing" and "knowledge" have long been of concern to philosophers, and epistemology (theory of knowledge) has traditionally been one of the main disciplines of philosophy. Yet we have encountered all sorts of problems with understanding "knowing" because of our confusion with it. Ryle maintained that we have confused "knowing that" and "knowing how." "Knowing how" is having the capacity to perform, being able to do, and so forth. But as Ryle pointed out, knowing that something is the case does not mean that we necessarily know how to *do* it. In the same way, to be able to perform or do does not mean that we necessarily understand the purposes and reasons for doing. All too often we have assumed that knowing and knowledge are too much on the side of "knowing that." This has resulted in the ignorant approach to formal education whereby we assume that after we "cram the heads" of students with facts and "knowledge," they will be able to go out into the world and perform successfully. A more healthy concept of knowing and knowledge would be that to know in the best sense is to "know that" *and* "know how."

Many problems go back to the mind–body dualism. These can even be traced back to Plato, who extolled the mental over the material; to the churchmen who extolled soul (mind) over body; and to Descartes, who devised the *cogito.* Ryle pointed out that the fault was not so much that of Descartes as it was of a long philosophical and theological tradition. Furthermore, he thought that such myths as the mind–body dualism have their uses. The creation of myths helps us get around many difficulties. It has often been observed that modern science would never have been accepted in Christendom if the Cartesian myth had not been developed, for it helped reconcile scientific findings with theological dogmas.

Perhaps we will need new myths to get around science's dogmas. New methods of investigation will need to be devised to replace our current ones. At any rate, Ryle's analysis is instructive in helping us wend our way through the linguistic confusions in which we find ourselves.

PHILOSOPHICAL ANALYSIS AND PHILOSOPHY OF EDUCATION

Although philosophical analysis is generally thought of as a relatively new development, all philosophies deal with the logical analysis of concepts, meanings, and problems to some extent. One can certainly see a great concern for analysis in the writings of Plato, Aristotle, Kant, and Descartes. The dialectic, for example, is not only a method for arriving at truth but also a method for eliminating contradictions that stand in the way of truth. Francis Bacon talked about the Idol of the Marketplace being the most troublesome of all; for as he put it, "Men believe that their reason governs words, but it is also true that words react on the understanding, and this it is that has rendered philosophy and the sciences sophistical and inactive."

The argument has been made many times that our thinking is governed in whole or in part by language and the meanings of words. It is difficult to conceive of thoughts without language, and what thinking we do can be expressed only in some kind of language. Some people believe that without language symbols (whether mathematical, verbal, written, pictured, or gestured), we would have no means of communication and hence no mind. Many analysts say that since thinking is so dependent on language, thinking problems are also language problems resulting from faulty usage and lack of clarity.

The use of analytic philosophy in education has some direct bearing on students, but perhaps it is most useful for educators in helping them clarify what *they* propose to do with students. The consequence of this use of analytic philosophy is not to develop some new educational "ism" or ideology but to help us to understand the meanings of our ideologies better. The benefits accrue to students as a result of a clarified and more meaningful approach to the educational process.

An illustrative example is the educator's confusion with the word *knowing,* an example given by Ryle. We have confused "knowing that" with the complete picture of knowing; consequently, once having "filled students' heads" with all kinds of data, we assume that our task is finished. Ryle pointed out, however, that knowing also includes "knowing how," or being able to do and perform with data. In one sense, this involves the old problem of the separation of theory ("knowing") from practice ("doing"), a problem to which John Dewey devoted much discussion. Dewey spoke of the philosophical dichotomy between knowledge and action, or knowing and doing. In other words, he maintained that knowing and doing have been artificially separated. The knowing side is similar to "knowing that," and the doing side similar to "knowing how." Dewey thought that these two should go together as much as possible, particularly with regard to the education of the young. The "learning by doing" slogan so often voiced by progressive educators has at least some of its roots in Dewey's thought. We learn or gain knowledge by becoming actively or physically involved with significant tasks. In fact, it could be said that the dichotomy goes back to the ancient Greeks, who talked about "areté" and "téchne" (virtue and skill).

Take, for example, the learning of bicycle riding. Prospective riders need to know that the vehicle is steered by turning the handlebars in the desired direction and shifting body weight to maintain balance. They must also know that the bicycle's momentum must be maintained at least at a particular minimum speed in order for the vehicle to remain operative. But so far, our prospective riders know only that certain things must be done in order to ride successfully. We may say they *know that* there are certain specific "principles" of bicycle riding. They have, so to speak, the "theory" of bicycle riding. All cyclists realize, however, that they must also know *how* to ride a bicycle—they must have a practical knowledge of cycling, and this involves the actual, out-of-doors *doing* of riding a bicycle. Educators have too often stopped with the "knowing that" aspect of knowing. Students get the theory but not the practice.

A more complex example would be the objective of producing democratic citizens, dear to the hearts of many Americans. American schools have largely accomplished the task by informing students that there is something called democracy and that in the United States this is usually associated with government, American history, and such things as the right to vote. As a general rule, however, very few students ever get to *be* democratic by *doing* things democratically. We require that they have hall passes, that they get permission to speak, and that they abide by restrictive rules that they usually have had no voice in constructing. They know that there is something called democracy, but they do not know how to be democratic. It is readily apparent why so little democracy is actually practiced in American life: most people have not had the opportunity to know *how*. In education, our usage of the term *knowing* has had a very narrow meaning. We have been confused about knowing because we have too arbitrarily restricted its meaning so as to exclude considerations about knowing extending far beyond a mere cognitive or intellectual knowing.

Thus, many analysts maintain that analytic philosophy has an important role to play in education because so much of education deals with logic and language. Teachers and students constantly deal in generalizations and value judgments about educational materials that need to be examined critically.

The analyst emphasizes that the role of language is learning and that there is a need to apply criteria for evaluating and clarifying the statements we make, a need which goes beyond the traditional studies of grammar. Some educators feel that language analysis should be the primary role with which philosophy of education is concerned. Their thesis is based on the idea that deliberate education should become more precise and scientific and that analysis offers one way to do this. They are quick to point out that other philosophies of education are usually based on highly questionable metaphysical assumptions and too often result in prescriptions that are more emotive than anything else. Such educational philosophers believe that students should study the language the students themselves use to describe and justify the meanings they apply in life.

Language is certainly important. It is doubtful that we could even think without language, since our thinking usually parallels language concepts. Bad thinking may be, in many cases, a poor use of language. Some educators protest that language analysis should be only a small part of philosophy, but philosophical analysts point out that the problems of language are so numerous, diffuse, and complex that the desired analytical study is a major undertaking of great significance. They contend that many educational problems are largely language problems and that if we can solve the language problems, we can, in effect, better solve the educational problems.

Language as an educational problem goes far beyond the confines of the school or classroom into practically all facets of life. Not only is language a prime concern for students in terms of curriculum, textbooks, and other conveyances of knowledge, but it is an integral concern in one's everyday life. Perhaps one of the special needs of modern life is a greater sensitivity to the place of language. People's behavior is heavily influenced by the language they encounter, for language stimulates all kinds of behavior. For example, Hitler came to power partly because of his ability to manipulate language. Contemporary totalitarian regimes maintain their power largely through a careful control of the language media, for they fear the consequences of an unfettered language.

George Orwell, in his novel *1984,* wrote about the creation of the Newspeak language, which was developed so that linguistic techniques could be used to control behavior. The Newspeak word *doublethink* means to believe two contradictory ideas at the same time. Thus, war is peace and love is hate. He also talked about *crimestop,* whereby people could be so conditioned to linguistic control that they could mentally prevent entertaining any idea hostile to the state or "Big Brother." One can find many examples of government officials using such techniques to try to cover up problems by using language (or corrupted versions of language) to protect their power and vested interests.

We can sympathize with the position of the philosophical analyst when we think of the barrage of advertising, sloganeering, and cliché thinking to which people are exposed daily. Since most people have had little training in logical thought, they are easy victims for the misuse of language to make them buy something, vote a certain way, or support a particular position. There are any number of language devices to which people are constantly exposed, many of which are effective in influencing their thinking. Determined persons representing vested interests have learned these devices and have found them so effective that they have used (or misused) them to persuade other people to behave in various ways. Books like Vance Packard's *The Hidden Persuaders* show how easily people can be manipulated and influenced by advertisers and politicians and how the methods used are often subtle and ingenious. Theodore White's *The Making of the President* points out how a variety of techniques, including the manipulation of language, can be used to help a candidate win election.

A further example is the term *the law*. Many people say that one should or should not do certain things because "it is the *law*." But what is the law? Laws change from time to time or differ from one country or state to another. Further, they are subject to interpretation, and thus a law as determined by one court may be overturned by another. In effect, it could be said that "the law" is an abstraction developed for a mythical person. Critics charge that lawyers prefer that the laws remain vague and abstract, for this gives them something to interpret and manipulate for clients, thus leading to an abundance of lengthy court cases.

Therefore, for reasons both practical and philosophical, analysts argue that we should be sensitive to language problems and attempt to make our language more precise and clear. This is a laudable goal but also very difficult to achieve, for words have as many meanings as users intend them to have.

Language usage affects students and teachers. Teachers often become unwilling tools of other interests as they use language in the educational process. The teacher teaches primarily with language and because of its many possibilities can use it in a variety of ways to influence the child. Teachers express ideas and information through language (including gestures), and the way they use it has a profound effect, often unrecognized, unintended, or even unconscious. Marxists have charged that teachers in capitalistic societies are so caught up in the system in which they are teaching that they cannot see that they are indoctrinating their students with the values inherent in a particular economic system.

By the time children reach adolescence, they are conditioned to the "language games" of education and may use language in similar ways to manipulate others. Language is employed in textbooks, in films, and other media; and the choice of words, the size of letters, and the kinds of grammatical construction (including what is left out) all contribute to a certain effect on a child's mental development. For example, many social studies texts omit critical discussions of various political, social, and economic policies because they might offend some pressure group by presenting such policies unfavorably. The textbooks children use in schools are not written in a vacuum and reflect many biases.

Educators themselves are victims of language devices contrived to get them to think or vote in certain ways and also to develop particular attitudes about education, children, and society. Teachers seem as susceptible to specious language devices concerning social issues as anyone else, and an enormous amount of sloganeering is generated in the educational profession. We talk about "the whole child" and "open schools" and use many other slogans. Some critics have asked: Who ever taught half a child? What does "open" really mean? We talk about "accountability" as if to show that we are businesslike and about having a "philosophy" when we generally mean a list of socially accepted maxims. We talk about the "democratic process" in instances where there is little or no democracy, about "individuality" when it is seldom allowed, and about "freedom" only within narrowly prescribed limits. Often, the case is similar to the sense of *1984:* we say "peace" when we mean war, "truth" when we mean falsehood, and "justice" when we mean injustice.

Aims of Education

Philosophical analysts are interested in improving both the educator's concepts about education and the ways in which these concepts are used. One of the first steps is to become acutely aware of language and its potential. Once we do this, the chances are better that we will have a greater concern for the sensitive use of language in the educational process. What the analytic philosopher is after is clarification. We must clarify what we propose to do in education in a philosophically adequate manner, and philosophical analysis is a major tool in accomplishing this task of clarification.

Analysts believe that educators should be attuned to the logical complexities of language. Language is a complex cultural development, and words have a variety of meanings and usages. What do such words as *knowing, mind, freedom,* and *education* really mean? While most analysts do not believe that words have inherent meanings, they do insist that we can use them in more precise ways to reflect accurately what is intended. Many concepts have an emotive effect that must be taken into consideration. Such words as *justice, patriotism, honor,* and *virtue* may give a "halo" or "hurrah" effect to statements about the aims of education.

For example, let us take the concept of *education.* Some analysts, such as R. S. Peters, insist that one cannot legitimately speak about the "aims" of education since if education is initiation into worthwhile activities, it already has all the aims it needs. Making statements about what education *should* do is to make prescriptions, an activity most analysts reject as outside the realm of analytic philosophy. Peters has questioned the use of the concept of "education" in general and has attempted to show how confusing the usage of the word has been. We have seen how Ryle attempted to show that the meaning of "knowing" could be more inclusive than the way it is ordinarily used by educators. Wittgenstein stated that words do not necessarily have an inherent, objective meaning; rather, they mean whatever the user intends them to mean. Peters, Ryle, and Wittgenstein cautioned us to examine the context and precision of our word usage. In short, the analysts do not attempt to prescribe any particular kind of education as much as they seek to clarify the conceptual devices employed by the educator, the processes of using them, their underlying presuppositions, and the purposes involved.

It seems that the use-value of words determines their meanings as much as any dictionary definition. In fact, dictionary definitions of words are altered periodically by practical use. Language itself is changing and evolving; one can neither define a word forever nor prescribe its meaning for everyone else. The educational consequence of this, the analysts claim, is that one must see concepts, word meanings, and statements about education in their practical context as opposed to a theoretical, prescriptive construction.

Teachers constantly call for practical solutions to educational problems. But this concern with "practicality" is itself open to analytic inquiry: just what does *practical* mean in this instance? Often, the "practical" teacher wants a technique, a gimmick, to apply to and solve a problem. It is reasonable, however, to observe that such "practical" solutions are often theoretical in the worst sense. Techniques are sometimes used indiscriminately. They are applied generally and universally in situations for which they were not designed; however, they are deemed "practical" because their mechanics are known and they can be acted upon.

"Achievement" is a talisman by which many educators swear, and the worth of any educational activity is judged upon students' achievement scores. "Achievement" in such instances is usually understood to be a "practical" outcome of education, but such emphasis may serve to retard one's education if the meaning of achievement is vague and unclear. Suppose one wants to learn how to play the piano, and the educator says that the "practical" approach is to proceed by achievement in learning to play scales. Such a method, however, may result in the student's learning to play scales but not in developing an ability to play the piano or in sustaining interest. We may pose the question: how "practical" is this approach?

Our use of words is intimately connected with the presuppositions underlying their use. In the case above, what was believed to be practical was not very practical at all. The proposition that one learns to play the piano by achievement in playing scales is itself theoretical and not always supported by factual circumstances (although playing the scales may *help* achieve the goal). Similar conditions exist with regard to numerous educational prescriptions.

Thus, rather than prescribing aims to be achieved in the educational process, the analyst prefers to look at what we mean by education in the first place and what advantages may accrue from a clarified concept of education. R. S. Peters spoke about the "justification" of education rather than mere aims. He pointed to at least four considerations that help us situate the meaning of education in order to arrive at better educational aims:

1. Education is more than mere specialized skills because it includes developing one's capacity to reason, justifying beliefs and conduct, knowing the *why* as well as the *what* of things, and organizing experience in terms of systematic conceptions.

2. Education is more than mere specialized knowledge and includes developing one's cognitive perspective, expanding moral understandings, and developing aesthetic appreciations.
3. Education includes doing and knowing things for their own sake, for the joy of doing and knowing.
4. Education is the process by which people are initiated into their particular life-styles.

Thus, in speaking about education, we must never forget that *means* figure in the meaning as well as *aims*. Peters aptly illustrated the problem of speaking about the aims of education when the meanings of education are so diverse. If we are truly going to be intelligent and reasonable in establishing aims in education, then we need to clear the ground to arrive at what we mean by education before we can reasonably construct particular aims. It may be that aims belong to particular teaching strategies and not to some esoteric word of confused meanings, such as *education*.

Dewey once said that "aim" was akin to a target and implied a definite goal or outcome. Peters agreed with Dewey and pointed out that if "aim" refers to specific outcomes, then it is ridiculous to speak of the "aims of education" as if these were universally agreed upon norms. It is more the case where, in any given historical period, the meanings of education have particular norms built into them by practical use. Thus, when people ask for the aims of education, they really are requesting clarification and specification of their particular contemporary norms. Any number of aims of education are possible depending upon the kinds of life people think are most important at any given time in history. Today, for instance, Peters says that there are some worthwhile overall aims, such as "growth" and "the self-realization of the individual." But aims of this sort have their roots within a cultural system that supports individualistic thought patterns. They point to autonomy and self-actualization as important, whereas another cultural epoch and historical period may view these as minor or not even recognize them at all.

Such analysts as Peters believe that we must separate the process of formulating aims in education from the general question, "What is *the* aim of education?" This question is not apt because its answer must be either conceptually true or persuasive. It falls into timeworn rubrics, such as "good citizenship is the proper aim of education" or "one of the cardinal aims of education is worthy home membership." The analyst thinks such statements only confuse the issue, for then we are pushed to define "good citizenship" or "worthy home membership." As Wittgenstein pointed out, we no sooner hear something uttered than we begin searching for its assumed objective or existing equivalent.

Israel Scheffler has critically analyzed how the word *relevance* has been misused or overused so as to complicate rather than clear up educational issues. Practically everybody would agree that education ought to be relevant. Being for relevance is like being for mother love and apple pie. But what is relevant? Scheffler maintains, in fact, that the primary task of education is not relevance; rather, it is to support and insure a society dedicated to ideals of free inquiry and rationality. Thus, it is not the aim of education we must seek but an understanding of what kinds of desirable aims there are, what the possibilities are of achieving them, and what kinds of consequences we may expect from acting on them. These latter considerations are not within the province of the philosopher of education as much as they are within the province of sociologists, psychologists, scientists, political leadership, and ordinary citizens. The analytic philosopher's role is simply to clarify and criticize meanings involved.

Methods of Education

Analysts are concerned that both the methods and materials of contemporary education undergo a serious analytical study. While most analysts avoid prescribing what should or should not go on in the educational process, they are very interested in seeing that both the educator and student critically examine the curriculum from the standpoint of materials, methods, policies, and procedures.

Analysts are aware that methods and media of all kinds educate the child in many ways. Although educators should understand that words and concepts are value laden, they do not always seem to operate with an awareness of this fact. When the McGuffey readers were used in the early 1900s, for example, they taught not only reading skills but also particular values concerning church, patriotism, and family. Books of the "Dick-and-Jane" type that came later supposedly attempted to provide a more neutral kind of material that was value free. Neutrality was not achieved, however, for "Dick-and-Jane" readers contained assumptions about gender roles, children's rights and their relationship to society, and dominant social class themes, such as the "work ethic" and respect for authority.

Analysts do not attempt to say whether a child should read McGuffey or Dick and Jane; rather, they examine the meaning of the claims made regarding the merits of such activities. Instead of saying what a child *should* read, think, study, or learn, the analyst examines what we mean by the words *think, read,* or *learn* and the statements we make regarding these words. Some analysts avoid not only prescriptive statements about what students ought or ought not do but also statements of value about the importance of such activities.

For example, there has been a great deal of concern in contemporary education about the "Right to Read" and the necessity of reading in adult life. The analysts would not question *whether* people should have a "right to read" but what is meant by the terminology and the statements made regarding this "right." There are a number of meanings involved in the way the words are used, and these must be viewed against the conditions and circumstances of contemporary society. It has been suggested that the "Right to Read" campaign is supported by the various publishing concerns who have vested interests in maintaining reading behavior. This support has to be considered in light of the great advances that have been made in the electronics media that modify the kinds and extent of reading skills needed. Another point of view is that the "Right to Read" campaign is fostered by reactionary political interests in order to take attention from more reform-minded social programs involved in education, such as the attempts to desegregate American society through educational means.

In addition, programs like the "Right to Read" campaign involve prescriptions that all children "ought" to read. When questioned about why children ought to read, advocates provide such answers as "to obtain a job," "to maintain a high standard of living," or for "leisure activities," all of which may or may not be desirable justifications. These "oughts" imply long-range considerations about the value of reading that may not withstand systematic scrutiny.

In regard to this particular slogan—the "Right to Read"—analysts are not primarily interested, philosophically speaking, about whether persons do or do not actually have such a moral "right." They are interested, rather, in what is meant by the slogan. Even though a particular analyst may personally agree that people should have the right to read, this is not an attempt to prescribe that right from the standpoint of philosophy itself. To the analyst, prescription is not the business of philosophy. Thus, in analyzing the meaning of "Right to Read," the analytic philosopher would seek to build an explanation of the various uses of the concept—the language "games" being played—showing inconsistencies, emotional reactions, contradictory assertions, and external influences that shed light on implied meanings.

Some analysts advocate devising *paradigms;* that is, constructing models of logic that serve to help us clarify and order our concepts. This resembles Wittgenstein's idea of "language games" in some respects but differs in that a paradigm has a rather specific use. It is tailored to particular kinds of problems. Gordon Eastwood has described an appropriate analytic paradigm as one that has "a syntactically and semantically appropriate language system" that should be prescriptive only to the extent that it "enable[s] the formation of hypotheses to guide research for facts not now known." In this regard, paradigms are useful for looking at educational problems in an objective, nonpartisan, and unemotive way.

Eastwood has even suggested that large-scale paradigms be used, and he has criticized many analytic philosophers of education who direct their attention to small (or what Eastwood calls insignificant) problems. Instead, philosophy of education must be concerned with theory building in education from the standpoint of emphasizing the logical foundations of theory, and Eastwood argues that we must envision this task from an appropriate paradigm standpoint to approach it adequately.

Jerome Popp has noted that one may choose different paradigms for different purposes, and it is unnecessary to choose global or universal paradigms. At the same time, however, he cautions that consistency seems preferable to wild eclecticism. Popp recognizes that the search for large-scale paradigms involves to some extent "world view" outlooks that are very close to old "grand manner" philosophy. It could be argued, for example, that the paradigm approach contains the seeds of destruction for the analytic approach to philosophy. It eschews the large-scale point of view but needs the larger picture to give coherence and meaning to its task.

Jonas Soltis has observed that, in the late 1950s and early 1960s, we underwent a shift from a "pragmatic paradigm" to an "analytic paradigm." Pragmatic philosophy could no longer deal adequately with urgent contemporary problems; so students of philosophy turned to the new paradigm of analysis, which seemed more in line with the concerns of the day. However, analysis is now apparently coming to suffer from similar shortcomings, and it must shift its focus from small-scale problems to larger, more encompassing ones.

Henry J. Perkinson talks about education in terms of various *functions:* intellectual, moral, emotional, aesthetic, political, and economic. Looking at education in such terms helps us to see all facets of education. Rather than viewing education as a confusing, conflicting series of activities, the paradigmatic approach helps us to isolate activities and examine specific aspects of those activities as we have never before been able to do. Thus, Eastwood's suggestion falls in line with the way science operates, but as Perkinson pointed out in *The Possibilities of Error: An Approach to Education,* there is no single critical method, only different approaches. The critical approach only looks for what is wrong. The use of paradigms can help us to examine existing theories, remove inconsistencies, modify actions, and replace institutions.

One of the areas with which analysts have spent much time is the activity of teaching. Paul Hirst has shown the need for empirical research on the effectiveness of various teaching methods. Most methods, he claims, are based on little more than hunches and personal prejudices. Hirst states that teachers need to be clear about the nature of the central activity in which they are professionally involved. How, for example, do we distinguish teaching from other activities? Are teachers teaching when they sharpen a few pencils and break up squabbles among the children? One must admit, says Hirst, that teaching is a "polymorphous" activity; it may take many different forms. To know that teaching is going on, we must clarify the aims and the intentions so that each activity is seen in a clear relationship to those aims.

Successful teaching seems to be teaching that brings about desired learning. Yet this desired learning could result from conditioning or indoctrination. If we wish to study the difference between conditioning and indoctrinating, we should postulate a perfect case of each in its most literal and ordinary use. Then we can understand the differences in the meaning of each term—that is, *conditioning* or *indoctrinating*. Even though there will be differences, there will also be similarities of meanings for each term with which everyone will agree, thus clarifying the meaning of each term. The clarified agreed-upon meanings become the different modes of teaching by which actual cases are compared. Thus, teaching methodologies are established based on teaching modes that serve as bench marks or standards of minimal performance. If one were to ask "How would you teach X to someone?" then reference could be made to the appropriate mode. Of course, disagreements as to proper modes could continue to arise so that there may be several other models on how to teach.

Analysis is an ongoing activity. Conclusions are not arrived at full-blown and axiomatic. They do not precede investigation but flow from it. The major thrust of analytic philosophy is to try to arrive at clarified principles, agreements, and conclusions rather than to start with them. In this sense, philosophical analysis follows in the footsteps of the Socratic view of philosophy as the search for wisdom.

Curriculum

Analysts, including Richard Pring, point out that such curriculum terms as *integrated studies, integrated curriculum, unified knowledge, broad fields of experience,* and *problem solving* are confusing and misleading. Such statements or phrases as "the seamless coat of learning" and "the unity of all knowledge" lack clarity of meaning and have no inherent value. Conversely, such terms as *traditional, subject matter,* and *compartmentalization* are not necessarily bad in and of themselves. These slogans and phrases dealing with curricula have been used to set up straw men polarized along conceptions of good and bad.

Curriculum used to be viewed as something established in order to achieve certain ends, but it seems that today the ends flow from the curriculum itself. Hugh Sockett maintains that throughout the literature on curriculum there is a great deal of talk about taking means to ends and conceiving of the relation between means and ends as contingent. Sockett argues that what must be maintained as central to any account of curriculum, aims, and objectives is human intentionality—our conception of what we are doing. Therefore, our conceptions must be clear.

Philosophical analysts are aghast at the flippant manner in which educational plans are made. Curriculum planning is too often superficial and badly done. Cultural bias is almost the only rationale one can discover in too many curriculum plans. There seems to be little systematic or careful planning. Often, this is not the fault of the persons involved so much as it is the faulty language, confused meanings, and unclear purposes involved. We not only need to examine present curricula in terms of these problems, but we also need to promote an ongoing critical attitude toward curriculum restructuring in which meanings and purposes are made clear.

Pring says that the foremost philosophical problems in curriculum and curriculum integration are what meanings are involved, what assumptions are made about knowledge, what the forms of knowledge are, what the interrelationship between these forms is, and what the structural unity of language is. Thus, we see that any concern with curriculum goes far beyond the idea of plugging subject areas into a switchboard of school programs. Unfortunately, today we have many people who see curriculum reform very narrowly and give little attention to the deeper questions involved. Analysts believe that greater attention must be given to the philosophical aspects, and they have encouraged greater work in this area.

CRITIQUE OF ANALYTIC PHILOSOPHY IN EDUCATION

Analysis has been an indispensable part of philosophy since its inception, and every serious philosopher has done some analysis. There is always a need for clarifying ideas and refining concepts. Much in the writings of philosophers from Plato to the present points to the need to use language carefully and to avoid inconsistency and illogic. It is undoubtedly true that a major problem is the confusion in understanding brought about by unclear or careless language. It is easy to document the misuse of many words and concepts, such as "liberal," "conservative," "God," and so forth. History is replete with instances of how the misuse of words and the misunderstanding of meanings have led to internal strife, religious differences, and even full-scale wars. Some analysts maintain that since language is so important to thinking, it is almost inconceivable that we could think at all without it. They further observe that confused thinking may well be the poor use of words in the thinking process.

One of the functions of philosophy is to develop a critical attitude toward language and meaning, and this is certainly something that analysts have fostered. Rather than accept ready-made answers, clichés, and slogans as solutions for educational and social problems, they have supported an approach that insists that all ideas and issues be examined every step along the way. Analysts are wary of "the grand manner of philosophizing" in which there is a cry for synthesis and simple solutions to complicated problems. They are skeptical of a utopian attitude toward problems in which emotive or predetermined ends may lead our thinking awry. They are also fearful of the emotional factors that may overshadow clear and dispassionate thinking. This is not to imply that analysts are cold and unemotional, but they are well aware of the dangers of passionate and fuzzy thinking.

Critics of analytic philosophy of education have pointed out that while analysis has helped educators clarify and define some educational problems better, this may be too limited a view to meet the demands of our changing, complex culture. Shying away from prescription has helped to make philosophers of education more wary of grandiose statements; but at the same time, some critics note that while philosophers have ceased to prescribe, many other people, such as psychologists and sociologists, continue to make grand prescriptions. There seems to be little evidence that these latter sources for contemporary educational prescriptions are necessarily superior to the philosophical sources. Indeed, some persons say that they are worse.

One of the things that frustrates critics of philosophical analysis is that it is difficult to ascertain what analysts really want in terms of education. In fairness to philosophical analysts, it should be emphasized that they have seldom claimed or pretended to introduce any prescriptive maxims for educational practice itself. Yet while analysts claim their only wish is to clarify concepts and language, it is extremely difficult for many critics to see that their work has really achieved any great clarification. Analysts have uncovered ambiguities and misconceptions in education. But where do we go from there? Wittgenstein wanted to "let the fly out of the bottle," but where does the fly go once it gets out?

Suppose we had a nicely clarified and precise language with regard to education. The purely descriptive and analytic approach may be able to give us positive clarity about what we are doing in education; but if we are doing the wrong things to begin with, the wrongness is not necessarily corrected simply by language clarification. To maintain that language clarification itself will reveal inhumane and wrong educational practice is, it seems, to express a mystical belief in the power of language at the expense of action. Nevertheless, we *should* clarify our ideas and statements. Clarification, however, does not rule out prescriptions and recommendations about the problems of life. Indeed, it should help us to arrive at better formulated and constructed recommendations for action.

Perhaps part of the critic's frustration lies in the efforts of some philosophical analysts to say that true philosophy can only be analytic or that analysis inevitably leads to the "death" of traditional philosophy. Where, then, do our visions come from? Surely, philosophy is not the only historical source for social renewal, and many philosophical recommendations and utopian schemes are nonsensical, unworkable, and even completely inhumane. However, it seems just as certain that philosophy has as great a role to play in formulating social and educational policy as any other intellectual pursuit. Dewey, in his quaint way, remarked that "while saints introspect, burly sinners rule the world." Analysts have seemed to be content to quarrel over the meanings of terms, phrases, and statements while the world around them paid respect to their efforts by simply ignoring them. It could be said that philosophical analysis is little more than a new form of scholasticism, where instead of arguing about how many angels can stand on the head of a pin, analysts debate about how the words *should* and *ought* may be used. One disgruntled critic charged that when someone points a finger at a problem, the analysts study the finger rather than the problem.

While analysts claim to eschew prescriptive and a priori assumptions, it seems that in general, philosophical analysis has its own underlying assumptions or prescriptions. The penchant for paradigmatic models of analysis betrays a hidden assumption that there are clear, certain, and specifiable ways of doing things, what Richard Rorty has criticized as the "mirror of nature" view of philosophy. This seems very close to philosophical realism's belief in a reality with its own inherent and universal principles. For example, Paul Hirst has stated that we need to know about the effectiveness of different teaching methods, but that "without the clearest concept of what teaching is, it is impossible to find appropriate behavioral criteria whereby to assess what goes on in the classroom." This assumes that a *clear* concept of teaching can be uncovered. It also assumes that teaching can be assessed on the basis of "appropriate" behavioral criteria. The assumptions are these: there is a clear form of teaching, there are appropriate teaching behaviors, and these things have an existence that can be studied, described, classified, and objectively duplicated. This is very close to the position of scientific realism.

The universalizing tendency in analytic philosophy has been a bone of contention for many postmodern thinkers, who attack all efforts to define the philosophical enterprise into a single approach. While postmodernists are sympathetic to analytic philosophy's sensitivities to language, they maintain that the chief value to come out of the tradition lies with Wittgenstein's approach—that is, to a fuller appreciation of the variety of usages language can have and to the interplay of meanings that are possible. On other points, however, postmodernists find analytic philosophy too constraining and too defining.

No doubt we can construct teaching models that can be taught and duplicated. This fact is no proof that such models are ethically desirable. Because something can be done is no grounds logically, morally, or socially for doing it. Clarity and logic do not equal rightness, perfection, or moral certainty because human problems, including the problems of education, seem to be contingent on many fluctuating variables. No sooner do we think we have arrived at a solution than intervening events push us off on another troublesome tangent.

The analysts have attacked pragmatists, existentialists, reconstructionists, and others because they recommend certain changes and make substantive judgments about social and educational policy. Pragmatism, for example, tried to make us sensitive to the means–ends continuum in achieving a more democratic society; that is, that the actual ends achieved in social and educational endeavors are continuous with, and contingent upon, the actual means used. Analytic approaches also may help us clarify both intended and actual means and ends, but their aversion to using philosophy in actively pursuing broad social and educational changes seems to some critics to be a classic case of the philosophical "failure of nerve" to meet the challenges we face today.

Analysts have attempted to redefine the work of philosophy by refuting the old "grand manner" or "systems" approach. This effort has had some very healthy effects because it helps us to stop thinking in terms of ultimate answers and sweeping conclusions. The Analytic Movement has helped philosophers develop and implement more refined linguistic and logical tools. The problem with analysis is, critics charge, that the tools seem to have become an end in themselves quite apart from the ethical and political uses to which they may be put.

MARTIN

ON THE REDUCTION OF "KNOWING THAT" TO "KNOWING HOW"

In this selection, Jane R. Martin, a contemporary American educator, further attempts to clarify Gilbert Ryle's famous distinction between "knowing that" and "knowing how." Martin demonstrates how the techniques of analytic philosophy may be used to examine crucial philosophical concepts in terms of education. She distinguishes between several kinds of knowing and suggests how they may enter into the teaching process. Without proposing what should be taught or who should teach it, Martin maintains that there are several kinds of "knowing that" and "knowing how," and she examines the further implications of Ryle's distinction for both theory and practice.

The distinction between "knowing how" and "knowing that," which Gilbert Ryle makes in Chapter 2 of *The Concept of Mind,* is the point of departure for this paper. Ryle's object in writing *The Concept of Mind* was to discredit once and for all Cartesian dualism, or what he calls "the Myth of the Ghost in the Machine." The particular aim of Chapter 2 is to show that there are many activities which directly display qualities of mind, yet are neither themselves intellectual operations nor yet effects of intellectual operations. When we describe such activities, we are not referring to a "second set of shadowy operations." According to Ryle, intelligent practice, that is, "knowing how," is not a "step-child of theory." On the contrary, theorizing, that is, "knowing that," is "one practice amongst others and is itself intelligently or stupidly conducted." In distinguishing between "knowing how" and "knowing

that" Ryle hopes to correct the intellectualist doctrine which tended to view all knowing as "knowing that." He strongly opposed the view that intelligent performance must be preceded by an intellectual acknowledgment of rules or criteria, that a person must "preach to himself before he can practice."

Ryle's distinction is clearly relevant to the problems of teaching and learning. For example, the learning of skills need not be preceded by knowledge of rules: men knew how to reason correctly before the rules of correct reasoning were formulated by Aristotle. Knowledge of rules is not sufficient for the performance of a skill: we do not say that a boy knows how to play chess if he can recite the rules but cannot make the required moves. In judging a performance we must look "beyond," not "behind," the performance. This does not mean we seek an occult cause for a skillful performance, but rather that a single sample of behavior is not sufficient to attribute "knowledge how" to an actor; we must take account of past record and subsequent performance as well.

Because of its simplicity and apparent obviousness, the distinction between "knowing how" and "knowing that" has great appeal, but like any dichotomy it gives rise to much controversy and perplexity. Hartland-Swann has argued that "knowing that" can be reduced to "knowing how." Let us grant that his reduction holds if "knowing how" and "knowing that" are used to refer to a rather limited range of dispositions. Once "knowing that" is reduced to "knowing how," however, a distinction must be made between two types of dispositions subsumed under "knowing how."

It is of practical importance to analyze the various types of "knowing how" and "knowing that" sentences in ordinary speech and to make such differentiations as are necessary, even if the simplicity of Ryle's dichotomy or Hartland-Swann's reduction is thereby lost. Just as Ryle has drawn our attention to the dangers to education inherent in the reduction of "knowing how" to "knowing that," one may point out dangers inherent in a reduction of "knowing that" to "knowing how" if analysis is discontinued at that point. It would seem no more desirable to teach mathematical or historical facts as if they were skills like swimming than to teach swimming as if it were Latin or geometry. And an equally grave mistake would be to teach moral judgments and rules of conduct as if they were either Latin or swimming.

Ryle's Distinction

In order to formulate Ryle's distinction between "knowing how" and "knowing that" as clearly as possible, it is necessary to ascertain the meaning of the terms "knowing how" and "knowing that." Ryle calls "know" a capacity verb, and thus it is safe to conclude that he would call both "knowing how" and "knowing that" capacities also. (Ryle differentiates capacities from tendencies, although both are dispositions. A tendency implies not only that something *could* be the case, but that it *would* be the case regularly when the appropriate conditions are realized; a capacity implies the ability to do something under specified conditions but does not imply frequency or regularity.) At no time does he say exactly what he means by the two types of knowing. From the examples he adduces and several of his statements, however, it is possible to determine that "knowing how" refers to skills or operations, for example, knowing how to play chess, knowing how to theorize, knowing how to speak Russian; and that "knowing that" refers to one's "cognitive repertoire," that is, to knowledge of factual propositions, as for instance, knowing that Sussex is a county in England, knowing that *Messer* is the German word for knife.

It is essential to note that Ryle assimilates all "knowing how" to the model "knowing how to perform a task" and all "knowing that" to the model "knowing that such and such is the case," for we then realize that his distinction is of a more limited nature than we might at first have thought. In ordinary language the phrase "knowing how" is often used when performances are not involved, and the phrase "knowing that" is found in sentences which do not refer to knowing factual propositions. For example, we say, "Johnny knows how a motor works," "I know how Eisenhower felt on election night," and "Jones knows how the accident happened." We also say, "Smith knows that he ought to be honest," "The child knows that he should be quiet when someone is speaking," and "Johnny knows that stealing is bad." None of these examples fits Ryle's paradigms for "knowing how" or "knowing that."

To summarize, Ryle's distinction between "knowing how" and "knowing that" is really a distinction between "knowing how to perform skills" and "knowing propositions of a factual nature." When Hartland-Swann discusses the question of the reducibility of "knowing that" to "knowing how," he too, I believe, is viewing "knowing how" and "knowing that" in this way. Thus in discussing his reduction one must not assume that it holds for all "knowing that" sentences. In fact, I think we will find that such sentences as "Johnny knows that he ought to be quiet" and "Jones knows that he should be honest" cannot be reduced to Ryle's and Hartland-Swann's "knowing how." This problem will be discussed in Section 3. First those sentences to which Hartland-Swann's reduction applies will be analyzed.

Two Kinds of "Knowing How"

Hartland-Swann maintains that Ryle's distinction between "knowing how" and "knowing that" proves to be unstable when subjected to analysis. Every case of "knowing that," he says, is a case of "knowing how." This follows from the fact that "know" is a dispositional term. If I understand him correctly, what he means is that if we call the statement "Johnny knows that Columbus discovered America" dispositional, then it must be translatable into some such form as "Johnny knows how to answer the question 'Who discovered America?' or 'What did Columbus discover?' correctly." The only alternative to this inclusion of "knowing that" in the "knowing how" category, Hartland-Swann feels, would be to give up the dispositional analysis of "know."

I think one must agree with Hartland-Swann that a dispositional analysis of "knowing that" entails a translation of a "knowing that" sentence into a "knowing how" sentence of the type illustrated above, that is, knowing how to answer a question or to state a fact. It would be a mistake, however, to end the analysis of "knowing" with this reduction, for granted that "knowing that" can be reduced to "knowing how," there is still a fundamental distinction to be made within Hartland-Swann's new, expanded "knowing how" category. The basis for this distinction lies in the fact that two very different sorts of dispositions are subsumed under "knowing how."

Let us consider for a moment the case of Jones who was witness to the murder of Y. Without doubt Jones knows that X murdered Y, and this, in turn, means he knows how to state that X murdered Y and knows how to answer the question "Who murdered Y?" Yet it seems intuitively obvious that there is an essential difference between his knowing how to answer the question "Who murdered Y?" and his knowing how to swim or speak French. That is to say, the difference between the capacity involved in knowing how to state that X murdered Y and the capacity involved in knowing how to swim is more basic than the difference between the capacities involved in knowing how to swim and knowing how to do logic, or in knowing how to ice skate and knowing how to play the violin.

I would like to suggest that the feature which distinguishes these two kinds of capacities from each other is *practice*. That is, "knowing how to swim" is a capacity which implies having learned how to swim through practice; "knowing how to answer the question 'Who murdered Y'" is a capacity which does not imply having learned how to answer the question through practice. When Jones was a witness to the murder, he knew immediately that X murdered Y and did not need to practice stating facts or answering questions. Similarly, when Jones looks out his window and sees rain falling, he knows that it is raining without any sort of practice in saying "It is raining" or answering the question "What is the weather like right now?" To be sure, if he knows that it is raining, he *is able* to state certain facts and answer certain questions, but his capacity to do so does not imply that he has practiced doing so. On the other hand, Jones could not know how to swim or speak French unless he had at some time practiced swimming or tried to speak French. If Jones tells us he knows how to swim we are justified in asking him if he has ever tried to swim. If he answers "No" to our query, his assertion will be discredited. But if Jones tells us that he knows that X murdered Y, it surely would be nonsensical for us to ask him if he has practiced that assertion or tried to answer questions on the subject before.

If, as I propose, the difference between the two types of capacities subsumed under "knowing how" is based on the notion of practice, some interesting consequences follow. If knowing how to swim requires learning to swim through practice, then we usually would not consider the practice itself to be swimming. The practice may consist in kicking and arm waving and, if all goes well, these will gradually approach swimming. Although the point at which the practice in swimming becomes swimming is not for us to determine, it is interesting to consider the case of the individual who practices just up to the point where he actually swims and then gets out of the water. I think we could say of him that he knows how to swim even though he has not yet actualized this capacity by swimming.

Just as there may be cases of knowing how to swim which are not cases of swimming, so there may be cases of swimming which are not cases of knowing how to swim. For example, it is conceivable that Jones falls into the water one day and swims to shore although he has never practiced or tried to swim before. We cannot deny that he is swimming, but we might well wish to deny that he knows how to swim. In the case of swimming, of course, it is logically possible but in fact unlikely that there would be a performance of the skill which had not been preceded by practice. If, however, we think of a skill such as hitting the target, we realize that it is not too unusual for a novice to hit the bull's-eye without any previous practice. In such a situation we would maintain that although he hit his mark he does not "know how" to hit it. For we would expect someone who knows how to hit the target to hit it again. In other words, hitting a target is an occurrence which may be due to accident or luck; knowing how to hit a target is a capacity, and we would be right to look for a certain degree of consistency of behavior.

"Practice," of course, is a vague term. Although I do not think its limits need be set here, it is important to realize that many skills are related and that practice for one skill may thus serve as practice for another. Hence, on those occasions when it appears that we know how to do something without having practiced it, upon reflection we will discover that we have had practice in a related skill. It is possible, also, for the accidental or lucky occurrence to serve as practice for a skill. For example, if Jones swims to shore although he has never had practice in swimming, this very swimming may provide him with practice.

It is not denied here that we do exhibit some patterns of behavior with consistency although we have not practiced them. Yawning, crying, sneezing are examples. We call these reflexes, not skills, however, and do not speak of "knowing how" to yawn, cry, or sneeze. The exception is the case of the actor who is able to perform these behaviors at will. We might actually say of him that he "knows how" to yawn, cry, or sneeze, but it is clear that he has learned to do so through practice.

It appears, then, that although Hartland-Swann's reduction of "knowing that" to "knowing how" is legitimate for those "knowing that" sentences which are cases of knowing factual propositions, there is still a basic distinction between these sentences and the kinds of "knowing how" sentences which are cases of knowing how to perform an operation. Whether or not it is agreed that the basis for the distinction is practice, I do not think the distinction itself can be denied.

Source: Jane Roland Martin, "On the Reduction of 'Knowing That' to 'Knowing How,'" in *Language and Concepts in Education*, edited by B. O. Smith and R. H. Ennis. Chicago: Rand McNally Company, 1961, pp. 399–404.

DOES THE QUESTION "WHAT IS EDUCATION?" MAKE SENSE?

Robin Barrow examines one of the important questions to be asked about education; and that is, what is it? He looks at education's historical use, as well as its activity. This article points to the use of analysis as a tool in looking at the fundamental concepts of education and shows the penchant of the philosophical analyst for exploring significant yet often assumed or passed-over educational questions. This is an example of a conceptual approach to analytical thinking as opposed to a purely linguistic one.

There are those who object to discussions about method and procedure in philosophy. Both Jim Gribble, for example, in his *Introduction to Philosophy of Education*, and more recently Janet Radcliffe Richards, in *The Sceptical Feminist*, have suggested that one should get on with philosophizing rather than begin with an account of what it involves. But since philosophy, unlike most other subjects, is defined in terms of its procedures and methods rather than its content, since doing philosophy is engaging in a process rather than examining a product, to have a fine appreciation of what the activity involves is to be more than halfway along the road to philosophizing. Furthermore, it seems clear to me that we have a particular need to get clear about the nature of philosophical analysis at the present time, since its lack of impact arises partly out of it being confused with other studies, such as that of semantics, and since different philosophers evidently see themselves as engaged in somewhat different tasks. The issue has been well highlighted in a recent exchange between John Wilson and Philip Snelders in the *Journal of Philosophy of Education*, where the former appears, as it were, from stage right with a barely modified Platonic theory of forms, and the latter comes to meet him from stage left with a handful of Protean concepts of no fixed shape. My own view, broadly, is that Wilson has the right of it in that we take too many silly alleged conceptual doubts seriously (the structure of British Trade Unions just isn't democratic; influencing people or teaching them the mathematics

tables is not indoctrination), but on the other hand Snelders has the right of it in seeing that nonetheless questions such as, "Is an educated man necessarily committed to the value of X and Y?" and "Does indoctrination necessarily presuppose intention?" cannot simply be dismissed on the grounds that education just *is* this, indoctrination just *is* that, and all sensible people know it.

So what is going on when one asks the question "What is education?" Does it make sense, or should it rather be rephrased in some other form, such as "What do you think education is?" "How is the word used in this society?" or "What do the professional educators mean by 'education'?" Is there an essence to education that cannot be ignored, or is one's conception just a matter of ideological perspective? In answering the central question I hope also to answer three others: "Can a concept be incorrect?", "Can a concept be invalid?" and "Does the claim that two conceptions of X are equally valid, imply that everything depends on your point of view?"

Let us start, unashamedly, with basics. A concept is a unifying principle. It is not to be identified with a mental image nor with a word. One has the concept of X when one appreciates what is common to all instances of X. How concepts are initially acquired is not my present concern, but it is evident that they are not all acquired in exactly the same way. Some, such as color and shape concepts, may arise through direct perception; others, such as the concept of house or philosopher, require understanding of function before they can be grasped. But still to have a concept of triangularity is to recognize particular triangles as such, just as to have a concept of house is to recognize cognitively that various seemingly dissimilar buildings perform the same particular set of functions, and to have a concept of happiness is to see the common factor between outwardly very different people contentedly at one or enmeshed with their situation.

As already noted, words and concepts are not the same thing. The same word may refer to more than one concept; one concept may be referred to by a number of synonymous words; things can be said about words that do not make sense in reference to concepts, and vice versa; in each of the above examples one might have the concept without having the word. Concepts, even when they refer to what we term concrete nouns, are by definition abstract and general. It is simply bad English to use the word concept in reference to particular instances, as in "my concept of Mrs. Thatcher" or "my concept of this desk."

So much is obvious. However, because as a matter of fact we use words to identify concepts and we can seldom, if ever, communicate except through words, there is both a temptation and a justification for trying to get at concepts by examining words. And this of course is what we are advised to do by a variety of linguistic philosophers. And they have a point. If we want to examine the concept of education, then surely we must start with the word "education," and surely it is significant in respect of understanding the concept that it appears to make little sense to say, for example, "His education improves every time he eats a chocolate pudding." On the other hand there are four serious problems with this procedure. First, if we are concerned with the use of the word either we must engage in the empirical task of finding out about and studying *all* uses of the word (which would make philosophy and linguistics indistinguishable), or we must judge some uses to be more central, more ordinary, or in some other way more acceptable than others, in which case we need criteria for making such judgments, which we do not in fact

have. Secondly, although it may be of some interest to know about the use of a particular word, it is not at all clear what significance or importance it is supposed to have. What hangs, for example, on the fact that the Greek word *areté* is used in very different ways from the English word "virtue" by which it is conventionally translated? What is such scrutiny telling us about virtue, which is to say the notion itself, as opposed to what the Greeks and we variously think about it? Or is this the crunch point: do we conclude here and now that there is nothing more to be considered than what various groups happen to think? Thirdly, if we do assume that the concept of virtue is to be identified with the use of the word "virtue" (whether this be a matter of definitional logic or practical necessity), it becomes logically impossible to have a revolutionary or original thought about a concept. Imagine that we live in a society that finds it inconceivable that non-human animals should be happy. Their conception of happiness, their use of the word "happy," in other words, makes it impossible for me to say correctly, "That dog is happy." But this makes it impossible for us to extend the application of our concepts. Moore traded, unknowingly, on just this muddle when he used the open question argument to show that good cannot be identified with anything since it is always possible to say, "I know this is X, but is it good?" Of course it is always possible to *say* that, because what we think it makes sense to say necessarily reflects our current views. But suppose we are just wrong? Suppose X and good *are* to be identified, and it doesn't make sense to say "I know this is X, but is it good?" All Moore's argument does is confirm our prejudices. (Indeed one might suggest that change in language presupposes a clear distinction between concepts and words. Words change their meanings, because people have original ideas that initially make ordinary language use inadequate or even wrong.) Fourthly, and most important of all, we have to remember that this link between words and concepts is only contingent. One can have a concept of beauty without the word "beauty" or any other word open to public scrutiny. And the truth is that many of us when we ask, "What is reality?" "What is free-will?" or "What is justice?" are manifestly not asking, "How do other people use the words 'real,' 'free will' and 'justice'?" which would at best tell us something about how other people would answer the questions, but are seeking to grapple with certain complex notions on which we have a tenuous hold.

The solution to the problem is very simple, although it has certain consequences which some seem unable to come to grips with. We should start with the word, allow usage to guide us to one or a set of target areas, and from that point on refuse to be bound by usage. For example, we may start with the word "education," make such observations as that it is a commendatory term, is sometimes used in somewhat unexpected contexts ("the educated left-jab of the boxer"), is generally presumed to imply something about knowledge and understanding, and so on. In doing that we are gaining something useful, for we are getting some hints and clues about what people in general think about what we call education. But we should remember (1) that this is only information about the use of the word and what people may therefore be presumed to think, and (2) that consequently we may get some contradictory or even incoherent hints and clues.

What will happen with many words is that a number of clearly distinguishable uses will emerge. In that case one settles on one such use (this is one of the target areas) and tries to gain a more complete and refined understanding of that use, that sense of the word, that idea or conception, if necessary making a positive contribution to knock shape into or shed light on it. At this stage no appeal is made to use, for we are trying to explicate in greater detail an idea that is already in our mind in response to a particular use of the word. The whole operation can be illustrated quite neatly by reference to creativity. Johnny, aged two, splashing paint about at will, is said by some to be creative. Fred, an adult, converting his attic into a habitable room, is regarded by his neighbors as creative. Beethoven glowering over the manuscript of the Ninth Symphony is once again in

creative mood. Now these are distinct cases. There may very well be points of contact between the examples, and some individuals might even want to call them all "creative" because they want to highlight some common denominator. Nonetheless the cases, as a whole, are indubitably distinct. Unless therefore someone does explicitly offer a lowest common denominator account of creativity, one may presume we are dealing with different, if related, uses of the word. They are different conceptions of creativity. To arrive at or note such different uses, to comment on the emotive meaning of the term in each case, to consider etymological origins, even to trace common denominators, are activities that belong to verbal analysis. But to concentrate on one use and to try to explicate the idea it refers to more precisely and clearly is to analyze a concept. Philosophical analysis no doubt should include both, but it seems to me that we have spent a disproportionate amount of time on verbal analysis and failed to appreciate that conceptual analysis soars away from usage. What I am trying to get at when I examine the notion of Beethoven as a creative artist should owe no more to how the word is used: I am alone with the notion seeking to giving an account of it that makes explicit what otherwise may remain a hazy accolade.

There are some immediate consequences of this view. The first is that conceptual analysis is a personal matter at rock bottom. You clear your mind. You are trying to clarify this idea of Beethoven being creative; you are trying to lay out a coherent account of what the idea involves for you. Of course the task does not have to be engaged in privately. We can have seminars and discussions and we can share conceptions. Very often we will, because, as has nowhere been denied, a lot of our concepts are initially acquired through a common language. But the fact that we are all brought up to use the word "democracy" with the same rough denotation, so that we are all contemplating the same target area, does not mean that any of us can give a decent explication of that concept. A second consequence of this view is that the phrase "*the* concept of X" needs explanation. Superficially it doesn't make sense, since there is no such thing as a unitary concept except contingently. Rather there are conceptions of democracy, education or whatever. However, the phrase can be taken as meaningful, if we interpret it to mean something such as "the conception dominant in Western culture" or "the conception in this circle."

A third consequence, as I have argued before, is that much philosophy of education is not engaging in *bona fide* conceptual analysis, and is as a partial result rather stultifying, besides providing a vulnerable point of attack for those who seek to dismiss philosophy altogether. Kevin Harris's book *Education and Knowledge,* for example, bases its entire attack on philosophy of education, on a misunderstanding of what conceptual analysis is for some of us, but in that he has been helped by the fact that some of what passes for conceptual analysis is in fact merely verbal analysis. Too many people seem to assume that when there's a word there's a paper to be written. But not all words refer to problematic or interesting concepts. In an otherwise most generous review of my *The Philosophy of Schooling,* I was recently taken to task by D. Bob Gowin for having failed to include a chapter on learning, which he suggests is one of the central concepts in the educational enterprise. I agree with him entirely about its centrality; I disagree with his view that it requires analysis. Learning, like play, teaching, and schooling itself, seems to me to be unproblematic as a concept. That is to say I know what learning is, even if I don't know various non-philosophical things such as how to facilitate it, in a way that I do not really know what my conception of free will amounts to, even though I quite often make claims about it. Naturally there is room for judgment over what concepts are problematic, and indeed it follows from the thesis I am arguing, that some concepts may be more problematic for one person than another. The important point here is the general one: we surely want to confine our attempts to explicate X to those cases where X, though often referred to, is really rather hazy, incoherent or ill-articulated in our minds. We want papers on moral personhood rather than

homo sapiens, on education rather than schooling.

I will not dwell here at any length on a point that I have made in the book just mentioned: given that conceptual analysis is a personal matter the criteria of success are essentially internal to the activity. Good conceptual analysis results in explications that are clear, coherent, internally consistent and implying nothing that the agent finds himself logically unable to accept at the same time as something else to which he is committed. (One cannot, for example, both hold that education and indoctrination are incompatible, and explicate the latter concept in terms that render it compatible with the former.) But I will add that it is, of course, a consequence of my view that conceptions of coherence and consistency might also vary. However, this does not seem to me to be problematic. As a matter of fact, because of our common linguistic background and because they happen to be relatively simple concepts, most of us share the same conceptions of coherence and consistency. But if someone were not to do so, if someone, for instance, regarded internal contradiction as quite compatible with coherence and consistency, I should merely have to clarify the issue by stating that the kind of conceptual analysis that I am advocating would be concerned with consistency in my sense of the word.

We are now in a position to answer the questions that I outlined at the beginning of this paper. It is clear that a person cannot in any ordinary sense of the word be said to be "wrong" when he offers his account of a concept, whatever he says. He may be criticized for attaching a word to an unusual concept (as, if he uses "refute" when he means reject) for having muddled or hazy concepts, for preoccupying himself with trivial concepts, or for having an idiosyncratic conception, but provided he can give a clear, coherent, consistent and compatible account of concept X, whatever name he gives to it, it is meaningless to say that his conception, as opposed to his use of language, is incorrect. The only way to retain the sentence "That is an incorrect conception" to any purpose, would be to interpret it to mean either "That is not my/our conception" or "That is an incoherent conception." Much the same has to be said in reply to the question "Can a concept be invalid?" Indeed I only include reference to this since misuses of the words "valid" and "invalid" seem to be on the increase, and it is not usually clear what precisely is meant. Validity is, strictly speaking, something that belongs exclusively to arguments. All we can say therefore is that if the claim that a concept is invalid is taken to mean that the concept is incoherent, unclear, inconsistent or incompatible, then obviously it may be invalid. If it is taken to mean that the wrong label is being attached to a concept, then it may be invalid. (In this sense the concept of validity here is invalid.) If it is taken to mean that the concept in question is morally repugnant to one, then it may be invalid. If it is taken to mean that the concept is not much entertained these days or is out of vogue, as one might say is the case with chivalry, then it may be invalid. Naturally if the invalidity of a concept is taken to be the same thing as its incorrectness, then we must conclude that the claim that a concept is invalid makes no sense.

Given that there are senses in which two concepts of X might be equally valid, acceptable or admissible, though different, does it follow that everything depends upon your point of view? The real question is what might be being suggested here. Suppose, for example, we have a conception of education that is bound up with breadth of understanding, and another that doesn't make reference to understanding at all. What can we say? At the verbal level we can say that the latter use of the label "education" is odd, possibly even incorrect in terms of standard English. At the conceptual level we might wish to criticize either conception for being insufficiently explicated. We are also at liberty to say that either one is more attractive as a concept to us, more morally acceptable perhaps, or more in line with our other goals. So the answer to the question is (1) the fact that no conception can be dismissed as wrong certainly doesn't necessarily imply that *everything* depends upon your point of view, and that you cannot be in any way brought into a public arena; rather, it just *entails* that your conception of X *is* your point of view on this matter, but (2) while you may entertain any idea you like, you may still be criticized on grounds of coherence, morality, practicality and wisdom.

Does the question "What is education?" make sense then? Not if it is taken to imply that there is an unalterable, imperishable idea that is always to answer to the name (or at any rate the English name) of "education." But certainly it makes sense provided that we interpret it either as a verbal question, requesting information about the use of the word amongst a given group, or as a way of asking one's interlocutor "What is *your* conception of education?"

Source: Robin Barrow, "Does the Question 'What Is Education?' Make Sense?" *Educational Theory*:191–195, Summer–Fall 1983.

SELECTED READINGS

Peters, R. S. *Ethics and Education.* London: Allen and Unwin, 1965. This book gives an analytical exploration of such concepts as freedom, authority, equality, and democracy. It sets forth an ethical position with a point of view regarding moral theory.

———, **ed.** *The Philosophy of Education.* New York: Oxford University Press, 1973. This collection brings together writings of such figures as Paul Hirst, Israel Scheffler, and D. W. Hamlyn. The various contributors analyze and attempt to clarify such important concepts as the aims of education, curriculum planning, and educational relevance.

Scheffler, Israel. *The Language of Education.* Springfield, IL: Charles Thomas, 1960. This work is a major statement by a leading analytic philosopher in the field of education. He examines the uses of language in education and the meanings of various educational concepts.

Soltis, Jonas F. *An Introduction to the Analysis of Educational Concepts.* 2d ed. Reading, MA: Addison-Wesley, 1977. A brief but well-written introduction to analytic philosophy in education. This book is more restricted in scope than some introductory works in the field. It is recommended as an excellent beginning treatise on the uses of analysis.

Marxism and Education

Of all the philosophies considered in this text, perhaps none has been more controversial than Marxism. The reasons for this are several. First of all, Karl Marx's ideas helped launch some of the most far-reaching social and political revolutions in the twentieth century. Second, Marxism played a significant role in the global competition called the Cold War, especially the contest between the United States and the former Soviet Union. Third, there is the historical Marx, whose numerous works reflected his intellectual development.

Marx's writings are sometimes divided into an earlier humanist period and a later revolutionary period. His later works greatly influenced communist revolutionaries at the turn of the century; his earlier, more humanistic works were mostly unpublished until the middle decades of the twentieth century. As a consequence, philosophical disputes have arisen over which is the "real" Marx—the humanistic social critic or the communist revolutionary.

A further complication is the confusing assortment of neo-Marxist doctrines that have developed, such as structural Marxism, phenomenological Marxism, feminist Marxism, critical Marxism, and several other varieties. Despite this diversity, some basic divisions of Marxist thought can provide insights into Marxist educational ideas. These include the original works of Marx, the theory of Marxism-Leninism, and "Western" or neo-Marxism.

ORIGINS OF MARXISM

Materialism

One of the distinguishing features of Marxism is the importance of materialistic ideas. Two materialist traditions (British and French) lie at the foundation of Marxism.

British Materialism

One of the chief architects of British materialism was Francis Bacon (1561–1626). He maintained that science is a tool for creating new knowledge that can be used to advance human well-being and progress. Marx drew considerably from Bacon's work, for he believed Bacon had emancipated science from theology. Bacon had taught that the senses are infallible and the source of all knowledge *if* guided by scientific method. Because of Bacon's work, Marx stated, "Matter smiled at man with poetical seasons of brightness."

Thomas Hobbes (1589–1679) systematized Bacon's materialism but made it more abstract. According to Hobbes, science is the process of discovering and studying the laws of motion and their effects on material bodies. He viewed moral philosophy as the science of the motion of human minds and rejected the spiritual dimension, holding that the universe simply is permeated by matter. His influence on Marx was not in terms of the universal law of motion (an idea Marx rejected), but rather in the idea that materialism should be used in arranging the practical affairs of humanity and civil society.

John Locke (1632–1704) also influenced Marx's thought, and his empiricism was one of its key ingredients. He held that human nature is malleable. The French took this view and made it into a "philosophy of progress"; for if human nature can be shaped, they reasoned, then it is possible to shape and direct human society and institutions.

French Materialism

According to Marx, French materialism "humanized" British materialism by placing it more squarely within a social context. French materialism had been influenced by René Descartes (1596–1650), who separated his physics from his highly idealistic metaphysics. From the standpoint of physics, he viewed motion as the driving force of matter and matter as the only basis of being and knowledge—a view that French materialists found supportive. However, the two most influential French materialists undergirding Marx's thought were Étienne Condillac (1715–1780) and Claude Adrien Helvétius (1715–1771).

Condillac used Locke's sense empiricism to oppose traditional ideas about a static human nature and an invariant human social order. In his "doctrine of sensationalism," Condillac maintained that human activities and thinking processes are matters of experience and habit; therefore, the whole development of humanity depends on education and environment. Helvétius pushed the idea even further by proclaiming that education could be used to bring about human perfection. Both he and Condillac argued that an individual's social class is simply a result of education and circumstance. For Helvétius, even individual differences in intelligence could be attributed to these factors. Human nature, he held, is neither good nor bad; circumstances, particularly education, make the individual, and the desired course is to arrange circumstances and education to produce human progress and a more satisfying life for all.

Marx drew from materialism a number of important ingredients. One was the view that science should be used to transform human circumstances. Allied to this was the view that human perception and knowledge are based on the sense experience of the material world. Finally, the notions of human perfectibility and the possibility of social progress through changes in the material world exerted a heavy influence on Marx.

Socialism

The word *socialism* first came into use in the late 1820s and was associated with the theories of such people as Henri Saint-Simon (1760–1825), Charles Fourier (1772–1837), and Robert Owen (1771–1858). Saint-Simon embraced industrialization and pushed for the scientific study of industry to serve the needs of society. He viewed industrial labor as *the* essential form of labor and held that industrialists rather than "idle aristocrats" should govern society. He called his theory the "industrial doctrine" and advocated progress in terms of society-wide improvement rather than simply individual improvement, a focus of great importance for Marx.

Charles Fourier believed in human perfectibility and called for new forms of social organization based on his theory of "perfection by association," a notion derived from Newton's law of gravitation. He believed that progress would occur through proper human association, the basic unit of association being anchored in a community of interest. Marx adopted many of Fourier's criticisms of capitalism's lack of social responsibility and its selfish absorption in the accumulation of wealth.

The leading socialist for Marx, however, was Robert Owen, who started as a child laborer in Manchester, England, and who eventually became a wealthy and important industrialist. In the textile mills of New Lanark, Scotland, he was instrumental in establishing shorter working hours, schools for child laborers, infant schools for the small children of working mothers, and improved housing and health conditions for all employees. Despite the initial fears of other mill owners, Owen's reforms actually increased the earnings of the mills. Owen tried to spread his ideas among other industrialists but had limited success. He eventually came to believe that radical social change was needed and that human progress would come about only through widespread fundamental changes in social and environmental conditions. Marx said that English communism began with Owen, for Owen took the lead in sowing the seeds of a cooperative social system.

Political Economy

The traditional discipline of political economy has been overshadowed by the contemporary discipline of economics, which relies on the analytic methodology of social science; but the study of political economy continues in some scholarly circles and is distinguished by a more full-blown reliance on socio-logical, political, historical, and philosophical thought. It was the customary manner of dealing with economic theory in the late eighteenth and early nineteenth centuries. One of its chief exponents was Adam Smith (1723–1790), a Scottish philosopher whose major treatise *The Wealth of Nations,* published in 1776, greatly influenced subsequent economic thought—particularly the theory of capitalism and the point of view that pro-motes minimum government regulation of economic life. Smith used the metaphor of the "invisible hand" to describe the way in which the economy is supposed to regulate itself if left to private individual initiative and market competition.

Another leading political economist was David Ricardo (1772–1823). Both Smith and Ricardo recognized productive labor as one of the prime bases of wealth, but Ricardo refined the definition of wages as the labor time it takes to produce a commodity. Marx thought that Smith and Ricardo had provided a valuable service in formulating new economic laws that advanced the production of wealth, but most of the policy implications he drew from them were the opposite of their intent. Marx used their ideas on labor as a basis of wealth, but he also added the notion of "surplus value"; that is, a worker produces *more* than his wage or the cost of production, and it is this surplus value from which profits are gained and by which workers are exploited.

THE PHILOSOPHY OF KARL MARX

Karl Marx (1818–1883)

Karl Heinrich Marx was born to comfortable middle-class circumstances in Trier, in the German Rhineland. His father was a lawyer and both parents were Jewish. The family converted to Christianity shortly before Marx's birth, at least in part because Jews could not otherwise legally enter the pro-fessions at that time. Although the father encouraged Marx's interest in phi-losophy, he wanted him to become a lawyer. Marx entered the University of Bonn to study law but soon transferred to the University of Berlin, where he studied history and philosophy.

Hegel, Feuerbach, and Materialism

When Marx arrived at the University of Berlin, the faculty and students were mostly followers of Hegel. Marx caught the enthusiasm of these "Young Hegelians", and although he later broke from it, Hegelianism made a lasting impression. Of the ideas that Marx gained from Hegelianism, at least two stand out: the concept of alienation and the process of the dialectic. Hegel thought that alienation came from our failure to recognize that truth is inti-mately connected with human thought. He rejected the realist position that truth is independent of the human mind and argued that alienation is the result of Spirit externalizing itself. This alienation will cease when people become self-conscious and realize that they are thinking beings and that truth is a facet of this self-consciousness. Humanity will realize that "objective" reality, such as culture and the human environment, is an emanation of Spirit.

Hegel maintained that reality could be comprehended through the dialectic, a system of logic with its triadic thesis, antithesis, and synthesis—in which logical contradictions could be dispelled and agreement eventually achieved in the synthesis of Absolute Idea (or Spirit). If a person thinks on a category, such as nature, he is forced to think of its opposite—history. In studying the development of the tension between nature and history in any given period, the thinker is led to the next era. Natural conditions shape what occurs in history, and the human activities that make up history have a way of transforming or altering natural conditions. The synthesis of ideas about nature and history in any given era is the creation of the beginning of a new era.

Marx rejected Hegel's idealism but kept both the concept of alienation and a dialectical version of history. In both cases, Marx retained the Hegelian conceptual apparatus but changed it from an idealistic to a materialistic philosophical base. Instead of humans being alienated from Spirit objectifying itself, Marx maintained that we become alienated from our own creations, such as society and the means of production. Rather than a dialectic occurring between ideas, Marx adopted the notion of a dialectic between economic conditions and human action, or what has been called "the materialist conception of history."

A second major influence on young Marx's philosophical development came from Ludwig Feuerbach (1804–1872). Where Hegel had maintained that human thought and action are determined by Spirit as it develops to any point in history, Feuerbach argued that the "spirit" of an era is nothing more than the totality of events and material conditions occurring during that era, for history is determined by the material influences on the thoughts and actions of real persons existing in a world of material conditions. This view greatly appealed to Marx, and while he later broke with Feuerbach by adhering to the position that human action *does* affect the course of history (how else could he advocate revolution?), he did maintain that material conditions exert the primary influence on humanity and its institutions.

Feuerbach also held that all ideologies, including religion, are usually an effort to construct an ideal world as a form of escape from the miseries of the material world. Marx, in turn, came to interpret religion as the fantasy of the alienated individual. In an oft-quoted statement, Marx called religion "the opium of the people," for, like Feuerbach, Marx felt that religion diverts people's attention from the necessity for reform and revolution in the here and now.

In his *Theses on Feuerbach*, however, Marx asserted that the older materialism had erred in viewing human beings as passive, for it failed to account for human action. For Marx, then, circumstances are changed only by human thought *and* practical action, and not by passive contemplation. This position is somewhat similar to the pragmatic view of the unity of thought and action. For Marx, however, the human action to be valued is "practical-critical" or revolutionary action (*praxis*), even violent revolutionary action.

The "Real" Marx

In his early years, as he was struggling with Hegelianism and developing his own views on socialism and reform, Marx wrote with a decidedly humanistic tendency. As he matured, he moved to revolutionary communism, particularly after he began collaborating with Friedrich Engels. He emerged as a severe critic of "bourgeois" capitalistic society and became a leading advocate of sweeping social revolution.

The debate within philosophical circles over the "real" Marx has been due, at least in part, to the fact that important early works were published only after such figures as Lenin, the leader of the Russian Revolution, had already formed views based on Marx's later works. Lenin's approach has been compared unfavorably with the early humanist writings of Marx. A rule of thumb for dividing the early period from the later period is the year 1848, when Marx and Engels' *Manifesto of the Communist Party* was published. Some critics have wondered whether Lenin's interpretation of Marx would have been so influential had the early works been widely available. Others, attracted to the power of revolutionary Marxism but repelled by the authoritarian and statist behavior of contemporary Marxist regimes, have sought to humanize Marxism. Jean-Paul Sartre attempted to do this by attaching his view of existentialism to a Marxist base. However, Adam Schaff, a Polish philosopher, held that Marx maintained his humanism throughout and that to understand Marx's thought, one must view it as a whole.

Part of the debate also relates to the nature of Marx's writing. Much of his work is difficult to understand, for he was not always consistent in his use of terms and meanings. Some of his writing was directed at specific issues of his day, and so they lack any precise bearing on the present. But more importantly, a great deal of Marx's work was in unfinished drafts, examples being the *Economic and Philosophical Manuscripts of 1844* (published in 1932), *The German Ideology* (written in 1845 and published in 1932), and the *Grundrisse* (written in 1857–1858 and published in 1941). Even his most important work, *Das Kapital* (*Capital*, first published in 1867), was envisioned as only the first part of a six-part work, the other parts never being completed. The *Grundrisse* is a sketch of what this massive work might have entailed.

In the "Preface to *A Critique of Political Economy*," written in 1859, Marx commented on his intellectual development. He called the "guiding thread" of his studies the conception that to really understand the nature of society, one has to go not to the Hegelian general development of the human mind but to the material conditions of life. It is in the ways that people produce necessities and create institutions that they become enmeshed in forces beyond their conscious wills. In order to understand how these forms of control come about, we must examine the way people produce material things. The sum of the material forces of production—agriculture, handicrafts, industry and so forth—is the *base*. All social relations—the class structure, institutions, legal and political authority and so forth—are the *superstructure*. The material base is the foundation on which the superstructure of society is built; hence, rather than looking first at the superstructure to understand society, one must go to the foundation, the material base. The ways of producing *material* things set the stage for social, political, and intellectual life. As Marx stated in the "Preface," this means that "It is not the consciousness of men that determines their lives, but, on the contrary, their social being that determines their consciousness."

According to Marx, at critical junctures in history, the material forces of production come into conflict with the social, political, and intellectual forces because material forces outpace institutional frameworks. Marx thought that the leading example of his own day was the way in which industrial development had outpaced social development. Industrial technology had grown by leaps and bounds, but society was still immersed in private property and monopolistic control of the many by the propertied few. Workers were enslaved in a system of subsistence wages, existing as little more than appendages to machines that produced wealth controlled and consumed by the few. The workers, the proletariat, would not accept such conditions indefinitely, and when the conflict between the forces of production and the outmoded superstructure of social institutions became severe enough, rapid social change would be almost inevitable. However, Marx thought that no superstructure ever changed until all the material forces of production underlying it had developed, and these material forces contained within themselves the bases for a new order. Therefore, industrial capitalism was a necessary condition to be built upon, for it provided the material base on which a new era of more expansive wealth could be realized.

Alienation

One of the best illustrations of Marx's humanism is the *Economic and Philosophical Manuscripts of 1844*, in which he described and analyzed the alienation of industrial workers. Under competitive capitalism, according to Marx, workers become reduced to little more than commodities, for they must sell their labor on the market like any other commodity and compete to sell their labor at the lowest price to those who own the means of production. The owners, in turn, are forced to compete in finding markets and in selling products at the lowest price. Owners must squeeze out the greatest amount of surplus value, and this means paying the lowest wages possible. In this system, the weak are overcome by the strong, and the result is the accumulation of wealth in the hands of the few and the reduction of the many to servile dependence. Society becomes divided into two great classes—property owners and the propertyless, or the "haves" and the "have-nots."

As Marx viewed it, labor becomes "objectified"; that is, both the worker's labor and the product he or she makes belong to someone else. The worker comes to view the product, which could give creative satisfaction, as an alien object belonging to another. Personal labor, which could give the worker a sense of power, is now only a means of securing a bare subsistence. The result is alienated labor and alienated people, for the workers become "strangers," not at home with themselves or their labor. As a consequence, they feel freely active only in their animal activities—eating, drinking, and procreating. These functions are essential to human life, but when they become divorced from creative production and participation in the more fulfilling aspects of cultural life, they become merely animal activities.

In this state of affairs, workers become separated from their humanity, or what Marx called their "species being." It is in their species being that people relate to themselves as members of a universal and free humanity and hence can relate to such ideas as "all men are created equal." Now, human beings are like all animals in being dependent on nature for food, shelter, and other material necessities of life; however, unlike other animals, they can create things beyond bare necessities and engage in art, science, and intellectual life—or what Marx called "conscious vital activity." These things, along with the raw materials of nature, are the objects of an individual's conscious existence and give human life its intellectual meanings. However, when workers' products—what they produce—are alien to them, and when their creative force—their labor—is alien, then the workers are alienated from their very species being. Their humanity, their species being, then becomes not a source of identity but just another object for survival. The worker is "objectified" and reduced to an animal-like existence.

According to Marx, private property is the cause of alienated labor. When the control of property, and hence the control of the means of productive life, is concentrated in the hands of a few, this results in alienated labor. If alienated labor robs people of their humanity, and if private property is the cause of alienated labor, then private property must be abolished. To emancipate society from private property, the worker must be emancipated, and to emancipate the worker is to emancipate humanity because the whole of human society is involved in the relationship of the worker to the product.

We can see from the foregoing how Marx's humanistic orientation led him to become more and more concerned about the impact of private property, which he thought was the key element in the superstructure of capitalism. His analysis of the problem incorporated not only philosophical criticism but a philosophy of history that was central to his mature thought.

The Materialist Interpretation of History

Much has been made of the "dialectical materialism" of Marxism. It has been characterized as a deterministic movement of humankind through various historical epochs until there is the inevitable triumph of communism over capitalism in the dialectic of history. Of course, Marx believed that communism would eventually triumph, but he did not think it was a mechanical inevitability of the dialectic of history. He was a dedicated revolutionary who believed that human resolve and action were necessary to bring about a new social order, but he did not see his view of history as any mechanical dialectic. Some of his philosophical descendants, however, have been more dogmatic, and *dialectical materialism* is a term they have frequently employed.

It has been suggested that perhaps the most appropriate term to describe Marx's view is "the materialist interpretation of history," where the dialectic is seen as an interpretive device rather than the deterministic structure and process of history itself. Marx thought that in producing the means of living, human beings made history. Roughly speaking, the stage of development of a people is seen in the level and type of its division of labor. Historically, this led first to the separation of industrial and commercial production from agricultural production, and hence to the separation of town and country—with its resulting clash of interests. Next came the separation of industrial production from commercial production and the divisions of labor within these categories. Thus, human history could be traced through the ever-increasing divisions of labor—the more "developed" a society became, the more division or specialization it experienced. The various stages of development were, in effect, just so many different forms of ownership, for the resulting divisions of labor determined the relations of individuals to each other regarding the materials, instruments, and products of labor.

Marx believed that humanity had advanced through five great stages of historical development. The original form of ownership was tribal ownership, a kind of naive communism in which the tribe functioned as an extended family and members cooperated in producing the means of subsistence. The second stage was the ancient city-state, where several tribes joined together for mutual benefit and where slavery and private ownership became more pronounced. The third stage came out of the breakdown of the city-states, when feudal kingdoms and empires emerged. Feudalism resulted in the division of labor into enserfed peasants, a nobility of landed estates, a proletariat of town-dwelling craftsmen, a small but growing class of lesser merchant-capitalists, and a few great merchant-capitalists.

The fourth stage was modern industrial "bourgeois" society. The "bourgeoisie," or modern capitalists, are akin to the city-dwelling merchant-capitalists (the "burghers" in the Middle Ages), who had their origins in the breakdown of the feudal order. The fifth stage was yet to come, and it would witness the rise of the proletariat, the industrial worker, in a new socialist era.

Marx thought that history could be interpreted as a history of class conflict, and he believed his own time would see the advent of the socialist era.

What characterized the epoch of the bourgeoisie, however, was that bourgeois domination, in effect, simplified class conflict. According to Marx, this was because society had become divided into two great classes of bourgeois capitalists (the "haves") and proletarian workers (the "have-nots"). Bourgeois society had developed through a series of revolutions in the methods of production, culminating in modern capitalistic industrialism. In this respect, then, the bourgeoisie had played a revolutionary role, for it had destroyed the old feudal order and had instituted a simplified social order of haves and have-nots.

For the modern bourgeoisie to maintain its preeminence, however, it must constantly reinvigorate the means of production. Based as it is on competition, the bourgeoisie must constantly expand its markets, and in doing so, it drags reactionary societies into its fold and transforms them into modern producing and consuming societies. It transcends national boundaries and establishes international forms of communication, production, and commerce. It builds immense cities, creates new forms of urban living, and transforms peasant populations into industrial and urban populations. According to Marx, to accomplish all this, the bourgeoisie must exploit labor and wring from it all the profits it can; however, such a society contains within itself the very means of its destruction, for bourgeois society is too narrow to encompass all the forces of production it has erected. It has created an immense new class of alienated labor that it cannot accommodate to its own internal structures, and this class will rise and overthrow it.

The triumph of the workers is not, however, a guaranteed result. The workers form an incoherent mass, divided among themselves by competition. Some small form of cohesion can be gained through such devices as trade unions, but this is not enough. The workers have to see that their strength lies in solidarity. Indeed, this was the end toward which Marx aimed in the publication of *The Manifesto of the Communist Party,* and this was behind the closing lines of that document where he proclaimed: "Let the ruling classes tremble at a communist revolution. The proletarians have nothing to lose but their chains. They have a world to win. Working men of all countries, unite!"

Interpretations of Marx

As is the case with most seminal thinkers, Marx attracted disciples, some of whom took his thought in directions that, had he lived to see them, he might have vigorously rejected. Even in his own lifetime, Marx is said to have declared that whatever else he might be, he was certainly not a Marxist. One of the reasons for the variety of "Marxisms" lies with Marx himself. He was ambiguous on many key points, and conditions changed sufficiently so that over the years his followers found it necessary to revise some of his basic conceptions.

Marxism-Leninism

Friedrich Engels (1820–1895), the son of a wealthy textile manufacturer, was born in Germany. After receiving a classical education, he moved to Manchester, England, to work in one of his father's mills. Influenced by the works of Owen and other reformers, he became convinced that radical social reforms were needed. He met Marx in 1844 and began a collaboration that lasted forty years. Because of his association with Marx and his interpretation of Marxist ideas after Marx's death, Engels gained within socialist circles an eminent position that enabled him to exercise great influence.

Engels was one of those who helped popularize "dialectical materialism." In Engels' view, history is *determined* by a dialectical process and material conditions are the deciding factor; therefore, the course of wisdom is for people to attune themselves to this historical process so that they are not at odds with it. As Engels viewed it, when science forsook the study of *things* and embraced the study of natural *processes*, it came nearer to discovering the universal laws of motion. Although he knew that human actions and social institutions are different from nature, where blind unconscious processes work on one another, Engels nonetheless held that history, too, has its own inner general laws. Human designs and individual actions often conflict, and so history works much like nature in effect—for many blind and unconscious human processes act against each other; consequently, as in the case of nature, history may be understood by discovering its inner general laws through dialectical materialism.

Engels gave history a deterministic twist that Marx never intended. As early as 1877, Engels was espousing determinism in *Anti-Dühring*, where he began formulating his idea of "scientific socialism." Although Marx had referred to his own view as "materialistic and thus scientific method," what Engels did, it has been charged, was to convert Marx's method into a *deterministic philosophy*. In short, Marx's "historical materialism" became in Engels' hands a variant of Hegelian philosophy where, in *The Dialectics of Nature*, "matter" is substituted for "Spirit" as the ontological or metaphysical foundation.

If Marx and Engels were men of theory, Vladimir Ilich Lenin (1870–1924) was a man of both theory and action. The son of a college professor, he was born with the surname of Ulyanov but took the name *Lenin* after joining the socialist movement. Lenin welded his own ideas to those of Marx and Engels so that the orthodox philosophy of the Soviet Union and several other countries was called "Marxism-Leninism." Lenin's view of materialism, following Engels, resulted in a type of naive realism, a "mirror image" epistemology that influenced subsequent views on education in the Soviet Union. As he expressed it in *Materialism and Empirio-Criticism*, "Our sensation, our consciousness is only *an image* of the external world, and it is obvious that an image cannot exist without the thing imaged, and the latter exists independently of that which images it." He rejected the Kantian dilemma about knowing the thing-in-itself and held that the only difference between the noumenon and the phenomenon is what is known and what is not yet known.

This penchant for cut-and-dried clarity (his critics would call it narrow dogmatism) is one of the hallmarks of Lenin's interpretation of Marx. In his conception of the state, Lenin followed Engels on the inevitability of dialectical materialism—that the state will eventually "wither away" after the establishment of the dictatorship of the proletariat. In *The State and Revolution*, Lenin interpreted Marx to mean that violent revolution to overthrow bourgeois forms of the state, including representative democracy, is part of this inevitability. This is clearly not Marx's view; although Marx did not shrink from violence, he maintained that in some of the more advanced industrial and democratic countries, such as England, Holland, and the United States, the proletariat could achieve its ends through peaceful means. As late as 1880, in a letter to the English socialist Henry Hyndman, Marx wrote: "If the unavoidable evolution turns into a revolution, it would not only be the fault of the ruling classes, but also of the working class." Lenin, however, argued that the dictatorship of the proletariat, "in accordance with the general rule, can only be brought about by violent revolution."

Lenin's view was no doubt influenced by the autocratic conditions in Russia at the time, and this may have compelled him to take what his critics allege to be a narrow view. These same critics maintain that, following the Russian Revolution, Lenin's ideas on the nature of the state and the need for a dictatorship controlled by a small, disciplined party apparatus led only to the establishment of a dictatorship by the official Communist Party. This party showed little sign of "withering away" until reforms led by Mikhail Gorbachev resulted in the dissolution of the Soviet Union. There has been an apparent rejection of Marxism-Leninism in favor of market economies in most of the former republics of the old Soviet Union, notably Russia under the leadership of Boris Yeltsin. However, whereas the old Soviet Union prided itself with achieving universal literacy and making education widely available to everyone, contemporary Russia is bogged down in political and economic problems and education seems to have taken a back seat to other issues.

WESTERN MARXISM AND THE ORIGINS OF "CRITICAL THEORY"

After Engels' death in 1893, the mantle of Marxist leadership was passed to the German Social Democratic Party, which became the leading organization of Marxist thought in the West. Western Marxism lost its revolutionary edge, however, after the changes in capitalist societies, in which workers' wages improved and "corporate" capitalism displaced the older individualistic type. Many Marxists concluded that the Western proletariat had lost the "will" for revolutionary *praxis*. In the East, Lenin and his followers launched the revolution that was to focus attention on Marxism-Leninism as the orthodox standard-bearer of Marxism. In the West, however, Georg Lukács (1885–1971) and Antonio Gramsci (1891–1937) developed Marxism further along lines that Marx had been associated with in his youth—the social criticism of the Young Hegelians. This theme was to be taken up by a group of philosophers and developed into a school of thought known as the Frankfurt School. Two distinguishing features of Western or neo-Marxism are its philosophical orientation and its efforts to move beyond material production and class conflict as the chief explanatory constructs of Marxist analysis and to move toward broad cultural explanations of power relations and conflict.

Marx was somewhat ambivalent about the role of philosophy. He thought it was a remnant of bourgeois culture, but he continued to criticize existing society in philosophical critiques that he claimed were "scientific." Lukács, however, took the unorthodox view that philosophy still had a role to play in mediating between changing capitalistic forms and the development of workers' understanding of their condition. According to Lukács, the failure of workers to take matters in hand was the result of (1) *reification*, that is, taking prevailing capitalistic ideas about the nature of society as the way things *must* be; (2) the division of labor that kept workers submerged; and (3) capitalist evolution and its accommodation to the less threatening demands of workers.

Italian philosopher Antonio Gramsci, building on Lukács' work, maintained that ideology as cultural *hegemony* (overriding cultural influence or authority) is an important aspect of power over society, even more than the modes of material production. It is through the *cultural* hegemony of ideology that workers *reify* (accept an idea or assumption as true) capitalistic ideas and acquiesce to them. Consequently, ideology is a powerful tool of capitalism (as it is in any "ism"), and for those who struggle against capitalism, the proper course is to question hegemonic bourgeois culture and its control over the consciousness of the proletariat. Lukács' and Gramsci's unorthodox views challenged some of the basic tenets of historical materialism itself, and they helped forge a new role for philosophy within Western Marxism.

The Frankfurt School

The term "critical theory" was probably first applied to the work of the Frankfurt School, the group of leftist scholars who gathered at the Institute for Social Research at the University of Frankfurt in 1923, many of whom later immigrated to the United States because of the threat of Hitler and the Nazis. This early critical theory was influenced by the work of several thinkers, including Kant, Hegel, Nietzsche, Freud, and Marx—to name a few. Central to the Frankfurt School's critical approach, however, is Marx's method of examining ideologies and showing their shortcomings. Some of the leading figures in the Frankfurt School were Max Horkheimer (1895–1971), Theodor Adorno (1903–1969), and Herbert Marcuse (1898–1979). A prominent recent figure in the movement is Jurgen Habermas (b. 1929).

Max Horkheimer studied the transformation of Western society from old-style capitalism to contemporary corporate or state capitalism. He held that individuality had been debased by bourgeois capitalism and that the centralizing capacities of capitalism threatened to eradicate individuality through "mass culture," fascism, and the fetishism of the technocratic consciousness. Horkheimer struck a decidedly pessimistic note, reflected in the titles of some of his works: *Eclipse of Reason* and *Dawn and Decline*. Horkheimer and Theodor Adorno coauthored *Dialectic of Enlightenment,* in which they expressed the belief that humane culture cannot prosper without reasoned thought; but because of centralization and authoritarianism in modern mass culture, there is a fear of theory and an elevation of technologism. Consequently, Horkheimer and Adorno believed that centralized planning and the authoritarian state should be the foci of critical or neo-Marxist philosophy.

According to Adorno, the use of various art and communication forms (such as radio, motion pictures, modern advertising and so forth) creates the preplanned, mass-produced social and cultural outlooks he called "mass culture." Such conditions overwhelm individual initiative and result in the "administered society," characterized by a "technological veil" behind which those in control hide facts and use them to dominate. The result is that people cannot think for themselves. Adorno distrusted the old Marxist notion of the "spontaneous power of the proletariat in the historical process," for he held that spontaneity is inadequate in the face of the domination that exists. Although he developed no single meaning for critical theory, in *Negative Dialectics* Adorno advocated dialectical thinking; that is, the thinker must try to envision the negation of things in order to create new alternatives.

Herbert Marcuse developed the Frankfurt School's themes about the eclipse of individuality into what he called "one dimensional man." In a work by that title, he described how technological consciousness and authoritarianism result in the paralysis of criticism and the inability to devise alternatives. "One dimensionality" results from the historical process by which the corporate, bureaucratic, scientific, and technological modes of organization have become so reified and entrenched that society as a whole mobilizes to protect them. The problem is that people apparently cannot move beyond this one dimension. For a time, Marcuse thought that the student radicalism of the 1960s would help bring about change because its "Great Refusal" showed the limits of the contemporary order. His work *An Essay on Liberation* was meant to further that movement toward a new socialism.

In some respects, Jurgen Habermas has taken neo-Marxist theory not only beyond more traditional Marxism but also beyond the Frankfurt School's approach. In *Communication and the Evolution of Society,* he attempts to develop an empirical philosophy of history with a practical (or political) intent, and he incorporates the developmental psychology of Jean Piaget and Lawrence Kohlberg into his theory. His interest in communication theory also incorporates elements of language analysis. He emphasizes, however, the Frankfurt School's view that sociocultural conditions are more significant than mere material forces of production. Rather than historical evolution springing only from material modes of production, it springs from social processes and structures produced by societies to maintain and enhance themselves.

From the standpoint of individuals, this occurs through individual learning capacities. In this sense, societies are dependent on individuals; however, individuals are dependent on the symbolic structures of the social world for their meanings and competence—that is, individuals need systems of language and behavioral expectations to communicate, organize, and resolve conflicts. For Habermas, then, material forces of production, while important, are not decisive for historical evolution. Forms of cooperation are just as decisive, and what is needed is not further clarification of the modes of production but more general principles of social organization.

As can be seen, Western Marxism and critical theory have taken Marxism away from some of the basic tenets of both Marx and Marxism-Leninism. Although Marx resisted describing any specific vision of the future of socialism, he did envision a society characterized by free association and self-management. However, as Stanley Aronowitz pointed out in *The Crisis in Historical Materialism,* what actually developed was authoritarian state socialism. Free association and self-management were still utopian dreams, not actualities; and the impulse for creative social theory eventually came from outside old-style Marxism itself in the form of feminism, the ecology movement, the drive for racial freedom, new nationalism, and even liberation theology. Yet, Aronowitz continued, Marx's thrust against domination, his dialectical theory of capitalist development, and his vision of social transformation may still serve as useful guideposts for those who seek to change the old order.

MARXISM AS A PHILOSOPHY OF EDUCATION

Although Marx himself did not write extensively about education, his educational ideas, coupled with his general theory, greatly influenced subsequent Marxist philosophers and educators. In the matter of subsequent Marxist theory, however, there have been several divergent directions. For example, the Marxist-Leninist version was dominant in such countries as the former Soviet Union and the former East Germany, but Marxism-Leninism has had little direct influence in the West. Western Marxism, while exerting some influence on the theory of education in the West, has had little or no direct effect on everyday policy and practice in such countries as the United States, although this may be changing. The point is that to understand Marxism's historic significance for philosophy of education, there must be a recognition not only of Marx's original works but also of divergent interpretations that may be at odds on some key points.

Aims of Education

The aims of Marxist education may be found in both the Marxist conception of history and in the critical analysis of existing conditions, for Marxist theory holds that human society must move from capitalism to socialism, and eventually to communism. In those countries where Marxism-Leninism once held sway, educational aims were viewed primarily in terms of this dialectical movement, and the immediate goals were to mold a socialist consciousness and a socialist society. This effort was greatly enhanced by providing an education to develop a new socialist human being.

The Socialist Consciousness

Marx wanted to overcome human alienation, which he felt was the direct result of private property and the control of production by an elite. The aim was to free conscious vital human activity by putting individuals back in control of their own labor. Marx felt that his particular task was to develop proper theoretical bases so that the working class would be aware of general directions to be taken. In this sense it could be said that Marx saw his role as educational.

In the 1840s, Marx criticized the education allowed the working classes of England and Germany as a paternalistic device used by the ruling classes to produce docile and obedient subjects. What public education should result in, he argued, was individual aims becoming public aims, natural independence becoming spiritual freedom, and raw drive becoming ethical drive. One bourgeois spokesman maintained that it was the neglected education of the working class that resulted in their unrest, because they failed to understand the "natural laws of commerce" that reduced them to pauperism. Marx had no patience for such attitudes; instead, it was the "brainlessness" of the bourgeoisie that led them to be "embarrassed" by the unrest among the working class.

Marx felt that the ruling classes would not provide a proper public education for working-class children because this would mean the eventual freeing of the proletariat and would result in the abolition of both pauperism and a subjugated proletariat. The bourgeois state, the organization of society by which the ruling classes maintained control, was based on the contradiction between public and private life. In order for the state to serve broad public needs and interests, the ruling classes would have to forego their advantage of private gain, and this they would not do. In short, the bourgeois state used education for ruling class ends and not for the ends of children or a freer, more humane society.

Perhaps Marx's conception of education is best represented in summary form in the *Theses on Feuerbach* where, in the third thesis, he separated his view of materialism from the older, more mechanistic view. The materialist doctrine that people are the product of circumstances and education, he stated, overlooks the fact that it is *people* who change *circumstances* and that "educators must themselves be educated"; that is, before one can purposefully educate others, that person must first be educated through some purposeful human activity. In other words, for Marx, human action is necessary to change socioeconomic circumstances. Likewise, the changing of educational processes and circumstances for better effect can be understood rationally only from the standpoint of purposeful human activity, or *praxis*.

In *The Holy Family*, Marx related how Locke, Condillac, and Helvétius had taught that the whole development of humankind depends on education and environment. Marx took this to mean that if people derive all knowledge and sensation from the world of sense experience, then it follows that the empirical world must be transformed and made suitable. If humans are by nature social beings, then they will develop their full humanity only in circumstances that are truly social. This further illustrates Marx's idea of revolutionary *praxis* and the part it would play in a new education as he envisioned it. The message is summed up in the eleventh thesis on Feuerbach: "The philosophers have only interpreted the world, in various ways; the point is to change it."

At least one approach to changing the world through the establishment of a socialist consciousness can be illustrated by going to the orthodox Marxist-Leninist approach as it was practiced in the former Soviet Union and the German Democratic Republic (or East Germany). In 1957, George Counts quoted Lenin as follows: "The school must become a weapon of the dictatorship of the proletariat." Stalin was even more direct: "Education is a weapon whose effect depends on who holds it in his hands and who is struck with it." According to Counts, the Soviet approach was to eradicate from the consciousness of the people all traces of antisocialist mentality and to instill the ideology of communism through an unremitting emphasis on communist morality. The Communist Party's view was that in order for the educational program to operate with maximum efficiency, it was necessary to "protect" the people from all competing ideologies and to educate them in the one true way.

Some two decades later, Susan Jacoby maintained that while communist political indoctrination was not so crude or abrasive as formerly, it was still "woven through every subject in the regular curriculum." It ranged from respect for Lenin to agreement with Marxist-Leninist economic principles. If the general values of identification with the group, muted individualism, and respect for authority were achieved, educators felt they had been successful. More recently, Mervyn Matthews, in his study of Soviet Education after Stalin, found that despite the moderate relaxation of Soviet dogma, the demands of Marxist-Leninist ideology still retained their preeminence. The efforts to build a socialist consciousness continued to be "exceptionally narrow and sectarian," and there was "hardly a trace of non-Marxist thought, or shift from long-standing anti-Western orientations."

A similar picture was found in the former German Democratic Republic. In her study of that country's educational system, Margrete Klein described how East German officialdom held Marxist-Leninist philosophy to be inherently correct and moral, but in actuality it led only to a lack of tolerance for other philosophical systems. Hence, in East Germany, as in the Soviet Union, the aim was to develop among the young a singular socialist consciousness characterized by dedication to such objectives as the communist cause, socialist patriotism, internationalism, conscientious labor, a high sense of public duty, and solidarity with the working class of all countries. Recent history indicates, however, that this aim (or at least the ways in which it was implemented) was hardly as successful as its adherents hoped, because when finally faced with a strong internal opposition, those Marxist-Leninist regimes crumpled. The former Soviet Union split into independent republics, and the two Germanies were reunited in alignment with the West.

Two Soviet educators who stood out in helping to shape orthodox Marxist-Leninist education were Nadezhda Krupskaya (1869–1939), who was also Lenin's wife, and Anton Makarenko (1888–1939). Both were important in developing an educational approach to help shape socialist consciousness. Krupskaya thought that this could best be achieved through an education that resulted in, among other things, "conscientious and organized communal instincts," and "a purposeful and well-thought-out world view." Makarenko advocated education by means of the collective; that is, one should develop group loyalties and identify oneself within a group context. The school served as the most important collective, where each member must realize his dependence and subordination of personal interests to the collective. This de-emphasis of individualism and the emphasis on the collective were drawn from Marx's distrust of capitalistic individualism, which he thought was socially irresponsible and based only on self-interest.

Orthodox Marxist-Leninists embraced the materialist doctrine that human beings are the product of education and environment. They took to heart Marx's admonition against allowing any intrusion of bourgeois principles into socialist education. If bourgeois indoctrination was banished, however, socialist indoctrination was not. Part of the explanation comes from the philosophy of Marxism-Leninism itself, for it was sure of its principles and took dogmatic positions on issues.

For a more complete view, however, it is necessary to examine Western Marxism from outside a Marxist-Leninist perspective. One such "outsider" is Paulo Freire, the Brazilian philosopher-educator, who has incorporated themes from both Western Marxism and phenomenology into his philosophy of education. In *Pedagogy of the Oppressed*, he set forth a view of education based on liberation and dialogue and is critical of traditional education, which he claims is based on the "banking concept." By the *banking concept*, Freire meant the approach to education in which the teacher chooses content and the student tries to absorb it. Knowledge is like a bank deposit placed in the care of the students. It is not theirs to create, appropriate, make over, or shape; rather, the students are under the power of the depositor or oppressor (the teacher and the social system that teacher represents). Thus, students are induced to reify—view as necessary and inevitable—the outlooks and values of the status quo. In such a system, the students are dependent on the oppressor for knowledge, and Freire believes that this approach annuls learners' creative potential and deadens their critical faculties. In the banking concept, the effort is made by the oppressor to change the *consciousness* of the learners without changing the social, political, and economic *conditions* in which they exist. In this manner, the oppressor can maintain hegemony over the oppressed by controlling how individual consciousness is formed.

Freire proposes a "problem-posing method" (not unlike Dewey's approach) that starts with the learner as an active rather than passive being. It takes its content from the actual experience of the learners or from learners' desires to expand their understanding. Thus, teachers and students work together in a dialogical relationship, learning about problems that begin within the domain of the student and then spread outward to the wider world. Freire believes that this approach helps create a critical consciousness because it helps learners see how they live and exist in the world, and it helps them see that the world is not static but in a process of becoming. Learners come to see themselves and the world as *becoming,* a dialectical relationship with the world through which the learner can exert some influence on surrounding conditions. As Freire maintained in *Education for Critical Consciousness,* once an individual perceives a challenge and understands the possible responses, constructive action to change objective conditions is then possible. In short, critical consciousness leads to critical action—to *praxis.*

The Socialist Society

If one aim of Marxist education is building a socialist consciousness, then perhaps an even greater aim is building a socialist society, for social conditions are an important part of the conditions that produce people with the desired consciousness. To repeat Marx's view, "It is not the consciousness of men that determines their being, but, on the contrary, their social being that determines their consciousness." Contemporary scholars, such as Stanley Aronowitz and Henry Giroux, have taken pains to point out that this is much more complex than it appears, and they have cautioned against the kind of mechanical determinism many Marxist advocates have championed.

If one goes to orthodox Marxist-Leninist theory, however, there apparently was a direct acceptance of such determinism. As Jacoby notes, Lenin felt that mass exposure to a single mind-set had many advantages for a revolutionary government attempting to build a new society. Typical practice in the former Soviet Union began with political indoctrination as early as nursery school and kindergarten, where children were told stories about Dyadya Lenin (Uncle Lenin) and his efforts on behalf of the workers. While in many respects this was not overly different from American practices concerning George Washington (the "Father of Our Country"), Jacoby maintains that the attention given to Lenin bordered on religious practice.

Joseph Zajda pointed out in his study of Soviet education that the emphasis on a strong national identity in Russian educational theory predated Lenin and the Revolution but the stress on communist morality in Soviet education was based on a Leninist interpretation of Marx's ethics and humanism. In this outlook, collectivism denoted communist morality and individualism denoted capitalist morality. In effect, in Marxist-Leninist educational theory, moral education and political socialization were inseparable, and the collective served as the backbone for both. The collective might be one's military unit, workplace, athletic team, or school at the local level; and it extended upward to identity with, for example, the Communist Party on a national basis or the working class on an international basis. In theory, every Soviet citizen was supposed to identify strongly with some collective aspect of life. Thus, collectivism and communist morality were the binding principles of Soviet society, although Marx envisioned the new socialist individual as issue-oriented and dedicated to rational principles rather than merely showing allegiance to persons or groups.

Western or neo-Marxist philosophy took a somewhat different approach, and an example of its impact on educational theory can be seen in *Schooling in Capitalistic America,* by Samuel Bowles and Herbert Gintis. They contended that liberal reform efforts in the United States have failed and that equalization of educational opportunity has not led to a noticeable economic equalization among individuals. This is because in capitalist societies, schools produce workers by reproducing the conditions of the workplace. The motivating force of the capitalist economy is profit, and since workers must satisfy their own economic needs, the capitalist system induces workers to enter the economic structure with their labor to produce profit (or surplus value). Under such conditions, the school has a dual function—it provides skills and knowledge that make workers more economically valuable, and it socializes people to existing economic structures by modeling the school after the workplace with its rules, lines of authority, and hierarchies. However, the educational experience gained in school also produces at least a few who question the existing social order. This presents a contradiction between capitalist educational goals and the actual educational outcome of at least a few "rebels" and "misfits" who question capitalism's principles.

According to Bowles and Gintis, under progressive liberalism, education became a panacea for social ills at a time when capitalism was really the root cause. The schooling process turned to changing *people* rather than changing the *economic system*. The resulting bureaucratic nature of schooling meant that the schools exerted socializing pressure through requiring obedience to existing norms and values. Therefore, rather than liberation, the schools promoted conformity to a set of authority relationships existing in the capitalistic economic system.

Bowles and Gintis maintained that progressive educational theory has basic flaws, for its objectives of integration, equality, and development contradict the economic principles of capitalism. For example, they charged that

Dewey erred in characterizing American society as democratic, when in fact capitalism, because of its hierarchical organization and division of labor, is authoritarian. Further, they charged that Dewey looked to technological solutions, when in reality the ills and their solutions are social and political. Perhaps they overlooked the fact that Dewey certainly advocated social and political changes and urged greater efforts toward achieving a more democratic society, but Bowles and Gintis took the classic Marxist position that the economy produces people, and capitalists have used education to produce a large pool of laborers, a kind of surplus value that capitalists may "invest" at their whim. Furthermore, since changes in the structure of production usually precede changes in the educational structure, there *is* a strong causal relationship between economic structure and educational structure. If the economy "produces" people (or people's consciousness or outlook), then the schools participate in this people-production process. If the production of people results in inequality, then the schools also participate in this. Changing schools will not necessarily change existing inequalities: at the most, it changes only people's perceptions or consciousness of conditions because the eradication of economic inequities is ultimately a *political* and not an educational question.

Bowles and Gintis argued that it follows from this that an equitable and liberating educational system can flow only from a broad-based transformation of economic life brought about by fundamental political changes, such as democratic control of production processes by working people. Bowles and Gintis' immediate goal for education is to continue the struggle for school reform as a contribution to the development of a democratic, revolutionary socialist movement. They agreed with Marx that a peaceful socialist revolution may be achieved in the United States and the strategy is to create a working-class consciousness. The initial phase of the revolution must occur by working through existing capitalistic institutions to enable people to remake oppressive institutions and to learn how to exercise power and make cooperative decisions. An egalitarian and liberating educational institution is an essential element of this process.

Methods and Curriculum

Marx did not look favorably on public education provided by the bourgeois capitalist state (or nation), primarily because he distrusted the curriculum it would include and the way in which this curriculum would be taught. Although Marx came out in favor of compulsory education in 1869, he was opposed to any curriculum based on class distinctions. Only such subjects as physical science and grammar were fit for schools, he believed, because the rules of grammar and the laws of physical science would be the same regardless of who taught them. He spoke out against a proposal that children should be taught "the laws that regulate the value of the produce of their labor," for he felt that this topic would only uphold bourgeois economic theories. He approved of nineteenth-century American public schools, where school boards composed of citizens at the local community level controlled the hiring of teachers and the curriculum. The only form of state (or national) control Marx favored was the idea of school inspectors to see that general school laws were obeyed. As late as 1875, he still found education by the state objectionable on the grounds that state control too often led to indoctrination in the interest of the bourgeoisie.

Marx objected to education under a *bourgeois* state—not a state under "the dictatorship of the proletariat." The *Manifesto* set forth a brief sketch of what this latter kind of state might institute, and free public education for all children was one of the recommendations.

Marx advocated technical and industrial education, but not narrow vocationalism. In a lecture entitled "Wages," delivered before a German workingmen's association in 1847, he noted how modern industry at that time used children to tend machinery, a simplified labor requiring virtually no education. Intellectual education, if the child or worker had any, made no difference in wages, for the kind of education advocated by the bourgeoisie was a narrow industrial education that made workers reluctant to challenge bourgeois interests. Marx approved a three-part curricular organization: mental education, physical education, and technological training, the latter including not only practical training in the trades but the general principles of production processes. This was meant to compensate for the deficiencies of apprentices, who learned only specific, task-oriented things. What was needed was a thorough understanding of the whole production process so that ignorance of the inner workings of the economic system would not be used as a way to hold the proletariat in industrial bondage.

Marx's views had a subsequent impact on education in Marxist-Leninist countries, particularly with regard to technological education. The attempt was to ensure the linkage of theory and practice and to avoid differentiations between intellectual and physical labor. In the early years after the Russian Revolution, Nadezhda Krupskaya advocated "polytechnical education" as a way of making people "masters of industry." As the word *polytechnical* indicates, the concept refers to preparing broadly in production processes. In Krupskaya's view, it should include both theoretical and practical emphases, as well as Marxist-Leninist philosophy. This was an inclusive concept and was difficult if not impossible to implement.

Margrete Klein, in her study of education in the former German Democratic Republic (East Germany), found that they followed the epistemological doctrines of Engels and Lenin that what is perceived is a copy or mirror image of objective reality. Learning and the acquisition of knowledge were seen as the process by which mind is raised from a level of ignorance to one of knowledge, and this was regarded as a dialectical process. In other words, there must be a dialectic of matter and motion in which one acts on his perception of material reality by seeking to alter, change, or transform matter in terms of its own internal laws. According to Lenin, each piecemeal action in this regard results in *relative* knowledge but the accumulation of these instances will eventually result in *absolute* knowledge revealed through practice.

This kind of certainty had some direct results for education under Marxist-Leninist systems of education. Lenin was certainly sympathetic to the plight of the proletariat, but he did not think that workers could launch and maintain a revolution without proper guidance. He believed that a small, disciplined party apparatus was needed to provide leadership for the proletariat. Lenin called this "democratic centralism," but the school curriculum he advocated was not simply what any group might establish but what the vested authority of the Party established. This resulted in an authoritarian view of knowledge and curriculum for the schools. It assured that political ideology was a central consideration, even in those areas of the curriculum that one might suppose to be free from it.

Perhaps the most notorious example of the pervasiveness of political ideology was the case of the theories of Trofim Lysenko, an agronomist during the Stalinist era. Contrary to Mendelian genetics, Lysenko argued that *acquired* characteristics could be *genetically* transferred. Because Stalin liked this theory, it was given official sanction and was taught in biology courses in Soviet schools for a number of years. Lysenko's ideas—and Stalin's insistence on following them—had disastrous results on Soviet agriculture during this period, yet the top-down authoritarian nature of deciding educational policy overcame all objections.

Despite the many drawbacks now so apparent in Marxist-Leninist educational theory, many scholars continue to find other variants of Marxist and neo-Marxist thought helpful in analyzing the problems of education in contemporary society. Several educational theorists have used elements of Western Marxist critical theory to analyze educational problems in capitalistic society and make recommendations for new forms of critical pedagogy and policy. In addition to Samuel Bowles and Herbert Gintis, there are Martin Carnoy, Henry Levin, Basil Bernstein, Michael Apple, and Henry Giroux, to name a few. Giroux's work serves as an example. In *Ideology, Culture, and the Process of Schooling*, Giroux develops the position that curriculum embodies dominant forms of culture in the way it reproduces the modes of knowing, learning, speaking, style, and manners of the dominant social classes. Furthermore, this is done in the guise of objectivity, fairness, and merit. In fact, the knowledge conveyed by schools reflects the principles of the dominant group, particularly with regard to political principles and technical knowledge needed to legitimize its power and enhance its capital accumulation. However, the things people learn sometimes help transform their perceptions and enable them more effectively to resist hegemony.

Giroux does not accept a simple correspondence theory of the relation of social being and consciousness, but he argues a neo-Marxist position that recognizes that there are many mediating influences between the two. In other words, the content of the curriculum and the way it is organized and learned may serve as mediating influences, and these influences may be unconsciously and passively received, or they may be purposefully organized for liberating effects.

The history–social studies curriculum may serve as an example. In recent years, there has been discussion about a crisis in historical consciousness, the "death of history," which has resulted in the development of an ahistorical outlook. People operate out of a set of assumptions that accepts (or as Lukács maintained, "reifies") conditions and ideas as they are received, without seeking explanations or understanding of the origins of those conditions and ideas. Under such conditions, people suffer from a social amnesia and lose sight of the changing nature of social processes by which hegemony is maintained.

Contemporary cultural hegemony reproduces itself in many ways. As Adorno showed, the mass-produced objects and messages of the culture industry make for a common public outlook; or there is the one-dimensional technological consciousness Marcuse described, a positivism that presents itself as the unalterable result of the gathering force of science and technology. Whereas at one time in American history, people looked on improvement as moral self-improvement and self-discipline, today improvement is seen in one-dimensional terms of improving material possessions or technological growth. These outlooks are tied to the present, denying the importance of historical consciousness. According to Giroux, such developments have removed political decisions from public discourse by removing "fact" and "solution" from social and historical contexts and making them simply technological concerns. This ahistorical consciousness has developed at the expense of the growth of independence of thought and a more rational mode of thinking among the public.

From Giroux's perspective, curriculum theory must become cognizant of the dialectic between sociocultural conditions and the active nature of human beings. Students must be seen as self-conscious agents who, with proper education resulting in heightened awareness of social and cultural realities, are enabled to move beyond an ahistorical consciousness and toward active participation and change.

Marxist Education in Retrospect

Marxism has had a major impact on the world and its education; but this impact, like the philosophy itself, is subject to various interpretations. The most direct impact has been in those countries living under a Marxist-Leninist system, but Marxism has also affected other countries. In the West, that impact was often negative in the sense that some countries attempted to construct educational policy to counteract what leaders saw as the threat of the Cold War and monolithic Marxist encroachment. Conversely, neo-Marxist adherents frequently found themselves in the position of having to "apologize" for the failure of existing Marxist regimes to match actions with Marxist humanistic rhetoric.

In recent years, neo-Marxist theory has exerted a different influence than the older Cold War attitudes. In the United States, elements of neo-Marxist theory have been used to analyze the nature of leading American educational policies and practices. This has not yet resulted in any large-scale policy redirection or widespread new instructional methodologies being adopted by local or state school systems, but it may show some results in the near future. Certainly, neo-Marxist ideas have been used by theorists to help gain new perspectives on education.

One of the characteristics of orthodox Marxism, and one to which Marx himself contributed, was the relegation of philosophy to the "dust bin of history." Theodor Adorno vigorously criticized this view and argued that Marx's criticism of philosophers talking about the world rather than changing it, and his call for the unification of theory and practice, led subsequent followers mistakenly to ignore the place of philosophical theory in human affairs. This was why orthodox Marxism, secure in its belief that dialectical materialism answered all the needs for philosophizing, became ossified. For Adorno, what was needed was more adequate theory, a position supported by the Frankfurt School.

This outlook has been important for some recent scholars in education who use Western Marxist or critical theory ideas in their work, but they are by no means of a single mind regarding the directions this should take. Their work is not generally within traditional philosophy; rather, they focus on a critical analysis of education from an interdisciplinary basis—that is, they use such disciplines as history, sociology, economics, and feminist studies, but often with philosophical emphases. For example, some scholars have used Marxist theory to help interpret the historical development of education, such as how business values influenced educational provisions in the United States or how many reforms were instituted for social control to protect power interests as much as for humanitarian purposes. Some studies suggest that any change in basic core values of a society result from a fundamental shift in the economic system.

Madan Sarup has urged that sociology of education needs a Marxist framework to deal with the problems of alienation, division of labor, and class. Marxism helps give sociology a more encompassing view of the ensemble of social relations, and it gives a basis for action in its emphasis on *praxis*.

Michael Apple has applied neo-Marxist ideas to curriculum theory and the ways schools reproduce knowledge to maintain existing social, economic, and political conditions. He holds that education functions not only as a way of reproducing social class and capital accumulation, it also reproduces sex stratification, the privileges of culturally dominant groups, and the limitations imposed by the structure of the state.

Martin Carnoy and Henry Levin are political economists who examine the traditional American justification of public education as the way to alleviate poverty and argue that the elimination of poverty and inequality, including racism, sexism, and unemployment, cannot progress very far in a capitalist-dominated society. Rather than being independent of the ills of society, the schools are an integral part of the capitalist system, and as such their potential for reform is severely limited. It is only with reform of the economic and political system that schooling can have a greater effect in bringing the dispossessed into their own.

Yet for all the analysis that has come out of the varieties of Marxist educational theory, it does not seem to have generated as yet a growing momentum among ordinary people to carry out the social and economic reforms the critics advocate. This is true not only in education but in the wider society as well. In the advanced industrial societies, Marxist theories and policy recommendations seem to get an indifferent reception or even hostile reactions from rank-and-file members of society. This has been recognized by such theorists as Henry Giroux, who noted that the failures of existing socialisms to elevate the working class to assume its envisioned role have dealt Marxism a fatal blow. What radical educators must do, he asserted, is to see Marxism not as a system valid for all times but as a "way of seeing" in which discourse is linked to the spirit of critical inquiry, a position that is clearly within the Western rationalist tradition of thought.

CRITIQUE OF MARXISM IN EDUCATION

One of the strengths of Marxism as a philosophy is that it provides a view of social transformation and promotes a view of purposeful human action to carry through on that transformation. It portrays a world where things are not fixed, and it strives for change. Because of these features, Marxism often appeals to those who see themselves as oppressed. In addition, Marxism emphasizes an ideal of social power for the lower classes. Thus, it has a strong appeal for those who live under regimes or in circumstances that show little regard for the dispossessed. Finally, Marxism offers a utopian vision of collective destiny.

Marxism also has the strength of its critical role, for it helps non-Marxist societies look at themselves in ways they would not ordinarily pursue. For example, it has been said that Marx's works have provided more insight into capitalism than capitalist theory itself. Whether this is true or not, Western Marxist critical analysis has issued warnings about alienation, technologism, bureaucratic centralization, mass culture, and presentism that are timely for most contemporary industrialized, consumerist societies. Its scholarly analysis of education from an interdisciplinary approach has offered alternative insights for education in capitalist societies.

Marxists have been major advocates of making resources available to everyone, and public education is one of the social goods they have advocated. In its educational theory, Marxism claims to blend theory and practice and to bring before learners the crucial need for rational activity and a sense of social responsibility needed for a more humane existence. Where Marxists have actually gained political control (and this has usually occurred in societies that are not industrially and technologically "advanced"), it has put a high premium on providing formal education for the population where virtually none existed before except for elites.

Some contemporary adherents of Marx, such as Robert F. Price, argue that there is still much fertile ground on education to explore in the works of Marx himself. Indeed, Price takes issue with some of the leading figures in the application of Marxist ideas to education, maintaining that they have too narrowly focused on education as a process of schooling the young, not on a more broad-based view of education as learning from all aspects of intellectual and practical life and across the life span—where culture, broadly defined, is the content that is learned.

Critics of Marxism abound, however, and not simply for what they see as major philosophical or theoretical weaknesses but for practical reasons as well. A glaring detraction of Marxism, of course, is the actual examples we have had of Marxist regimes in action. In those countries where exponents of Marxism gained the upper hand, the actual model of education presented seldom seems to have demonstrated the theoretical humanistic ideals Marxist theory espouses. Governments that have advocated Marxism have been characterized by an elite party structure, bureaucratic authoritarianism, rigid state control, and the lack of personal freedom. Marxist-Leninist education in the former Soviet Union, for example, showed this rigidity, for its theory and practice were not combined in constructive ways. It embraced rampant indoctrination, rigid curriculum control, and a disregard for intellectual freedom.

These drawbacks may be endemic to theoretical Marxism, whether of the orthodox or "neo-" varieties, and this has led many of the latter persuasion to attempt fundamental reconstructions of basic Marxist tenets in efforts to go beyond Marxism. Historically speaking, the Marxist belief that there is no neutral education led orthodox proponents to indoctrinate single-mindedly, while critical Western Marxists who drew back from indoctrination and violent revolution were left only with a role of critics on the fringes. Today, they decry the crisis in Marxist theory and cast about for new directions.

For example, "postmodern" critical theorists, such as Stanley Aronowitz and Henry Giroux, have each drawn considerably from the Marxist tradition but are also critical of some of its chief features. Aronowitz, in *The Crisis in Historical Materialism*, chronicled how Western Marxists of various hues became aware of the gap between Marx's intellectual vision and the blunt actualities of Marxist-based regimes. Indeed, many revolutionary movements today explicitly reject Marxism, such as the fundamentalist Islamic movements in the Middle East and in Afghanistan.

Marxists have also been reluctant to push some issues to the extent they have pushed those of a political nature, and they argue that Marxism's weaknesses lie in strategy rather than facing the prospect of poor theoretical dimensions. Giroux, in *Border Crossings*, noted that while Marxist analyses energized radical education in the late 1970s, he doubted that Marxism is the primary influence on radical education today. Giroux found that Marxism can be reductionist and one-dimensional in its emphasis on class conflict and its structures. He argued that Marxism's flaws cast serious doubt on its appropriateness as a guiding theory, but he also maintained that educators still should understand the Marxist tradition and its insight into the politicized nature of schools and how they reproduce the dominant social consciousness. In Giroux's opinion, Marxism's role today is more in terms of historical background or setting, not guiding vision.

Michael Apple has faulted postmodern critical theory for its disillusionment with the Marxist concentration on structural tensions and material conditions. In *Official Knowledge: Democratic Education in a Conservative Age* (1993), Apple continued to give attention to structures that promote domination and inequalities. He maintained that class should not be dismissed too quickly and that attention should still be given to the material conditions that shape life chances. To back his contention, Apple scored what he sees as the growing dominance of official policy through tighter accountability and control of education, the privatization movement, and national curricula and assessment. He says that the issue comes down to a recurring conflict between property rights and personal rights, and so his basic argument runs counter to the postmodernist disillusionment with Marxist concepts.

Marxism and its critical perspectives have played important roles in helping people see shortcomings and weaknesses in the social systems they have. But as some observers may note, adherents of that perspective still seem to have a Marxist agenda they want implemented in education: a movement toward a socialist society and a continuing strong distrust for any aspects of capitalism, characteristics that some critics find questionable. These critics maintain that Marxists and neo-Marxists alike show a lack of sensitivity to the positive changes that nonsocialist industrial economies have undergone. They also note that *praxis* or purposeful human action may apply in nonsocialist theories and systems and that the dialectic of history—or historical evolution—may not be only a socialist or a materialist development.

ON EDUCATION

Karl Marx never wrote extended treatments of education, but his works are sprinkled with references to the importance of education. Marx thought that while modern industry had brought untold misery, it could also provide a new means for a better life for all; however, this possibility was thwarted by capitalist thinking that went to any lengths to make profit, including the vicious exploitation of children. The following selections provide examples of Marx's views on education. Note how he differentiates between modern industry and capitalism and how his commentary interweaves concern for how children are exploited with his concern for children to be properly educated.

Circumstances Change Education

[From "Theses on Feuerbach," written in 1845, section 3].

The materialist doctrine that men are the products of circumstances and education, hence changed men are the products of different circumstances and changed education, forgets that these circumstances are changed by men and that the educator himself must be educated. Necessarily, therefore, it divides society into two parts, of which one is superior to society (for example, Robert Owen).

The coincidence of the changing of circumstances and of human activity can be understood only as *revolutionary practice*.

Education and Environment

[From Marx and Engels, The Holy Family *(1845), Chapter IV].*

Condillac, Locke's immediate follower and French translator, at once opposed Locke's sensualism in favor of seventeenth century metaphysics. . . .

In his *Essai sur l'Origine des Connaissances Humaines* [Amsterdam, 1746] he consummated Locke's ideas and proved that not only the soul but also the senses, not only the art of creating ideas but also the art of sensuous perception, are matters of *experience* and *habit*. Hence the whole development of man depends on *education* and *environment*. It was only by the *eclectic* philosophy that Condillac was supplanted in the French schools.

The difference between French and English materialism is the same as the difference between the two nations. The French endowed English materialism with wit, flesh, blood, and eloquence. They imparted to it the temperament and grace it had lacked. They *civilized* it.

In Helvétius, who likewise derives from Locke, materialism receives its proper French character. He conceived it primarily in connection with social life (Helvétius, *De l'Homme, de ses Facultés intellectuels et de son éducation* [London, 1775]). Sensuous qualities and self-love, enjoyment of understood personal interest, are the basis of all morality. The natural equality of human intelligence, the unity of the progress of reason and the progress of industry, the natural goodness of man, and the omnipotence of education are the main factors of his system. . . .

It requires no great acuteness to see from the teachings of materialism on such matters as the original goodness and equal intellectual endowment of men, the omnipotence of experience, habit, education, and the influence of environment on man, the great importance of industry, the justification of enjoyment, etc., that there is a necessary connection between materialism and communism and socialism. If man derives all knowledge, sensation, etc., from the world of the senses and sense experience, it follows that the empirical world must be so constructed that in it he experiences the truly human and becomes aware of himself as a man. If properly understood interest is the principle of all morality, it follows that the private interests of men coincide with the interests of humanity. If man is unfree in the material sense, that is, free, not through the negative power of avoiding this or that, but through the positive power of asserting his true individuality, it follows that crime must not be punished in the individual but that antisocial sources of crime must be destroyed and each man given the social scope for his essential life-expression. If man is by nature social, he will develop his true nature only in society, and the power of his nature must be measured not by the power of separate individuals but by the power of society.

Education for the Worker

[From "Wages," lectures delivered before the German Working Men's Association in Brussels, December 1847, and printed in the Neue Rheinische Zeitung, *April 5, 6, 7, and 11, 1849].*

Another very favorite bourgeois proposal is *education*, especially many-sided *industrial education*.

We will not call attention to its trite contradiction, which lies in the fact that modern industry constantly replaces complicated work with more simple labor which requires no education. We will not call attention to the fact that it throws ever more children, from the age of seven up, behind the machine and makes them sources of profit not only for the bourgeois class but also for their own proletarian parents. The factory system frustrates the school laws—for example in Prussia. We will not call attention to the fact that intellectual education, if the worker possesses it, has no direct effect at all on his wages, that education altogether depends on life conditions, that by moral education the bourgeois understands the drumming into the head of bourgeois principles, and that, finally, the bourgeois class has neither the means nor, assuming it had them, (even the

desire to) apply them so as to offer the people a real education.

We confine ourselves merely to raising a purely economic point.

The actual meaning of education in the minds of philanthropic economists is this: Every worker should learn as many branches of labor as possible, so that if, either through the application of new machinery or through a changed division of labor, he is thrown out of one branch, he can easily be accommodated in another.

Education and Juvenile and Child Labor

[From "Instructions for the Delegates of the Provisional General Council (of the First International). The Different Questions." Written in English at the end of August 1866; published in the International Courier, *February 20 and March 13, 1867].*

We consider the tendency of modern industry to make children and juvenile persons of both sexes cooperate in the great work of social production as a progressive, sound, and legitimate tendency, although under capital it was distorted into an abomination. In a rational state of society *every child whatever,* from the age of 9 years, ought to become a productive laborer in the same way that no able-bodied adult person ought to be exempted from the general law of nature, viz., to work in order to be able to eat, and work not only with the brain but with the hands too.

However, for the present, we have only to deal with the children and young persons of both sexes belonging to the working people. They ought to be divided into three *classes,* to be treated differently; the first class to range from 9 to 12; the second from 13 to 15 years; and the third to comprise of ages 16 and 17 years. We propose that the employment of the first class in any workshop or housework be legally restricted to *two;* that of the second, to *four;* and that of the third, to *six* hours. For the third class, there must be a break of at least one hour for meals and relaxation.

It may be desirable to begin elementary school instruction before the age of 9 years; but we deal here only with the most indispensable antidotes against the tendencies of a social system which degrades the workingman into a mere instrument for the accumulation of capital, and transforms parents by their necessities into slaveholders, sellers of their own children. The *right* of children and juvenile persons must be vindicated. They are unable to act for themselves. It is, therefore, the duty of society to act on their behalf

If the middle and higher classes neglect their duties toward their children, it is their own fault. Sharing the privileges of these classes, the child is condemned to suffer from their prejudices.

The case of the working class stands quite different. The working man is no free agent. In too many cases he is even too ignorant to understand the true interest of his child, or the normal condition of human development. However, the more enlightened part of the working class fully understands that the future of its class, and, therefore, of mankind, altogether depends upon the formation of the rising working generation. They know that, before everything else, the children and juvenile workers must be saved from the crushing effects of the present system. This can only be effected by converting *social reason into social force*, and, under given circumstances, there exists no other method of doing so than through *general laws*, enforced by the power of the state. In enforcing such laws the working class does not fortify governmental power. On the contrary, they transform that power, now used against them, into their own agency. They effect by a general act what they would vainly attempt by a multitude of isolated individual efforts.

Proceeding from this standpoint we say that no parent and no employer ought to be allowed to use juvenile labor except when combined with education.

By education we understand three things.

Firstly: *Mental education.*

Secondly: *Bodily education,* such as is given in schools of gymnastics, and by military training.

Thirdly: *Technological training,* which imparts the general principles of all processes of production, and, simultaneously, initiates the child and young person in the practical use and handling of the elementary instruments of all trades.

A gradual and progressive course of mental, gymnastic, and technological training ought to correspond to the classification of the juvenile laborers. The cost of the technological schools ought to be partly met by the sale of their products.

The combination of paid productive labor, mental education, bodily exercises, and polytechnic training will raise the working class far above the level of the higher and middle classes.

It is self-understood that the employment of all persons from 9 and to 17 years (inclusively) in nightwork and all health-injuring trades must be strictly prohibited by law.

Elementary Education and Children in Factories

[From Capital *(1887), Vol. 1, Chapter 15, Section 9]*

. . . From the factory system budded, as Robert Owen has shown us in detail, the germ of the education of the future, an education that will, in the case of every child over a given age, combine productive labor with instruction and gymnastics, not only as one of the methods of adding to the efficiency of production, but as the only method of producing fully developed human beings.

Modern Industry, as we have seen, sweeps away by technical means the manufacturing division of labor, under which each man is bound hand and foot to a single detail operation. At the same time, the capitalistic form of that industry reproduces this same division of labor in a still more monstrous shape; in the factory proper, by converting the workman into a living appendage of the machine; and everywhere outside the factory [in small-scale operations and cottage industries where machines are hand-driven rather than power-driven], partly by reestablishing the division of labor on a fresh basis by the general introduction of the labor of women and children, and of the cheap unskilled labor.

The antagonism between the manufacturing division of labor and the methods of Modern Industry makes itself forcibly felt. It manifests itself, amongst other ways, in the frightful fact that a great part of the children employed in modern factories and manufactures are from their earliest years riveted to the most simple manipulations and exploited for years without being taught a single sort of work that would afterwards make them of use, even in the same manufactory or factory. In the English letter-press printing trade, for example, there existed formerly a system, corresponding to that in the old manufactures and handicrafts, of advancing the apprentices from the easy to more and more difficult work. They went through a course of teaching till they were finished printers. To be able to read and write was for every one of them a requirement of their trade. All this was changed by the printing machine. It employs two sorts of laborers, one grown up, tenters, the other, boys mostly from 11 to 17 years of age whose sole business is either to spread the sheets of paper under the machine or to take from it the printed sheets. They perform this weary task, in London especially, for 14, 15, and 16 hours at a stretch, during several days in the week, and frequently for 36 hours, with only 2 hours' rest for meals and sleep. A great part of them cannot read, and they are, as a rule, utter savages and very extraordinary creatures.... As soon as they get too old for such child's work, that is about 17 at the latest, they are discharged from the printing establishment. They become recruits of crime. Several attempts to procure them employment elsewhere were rendered to no avail by their ignorance and brutality, and by their mental and bodily degradation.

As with the division of labor in the interior of the manufacturing workshops, so it is with the division of labor in the interior of society. So long as handicraft and manufacture form the general groundwork of social production, the subjection of the producer to one branch exclusively, the breaking up of the multifari-

ousness of his employment, is a necessary step in the development. On that groundwork each separate branch of production acquires empirically the form that is technically suited to it, slowly perfects it, and, as soon as a given degree of maturity has been reached, rapidly crystallizes that form. The only thing that here and there causes a change, besides new raw material supplied by commerce, is the gradual alteration of the instruments of labor. But their form, too, once definitely settled by experience, petrifies, as is proved by their being in many cases handed down in the same form by one generation to another during thousands of years. A characteristic feature is, that, even down into the eighteenth century, the different trades were called "mysteries" (*mystères*); into their secrets none but those duly initiated could penetrate. Modern Industry rent the veil that concealed from men their own social processes of production, and that turned the various spontaneously divided branches of production into so many riddles, not only to outsiders, but even to the initiated. The principle which is pursued, of resolving each process into its constituent movements, without any regard to their possible execution by the hand of man, created the new science of technology. The varied, apparently unconnected, and petrified forms of the industrial processes now resolved themselves into so many conscious and systematic applications of natural sciences to the attainment of given useful effects. Technology also discovered the few main fundamental forms of motion, which, despite the diversity of the instruments used, are necessarily taken by every productive action of the human body; just as the science of mechanics sees in the most complicated machinery nothing but the continual repetition of the simple mechanical powers.

Modern Industry never looks upon and treats the existing form of a process as final. The technical basis of that industry is therefore revolutionary, while all earlier modes of production were essentially conservative. By means of machinery, chemical processes and other methods, it is continually causing changes not only in the technical basis of production, but also in the functions of the laborer, and in the social combinations of the labor process. At the same time, it thereby also revolutionizes the division of labor within the society, and incessantly launches masses of capital and of workpeople from one branch of production to another. But if Modern Industry, by its very nature, therefore necessitates variation of labor, fluency of function, universal mobility of the laborer, on the other hand, in its capitalistic form, it reproduces the old division of labor with its ossified particularizations. We have seen how this absolute contradiction between the technical necessities of Modern Industry, and the social character inherent in its capitalistic form, dispels all fixity and security in the situation of the laborer; how it constantly threatens, by taking away the instruments of labor, to snatch from his hands his means of subsistence, and, by suppressing his detail function, to make him superfluous. We have seen, too, how this antagonism vents its rage in the creation of that monstrosity, an industrial reserve army [of the unemployed], kept in misery in order to be always at the disposal of capital; in the incessant human sacrifices from among the working class, in the most reckless squandering of labor power, and in the devastation caused by a social anarchy which turns every economic progress into a social calamity. This is the negative side. But if, on the one hand, variation of work at present imposes itself after the manner of an overpowering natural law, and with the blindly destructive action of a natural law that meets with resistance at all points, Modern Industry, on the other hand, through its catastrophes imposes the necessity of recognizing, as a fundamental law of production, variation of work, consequently fitness of the laborer for varied work, consequently the greatest possible development of his varied aptitudes. It becomes a question of life and death of this law. Modern Industry, indeed, compels society, under penalty of death, to replace the detail worker of today, crippled by lifelong repetition of one and the same trivial operation, and thus reduced to the mere fragment of a man, by the fully developed individual, fit for a variety of labors, ready to face any change of production, and to whom the different social functions he performs are

but so many modes of giving free scope to his own natural and acquired powers.

One step already spontaneously taken toward effecting this revolution is the establishment of technical and agricultural schools, and of "*écoles d'enseignement professionnel,*" in which the children of the workingmen receive some little instruction in technology and in the practical handling of the various implements of labor. Though the [English] Factory Act, that first and meager concession wrung from capital, is limited to combining elementary education with work in the factory, there can be no doubt that when the working class comes into power, as inevitably it must, technical instruction, both theoretical and practical, will take its proper place in the working-class schools. There is also no doubt that such revolutionary ferments, the final result of which is the abolition of the old division of labor, are diametrically opposed to the capitalistic form of production, and to the economic status of the laborer corresponding to that form. But the historical development of the antagonisms, immanent in a given form of production, is the only way in which that form of production can be dissolved and a new form established. . . .[H]andicraft wisdom became sheer nonsense from the moment the watchmaker Watt invented the stream engine, the barber Arkwright the throstle, and the working jeweller, Fulton, the steamship.

So long as Factory legislation is confined to regulating the labor in factories, manufactories, etc., it is regarded as a mere interference with the exploiting rights of capital. But when it comes to regulating the so-called "home labor," it is immediately viewed as a direct attack on the *patria potestas*, on parental authority. The tender-hearted English Parliament long affected to shrink from taking this step. The force of facts, however, compelled it at last to acknowledge that modern industry, in overturning the economic foundation on which was based the traditional family, and the family labor corresponding to it, had also unloosed all traditional family ties. The rights of the children had to be proclaimed. The final report of the Ch[ildren's] Empl[oyment] Comm[ission] of 1866, states: "It is, unhappily, to a painful degree apparent throughout the whole of the evidence, that against no persons do the children of both sexes so much require protection as against their parents." The system of unlimited exploitation of children's labor in general and the so-called home labor in particular is "maintained only because the parents are able, without check or control, to exercise this arbitrary and mischievous power over their young and tender offspring. . . . Parents must not posses the absolute power of making their children mere 'machines to earn so much weekly wage.' . . . The children and young persons, therefore, in all such cases may justifiably claim from the legislature, as a natural right, that an exemption should be secured to them, from what destroys prematurely their physical strength, and lowers them in the scale of intellectual and moral beings." It was not, however, the misuse of parental authority that created the capitalistic exploitation, whether direct of indirect, of children's labor; but, on the contrary, it was the capitalistic mode of exploitation which, by sweeping away the economic basis of parental authority, made its exercise degenerate into a mischievous misuse of power. However terrible and disgusting the dissolution, under the capitalist system, of the old family ties may appear, nevertheless, modern industry, by assigning as it does an important part in the process of production, outside the domestic sphere, to women, to young persons, and to children of both sexes, creates a new economic foundation for a higher form of the family and of the relations between the sexes. It is, of course, just as absurd to hold the Teutonic-Christian form of the family to be absolute and final as it would be to apply that character to the ancient Roman, the ancient Greek, or the Eastern forms which, moreover, taken together form a series in historical development. Moreover, it is obvious that the fact of the collective working group being composed of individuals of both sexes and all ages must necessarily, under suitable conditions, become a source of humane development; although in its spontaneously developed, brutal, capitalistic form, where the laborer exists for the process of production, and not the process of production for the laborer, that fact is a pestiferous source of corruption and slavery.

Karl Marx, *On Education, Women, and Children* (1975), Vol. 6 of The Karl Marx Library, edited by Saul K. Padover. Pp. 20, 21-22, 25, 91-92, 112-113, and 114-118.

· · · · · · · · · · S C H R A G · · · · · · · · · ·

EDUCATION AND HISTORICAL MATERIALISM

Francis Schrag is critical of contemporary educational theorists writing in the Marxist tradition, primarily because he believes they misunderstand or misconstrue Marx's theory of historical materialism. This does not mean, however, that Schrag does not see much to be gained from Marx's views. He advocates that we learn from the insights of Marx and historical materialism but that we take care in how Marxist theory is applied to interpreting contemporary educational developments.

The intimate connection between schooling and the growth of the productive forces does not require us to deny the role played by schools in the reproduction of the relations of production. According to M. Apple, whatever their differences, Marxist educational writers agree on "the important role schools . . . play in reproducing a stratified social order that remains strikingly unequal by class, gender, and race. . . . The educational and cultural system is an exceptionally important element in the maintenance of existing relations of domination and exploitation in these [i.e., France, Italy, Sweden, England, U.S.] societies."

When they speak of the reproduction of the relations of production, Marxists may mean one of two different things which they do not always distinguish. Nicos Poulantzas, for one, does.

> First, there is the extended reproduction of the places occupied by the agents ... Secondly, there is the reproduction and distribution of the agents themselves to these places.

I shall speak about the second aspect first because most Marxists appear to focus on this. They contend that, despite a few exceptions, the children of the proletariat become proletarians while the ruling class transmits its privileges to its own descendants. The school is seen as both sorter and legitimator of this process. I do not deny that schools and school systems favor certain groups and classes. Perhaps in some times and places, the ruling classes have consciously used the schools to secure continuing dominance for their children. Perhaps we are even in such a place and time. Despite all this, I would claim that the *trend* of the last century in Capitalist society towards more equal educational opportunity is not only *not* inconsistent with, but indeed, *required* by historical materialism. Assuming, as Marxists do, that the ruling class is small in number relative to the proletariat and that talent is distributed equally in all strata, the society which fails to identify, nurture, and reward talent, especially scientific talent, regardless of social origin, will sooner or later be at a disadvantage. The gradual extension of the education franchise in Western countries to Jews, orientals, blacks and to other minority groups and women is precisely what historical materialism *would predict*. Those societies which can best mobilize their intellectual resources for technological development will be most likely to further the development of the productive forces. An objection might go like this: "You talk as if the development of the productive forces requires that an entire population

receive excellent schooling, yet you say that the development takes place primarily in a few dozen laboratories which collectively employ no more than a few thousand workers." My response: First, the successful operation of a modern industrial system requires the advanced technical training of a much larger proportion of the population than you suggest. (This is one of the lessons the People's Republic of China learned from the failure of its cultural revolution.) But more important, those few thousands in whose hands the development of the forces rests must be the most talented and the most superbly trained that the society can support. The identification and the nurture of such talent require a school system which is reasonably effective for all and reasonably open to all.

Marxists sometimes write as if an ineffective mass educational system were exactly what capitalism demanded. They should spend more time reading *Fortune*, and less reading *Telos*. The spokespersons for the leading industrial corporations understand the implications of historical materialism far better than many Marxists. Consider, for example, a statement from the recent, widely published report, *A Nation at Risk*, hardly a manifesto of the political left:

> Knowledge, learning, information, and skilled intelligence are the new raw materials of international commerce and are today spreading throughout the world as vigorously as miracle drugs, synthetic fertilizer and blue jeans did earlier.... Learning is the indispensable investment for success in the 'information age' we are entering.

I turn now to the second meaning of reproduction, the reproduction of the *places* occupied by agents. Marxists have several 'theories' about this process. One, associated with S. Bowles and H. Gintis, depends on the alleged structural correspondence between the two institutions. Briefly stated, the idea is that in capitalist society, a hierarchical organization in the school with a ruling class (the staff) and a subordinate class (students), reproduces and hence prepares students for the hierarchical capitalist workplace. Success in the school, it is alleged, requires the kind of deference and docility which is required for 'success' in the workplace.

It has become fashionable among some contemporary Marxists to criticize Bowles' and Gintis' functionalism as vulgar and outmoded. But when it comes to explaining how the school serves to "maintain hegemony" even so "emancipated" a scholar as Roger Dale falls back on the same kinds of characteristics: schools "emphasize things like rule following, punctuality and hierarchy. They divide the mass of children into groups on a more or less arbitrary basis. . . ." Schools reflect the "reward system of capitalism—individual 'payment' for individual work." This 'theory' has always struck me as wildly implausible. First of all, the hierarchical structure of the school and the classroom is a feature of schools in every society. It is no less true of schools in contemporary China or Hungary than of those in the United States, no less true of 17th Century Italian or English schools than of 20th Century California schools. So if the school plays a central role in reproducing capitalist social relationships in the United States, one can only wonder how it avoids playing the same role in the socialist countries. Moreover, since the roles to be played and the dispositions needed by capitalists and proletarians are so discrepant, it is nothing short of amazing that the comprehensive, relatively undifferentiated, schools of the United States (compared with most of capitalist Europe, for example) are so well suited to reproduce members of *both* classes. We have, moreover, good reason to believe that Bowles' and Gintis' hypotheses concerning the nature and outcomes of schooling will not withstand serious empirical scrutiny.

The difficulty with every theory which depends on parallels between the school and the *capitalist* workplace is simply this: any feature of schooling which figures in the *explanans* must be characteristic of schools under capitalism *only*. No such feature has yet been identified. The presence of hierarchical relations in school is surely just the *wrong* kind of characteristic to figure in a correct account. One might, indeed, suspect that hierarchies in

the workplace (whether under capitalism or socialism) *derive* from the much more fundamental hierarchy present in every socialization setting, that of adult and child.

An alternative theory, deriving from Marx's contrast between mental and manual labor, is adumbrated by Poulantzas, H. Svi Shapiro, and others. On one reading, different schools or different tracks (within the same school) reflect and prepare students for dominant or subordinate roles in the production process. On Poulantzas' reading, based on the European context where virtually all schooling is academic,

> the school reproduces the mental/manual division within itself through its training of mental labour: the 'training' of manual labour consists, within the school, in excluding it from mental labour, the very condition of the training of mental labour by the school being this internalized exclusion of manual labour (keeping it in its proper place).

This theory is not very plausible either for two reasons: first, the tendency of the school to 'train' mental labor seems to be ubiquitous. Even in Communist nations where schooling is combined with productive labor or where technical skills are taught within the school, the separation between academic training in mathematics, history, etc. on the one hand, and auto mechanics, construction, farming, etc. on the other, is maintained. Second, the mental/manual division is not readily correlated with class divisions in capitalist society. Of course the concept and definition of class is hotly contested in both Marxist and non-Marxist circles; still it is clear, I think, that in virtue both of their role in the production process and their relationship to the means of production, some of those (e.g., engineers) who merit inclusion in the proletariat clearly belong on the mental labor side of the divide.

In recent years, some Marxist educational writers have "gone beyond" theories of reproduction. They see these as tainted by functionalist explanatory paradigms and vulgar materialism. These writers tend to down play the primacy of the economy. They argue for the "relative autonomy" of the school, contending that it is merely a site where "resistance" against domination occurs. Gender and race join class as bases of domination and subordination; the victory of capital is by no means certain.

This position is not, as it purports to be, a liberated Marxism, but rather a liberation *from Marxism*, certainly from historical materialism. The school may, indeed, be "*relatively autonomous*" (a phrase brilliantly coined to resist refutation) but if it is, then its workings lie *beyond* the scope of historical materialism. Gender and race certainly are bases of inequality, but from the point of view of historical materialism these categories *must* be derivative of class relationships. Those Marxists who refuse to accord primacy to the economy need to be reminded that, in the words of the Italian Marxist, S. Timpanaro,

> Marxism was born as an affirmation of the *decisive primacy* of the socioeconomic level over juridical, political and cultural phenomena. It might be said that in the expression 'historical materialism,' the noun was a polemic against Hegel and a whole philosophical tradition which affirmed the primacy of the spirit over any economic structure, whereas the adjective was a polemic against Feuerbach and English classical economics, in short against any statically naturalist conception of human society.

Historical materialism tries to account for the most massive and general transformations in society, transformations which occur over centuries. The transition from feudalism to capitalism is the paradigm case. According to the view Marx shares with others influenced by evolutionary theory, there are some very general, very pervasive patterns which may be discerned amid the myriad experiments, the rises and falls, the zigs and zags which comprise the historical process. In education the general decline in the value of the liberal arts, and belles lettres, the rise to respectability and prominence of institutions for the training of scientists and engineers, the expansion of the educational franchise, the evolution of the

screening process to identify the intellectually able, the ephemeral nature of so many educational reforms—these are the long term developments which historical materialism would predict and explain.

Although some of the large-scale trends in the evolution of educational systems may be explained by historical materialism, that theory has little explanatory value so far as the organization of classrooms, the selection of subject matter, or the mode of pedagogy is concerned. A materialist approach to the history of education deriving from the insights (though not the theory) of Marx would, however, have much to contribute to our understanding of the transformation, but more important, the long periods of stability which are such a salient feature of the history of schooling.

Such a theory would see both what is taught (the manifest curriculum), and the educational relations between teacher and student (which forms so central a part of the 'hidden curriculum'), as constrained *primarily* by the technology of communication available during a particular epoch. The history of education would be seen as involving a dialectical relationship between the "forces" and "relations" of communication. The principal landmarks for such a history are: the invention of the alphabet, the invention of print, the evolution of the mass media, and possibly the invention of photocopiers and microcomputers. Space forbids more than a couple of brief illustrations of the kinds of relationships such a history would focus on.

(1) Walter Ong describes the way in which education throughout the Middle Ages and Renaissance retained a "dominantly oral-aural bent."

The student in the university proved his ability in logic, physics, or natural philosophy, ethics, metaphysics, law, or medicine as well as theology by disputation and possibly a final oral examination in a disputation-like form.

This emphasis on disputation was only gradually eroded by the development of new "forces" of communication dependent on the invention of print.

With print came the catechism and the textbook, less discursive and less disputatious ... catechisms and textbooks presented facts or their equivalents: memorizable, flat statements that told straightforwardly and inclusively how matters stood in a given field.

Ironically, technological advance increased student passivity and dependence on authority.

(2) It is almost impossible to imagine a textbook in biology or architecture which is not replete with technical illustrations and diagrams, for learning in such fields depends on the description of processes and phenomena which are hard to capture in words alone. Hand-done technical drawings tend to deteriorate when recopied. Not until the middle of the 15th Century were woodcuts and engravings produced which could be used to convey systematically accurate *information* to large numbers of people. Of course, the transmission of knowledge about plants and building did not begin in the 15th Century, but prior to that, not much useful learning in such fields could take place *in school*.

A materialist history of education drawing on the work of scholars like Walter Ong and Jack Goody will help explain both the profound changes which have occurred over the last three thousand years and the long periods of apparent stability. Such a history will agree with recent Marxists that decisions to teach this or that subject matter are often less significant than contemporary rhetoric suggests. But the materialist historian will trace the apparent persistence of more fundamental "lessons" concerning social structure not to a "capitalist logic" but to the persistence of "educational relations" which are themselves determined by the level of development of the "educational forces" during a particular epoch.

Marx's materialism captures a profound insight into the historical process. It is just this insight which so many contemporary educational Marxists seem bent on denying.

Source: Francis Schrag, "Education and Historical Materialism," in *Philosophy of Education, 1984, Proceedings of the Fortieth Annual Meeting of the Philosophy of Education Society.* Normal, IL: Philosophy of Education Society, 1985, pp. 255–263.

SELECTED READINGS

Apple, Michael. *Official Knowledge: Democratic Education in a Conservative Age.* New York: Routledge, 1993. The author uses a philosophical perspective that draws considerably from Marxist critical theory to develop what he believes is a more adequate educational theory to meet the challenge of contemporary conservatism. Apple stresses the need for attention to race, class, and gender issues, and he urges resistance to the educational policies of an aggressive conservative ideology.

Bowles, Samuel, and Gintis, Herbert. *Schooling in Capitalist America: Educational Reform and the Contradictions of Economic Life.* New York: Basic Books, 1976. A leading example of the application of Marxist ideas to education in the United States, this study has stimulated much commentary and critical analysis. The authors articulate the point of view that the schools serve capitalistic society by reproducing essential elements and values of the workplace.

Brosio, Richard A. Capitalism's Emerging World Order: The Continuing Need for Theory and Brave Action by Citizen-Educators. *Educational Theory* 43(4):467–482, Fall 1993. The author finds continuing food for thought within Marxist theory to shed light on the socioeconomic and political realities that shape our lives in the so-called "new world order." He believes that present-day capitalism presents a particular challenge to sober thought on what needs to be done.

Freire, Paulo. *Pedagogy of the Oppressed,* translated by Myra Bergman Ramos. New York: The Seabury Press, 1970. Although Freire uses Marxist concepts, such as *praxis,* he also weaves existential and phenomenological themes into his philosophical point of view. This particular work is a philosophical treatise on the education of illiterate people in underdeveloped countries and is oriented toward adult education as much as the education of the young.

Giroux, Henry. Marxism and Schooling: The Limits of Radical Discourse. *Educational Theory* 34(2):113–135, Spring 1984. The author analyzes contemporary Marxist educational theory and finds it wanting. He notes that hegemony is more than class domination and argues that radical educators must better understand other social and cultural forces at work in modern society if they want to effect educational change.

Margonis, Frank. Marxism, Liberalism, and Educational Theory. *Educational Theory* 43(4):449–465, Fall 1993. The author maintains that present views that Marxism is dead are premature. Despite the theory's deficiencies in interpreting human differences and contemporary political movements, Marxism still has merit because we have not gone beyond the conditions that spawned it.

Marx, Karl. *On Education, Women, and Children. The Karl Marx Library,* vol. 6, arranged, edited, with an introduction and new translations by Saul K. Padover. New York: McGraw-Hill, 1975. Selections of Marx's writings on education and related topics, this volume shows Marx's polemical style and illustrates his biting criticism of the educational practices of his time. It also illustrates how Marx used statistics and documentary evidence to bolster his argument.

———; **Engels, Frederick; and Lenin, V. I.** *The Essential Left: Four Classic Texts on the Principles of Socialism.* New York: Barnes and Noble, 1965. Selections of some of the most important works of Marxist philosophy, including the *Manifesto of the Communist Party,* by Marx and Engels, and Lenin's *The State and Revolution.*

Philosophy, Education, and the Challenge of Postmodernism

At present, a disaffection with the modern is prominent, and words with the prefix *post* are tossed around—"postindustrial," "postliberal," "poststructural," and even "postphilosophy"—but the general term is "postmodern." Some observers claim that what is called postmodern is simply a part of the modern, while others claim it is something new and different. A historian might say that the trouble with such claims is that we contemporaries are simply too close to what is happening and that time must pass before we can look back and properly judge the significance of postmodernism.

Nevertheless, proclamations about the postmodern have filled the air, and the way the term is used often creates confusion: does it mean that we are entering a new historical epoch *after* the modern, something akin to the great watershed in history that came with industrialization and the scientific-technological revolution? Or does it mean a change in artistic and literary styles within the modern era itself, such as occurred with the rise of modern art and the modern novel? Or is postmodernism something else, an in-between period in which old ways of thinking are being questioned and a new era is hidden beyond the horizon, yet to be born? In other words, reasonable questions may be raised about whether the modern era is dead or dying, whether postmodernism is truly an epochal watershed in human thought and culture, or whether the apparent change is merely a periodic fluctuation in, say, the artistic, literary, and theoretical tastes of intellectuals. Whatever the case, an intellectual upheaval is occurring, and it needs to be studied for what it portends.

POSTMODERN VARIETY

In virtually any scholarly journal devoted to literary or social criticism within the past decade or two are numerous writings about something called "the postmodern," but the term itself is not easily defined or described. In *The Ideologies of Theory* (1988) Frederic Jameson noted that postmodernism is a hotly contested concept and the main difficulty lies in its parasitical relationship with modernism. Indeed, practically any characteristic of the postmodern can as easily be attributed to the modern, but Jameson argued that an important factor in the arrival of postmodernism was the upheavals of the 1960s, when the assumed truths of the time were brought into question and various experiments in "offensive" life-styles and outlooks became prominent. For example, Third World "natives" threw off the yokes of colonialism, and new identities were taken on by minorities and marginal people. It was a time when old-style communism began its slide to oblivion under de-Stalinization and hopes rose for a new left and new communism, and when opposition in the United States to the Vietnam War set a new generation on radical social and political paths.

Today, however, we can see that the promised liberation of the Third World was an oversimplification, that the new communist and leftist movements have retreated or died in the face of aggressive neoconservatism, that the Vietnam War opposition and its radical intensity are now but a memory, and that many of the "offensive" life-styles so prominent in the abrasive 1960s, the art forms and modes of thought that served as a kind of high culture, are now brought down to the level of the mass production of commodities and have become ordinary aspects of daily life. In Jameson's view, then, what at first held so much promise had by the 1980s been coopted, sidetracked, or made banal. Disillusionment and exhaustion seemed to follow.

From Todd Gitlin's perspective in 1989, the amount and level of commentary on the postmodern show that it truly matters and that anxiety about it is abundant. Gitlin observed that the term is usually applied to a variety of styles dealing with a sense of artistic or intellectual exhaustion and a concern with irony, contingency, and popular culture. The postmodern outlook draws sustenance from European intellectuals, such as Michel Foucault, Jacques Derrida, Jean Baudrillard, Jacques Lacan, and Jean-François Lyotard; and among its chief concerns are how to live, feel, and think in a world of nuclear proliferation, economic uncertainty, and political instability. Gitlin distinguished *premodern* and *modern* perspectives from the *postmodern*. Premodernism was devoted to a unity of voice, as in the Renaissance when a classically oriented high culture was extolled over popular culture. When modernism arrived, it still aspired to unity but as a struggle against the disintegration of the older unity; and while there was nostalgia for the assumed wholeness in the past, there was ambivalence toward traditional authority and a search for new authority, such as the authority of science over religion. In postmodernism, however, the search for unity has apparently been abandoned and a bewildering array of styles and interpretations are present. Pastiche, difference, and juxtaposition are prominent, and traditional claims to universality are deconstructed and made to appear superfluous. If modernism destroyed an older unity and is itself now disintegrating, Gitlin argued, postmodernism seems to be fascinated with the pieces of residue.

In general, the postmodern consciousness perceives a crisis existing in culture and embraces the belief that no single cultural tradition or mode of thought can serve as a *meta*narrative, a universal voice for all human experience. As Jean-François Lyotard put it in *The Postmodern Condition* (1984), a simple definition of the postmodern is "incredulity toward metanarratives." One of the views postmodernism has most called into question is the modernist Eurocentric metanarrative of universal rational structures serving as the yardsticks against which to judge what counts as the good, the true, or the beautiful. In philosophy, this outlook is what Richard Rorty attacked in *Philosophy and the Mirror of Nature* (1979), when he declared that philosophy simply cannot serve as an objective "mirror of Nature" against which all knowledge claims are measured. In a similar vein, in *Paradigms Lost: Images of Man in the Mirror of Science* (1989), John Casti critiqued scientific rationalism for its claims of detached objectivity when actual scientific investigation relies to a considerable degree on hunches, intuition, and even aesthetic enjoyment rather than pure methodological procedure.

Thus, what postmodernism sees is a crisis in culture, what it celebrates is an iconoclastic outlook that breaks with claims of universality, and what it rejects is objective certainty that seeks to end discussion and debate. One result is that the defining boundaries that once seemed so clear now appear to be fading, including the knowledge boundaries between the academic disciplines. A case in point is how recent philosophical study has had an impact on other disciplines and how those disciplines have affected philosophy. Such cross-fertilization has been perhaps most notable in the interchange between philosophy and the social sciences, history, and language and literature; but it has also spread to the theory of education as well.

If education has experienced the postmodern scrutiny, perhaps the strongest source has been from adherents of critical theory, although it is not limited solely to that source. For example, Stanley Aronowitz and Henry Giroux, in *Postmodern Education: Politics, Culture, and Social Criticism* (1991), wrote that part of the difficulty in clarifying postmodernism is the ambivalence of postmodern conditions. They, too, see a crisis in culture, and they propose an emancipatory postmodern education that answers for its choices, however provisional those choices may be. One feature that Aronowitz and Giroux offer is a radical approach to education and democracy to replace old-style master narratives found in the liberal arts, modern science, and philosophical positivism.

Traditions of knowledge that ground the curriculum in canons of a particular cultural tradition, in "scientific laws" or first principles, are challenged as forms of continuing domination. As a remedy, Aronowitz and Giroux promote a curriculum that includes marginal knowledge and discourses of difference, particularly around gender, race, ethnic, and class identities. They advocate an education that elevates these marginal voices to equitable or even superior standing with traditional canons. Traditional knowledge is not ignored, but when it is studied, the effort should be to examine the content—to "deconstruct" the "text"—to see how it shapes our notions of difference (race, gender, and so on) and contributes to elevating some segments of society to power and affluence while reducing others to subaltern status.

POSTMODERNISM AND PHILOSOPHY

Postmodernism is not primarily a brainchild of philosophers, but certainly philosophers have contributed a fair share to its genesis and development. Many postmoderns prefer the word "theory" over "philosophy" because they want to avoid traditional metanarratives and false separations between fields of knowledge that the boundary lines between academic disciplines promote. Nevertheless, it seems fair to speak of postmodern philosophy if it is understood that postmodernism is characterized by variety and pastiche, and that "postmodern philosophy" does not signify an overriding agreement or unity of thought. If the postmodern is parasitic on the modern, this is no less true of postmodern philosophy, which seems fascinated with what modern philosophy has wrought. So, a brief review sketch is in order to provide a context.

Chapter 4 examined the philosophy of pragmatism, which rejects metaphysical views of a block universe, recognizes that knowledge is provisional and uncertain, and involves a commitment to ameliorating or solving human problems, a commitment in which education takes a central role. Its chief proponents were Charles S. Peirce, William James, and John Dewey, and their optimistic hope for the future and the need for action to solve problems are among pragmatism's hallmarks. Pragmatism went into decline by mid century, but in its resurgence, the new pragmatic outlook resonates with certain postmodern themes in philosophy and education, such as rejection of metanarratives and aversion to objective certainty. Richard Bernstein, Richard Rorty, and Cornel West are among the chief exponents of neopragmatism, and Rorty in particular has been identified with postmodern philosophy.

The postmodern consciousness responds negatively to behaviorism (Chapter 6) for its totalizing view of scientific objectivity and its reduction of human intentions and actions to a technology of behavior. Postmodernism also responds negatively to analytic philosophy (Chapter 8) because of its affinity with positivism and objectivism. However, postmodernists respond positively to analytic philosophy's sensitivities to language, particularly the later work of Ludwig Wittgenstein, who saw language as having a multiplicity of usages and who celebrated the interplay of meanings.

The influence of existentialism, phenomenology, and hermeneutics was explored in Chapter 7. Figures from these perspectives include Friedrich Wilhelm Nietzsche, Martin Heidegger, and Jean-Paul Sartre. Nietzsche's challenge to conventional philosophy and his important moral and political insights influenced existentialism and other philosophical perspectives.

Heidegger's dasein analysis and hermeneutics promoted the examination of singularity and particularity, not history writ large as Hegel or Marx would have it. Sartre developed the view that we must fashion our own meaning in the world, and his acceptance of Marxism was accompanied with an insistence that there is no objective determinism. Postmodernists find much support in these views, particularly the challenge to conventional philosophy, the emphasis on singularity and particularity, and the distrust of objective determinism. These themes find sympathetic reception in postmodern philosophy and philosophy of education.

Chapter 9 sketched a picture of Marxism and described how, in the West, the mantle of Marx was eventually passed to the Frankfurt School and critical theory. Some of this evolution occurred because of changes in Western capitalism and some because of disillusionment with old-style "vulgar" Marxism. Such thinkers as Georg Lukács provided critical analyses of structural changes in Western societies, while others, such as Antonio Gramsci, took Marxism away from binary class conflict to cultural hegemony and conflict between dominant and subordinate cultural groups. The Frankfurt School, led by Theodor Adorno and Max Horkheimer, developed new interdisciplinary approaches to study society and culture, and the term "critical theory" came to be applied. In turn, critical theory has been of great importance to postmodern philosophy and educational theory.

For the most part, modern philosophy presents themes and ideas from which many postmodernists draw sustenance, although there is disagreement and repulsion to be sure. With this background in mind, it is possible to better understand the context for postmodern philosophers, because they both criticize and adopt elements from their predecessors.

Postmodern Philosophy and Its European Backgrounds

Although the term *postmodern* itself is primarily an American usage, most of the generative postmodern ideas have come out of European philosophy, particularly from France. Many philosophers have contributed important elements to the postmodern thrust, but for purposes of illustration, the work of two leading French philosophers will be briefly considered. They are Michel Foucault and Jacques Derrida. While each of them rarely if ever referred to his own work as postmodern, their ideas have generated a great deal of commentary and stimulated philosophical thought that is characteristic of postmodern philosophy.

Michel Foucault (1926–1984)

Michel Foucault is perhaps best known for writing philosophical histories, primarily on how notions of truth have their origins in historical conflict and struggle and how these notions exercise power over institutions, social systems, and personal identities. For example, in *The Order of Things* (1973),

Foucault conducted an "archaeology of the human sciences" (psychology, sociology, and anthropology) to show how our modern view of "man" developed, not as a child of God or as a thinking being but as an object of study with predictable traits of behavior. This view did not appear until the concepts and methods of modern science were applied to the human sciences in the nineteenth century. In part, it was an outgrowth of the norms demanded by industrial society, but it was also a result of changing views on what counted as objective knowledge and truth. Foucault suggested that the modern concept of man may have run its course because the human sciences that give it universality and objectivity mask all sorts of modern techniques of manipulation, domination, and power—techniques that control how we see ourselves and discipline ourselves to fit into various roles demanded by the modern political, social, and economic order.

In other studies, Foucault examined the truth/power connection in specific contexts, conducting what he called a "genealogy" of how we use techniques of power and control to constitute ourselves as both subjects (selves) and objects of knowledge (things). His approach develops historical understandings from within specific historical events, or what he called "eventalization." Rather than attempting to find a uniform principle or anthropological trait to explain history as the way it necessarily had to occur, eventalization looks at breaches in the historical flow, singular occurrences that become significant in how we define and organize ourselves. For example, in *Madness and Civilization* (1973), he examined how we came to define insanity and built asylums to treat it; and in *Discipline and Punish* (1979), he did the same with criminality and prisons. His intent was to reveal how we developed institutions around the notions of insanity and criminality when other ways of seeing these conditions might have been chosen. Thus, Foucault attempted to understand how connections, strategies, forces, blockages and social processes come together in historical events to send us in certain directions rather than others.

By emphasizing singular events, Foucault was not looking simply for breaks in an otherwise seamless weave of history; rather, events are made by multiple processes, including past practices and present variations or inventiveness. Rather than trying to find universal causal forces to explain history, the task is to look for multiple influences within events or periods. For example, in his study of criminality and imprisonment, Foucault maintained that people related imprisonment to schooling practices and military discipline. It is not that one of these influences "caused" the other (the existence of schools did not "cause" prisons to appear); rather, analysis of the processes internal to the historical event of prison development leads not to causes, but to a "polymorphism" of relations that induce people to conduct and govern themselves within that context.

Prisons came about in relation to several factors: technologies, such as architecture that permitted surveillance and incarceration; tactics, such as strategies to control criminality; aversions, such as the fear of violence and disorder at public executions; and theoretical schemata, such as the application of ideas about reform and rehabilitation to criminals. These techniques, practices, and ideas were related to existing customs of schooling and military discipline as possibly effective ways to organize and operate prisons and to treat those incarcerated in prisons. Thus, Foucault maintained that the development of prisons did not come about by some external causal force of history; instead, they were rationally constructed programs and calculated measures related to prevailing conceptions of knowledge and truth, and they were meant to address perceived needs within specific historical events. Existing ideas were reshuffled into new perspectives that formed new narratives or discourses about what counts as truth and knowledge. The result was a "regime of truth" that exercised power and control over people and institutions.   Power in this sense is not something people possess, nor is it imposed from without; rather, it is found in ways people conduct and govern themselves and how they perceive and define themselves and the society in which they live.

It could be argued that Foucault merely created another narrative about human history and how historical events shape and are shaped by notions of truth and power, but the way in which he uncovered the subtleties of the relations of truth/knowledge and power, and how individual and social identities are formed, provided new ways to view historical process not burdened by metanarratives of unfolding causal forces, such as Hegel or Marx envisioned. Postmoderns take Foucault to mean that the situations we face today, such as power regimes that pass themselves off as necessary and historically determined, are not the result of inevitable destiny but of human invention within specific historical contexts. If conditions are to be changed, they must be changed by human invention, and this involves what we consider at the time to be knowledge and truth and how we define and exercise power as a result.

Jacques Derrida (b. 1930)

Jacques Derrida has contributed significant philosophical critiques of the *logocentrism* of Western philosophy, and he has had an important influence on several fields, such as literature and literary criticism. In *Of Grammatology* (1976), Derrida held that the philosophical quest of metaphysics is to understand *logos* (from the Greek: speech, word, or reason; the central controlling rational principle of the universe). Philosophers have assumed at least since Aristotle that the human mind has a direct representational relationship with the external world, and logos is the organizing rational principle of that world. Philosophers (or any speaker or writer for that matter) use speech and writing to signify or represent something. Words and combinations of words are the *signs* or *representations* of things, ideas, objects of thought and so on. So, philosophers provide analyses and orderings for what they purport to be accurate representations of logos; that is, what appears to the mind or intellect is reported or described as representative of logos.

The problem is that the metaphysical quest has resulted in contradictions and paradoxes. As Derrida sees it, this is because philosophers' representations do not belong to some external logos hidden from the rest of us, but to the language we use—that is, to discourses, writings, or texts. To put it simply, all we have is text and nothing more. What is needed then is to "deconstruct" texts rather than try to make them accurately reflect logos. The critic must work from inside a text, not in order to get an external and objective view of logos or even of what the speaker/author/philosopher "really" meant; rather, the critic looks at how the vagaries of language confuse central meanings in texts. Part of the difficulty is that we are never fully in control of the language we use because words are representations with variable shades or tones of meaning. When we define a word, we recognize that it may have several meanings, and we find that it also relates to other words and their meanings. Both the author and readers/listeners bring to a discourse their own emphases and shades of meanings shaped by experience, and the context in which the writing and reading occurs may also influence understanding. In other words, what we get when we read a text is not an objective account of logos or even what the author really meant, but our present interpretation or understanding of the text itself. This understanding becomes, so to speak, our own "text" of the text.

A Derridian scenario may be stated this way: consider that someone is thinking, trying to shape an idea or understanding. As the thinker grasps the essential understanding she wants, she tries to put it into words. As she struggles with the project, she is confronted with choosing exactly the right words to convey as precisely as possible just how she perceives the matter, but as soon as she chooses a word, she finds that it only implies or relates to other words. She may feel the need to talk with other people, to reflect aloud and receive criticism. In the process of discussion, she revises, discards, and changes words and descriptions and receives suggestions for additional changes. She may next try to commit her thoughts to paper, and once again she confronts words and slippery meanings. If our thinker is like most, she will probably not be satisfied. She may put the paper aside and resolve to come back to it later; but even here, the words she has already written may strike her with variant meanings, and so she revises more.

At each step, her "picture" changes, but now it is composed of written words; and chances are that when she stops, her words convey something different from her original thought. As soon as she chooses a word, it suggests other words, and the meaning gets broadened, restricted, or redirected. Now suppose she publishes her work or orally delivers it before an audience. Will her audience grasp what she "really" meant? Not likely, because her readers will each bring a set of experiences, a fund of related meanings, to the encounter. Her words will strike them in somewhat different ways than she intends, and they will impute their own shades of meaning and inference, perhaps discuss with their friends her remarks, and may even be inventive and enlarge her remarks to suit their own contexts. As Derrida put it in *Of*

Grammatology, in this kind of situation the writing has become "enlarged and radicalized"; it "no longer issues from a logos." What happens is that our thinker's assumed apprehension of a logos, including her original thought and its later refinements, has been "deconstructed" of its original "truth."

Derrida has coined a term for this kind of dilemma: *differance*. It is a combination of "difference" and "defer". It is used to indicate how our efforts at speech and writing always confront differences in interpretation and the relations of meanings, not only in how one word implies other words, but also how people understand or use words; and this indicates the need to defer to the complexities and interplay of meanings encountered in any attempt to establish a central meaning in a system of signs and symbols—language—that simply cannot accomplish the task with precision. In their efforts to find central principles and structures (or logos), what philosophers have done is, in effect, play with words and substitute one version of logos for another. The result has been interminable disputes about nature and culture, mind and body, subject and object, being and becoming and so on.

From Derrida's standpoint, what philosophers have done is to celebrate the *signifier* (reason, mind, consciousness) over the *signified* (words, signs, language), when it is the signified—the words and signs—that shape our thinking. In other words, philosophers have gotten it backwards, or at least out of kilter. Think of it this way: philosophers have assumed a "metaphysics of presence" where the mind, the rational "organ," has a presence to logos such that it can apprehend it and "read" its intelligible features. Language is seen, then, as merely a tool, a medium by which to report philosophical findings about logos. The assumption is that mind precedes language or words and signs, but as Derrida might put it, what would happen if we assumed that language precedes minds—that is, that we have minds because we have language? Another way of putting it is that what we call *mind* comes from our cultural texts and how we read or interpret them: all we have is text, and all we know is text.

Critics may say that Derrida merely elevates language over thought and that the "deconstruction" of cultural texts only reduces down to their "destruction." As some critics of postmodernism point out, the postmodern consciousness seems too prone to nihilism and relativism, too ready to say that since there is no central truth, everything is relative and any interpretation is legitimate; it leads to ethical relativism, where anything is permissible. However, this does not reflect what Derrida seems to be saying in his extensive writings. What he pushes is a greater sensitivity to the dispersal and interplay of meanings throughout language, of how words refer to other words and meanings, and how each of us interprets as a result.

Furthermore, the very thoughts people have arise out of their historic context, their cultural epoch, their language and fund of meanings, and the uses to which they put these things. In short, what we think we know is unstable; but this does not mean that we cannot develop understandings and take moral positions on issues we deem important—rather, our understandings and positions have no special privileged status over others. It does not mean we cannot communicate with each other, but it does mean that communication is problematic and inexact.

The Challenge of Neopragmatism

In some respects, key postmodern themes are echoes of what the pragmatists were saying as far back as the late nineteenth and early twentieth centuries, but where postmodernism seems to offer mainly negative perspectives, neopragmatism projects a more optimistic countenance. While the neopragmatists share a great deal with the postmodern outlook, they also disagree with some of its themes. Perhaps this is only an instance of postmodern variety, but it also indicates that pragmatism has its own features that give it a unique standing in philosophical discourse.

Richard J. Bernstein, in *The New Constellation* (1992), examined the variety of modern–postmodern philosophical perspectives and the difficulty of finding common ground to meet what he sees as contemporary "ethical–political" needs. Postmoderns see a break in philosophical thought, a rupture that undercuts traditional humanism as Foucault did in his archaeology of the human sciences or as Derrida did with his deconstruction of Western logocentrism. Yet, while Bernstein finds this frustrating, he also sees it as a hopeful sign rather than a cause for gloom. His hope is that philosophers of many persuasions will begin seriously to examine each other's work for what they can learn, not for who has the best corner on the truth. The postmodern emphasis on crossing disciplinary boundaries may be another indication of intellectual health, a breaking down of the artificial boundaries that have categorized academic and intellectual endeavor. Still, the concentration on ruptures poses the danger of specialized vocabularies that talk past each other and that fragment the healthy interchange philosophical discourse might have.

Bernstein does not want a "substantive philosophical consensus" where a school of thought tries to gain the upper hand; rather, he calls for less confrontation and more dialogical encounter. He suggests that the present need is for philosophers—as the classic pragmatists did—to think of themselves as participating in an engaged community of inquirers who understand their fallibility and recognize their difference but who respond to the conflicts of the day as part of an "engaged fallibilistic pluralism." He suggests that there are ample and pressing ethical and political issues about which philosophers may engage fruitfully in dialogue and learn from each other, even if there can be no final agreement among the constellation of outlooks in contemporary philosophy. Despite the odds, Bernstein promotes an upbeat outlook in philosophy that runs counter to contemporary pessimism.

The affirmative character of American pragmatism is also found in the work of Cornel West, who is clearly in tune with the themes of difference, marginality, and otherness explored by the postmoderns. In *The American Evasion of Philosophy* (1989), he maintained that too much of the postmodernist treatment continues to hold a narrow Eurocentric focus and that the reliance on the works of such thinkers as Lyotard, Derrida, and Foucault demonstrates this focus. As a corrective, West suggests that neopragmatism can broaden the postmodernist thrust with a helpful American response. While American culture certainly has deep roots in Europe, West believes that the American immigrant experience with cultural diversity, and such developments as the inclusion into academic life of marginal groups (e.g., people of color, the working class, and women), have given American culture a different focus. As a result, neopragmatism stands as a form of American left-leaning thought that fits the postmodern moment, an outlook indebted to Europe but remaining in "the American grain." It retains the "evasive" American philosophical tradition, a view that is committed to serious thought and moral action without a totalizing philosophical system, and it promotes cultural criticism and political engagement in the service of creative democracy.

Of all the neopragmatists, perhaps Richard Rorty has been most identified with the postmodern temper. In the influential *Philosophy and the Mirror of Nature* (1979), he attacked the foundational ambitions of modern philosophy, particularly positivistic and analytic efforts to define and unify philosophy under a central rubric. He opted for "edifying" philosophy rather than foundational Philosophy (with a capital *P*). In *Contingency, Irony, and Solidarity* (1989), he further disparaged the philosophic effort to force unity when contingency, irony, and incommensurability are realities we must face. Thus, Rorty offers little support for the failed attempts to universalize human thought (attempts that characterize most of the history of philosophy), and he maintains that no theory in philosophy (or any other discipline) about "the nature of Man or Society or Rationality" is going to synthesize the great diversity found in human thought. The best we can hope for is solidarity in our commitments to overcome cruelty in the world, and such solidarity is a goal to be achieved, not some trait of human nature buried deep down within us.

Rorty argues that rather than trying to find some human nature within us that stands outside history, we need to affirm that beliefs can be acted upon but understand that those beliefs are themselves contingent upon the historical circumstance and place in which we are located. Solidarity involves a group of like-minded people committed to a course of action against some grating cruelty, usually perpetrated by some other group. This suggests that great care must be taken with the moral and ethical dimensions of separating the *we* from the *they*. Rorty recognizes this, and he also recognizes the irony that no universal philosophical principle or universal mode of reasoning will relieve us of the moral dilemmas involved. We are thrown back on our own resources, which are contingent to our particular historic time and place.

We may push the boundaries of solidarity outward to include suffering marginal groups formerly occupying a "they" position, and we may look inward to include those at the bottom of our own group who suffer from our own cruelties. Solidarity is not a given feature of humanity; we have to recognize it, affirm it, work for it, and struggle to sustain it. There is no true and universal philosophy of democracy, for example, that will stimulate and direct our actions. We may borrow from history, and we may use philosophy as a contribution in the service of solidarity, but this involves philosophical arguments to be made and tested for how well they help in specific situations, not for how well they represent the universal. Rorty's point is that there is room for hope and optimism, with the understanding that we have to start where we are and struggle with contingency, irony, and incommensurability to overcome cruelties and relieve human suffering located not in eternity but in our own historical moment and place.

Neopragmatism's optimistic qualities do not prevent it from offering some challenging criticism to postmodernism, some of which is suggested by West's comment on the lingering Eurocentric bias in postmodernism. For example, in "The Resurgence of Pragmatism" (1992), Bernstein questioned the tendency of "radical postmoderns" to use a "sophisticated" and "transgressive" jargon lifted out of Western Marxism and critical theory, which is barely intelligible to academic colleagues, much less the general public. In Bernstein's view, neopragmatists must use a moral and political vocabulary shared by both the educated and uneducated if they truly want to promote democratic communal life and oppose injustices. Bernstein is also sensitive to the American roots of pragmatism; he does not want to support undesirable ethnocentrism and nationalism, but he wants to avoid an opposite danger in ignoring the cultural context in which philosophical endeavor must occur. He argues that postmodern pragmatists must be sensitive to specific cultural contexts while also recognizing, as the classic pragmatists did, that the idea of a community of inquirers has a universal quality that is incompatible with nationalistic or ethnocentric bias.

To bolster his observations, Bernstein cited Jurgen Habermas who, in *The Philosophical Discourse of Modernity* (1987), criticized Heidegger, Adorno, and Derrida for believing that they had "to tear philosophy away from the madness of expounding a theory that has the last word." Habermas observes a tendency that runs deep in the postmodern concern with fragmentation and its attacks on rationalism, a tendency that seduces us into misleading "either-or" thinking. This kind of flaw can be seen in Lyotard who, in *The Postmodern Condition*, urged us to escape our nostalgia for wholeness and to "wage a war on totality." Habermas maintains that the suspicion of totality may be good, but this suspicion is hardly new because the fallibilistic consciousness caught up with philosophy long ago when the classic pragmatists warned against block universe views (or "foundationalism" and "metanarratives" to postmoderns).

Bernstein agrees with Habermas and points out that if postmodernism is skeptical of binary oppositions (or "dualisms" to the pragmatists), it is also true that from the late nineteenth century to the end of his career in the mid-twentieth century, John Dewey warred against dualisms, too. Paradoxically, postmodernists slip into crude binary thinking when they condemn universality and praise divergency. As Bernstein sees it, what the pragmatists wanted was to reconstruct (not deconstruct) philosophy to recognize fallibility, contingency, and the radical plurality of experience. Thus, the classic pragmatists were better postmodernists than many so-called postmoderns because the pragmatists wanted to understand both universality *and* particularity, identity *and* difference, and wholeness *and* fragmentation. As Bernstein puts it, we should learn to live with contingency and ambiguity, not ignore it or wallow in it. He is particularly critical of postmodernists who dismiss ethical-political commitment by throwing it into an abyss of deconstruction, because even Derrida recognized that criticism is always motivated by some affirmation.

The classic pragmatists recognized fallibility, but they also committed themselves to democratic pluralism and experiment rather than cynical despair. They were ahead of their times, for they already had a sense of what we now call "modern/postmodern" controversies, and they sought creative responses to those controversies. Bernstein concludes that the dialectics of the postmodernists are now catching up with where the pragmatists have been all along.

Richard Rorty's postmodernist features are obvious, yet in "Two Cheers for the Cultural Left" (1990), he takes postmodern leftists to task for saying that American society is unreasonable rather than showing how it has betrayed its democratic traditions. In their determination to revolutionize society rather than reform it, radical leftists are so afraid of complicity with "bourgeois liberalism" that they have forgotten to fear political impotence.

This criticism is extended in "Intellectuals in Politics: Too Far In? Too Far Out?" (1991), where Rorty chastised postmodern leftists for abandoning electoral politics in favor of cultural politics. Their concern with class, race, and gender is admirable; but in their "politics of difference" and their fear of complicity with bourgeois liberalism, they have forgotten the mundane world of "real politics," where the evils of "the strong depriving the weak" and "the rich ripping off the poor" must be fought. The result is that they have given up on democratic politics and have withdrawn membership in a functioning democracy because they think "the system" is irredeemable. As a result, they have become like cynical outsiders who always knew that democracy simply was not going to work.

As can be seen, *postmodern philosophy* is not a name for a singular development or a particularly unified philosophical perspective; rather, it reflects something akin to William James's observation that human consciousness could be a blooming, buzzing confusion. Yet, this metaphor, which brings to mind a bright and happy image of flowers and bees, is hardly the image postmodernism brings to mind; rather, it projects an unhappy consciousness, a mood or frame of mind without a definite sense of direction or outcome.

POSTMODERN PHILOSOPHY AND EDUCATION

Variety is characteristic of postmodern philosophy of education, although its strongest element seems to be derived from the Marxist tradition of critical theory. Henry Giroux is among the most prominent exponents of postmodern critical theory in philosophy of education, including his work in collaboration with Stanley Aronowitz. In addition, Peter McLaren has developed an ethnographic approach closely aligned with Giroux; McLaren calls this approach "critical pedagogy." Others in the postmodern vein include Cleo Cherryholmes, who developed a poststructuralist critical pragmatism, and C. A. Bowers, who distances himself from critical theory and champions what he calls postliberalism. Numerous other contributors to postmodern education could be included, such as William Stanley, who joins postmodern critical pedagogy to the social reconstructionist tradition in education, but the works of the above persons are representative of postmodern variety in philosophy of education.

The bulk of literature on postmodern education has been generated from the critical theory perspective. There are strong elements of Marxism in critical theory, of course; but the postmodern suspicion of metanarratives is also directed at Marxist thought, and so postmodern critical theory has made some adjustment in that regard. Henry Giroux's account of the changes serve as an illustration. In *Border Crossings* (1992), Giroux credited Samuel Bowles and Herbert Gintis for energizing radical education in the late 1970s with their Marxist interpretation of education as a form of social reproduction. Pierre Bourdieu provided a similar influence with his Gramscian perspective that schools reproduce "cultural capital" for those occupying positions of advantage. In Giroux's opinion, both views were too heavy on Marxist theories of class conflict as the explanatory principle for domination and they lacked a larger view of power along the lines of Foucault. Marxism's influence has receded because of its internal flaws, but Giroux maintains that it is still important to understand the Marxist tradition in order to develop an effective criticism of modernism, even as it is necessary to avoid the totalizing language of Marxism.

From Giroux's perspective, the philosophical task is to rethink the purpose and meaning of education as a convergence of modernism and postmodernism. On the one hand, he wants to retain modernism's belief in human reasoning to overcome suffering (but without its pretensions to universality) and its emphasis on ethical, historical, and political discourse. On the other hand, he wants to include marginal discourses and the politics of difference in order to redefine relations between the margins and the center for social change and justice.

Critical theorist Michael Apple would likely take exception to Giroux's conclusions about neo-Marxism. Apple maintains that class is more significant than postmodernists recognize and that gender and race cannot be separated from class. For example, in *Official Knowledge* he noted that a significant factor among marginal people in the United States is that the greater percentage of low income or unemployed people are women and people of color. This shows that race and gender are not separate from class, and postmodernists err when they fail to recognize this. From Apple's more Marxist perspective, then, attention to material conditions, class conflict, and the social structures that support them are important, and educational theory that skirts such issues is thereby weakened.

Peter McLaren notes that while critical theorists have much in common, such as a Marxist background, there is also divergence—particularly the difference between the highly theoretical approaches of Aronowitz and Giroux and McLaren's ethnographic approach, which he prefers to call critical pedagogy. In *Life in Schools* (1994), Mclaren argued that critical pedagogy is not a singular set of ideas; rather, its common objective is to empower the powerless and to overcome inequities and injustices. Critical pedagogy challenges the way schools support dominant power and maintain existing inequities, and it envisions schools as agencies where self and social empowerment can be enhanced. Thus, critical pedagogy is "irrevocably committed to the side of the oppressed." It opposes positivistic, ahistorical, and depoliticized education and is particularly attuned to the politics of power relations found in schools that are part of the larger society.

Cleo Cherryholmes prefers the term *poststructuralism* over *postmodernism*, primarily because he sees structuralism as the major obstacle to overcome in modern education, an argument he developed in *Power and Criticism: Poststructural Investigations in Education* (1988). As Cherryholmes sees it, structuralism is a form of positivism with its roots in the Enlightenment tradition of rational control over human affairs. Structuralism presents the larger problem because it has been so intrusive in modern education, with its theory of rational linear progress and control. This is seen in the emphasis on a rigidly structured curriculum, the reliance on testing and sorting, and the extent of bureaucratic control. Simply described, structuralist theory defines social systems by the interconnections of the various parts with each other and with the whole, and it seeks to uncover the rational principles for the structural framework of social systems and schools. As such, structuralism is a metanarrative that says that structure is the key to logos.

Cherryholmes' version of poststructuralist thought, on the contrary, uses the work of Foucault and Derrida to analyze and deconstruct the assumptions of structuralism. There is the need to go beyond mere negation, however, and Cherryholmes uses elements of Dewey and Rorty to develop what he calls "critical pragmatism" as a possible response to structuralist assumptions in education. He differentiates critical pragmatism from the "vulgar" pragmatism that uncritically accepts conventional discourses and uses education for functional utilitarian purposes. Critical pragmatism emphasizes a sense of postmodern crisis, and it emphasizes a thoroughgoing examination of standards of value and belief, how institutions are organized and conducted, and how we perceive and treat others.

C. A. Bowers takes a different stance from the other authors, and while he stands outside the tenor of the postmodern radical left, he may be placed under the postmodern umbrella of variety. In *Elements of a Post-Liberal Theory of Education* (1987), he examined the works of Carl Rogers, B. F. Skinner, Paulo Freire, and John Dewey, a divergent group of individuals he believes represent various points within the liberal spectrum. Although he recognizes important contributions of liberalism, he claims it stands as a "regime of truth," like those Foucault criticized. Bowers' intent is to go beyond liberalism because he believes that its conceptual framework is too limiting and may actually contribute to the crisis in our sense of social purpose and cultural authority. This gives his thought a postmodern thrust but one that includes cultural conservation as well as negation. He attempts to update liberalism by using its "language of possibility" in contexts unknown to its founders, such as the ecological crisis.

Like the critical theorists, Bowers wants a "language of empowerment," but he distances himself from the neo-Marxist critical theory approach because he believes it is untested and inadequate to provide a basis for the radical empowerment needed today. He accepts Dewey's view of social intelligence, and he wants to preserve progressive liberal achievements in politics and education; but he believes that liberal individualism encourages the pursuit of self-interest, which accounts for such problems as the ecological crisis. What Bowers wants is a theory of education that conserves the "community of memory" of significant cultural achievements and that builds a reflective community that looks to the future. This includes a new conception of individualism based on political participation and the common good.

Aims of Education

Henry Giroux stresses that ethics must be a central concern to critical education, particularly the different ethical discourses that offer students a richer fund of meanings and that help them relate to diversity in the wider society. This helps students understand how individual experience is influenced by different ethical discourses and how ethical relations are formed between the self and others, including others of very different background, origin, and perspective. The basic function is to engage students in *social discourse* that helps them reject needless human suffering and exploitation, and the purpose is to develop a social sense of responsibility for others, including those considered "outsiders" on the margins of social life. Put another way, the aim is to develop student identities that enable them to struggle against inequality and to expand basic human rights. In this sense, then, the aim of education is emancipation from oppression.

Social discourse is a crucial consideration. In *Border Crossings*, Giroux maintained that postmodern critical theory looks to the production of meaning as more important than the production of labor in shaping the boundaries of human existence. The Marxist notion of labor–capital conflict fails to explain human circumstances sufficiently because social conditions based on religion, gender, race, and ethnicity have dynamics that cannot be reduced simply to the logic of class conflict. How personal identities are influenced by language—by narratives and discourses—is more significant, so postmodernist critical theory concentrates on "the world of the discursive," where signifying terms and practices affect how persons relate to themselves, to others, and to the surrounding physical and cultural environment. In this sense, then, the world of our conscious life is a "textual" world, a "text" or discourse that can be interpreted, analyzed, and reshaped or "reinvented." It is a text from which people develop their sense of self and their sense of social and cultural relations.

The discursive world is complex, not a world that can be neatly explained by binary oppositions or the rule-bound determinism found in the "laws" of science and economics. Recognition of the importance of signs and meanings does not imply ignoring political and economic forces; instead, it means giving the discursive an important place in understanding how personal and social identities and meanings are made and how they play powerful roles in shaping privilege, oppression, and conflict. In Giroux's perspective, the postmodernist aim of emancipation from oppression strives "to deterritorialize the map of dominant cultural understanding."

Peter McLaren makes the point this way: education should result in self- and social empowerment. In *Life in Schools*, McLaren criticized the American tradition that schools develop a democratic and egalitarian society, with the traditional humanities curriculum informing students about humane values and ethical standards. As McLaren sees it, contemporary schools do precious little to promote even the Western humanist tradition, and the assumption that schooling produces social and economic mobility must be compared against an actual record of serving the interests of the affluent. This latter condition is seen in recent conservative reforms, where aims and curriculum were geared to the marketplace and international economic competition.

Current interests that dominate education assume that existing educational arrangements are necessary and that teachers and intellectuals should serve the status quo and rely on scientific predictability and measurement to direct educational policies and practices. They believe that students need to become educated in social and technical knowledge before they can become effective as moral agents. Critical pedagogy, on the contrary, assumes that education for self- and social empowerment is *ethically prior* to accumulation of knowledge, although knowledge acquisition occurs along with empowerment. McLaren's point is that the primary aim of self- and social empowerment is to develop students' commitment to a social transformation that elevates marginalized groups, particularly the oppressed poor.

Cleo Cherryholmes also sees emancipation from oppression as an important aim of education, but in *Power and Criticism* (1988), he noted some expressions of caution in the work of Foucault (who stressed that knowledge and truth claims are historically relative) and Derrida (who showed that meanings are dispersed and in constant play). Cherryholmes developed his argument along these lines: Claims that current educational arrangements are necessary are tied to knowledge and truth claims that support existing political power. The prevailing discourse, the rhetoric of meanings and explanations that support the necessity of current educational arrangements, is simply unstable ideology, not timeless truth and knowledge. For Cherryholmes, then, an appropriate education would be concerned with prevailing discourses to uncover the claims and instabilities of the dominant order and to recognize both the conditions that oppress and those that may be built upon to liberate and expand human possibilities. He cautions, however, that combating oppression may involve other kinds of oppression and coercion. People who are privileged by power and status may not want to relinquish those privileges. Overcoming a discourse of power and its knowledge/truth claims may involve creating new discourses of power and privilege that themselves become oppressive regimes of truth, as Foucault stressed. Derrida's conclusions about the instabilities of meanings and discourses should serve to alert us that emancipation from oppressive discourses may lead to new oppressive discourses, too. Thus, Cherryholmes' critical pragmatism emphasizes helping students reflect on received and marginal knowledge and truth and is committed to helping students develop new discourses of emancipation, but it emphasizes John Dewey's view of the "experimental" nature of education and human fallibility—that is, the conclusions we draw and the choices we make have political, moral, and ethical consequences. Those conclusions and choices must be subjected to frequent evaluation and readjustment or reconstruction.

C. A. Bowers advocated the restoration of community as the essential aim of education in *Elements of a Post-Liberal Theory of Education* (1987). His examination of the historical tradition of liberalism presents a more culturally conservative analysis than the radical criticism provided by some postmodernists, but he also promotes a radical "bioregional" education that emphasizes empowerment and building a culture that lives in harmony with the natural environment. Bowers includes educational objectives concerned with knowledge, such as tacit knowledge of worthwhile cultural traditions for a "community of memory." Explicit knowledge necessary for understanding the self as a social being, which includes understanding the forces that constitute personal identity and social consciousness. His emphasis, however, is not on the liberal notion of freeing the self but on educating individuals for effective membership in a social and natural ecological community. He stresses the need to move beyond the liberal view of the autonomous individual to a view of the individual as a social-cultural being. In this view, language is the constituting ground of individual being and it should be the starting point for education.

For Bowers, one of the things from which we need to be freed is the oppression of symbolic knowledge as it is taught in schools because it makes literacy the defining feature of knowledge and learning; instead, oral communication should be included along with literacy, and the emphasis should be placed on a shared language, on how we use language and how it uses us, and on communicative competence as preparation for membership in a political community.

Curriculum

Generally speaking, postmodernists hold that the curriculum should not be viewed as discrete subjects and disciplines; instead, curriculum should include issues of power, history, personal and group identities, cultural politics, and social criticism leading to collective action. Rather than pretending that education has no connection with politics, postmodernism connects educational materials and processes (means) to the imperatives of a democratic community (ends). They envision a curriculum that is successful when it empowers people and transforms society, not when it maintains privileged economic and political interests. It is a curriculum that organizes itself from the inside out, so to speak—that is, from the concrete personal identities, histories, and ordinary experiences of students outward to the more abstract meanings of culture, history, and politics rather than the other way around.

Aronowitz and Giroux have extensively treated the debate over education between conservatives, liberals, and radicals in *Education Under Siege* (1985) and in *Postmodern Education* (1991). They note an aggressive conservatism in the 1980s that took the initiative in education, one that redefined the curriculum by waging a "cultural war" in the schools against liberal and leftist ideas. Conservatives understood the school as a political site they could use to help make their ideas dominant across the culture. For example, Allan Bloom in *The Closing of the American Mind* (1987) promoted the immersion of students in a higher education curriculum that would, in his own words, be "universalistic" and "imperialistic" and whose main reason for existence would be to preserve Western culture. In Giroux's opinion (in *Border Crossings*, 1992), works like Bloom's were unwittingly helpful to the radical left because the neoconservative political agenda helped educators see schools as *active arenas of cultural politics* rather than simply places where cultural domination and hegemony are reproduced. The conservative ascendancy led to school reforms that reaffirmed the traditional curriculum, cut back school budgets, and demanded that schools cater to business needs. As a result, the school as a site for cultural politics has taken on added meaning for postmodern radical educators who question the conservative reforms, just as they question the status of the scientific paradigm of thought in curriculum and evaluation. They reject distinctions between high and low culture and maintain that the popular culture (such as the entertainment media, popular novels, and rock music) is itself deserving of study—not for the purposes of emulation, but as material that can be analyzed and deconstructed to show how it helps or hurts.

Since postmodernists reject master narratives, they favor including the particular and specific narratives of those who suffer subordination because of race, gender, class, and sexual orientation. They value the study of people on the margins of culture for the specific histories and cultural contributions each can bring to the educational setting. These inclusions help students to understand the boundaries that may affect personal and social well-being. In addition, postmodernists spurn intellectual elites who set themselves above history and attempt to "get it right" for the rest of us, and so they promote a plurality of voices in the curriculum by including marginal narratives that, in Giroux's words, "represent the unrepresentable." Along with Foucault, they see reason and knowledge from within particular historical contexts of status and power, and students are encouraged to identify themselves in relation to the human struggles of those contexts. They want a variety of narratives to be included in the curriculum to help enlighten and liberate human possibilities.

An important aspect of curriculum from the critical pedagogy perspective is the inclusion of the ordinary experience of students as legitimate parts of the curriculum. This view of curriculum includes the competing identities, cultural traditions, and political outlooks students bring with them; and it refuses to reduce the issues of power, justice, and equality to a single master discourse. Critical pedagogy recognizes that students' personal identities develop over time and are influenced by many factors, including personal experience. Thus, the everyday world and ordinary experience of students can be used (in addition to officially sanctioned forms of traditional knowledge) as serious objects of study. In critical education, the curriculum is developed as part of the ongoing engagement of students with a variety of narratives that can be reinterpreted and reformulated, both culturally and politically.

From a postmodernist critical perspective, then, the issue in curriculum is not simply an argument for or against established canons of knowledge but one that remakes the meaning and use of canons of knowledge. Generally speaking, critical pedagogy emphasizes the need to break down traditional disciplinary boundaries in favor of an interdisciplinary approach. Perhaps a better way of stating it is the need to create a new conception of knowledge that does not depend upon disciplinary boundaries. In some respects, this resembles what the pragmatists recommended, especially what some progressives advocated in their "problems" approach to the curriculum, where knowledge is drawn from many disciplines and integrated around a particular problem or issue. As Giroux saw it in *Border Crossings*, however, the curriculum must be "reclaimed as a cultural politics" and "a form of social memory." Of course, the traditional disciplines of history and literature, for example, with their variety of historiographical theories and interpretation of literary genres, have always served as forms of cultural politics and social memory. But from Giroux's perspective, cultural politics involves understanding the production, creation, and interpretation of knowledge as part of a broader attempt to create public cultures. What is meant by "social memory" is to start with the everyday and the particular as a basis for learning and then proceed to traditional knowledge and popular culture as elements for study and critical evaluation to inform personal experience. A very important consideration, however, and the one that is crucial to postmodernist critical theory, is that such a curriculum must elevate the "silenced" narratives on the margins to avoid a totalizing outcome that maintains existing arrangements of power and privilege. Teaching and learning a curriculum of this kind creates in students a social memory that is neither singular nor totalizing but an enlarged understanding that includes voices from the center of culture to the very margins.

A major concern of postmodern critical pedagogy is to overcome the Enlightenment belief that the "universal laws of Nature" can, with the cold light of reason, be read from the face of an intelligible universe. According to Giroux, such a view of reason is not innocent because it promotes a "hidden curriculum" that exercises a totalizing form of power over thought and knowledge. Critical pedagogy urges educators to be skeptical of claims to "objective" knowledge purported to be outside time and ideology because this places knowledge outside history or changes in human experience and puts such knowledge claims beyond criticism and dialogue. This is why Giroux argues that we must regain a sense of alternatives by combining a language of critique and possibility. He believes that postmodern feminism exemplifies this sense of alternatives. Its critique of patriarchy has opened many eyes to inequalities based on gender, and it has provided new forms of identity and social relations for women. This kind of critique helps extend our understanding of both individual freedom and social responsibility, just as it awakens us to new understandings of the oppression of individuals and social groups based on gender. Such critiques help promote useful utopian thought, not a disutopianism that looks only backward and offers no viable notion of how to extend human freedom and social responsibility in the present and future. Through a critical approach, the future is kept open with new possibilities, not frozen over by views that are ahistorical and closed.

Bowers combines elements of Paulo Freire and John Dewey into a perspective that recognizes the danger of accepting received knowledge and existing conditions as inevitable. Unlike the radical perspective of the critical theorists, however, Bowers gives greater emphasis to cultural conservation, although he recognizes that this must be accomplished with care and that education in critical awareness must accompany the emphasis on social responsibility. He faults both Dewey and Freire for their emphasis on "living forward" at the expense of historical understanding and appreciation of what he calls "the community of memory." He argues that this continuous forward movement is a weakness of liberalism generally because it encourages individuals to escape community restraints and make moral judgments merely a concern of relative individual interpretation.

The liberal view promotes a view of individuality as self-interest, and the pursuit of self-interest, in turn, has led to the exploitation of other people and the environment. Instead, Bowers wants the authority of substantive traditions and community norms in the community of memory to be joined with critical reflection as an integral element in the making of moral judgments. This recognizes the relation of knowledge/truth and power in Foucault's sense because individuals are located in historical events or contexts. This differs from Giroux's notion of social memory because Bowers is not nearly so intent on the radical liberation of self and because he wants the community of memory to provide restraints imposed by substantive values. He differentiates his view of cultural conservatism from conservative extremism because the community of memory, with its expansive fund of useful meanings, also liberates the empowerment of self.

Role of the Teacher

As Giroux wrote in *Border Crossings*, Antonio Gramsci helped pave the way for seeing the significance of hegemonic power in culture and more recently such figures as Pierre Bourdieu have reintroduced it. Gramsci's theory showed how dominant interests depend less on overt force than on hegemonic leadership that wins the consent of subordinate groups to maintain the existing social order. This consent is organized in many ways, but in schools, it is found in how curriculum and pedagogical processes are managed and used. To counter this, teachers should use the issue of difference in an ethically challenging and politically transforming way. For example, personal-social differences can be incorporated into critical pedagogy to foster understanding of how personal identities are constructed in multiple and contradictory ways. This involves students exploring their own individual histories, including self-reflection on race, gender, and class, to show how human experiences and identities are made in different historical and social formations. Critical pedagogy focuses on how group identities are developed in social relations, how they are defined around differences, how these factors become significant, and how such differences affect a democratic society.

In *Teachers As Intellectuals* (1988), Giroux calls for a critical pedagogy that views educators as cultural workers who are "transformative intellectuals" occupying special political and social roles. Rather than defining the teacher in terms of a narrow language of technical professionalism, critical pedagogy helps clarify the role of teachers as thinkers and as cultural workers producing more appropriate ideologies and social practices. In this view, teachers are both scholars and practitioners and their role is not simply to teach a body of knowledge but to help students see the ideological and political interests that curricular knowledge may serve in various ways. It not only involves how knowledge can be used to totalize and objectify but also how it can be used to liberate students to become critical and responsible members of a democracy. For example, feminist scholarship has made persuasive arguments that politics is local and personal and this can be combined with politics in its more global aspects. This is not simply collapsing the political into the personal or exploding it to the global sense but using a political focus to help students bridge gaps between the personal and the political and to understand themselves in relation to such forces as institutional forms of racism, sexism, and class exploitation of the wider society. Thus, to be a transformative intellectual involves helping the student develop a critical consciousness that connects schooling with the public spheres of culture, history, and politics.

From another perspective, Cleo Cherryholmes looks at classroom interaction between students and teachers as a crucial consideration in teaching. He notes that an asymmetry exists because teachers have authority by virtue of their official position and greater education, training, and experience, and these factors militate against symmetry in the teacher–student relation. From a critical pragmatism perspective, however, greater symmetry is needed for students to learn to express themselves and to gain the confidence to explore, experiment, and take responsibility. A primary condition for improving the symmetry is for teachers to be committed to critical discourse with and among students. This involves helping students move beyond reliance upon positivistic knowledge received on authority and thence to genuine experiment, critical reflection, and judgment. Teachers do not relinquish responsibility for management; rather, they discourage reification or reliance on authoritative knowledge and encourage students to analyze received arguments to help make their own arguments and judgments. Cherryholmes points to the need for *good* arguments and judgments based on the Deweyan view of helping students take responsible concern for the daily problems of the community. Making good arguments and judgments involves substantive values as standards necessary for a democratic community, such as human dignity, liberty, equality, and concern for others.

The concern with teacher–student interaction is also important for Bowers, and he highlights the role of primary socialization schooling now serves. Historically, primary socialization of the young was conducted mostly in familial, religious, or occupational settings, such as the apprenticeship, and socialization was conducted in accordance with the authority governing those settings. Today, schools carry the larger burden of primary socialization; and Bowers sees this as a unique opportunity for teachers to help students question prevailing assumptions, explore and test complex understandings, and negotiate and shape perceptions. Success in this opportunity, however, depends to a large extent on teachers understanding their roles and the political nature of education.

A major concern is teachers being sensitive to their influence over the language process and how it shapes the way students think and conceptualize, because teaching and language have important political dimensions in educating for what Bowers calls *communicative competence*. Teaching includes not only explicit knowledge and spoken and written language but body language and attitudinal expressions of approval and disapproval, all of which transmit culture and influence student socialization. The essential functions of teaching include helping students become competent communicators, conserve meaningful traditions, question received knowledge, make explicit the beliefs and practices that are socially and individually harmful, and think about social and cultural problems that make up the crises we face today.

CRITIQUE OF POSTMODERNISM IN EDUCATION

The confusing nature of postmodernism and its relative newness make assessment difficult. Critics may note that postmodern educational recommendations are largely untested as yet, but this judgment could be made against many theoretical perspectives in education. Despite its newness, the postmodern view has some obvious strengths. One is the attention given to moral and ethical education, such as the stance by Giroux and McLaren on the inclusion of difference and marginality and how "the other" (the outcasts on the margins of culture) can add important dimensions to a learning community.

The emphasis on social discourse adds a powerful moral dimension by including students from the center to the margins—not to indoctrinate in a single culture but to develop personal and social identities based on deeper understandings of cultural differences. The emphasis on diversity and social discourse has the additional virtue of promoting education for a pluralistic democratic community that can counteract the development of socially destructive self-interest.

The sense of postmodern crisis applies not only to culture but to the environment as well, and sensitivity to ecology is an added dimension for developing social responsibility. Postmodern approaches to education promise to encourage a sense of personal, social, and ecological responsibility that is missing from many other educational perspectives.

The attention given to the political nature of education is another strength, but connections between education and politics have been recognized for a long time. Plato's *Republic* is an early example of the use of education for political ends, and Marxist theory has promoted a political view of education. However, the postmodern emphasis on the politics of difference (race, class, and gender) is joined to a view of the curriculum as a type of cultural politics. Attention given to the political nature of schooling and the relations of power within the schooling process provide some essential new insights. They shed light on how personal and social identities are formed, not simply by overt dominance, but by the subtle power narratives in the curriculum and the school structure. New understandings gained from these insights may help liberate students more adequately, just as it may also help educators become sensitive to the broader dimensions of their work.

The postmodern attention to language, to discourse and narrative that shape people's minds, calls for greater attention to how the curriculum and the teaching-learning process may serve to liberate or oppress. However, the view expressed by Cherryholmes that discourses of difference may lead to new regimes of truth that oppress is a healthy reminder to postmoderns for constant attention to ethical and moral reflection on the directions discourses in education may take. Developing students' sense of membership in a political community, including a community that understands and protects the bioregion and one that is dedicated to empowerment and freedom from cultural oppression, has strong potential for enhancing ethical and political growth.

Finally, the views on the crucial role of the teacher as a transformative intellectual whose role is to help students take personal and social responsibility for their futures is an important ingredient in the postmodern view of education. The tension between the radical views of Giroux and McLaren on social memory and the conservative view of Bowers on the community of memory illustrates postmodern variety, but in other respects, this brings attention to the crucial role teachers play in helping students develop identity and a sense of historical place. The emphasis on transformation points to a key element of postmodern thought in education, and this is the need to go beyond the mere transmittal of received knowledge to an activist stance on possibility and future directions. Despite the variety, the postmodern emphasis on empowering students to understand their past and present circumstances and on preparing them with articulated goals for the future are clearly strengths.

There are also some troubling weaknesses. Postmoderns highlight the crisis in culture and promote student identity with those who are different and on the margins, but their language of possibility is academic and, as critics frequently point out, difficult to decipher. One wonders how well people on the margins can identify with it, not to mention those in the mainstream culture who control policy and perhaps could be persuaded to the strengths of their arguments. For postmodern philosophy of education to have an impact on the "real" world of education, attention must be given to a public language that communicates and persuades.

In some respects, postmoderns seem to be more conscious of what they oppose than what they promote; this is revealed in the lack of attention to the sometimes overwhelmingly negative tone of their delivery. Greater attention to the positive aspects of their message and to making that language more in tune with normal discourse may add to the attractiveness of their proposals for ordinary citizens. The "real" world of education is indeed a political world in which the power of persuasion is also a form of empowerment for those who advocate new directions.

Another troublesome feature is the desire of postmodern critical theorists to politicize schooling. Certainly the existing forms of control over education represent entrenched power interests, but as Cherryholmes notes, if we learn anything from Foucault and Derrida it is that the creation of new truth regimes and power discourses may lead to unforeseen and undesirable outcomes. Postmodern critical theory seems to maintain a lingering traditional Marxism that claims that all views except its own are ideology. Thus, they critique other viewpoints as "totalizing theories" or "ideologies of power and control" and place themselves on the moral high ground. Perhaps this is an inevitable outcome of any sort of theory, but postmodernism may be strengthened by more attention to these kinds of problems.

The sensitivity to human differences and lifting up the oppressed are among postmodernism's strongest moral qualities; but in celebrating human differences, postmodernists may fail to recognize important commonalities. Perhaps their fascination with ruptures and fragmentation blinds them to the characteristics human beings hold in common. The rejection of totalizing metanarratives of universal human nature need not imply a rejection of commonalities that exist across the human spectrum. Certainly postmodernists, in their rejection of universals and their recognition of human divergency, would not want to suggest that human differences imply species differences. The emphasis on difference may serve to extend fragmentation and separateness, not a healthy recognition of common human bonds. Indeed, the postmodern desire for empowerment and freedom from oppression seems to have a "universal" ring to it, as does its emphasis on "the world of the discursive."

It seems to be no stretch of reason to suggest that *all* people need a sense of personal and social worth nurtured in a democratic community, a reasonable sense of security in safety and health, and opportunities to fulfill basic needs for food, clothing, and shelter. There may be variations from one part of a community to another (or from one part of the globe to another) on what are preferable ways to meet these needs, but it seems pointless to deny that there is a great deal that humanity has in common, and this commonality has a "universal" significance that postmodernism, particularly the critical theory version of it, seems to repress in its own discourses. Moreover, a discourse that minimizes or ignores the common bonds of humanity may itself become a form of totalizing narrative because it marginalizes or discounts the topic.

BORDER PEDAGOGY AS POSTMODERN RESISTANCE

In the following selection, Henry A. Giroux provides a context in which postmodern thought can have an impact on education. Although he speaks specifically to the issue of racism, his comments may also be extended to additional forms of "Otherness," including gender and class identities. Note his emphasis on how the totalizing nature of Eurocentric discourse freezes out other discourses and how inclusion of the voices of Others may enrich not only the lives of students but the lives of teachers and the larger society as well.

Within the current historical conjuncture, the political and cultural boundaries that have long constituted the meaning of race and culture are beginning to shift.... First, the population of America's subordinate groups are changing the landscapes of our urban centers.... Second, while people of color are redrawing the cultural demographic boundaries of the urban centers, the boundaries of power appear to be solidifying in favor of rich, white, middle and upper classes....

The dominant discourses of modernity have rarely been able to address race and ethnicity as an ethical, political, and cultural marker in order to understand or self-consciously examine the notions of justice inscribed in the modernist belief in change and the progressive unfolding of history. In fact, race and ethnicity have been generally reduced to a discourse of the Other, a discourse that regardless of its emancipatory or reactionary intent, often essentialized and reproduced the distance between the centers and margins of power. Within the discourse of modernity, the Other not only sometimes ceases to be a historical agent, but is often defined within totalizing and universalistic theories that create a transcendental rational white, male, Eurocentric subject that both occupies the centers of power while simultaneously appearing to exist outside time and space. Read against this Eurocentric transcendental subject, the Other is shown to lack any redeeming community tradi-

tions, collective voice, or historical weight–and is reduced to the imagery of the colonizer....

If the construction of anti-racist pedagogy is to escape from a notion of difference that is silent about other social antagonisms and forms of struggle, it must be developed as part of a wider public disclosure that is simultaneously about the discourse of an engaged plurality and the formation of critical citizenship. This must be a discourse that breathes life into the notion of democracy by stressing a notion of lived community that is *not* at odds with the principals of justice, liberty, and equality. Such a discourse must be informed by a postmodern concern with establishing the material and ideological conditions that allow multiple, specific, and heterogeneous ways of life to come into play as part of a border pedagogy of postmodern resistance. This points to the need for educators to prepare students for a type of citizenship that does not separate abstract rights from the realm of the everyday, and does not define community as the legitimate and unifying practice of a one-dimensional historical and cultural narrative. Postmodernism radicalizes the emancipatory possibilities of teaching and learning as a part of a wider struggle for democratic public life and critical citizenship. It does this by refusing forms of knowledge and pedagogy wrapped in the legitimizing discourse of the sacred and the priestly; its rejecting universal reason as a foundation for human affairs; claiming that all narratives are partial; and performing a critical reading on all scientific, cultural, and social texts as historical and political constructions.

In this view, the broader parameters of an anti-racist pedagogy are informed by a political project that links the creation of critical citizens to the development of a radical democracy; that is, a political project that ties education to the broader struggle for a public life in which dialogue, vision, and compassion remain critically attentive to the rights and conditions that organize public space as a democratic social reform rather than a regime of terror and oppression. It is important to emphasize that difference and pluralism in this view do not mean reducing democracy to the equivalency of diverse interests; on the contrary, what is being argued for is a language in which different voices and traditions exist and flourish to the degree that they listen to the voices of others, engage in an ongoing attempt to eliminate forms of subjective and objective suffering, and maintain those conditions in which the act of communicating and living extends rather than restricts the creation of democratic public spheres. This is as much a political as it is a pedagogical project, one that demands that anti-racist pedagogical practices be developed within a discourse that combines a democratic public philosophy with a postmodern theory of resistance.

What is being called for here is a notion of border pedagogy that provides educators with the opportunity to rethink the relationship between the centers and the margins of power. That is, such a pedagogy must address the issue of racism as one that calls into question not only forms of subordination that create inequities among different groups as they live out their lives but, as I have mentioned previously, also challenges those institutional and ideological boundaries that have historically masked their own relations of power behind complex forms of distinction and privilege. What does this suggest for the way we develop the basic elements of an anti-racist pedagogy?

First, the notion of border pedagogy offers students the opportunity to engage the multiple references that constitute different cultural codes, experiences, and languages. This means providing the learning opportunities for students to become media literate in a world of changing representations. It means offering students the knowledge and social relations that enable them to read critically not only how cultural texts are regulated by various discursive codes, but also how such texts express and represent different ideological interests. In this case, border pedagogy establishes conditions of learning that define literacy inside the categories of power and authority. This suggests developing pedagogical practices that address texts as social and historical constructions; it also suggests developing pedagogical practices that allow students to analyze texts in terms of their presences and absences; and most important, such practices should provide students with the opportunity to read texts dialogically through a configuration of many voices, some of which offer up resistance, some of which provide support.

Border pedagogy also stresses the necessity for providing students with the opportunity to engage critically the strengths and limitations of the cultural and social codes that define their own histories and narratives. Partiality becomes, in this case, the basis for recognizing the limits built into all disclosures. At issue here is not merely the need for students to develop a healthy skepticism towards all discourses of authority, but also to recognize how authority and power can be transformed in the interest of creating a democratic society.

Within this disclosure, students engage knowledge as a border-crosser, as a person moving in and out of borders constructed around coordinates of difference and power. These are not only physical borders, they are cultural borders historically constructed and socially organized within maps of rules and regulations that serve to either limit or enable particular identities, individual capacities, and social forms. In this case, students cross over into borders of meaning, maps of knowledge, social relations, and values that are increasingly being negotiated and rewritten as the codes and regulations which organize then become destabilized and reshaped. Border pedagogy decenters as it remaps. The terrain of learning becomes inextricably linked to the shifting parameters of place, identity, history, and power. By reconstructing the traditional radical emphasis of mapping domination to the politically strategic issue of engaging the ways in which knowledge can be remapped, reterritorialized, and decentered, in the wider interests of rewriting the borders and coordinates of an oppositional cultural politics, educators can redefine the teacher–student relationship in ways that allow students to draw upon their own personal experiences as real knowledge.

At one level this means giving students the opportunity to speak, to locate themselves in history, and to become subjects in the construction of their identities and the wider society. It also means defining voice not merely as an opportunity to speak, but to engage critically with the ideology and substance of speech, writing, and other forms of cultural production. In this case, "coming to voice" for students from both dominant and subordinate cultures means engaging in rigorous discussions of various cultural texts, drawing upon one's personal experience, and confronting the process through which ethnicity and power can be rethought as a political narrative that challenges racism as part of broader struggle to democratize social, political, and economic life. In part, this means looking at the various ways in which race implicates relations of domination, resistance, suffering, and power within various social practices and how these are taken up in multiple ways by students who occupy different ethnic, social, and gender locations. In this way, race is never discussed outside broader articulations, nor is it merely about people of color.

Second, a border pedagogy of postmodern resistance needs to do more than educate students to perform ideological surgery on master-narratives based on white, patriarchal, and class-specific interests. If the master-narratives of domination are to be effectively deterritorialized, it is important for educators to understand how such narratives are taken up as part of an investment of feeling, pleasure, and desire. There is a need to rethink the syntax of learning and behavior outside the geography of rationality and reason. For example, this means that racism cannot be dealt with in a

purely limited, analytical way. An anti-racist pedagogy must engage how and why students make particular ideological and affective investments and occupy particular subject positions in regard to issues concerning race and racism. This means attempting to understand the historical context and substance of the social and cultural forms that produce in diverse and multiple ways the often contradictory subject positions that give students a sense of meaning, purpose, and delight. As Stuart Hall argues, this means uncovering both for ourselves as teachers as well as for the students we are teaching "the deep structural factors which have a tendency persistently not only to generate racial practices and structures but to reproduce them through time and which therefore account for their extraordinarily immovable character." In addition to engaging racism within a politics of representation, ideology, and pleasure, it is also important to stress that any serious analyses of racism also has to be historical and structural. It has to chart out how racist practices develop, where they come from, how they are sustained, how they affect dominant and subordinate groups, and how they can be challenged. This is not a discourse about personal preferences or dominant tastes but a discourse about economics, culture, politics, and power.

Third, a border pedagogy offers the opportunity for students to air their feelings about race from the perspective of the subject positions they experience as constitutive of their own identities. Ideology in this sense is treated not merely as an abstraction but as part of the student's lived experience. This does not mean that teachers reduce their role to that of an intellectual voyeur or collapse his or her authority into a shabby form of relativism. Nor does it suggest that students merely express or assess their own experiences. Rather, it points to a particular form of teacher authority grounded in a respect for a radically decentered notion of democratic public life. This is a view of authority that rejects the notion that all forms of authority are expressions of unwarranted power and oppression. Instead, it argues for forms of authority that are rooted in democratic interests and emancipatory social relations, forms of authority that, in this case, begins from a standpoint from which to develop an educational project that reflects politics as aesthetics, that retains instead the significance of the knowledge/power relationship as a discourse of criticism and politics necessary for the achievement of equality, freedom, and struggle. This is not a form of authority based on an appeal to universal truths, it is a form of authority that recognizes its own partiality while simultaneously asserting a standpoint from which to engage the discourses and practices of democracy, freedom, and domination. Put another way, this is a notion of authority rooted in a political project that ties education to the broader struggle for public life in which dialogue, vision, and compassion remain critically attentive to the liberating and dominating relations that organize various aspects of everyday life.

This suggests that teachers use their authority to establish classroom conditions in which different views about race can be aired but not treated as simply an expression of individual views or feelings.... An anti-racist pedagogy must demonstrate that the views we hold about race have different historical and ideological weight, forged in asymmetrical relations of power, and that they always embody interests that shape social practices in particular ways. In other words, an anti-racist pedagogy cannot treat ideologies as simply individual expressions of feeling, but as historical, cultural, and social practices that serve to either undermine or reconstruct democratic public life. These views must be engaged without silencing students, but they must also be interrogated next to a public philosophy that names racism for what it is and calls racist ideologies and practices into account on political and ethical terms.

Fourth, educators need to understand how the experience of marginality at the level of everyday life lends itself to forms of oppositional and transformative consciousness. For those designated as Others need to both reclaim and remake their histories, voices, and visions as part of a wider struggle to change those material and social relations that deny radical plural-ism as the basis of democratic political community. It is only through such an understanding that teachers can develop a border pedagogy which opens up the possibility for students to reclaim their voices as part of a process of empowerment and not merely what some have called an initiation into the culture of power. It is not enough for students to learn how the dominant culture works to exercise power, they must also understand how to resist power which is oppressive, which names them in a way that undermines their ability to govern rather than serve, and prevents them from struggling against forms of power that subjugate and exploit.... This is not to suggest that the authority of white dominant culture is all of one piece, nor is this meant to imply that it should not be the object of study. What is at stake here is forging a notion of power that does not collapse into a form of domination, but is critical and emancipatory, that allows students to both locate themselves in history and to critically, not slavishly, appropriate the cultural and political codes of their own and other traditions. Moreover, students who have to disavow their own racial heritage in order to succeed are ... being positioned to accept subject positions that are the source of power for a white, dominant culture. The ability of white, male, Eurocentric culture to normalize and universalize its own interests works so well ... as a site of dominant narratives, [that it prevents] ... black students from speaking through their own memories, histories, and experiences.... [We must illuminate] more clearly how power works in this society within the schools to secure and conceal various forms of racism and subjugation. Power is multifaceted and we need a better understanding of how it works not simply as a force for oppression but also a basis for resistance and self and social empowerment. Educators need to fashion a critical postmodern notion of authority, one that decenters essentialist claims to power while at the same time fighting for relations of authority and power that allow many voices to speak so as to initiate students into a culture that multiplies rather than restricts democratic practices and social relations as part of a wider struggle for democratic public life.

Fifth, educators need to analyze racism not only as a structural and ideological force, but also in the diverse and historically specific ways in which it emerges. This is particularly true of the most recent and newest expressions of racism developing in the United States and abroad among youth in popular culture, and in its resurgence in the highest reaches of the American government. This also suggests that any notion of an anti-racist pedagogy must arise out of specific settings and contexts. Such a pedagogy must allow its own character to be defined, in part, by the historically specific and contextual boundaries in which it emerges. At the same time, such a pedagogy must disavow all claims to scientific method or for that matter to any objective or transhistorical claims. As a political practice, an anti-racist pedagogy has to be constructed not on the basis of essentialist or universal claims but on the concreteness of its specific encounters, struggles, and engagements. . . .

Sixth, an anti-racist border pedagogy must redefine how the circuits of power move in a dialectical fashion among various sites of cultural production. We need a clearer understanding of how ideologies and other social practices which bear down on classroom relations emerge from and articulate with other spheres of social life. As educators, we need a clearer understanding of how the grounds for the production and organization of knowledge is related to forms of authority situated in political economy, the state, and other material practices. We also need to understand how circuits of power produce forms of textual authority that offer readers particular subject positions, that is, ideological references that provide but do not rigidly determine particular views of the world. In addition, educators need to explore how the reading of texts [is] linked to the forms of knowledge and social relations that students bring to the classroom. In other words, we need to understand in terms of function and substance those social and cultural forms outside the classroom that produce the multiple and often contradictory subject posi-

tions that students learn and express in their interaction with the dominant cultural capital of American schools.

Finally, central to the notion of border pedagogy are a number of important pedagogical issues regarding the role that teachers might take up in making a commitment to fighting racism in their classrooms, schools, communities, and the wider society. The concept of border pedagogy also helps to locate teachers within social, political, and cultural boundaries that define and mediate in complex ways how they function as intellectuals who exercise particular forms of moral and social regulation. Border pedagogy calls attention to both the ideological and the partial as central elements in the construction of teacher discourse and practice. In part, this suggests that to the degree that teachers make the construction of their own voices, histories, and ideologies problematic they become more attentive to Otherness as a deeply political and pedagogical issue. In other words, by deconstructing the underlying principles which inform their own lives and pedagogy, educators can begin to recognize the limits underlying the partiality of their own views. Such a recognition offers the promise of allowing teachers to restructure their pedagogical relations in order to engage in open and critical dialogue questions regarding the knowledge taught, how it relates to students' lives, how students can engage with such knowledge, and how such practices actually relate to empowering both teachers and students. Within dominant models of pedagogy, teachers are often silenced through a refusal or inability to make problematic with students the values that inform how they teach and engage the multifaceted relationship between knowledge and power. Without the benefit of dialogue, an understanding of the partiality of their own beliefs, they are cut off from any understanding of the effects their pedagogies have on students. In effect, their infatuation with certainty and control serves to limit the possibilities inherent in their own voices and visions. In this case, dominant pedagogy serves not only to disempower students, but teachers as well. In short, teachers need to take up a pedagogy that provides a more dialectical understanding of their own politics and values; they need to break down pedagogical boundaries that silence them in the name of methodological rigor or pedagogical absolutes; more important, they need to develop a power-sensitive discourse that allows them to open up their interactions with the discourses of various Others so that their classrooms can engage rather than block out the multiple positions and experiences that allow teachers and students to speak in and with many complex and different voices.

Source: Henry A. Giroux, "Postmodernism as Border Pedagogy: Redefining the Boundaries of Race and Ethnicity," in *Postmodernism, Feminism, and Cultural Politics*, edited by Henry A. Giroux. Albany: State University of New York Press, copyright © 1991, pp. 217, 218, 245, 246, 247–254. Reprinted by permission of the publisher.

. . . .

SELECTED READINGS

Aronowitz, Stanley, and Giroux, Henry A. *Postmodern Education: Politics, Culture, and Social Criticism.* Minneapolis: University of Minnesota Press, 1991. One of the leading statements on postmodern educational theory, this work seeks to develop a radical discourse in opposition to the dominant narratives that tend to define the issues of the day, particularly current educational reform that is driven by market needs rather than focused on the needs of the community.

Baynes, Kenneth, et al. *After Philosophy: End or Transformation?* Cambridge, MA: MIT Press, 1987. A collection of selections from leading philosophers who have influenced postmodern thinking. The book contains some classic selections as well as interviews of philosophers explaining their philosophical projects.

Giroux, Henry. *Border Crossings: Cultural Workers and the Politics of Education.* New York: Routledge, 1992. A major recent example of Henry Giroux's approach to philosophy of education from a postmodern critical perspective. Giroux explores the postmodern determination to break through the barriers and boundaries established by modernist thought on educational theory.

LeCompte, Margaret D., and deMarrais, Kathleen Bennett. The Disempowering of Empowerment: Out of the Revolution and into the Classroom. *Educational Foundations* 6(3):5–31, Summer 1992. The authors question current tendencies to make "empowerment" into simply another movement and thereby to coopt the liberating potential of the concept. What is needed is greater engagement in genuine efforts to empower the dispossessed.

Stout, Maureen. Rethinking the Concept of "The Popular" in Critical and Poststructural Social and Educational Theory, *Educational Foundations* 6(3):51–66, Summer 1992. An appeal to understand the postmodern concern for popular culture not as merely working class culture but as the cultures of marginalized groups. Such a conceptualization should help educators understand the nature of partial knowledge(s) and incomplete understanding(s) in shaping a new sense of democratic community.

Selected Bibliography

Adler, Mortimer J. *Paideia Problems and Possibilities.* New York: Macmillan, 1982.

———. *The Paideia Proposal: An Educational Manifesto.* New York: Macmillan, 1982.

———, **and Mayer, Milton.** *The Revolution in Education.* Chicago: University of Chicago Press, 1958.

Alcott, Amos Bronson. *Journals.* Boston: Little, Brown, 1938.

Alinsky, Saul. *Rules for Radicals.* New York: Random House, 1971.

Apple, Michael W., ed. *Cultural and Economic Reproduction in Education: Essays on Class, Ideology, and the State.* New York: Routledge and Kegan Paul, 1982.

———. Education, Culture, and Class Power: Basil Bernstein and the Neo-Marxist Sociology of Education. *Educational Theory* 42(2):127–146, Spring 1992.

———. *Official Knowledge: Democratic Education in a Conservative Age.* New York: Routledge, 1993.

Aquinas, Thomas. *Basic Writings.* New York: Random House, 1905.

———. *Summa Theologica,* vol. 1–3, translated by Fathers of the English Dominican Province. New York: Benziger Brothers, 1947.

———. *The Teacher—The Mind.* Chicago: Henry Regnery, 1953.

Arato, Andrew, and Gebhardt, Eike, eds. *The Essential Frankfurt School Reader.* New York: Urizen Books, 1978.

Aristotle. *The Nicomachean Ethics of Aristotle,* translated by David Ross. New York: Oxford University Press, 1975.

———. *Politics,* translated by Benjamin Jowett. New York: Colonial Press, 1899.

Aronowitz, Stanley. *The Crisis in Historical Materialism: Class, Politics, and Culture in Marxist Theory,* 2d ed. Minneapolis: University of Minnesota Press, 1990.

———. *The Politics of Identity: Class, Culture, Social Movements.* New York: Routledge, 1992.

———, **and Giroux, Henry A.** *Education Under Siege: The Conservative, Liberal, and Radical Debate Over Schooling.* Westport, CT: Bergin and Garvey, 1985.

————, and **Giroux, Henry A.** *Postmodern Education: Politics, Culture, and Social Criticism.* Minneapolis: University of Minnesota Press, 1991.

Augustine. *Concerning the Teacher,* translated by George G. Leckie. New York: Appleton-Century-Crofts, 1938.

————. *Confessions,* translated by Edward B. Pusey. New York: Modern Library, 1949.

Aurelius, Marcus. *Meditations,* translated by Maxwell Staniforth. Baltimore: Penguin, 1964.

Ayer, Alfred Jules. *Language, Truth and Logic.* New York: Dover, 1952.

————. *Russell and Moore.* Cambridge, MA: Harvard University Press, 1971.

Bach, Marcus. *Major Religions of the World.* Nashville, TN: Abingdon Press, 1959.

Bacon, Francis. *Advancement of Learning and Novum Organum.* New York: Colonial, 1889.

Baird, Robert D., and Bloom, Alfred. *Indian and Far Eastern Religious Traditions.* New York: Harper & Row, 1972.

Banerjee, M. *Invitation to Hinduism.* New Delhi: Printsman, 1978.

Bayles, Ernest. *Pragmatism and Education.* New York: Harper & Row, 1966.

Baynes, Kenneth, et al. *After Philosophy: End or Transformation?* Cambridge, MA: MIT Press, 1987.

Beck, Clive. *Educational Philosophy and Theory: An Introduction.* Boston: Little, Brown, 1974.

Bell, Daniel. *The End of Ideology: On the Exhaustion of Political Ideas in the Fifties.* New York: The Free Press, 1960.

Bellah, Robert N., et al. *The Good Society.* New York: Alfred A. Knopf, 1991.

Bender, Frederic L., ed. *The Betrayal of Marx.* New York: Harper & Row, 1975.

Bereiter, Carl, and Engelmann, S. *Teaching Disadvantaged Children in the Pre-School.* Englewood Cliffs, NJ: Prentice-Hall, 1966.

Bergson, Henri. *Creative Evolution,* translated by Arthur Mitchell. New York: Modern Library, 1944.

Berkeley, George. *Principles of Human Knowledge.* New York: E. P. Dutton, 1910.

Berlin, Isaiah. *Karl Marx: His Life and Environment. The Home University Library of Modern Knowledge, No. 189,* 3d ed. London: Oxford University Press, 1963.

Bernstein, Richard J. *The New Constellation: The Ethical-Political Horizons of Modernity/Postmodernity.* Cambridge, MA: MIT Press, 1992.

————. *Philosophical Profiles.* Cambridge, England: Polity Press, 1986.

————. *Praxis and Action: Contemporary Philosophies of Human Activity.* Philadelphia: University of Pennsylvania Press, 1971.

————. The Resurgence of Pragmatism. *Social Research* 59(4):813–840, Winter 1992.

————. Varieties of Pluralism. *American Journal of Education* 95(4):509–525, August 1987.

Berry, Thomas. *Religions of India: Hinduism, Yoga, Buddhism.* New York: Bruce Publishing Co., 1971.

Bloom, Allan. *The Closing of the American Mind.* New York: Simon and Schuster, 1987.

Bode, Boyd. *Progressive Education at the Crossroads.* New York: Newson, 1938.

Bowers, C. A. *Elements of a Post-Liberal Theory of Education.* New York: Teachers College Press, 1987.

Bowes, Pratima. *Hindu Intellectual Tradition.* Columbia, MO: South Asia Books, 1977.

Bowles, Samuel, and Gintis, Herbert. *Schooling in Capitalist America: Educational Reform and the Contradictions of Economic Life.* New York: Basic Books, 1977.

Brameld, Theodore. *Education as Power.* New York: Holt, Rinehart and Winston, 1965.

————. *Patterns of Educational Philosophy.* New York: Holt, Rinehart and Winston, 1971.

————. *Toward a Reconstructed Philosophy of Education.* New York: Dryden, 1956.

Brosio, Richard A. Capitalism's Emerging World Order: The Continuing Need for Theory and Brave Action by Citizen-Educators. *Educational Theory* 43(4):467–482, Fall 1993.

Broudy, Harry S. *Building a Philosophy of Education.* Englewood Cliffs, NJ: Prentice-Hall, 1961.

————. Philosophy of Education Between Yearbooks. *Teachers College Record* 81:130–144, 1979.

————. *The Real World of the Public Schools.* New York: Harcourt Brace Jovanovich, 1972.

Brubacher, John S. The Challenge to Philosophize About Education, in *Modern Philosophies and Education. The Fifty-Fourth Yearbook of the National Society for the Study of Education,* part I, chapter VII. Chicago: National Society for the Study of Education, 1942, pp. 289–322.

————. *Modern Philosophies of Education.* New York: McGraw-Hill, 1939.

Buber, Martin. *I and Thou,* translated by Ronald G. Smith. New York: Charles Scribner's, 1958.

Burnett, Joe E. Some Observations on the Logical Implications of Philosophic Theory for Educational Theory and Practice, in *Philosophy of Education, 1958. Proceedings of the Fourteenth Annual Meeting of the Philosophy of Education Society.* Edwardsville, IL: The Philosophy of Education Society, 1958.

Burns, Hobart W. The Logic of the "Educational Implication." *Educational Theory* 12:53–63, 1962.

Butler, J. Donald. *Four Philosophies.* New York: Harper, 1951.

————. *Idealism in Education.* New York: Harper & Row, 1966.

Camus, Albert. *The Myth of Sisyphus,* translated by Justin O'Brien. New York: Alfred A. Knopf, 1955.

————. *The Rebel,* translated by Anthony Bower. New York: Alfred A. Knopf, 1978.

Carnoy, Martin, ed. *Schooling in a Corporate Society: The Political Economy of Education in America.* New York: David McKay Co., 1972.

————, and **Levin, Henry M.** *The Limits of Educational Reform.* New York: David McKay Co., 1976.

Casti, John L. *Paradigms Lost: Images of Man in the Mirror of Science.* New York: William Morrow and Co., 1989.

Chai, Ch'u, and Chai, Winberg. *The Story of Chinese Philosophy.* New York: Washington Square Press, 1961.

Chamberlin, Gordon. *The Educating Act: A Phenomenological View.* Lanham, MD: University Press of America, 1981.

Chennakesavan, Sarasauti. *A Critical Study of Hinduism.* New York: Asia Publishing House, 1974.

Cherryholmes, Cleo. *Power and Criticism: Poststructural Investigations in Education.* New York: Teachers College Press, 1988.

Childs, John Lawrence. *American Pragmatism and Education.* New York: Holt, Rinehart and Winston, 1956.

————. *Education and the Philosophy of Experimentalism.* New York: Appleton-Century, 1931.

Chuang Tzu. *Chuang Tzu: Basic Writings,* translated by Durton Watson. New York: Columbia University Press, 1964.

Code, Lorraine. *Epistemic Responsibility.* Hanover, NH: University Press of New England, 1987.

College Entrance Examination Board. *Academic Preparation for College: What Students Need to Know and Be Able to Do.* New York: College Board, 1983.

Comte, Auguste. *A General View of Positivism,* translated by J. H. Bridges. New York: R. Speller, 1957.

Conant, James. *Education and Liberty.* Cambridge, MA: Harvard University Press, 1953.

Conze, Edward. *A Short History of Buddhism.* New York: George Allen & Unwin, 1980.

Copernicus, Nicolaus. *The Revolutions of the Heavenly Spheres,* translated by A. M. Duncan. New York: Barnes and Noble, 1976.

Counts, George S. *The Challenge of Soviet Education.* Westport, CT: McGraw-Hill, 1957.

————. *Dare the Schools Build a New Social Order?* New York: Arno Press, 1969.

Creel, Herrlee G. *Chinese Thought: From Confucius to Mao Tse-Tung.* New York: The New American Library, 1953.

————. *What Is Taoism? (and Other Studies in Chinese Cultural History).* Chicago: University of Chicago Press, 1970.

Crowley, Sharon. *A Teacher's Introduction to Deconstructionism. NCTE Teacher's Introduction Series.* Urbana, IL: National Council of Teachers of English, 1989.

D'Amico, Robert. *Marx and Philosophy of Culture.* Gainesville: University Presses of Florida, 1981.

Daniels, Robert V., ed. *A Documentary History of Communism,* vol. 1 and 2. New York: Vintage Books, 1960.

Darwin, Charles R. *The Origin of Species by Means of Natural Selection.* New York: Oxford University Press, 1958.

Dasgupta, Shashi Bhusan. *Aspects of Indian Religious Thought.* Calcutta, India: Firma Kim Private, 1957.

David-Neel, Alexandra. *Buddhism: Its Doctrines and Its Methods.* New York: St. Martin's Press, 1977.

Dawson, Miles Menander. *The Basic Thoughts of Confucius.* New York: Garden City Publishing Co., 1939.

DeBacy, Theodore, ed. *The Buddhist Tradition in India, China, and Japan.* New York: The Modern Library, 1969.

Derrida, Jacques. *Of Grammatology,* translated by Gayatri Chakravorty Spivak. Baltimore: Johns Hopkins University Press, 1976.

Descartes, René. *A Discourse on Method and Meditations,* translated by Laurence J. Lofleur. Indianapolis: Bobbs-Merrill, 1960.

Dewey, John. *A Common Faith.* New Haven: Yale University Press, 1934.

———. *Art as Experience.* New York: Capricorn, 1959.

———. *The Child and the Curriculum and the School and Society.* Chicago: University of Chicago Press, 1990.

———. *Democracy and Education.* New York: Macmillan, 1916.

———. *Essays in Experimental Logic.* New York: Dover, 1953.

———. *Experience and Education.* New York: Macmillan, 1938.

———. *Experience and Nature.* LaSalle, IL: Open Court, 1929.

———. *How We Think.* Boston: D. C. Heath, 1933.

———. *Human Nature and Conduct.* Carbondale: Southern Illinois University Press, 1988.

———. *The Influence of Darwin on Philosophy and Other Essays in Contemporary Thought.* New York: Henry Holt, 1910.

———. *Moral Principles in Education.* Carbondale: Southern Illinois University Press, Arcturus Books Edition, 1975.

———. My Pedagogic Creed. *The School Journal* 54(3):77-80, January 16, 1897.

———. The Need for a Recovery in Philosophy, in *On Experience, Nature, and Freedom: Representative Selections,* edited by Richard J. Bernstein. New York: The Library of Liberal Arts, Bobbs-Merrill, 1960, pp. 16–69.

———. *The School and Society.* Chicago: University of Chicago Press, 1915.

———. *Theory of the Moral Life.* New York: Holt, Rinehart, and Winston, 1960.

Durkheim, Émile. *Socialism and Saint-Simon,* edited by Alvin W. Gouldner and translated by Charlotte Satler. Yellow Springs, OH: Antioch Press, 1958.

Eastwood, Gordon. Paradigms, Anomalies, and Analysis: Response to Jonas Soltis, in *Philosophy of Education, 1971. Proceedings of the Twenty-Seventh Annual Meeting of the Philosophy of Education Society.* Edwardsville, IL: Philosophy of Education Society, 1971, pp. 47–54.

Edel, Abraham. Analytic Philosophy of Education at the Crossroads. *Educational Theory* 22:131–153, 1972.

Emerson, Ralph Waldo. *Essays.* New York: Houghton Mifflin, 1883.

Epstein, Isidore. *Judaism: A Historical Presentation.* Baltimore: Penguin Books, 1959.

Erasmus, Desiderius. *The Education of a Christian Prince,* translated by Lester K. Born. New York: Columbia University Press, 1924.

Feibleman, James K. *Understanding Oriental Philosophy.* New York: Horizon Press, 1976.

Feinberg, Walter. *Understanding Education: Toward a Reconstruction of Educational Inquiry.* New York: Cambridge University Press, 1983.

Fischer, Ernst, and Marek, Franz, eds. *The Essential Lenin,* translated by Anna Bostock. New York: Herder and Herder, 1972.

Foucault, Michel. *Discipline and Punish.* New York: Vantage Books, 1979.

———. *Madness and Civilization: A History of Insanity in the Age of Reason.* New York: Vintage Books, 1973.

———. *The Order of Things: An Archaeology of the Human Sciences.* New York: Vintage Books, 1973.

Freire, Paulo. *Education for a Critical Consciousness.* New York: The Seabury Press, 1973.

———. *Pedagogy of the Oppressed,* translated by Myra Bergman Ramos. New York: The Seabury Press, 1970.

Freud, Sigmund. *Civilization and Its Discontents,* translated by James Strachey. New York: W. W. Norton, 1962.

Froebel, Friedrich. *The Education of Man,* translated by W. N. Hailman. New York: A. M. Kelley, 1974.

Fung, Yu-Lan. *The Spirit of Chinese Philosophy.* Westport, CT: Greenwood Press, 1947.

Gaer, Joseph. *What the Great Religions Believe.* New York: NAL/Dutton, 1964.

Gard, Richard A. *Buddhism.* New York: George Braziller, 1914.

Gavin, William J., ed. *Context Over Foundation: Dewey and Marx.* Norwell, MA: Kluwer, 1988.

Gentile, G. *The Reform of Education.* New York: Harcourt, Brace, 1922.

George, Paul S. *The Theory Z School: Beyond Effectiveness.* Columbus, OH: National Middle School Assoc., 1983.

Geuss, Raymond. *The Idea of Critical Theory: Habermas and the Frankfurt School. Modern European Philosophy.* New York: Cambridge University Press, 1981.

Gibb, H. A. R. *Modern Trends in Islam.* Chicago: University of Chicago Press, 1947.

Gibson, Etienne. *The Spirit of Medieval Philosophy.* New York: Charles Scribner's, 1940.

Giroux, Henry A. *Border Crossings: Cultural Workers and the Politics of Education.* New York: Routledge, 1992.

———. *Ideology, Culture, and the Process of Schooling.* Philadelphia: Temple University Press, 1981.

———. Marxism and Schooling: The Limits of Radical Discourse. *Educational Theory* 34(2):113–136, Spring 1984.

———. *Teachers As Intellectuals: Toward a Critical Pedagogy of Learning.* New York: Bergin and Garvey, 1988.

Gitlin, Todd. Postmodernism: Roots and Practices. *Dissent* 36:100–108, Winter 1989.

Goodlad, John I. *A Place Called School: Prospects for the Future.* New York: McGraw-Hill, 1984.

Gopalan, S. *Outlines of Jainism.* New York: John Wiley & Sons, 1973.

Gramsci, Antonio. *Selections from the Prison Notebooks of Antonio Gramsci,* edited by Quintin Hoare and Geoffrey N. Smith. New York: International Publishers, 1971.

Greene, Maxine. *Landscapes of Learning.* New York: Teachers College Press, 1978.

———. *Teacher as Stranger: Educational Philosophy for the Modern Age.* Belmont, CA: Wadsworth, 1973.

Guillaume, Alfred. *Islam.* New York: Penguin Books, 1954.

Habermas, Jurgen. *Communication and the Evolution of Society,* translated and with an introduction by Thomas McCarthy. Boston: Beacon Press, 1979.

———. *On the Logic of the Social Sciences,* translated by Shierry Weber Nicholsen and Jerry A. Stark. Cambridge, MA: MIT Press, 1988.

———. *The Philosophical Discourse of Modernity.* Cambridge, MA: MIT Press, 1987.

———. *Theory and Practice.* Boston: Beacon Press, 1973.

Hackett, Stuart C. *Oriental Philosophy.* Madison: The University of Wisconsin Press, 1979.

Hamm, Russell L. *Philosophy and Education: Alternatives in Theory and Practice.* Danville, IL: Interstate, 1974.

Harris, William Torrey. Moral Education in the Common Schools, in *Modern Philosophies of Education.* New York: Random House, 1971.

Harshbarger, Luther H., and Mourant, John A. *Judaism and Christianity: Perspectives and Traditions.* Boston: Allyn and Bacon, 1968.

Hegel, Georg W. F. *The Logic of Hegel, Translated from the Encyclopaedia of Philosophical Sciences,* translated by William Wallace. New York: Oxford University Press, 1892.

———. *The Phenomenology of Mind,* translated by J. B. Baillie. New York: Allen Unwin, 1949.

———. *Philosophy of Right,* translated by T. M. Knox. New York: Clarendon, 1957.

Heidegger, Martin. *The Basic Problems of Phenomenology.* Bloomington: Indiana University Press, 1982.

———. *Existence and Being,* translated by Werner Brock. Chicago: Henry Regnery, 1968.

Herndon, James. *How to Survive in Your Native Land.* New York: Bantam Books, 1971.

Hinnells, J. R., and Sharpe, E. J. *Hinduism.* New Castle upon Tyne, England: Oriel Press, 1972.

Hirsch, E. D. Jr. *Cultural Literacy: What Every American Needs to Know.* Boston: Houghton Mifflin, 1987.

Hobbes, Thomas. *Selections,* edited by Frederick J. E. Woodbridge. New York: Charles Scribner's, 1930.

Hook, Sidney. *Education for Modern Man.* New York: Knopf, 1963.

Horkheimer, Max. *Dawn and Decline.* New York: Continuum, 1978.

———. *Eclipse of Reason.* New York: Continuum, 1973.

———, **and Adorno, Theodor.** *Dialectic of Enlightenment,* translated by John Cumming. New York: Herder and Herder, 1969.

Horne, Herman H. *The Democratic Philosophy of Education.* New York: Macmillan, 1935.

Howard, Dick. *The Development of the Marxist Dialectic.* Carbondale: Southern Illinois University Press, 1972.

Hullfish, Henry Gordon, and Smith, Philip G. *Reflective Thinking: The Method of Education.* New York: Dodd, Mead, 1961.

Hume, David. *Treatise Upon Human Nature.* New York: Oxford University Press, 1941.

Husserl, Edmund. *Ideas.* New York: Macmillan, 1962.

Hutchins, Robert Maynard. *The Conflict in Education.* New York: Harper & Row, 1953.

———. *Great Books, The Foundations of a Liberal Education.* New York: Simon and Schuster, 1954.

Huxley, Aldous. *Brave New World.* New York: Bantam, 1932.

———. *Tomorrow and Tomorrow and Tomorrow.* New York: Harper, 1956.

Hyppolite, Jean. *Studies on Marx and Hegel,* translated with introduction, notes, and bibliography by John O'Neill. New York: Basic Books, 1969.

Illich, Ivan. *Deschooling Society.* New York: Harper & Row, 1970.

Jacoby, Susan. *Inside Soviet Schools.* New York: Hill and Wang, 1974.

Jaini, Padmanabh S. *The Jaina Path of Purification.* Berkeley: University of California Press, 1979.

James, William. *Pragmatism, a New Name for Some Old Ways of Thinking.* New York: Longmans, Green, 1931.

———. *Talks to Teachers.* New York: Holt, Rinehart and Winston, 1899.

———. *The Varieties of Religious Experience.* New York: Longmans, Green, 1902.

Jameson, Frederic. *The Ideologies of Theory: Essays 1971–1986. Theory and History of Literature,* vol. 48 and 49, edited by Wlad Godzich and Jochen Schulte-Sasse. Minneapolis: University of Minnesota Press, 1988.

Jaspers, Karl. *Philosophy of Existence,* translated by Richard F. Grabau. Philadelphia: University of Pennsylvania Press, 1971.

Jencks, Christopher. *Inequality: A Reassessment of the Effect of Family and Schooling in America.* New York: Basic Books, 1972.

Jervis, Kathe, and Montag, Carol, eds. *Progressive Education for the 1990s: Transforming Practice.* New York: Teachers College Press, 1991.

Jurji, Edward J. *The Great Religions of the Modern World.* Princeton, NJ: Princeton University Press, 1946.

Kallen, Horace. *Culture and Democracy in the United States.* New York: Boni and Liveright, 1924.

Kant, Immanuel. *Critique of Practical Reason,* translated by Lewis White Beck. New York: Liberal Arts Press, 1956.

———. *Critique of Pure Reason.* Chicago: University of Chicago Press, 1949.

———. *Education,* translated by Annette Churton. Ann Arbor: University of Michigan Press, 1960.

Kellner, Douglas. *Critical Theory, Marxism, and Modernity.* Baltimore: Johns Hopkins University Press, 1989.

Kierkegaard, Søren Aabye. *Attack on "Christendom,"* translated by Walter Lowrie. Princeton, NJ: Princeton University Press, 1944.

———. *Fear and Trembling, and the Sickness unto Death,* translated by Walter Lowrie. Princeton, NJ: Princeton University Press, 1954.

Kilpatrick, William Heard. *Education for a Changing Civilization.* New York: Macmillan, 1927.

Kim, Yong Choon. *Oriental Thought.* Lanham, MD: Rowman and Littlefield, 1973.

Klein, Margrete S. *The Challenge of Communist Education: A Look at the German Democratic Republic. East European Monographs.* New York: Columbia University Press, 1980.

Kneller, George F. *Existentialism and Education.* New York: John Wiley, 1958.

———. *Introduction to Philosophy of Education.* New York: John Wiley & Sons, 1971.

Kohlberg, Lawrence. Moral Education Reappraised. *The Humanist* 38(6), November/December 1978.

———. Stages of Moral Development as a Basis for Moral Education, in *Moral Education: Interdisciplinary Approaches,* edited by Clive M. Beck et al. Toronto: University of Toronto Press, 1971.

Koller, John M. *Oriental Philosophies.* New York: Charles Scribner's Sons, 1970.

Kuhn, Thomas. *The Structure of Scientific Revolutions,* 2d ed. Chicago: University of Chicago Press, 1970.

LeCompte, Margaret D., and deMarrais, Kathleen Bennett. The Disempowering of Empowerment: Out of the Revolution and into the Classroom. *Educational Foundations* 6(3):5–32, Summer 1992.

Lenin, Vladimir I. *Materialism and Empirio-Criticism.* New York: International Publishers Co., 1970.

Locke, John. *An Essay Concerning Human Understanding.* New York: E. P. Dutton, 1961.

———. *John Locke on Education,* edited by Peter Gay. New York: Teachers College Press, 1964.

————. *Some Thoughts Concerning Education,* edited by F. W. Goforth. New York: Barron's Educational Series, 1964.

Lodge, R. C. *Philosophy of Education.* New York: Harper, 1937.

Lyotard, Jean-François. *The Postmodern Condition.* Minneapolis: University of Minnesota Press, 1984.

Mager, Robert F. *Developing Attitude Toward Learning,* 2d ed. Belmont, CA: Lake Publishing, 1984.

Marcel, Gabriel. *The Philosophy of Existentialism,* translated by Manya Harari. New York: The Citadel Press, 1968.

Marcuse, Herbert. *An Essay on Liberation.* Boston: Beacon Press, 1969.

————. *One Dimensional Man.* Boston: Beacon Press, 1964.

————. *Reason and Revolution: Hegel and the Rise of Social Theory.* Boston: Beacon Press, 1960.

Margonis, Frank. Marxism, Liberalism, and Educational Theory. *Educational Theory* 43(4):449–465, Fall 1993.

Maritain, Jacques. *Education at the Crossroads.* New Haven, CT: Yale University Press, 1943.

Marler, Charles D. *Philosophy and Schooling.* Boston: Allyn and Bacon, 1975.

Marx, Karl. *Capital: A Critique of Political Economy. Vol. I. The Process of Capitalist Production,* edited by Friedrich Engels and translated from the third German edition by Samuel Moore and Edward Aveling. London: Lawrence and Wishart, 1965.

————. *The Communist Manifesto,* translated by Samuel Moore. London: Penguin, 1967.

————. *Karl Marx: Selected Writings.* London: Oxford University Press, 1977.

————. *On Education, Women, and Children: The Karl Marx Library,* vol. 6, edited by Saul K. Padover. New York: McGraw-Hill, 1975.

————. *On Society and Social Change, with Selections by Frederick Engels,* edited by Neil J. Smelder. Chicago: University of Chicago Press, 1973.

————. *The Portable Karl Marx,* selected, translated in part, and with an introduction by Eugene Kamenka. New York: The Viking Press, 1983.

————. *Writings of the Young Marx on Philosophy and Society,* translated and edited by Lloyd D. Easton and Kurt H. Guddat. Garden City, NY: Anchor Books, 1967.

————; **Engels, Frederick; and Lenin, V. I.** *The Essential Left: Four Classic Texts on the Principles of Socialism.* New York: Barnes and Noble, 1965.

Matthews, Mervyn. *Education in the Soviet Union: Policies and Institutions Since Stalin.* London: Allen and Unwin, 1982.

Maurer, Armand. *Medieval Philosophy.* New York: Random House, 1962.

May, Rollo. *Existence: A New Dimension in Psychiatry and Psychology.* New York: Basic Books, 1958.

Mays, Wolfe. Linguistic Analysis and the Philosophy of Education. *Educational Theory* 20:269–283, 1970.

McClellan, James E. In Reply to Professor Soltis, in *Philosophy of Education, 1971. Proceedings of the Twenty-Seventh Annual Meeting of the Philosophy of Education Society.* Edwardsville, IL: Philosophy of Education Society, 1971, pp. 55–59.

McLaren, Peter. *Life in Schools: An Introduction to Critical Pedagogy in the Foundations of Education.* New York: Longmans, 1994.

Meadows, Donella H., et al. *The Limits of Growth.* New York: Universe Books, 1972.

Meichenbaum, Donald. *Cognitive-Behavior Modification.* New York: Plenum Press, 1977.

Merleau-Ponty, Maurice. *Phenomenology of Perception,* translated by Colin Smith. Atlantic Highlands, NJ: Humanities Press International, 1981.

————. *Primacy of Perception,* edited by James M. Edie and translated by William Cobb et al. Evanston, IL: Northwestern University Press, 1964.

Mesarovic, Mihajlo D. and Pestel, Eduard. *Mankind at the Turning Point: The Second Report to the Club of Rome.* New York: Dutton, 1974.

Montessori, Maria. *The Secret of Childhood,* translated by Barbara Barclay Carter. New York: Longmans, Green, 1936.

Moore, George E. *Philosophical Papers.* New York: Allen and Unwin, 1959.

Morris, Van Cleve. *Existentialism in Education.* New York: Harper & Row, 1966.

————, **and Pai, Young.** *Philosophy and the American School.* 2d ed. Boston: Houghton Mifflin, 1976.

Nakamura, Hajime. *Ways of Thinking of Eastern Peoples: India, China, Tibet, Japan,* rev. ed. Edited by Philip P. Wiener. Honolulu: Eastwest Center Press, 1964.

National Commission on Excellence in Education. *A Nation at Risk: The Imperative for Educational Reform.* Washington, D.C.: Government Printing Office, 1983.

National Society for the Study of Education. *Modern Philosophies of Education. The Fifty-Fourth Yearbook of the National Society for the Study of Education,* edited by Nelson B. Henry. Chicago: National Society for the Study of Education, 1955.

————. *Philosophies of Education. The Forty-First Yearbook of the National Society for the Study of Education,* edited by Nelson B. Henry. Chicago: National Society for the Study of Education, 1942.

————. *Philosophy and Education: The Eightieth Yearbook of the National Society for the Study of Education,* edited by Jonas Soltis. Chicago: National Society for the Study of Education, 1981.

Neill, A. S. *Summerhill.* New York: Hart, 1960.

Nietzsche, Friedrich. *Beyond Good and Evil.* New York: Viking Penguin, 1990.

————. *Thus Spake Zarathustra,* translated by A. Tille. New York: E. P. Dutton, 1958.

————. *The Will to Power,* translated by Walter Kaufmann and R. J. Hollingdale. New York: Random House, 1967.

Oldenberg, Hermann. *Buddha: His Life, His Doctrine, His Order.* Delhi: Indologial Book House, 1971.

Organ, Troy Wilson. *Western Approaches to Eastern Philosophy.* Athens, OH: Ohio University Press, 1975.

Orwell, George. *1984.* New York: Harcourt, Brace, 1949.

Ozmon, Howard. *Contemporary Critics of Education.* Danville, IL: Interstate, 1970.

———. *Dialogue in Philosophy of Education.* Columbus, OH: Merrill Publishing Co., 1972.

———. *Utopias and Education.* Minneapolis: Burgess, 1969.

Pacheco, Arturo. Marx, Philosophy, and Education, in *Philosophy of Education, 1978. Proceedings of the Philosophy of Education Society.* Champaign, IL: Philosophy of Education Society and University of Illinois, 1979, pp. 208–220.

Packard, Vance Oakley. *The Hidden Persuaders.* New York: Pocket Books, 1981.

Paringer, William Andrew. *John Dewey and the Paradox of Liberal Reform.* Albany: State University of New York Press, 1990.

Pavlov, Ivan Petrovich. *Conditioned Reflexes,* translated by G. V. Anrap. New York: Dover Press, 1960.

Peddiwell, J. Abner [pseud.]. *The Saber-Tooth Curriculum.* New York: McGraw-Hill, 1939.

Peirce, Charles S. *Philosophy and Human Nature.* New York: New York University Press, 1971.

Perkinson, Henry J. *The Possibilities of Error: An Approach to Education.* New York: David McKay, 1971.

———. *Teachers Without Goals, Students Without Knowledge.* New York: McGraw-Hill, 1993.

Pestalozzi, Johann H. *How Gertrude Teaches Her Children,* translated by Lucy E. Holland and Francis C. Turner. Syracuse, NY: George Allen and Unwin, 1894.

Peters, R. S. *Ethics and Education.* London: Allen and Unwin, 1965.

———. *The Philosophy of Education.* London: Oxford University Press, 1973.

Planhol, Xavier de. *The World of Islam.* New York: Cornell University Press, 1957.

Plato. *The Laws,* vol. 1 and 2, translated by R. G. Bury. New York: G. P. Putnam's, 1926.

———. *The Meno of Plato,* edited by E. Seymer Thompson. New York: Macmillan, 1901.

———. *The Republic,* translated by B. Jowett. New York: Modern Library, 1941.

Plotinus. *The Enneads,* edited by John Dillon and translated by Stephen MacKenna. New York: Viking Penguin, 1991.

Popp, Jerome A. Philosophy of Education and the Education of Teachers, in *Philosophy of Education, 1972. Proceedings of the Twenty-Eighth Annual Meeting of the Philosophy of Education Society.* Edwardsville, IL: Philosophy of Education Society, 1972, pp. 222–229.

Popper, Karl. *The Open Society and Its Enemies.* Princeton, NJ: Princeton University Press, 1966.

Pratte, Richard. Analytic Philosophy of Education: A Historical Perspective. *Teachers College Record* 81:145–165, 1979.

———. *Contemporary Theories of Education.* Scranton, PA: International Textbook, 1971.

———. *Ideology and Education.* New York: David McKay, 1977.

Price, Ronald F. *Marx and Education in Late Capitalism.* London: Croom Helm, 1986.

———. *Marx and Education in Russia and China.* Totowa, NJ: Roman and Littlefield, 1977.

Putnam, Hilary. *The Many Faces of Realism: The Paul Carus Lectures.* LaSalle, IL: Open Court, 1987.

Putnam, Hilary, and Putnam, Ruth. Education in a Multicultural Democracy: Two Deweyan Perspectives. *Educational Theory* 43(4):361–376, Fall 1993.

Quintilian, Marcus F. *Institute of Oratory,* translated by H. E. Butler. London: W. Heinemann, 1921.

Rader, Melvin. *Marx's Interpretation of History.* New York: Oxford University Press, 1979.

Radhakrishnan, Sarvepalli, ed. *History of Philosophy—Eastern and Western,* vol. 1. London: Bradford and Dickens, Drayton House, 1952.

Rafferty, Max. *Suffer Little Children.* New York: Devin-Adair, 1962.

———. *What Are They Doing to Your Children?* New York: New American Library, 1963.

Redl, Helen, ed. and trans. *Soviet Educators on Soviet Education.* New York: The Free Press, 1964.

Reich, Charles. *The Greening of America.* New York: Random House, 1970.

Reitman, Sanford W. *The Educational Messiah Complex: American Faith in the Culturally Redemptive Power of Schooling.* Sacramento: Caddo Gap Press, 1992.

Rickover, Hyman G. *Education and Freedom.* New York: New American Library, 1963.

Rogers, Carl. *Freedom to Learn.* Columbus, OH: Merrill Publishing Co., 1969.

Rorty, Richard. *Consequences of Pragmatism (Essays: 1972–1980).* Minneapolis: University of Minnesota Press, 1982.

———. *Contingency, Irony, and Solidarity.* New York: Cambridge University Press, 1989.

———. Intellectuals in Politics: Too Far In? To Far Out? *Dissent* 38:483–490, Fall 1991.

———. *Philosophical Papers,* vol. 1 and 2. Cambridge: University of Cambridge Press, 1991.

———. *Philosophy and the Mirror of Nature.* Princeton: Princeton University Press, 1979.

———. Two Cheers for the Cultural Left. *South Atlantic Quarterly* 89:227–234, Winter 1990.

Roshi, Eido Shimano. *Golden Wind.* Tokyo: Japan Publications, 1979.

Roszak, Theodore. *Making of a Counter Culture.* New York: Doubleday, 1969.

Rousseau, Jean-Jacques. *Émile,* translated by Alan Bloom. New York: Basic Books, 1979.

———. *On the Social Contract,* edited by Roger D. Masters and translated by Judith R. Masters. New York: St. Martin, 1978.

Royce, Josiah. *Lecture on Modern Idealism.* New Haven, CT: Yale University Press, 1964.

Rugg, Harold O. *The Great Technology.* New York: John Day, 1933.

Russell, Bertrand. *Education and the Modern World.* New York: W. W. Norton, 1932.

———. *Education and the Social Order.* London: Allen and Unwin, 1932.

———. *Our Knowledge of the External World as a Field for Scientific Method in Philosophy.* London: Allen and Unwin, 1926.

———. *Principles of Social Reconstruction.* London: Allen and Unwin, 1916.

———. *Religion and Science.* New York: Oxford University Press, 1935.

Ryle, Gilbert. *Collected Papers,* vol. 1 and 2. New York: Barnes and Noble, 1971.

———. *Concept of Mind.* New York: Barnes and Noble, 1949.

Saksena, Shri Krishna. *Essays on Indian Philosophy.* Honolulu: University of Hawaii Press, 1970.

Sarup, Madan. *Marxism and Education.* New York: Routledge Kegan Paul, 1978.

———. *Marxism/Structuralism/Education: Theoretical Developments in the Sociology of Education.* London: Falmer Press, 1983.

Sartre, Jean-Paul. *Being and Nothingness,* translated by Hazel Barnes. New York: Philosophical Library, 1956.

———. *Critique of Dialectical Reason,* translated by Alan Sheridan-Smith. New York: Schocken Books, 1976.

———. *Existentialism and Human Emotions,* translated by Hazel Barnes. New York: Philosophical Library, 1947.

———. *Search for a Method,* translated by Hazel Barnes. New York: Random House, 1968.

Schaff, Adam. *Marxism and the Human Individual,* edited by Robert Cohen and translated by Olgierd Wojtasiewicz. New York: McGraw-Hill, 1970.

Scheffler, Israel. *Conditions of Knowledge: An Introduction to Epistemology and Education.* Chicago: University of Chicago Press, 1983.

———. *The Language of Education.* Springfield, IL: Charles Thomas, 1960.

Schubring, Walther. *The Doctrine of the Jainas,* translated by Wolfgang Buerlen. Delhi: Motilal Banarsidass, 1962.

Shimahara, Nobuo, ed. *Educational Reconstruction: Promise and Challenge.* Columbus, OH: Merrill Publishing Co., 1973.

Shourie, Arun. *Hinduism: Essence and Consequence.* New Delhi: Vikas Publishing House, 1979.

Sizer, Theodore. *Horace's Compromise: The Dilemma of the American High School.* Boston: Houghton-Mifflin, 1992.

Skinner, B. F. *Beyond Freedom and Dignity.* New York: Alfred A. Knopf, 1971.

———. *Walden Two.* New York: Macmillan, 1976.

Soll, Ivan. Hegel as a Philosopher of Education. *Educational Theory* 22:26–33, Winter 1973.

Soltis, Jonas F. Analysis and Anomalies in Philosophy of Education, in *Philosophy of Education, 1971. Proceedings of the Twenty-Seventh Annual Meeting of the Philosophy of Education Society.* Edwardsville, IL: Philosophy of Education Society, 1971, pp. 28–46.

————. *An Introduction to the Analysis of Educational Concepts*, 2d ed. Reading, MA: Addison-Wesley, 1977.

————. Philosophy of Education for Educators: The Eightieth NSSE Yearbook. *Teachers College Record* 81:225–247, 1979.

————. Philosophy of Education: Retrospect and Prospect, in *Philosophy of Education, 1975. Proceedings of the Thirty-First Annual Meeting of the Philosophy of Education Society*. San Jose, CA: Philosophy of Education Society, 1975, pp. 7–24.

————. Philosophy of Education Since Mid-Century. *Teachers College Record* 81:127–129, 1979.

Spencer, Herbert. *Education: Intellectual, Moral, Spiritual.* Paterson, NJ: Littlefield, Adams, 1963.

————. *Herbert Spencer on Education*, edited and with an introduction by Andreas Kazamias. New York: Teachers College Press, 1966.

Stanley, William B. *Curriculum for Utopia: Social Reconstructionism and Critical Pedagogy in the Postmodern Era.* Albany: State University of New York Press, 1992.

Stout, Maureen. Rethinking the Concept of "The Popular" in Critical and Poststructural Social and Educational Theory. *Educational Foundations* 6(3):51–66, Summer 1992.

Strain, John Paul. Idealism: A Clarification of an Educational Philosophy. *Educational Theory* 25:263–271, 1975.

Suda, J. P. *Religions in India: A Study of Their Essential Unity.* New Delhi: Sterling Publishers Pvt., 1978.

Suzuki, Daisetz T. *The Awakening of Zen*, edited by Christmas Humphreys. Boulder, CO: Prajna Press, 1980.

————. *The Essentials of Zen Buddhism.* Westport, CT: Greenwood Press, 1962.

Ta Hui. *Swampland Flowers: The Letters and Lectures of Zen Master Ta Hui*, translated by Christopher Cleary. New York: Grove Press, 1977.

Task Force on Education for Economic Growth. *Action for Excellence: A Comprehensive Plan to Improve Our Nation's Schools.* Denver, CO: Education Commission of the States, 1983.

Task Force on Federal Elementary and Secondary Education Policy. *Making the Grade: Report of the Twentieth Century Fund Task Force on Federal Elementary and Secondary Education Policy*, with a background paper by Paul E. Peterson. New York: Twentieth Century Fund, 1983.

Thomas, Edward J. *The History of Buddhist Thought.* New York: Barnes and Noble, 1951.

Thompson, Lawrence G. *Chinese Religion: An Introduction.* Belmont, CA: Dickenson Publishing Co., 1969.

Thoreau, Henry David. *Walden and Civil Disobedience.* New York: Norton, 1966.

Thorensen, Carl E., ed. *Behavior Modification in Education. The Seventy-Second Yearbook of the National Society for the Study of Education*, part I. Chicago: National Society for the Study of Education, 1973.

Tillich, Paul. *The Courage To Be.* New Haven, CT: Yale University Press, 1952.

Toffler, Alvin. *Future Shock.* New York: Random House, 1970.

———. *Learning for Tomorrow: The Role of the Future in Education.* New York: Vintage Books, 1974.

———. *The Third Wave.* New York: William Morrow and Co., 1980.

Troutner, Lee. Making Sense out of "Existential Thought and Education": A Search for the Interface, in *Philosophy of Education, 1975. Proceedings of the Thirty-First Annual Meeting of the Philosophy of Education Society.* San Jose, CA: Philosophy of Education Society, 1975, pp. 185–199.

Tucker, Robert C. *Philosophy and Myth in Karl Marx.* New York: Cambridge University Press, 1961.

Vandenberg, Donald. *Being and Education: An Essay in Existential Phenomenology.* Englewood Cliffs, NJ: Prentice-Hall, 1971.

———. Existential and Phenomenological Influence in Education. *Teachers College Record* 81:166–191, 1979.

Watson, John Broadus. *Behaviorism.* Chicago: University of Chicago Press, 1957.

Watt, W. Montgomery. *Muhammad, Prophet and Statesman.* New York: Oxford University Press, 1961.

Weber, Max. *The Religion of India.* New York: The Free Press, 1958.

Werner, Harold D. *Cognitive Therapy.* New York: The Free Press, 1982.

West, Cornel. *The American Evasion of Philosophy: A Genealogy of Pragmatism.* Madison: University of Wisconsin Press, 1989.

Whitehead, Alfred North. *The Aims of Education and Other Essays.* New York: Macmillan, 1929.

———. *Science and the Modern World.* New York: Macmillan, 1967.

———, **and Russell, Bertrand.** *Principia Mathematica.* New York: Cambridge University Press, 1968.

Wittgenstein, Ludwig. *Blue and Brown Books.* New York: Barnes and Noble, 1969.

———. *Philosophical Investigations,* translated by G. E. M. Anscombe. New York: Macmillan, 1968.

———. *Tractatus Logico-Philosophicus,* translated by D. F. Pears and B. F. McGuinness. New York: Humanities Press, 1961.

Yang, C. K. *Religion in Chinese Society.* Berkeley: University of California Press, 1961.

Zajda, Joseph. *Education in the USSR.* New York: Pergamon Press, 1980.

Zeldin, David. *The Educational Ideas of Charles Fourier.* New York: A. M. Kelley, 1969.

Name Index

Subject Index